Vietnam: The Naval Story

VIETNAM:
THE NAVAL STORY

Edited by Frank Uhlig, Jr.

NAVAL INSTITUTE PRESS   ANNAPOLIS, MARYLAND

Copyright © 1986
by the United States Naval Institute
Annapolis, Maryland

Library of Congress Cataloging-in-Publication Data
Vietnam: the naval story.
    Includes index.
    1. Vietnamese Conflict, 1961–1975—Naval operations,
American.   2. United States. Navy—History—Vietnamese
Conflict, 1961–1975. I. Uhlig, Frank, 1927–
DS558.7.V52   1986   959.704′345   86–16345

ISBN: 0-87021-014-9

Printed in the United States of America

9   8   7   6   5   4   3   111456

Contents

Preface

During an impromptu lunch at the Harbour House restaurant in Annapolis in 1961 Professor Ellery Clark of the U. S. Naval Academy's history faculty proposed that the Naval Institute publish annually a book of essays on topics chosen by the Institute. Roger Taylor, then the Institute's managing editor, carried the idea forward, obtained approval of the Board of Control that May to bring the idea to fruition, and appointed me to do that.

Our aim was, through the "processes of scrutiny, analysis, and discussion," to help the Navy "recognize tomorrow's requirements today and permit the Service to adjust the course without reducing speed." To do that we asked "men varying widely in experience and temperament, but all knowledgeable in their own specialities, to analyze critically one aspect or another of the Navy and the world situation in which the Navy must operate. Each author was asked to consider many questions about his subject and each was free to consider as many more as he desired.... Each was charged with expressing his views on his subject, whatever they might be."[1]

It seemed reasonable then, when the war in Vietnam took on a substantial American character, to ask the people who knew most about it—those in command or in responsible staff positions—to tell their professional peers some of the important and interesting things they had done and knew about. Hence, shortly after the first major American victory, that won by the 7th Marines on the Van Tuong Peninsula near Chu Lai in August 1965, the victorious commander, Colonel (later Brigadier General) Oscar Peatross, USMC, was asked, and agreed, to write a description of the action for *Naval Review 1967*, which then was in the planning stage. The Institute published that issue in the fall of 1966.

Early in 1966, in order to find out what was happening in the naval parts of

1. All the quotations are from the preface to *Naval Review 1962–1963* (Annapolis, MD: U. S. Naval Institute, 1962), pp. ix–xi.

the war, who was doing it, what should be written about, and who had something to say, the Institute's secretary-treasurer, Commander R. T. E. Bowler, Jr., sent this editor to Vietnam for three weeks. A year later I was sent back for another three weeks. Most of the rest of the essays published herein stemmed directly or indirectly from those visits.

Every issue of the *Naval Review* was the product of many people's skill. The assistant editors and editorial assistants involved in the early issues from which the essays in this book were taken were Mary Veronica Amoss, Christine R. Ulrich, Jan Snouck-Hurgronje, and Tomi Johnston. Beginning in 1970 the *Naval Review* took on additional duty as the May issue of the U. S. Naval Institute *Proceedings*. So for the issues of 1971 and 1972, those editorial tasks were taken on by Clayton R. Barrow, Robert A. Cohen, and Katherine McInnis of the *Proceedings* staff. Each issue had its designer. Alas! There is no evidence in this book of their work, but there is in each of the original issues, and therein the contribution of each is acknowledged. The general size and layout of the *Naval Review*, and the *Proceedings* as well, however, are the work of David Q. Scott, who was the Institute's first art director. David's artistic influence pervades even this book, published long after his death in an airplane crash.

The present book was proposed by Deborah Guberti Estes, manager, acquisitions and subsidiary rights, at the Institute's vigorous book-publishing division, the Naval Institute Press. Carol Swartz was the manuscript editor and Moira Megargee, the designer. Each in her own way, Marjorie Whittington of the book department and Patty Maddocks, the Institute's photo librarian, were extremely helpful. I would also like to thank Roy Carson for his careful proofreading and Susan Sweeney for doing the index. In the background presiding over the entire effort, was Tom Epley, director of the Naval Institute Press. Still further back were Commander Bowler and his successor, Captain James A. Barber, Jr. And, over the horizon, lay the Board of Control. They all hold responsibility, the largest part of which was to put their faith in me.

FRANK UHLIG, JR.

Vietnam: The Naval Story

Introduction

"Communications dominate war," wrote Alfred Thayer Mahan; "broadly considered," he continued, "they are the most important single element in strategy, political or military."[1] By communications, he meant not only "all the routes . . . which connect an operating military force with a base of operations and along which supplies and military forces move," but also those routes that connect a warring nation with other nations.[2]

According to the U. S. Navy's brief history of the war in Vietnam, "over 85 percent" of North Vietnam's military imports passed through Haiphong."[3]

And, as General Bruce Palmer, who for a time commanded II Field Force in Vietnam, tells us, between December 1966 and the spring of 1970, military supplies from North Vietnam to that side's forces in the II, III, and IV Corps areas of South Vietnam, that is, in most of South Vietnam, "came mostly by sea through the port of Sihanoukville and thence cross-country to the border bases in Cambodia and Laos."[4]

It is for the reason given long ago by Captain Mahan that countries build and maintain navies. Though not always understood in this country, it is why for so many years the United States has possessed the world's most powerful navy. In contrast, at the time of the Tonkin Gulf incidents in August 1964, the navy of North Vietnam consisted of only a few dozen motor torpedo boats and smaller craft, most of which were soon destroyed by the U. S. Navy's carrier-based air attacks on their bases.

What did the United States do about these facts? How well did we employ our huge navy in the Vietnamese war? How well did that navy perform? The answers, in the same order, are very little, badly, and very well.

It is clear that not enough of the people in South Vietnam were prepared soon enough to make effort enough to resist North Vietnam's campaign to conquer them. The Northerners, in contrast, were from first to last determined to prevail. And so they did.

Ideally, the main American effort in the war would have been diplomatic in nature, with the aim of exploiting the many already existing differences between the Soviet Union and China, while a complementary effort ought to have been made to exploit the enmity that lay latent between the Chinese and the North Vietnamese. Success in such efforts would have denied the Soviets the use of overland routes of communication to North Vietnam through China, would have forestalled any Chinese opposition to an American blockade of North Vietnam (if, under the circumstances, a blockade even would have been necessary), and would have reduced substantially the fears in this country of a Soviet-Chinese Marxist march to the Strait of Malacca. It might even have made the outcome of a struggle between North and South Vietnam so clearly unimportant that the United States could comfortably have refrained from engaging directly in that struggle.

These are not the things that happened, and perhaps they could not have happened. In our country the notion of monolithic communism, as well as the forces opposed to accurate knowledge and clear analysis that are often associated with the name of Senator Joseph McCarthy, were powerful—perhaps too powerful to have permitted such diplomatic maneuvers. In China, Mao Zedong and his veterans of the Long March, peasants clinging for dear life to the one idea that had passed their way, were firmly in power. Though they may have scorned the Vietnamese and feared the Soviets, they did not love the Americans.

By early 1972 that which, had it happened earlier would have been a blessing, actually came to pass. The United States and China began the process that eventually led to China's assumption of a stance less distant from the United States than from the Soviet Union. Because of this, the war in Vietnam lost what little purpose it still had for the United States, and this country hastened the already-begun withdrawal of its forces.

By then the South Vietnamese appeared finally to have been almost ready to stand on their own, though they were dependent upon the United States for their armaments just as the North Vietnamese were dependent for their armaments upon the Soviet Union. What happened was that the United States not only withdrew its forces from Vietnam but also dried up South Vietnam's supply of arms. In contrast, the Soviets, who had never committed their troops to North Vietnam, continued their generous supply of weaponry and support to their client state. Then, in a powerful invasion from across the border in 1975, North Vietnam's large army overwhelmed the smaller, less well supplied, and less well commanded army of the South, and in a short while South Vietnam was no more.

When in 1964 and 1965 the United States chose to send its combat forces into war, many people, both within the Navy and without, called for the blockade of North Vietnam's ports, of which by far the most important was Haiphong. By themselves blockades are not enough. A resourceful enemy always seems to get a portion of what the blockader would like to stop, and he learns to do without a lot of the rest. Still, vast amounts of arms and other military goods, as well as civilian cargoes, were entering North Vietnam by sea. Everything that could be kept from entering North Vietnam would be to the advantage of the U. S. and South Vietnamese forces fighting on the other side of the Demilitarized Zone. Nonetheless, the U. S. government chose not to blockade.

From that decision a good deal flowed. For example, the interdiction of coastal and inshore shipping off South Vietnam became necessary. That is, if we would not interfere with the shipping of our chosen enemies, we would have to interfere with that of our chosen friends. "Market Time," as the interdiction effort was called, appears to have been a success. At least, few enemy attempts seem to have been made to pierce the screen of aircraft, ships, and boats erected by the U. S. Navy and Coast Guard (and, to a lesser extent, by the South Vietnamese Navy) off the coast of South Vietnam, and of those attempts, hardly any succeeded.

One reason for this modest North Vietnamese effort was that the screen, if its execution was arduous for the naval interdictors and a nuisance to the South Vietnamese fishermen, merchants, and other mariners, was, for the North Vietnamese, hard to pierce. Another reason, as General Palmer tells us, is that for more than three years, apparently as a result of a massive American intelligence failure, the enemy freely used Cambodian ports for the supply of his armies in the field. A clear perception of the facts could have permitted a short extension of Market Time's patrols to cover Sihanoukville (now Kompong Som), Cambodia's major port.

A blockade of North Vietnam, which would have halted outbound as well as inbound traffic, might have made the intelligence failure a matter of inconsequence, instead of a matter of central importance. It might also have permitted Market Time and the substantial U. S. naval campaigns in the Mekong Delta to have been as successful as they were at far less cost if, indeed, they would have been necessary at all.

In his "sea power commentary" in *Naval Review 1967* Rear Admiral John D. Hayes, noting that the United States had chosen to bomb the enemy rather than blockade him, observed that "this decision was an admission by the United States that, in undeclared limited war, it would not avail itself of belligerent rights at sea, and its powerful Navy is, therefore, unable to deny the use of the seas to an enemy. In the Cold War, the concept of freedom of the seas has triumphed over that of control of the seas."[5]

Three years later, in his sea power commentary in *Naval Review 1970*, Admiral Hayes quoted the perceptive early twentieth century British naval historian Sir Julian Corbett to the effect that "freedom of the seas cannot exist so long as naval warfare is allowed to exist, since without substantial permission to command the seas, navies, except as mere adjuncts to armies, cease to have meaning."[6]

And in his "Theory of Naval Strategy in the Nuclear Age" published in *Naval Review 1972*, Rear Admiral Edward Wegener of the Federal German Navy wrote that "history will judge" whether the decision not to blockade "was a wise one, or whether it was a serious, perhaps the crucial, mistake of the whole Vietnam war."[7]

In any event, it was as a "mere adjunct" to its army that the world's most powerful navy energetically, bravely, and at great cost to itself tried to carry out a difficult task that ought to have been easy, an expensive task that ought to have been cheap. The result was failure in an effort that ought to have been a success.

To be sure, in May 1972 the U. S. Seventh Fleet at last was permitted to mine the approaches to Haiphong and the other North Vietnamese harbors. The result of this small, easily and cheaply conducted action was dramatic. Thereafter, until U. S. forces swept the channels following the agreement upon a ceasefire in January 1973, no large merchant ships either entered or left Haiphong. But, by this time "there were ample overland rail and road links to North Vietnam from China to maintain the flow of supplies provided by the Soviet Union and China. Unfortunately . . . the bold action came years too late."[8] Obviously, while President Nixon had managed to open China's door to the United States, he had not been able to close her doors to the Soviet Union and Vietnam. Even so, it is not clear how much of the cargo that would have been carried in ships whose voyages had been frustrated by the mines off Haiphong ever made it into North Vietnam by way of China's roads and railroads.

Aside from what was close to a self-blockade of South Vietnam, how did the Navy attempt to help out in the war? Not only was blockade of the North in any form forbidden, but so was invasion, whether overland across the narrow Demilitarized Zone, or DMZ, or by sea somewhere on North Vietnam's long coast. All that was left for the Navy was bombardment, chiefly of North Vietnam, and chiefly by carrier-based aircraft. The targets were the enemy's minuscule industrial plant, and his people, trucks, trains, and boats carrying arms southward to the northernmost provinces of South Vietnam. (Flying mainly from bases in Thailand the U. S. Air Force was engaged in the same sort of activity and at about the same scale as the Navy was.)

From its beginning in 1964 the effort, one not likely to be successful anyway, was hobbled by overbearing direction from Washington, which chose to control military matters down to the most minute detail. Thus, as Admiral Hayes wrote in *Naval Review 1968*, "used as it was in Vietnam, the naval power of the United States did not succeed either in improving the military and political situation there or in reducing the cost of the war."[9]

With specific reference to blockade, Sir Basil Liddell Hart wrote that "helplessness induces hopelessness, and history attests that loss of hope and not loss of lives is what decides the issue of war."[10] In place of the silent, bloodless blockade, conducted by ships far beyond the reach of those they affected, we chose to bomb the enemy's supplies while they were in his towns, on his roads, or piled up under the jungle's triple canopy. The enemy was not helpless to counter that, and knew he was not, for he could see the wreckage of the hundreds of our aircraft he shot down.

Indeed, between 1965 and 1968, 421 of the Fleet's fixed-wing aircraft were shot down by the enemy and 450 aviators were lost, many of whom became prisoners of war.[11]

The cost of our bombing effort, its apparent ineffectiveness, and perhaps a growing revulsion against the bombing of any targets that could be termed civilian resulted in an interesting reversal of the effect on morale that we were told to expect from a bombing campaign against our enemies. It was not the enemy's willingness to fight that crumbled, but ours.

In April 1968 President Johnson halted bombing in most of North Vietnam, and that November he ended it in nearly all the rest. Thereafter naval aircraft attacked targets only in a small part of North Vietnam and in Laos and South Vietnam, though hardly without cost, for 130 more aircraft were lost in this effort.[12] In 1972, in response to a massive enemy offensive across the DMZ, the bombers returned to all of North Vietnam, this time under local, rather than distant, tactical control. The results were better. After it became clear that the North Vietnamese were using peace negotiations as a screen to rebuild their forces, for eleven days beginning in mid-December 1972 the Air Force and Navy attacked Hanoi heavily. They did great damage but at heavy cost to themselves. So "they focused on the enemy's missile defense network including command and control facilities, missile assembly and transportation points, and the missile batteries themselves. . . . By 29 December . . . the surface-to-air missile system had been neutralized and U. S. losses reduced to a minimum. At the end of the year, the North Vietnamese resumed serious discussions in Paris and on 15 January 1973, combat operations in the North were halted."[13]

It seems as if the heavy bombing caused the enemy to return to the peace table, though it is evident he was no more serious about peace in January than he had been in November. What he wanted, and got, was an end to the pain which, without SAMs, he could no longer ameliorate. One must recognize that the main source of that pain was the big B-52 bomber, a direct descendant of the B-17, B-24, and B-29 that a generation before had laid waste the cities of Germany and Japan. Neither the carrier-based attack planes nor the similar "fighter-bombers" of the Air Force could in any way match the load-carrying capacity of the big B-52.

One of the unforeseen results of the bombing of North Vietnam was that the U. S. pilots and aircrewmen who became prisoners of war also became a weapon for the enemy to use against us. When the people of the United States realized the savage conditions under which the prisoners existed year after year, their release became a principal U. S. war aim. As part of the cease-fire agreement of January 1973, the North Vietnamese gave them up "in exchange for U. S. military withdrawal from South Vietnam and the clearing by the U. S. Navy of mines from North Vietnamese waters."[14]

Justly, the returned prisoners became public heroes. Unjustly, until many years later they were the only veterans of the Vietnam war who were recognized publicly as heroes.

The influence of the prisoner of war issue remains with us. When a U. S. naval officer was imprisoned in December 1983 after his aircraft had been shot down over Lebanon, there was intense public concern for his safety. By bringing that officer back to this country, a little-known but enterprising politician, the Reverend Jesse Jackson, made himself into a national figure. More importantly, hereafter the POW issue may influence the tactical decisions of those commanders who must engage foes in parts of the world where prisoners of war can expect nothing but the most barbarous treatment, especially when the foe knows that their release is likely to become a domestic U. S. political issue and that for their release he can gain concessions from the United States.

Still more serious than the POW issue or any of its aspects is the fact that at a time when the United States had incomparably the most powerful navy in the world, it permitted a foe who in effect had no navy at all to have equal access to the sea and thus both to his own distant forces and to his even more distant sources of arms, ammunition, and the other goods of war. Perhaps during the war we were numbed by that fact. But now, with the war long past, we should feel shocked and outraged at ourselves.

Before we engage in any similar war we must be sure, among other things, that we can use our sea power properly. If for any reason we find that we will be unable to do that, or even are in doubt about it, we owe it to ourselves to find a solution to our problem other than war.

Notes

1. Mahan, A. T., in Westcott, ed., *Mahan on Naval Warfare; Selections from the Writings of Rear Admiral Alfred T. Mahan* (Boston, 1918), 71.

2. Slightly shortened, this is the definition for "Lines of Communication" in the *Dictionary of Military and Associated Terms* (JCS Pub 1) (Washington, D.C., 1972), 176. This dictionary is published, and every so often updated, by the Joint Chiefs of Staff.

3. Marolda, Edward J., and J. Wesley Pryce III, *A Short History of the United States Navy and the Southeast Asian Conflict 1950–1975* (Washington, D.C., 1984), 88.

4. Palmer, Bruce, Jr., *The 25-Year War, America's Military Role in Vietnam* (Lexington, Ky., 1984), 98–99.

5. Hayes, John D., "Sea Power, July 1965–June 1966: A Commentary" in *Naval Review 1967* (Annapolis, Md., 1966), 265.

6. Hayes, John D., "Sea Power: A Commentary, Patterns of American Sea Power, 1945–56. Their Portents for the Seventies," *Naval Review 1970* (Annapolis, Md., 1970), 349. Beginning with this issue the annual *Naval Review* took on additional duty and thereafter also appeared as the May issue of the U. S. Naval Institute *Proceedings*.

7. Wegener, Edward, "Theory of Naval Strategy in the Nuclear Age," *Naval Review 1972* (Annapolis, Md., 1972), 202. In his 1970 essay cited above, Admiral Hayes, who had seen an early translation of Admiral Wegener's article, called it "one of the most perceptive pieces of naval writing since World War II." In its original version, in German, it appeared in *Marine Rundschau* for October 1968.

8. Palmer, *op. cit.*, 122.

9. Hayes, John D., "Sea Power, July 1966–June 1967: A Commentary," *Naval Review 1968* (Annapolis, Md., 1968), 282.

10. Liddell Hart, B. H., *Strategy* (New York, 1967), 202.
11. Marolda and Pryce, *op. cit.*, 31.
12. Marolda and Pryce, *op. cit.*, 81.
13. Marolda and Pryce, *op. cit.*, 91.
14. Marolda and Pryce, *op. cit.*, 91.

The Choice Taken:
The Aerial Bombardment of
North Vietnam

Task Force 77 was made up chiefly of light and medium bombers, fighters, electronic combatants of various types, and the carriers from which they flew. In his examination of "Task Force 77 in Action off Vietnam," written in the autumn of 1970, Vice Admiral Cagle focuses on the difficult and unrewarding period from the beginning of August 1964 to the end of March 1968—that is, from the Tonkin Gulf episodes that provided President Lyndon Johnson with one of the reasons for beginning the aerial bombing of North Vietnam to that same president's public announcement of his decision to halt the bombing he had begun of Hanoi, Haiphong, and most of the rest of North Vietnam.

In our effort to help the South Vietnamese (and the Laotians) to prevent a conquest by the North Vietnamese, the United States had been engaged for years in advisory, clandestine, and other small military activities in and about those countries. Latterly, these had included low-level reconnaissance flights both from ashore and afloat to determine what the North Vietnamese secretly were trying to accomplish in the lands of their intended victims. Some of the reconnaissance aircraft had been shot down, their pilots and crews killed or captured, including a few from the carriers.

Since 1971 a lot has been written about the Tonkin Gulf episodes. We now know that while the first, or daylight "battle," on 2 August 1964, actually happened, the second, on the night of 4 August, occurred only in the excited imaginations of tense and tired men misled by their own sensors. A naval aviator, Vice Admiral James B. Stockdale, who, as a commander, was present on both occasions, has recently provided an interesting account of these events. Almost from the start he knew that the second "battle" was no such thing at all.[1]

When Captain J. J. Herrick, the destroyer division commodore, realized that his report of having been under attack probably was mistaken, he reported that, too. But corrective news seldom catches up with an erroneous report. Perhaps intent on punishing those whom he believed highly deserving of punishment, President Johnson allowed his orders for a retaliatory strike, based on the mistaken information, to stand. Stockdale took part in that event, too.[2]

As we have seen, the bombing of North Vietnam by the Navy and Air Force was conducted, not in conjunction with other actions, such as a blockade and a counter-invasion, but as a substitute for them. There was little empirical evidence that such an effort could succeed in halting the movement of North Vietnamese troops, arms, and supplies into South Vietnam. And there was no experience that suggested it could break the will of a determined foe. With so chancy an enterprise, it was up to those who made the decision to bomb to ease the work of those who had to carry it out. But, as Admiral Cagle makes plain, that did not happen.

In addition to the carriers' aircraft, the fleet's surface ships also engaged the enemy, though they did not do so as elements of Task Force 77. Their work is worth a few words.

It was not until October 1966, long after the air war had begun, that surface ships were allowed to fire on any targets in North Vietnam. And, like the carriers, the surface combatants fought under substantial restraints. None, for example, were allowed to fire on targets north of 17°31″ North (that is, only 31 miles north of the DMZ) until February 1967, and it wasn't until 1972 that they were permitted to shoot at targets near Hanoi and Haiphong.[3] Though none were sunk, quite a few surface combatants were hit by enemy fire from ashore and one, the destroyer *Higbee*, was hit by a bomb dropped by a MiG.[4]

In any event, most of the bombarding ships were destroyers whose 5-inch guns were too small to do much damage ashore and too short-ranged to do it far inland. Cruisers, of which there were not many, could reach a bit farther inland with their 6-inch or 8-inch guns, and they could hit harder. But it was not until long after the bombing halt of March 1968 that a really effective gunfire ship appeared on the scene, the battleship *New Jersey*. But seldom, if ever, was that ship given work near the upper end of her abilities. Once she left the scene, she never returned. One wonders if a more aggressive use of that ship and her sisters (none of which were recommissioned during that war) against the many North Vietnamese targets within range of 16-inch guns mightn't have accomplished far more for us, and at a far less cost in pilots killed, wounded, or made prisoners of war, and in aircraft destroyed, than we in fact experienced. Now that the *New Jersey* and her sisters are back in, or are coming back into, commission, it is reasonable to hope that the research into longer gun range and greater gun accuracy, which 20 years ago we spurned, will no longer be delayed. Against targets at sea the big gun was a vastly overrated instrument. Against those ashore it has the potential for being, within limits still unclear, indispensable.

The carrier-based air campaigns off Vietnam, fought 20 to 30 years after those of World War II, were quite different from their forerunners. Now another 15 or 20 years have gone by. How carrier-based aviation might be used in any future war is not altogether clear. What is clear is that, while carrier aviation is likely to be very useful, it will fight in a far different fashion from the way it was required to during the Vietnamese war. For that we should be thankful.

Notes

1. Stockdale, Jim and Sybil, *In Love and War: The Story of a Family's Ordeal during the Vietnam Years* (New York: Harper & Row, 1984), 3–24.

2. Ibid., 24–36.

3. Marolda, Edward J. and G. Wesley Pryce III, *A Short History of the United States Navy and Conflict 1950–1975* (Washington, D.C.: Naval Historical Center, 1984), 28–29, 88–89.

4. Ibid., 29, 89.

Task Force 77 in Action Off Vietnam

Vice Admiral Malcolm W. Cagle, U.S. Navy

The floating airfields of the U. S. Navy in the Western Pacific, the carriers of Task Force 77, first saw action in Vietnam on 2 August 1964 in response to an emergency call from the destroyer *Maddox* (DD-731)[1] following an unprovoked attack by North Vietnamese torpedo boats. Task Force 77's aircraft also initiated the 37-month bombing effort of North Vietnam on 7 February 1965. As on many other occasions, carrier aircraft were first at the scene of trouble.

It was the beginning of a 37-month long carrot-and-stick campaign to persuade Hanoi to cease its aggression against South Vietnam. It was always to be a restrained, graduated, strategic bombing effort on carefully selected targets, a stop—listen—and talk interdiction campaign. Until President Johnson's dramatic announcement on 31 March 1968 that there would be no more bombing of North Vietnam above the 20th parallel, the carriers of Task Force 77 would cruise in the waters of the Gulf of Tonkin as close as 60 miles to the enemy's coast.

What were the lessons, the mistakes, the accomplishments of that campaign? What did the campaign teach us?

This article will analyze the actions and accomplishments of Task Force 77, the attack aircraft carrier force at "Yankee" and "Dixie" Stations, beginning with the punitive attacks in August 1964 and closing with the start of the bombing curtailment on 1 April 1968, from which point the U. S. withdrawal from Vietnam can be measured.

Air Interdiction Strategy

From the beginning, the U. S. objective in South Vietnam was to preserve the South Vietnamese government as an independent, stable government that would deserve and receive popular support. In 1965, however, the Republic of South Vietnam was on the ragged edge of collapse. The Viet Cong, supported by North Vietnam and the North Vietnamese Army, had occupied large parts of the country and were subjecting the people to armed attacks and acts of terrorism, including assassination. Although the South Vietnamese government was functioning under a constitution, the Communist pressure had created such political instability that coups d'état had been taking place with regularity since the fall of 1964. Animosity between Buddhists and Catholics was high, and attempts to resolve political differences among the religious factions were at an impasse.

The U. S. military strategy to preserve South Vietnam had two interlocking objectives: inside that country, a ground and air campaign

Half a dozen bombs spill from beneath the wings of a carrier-based A-4 light attack plane as, early in the war, it attacks an enemy target in South Vietnam. Until the Air Force had established sufficient bases ashore, the Navy normally kept a carrier on "Dixie Station" to support operations in the South.

to defeat the enemy, or force their withdrawal; and, outside that country, an air and naval offensive against North Vietnam to force her to stop her aggression. In the beginning, it was fondly hoped and believed that Ho Chi Minh would conclude that, against such American military involvement, he could not succeed.

The air bombing campaign against North Vietnam was initiated on the assumption that most North Vietnamese and Viet Cong war-making material came overland into South Vietnam; until February 1965, it was not believed that much of it came be sea. With the use

of highly selective air power and, very shortly, by creating an effective anti-infiltration barrier along the South Vietnamese coast, the belief was that North Vietnam would be prevented from sustaining the war inside South Vietnam. The United States hoped that the aggression could be choked off by selective and gradually increasing attacks on North Vietnam's military installations and power plants, her petroleum products, her logistic storage areas, her war-supporting industrial facilities, and the vehicles, roads, and bridges by which war material moved south.

Throughout the campaign a fundamental principle was to avoid damaging nonmilitary targets and to avoid harm to noncombatants.

From the beginning, the air interdiction effort was inhibited by major restrictions. One of these was the unpredictability of the weather in the monsoon season of Southeast Asia, which greatly favored the enemy. Since Washington maintained control of the war from afar, the fighting forces' ability to react to changes in the weather was severely handicapped. The other major restrictions were political and they were self-imposed. The sanctuaries, base camps, and supply depots in Cambodia were declared off limits to our aircraft. Immediate pursuit of the enemy was forbidden. Haiphong, the key port of North Vietnam, through which 85% of North Vietnam's imports flowed, was never mined or blockaded or made to suffer major or crippling damage from air attacks. Instead, during the days the weather was good enough for such precision attacks, and often at night in hazardous low-level attacks under the flickering illumination of flares, shiploads of materials which had been unloaded at Haiphong were sought out and bombed on their journey south. Truck by truck and storage site by storage site—if they could be found under the dense canopy of jungle and camouflage—they were destroyed.

The Initial Involvement

Task Force 77's involvement against North Vietnam can be dated from 2 August 1964, the day North Vietnamese torpedo boats attacked the destroyer *Maddox* while that ship was on a routine reconnaissance patrol in international waters. Such patrols had taken place before, and the ships had always operated in international waters off the North Vietnamese coast, observing junk traffic and naval activity, and collecting hydrographic data and electronic intelligence.

During the sunny forenoon of 2 August, 28 miles off the coast of North Vietnam, the *Maddox*'s radar detected three contacts closing at approximately 40 knots. At such speeds, they could only be torpedo boats. For two hours, Commander Herbert L. Ogier, the destroyer's Commanding Officer, and his CIC team, with the embarked destroyer division commander, Captain J. J. Herrick, the on-scene commander, watched the approaching boats. Despite the *Maddox*'s evasive action and increased speed, they continued to close her until visual identification became possible. The trio were indeed torpedo boats—82-foot, aluminum-hulled craft of the Soviet-built P-4 class, each armed with two 18-inch torpedoes and capable of 40 knots. There could be no mistaking their hostile intent. Nor, in the clear afternoon skies, could the North Vietnamese mistake the *Maddox* for anything other than a U. S. man-of-war.

The *Maddox* fired three warning shots. When these were ignored, Commander Ogier ordered destructive fire. One North Vietnamese boat was probably hit, but fired two torpedoes, both of which missed.[2] The second boat retired to the north. The third boat, believed hit at least once, passed approximately 1,700 yards astern of the *Maddox*, firing a machine gun. (Only one of the 12.7-millimeter bullets hit. It penetrated the destroyer's Mk-56 director foundation and ricocheted into a ready service locker.) The *Maddox* broke off further pursuit and retired from the area.

Meanwhile, four F-8E aircraft from the *Ticonderoga* (CVA-14) joined the action.

"We had launched at 1415 from 'Tico'," said Commander R. F. Mohrhardt, "on a training mission to conduct a practice coordinated strike in the vicinity of the ship with other CVW-5 aircraft. At time of takeoff we weren't aware that *Maddox* was under attack.

"At approximately 1500, we were vectored north to assist *Maddox*, then about 300 miles north of us. The weather was good, but it took us almost 30 minutes to get to the scene. *Mad-*

dox's air search radar and UHF/DF gear were not working, and she wasn't TACAN equipped, so we had to depend on our own UHF/ADF gear. Some miles out, my wingman picked up *Maddox* on his AI [airborne intercept] radar and a few minutes later we made a visual sighting.

"During our flight north, we switched to *Maddox*'s control and Commodore Herrick gave us a running sitrep on what had happened and was happening. He made it clear that *Maddox* had been attacked, that he was on-scene commander, and that our orders were to take the PTs under attack as soon as possible and destroy them.

"As we approached, I could see *Maddox* headed south at flank speed, and about a mile or so to the north, 3 P-4 boats heading north at high speed, about 30 miles off the coast. They were in a line abreast with one boat trailing slightly. We charged our guns, got into position to attack, and since my section was lowest on fuel, I agreed that my section would attack the trailing PT boat, while the other would work over the lead pair. My wingman and I made our first pass and got off our Zunis. Mine hit in the wake astern and his hit right in front of the PT's bow. As we 'bent it' around to make a strafing pass, I could see that the trailing boat was now dead in the water. Numerous 20-mm. hits were scored on the strafing runs and, as I pulled off, I saw the boat burning and smoking heavily at the stern and the crew throwing gear and smoke lights over the side, probably to mark their position. In my opinion, our attack sank that third P-4."

As the *Maddox* left the area, it was obvious that an unprovoked, premeditated, daylight attack had been made on a U. S. ship on the high seas, an attack which quickly led to direct American intervention.

President Johnson warned North Vietnam the next day that "United States ships have traditionally operated freely on the high seas in accordance with the rights guaranteed by international law. . . . They will continue to do so," he said, "and will take whatever measures are appropriate for their defense." He further warned North Vietnam to be under "no misapprehension as to the grave consequences which would inevitably result from any further unprovoked military action against United States forces."

By presidential order, the Tonkin Gulf patrol was reinforced by a second destroyer, the *Turner Joy* (DD-951). The other carrier in the Western Pacific, the *Constellation* (CVA-64), left Hong Kong, 400-odd nautical miles distant, and, in difficult weather, headed for the Gulf. During daylight hours a combat air patrol from the nearby *Ticonderoga* (Captain D. W. Cooper), with CTF 77, Rear Admiral R. B. Moore, embarked, protected the two destroyers. To reduce the risk of night torpedo boat attacks, the two ships retired each afternoon to a "night steaming area" about 100 miles offshore.

On 3 August the *Maddox*, now accompanied by the *Turner Joy* (Commander R. C. Barnhart), again entered the Gulf of Tonkin with orders to fire only in self defense and with restrictions against immediate pursuit. But there was no response.

On the night of 4 August 1964, however, while the destroyers were proceeding easterly at a speed of about 20 knots, the *Maddox* spotted and tracked at least 5 high-speed radar contacts 36 miles away. The night of 4–5 August was perfect for attack by torpedo craft. There were many low clouds, no moon, and very poor visibility. Because of the high closure rate, and a similarity to the 2 August attack, the "blips" were evaluated as probable torpedo boats. The *Maddox* and the *Turner Joy* changed course and increased speed.

About an hour later, with the ships then 60 miles off the North Vietnamese coast, both held radar contacts 14 miles to the east. To

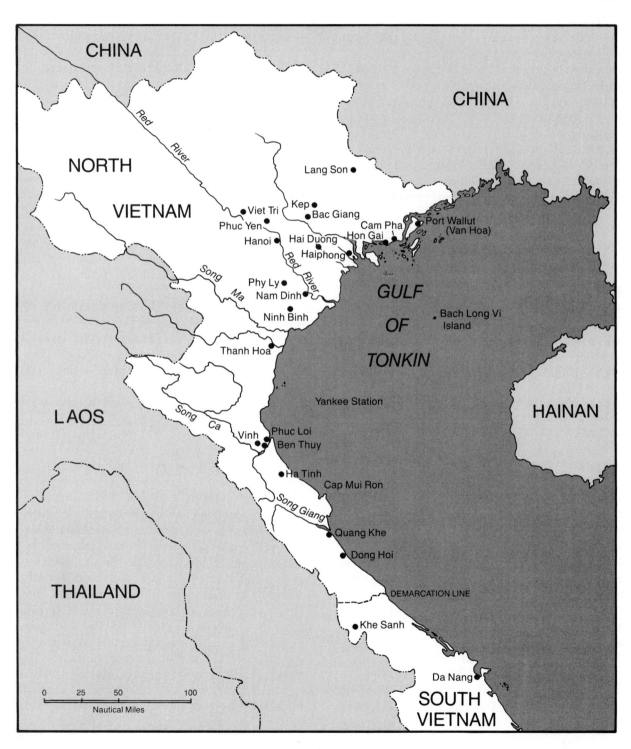

CHINA

NORTH

VIETNAM

Red River

Lang Son

Viet Tri
Kep
Bac Giang
Phuc Yen
Cam Pha
Hon Gai
Port Wallut
(Van Hoa)
Hanoi
Hai Duong
Haiphong
Red River
Phy Ly
Nam Dinh
Ninh Binh

Song Ma

Thanh Hoa

LAOS

Song Ca

Vinh
Phuc Loi
Ben Thuy

Ha Tinh
Cap Mui Ron

Song Giang

Quang Khe

Dong Hoi

THAILAND

DEMARCATION LINE

Khe Sanh

Da Nang

SOUTH
VIETNAM

CHINA

GULF
OF
TONKIN

Bach Long Vi
Island

Yankee Station

HAINAN

0   25   50   100
Nautical Miles

those watching the radar, it soon became evident from the maneuvers of the approaching blips that they were pressing an attack. On Commodore Herrick's command, both destroyers opened fire at a range of 6,000 yards. Torpedo noises were then heard on the *Maddox*'s sonar and this information was immediately passed to her companion. In the nick of time, both ships twisted to avoid the torpedo, and seconds later a wake was sighted passing 300 feet to port of the *Turner Joy*.

One boat, taken under fire by the *Turner Joy*, was hit several times and disappeared from all radars.

Meanwhile, despite the very bad weather, aircraft from CVW-5 on the USS *Ticonderoga*, 120 miles away, were approaching to lend assistance. Two A-1 Skyraiders from VA-52, flown by Commander G. H. Edmondson and Lieutenant J. A. Barton, dropped flares, then made passes at 700 and 1,500 feet altitude, respectively, sighting gun flashes on the surface of the water. During one pass over the two destroyers, both pilots sighted a "snakey" high speed wake one and one-half miles ahead of the *Maddox*.

At midnight, all radar contact was lost and the action ended.

Less than half an hour after the second attack, Admiral U. S. G. Sharp, Jr., Commander-in-Chief, Pacific, recommended immediate punitive air strikes by TF 77 against the North Vietnamese torpedo boat bases. Two hours later, a presidential decision, relayed from Secretary of Defense Robert S. McNamara through the Joint Chiefs of Staff, ordered strikes at first light the following day. The assigned targets were four North Vietnamese torpedo boat bases plus the oil storage facilities at Phuc Loi and Vinh.

Meanwhile the *Constellation* pushed through heavy weather to join the *Ticonderoga*.

It was a frantic day on the two carriers. The JCS "execute" message for Operation "Pierce Arrow," initially ordered an attack at 0700 local time (1900 Washington time). Bombs were loaded, pilots were briefed, and an early morning attack was readied.

At 2340 on 4 August, Washington time (1140 on 5 August in the Gulf of Tonkin) the President announced to the public that the United States was making a measured response to the North Vietnamese aggression:

"My fellow Americans," he said, "as President and Commander in Chief, it is my duty to the American people to report that renewed hostile actions against United States' ships in the high seas in the Gulf of Tonkin have today required me to order the military forces of the United States to take action in reply. . . .

"That reply is now being given, as I speak to you tonight. Air action is now in execution[3] against gun boats and certain supporting facilities in North Vietnam which have been used in these hostile operations. . . .

"Our response for the present will be limited and fitting. . . .

"We Americans know—although others appear to forget—the risk of spreading the conflict. We still seek no wider war . . ."

Commencing at approximately 1230 local time, 64 strike aircraft were launched from the *Ticonderoga* and *Constellation* and were over their targets about 1315.[4] Ten of the *Constellation*'s A-1s, led by Commander H. F. Griffith, plus two F-4s and 8 A-4s from the same ship, struck PT boat bases at the northernmost target, at Hon Gai. Further south, 5 other "Connie" A-4s, 3 F-4s, and 4 A-1s struck the PT boat bases at Loc Chao. Six F-8s from the "Tico" led by Commander Mohrhardt (VF-53) hit the PT boats at Quang Khe, and 26 other Tico aircraft attacked the two oil-storage dumps at Vinh. This attack, led by Commander Wesley L. McDonald (Commanding Officer, VA-56), and Commander W. E. Carman (Commanding Officer, VF-53), was over in minutes.[5] Smoke from the 10 Vinh petroleum storage tanks rose to 14,000 feet and damage was estimated at 90%. Eight gunboats and torpedo boats were destroyed and 21 damaged. Thus, the North Vietnamese Navy paid a high price for the ineffective efforts of their torpedo craft. Significantly, U. S. retaliation had come from the sea, where American power was all powerful and unhampered by the need to coordinate the response with foreign states.

But the retaliation was not without cost. Two of the *Constellation*'s aircraft were lost to AAA fire at Hon Gai. Lieutenant (j.g.) Richard Sather, flying a VA-145 Skyraider, was shot down and killed over Loc Chao; Lieutenant (j.g.) Everett Alvarez, flying an A-4C, was shot down over Hon Gai and became the first U. S. pilot to be captured by the North Vietnamese. At this writing he remains a prisoner. Two other "Connie" aircraft were hit but were recovered safely.

Six days later, on 10 August 1964, Congress passed a joint resolution—later to be called the Gulf of Tonkin resolution—that termed the attacks on the destroyers a part of a "deliberate and systematic campaign of aggression that the Communist regime in North Vietnam had been waging against its neighbors and the nations joined with them." The resolution approved the nation's determination to "take all necessary measures to repel any armed attack . . ." and to prevent any further aggression until the President determined that "peace and security of the area is reasonably assured."

"For the next six months (until the retaliatory strikes beginning 7 February 1965)," said Rear Admiral H. L. Miller, CTF 77, "the operations of Task Force 77 consisted of standing by for retaliatory strikes over North Vietnam with various bomb loads and missiles. Photographic flights were made over South Vietnam and Laos watching for buildups of Viet Cong and the infiltration of North Vietnamese along the Ho Chi Minh trail. Strikes by small groups of carrier aircraft were made on trucks and material storage areas in South Vietnam whenever they were found."

The Start of Naval Air Interdiction (1965)

The attacks just described were punitive. The routine bombing of North Vietnam by TF 77 aircraft did not begin until 7 February 1965. The original nickname, Flaming Dart, was given to a plan for retaliatory air strikes if overt acts of Viet Cong aggression against American forces in South Vietnam continued. Such attacks (for example, a Christmas Eve attack on a hotel used as an officers' quarters in downtown Saigon) did continue.

On 7 February, the Viet Cong launched a heavy mortar attack on United States forces and billets at the Pleiku Airbase and nearby Camp Holloway. Eight Americans were killed and 109 were wounded.

Following this attack, TF 77 was alerted and Flaming Dart was readied for execution. Rear Admiral Miller, embarked in the *Ranger* (CVA-61), received orders at 0621 on 7 February 1965 to assemble TF77 and to prepare for retaliatory strikes on North Vietnam. Two other carriers, the *Coral Sea* (CVA-43) and the *Hancock* (CVA-19), then en route to Cubi Point in the Philippines, reversed course and joined the *Ranger* in the early afternoon. The pace was intense aboard the three ships as magazines were opened, pilots were briefed, and bomb racks loaded. Commander Warren H. Sells, Commander Carrier Air Wing 21, aboard the *Hancock*, would be airborne coordinator for the strike.

At 1240, orders to attack were received. Despite very poor weather over the targets, the *Coral Sea* and *Hancock* catapulted off 20 and 29 aircraft, respectively, for strikes against the North Vietnamese army barracks and port facilities at Dong Hoi, just north of the Demilitarized Zone (DMZ). TF 77 was in action in less than nine hours after the first alerting message.

Simultaneously, the *Ranger* launched a 34-plane strike against the Vit Thu Lu barracks, 15 miles inland and 5 miles north of the Demilitarized Zone, but the northeast monsoon prevented her attacks, as well as others by the U. S. Air Force and the South Vietnamese Air Force, from being carried out.

"At this stage of the war," said Rear Admiral Miller, "attack groups were assigned a specific target, as in this case for *Ranger*. If that target was closed at the time of attack, there was no recourse but to drop the ordnance in the water."

At Dong Hoi, ten buildings were destroyed, two others heavily damaged, and an undetermined number left burning by aircraft from the *Coral Sea* and the *Hancock*. One A-4E from the *Coral Sea* was lost, three others were damaged, and five of the *Hancock*'s aircraft were also damaged. The downed Skyhawk, flown by Lieutenant Edward A. Dickson of VA-155, was hit in the port wing. Lieutenant Dickson, however, gallantly pressed home his attack and dropped his ordnance before turning toward the safety of the sea. He was seen to eject above a cloud bank one to two miles off the coast but, despite a 48-hour search, he was not found.

The enemy's response was not long in coming. On 10 February the enemy blew up a United States enlisted men's billet at Qui Nhon, killing 23 men and wounding 21 others. Again, Admiral Sharp recommended prompt and emphatic retaliation.

Flaming Dart Two began on 11 February. The *Coral Sea*, *Hancock*, and *Ranger* were ordered to strike the Chanh Hoa barracks. The selected times-over-target (0900 for CVW-9, 0915 for CVW-21 and 0930 for CVW-15) were chosen at the Washington level in order to

coincide with a statement made by President Johnson in Washington announcing the retaliation. Tactically, the choice of time was poor, for in February, the "crachin" fog, rain, and low visibility characteristic of the northeast monsoon would almost certainly be present in the early morning.

Ninety-nine aircraft were launched by the three carriers. The predictably bad weather was present, with clouds as low as 500 feet and visibility less than a mile, and it gave the pilots trouble. The knowledge that the weather would be bad determined the choice of weapons. In this case "Snakeye," a retarded bomb, had to be used in order to provide bomb-blast escape distances. Moreover, the precise numbers of attacking and support aircraft, and the number, types, and fuzing of weapons were specified by Washington. The use of napalm was forbidden. The *Ranger*, *Coral Sea*, and *Hancock* made their attacks in scud clouds at 500 feet, with a cloud layer at 1,000 feet and the visibility less than a mile. Three aircraft from the *Coral Sea* were lost and several others were hit by antiaircraft artillery.[6] Two of the three pilots were recovered, but the third was captured when his F-8D was crippled by ground fire. The accuracy and vigor of North Vietnamese antiaircraft defense response was clearly evident.

It was evident, too, that such tight tactical restrictions on bombing, together with tactical operational decisions made at long distance for political purposes, would not achieve the desired result. This type of tit-for-tat response was not likely to deter the Communists from further attacks inside South Vietnam. Indeed, it did not. The Viet Cong continued and increased their hit-and-run attacks on U. S. forces and bases. On 30 March, for example, they bombed the U. S. Embassy in Saigon.

As Viet Cong pressure mounted in South Vietnam, Washington deemed it appropriate to provide more and better protection for U. S. installations ashore. Accordingly, on 8–10 March 1965, Marines from the Seventh Fleet were landed at Da Nang. CTF 77 provided combat air patrol and photographic coverage for this landing.

President Johnson's speech at Baltimore on 7 April 1965 put American objectives in Southeast Asia in an eloquent frame for the long campaign which was about to open:

"Our objective is the independence of South Vietnam and its freedom from attack. . . . We will do everything necessary to reach that objective, and we will do only what is absolutely necessary.

"We will not be defeated.

"We will not grow tired.

"We will not withdraw, either openly or under the cloak of a meaningless agreement.

". . . And we remain ready . . . for unconditional discussion."

Early Rolling Thunder Raids

The bombing of North Vietnam, no longer limited to punitive raids, now began under a new notion (at this stage of the war it could not yet be called a concept) called Rolling Thunder and, like thunder, it was to be spasmodic. In the beginning the general thinking was to draw a bombing line somewhere across the southern part of North Vietnam and move the line northward very slowly. As the line neared Hanoi, it was believed that the North Vietnamese would capitulate to save their capital. As we shall see, however, this scheme was never followed. As the months rolled by and the war drew nearer to Hanoi, a sanctuary zone was placed around both Hanoi and Haiphong. Strikes in these sanctuaries were permitted only on special occasions.

Rolling Thunder operations were always conducted under strict controls and with specific guidance from the highest levels of government—targeting by remote control. As on the previous occasions, commanders were told on which day to strike; in many cases they were told the hour of attack (which ignored weather conditions). They were told by Washington the number of sorties by task and by target; the type, number, and fuzing of weapons to be used; and, sometimes, even the direction of attack. Attacks were limited to primary targets or one of two alternates. Unexpended ordnance had to be dumped into the South China Sea. Pre-strike reconnaissance was not permitted. Bomb damage assessment (photographic) aircraft were to accompany strike aircraft or follow them immediately; subsequent bomb damage assessment was to be conducted by these aircraft, unescorted, flying at medium altitudes only. No aircraft was to be re-loaded and returned for a second attack. If the target weather was bad on the approved day, the mission could not be rescheduled without repeating the elaborate process of gaining approval from Washington. Enemy aircraft had to be positively identified before shooting, a tough requirement for aircraft flying at Mach 1. Rules were so stringent that only military trucks could be hit, and these had to be moving on highways, not parked in villages. (Later this rule was relaxed to allow trucks within 100 meters, and later still, within 300 meters, of the roads to be attacked, but never in the village sanctuaries.) No one explained to the pilots how to distinguish a *military* truck from a *nonmilitary* one.

To facilitate the initial Rolling Thunder coordination between the U. S. Air Force and the Seventh Fleet, target times were assigned to each. But this was difficult to coordinate and soon this system was replaced by the division of North Vietnam into geographical areas known as "route packages." By this system, interference between TF 77 and the Seventh Air Force was lessened and, in addition, it became possible to assign responsibility to each Service for target development, intelligence data collection, and target analysis in its own areas.

A geographic point in the Gulf of Tonkin was selected as the locus of operations for TF 77 and was given the code name, Yankee Station.[7]

As the air campaign progressed, Admiral Sharp reminded his operational commanders and pilots that Rolling Thunder was unusual. "It does not seek to inflict maximum damage on the enemy," he said. "Instead, it is a precise application of military pressure for the specific purpose of halting aggression in South Vietnam."

Task Force 77 pitched in with vigor to carry out the orders. On 18 March 1965, aircraft from the *Coral Sea* and the *Hancock* hit supply buildings at Phu Van and Vinh Son army supply depots. Several aircraft sustained light damage from antiaircraft artillery, but none was lost.

Eight days later, on 26 March, 70 aircraft from the same two carriers struck four North Vietnamese radar sites at Vinh Son, Cap Mui Ron, Ha Tinh, and Bach Long Vi Island, causing heavy damage. Both pilots were safely recovered from an A-4 and an F-8 which were hit.

On 29 March, the two carriers again launched 70 aircraft. This time they struck radar and communication facilities on Bach Long Vi, a small island strategically located in the Gulf of Tonkin. Weather and visibility were poor, with a ragged 5,000-foot ceiling. Four of the first six aircraft over the target—three of them squadron commanders—were hit and three of them shot down. Commander Jack H. Harris, Commanding Officer of VA-155, had a flameout and ejected into the sea, but was rescued. Commander W. N. Donnelly, Commanding Officer of VF-154, was also hit and landed in the water four miles north of the island. The low altitude, upsidedown ejection at 400 knots dislocated his shoulder and fractured a neck vertebra. (He spent 45 hours in a raft before being rescued by an Air Force HU-16 Albatross.

Twice during the first night, Commander Donnelly crawled painfully under his life raft when an unidentified destroyer-type vessel without flag or running lights passed as near as 300 yards to him.) Lieutenant Commander Kenneth E. Hume, also from VF-154, was killed during a run on the target. The fourth, Commander Peter Mongilardi, Commanding Officer of VA-153, took a hit in his wing and was "towed" home by a tanker aircraft, pumping fuel overboard as fast as the tanker could give it to him. However, he was recovered aboard the *Coral Sea* safely.

At 1600, 31 March, 60 aircraft from the *Coral Sea* and the *Hancock* again hit radar installations at Cap Mui Ron, 78 nautical miles northwest of the DMZ.

In the closest attack yet to Hanoi, on 3 April, the two carriers conducted two strikes—one in the morning, one in the afternoon, hitting and wrecking a bridge at Dong Phuong Thong, 70 miles south of the enemy capital, with 60 tons of ordnance. The attacks were led by the two air wing commanders, Commander H. P. Glindeman, Jr., and Commander W. H. Sells.

As a result of this early interdiction effort, the countermoves of the North Vietnamese soon became apparent. Instead of moving by companies, battalions, or regiments, the enemy soldiers traveled in small units along what formerly were little-used roads and trails hidden beneath the heavy jungle foliage. Collectively these are called the Ho Chi Minh trail. New parallel land routes for trucks were opened and trucks were imported from Communist countries to use on the growing road system to replace trains. The new transportation network was complete with many supply dumps, rest camps, truck depots, and repair facilities along the way. Trucks moved war materials largely at night. Because our rules forbade attacks on villages, the enemy began to park trucks in the villages during daylight where they could not be attacked. Bomb damage was quickly repaired—a bomb crater in an hour, a bridge in a day. Camouflage was employed extensively and new construction put factories, oil lines, and supply dumps underground or in caves. Inland waterways and canals were also used, as were thousands of bicycles for shuttling supplies southward.

Establishment of Dixie Station

In April 1965, Task Force 77 pilots drew still another role—a role which for the nth time reflected their value—flying regular close support missions against the Viet Cong in South Vietnam. The initial effort by aircraft from the *Midway* and the *Coral Sea*, plus Marine F-8Es from VMF-212 flying from the *Oriskany* with CVW-16, was so successful that General Westmoreland requested the permanent assignment of a carrier stationed off the northern half of South Vietnam to support his ground forces. Since land bases for tactical air were not available and could not be produced quickly enough, CinCPacFlt directed on 16 May the establishment of Dixie Station, about 100 miles southeast of Cam Ranh Bay. This assignment would last for 15 months until land-based aviation had been established sufficiently so as to be able to handle the bombing load within South Vietnam.

But this new assignment meant that three of the four deployed carriers, one ship at Dixie Station and two at Yankee Station, had to spend a grueling and unacceptable 80% of their time at sea, with precious little time for rest and maintenance.[8] On 5 June, therefore, the deployment of five carriers to the Western Pacific was begun. (Even so, for the remainder of the war, the deployed carriers averaged 75% of their time at sea.)

The Growth of the Enemy's Defenses

In the fall of 1964, the air defense system of North Vietnam was weak. As the war became hotter, however, a dramatic and ominous buildup was observed in all four parts of North Vietnam's air defense system—radar networks, surface-to-air missile (SAM) defenses, MiG fighter aircraft, and automatic antiaircraft (AAA) guns.

On 5 April 1965, photography revealed the first North Vietnamese surface-to-air missile site under construction, some 15 miles southeast of Hanoi. The pictures came from the cameras of an RF-8 Crusader from the *Coral Sea* on an early reconnaissance mission. The wet prints were rushed to Rear Admiral Edward C. Outlaw, who had relieved Admiral Miller as CTF 77.

Said Admiral Outlaw: "It was the first confirmation of the enemy missile buildup, which we had expected for some time. I immediately flew to Saigon to show the pictures to Major General J. H. Moore, Commanding General, Seventh Air Force, and his staff.*

The second SAM-occupied site appeared about a month later and, by mid-July 1965, several more sites were photographed in various stages of construction, forming an irregu-

*EDITOR'S NOTE: Writing in the *New York Times* for 8 April 1971, Admiral Outlaw reported that "In the spring of 1965 a photographic reconnaissance plane returned to the flagship with photos which were immediately identified as a surface-to-air missile site. This was the first clear proof that SAM sites were under construction. That same day the planning members of my staff and I flew to Saigon to confer with the Commander, 7th Air Force, and to plan a joint Air Force/Navy strike against this first site, which was not yet completed. The joint plan was proposed through the chain of command and, after what seemed an inordinate delay, the proposal was returned disapproved.

"Such a refusal was beyond my comprehension. It was feasible to have destroyed this site and all others still under construction which were ultimately completed. It was not until the North Vietnamese had shot down some numbers of our aircraft that our combined air forces were permitted to strike back at these, now well-established, defensive sites. Since then approximately 115 of our planes have been destroyed by surface-to-air missiles launched from pads which I believe could have been destroyed at a minimum risk before they became operational."

In the same article, the Admiral wrote that "we were restrained to carrying out a campaign which seemed designed *not* to win."

lar ring around Hanoi and Haiphong. But still the authority to attack them could not be obtained.

The hesitation in Washington was partly due, of course, to a fear that if the missile sites were attacked, Russian technicians might be killed. Others insisted that the SAM batteries were defensive only; that if American aircraft did not attack Hanoi and Haiphong, the enemy would not fire at them. Still others feared that such attacks might be regarded as U. S. escalation.

Permission to attack the missile sites did not come for many weeks, until after a SAM had destroyed an Air Force F-4C on 24 July, by which time numerous sites were under construction. Three days later the Air Force was authorized to hit two SAM sites northwest of Hanoi in retaliation. The attacks were to be made on one day only, and the pilots were specifically forbidden to attack any air base from which enemy MiGs might oppose the mission.

Fifty-five Air Force aircraft attacked the SAM sites and the guns protecting them; the price paid was four aircraft lost. Another strike was ordered by Washington, and while photography taken on 8 August showed the mobile SAMs still in place at the two sites, the strike group found the sites empty the following day. It was an early and convincing demonstration of the mobility of the Soviet SA-2 missiles, and a preview of how the enemy would move his weapons in the months ahead.

The use of missiles by Hanoi led to the establishment on 12 August 1965 of Operation Iron Hand,[9] an anti-SAM campaign using the Navy-developed Shrike missile, which could identify and home on a SAM battery's guidance radar.

On the night of 11–12 August, in fact, the Navy lost its first aircraft to SAMs. Two A-4Es, from VA-23, flying off the *Midway*, were at 9,000 feet, on a road recce mission 60 miles south of Hanoi. The flight leader, Lieutenant

Commander D. Roberge, and his wingman, Lieutenant (j.g.) Donald H. Brown, Jr., observed what appeared to be two flares glowing eerily beneath the clouds 15 miles north of their position. They watched what appeared to be two "hunting" spots of light come out of the clouds and move closer and closer. In sudden recognition of danger, both pilots pushed over and added full power. It was too late. Seconds later the SAMs exploded, destroying Lieutenant (j.g.) Brown's aircraft and damaging Lieutenant Commander Roberge's. Although his plane was on fire, the latter managed to limp back and land aboard the *Midway*, his Skyhawk's belly scorched, wrinkled, and peppered with more than 50 holes.

A new era of warfare for naval aviation had begun.

Task Force 77 reacted promptly in an effort to find and destroy the enemy missile batteries. As directed, on 12 and 13 August, 76 missions searched at low levels for the sites. Five planes and two pilots were lost to AAA, and seven other planes were damaged, but no SAMs were found. It was truly a black Friday the 13th for TF 77.

It was also a disillusioning experience and a foretaste of increased difficulties. First, it was a problem to find the highly mobile SAMs, which could pack up and move by truck and van in three hours. Whenever overflown, the SAM batteries always moved immediately, so that the next flight would find the site empty.[10] Second, the very existence of missiles forced a change in bombing tactics and results. Hereafter, the pilots must either release at higher altitudes than before (5,000 to 6,000 feet), which meant greater miss distances, or at very low altitudes, which meant exposure to the increasingly accurate, visually controlled guns and heavy small arms fire.

It was not until the morning of 17 October 1965, in fact, that an Iron Hand flight of four A-4Es, led by an A-6 Intruder from the *Inde-*

pendence's CVW-7 (flown by Lieutenant Commander Cecil E. "Pete" Garber, VA-75), destroyed the first occupied and operational SAM site, one near Kep airfield 52 miles northeast of Hanoi. Commander H. B. Southworth, Commanding Officer, VA-72, leading the Skyhawks, saw three separate fires among the radar vans, ten vehicles burning, and one SA-2 missile broken and burning, while a second snaked over the ground burning itself out.

"After so many weeks of disappointment," said Rear Admiral James R. Reedy, who had taken over recently as CTF 77, "it was heartening news, and a reward for persistence in sending an Iron Hand group with each big strike since September 20."

The second element of the North Vietnamese air defense system was also mushrooming—the automatic antiaircraft weapons and antiaircraft artillery. As the SA-2 missiles forced our aircraft to fly at lower levels, these AAA weapons became increasingly effective.

In 1965, North Vietnam was also rapidly building early warning and height-finding radar sites. A ground-controlled intercept (GCI) capability was established in both the northern and southern portions of the country, which also covered the Gulf of Tonkin.

As SAM defenses were increased and perfected, so was North Vietnam's aircraft inventory. Late in May 1965, some Il-28 jet light bombers were identified at Phuc Yen airfield. By mid-June, the number of MiG-15 and MiG-17 fighter aircraft had climbed to almost 70. At Phuc Yen, the presence of unpacked crates indicated that there were more aircraft awaiting assembly. And by the end of 1965, North Vietnam was operating 75 MiGs and the eight Il-28 light bombers. Repeated but fruitless recommendations to attack these aircraft and the main North Vietnamese airfields were made.

Naval air's first MiG kills came in June 1965—the first on 17 June when F-4s from the

Midway's VF-21, flown by Commander Louis C. Page and his radar intercept officer (RIO), Lieutenant John C. Smith, and Lieutenant Jack E. D. Batson and his RIO, downed two MiGs 50 miles south of Hanoi. At 1026, while headed northeast, Commander Page picked up bogies on his radar miles ahead. The two Phantoms and four MiGs approached each other head-on at a 1,000-knot closure speed—a mile every three and one-half seconds. The F-4s were ready to fire their long-range Sparrows. Commander Page finally spotted the characteristic huge nose intakes, mid-wings and prominent bubble canopies of the silver MiG-17 "Frescoes" and pickled off his missile at the second of the four MiGs, which were flying in a ragged single file. Lieutenant Batson fired at the third—and both MiGs burned in puffs of orange flame and black smoke.

On 20 June, the third MiG was bagged—this time by propeller-driven A-1 "Skyraiders." The flight of four "Spads," led by Lieutenant Commander E. A. Greathouse from VA-125, also aboard the *Midway*, were on a rescue combat air patrol (ResCAP) mission when jumped by two MiG-17s. Maintaining tight air discipline, the Skyraiders dove for the deck and "scissored" defensively just above the treetops. In a series of turns and reverses, during a dogfight which lasted five minutes, the four prop pilots succeeded in out-turning and out-maneuvering the MiGs. Two of them, Lieutenant Clinton B. Johnson and Lieutenant (j.g.) Charles W. Hartman, finally got a tail-on shot—and watched one MiG go down under their chattering 20-mm. guns. (Back at Yankee Station all ears in every ready room and CIC were glued to the Tactical Air Control net listening to the four Spad pilots' account of their unusual but successful air encounter.)

These were the kind of victories that made naval aviators' spirits and morale soar. On board the *Midway* for a routine visit, the

Secretary of the Navy, Paul Nitze, made the victory announcement of the first kill to the ship's crew.

1965 Results

The Rolling Thunder air operations expenditure in 1965 would grow eightfold in 1966, as more lucrative targets were authorized. Ten different attack carriers had participated in operations at Yankee Station. Eight hundred trucks and 650 pieces of railroad rolling stock had been damaged or destroyed. The Navy had flown more than 30,993 combat and combat-support sorties over North Vietnam and 25,895 more over South Vietnam. Over one hundred Navy aircraft were lost, and 82 crewmen had been killed, captured, or reported missing. Forty-six others had been rescued after the loss of their aircraft. Attacks had largely been concentrated on military barracks, rails, roads and bridges, but not on the really worthwhile targets.

These first 11 months of combat of 1965 revealed the development of the strategy of gradualism—applying military pressure in small doses—a strategy that was to continue for 26 more months, interspersed with other self-imposed bombing pauses, self-inflicted restrictions, and self-designated sanctuaries. This strategy assumed that our direct military involvement in South Vietnam, and our selective use of our overwhelming airpower against North Vietnam, would force the North Vietnamese to the peace table. By applying gradual military pressure, we believed we could "get the signal through to Hanoi," to use a favorite State Department term, to convince North Vietnam to stop attacking its neighbor, and in so doing, we would not risk escalating the conflict.

The year 1965 saw another result which would become a way of life for the entire war—the tendency to measure effort and accom-

plishment by the number of sorties flown. "We tried to counter this unfortunate tendency," said Admiral Roy L. Johnson, then Commander Seventh Fleet, "by emphasizing quality of effort based on the best possible BDA [bomb damage assessment]. Admittedly, BDA was often difficult to obtain. But we recognized that Secretary McNamara had to have some way of measuring effort, and in particular, for controlling the air effort. Controlling and limiting the number of missions was his method."

During 1965, several significant developments had occurred in TF 77. In June the *Independence* (CVA-62), an Atlantic Fleet carrier, had arrived at Yankee Station, bringing a squadron of the new A-6A Grumman Intruder aircraft, the world's first truly all-weather tactical bomber with its sophisticated computerized electronic system. In November, the *Kitty Hawk* (CVA-63) arrived with her new Naval Tactical Data System and with the twin turboprop E-2A Hawkeye early-warning aircraft aboard. This computerized defense system was designed to provide greatly improved surveillance and automatic tracking and aircraft interception. And on 2 December, with Rear Admiral Henry Miller back in command of TF 77, the eight nuclear reactors of the *Enterprise* (CVAN-65) drove her smartly onto Yankee Station. In escort position off her bow steamed the nuclear-powered *Bainbridge* (DLGN-25). The long history of war at sea had entered a new era with nuclear warships in action for the first time.

One of the final 1965 strikes against North Vietnam was to be a big one, and the next to the last for almost seven weeks. On 22 December, the *Enterprise, Kitty Hawk*, and *Ticonderoga* launched more than 100 planes in a combined strike against the Uong Bi thermal power plant, 15 miles north-northeast of Haiphong, the first industrial target authorized by the

An F-8 Crusader from the Oriskany *zooms past a V.C. position still smoking from direct hits by 2.75-inch rockets. The Crusader attacked the V.C. emplacement about 10 miles SW of Hue, South Vietnam, on 12 November 1965. An excellent fighter, the single-place F-8 was far from an ideal attack plane.*

JCS. The three carriers' aircraft were assigned times to be over target which were 30 minutes apart, beginning at 1500.

The attacks by the *Enterprise* came in from the north, while the *Kitty Hawk*'s and *Ticonderoga*'s aircraft approached from the south. Flak was heavy, especially at 3,000 feet, and

two A-4s from the *Enterprise* were lost to ground fire. But the attack caused severe damage to the boiler house, and the pilots saw smoke pouring from both ends of the generator hall, observed the fuel-oil supply burning, and saw the administration building collapse. The petroleum storage area was engulfed in flames, the coal treatment center demolished, and the twelve storage buildings were struck. Uong Bi would supply little electrical power to the Hanoi-Haiphong electrical power network for many weeks.

The year ended with a U. S. suspension of the bombing commencing Christmas Day which, Secretary of State Rusk said, could lead to peace negotiations if the enemy would show constraint.

A memorable year thus ended for TF 77. New methods of visual bombing at night had been developed. New eras of electronic and missile warfare had begun. Supersonic fighter and reconnaissance jet aircraft had seen action for the first time. A true, effective all-weather tactical attack aircraft (the A-6) had arrived. And nuclear power ships had seen combat.

1966

As 1966 opened, and during the 37-day bombing standdown which followed, a massive attempt was made to bring Hanoi to the peace table.[11] The United States stated that it would welcome a conference on Southeast Asia—or any part of it. We said again that we wanted no U. S. bases in Southeast Asia, and that we did not desire to retain troops in South Vietnam after peace was assured. If the countries of Southeast Asia wanted to be nonaligned or neutral, we wouldn't object. If the North Vietnamese would agree to peace, we would be prepared to contribute $1 billion to the economic reconstruction of Southeast Asia. We told Hanoi we would allow the Viet Cong to be represented at the peace table and to express their views if Hanoi would cease its aggression. And, repeatedly, we said we would stop the bombing of North Vietnam if there were reciprocation.

Hanoi, however, stood fast, spurned every peace effort, and responded to the U. S. presentation before the United Nations by saying that any resolutions made by that body would be considered null and void. Also, the United States was being bombarded from all sides not to resume the bombing—from the U.N., from allies in Europe, and from doves at home. Hanoi applauded every such effort.

Indeed, while the various peace initiatives were being pushed, Hanoi was taking maximum advantage of the bombing pause in anticipation of the resumption of bombing. Photographic reconnaissance during the pause showed the enemy reconstructing and improving his roads and bridges, improving and increasing the air defense of important areas, digging his POL system underground and into caves, dispersing his military support base, and pushing large numbers of loaded trucks toward the DMZ and the infiltration routes which fed the Ho Chi Minh trail. As many as 40 additional antiaircraft gun positions were photographed near the northwest rail line between Hanoi and Communist China, and an increase of over 25 big guns below Vinh was noted. Altogether, the enemy had used the standdown to add a total of almost 20 early warning and fire control radars, many SAM sites, and some 400 antiaircraft emplacements to his defense network.

During the standdown, Admiral Sharp told the JCS that if the bombing effort was to succeed, North Vietnam must be denied access to external assistance from Russia, Communist China, and other Bloc nations, whether by sea or by rail. Military supplies already stockpiled in North Vietnam had to be destroyed, he said. All known military material and facilities should be destroyed and military activities and movements should be continuously ha-

rassed and disrupted. All this, he said, would require air bombing operations quite different from those in 1965.

"It was obvious," said Admiral Sharp, "that our air operations in 1965 had not achieved their goal and that the nature of the war had changed since the air campaign began. We had not forced Hanoi to the peace table. We had not scared Hanoi out of the war. We had not caused any diminution whatsoever of his carrying the war into South Vietnam. In fact, the reverse was true. It was evident to me that Ho Chi Minh intended to continue to support the Viet Cong until he was denied the capability to do so.

"I felt that a properly oriented bombing effort could either bring the enemy to the conference table or cause the insurgency to wither from lack of support. The alternative would be a long and costly war—costly in lives and material resources—a long war which even in early 1966 was already becoming distasteful to some Americans."

Rolling Thunder Operations Resumed

When Rolling Thunder operations were resumed on 31 January, however, the same pattern as before Christmas was followed, not the revised strategy recommended by CinCPac. Targets were still largely limited to the southern portion of North Vietnam. The airfields, the MiGs, the closure of Haiphong, the industrial targets in the northeast, the electrical and petroleum targets, all remained off limits. However, the objective of Rolling Thunder was slowly shifting (perhaps not consciously) from punishment to interdiction in order to shut off the supply of men and materials to South Vietnam, which should induce Hanoi to seek a political settlement at the peace table.

Largely unappreciated, as the interdiction effort unfolded, were the restrictions of the monsoon weather, which caused a high percentage of sortie cancellations or diversions and greatly limited the information obtained from bomb damage photography. At the decision levels in Washington, it was not appreciated that at night and during the bad weather periods of the northeast monsoon, the enemy would always be able to move his war supplies.

The buildup of SAM missiles, radars, MiGs, and AAA guns began to take an increasingly heavy toll of American aircraft, with AAA guns taking the most. Six aircraft and five crewmen were lost in January 1966 (two over South Vietnam, one over North Vietnam, and three at sea) and ten aircraft and ten air crewmen in February. From time to time, the flurries of SAMs damaged or downed an airplane. On 9 February, an A-4C from the *Ticonderoga* was damaged 20 miles southwest of Thanh Hoa, but the pilot, Commander Jack L. Snyder, the air wing commander of CVW-5, managed to get over the Gulf before ejecting, to be picked up by the USS *England* (DLG-22). Pilots described the SAMs as looking like telephone poles, slightly tapered at the nose, and trailed by a bright orange flame.

At first, the best defense against the Soviet supplied SA-2 missiles (which were now arriving in North Vietnam in abundance) was to fly below their envelope. However, such low-altitude flight required more fuel and placed the aircraft within the kill envelope of small arms, automatic weapons, and light antiaircraft artillery.

An early set of rules for defending against SAMs was developed by Air Wing 21 aboard the *Hancock* (CVA-19), of which perhaps the most important was that pilots should not operate at mid- or high altitudes in a SAM environment.

It was the beginning of a new style of aerial combat.

Early in 1966 shortages began to appear— ammunition, rockets and bombs, personal survival radios, F-4 aircraft, and pilots. Walter Cronkite, of CBS news, stated that the Navy was short of attack pilots, and this touched off a Department of Defense investigation. The investigation showed that while a few pilots might be flying as many as 28 missions per month over North Vietnam, the average was between 16 and 22. But the investigation did establish some "exposure" limits. The Chief of Naval Operations stated that no naval aviator would fly more than two complete combat deployments over a 14-month period. A pilot having 12 months of exposure would not commence a deployment, while a pilot with less than 12 months would start a deployment, but be ordered out of the combat area when his 14th month was completed.[12]

To keep the cockpits manned, however, the pilot-training output was raised, though that took 18 months to become effective. More immediately, many shore billets and staff aviator jobs were eliminated in order to put more pilots into cockpits, the input of pilots into postgraduate school was minimized, and the pilot-to-seat ratio was held at 1.4 rather than the recommended 1.7. (For example, 20 pilots in a 14-plane A-4 squadron rather than the desired 24.) By such actions, the analysts "solved" the pilot shortage problem.

In like manner were ammunition shortages solved. For example, if the number of bomb "bodies" was sufficient, then the systems analysts stated that no shortage existed even though there might be only enough bomb "tails" for two-thirds of the bodies. The leftover stockpiles of World War II "fat" bombs, although not ideal for jet aircraft, proved to be adequate, but these supplies dwindled steadily as the bombing effort increased. Production of all types of ammunition had been stepped up, but it had not yet met the demand. The Pacific command listed various ordnance items as critical and established a control and rationing system over many types of bombs and over assorted rockets, flares, and warheads.

March weather was slightly better than

February's, with an occasional day of good visibility throughout the Rolling Thunder area. More often, however, pilots found an almost 100% cloud cover with cloud bases below 1,500 feet. This caused a high rate of sortie cancellations, especially over North Vietnam where the monsoon weather was still in full swing. Even so, the rate of damage to fleeting targets in the Rolling Thunder area improved significantly.

Pilots from TF 77 flew 6,500 sorties in March in North and South Vietnam. Eleven aircraft were lost, with ten air crewmen lost or missing.

April was to be TF 77's worst month yet—21 aircraft lost with 15 air crewmen. Much of the carriers' effort was in the Vinh-Ben Thuy complex because of poorer weather farther north. However, for the first time since the Christmas bombing pause, the Northeast quadrant could be hit when weather permitted.

On 18 April, as the northeast monsoon eased off, TF 77 got a chance to hit an important industrial target for the second time—the Uong Bi thermal power plant near Haiphong. The plant supplied one-third of Hanoi's power and nearly all of Haiphong's. Since the first attack by TF 77 on 22 December, extensive repairs had been made to the plant, and it was time for another visit.

Just before midnight, two A-6As from the *Kitty Hawk*, flown by Commander Ronald J. Hays and Lieutenant John T. Been, and Lieutenant Eric M. Roemish and his RIO, all of VA-85, executed an imaginative low-level radar attack. Each of the A-6s carried 13 1,000-pound bombs.

The approach to the target was one which would both optimize the radar return from the power plant and avoid much of the enemy defenses.

Commander Hays and Lieutenant Roemish were launched near midnight. The two A-6s joined up, updated their navigation systems, verified the operation of their weapon systems, and set course to the target. The attack plan called for remaining below the enemy's radar envelope as long as possible from Yankee Station to landfall.

The landfall was made exactly as planned and the two aircraft then took lateral separation. Each pilot acquired the target separately and made his own run. Both aircraft were on and off the target within seconds of one another. The 26 one-thousand-pound bombs hit the power plant. The success of the mission was readily apparent as huge secondary explosions occurred and showers of flashes from the resulting electrical shorts could be seen. It was not until after the crews released their bombs that the enemy started firing, lighting the night sky and filling the air with flak. The attack was not only a complete success but also a complete surprise.[13] Subsequent photographs showed all 26 bombs had impacted inside the perimeter fence of the power plant. In fact, one or two bombs had hit the 250-foot-high smoke stack and leveled it.

The next day, three previously restricted targets at Cam Pha—only 35 miles from the Red China border—were hit by the *Kitty Hawk*—the railroad yards, the water pumping station, and a coal treatment plant. Some 50 tons of ordnance were delivered by 24 aircraft in three surprise raids. There were many hits on the web of railroad tracks, the large repair building, the coal treatment plant, and the approaches to the coal loading piers: the largest building in the area disintegrated with a large secondary explosion. A score of fires was started and smoke and debris soared above 2,000 feet. Flak suppression F-4 Phantoms quickly silenced most enemy opposition and there were no aircraft losses.

However, this strike on Cam Pha, a small and insignificant harbor, stirred up a hornet's nest in Washington.

"We had launched the strike against Cam

Pha within 90 minutes after its appearance on the target list," said Rear Admiral J. R. Reedy, once again Commander TF 77, "for it was a key target we had repeatedly asked to hit, and always before, the answer had been no.

"On this occasion, however, there happened to be a Polish merchant ship taking on coal at the loading pier. Our pilots had been carefully directed not to attack foreign shipping—and they didn't, even though our pilots saw the Polish merchant ship firing machine guns at them.

"During the course of the attack, one bomb landed about 300 feet from the Polish ship—whose Master later charged that his ship had been bombed.

"For several days afterwards, the messages from Washington came thick and fast asking for details, analysis, statements and proof that we hadn't attacked the Polish ship."

Between 13 and 19 April, *Kitty Hawk* and *Ticonderoga* aircraft dropped two important bridges—each over 1,000 feet long—at Haiphong and Hai Duong.

Commander David B. Miller, CO of VA-144 on the *Ticonderoga*, was strike leader of 11 A-4s and four F-8s against the Haiphong highway bridge, one of the largest bridges leading into that city from Red China. Earlier in the day, Commander Miller had flown a mission in the same area and had observed the marginal weather and enemy defenses. He became convinced that a small, "clean wing," maximum-load attack could be successful. The drop tanks were removed from the A-4s and the ship's launch point was moved well to the north by Captain Robert Miller, the *Ticonderoga*'s skipper.

As the strike group approached the target from behind the ridge to the north, two SAMs were fired at them from Haiphong; but the flight avoided them. Climbing again after the missiles passed, the group came under heavy flak. Two aircraft were hit—an F-8 escort, pi-

loted by Commander Mohrhardt of VF-53, and Commander Miller's A-4. A 37-mm. projectile had hit the dorsal fin of Miller's aircraft, leaving a large hole. Despite this damage, and two more SAMs fired at the group, Commander Miller and the *Ticonderoga* flight pressed their attack and dropped five of the twenty-one spans of the bridge. Commander Mohrhardt was able to fly his burning F-8 out to sea where he was picked up safely by helicopter.

April also saw a modification of the manner in which Rolling Thunder targets were assigned.[14] Until this time, the Air Force and the Navy had shared the air over North Vietnam on a time basis, alternating the six areas every week. But this system of fixed times on target didn't work well for the carriers, which were launching and recovering aircraft every 90 minutes. So the six route package areas were now permanently divided. This placed the coastal areas, including Haiphong, in the Navy's area, leaving the area north of the DMZ, Hanoi, and the country to the west for the Air Force. However, some route package areas were major off-limit sanctuaries which contained the most lucrative targets. In addition, there was a buffer zone along the entire border between North Vietnam and Red China, which was kept immune from bombing.

The assignment of permanent areas of responsibility to the Air Force and the Navy had one immediate effect, a reduction in aircraft and aircrew losses. This was because pilots became very familiar with their assigned target areas, since they flew over them repeatedly and got to know the enemy's defenses and the best directions for attack. Furthermore, pilots became so familiar with the areas that they could detect meaningful changes.

One particular mission on 27 April by a VA-85 A-6 from the *Kitty Hawk* deserves recognition. The Intruder was flown by Lieutenant William R. Westerman and his Bombardier/

Navigator was Lieutenant (j.g.) Brian E. Westin. While making a run on numerous barges in a canal north of Vinh, the A-6 took a direct hit and Lieutenant Westerman was badly wounded.

Westin guided his wounded pilot out to sea both by oral assurances and by releasing his own shoulder straps, stretching across the mid-cockpit console, and controlling the aircraft from the right seat. When safely at sea, Westin insisted that the semi-conscious pilot eject himself first, a reversal of the normal procedure. After the wounded pilot was successfully out, Westin then ejected himself from the now pilotless aircraft. By chance, Westin was recovered first by the nearby SAR helicopter. He then helped direct the helicopter to the downed pilot. Upon arrival over Westerman, Westin noted that the wounded pilot, weak from loss of blood, lacked the strength to get into the recovery sling. Westin jumped back into the water, assisted Westerman into the sling, and in view of his immediate need for medical attention, waved the SAR helicopter to take the pilot back to the SAR destroyer. Westin awaited the arrival of a second SAR helicopter. For his courage and selflessness, Westin was awarded the Navy Cross.

Throughout May, the four TF 77 carriers kept flying hard, the *Ranger*, the *Hancock*, and the *Enterprise* at Yankee Station, with the *Intrepid* (CVS-11) at Dixie Station supporting General Westmoreland's four search-and-destroy operations then underway: Lexington, Hardihood, Reno, and Makiki. The *Intrepid* (Captain G. Macri) had arrived at Dixie Station on 15 May to relieve the *Hancock*. On her decks were 32 A-4s and 24 A-1s of CVW-10, but no fighters. Once an attack carrier, but an ASW carrier since 1964, she temporarily resumed her old role and, as the U. S. Navy's 16th attack carrier, helped to ease the strain of keeping five attack carriers continuously deployed to West-Pac and two in the Mediterranean. It was a

killing deployment schedule for the 16 ships, 7 months out, 5 months at home at the best, a schedule which would slowly erode the reenlistment rate and depress the pilot retention rate.

With five attack carriers on station in the Western Pacific, three of them constantly at Yankee Station, the air war had now reached a high level. Attack sorties on North Vietnam continued to grow.

	Attack Sorties		Aircraft/ Pilot Losses
	NVN	SVN	
March	1923	3474	11/9
April	2780	3184	21/15
May	2568	2810	9/2
June	3078	2597	9/9

By the end of May, the enemy's SAM network had been extended south and west, and more than 100 SAM sites protected North Vietnam. Hanoi and Haiphong had become the most heavily defended targets in the world.

MiG activity was also growing. TF 77's electronic warning aircraft, EA-3Bs, supported by EC-121M Big Look aircraft based at Da Nang, issued 141 SAM warnings and 38 MiG warnings. The presence of all-weather MiG-21 Fishbeds at North Vietnamese airfields was also confirmed. A total of 70 MiGs was now credited in the enemy's air order of battle, plus 6 Il-28 Beagles.

The number of supply ships arriving in Haiphong harbor was also growing. Nineteen ships arrived in April, 25 in May, and 28 in June. Pilots circling in the Gulf of Tonkin flew past loaded Soviet ships and tankers. On their decks could be seen trucks, missile equipment, and oil drums. The pilots knew they would be hunting these same trucks and missile trailers, one by one, in subsequent weeks.

There were 12 Navy engagements with MiGs in June and two MiG-17s were destroyed, two others damaged. In addition, one North

Vietnamese prop aircraft was destroyed and another damaged. The price was one F-8E lost. The engagement on 12 June, involving four F-8s from the *Hancock*, and four MiG-17s, was typical, since it showed the hit-and-run tactics of the enemy pilots and demonstrated the superior airmanship and aggressiveness of the U. S. Navy fighter pilots.

The four F-8s were flying cover for an attack group of A-4s who were bombing the Dai Tan military area, 24 miles northwest of Haiphong.

"We first spotted the four MiG-17s starting a low run attack from below," said Commander Harold L. Marr, Commanding Officer VF-211. "We broke into them and made them overshoot." Commander Marr fired one Sidewinder which failed to home properly, but his second missile went straight and true, blowing up the MiG at an altitude of 50 feet.

"We were able to outmaneuver the MiGs," said Commander Marr, "and it was pretty obvious we could outfly them. To the best of my knowledge, they never fired a shot at us."

Nine days later, Commander Marr's wingman, Lieutenant (j.g.) Phillip W. Vampatella, bagged one for himself. On this occasion, Vampatella was flying cover for a downed pilot, and during the mission his F-8 had been hit and damaged in the tail section. Vampatella headed his crippled aircraft back for the *Hancock*. As he turned seaward, one of the MiGs followed him and began an attack. Vampatella added afterburner power for speed, and maneuvered his damaged craft as best he could to avoid the MiG's cannon fire. As they neared the Gulf, Vampatella noted the MiG reversing course, whereupon he also reversed, got on the MiG's tail, fired a Sidewinder, and watched it disappear and explode in the MiG's tail pipe.

It was during this period that an effective method of attacking North Vietnamese trucks was perfected, the use of flares for visual night attacks at low level. "The pioneer of this technique was Commander Harry Thomas, Com-

manding Officer, VA-153," said Commander David E. Leue. "He had had considerable night attack experience during the Korean War. He taught us in mid-1965 how to find and destroy trucks at night—at ferry crossings and at downed bridges."[15]

The tactic called for pairs of A-4 Skyhawks, one flying 1,000 feet above the other and carrying flares, the second and lower aircraft watching the roads, ferry crossings and bridges, and calling for flares.

"Using this tactic," said Commander Leue, "we finished out *Coral Sea*'s 1965 cruise by burning trucks on most nights of our last two line periods."

During the 1966 period, two squadrons, VA-153 and VA-155, continued and expanded the technique, and were aided by the E-2 Hawkeye aircraft, for navigational assistance, as well as by the new Mk 4 gun pod. It was risky but effective work, and demolished trucks could be seen by daylight on many of North Vietnam's principal roads.

"A notable night was in July 1966," said Commander Leue,[16] "when my wingman, Lieutenant (j.g.) R. Harrell, and I found a nose-to-tail convoy of trucks two miles long just south of Thanh Hoa. It was an hour after midnight, clear and black. We caught these particular trucks with their lights on, an unusual circumstance which I attribute to another pair of A-4s ten miles away being shot at. The noise must have diverted the attention of these truck drivers, for apparently they did not hear us coming and did not turn off their lights. Our first strafing run was made without flares, and several trucks were set afire. We then used flares and Commander Edmund W. Ingley, Commanding Officer, VA-155, and his wingman joined the fray. Before we left the area, it was almost IFR (instrument flight rules) in smoke from burning trucks."

This dangerous but effective kind of night mission demanded discipline, courage, and airmanship of a high order, especially in the mountainous terrain of North Vietnam.

One of the most unorthodox recoveries in the history of aircraft carriers occurred on 3 June 1966. Commander Milton J. Chewning, Commanding Officer of VA-55, while on his eleventh strike mission over North Vietnam, took a burst of AA fire just forward of the starboard wing. The exploding shell peppered the cockpit with fragments, and several of them hit and incapacitated Commander Chewning's right arm. He calmly locked his throttle and adjusted his cabin environmental controls to compensate for the loss of air pressure in the cockpit. He then flew 150 miles to the *Ranger* left-handed, reporting by radio once or twice that he felt "woozy."

On board the *Ranger*, there was a hurried conference. Should a landing be tried? Was the pilot so badly wounded he couldn't make it? Might not his landing endanger men on the flight deck? After listening to Mike on the radio, and assessing his condition, it was quickly decided to give him the chance to land aboard.

While Commander Chewning was making the 20-minute flight to the carrier, Captain Leo B. McCuddin, the *Ranger*'s Commanding Officer, ordered the flight deck cleared of all unnecessary equipment. A flight surgeon was launched in a helo in case Commander Chewning chose to eject, and a second doctor was positioned on the flight deck with all emergency equipment.

"I stood in CIC monitoring Mike's voice," said Commander Fred Palmer, Commander Air Wing 14, "and I was prepared to order him to eject if he again reported that he felt 'woozy.'" He didn't, however. As Mike got within sight of the ship, Commander Paul Russell, *Ranger*'s operations officer, stood in the doorway between CIC and CATTC monitoring his approach on the scopes, and at the same time talking directly by telephone to Captain

McCuddin on the bridge. Captain McCuddin had already begun turning the ship into the wind, and when Mike's A-4E appeared on the CATTC radar astern of *Ranger*, even before Mike's plane could be seen from the ship, Captain McCuddin stopped the turn. The ship was still 30 degrees out of the wind, but this way Mike got a 'straight-in' approach to the deck.

"Mike rolled out in the groove and headed for the deck with a locked throttle," continued Commander Palmer. "The LSO, Lieutenant Commander 'Pon' Johnson, spoke gentle words to him. Mike's pass was actually FAB[17], but Lieutenant Commander Johnson's LSO record book said, 'O.K. pass, #3 wire.'

"Who says LSOs—and ship's skippers—don't have a heart?"

Rushed to sickbay, Commander Chewning was operated on for the removal of the several chunks of shrapnel in his arm, and later flown ashore for further treatment.

For his courage and airmanship, Commander Chewning was awarded the Silver Star Medal.

While light attack aircraft were attacking North Vietnam's trucks, A-6s from VA-65 aboard the *Constellation* were going against the fuel storage sites which supported them. One visible success was a flight of two Intruders led by Commander Frank Cramblet which struck the Yen Hau petroleum storage depot south of Vinh late in July. Billowing smoke visible from Yen Hau could be seen from the flight deck of the *Constellation*, some 60 miles to the east.

The Hai Duong bridge, a major link between Hanoi and Haiphong, was dropped by a single A-6 crew on a night raid. Lieutenant Commander Bernie Deibert and his B/N, Lieutenant Commander Dale Purdy, executed the imaginative strike on 12 August 1966 while operating with VA-65. The Intruder crew caught the North Vietnamese completely by surprise in one of their most highly defended areas. The five Mk-84, 2,000-pound bombs they released demolished the center span of the bridge.

It was also during this period that Lieutenant R. S. Williams and his B/N, Lieutenant J. E. Diselrod, developed a unique air-to-air defense tactic for night Intruder strikes. While retiring from their target area 40 miles into North Vietnam, Lieutenant Diselrod noted indications of an enemy fighter. When evasive maneuvers appeared futile, the A-6 crew intentionally overflew Nam Dinh, an area noted for its intensive AAA fire. The barrage discharged at the unidentified aircraft proved sufficient to discourage the trailing North Vietnamese pilot, and a successful termination of intercept tracking was achieved. This particular tactic became known as the "Willard Egress" to the flight crews of VA-65 and CVW-15.

Early in September 1966, Rear Admiral D. C. Richardson, then CTF 77, put into effect a new interdiction campaign based on a careful study of the enemy's targets and geography.[18]

"We were dealing with a dynamic situation," said Admiral Richardson, "and, although we had the initiative, routes and areas had to be carefully analyzed and our attacks concentrated in certain areas to cause traffic to bunch.

"By so doing," he said, "targets of opportunity were created and our damage took longer to repair.

"It was a systems approach to targeting," he continued. "No single target by itself was all-important, but rather the relationship of one target to other targets in a grouping. I was not interested in damage just for damage's sake, nor in the statistical summaries of so many downed bridges, damaged approaches, destroyed locomotives, and the like.... Nor was I interested in striking large target complexes because they were large, nor big bridges because they were big. Rather, our goal was to stop the enemy from functioning in some part

of his transportation system, to force him to ship his supplies by some alternate means around a stricken complex, and thereby slow down his war effort in South Vietnam."

Admiral Richardson put his new interdiction plan to work by closing the rail line south of Thanh Hoa and temporarily choking train movement at the rail yards of the Ninh Binh, Thanh Hoa, and Phy Ly complexes. All bridges south of Thanh Hoa were destroyed.[19] The idea paid off. As soon as the rail line was closed, an immediate buildup of trains was noticed. Multiple carrier strikes were directed against the trapped rolling stock, and more than 100 railroad cars were destroyed at Ninh Binh, and 80 more at Thanh Hoa. The North Vietnamese countered by bringing numerous trucks into the rail yards to offload supplies from the stalled railroad cars which had not been destroyed. Not in weeks had pilots seen so many trucks in the open and in daylight. Task Force 77 immediately made strikes against what the pilots called "luctars" (lucrative targets). Thirty trucks of a 60-truck convoy were destroyed during one such attack at Ninh Binh.

This was the kind of damage that pilots could clearly see for themselves. In September, 872 pieces of rolling stock and 729 trucks were damaged or destroyed as the result of the Navy's concentrated "attrition-interdiction" campaign.

Oriskany Fire

On the morning of 26 October 1966, TF 77 suffered its most grievous loss in the war to date when a fire broke out on board the *Oriskany* (CVA-34). The bad weather over North Vietnam forced the cancellation of the morning mission, so the ordnance from the strike aircraft was removed from the planes and carried back to the magazines. Among the ordnance being returned was a large number of magnesium parachute flares. Two seamen, one handing the flares from an ammo cart in a passageway to his buddy at the storage locker, mishandled a flare. Ignition took place in the locker and quickly set off about 700 other flares stored in the locker. The resulting fire killed 44 officers and men, including 25 pilots, most by asphyxiation, and injured 38. Two helicopters were jettisoned, four A-4s received major damage, and nine others suffered minor salt water damage. Valiant and tireless efforts by the crew of the *Oriskany* prevented further loss of life or greater damage to the ship and won the praise of all. Particularly noteworthy was the heroic action of the crew in removing bombs, some of which were already engulfed in flames. A total of 343 bombs, some 1,000 pounds and 2,000 pounds in size, and all subject to cook-off, was jettisoned from the hangar and flight decks in a massive effort that saved the ship and hundreds of lives. There were also many heroic and daring actions which saved the lives of many officers and men trapped in burning, smoke-filled staterooms and compartments.

The POL Campaign

By Asian standards, North Vietnam possessed a good petroleum, oil, and lubricants (POL) storage and distribution system to meet the needs of its industrial, transportation, and military consumers. Its wartime POL requirements were estimated to be 15,000 to 20,000 metric tons a month, an amount which two small tankers or 170 railroad tank cars bringing oil from Red China could supply.

As the American bombing effort stepped up, Hanoi only had to look at history—World War II in Germany and Japan—to anticipate the bombing of their POL system, which was above ground and exposed.[20] By June 1966 air bombing in the southern part of North Vietnam had eliminated Nam Dinh and Phu Qui as POL storage centers, and the storage capacity at Vinh had been cut by two-thirds.

But the major part of the POL system, located near Hanoi and Haiphong, remained untouched. In late 1965 and early 1966, new POL farms with buried or bunkered tanks were sighted or photographed all over the country, the majority of them in or near the major military and industrial centers. Also, extremely large numbers of 55 gallon-type petroleum drums were visible.

In April 1966, a new bombing plan, known as Rolling Thunder 50, was released for planning—not execution—by the Secretary of Defense. It contained two major target systems—the major industries in the Northeast quadrant and the entire POL system. Authority was granted to plan attacks against eleven specific targets: the Viet-Tri Railroad-Highway Bridge, the Haiphong Thermal Power Plant, the Haiphong Cement Plant, and the early warning-ground control intercept radar at Kep airfield (a key facility which supported Northeast's entire air defense); and seven POL storages, at Haiphong, Hanoi, Nguyen Ke, Bac Giang, Do Son, Phuc Yen, and Duong Nham. After close cooperation with and joint planning between the U. S. Seventh Air Force and Commander Seventh Fleet, attacks against the POL system were begun.

They were scheduled for late April, but a delay developed.

The only reason for the delay was uncertainty on Washington's part that *only* these eleven targets would be hit, that no collateral damage on other targets such as third country shipping or civilians would occur.

An intensive search was begun for techniques that would minimize these risks.

After two months of consultation and analyses, Secretary McNamara ordered attacks to begin on the seven POL storage facilities on 23 June, including those at Hanoi and Haiphong, plus the Kep airfield radar. He directed that special care be taken to avoid damaging Russian, Red Chinese, or Communist Bloc shipping in Haiphong. Special care was also to be taken to minimize casualties among enemy civilians. He directed that the most experienced pilots should be used, that good weather should be selected in order to promote visual accuracy, and that careful selection of the attack axis should be made.

Navy pilots attacking the Haiphong POL storage area were ordered not to make attacks on any craft in the harbor unless they were first fired on, and "only if the craft is clearly of North Vietnam registry." In addition, "piers servicing the Haiphong POL storage will not be attacked if a tanker is berthed off the end of the pier."

At the very last minute, still another delay developed: a news leak. In the United States, newspaper stories appeared which said that North Vietnam's POL system would be struck very soon and giving essential strike details. This publicity, appearing at almost the same time that the POL strikes were being authorized, caused another week's postponement.

Finally, on 29 June 1966, more than a year after Rolling Thunder had commenced, the bombing program against POL facilities got under way with strikes on Hanoi and Haiphong. Twenty-eight of the *Ranger*'s aircraft, including anti-MiG, anti-SAM, and anti-flak elements, led by Commander Frederick F. Palmer, Commander Air Wing 14, went against the Haiphong POL complex, the country's largest, and turned it into three huge fireballs and many columns of smoke which rose to 20,000 feet. "I put the A-4Cs, slowest of the jets in the attack group, in the van," said Palmer. "Commander Al 'Shoes' Shaufelberger, Commanding Officer of VA-146 (Blue Diamonds), did a perfect job of navigating to the target area, and the fireball from his bombs provided an interesting obstacle for subsequent attackers during their pull-out. Commander Bob Holt, leading the War Horses of VA-55, peppered and ignited several tanks with his load of 2.75-inch Mighty Mouse rockets. The flak was heavy, initially, in the target

area, but flak suppressors—F-4s of VF-142 led by Commander Jim Brown—were so accurate in placing their bombs that it seemed as if a switch had suddenly 'turned off' the heavy caliber antiaircraft fire. Finally, Fighting 143, led by Commander Walt Spangenberg, positioned their Phantoms between the MiG bases and the attack group. There were no takers."

Meanwhile, the *Constellation*'s aircraft went against the Do Son POL on the tip of the peninsula which forms the southeast arm of Haiphong harbor. On 30 June, *Hancock* and *Constellation* aircraft struck the Bac Giang POL storage. On 1 July it was *Constellation* and *Hancock* against Dong Nham, 13 miles northwest of Haiphong where 7 POL tanks and 4 support buildings were destroyed. The *Hancock* sent 18 of her airplanes far inland up the valleys to smash the Bac Giang POL storage north of Hanoi a second time.

Back in the office of the Secretary of Defense, there was a tense air of expectancy, a mixture of fear and hope—fear that the bombs might fall on Soviet or Red Chinese merchant ships in Haiphong or, despite all the precautions and restrictions, into the heavily populated civilian areas of the cities—perhaps even the embassies, hospitals, and schools. There was also fear that this "escalation" might trigger some Soviet or Communist reaction. But there was also hope—hope that this new blow might persuade Hanoi to bid for peace. Rear Admiral J. R. Reedy, CTF 77, was under specific orders to send back detailed information on the strikes on an "as occurring" basis and to mark his messages personally for Secretary McNamara, Chairman of the JCS General Wheeler, and Admiral Sharp, CinCPac.

Several key offices in the Pentagon, including the Chairman of the JCS, remained manned that first night awaiting the initial strike results.

Nothing happened. Except for the usual Communist rhetoric, there was no North Vietnam response or reaction—nor was there any collateral damage. The precision and skillful airmanship asked for had been delivered.

On 7 July 1966, the Haiphong petroleum storage area was struck again, with particular emphasis against the pumping machinery as well as the storage tanks. Pilots from the *Constellation* reported dense black smoke rising to 20,000 feet and secondary explosions. One A-4C from the *Hancock* was hit, but the pilot ejected safely southeast of Haiphong and was rescued.

On 9 July, the Thanh Hoa storage was hit again, and on 12 July, the Haiphong POL was blasted for the third time.

The Vinh POL storage was hit on 23 July, resulting in a spectacular fire with four large fireballs. During this attack, Commander Wynne F. Foster, Commanding Officer of VA-163, flying an A-4E, took a 57-mm. hit through the starboard side of the cockpit, which almost severed his right arm below the shoulder. Radioing that he was bleeding badly, he managed to steer the crippled Skyhawk with his knees while holding the stump of his shattered arm and restricting the gush of blood. When over water near the USS *Reeves* (DLG-24), and growing faint, he succeeded in making a left-handed ejection and was rescued by the ship's whaleboat, then evacuated to the *Oriskany* by helicopter where his arm was amputated.[21] (His change of command ceremony, held on the *Oriskany* in Subic Bay a few days later, was conducted from a stretcher, concluding with the traditional, but left-handed, salute.)

By the end of July, the first effects of the POL strikes were becoming apparent.[22] No Soviet tankers arrived at Haiphong in July. They showed up again in August but, then and thereafter, were loaded with drums rather than bulk fuel. Two Soviet tankers, scheduled to unload at Haiphong, unloaded instead in Red China and their cargo was transshipped to North Vietnam by tank car.

After the attacks on the Haiphong POL storage and oil tank barges, the North Vietnamese quickly realized that though their diesel-powered barges, each able to carry 600 metric tons, were fair game, ships of other nations were not. Thereafter it became a contest between the pilots and the barge crews. The latter would nestle their 150-foot craft alongside tankers of other nations anchored in the roadsteads off Haiphong and Hon Gai. When darkness or bad weather came, these barges would dash for the ports which were off limits to U. S. aircraft. Thus it remained for the A-6 crews, with their all-weather attack systems, and the A-4 crews, working under flares at night, to prevent or inhibit the "last mile" of transport for vital petroleum to North Vietnam.

Strikes on 1 and 4 August 1966 destroyed or damaged four, and possibly six, of the ten tank barges owned by North Vietnam.

After the destruction of the storage tanks and the oil in them, the Soviets nearly doubled their efforts.

Other parts of the POL system attacked by TF 77 aircraft were railroad tank cars and river barges.

By Christmas 1966, the long POL campaign had wrecked all the above ground POL storage sites, including the largest facility, in Hanoi. The Haiphong receiving terminal had been reduced to marginal levels, from a capacity of four tanker shiploads to less than one-third of one shipload per month. Most of the oil barges and oil tank cars had been destroyed. Notwithstanding this damage, North Vietnam retained sufficient oil reserves dispersed in drums and buried or hidden in caves to maintain its military and economic activity for up to four months.

The POL campaign had come too late. The 15-month delay,[23] and the 37-day bombing pause following Christmas, 1965, had given the enemy time to disperse his stocks and to shift from transporting oil by rail to moving it in trucks, and even to commence the construction of an underground pipeline system.

As 1966 ended, it was evident that the interdiction campaign was causing Hanoi extreme hardships. The effect of heavier air strikes was reflected in North Vietnam's public outcries and their insistence that "stop the bombing" was a first prerequisite to any negotiations. The entire population of North Vietnam had been mobilized to support the war effort, and it was estimated that more than 300,000 people were required just to keep the lines of communication open. Admiral Sharp gave this evaluation in his year-end report:

"Despite our interdiction, the enemy has accommodated to our LOC (lines of communications) attacks by ingeniously hiding and dispersing his logistic activity. His recuperative capability along these lines has been remarkable."

General Westmoreland added his P.S. ". . . there is no lessening of enemy determination," he said.

Task Force 77 counted up the year's effort: more than 30,000 attack sorties against North Vietnam and 20,000 against the enemy in South Vietnam. Eighty-nine airmen had been killed, captured, or reported missing, and over 120 aircraft had been lost on combat missions.

1967

As 1967 opened, Admiral Sharp made a fresh attempt to have the character of the air interdiction campaign changed. Since the objective of the U. S. military effort was neither to defeat nor to destroy North Vietnam but to cause North Vietnam to stop supporting, controlling, and directing insurgencies in Southeast Asia, three tasks had to be accomplished: (1) to deny North Vietnam access to the flow of external assistance, primarily from Communist China and Russia, (2) to curtail the flow of men and supplies from North Vietnam into Laos and South Vietnam, and (3) to destroy in depth those resources in North Vietnam that contributed to support of the aggression.

"There were six basic target systems in North Vietnam," said Admiral Sharp, "electric power, war supporting industry, transportation support facilities, military complexes, petroleum storage, and air defense."

Admiral Sharp felt that accomplishment of these three tasks was dependent on applying continuous and steadily increasing pressures against these target systems, rather than on individually selected targets on a stop-and-go basis. "The application of steadily increasing pressure had been denied us in 1966," he said, "because of operational restrictions."

"I had informed Washington in December that the no-bombing zone placed around Hanoi should be relaxed. I told them that we were just starting to put some real pressure on Hanoi with our air strikes on the Hanoi rail yard and vehicle depot—hitting them where it hurt. Hanoi had complained that these early attacks had killed civilians. They were hoping for a favorable reaction—and they got it. Not only did our government say we regretted that civilians were killed, but we also stopped our pilots from striking targets near Hanoi. So the North Vietnamese were successful once again in getting the bombing pressure removed, and this success encouraged them to continue their aggression. With nearly 400,000 U. S. fighting men in country, it was apparent to Hanoi they couldn't take over South Vietnam by force—but they *could* fight a protracted war, terrorize the countryside, make our revolutionary development plan difficult, and kill a lot of people, including Americans. This type of war, I felt, might continue a long time, and my personal feeling, based on a limited sounding of public opinion, including the thoughts of quite a few members of Congress, led me to the conclusion we should end this war successfully as soon as possible.

"It was this background," he continued, "that caused me to recommend on 18 January 1967 that all targets in each of the six target systems which required approval by higher authority be approved as a package—not doled out a few at a time.[24] This would give me maximum flexibility in the timing of strikes, taking into consideration intelligence and weather factors. I asked for authority to hit 15 new targets each month. In this way, I could apply the needed pressure and avoid peaks and depressions. If we were to increase the pressure on Hanoi, a steady program of disruption against the basic target systems was necessary. The six target systems should be considered as a single package, with each system interrelated to the other, and elements of each system should be attacked, rather than one system at a time."

The recommendations won some success, for in late January and again in late February, strikes were authorized against 16 fixed targets in the northeast quadrant. But the policy of piecemeal approval of targets and tactical restrictions continued.

In mid-April, ten targets were authorized by Washington, a power transformer station, a cement plant, three bridges, a rail repair shop, an ammunition depot, a POL storage area, and two MiG airfields near Hanoi. Certain targets within ten miles of Hanoi were authorized for attack.

On 2 May, ten more targets were added—targets along the highway and railroad transportation systems from Communist China, and enemy aircraft at their home bases.

On 23 May, a ten-mile no-bombing circle was placed around Hanoi.

On 5 July 1967, in Saigon, a crucial briefing was given to Secretary McNamara, which determined the future direction of the air interdiction campaign. (Also present at this meeting were Under Secretary of State Katzenbach; the U. S. Ambassador to South Vietnam, Ellsworth Bunker; Admiral Sharp; General Westmoreland, ComUSMACV; General William W. Momyer, Commander Seventh

Air Force; Vice Admiral Hyland, Commander Seventh Fleet; and several staff members from State, Defense, and JCS staffs.)

Admiral Sharp led off the briefing with a summary of the Rolling Thunder campaign up to that point and explained the concept of denying North Vietnam access to external aid, cutting down the enemy's movement of war material into South Vietnam, and the need for vigorous, unremitting attacks on the six primary target systems of North Vietnam. Admiral Sharp described the several results which had occurred during the recent months of the air bombing campaign—that the enemy was no longer using his MiGs to challenge our attacks, that the effectiveness of his SAMs had diminished, that our new bombs, rockets, and missiles were showing greater effectiveness, that Hanoi's problems were increasing, the evidence being their drawdown on manpower, the increase in ship offloading time, the impairment of their transportation system, the pile-up of supplies, and the like. In short, Admiral Sharp said that the trend of the war had changed in our favor, and he recommended that the pace of the bombing be stepped up.[25]

On 20 July 1967, 16 new targets in the northeast sector, mostly railroad and highway bridges, were added, bringing the approved total to 46. Of the 46, thirty were in the Hanoi-Haiphong area.

In August, several targets in the so-called Chinese buffer zone, some only eight miles from the border, were authorized: the Port Wallut naval base, the Lang Son railroad bridge, and the Na Phuoc railroad yard, were naval targets. However, that same month all targets in the central Hanoi area were again placed off limits, a restriction that continued for two months.

On 30 August, the coal handling resources at Cam Pha and the Hon Gai port facilities were authorized for attack whenever foreign shipping was not present. The Communists quickly took advantage of this rule, and only on rare occasions thereafter was a foreign ship *not* tied up to the Cam Pha coal piers.

The restrictions placed against North Vietnam's coal loading port of Cam Pha are indicative of Washington's sensitivity to attacks on third country shipping. The TF 77 attack on Cam Pha in April 1966, which resulted in a charge that a Polish ship had been bombed, has been described. This attack put Cam Pha back on the restricted list until August.

Meanwhile, in June 1967, another bombing incident occurred at Cam Pha. The Soviets charged that their merchant vessel *Turkestan* had been attacked on 2 June, killing one crewman and injuring others. A full scale investigation of the incident revealed that two flights of Seventh Air Force F-105s had attacked Cam Pha on 2 June, but Washington flatly denied that these aircraft had attacked the *Turkestan*. Indeed, they had not. But about two weeks later, new information arrived in Washington that a third flight of Seventh Air Force fighters, after attacking Bac Giang rail yard 65 miles from Cam Pha, and while en route home, had passed over the harbor, had been fired upon by Cam Pha gun batteries, and had attacked the guns. Apparently the Soviet ship had been struck by this fire. Premier Kosygin later brought a 20-mm. projectile with U. S. Air Force markings from the *Turkestan* to the United States for his meeting with President Johnson at Glassboro, New Jersey.[26]

In any case, the coal mines and mining facilities of North Vietnam, which supplied coal to the electric power plants of North Vietnam, were never authorized for attack.

August passed. In September, 17 new targets were added, and in October, eight more, seven in the Haiphong port area, including three shipyards. In November, 14 new targets were added, bringing the approved to-

tal to 85. Thus, the tightly supervised and limited bombing campaign was continued.

Combat SAR—the Rescue of Pilots

One of the truly great success stories of TF 77 operations in the Gulf of Tonkin is the development, by Rear Admiral J. R. Reedy and his staff, of a combat Search and Rescue (SAR) capability for rescuing pilots not only from the water, but from the enemy's territory. There had been, of course, many helicopter rescues of downed pilots from enemy territory during the Korean War, but the system, procedures, hardware, and communications in 1950–53 had never been elaborate.

The overriding reasons for a well-developed and aggressive combat SAR capability in Southeast Asia were, of course, to prevent pilots from being captured and to sustain pilot morale. To fly day after day deep into the high-threat areas of Vinh, Thanh Hoa, Hanoi, Haiphong, and the Red River Valley, to dodge SAMs and endure history's heaviest and most accurate barrage of gunfire, often in marginal weather or at night, demanded the highest order of courage, airmanship, devotion to duty, and self-discipline on the part of the aviators. If they were shot down and survived, but could not be rescued, they knew that they faced unnumbered years of prison, isolation, and hunger—even torture or death.

Thus, the pilots looked upon the combat SAR machinery as the best life insurance they could have. If they knew (and they *did* know) that every possible effort would be made to rescue them, their morale would be strengthened and their fortitude increased.

There were lesser, but still important, reasons for a combat SAR system—to prevent the enemy from exploiting downed pilots either as sources of intelligence or as political hostages; and to protect a costly resource, since a highly trained pilot flying jets costs hundreds of thousands of dollars to replace.

At first, in 1965–66, the SAR system consisted of an Air Force Grumman amphibian aircraft which remained airborne in the Gulf from sunrise to sunset. To this the Navy added an armed two-plane A-1 Skyraider rescue patrol (ResCAP), and a roving SAR destroyer. The Skyraiders were ideally suited for SAR and helo escort duty. They could fly slowly enough to remain with the rescue helos, and their ordnance lifting capacity enabled them to carry a heavy load of bombs and ammunition for suppressing enemy ground fire. (Later, when the A-1s left the Fleet, they were replaced as SAR aircraft by A-4s and A-7s.)

In April 1965, Rear Admiral M. F. Weisner established a second SAR station using a UH-2A/B Seasprite helicopter from the *Ranger* in the destroyer *England*. The northern station, lacking a helo, had a Tacan-equipped DDG and an accompanying shotgun destroyer. The southern, or combat, SAR station was east of Vinh with a DD and a DLG, the latter fitted with both Tacan and a helo platform. The UH-2 helo (then nicknamed "Angel") aboard the DLG had no armor plating, but the pilots and crew wore flak jackets and had a .30-caliber machine gun mounted in the cabin.

The first overland rescue from North Vietnam of a Navy pilot by a Navy helo occurred on 20 September 1965 when an A-4E flown by Lieutenant (j.g.) John R. Harris of VA-72, aboard the *Independence*, was downed 20 miles east of Hanoi. Harris was recovered by a UH-1B helo which landed aboard the cruiser *Galveston* (CLG-3).

In November 1965, as a result of a recommendation by Rear Admiral E. P. Aurand to Rear Admiral Reedy, the first SH-3 Sea King helicopter arrived at Yankee Station. The Sea Kings, much larger helos than the Seasprites, were temporarily stripped of their ASW equipment. The reliability of their two engines, and their larger payload and longer range as compared to the Seasprites, made them ideal rescue vehicles and cargo carriers for the destroyers. Because of their size, the Sea Kings were kept aboard the attack carriers or, if one were present, aboard the ASW carrier. These helos were known as "Fetch."

In December 1965, the UH-2 aboard the DLG was replaced by one with armor plate around the pilot, crewmen, engine, and main transmission. It had self-sealing oil lines and fuel cells, and had a higher power T-58 engine. It was armed with M-60 machine guns and was painted in camouflage colors.

After the Yankee Station carriers moved farther north in the Gulf, two combat SAR stations (North and South) were formally established, in April 1966. Each had a DLG (with Tacan and a combat SAR UH-2) and a "Shotgun" DD. At this time, the UH-2's nickname changed from "Angel" to "Clementine"—number 1 for North and number 2 for South Combat SAR Station.

In May 1966, specially equipped and armored SH-3s, known as "Big Mothers," arrived in the Gulf, armed with two M-60 machine guns. Prior to each in-country air strike, one or more Big Mothers would be dispatched to the combat SAR station nearest the assigned targets. In 1966, whenever an actual rescue was in progress, four A-1 Skyraiders always accompanied each UH-2 or SH-3 to give suppressive ground support to a downed pilot and to protect the rescue helicopter.

The destroyers assigned to North and South SAR were provided with a "High Drink" (helicopter inflight refueling) capability—to permit a helicopter to hover over the fantail, lower its hoist to the deck, and retrieve a refueling hose and refuel while remaining airborne. This required that the destroyers be equipped with JP-5 tanks, hoses, and fuel testing equipment.

By refueling every two to three hours the SAR helo could remain on station for up to 12 hours and always have enough fuel to make a run in-country for a rescue if necessary.

In December 1966, the Air Force replaced its HU-16 amphibian with a C-13OE, which was capable of longer-ranged communication and greater on-station time.

Prearranged airborne teams of rescue helicopters and armed escorts (A-1s initially, A-4s, or A-7s) flew near the egress routes of the Alpha strikes. When a pilot was shot down, the strike leader, or wingman, became "on-scene commander" to coordinate and direct the rescue attempt. Aboard either the North or South SAR station, a destroyer squadron commander would serve as SAR Coordinator. The Commodore would have the latest information on enemy aircraft and missile defenses, the targets being struck, a complete list of all rescue vehicles, and a careful plot of the enemy gun and missile defenses. It was the SAR coordinator's decision, in conjunction with recommendations from the on-scene commander, to either attempt a rescue or not. If a pilot could be seen on the ground, or if he used his rescue radio, the attempt would normally be made.

How well did the system work? From the start of the war until October 1966, 269 naval and Air Force pilots and air crewmen were shot down or forced to abandon their aircraft over North Vietnam. Of these, 103 (more than half of them from the Air Force) were recovered, 75 were known to have been killed, 46 were made prisoners, and the fate of the remaining 45 is not known.

The statistics were clear in one particular—if a pilot could get his damaged aircraft over the sea before he "punched out," his chances of rescue were better than 90%. If he bailed out over North Vietnam in 1966, however, his chances were considerably less—and this percentage would drop steadily for the remainder of the war, especially in the "Iron Triangle" of Haiphong, Hanoi, and Thanh Hoa. The North Vietnamese made vigorous efforts to capture every downed pilot, even those close to their shores—and the reward for doing so was high. Junk fishermen were paid $200 per pilot—a fortune for them.

It became evident that speed in rescues was all important, for after 30 minutes a downed pilot's chances of rescue began dropping rapidly. It also became apparent that any SAR effort which lasted for several hours, or which continued the following day, could be converted into an ambush for rescue aircraft and helos. The enemy often spread parachutes to attract attention and get pilots to fly low. The enemy also made use of captured "beeper" radios carried by all pilots to decoy a rescue helo into an ambush.

The effectiveness, speed, teamwork, and heroism of the combat SAR system can best be told by recounting three rescues, one on the coast, one deep inside Haiphong harbor, and one at night. Each is typical of the aggressive determination to bring home every pilot who had any chance of being rescued. These rescues will be capsuled in the words of the principals, taken from official records:

The Coastline Rescue took place on 20 March 1966. The downed pilot was Lieutenant James S. Greenwood and the rescue helo pilot was Lieutenant Commander David J. McCracken.

Greenwood: "I was flying an F-4B Phantom from VF-92 aboard *Enterprise*. With another VF-92 F-4B, we launched at 1715 to attack a bridge 40 miles south of Vinh. Approaching the target we encountered heavy antiaircraft fire. Both our planes were hit immediately. My aircraft, voice call Silverkite 202, developed fires in both engines and became uncontrolled, so I ordered my RIO to eject . . . I soon followed him. As I descended in my parachute through a solid overcast between 500 and 1,000 feet, I could see that my RIO would land only 100 yards from the beach, and I roughly one-half mile out. Just before I hit the water, I noticed one enemy junk about two miles north of us, and many people gathering near the beach near the point where my RIO was descending. I considered him too close to the beach to even think of an attempt to swim for open water. . . ."

McCracken: "After I lifted off USS *Worden* (DLG-18), it took me about 15 minutes to reach the general area of the downed pilot. The area had been marked by an orange flare dropped by Crown Bravo [the USAF rescue Grumman Albatross]. The pilot of Crown Bravo told me that his airplane had been hit by heavy AAA fire from the nearby beach and that he couldn't land because of holes in his fuselage. He also told me to hurry because enemy junks were closing in on the downed pilot.

"I flew in toward what I thought was the flare, got too close to some junks near the beach, and they opened fire on me. The smoke I saw wasn't from the marker flare, however, but from a burning belly tank. So I turned away from the shore, heading east, when AMH2 G. E. McCormack, my second crewman, opened up on a nearby junk which had commenced shooting at us. About the same time, my co-pilot, Ensign R. H. Clark, Jr., spotted the downed pilot. He grabbed a Thompson .45-caliber machine gun and joined McCormack firing at the junk, only 100–150 yards away."

Clark: "When Mr. McCracken started in to make the pickup, the four A-4s [from the *Enterprise*] started making strafing attacks on the junk. About half the crew of the junk jumped in the water, while the remainder continued shooting at us. When we reached the downed pilot, he grabbed the horse collar, and before he could get into it, Chief Davis, the first crewman, started hoisting him up. The pickup didn't take 30 seconds."

Davis: "Whenever the A-4s made a strafing pass, the junks would stop firing at us, but we kept the junk under fire with the Thompson and the M-60 all the time. [Chief Davis didn't know it at the time, but several guns, both tracer fire and mortars, were being fired at the helo from the beach.] As we pulled into a hover, the survivor was waving his arms indicating he was not injured, so I lowered the sling to him. He grabbed it in a death grip and nodded his head to bring him up, so I raised him as he hung on."

McCracken: "Just as Chief Davis grabbed the survivor and lifted him bodily into the helo, a mortar round hit the water behind us, and another one hit forward. The splash of the first round lifted the tail and put us into forward flight. [McCracken didn't know it but the first round damaged his hoist and tail assembly.] Getting out of there was my intention anyway—but not in so violent a maneuver!"

Later, in a message to McCracken, Vice Admiral John J. Hyland, Commander Seventh Fleet, expressed the feelings of all TF 77 pilots. ". . . the courage, determination, and tenacity of pilots and crew of your helo is again deserving of widest recognition and official commendation." Only six days earlier, McCracken had received his first Silver Star for heroism for a helo rescue under fire of an Air Force pilot.

The Haiphong Harbor rescue of Lieutenant Commander Thomas Tucker took place on 31 August 1966. The rescue helo pilot was Commander Robert S. Vermilya, Commanding Officer of HS-6.

Tucker: "I was flying a BDA (Bomb Damage Assessment) mission 31 August 1966 from *Oriskany* for strikes being conducted in the Haiphong area. About 1450, I was hit by a 37-mm. projectile and I experienced immediate loss of aileron and elevator control. With just my rudder, I managed to head toward the ocean, but within a minute after being hit, the bird became uncontrollable, pitched nose up and then rolled inverted. By the time I was finally able to eject at 1,500 feet, the Crusader

LCdr. Thomas Tucker is hauled up from Haiphong Harbor.

was in a steep dive. After getting out, I blacked out for a few seconds, and when I came to, I was about 1,000 feet above the harbor and several guns were firing at me, for I could hear the bullets whistling past.''

Tucker landed in Haiphong's secondary ship channel, about 150 yards off the beach, three miles from the city itself, and in an area where many junks and sampans were present.

Vermilya: "I was pilot of 'Indian Girl 68' with Ensign William E. Runyon co-pilot, Chief Tom Grisham and ADR2 Jerry Dunford as

crew. We had taken off from *Kearsarge* two hours earlier, and for this mission, north SAR consisted of *Towers* and *Wiltsie*. We heard the Mayday call, and the pilot calling out, 'I'm hit, I'm hit, I'm hit.'

"At the time, we were orbiting near the coast-out point, so I picked up speed and took up a heading for Haiphong. My escorts hadn't yet shown up, but the on-scene commander (Lieutenant Foster Teague, flying another *Oriskany* F-8 from VF-111) told me that if I waited any longer, I'd never make it. He said it was either now or never." Lieutenant Teague, meanwhile, was himself dodging SAMs being fired at his aircraft.

"So I descended to 60 feet altitude and headed up the long channel to Haiphong itself. As I got close to the area, the smoke stacks of several factories in Haiphong were visible." Vermilya and his crew, being preoccupied with the search for Tucker, knew they were being fired at, but they did not appreciate the volume or intensity of the enemy's fire. Tucker, now in his life raft 100 yards from the shoreline, could see splashes from artillery passing *above* the incoming helo and splashing into the water beyond. Before the helo came into view, in fact, the same guns had been firing at him; he also saw several sampans headed toward him to make the capture.

"The sampans were getting close to the downed pilot," continued Vermilya, "until Lieutenant Teague made a strafing pass and blew one up and set another on fire—after this, the rest of the boats started going the other way.

"We didn't see the downed pilot until he lighted off an orange flare—then we could see that a lot of rifle and automatic weapon fire was splashing near him. So I made a sharp turn back, made an emergency hover at 30 feet, dropped the "horse collar" for about ten seconds, and Jerry Dunford winched him aboard."

Commander Vermilya had spent 20 minutes flying the big helo up the harbor channel through a curtain of fire, but the ten-second hover was the most dangerous part of the mission—every gun in the harbor which could bear was firing at the "Big Mother." But not a single projectile hit the helo.

This is one of the three rescues of naval pilots from Haiphong harbor which occurred during the war. On 7 July 1966, Lieutenant Commander William Isenhour of VA-216 aboard *Hancock*, was rescued from the mouth of the Haiphong River. "This rescue happened during a re-strike of the Haiphong POL site," said Rear Admiral Reedy. "I was in the war room listening on the strike frequency relayed by Middleman. Lieutenant Commander Isenhour headed out to sea, and just before ejecting he told his buddies, 'Keep those goddamn sampans away from me after I get in the water.' He sounded as calm as if he'd said it over morning coffee."

Almost a year later, Lieutenant (j.g.) J. W. Cain of VA-192 was forced to eject from his A-4 Skyhawk. He landed in the water near Haiphong harbor and was immediately taken under small arms fire. Said Commander Billy Phillips, Cain's air group commander: "The one aspect of the rescue that impressed me was the effectiveness of the F-8s whose repeated strafing attacks subdued fire from the beach against Lieutenant (j.g.) Cain. Commander Bill Conklin, Commanding Officer of VF-194, was the on-scene commander, and he mustered twelve F-8s at the scene. Four of these made close-interval attacks until they ran out of ammo, then Bill called in four more. This process continued until 10 of the F-8s had been utilized and the helo escorted by two A-1s from VA-52 had rescued Lieutenant (j.g.) Cain."

After 20 minutes, Cain was rescued by a helo flown by Lieutenant S. T. Milliken and Lieutenant (j.g.) T. E. Pettis, who received intense mortar and AAA fire including two SAMs.

The night rescue of Lieutenant Commander John W. Holtzclaw and his RIO Lieutenant Commander John A. Burns, both of VF-33, took place on 19 June 1968. The rescue helo pilot was Lieutenant Clyde E. Lassen of HC-7.

Ten minutes after midnight on 19 June 1968, an F-4B from the USS *America* (CVA-66) was destroyed by a SAM missile. Its two crewmen, Lieutenant Commander Holtzclaw and Lieutenant Commander Burns, were able to eject from the tumbling wreckage, but they were down 20 miles inland, south of Hanoi, and in a densely inhabited area. Their parachutes fell into a rice paddy area between two villages. During the next 45 minutes, Holtzclaw and Burns slowly made their way across the rice paddies to a small densely foliaged karst hill nearby. The hill was flanked on three sides by rice paddies and on the fourth by a mountain range.

The rescue attempt started from southern SAR station when a UH-2A Seasprite helicopter lifted off the deck of the USS *Preble* (DLG-15) and headed through the dark, moonless night. Its crew consisted of pilot Lieutenant Clyde E. Lassen, co-pilot Lieutenant (j.g.) Clarence L. Cook, and crewmen AE2 Bruce B. Dallas and ADJ3 Donald West.

"For the first hour," said Holtzclaw, "we heard no airplanes overhead. We made our way up the hill to an extremely dense section of jungle, where we first heard the sound of airplanes. We used our walkie-talkies and were told "Clementine Two" was on the way to get us. Lieutenant Commander Burns and I tried to find a clear area on the hillside for pick-up but couldn't find one."

As the Seasprite neared the rescue area, two "balls of flame," possibly SAMs, streaked past the helicopter. A minute later, Lieutenant (j.g.) Cook sighted the flaming wreckage of the F-4 and located the general position of the survivors who were now about three miles from the crashed aircraft. Difficult terrain, a dark, overcast night, and heavy enemy small arms and automatic weapons fire were factors making the rescue of the F-4 crew extremely difficult.

Lieutenant Lassen made his first landing in a rice paddy below the hill and 600 feet from the downed pilots.

As the helo touched down, the waiting enemy opened up with small arms and automatic weapons fire. Lassen immediately lifted off and orbited the area.

Meanwhile, other aircraft had arrived from TF 77 and began dropping flares.

"The survivors were between two large trees about 150 feet apart," said Lieutenant Lassen, "and other fairly tall trees were also in the area, but I decided that by the light of the flares, I'd try to pick them up from the hillside."

As Lieutenant Lassen approached, in a 50-foot high hover between the trees, Petty Officer Dallas began lowering the rescue sling.

Suddenly the flares burned out, leaving the area in pitch darkness and Lieutenant Lassen with no visual ground reference.

"Dallas yelled that we were going to hit a tree," Lieutenant Lassen said. "I added power and was just starting a climb when I hit it. The jolt was terrific. The helo pitched nose down and went into a tight starboard turn. I regained control and waved off. I then told the rescue aircraft orbiting overhead that we had struck a tree and that I was experiencing fairly heavy vibration. We requested more flares and were told that no more were available but that some were on the way. Also, I told the survivors that they would have to get down off that hill and into the clearing."

In the rear of the helicopter, the crewman, Dallas, was also having his troubles in recovering the hoist.

"I started retracting the hoist as fast as possible," he said, "and in the process the helo hit a tree on the right side. I was leaning out of

the open door at the time, and I was hit on the face as the tree went by. As soon as the limb hit me, I yelled 'get up! get up!'—and we were out of there and climbing. Nothing but Mr. Lassen's skill and experience saved us from crashing."

The helicopter developed a fairly heavy vibration immediately after the collision which damaged the horizontal stabilizer, the tail rotor, the antenna, and the door.

Shaken but undeterred by the narrow escape, Lieutenant Lassen made pass after pass over the area while Cook and Dallas fired at the gun flashes below.

In the darkness of the tangled, vine-covered hillside, Holtzclaw and Burns, the latter hampered by a sprained left ankle and an injured knee as a result of the ejection, were stumbling downhill toward the rice paddy area below. As they reached the flat area, Lieutenant Lassen made his second approach for the pick-up. As the UH-2 touched down, he spotted the survivors struggling across the rice paddies but still too far away. Enemy fire was also steadily increasing. He took off again, circled the area and headed in for his third landing. Another SAM went by, narrowly missing the UH-2, but the pilot continued to drop lower until finally he held the helo in a hover with the wheels just touching the soft ground.

"While we were on the edge of the clearing," said Burns, "we both could hear the North Vietnamese search party noisily crashing through the jungle a short distance away."

For three minutes the helicopter hung there with its floodlight on as Holtzclaw and Burns frantically stumbled and fell their way across the paddy with its criss-crossing dikes. The UH-2 was under fire from two sides at first, and then from a third, as the enemy closed in on the area vacated a minute before by the men being rescued. Returning the fire, the helicopter crew silenced at least one position and managed to keep the enemy down until the exhausted, mud-spattered survivors clambered aboard.

Lieutenant Lassen immediately lifted off and headed the badly damaged and vibrating helicopter for the sea. The helicopter had been overland for 56 minutes and under fire for 45 minutes while pressing the rescue attempt. Even yet, they were not out of danger, for as Lieutenant Lassen neared the coast, the Seasprite once again ran into heavy flak and automatic fire, and during subsequent evasive maneuvers, the damaged door was torn off.

Finally over the water, the success of the rescue now depended on how much fuel remained. With every available radio in TF 77 listening and all hands praying, the Seasprite finally landed aboard the *Jouett* (DLG-29) with only five minutes of fuel remaining.

For his intrepidity and conspicuous gallantry, Lieutenant Lassen was later awarded the Medal of Honor by President Johnson.

The Effects of the Weather

One of the key factors in the bombing interdiction effort against North Vietnam was the monsoon weather, which often precluded full-scale attacks on fixed targets and greatly reduced armed reconnaissance.

The heavy, often torrential rain, low clouds, and poor visibility, served to hide the enemy's missiles and guns, and to provide early concealment for the launching and inflight trajectory of the missiles. This forced our aircraft below the cloud layers and down into the effective range of radar controlled guns and small arms. When these weather handicaps were added to the cover of night, when the only aircraft which could find a target without the use of flares, fly low enough to hit it, and maneuver to avoid the mountain tops, missiles, and flak, was the A-6 Intruder, it can be understood why bombing aircraft usually could locate their targets over North Vietnam less than one-third of the time.

But more important, under cover of clouds and darkness the enemy could repair his roads and bridges, fill in the bomb craters, repair the rail lines, and construct the pontoon bridges and bypasses to keep his supply pipelines into South Vietnam filled.

When the southwest monsoon blew, from late April until mid-October, North Vietnam's weather could be expected to be reasonably good, with June, July, and August providing the best visibility and the clearest skies. During the remainder of the year, as the monsoon winds reversed and blew from the northeast, the weather over North Vietnam could be expected to be both poor and unpredictable. The 60-day periods of March–April and September-October were especially uncertain, as the cold fronts and low pressure centers associated with the transition from southwest to northeast monsoons occurred. By November, the northeast monsoon would usually be well developed, and the onshore flow of moist air could be expected to produce extremely poor weather until the following spring.

If the air interdiction campaign was to be effective, therefore, a concerted, all-out effort had to be made during the few months of good weather.

In effect, the monsoon weather forced Task Force 77 to be alert for, and ready to react to, unseasonal and unpredicted breaks in the weather. For example, on 19 to 23 January 1967, there was a four-day period of relatively clear weather over North Vietnam. It was a golden opportunity for coordinated three-carrier strikes, and in three days eight hundred sorties were flown into the North. Then the monsoon closed in again and, except for a short break on 27 January, coordinated attacks could not be undertaken again until 4 February when, once again, the weather broke briefly. Then it reclosed until the second week of March, when one thousand Rolling Thunder sorties were flown. On 1 March 1967, in fact, Task Force 77 was instructed not to fly over North Vietnam in marginal weather. Loss of aircraft in February and March, in both 1965 and 1966, had been high and the poor monsoon weather had certainly been a factor.

In addition to the unpredictable weather, there were typhoons to worry about. In 1967, for example, it was Typhoon Billie in July, tropical storms Fran and Kate in August, and typhoons Emma and Gilda in November. These storms caused the loss of several days' strike effort because of the necessity for ships to take evasive action.

In summary, the uncertainty, unpredictability, and caprice of the Vietnamese weather was a factor heavily favoring the enemy. "The nature of the weather in Vietnam was also a vital factor in the interdiction campaign that was never fully appreciated by Washington," said Vice Admiral David C. Richardson, CTF 77 in 1966–67. "With the centralized control of the war from afar," he said, "Washington could not keep in touch with the ever-changing weather which often required on-the-scene changes in target and weapon assignments."

Mining of North Vietnamese Waters

It was never fully appreciated in Washington that about 50% of the enemy's cargo moved on the internal waterways.

During 1966, as the road and rail systems of North Vietnam were attacked by TF 77, the enemy made increasing use of barges and sampans (waterborne logistic craft[27]) to transport men and supplies southward. This trend had first been noted early in 1966, and recommendations had been made to close the river mouths to the barges by mining. Finally, on 23 February 1967, the mining from the air of selected areas of North Vietnam—not Haiphong, of course—was authorized by higher authority. The use of air-delivered mines in selected river areas was determined to be an effective method of reducing North Vietnamese coastal traffic.

The first use of mines commenced on 26 February when seven A-6As from the carrier *Enterprise*, led by Commander A. H. Barie, Commanding Officer of VA-35, planted two fields in the mouths of the Song Ca and South Giang rivers. The mines were dropped from a very low altitude, and although some flak was noted in the vicinity of Vinh, no SAMs were fired.

In March, three new minefields were sown in the mouths of the Song Ma, Kien Giang, and Cua Sot rivers, this time by A-6s from the carrier *Kitty Hawk*. In view of the need to make very precise drops, the aircraft had to make straight-in, low-level passes. This necessitated nighttime runs using a radar-significant target. Though moonlight was a help when it was available, most missions were flown in bad weather. It was a demanding and dangerous assignment.

By mid-April, all the minefields authorized, five in number, had been planted. North Vietnam's three main deep water ports of Haiphong, Hon Gai, and Cam Pha, however, were not authorized.

A careful watch was made to see what effect the mining campaign had.

The first indication came in April, in the Song Giang, when several boats conducting minesweeping operations were photographed. Soon it became apparent that little, if any, traffic was entering or leaving the river mouths. Three sunken boats were noted in the Song Giang on 23 May.

The traffic across the river mouths slowly dried up. And just as the enemy had abandoned truck and rail traffic on the exposed coastal highway, so now did he stop moving war supplies by coastal barges. The enemy simply accepted his losses and the fact that in this area he was beaten. He moved inland, using more trucks, mainly at night, over the unpaved roads hidden under the heavy canopy of the jungle.

The *Forrestal* Fire

On 29 July, TF 77 suffered its second and most serious accident—a severe fire on board the *Forrestal* (CVA-59). This carrier from the Atlantic Fleet had arrived at Yankee Station only five days earlier, and was preparing to launch her second strike of the day, when a Zuni rocket was inadvertently fired from a parked F-4B on the after starboard quarter of the flight deck. The rocket warhead struck the fuel tank of a nearby A-4 Skyhawk being readied for flight and, within seconds, the after half of the flight deck was a holocaust of flames. Fire fighters charged selflessly into the inferno to be met by the blast of exploding bombs, which killed several men and further spread the fire. The flight deck fire was under control in about an hour, but it took another twelve and one-half hours to extinguish all below-deck fires. The tragedy cost 134 lives and hospitalized 60. It caused the loss of 21 aircraft, and damage to 41 others, and put the great carrier, the first of her class, back in the shipyard for nearly seven months of repairs.

The Effort to Isolate Haiphong

The key to forcing Hanoi to stop supporting and directing the aggression in South Vietnam, as Admiral Sharp had often noted, was to deny North Vietnam access to external military and economic assistance. This assistance came largely by sea, primarily into the main port of Haiphong, through which it was estimated that 85% of the country's imports passed, although some came into the ports of Cam Pha and Hon Gai. The remainder came by rail and road from Red China or by rail from Soviet Russia through China.

The quick and easy way to snuff out the war would have been to blockade Haiphong—or to use the term of the 1962 Cuban missile crisis, to "quarantine" it. But this recommendation was repeatedly rejected because of the risk of damage to third-country shipping.

But, if closing Haiphong harbor from seaward by mining or blockading was forbidden, could not the port city be isolated by bombing? To do this would require the destruction of the major bridges, the mining of the transshipment points near the city, and the cutting of the rail lines between Hanoi and Haiphong. Obviously, this was a much more difficult, costly, less efficient alternative than either blockading, quarantining, or mining the port—but it was all that was left, so an intensive effort would be made.

The effort got under way on 30 August 1967, as a result of a visit to Washington by Admiral Sharp which included discussions with key members of Congress.

The Haiphong highway bridge, south-southeast of the city, was the initial isolation target. The *Oriskany*'s air wing, led by Commander Burton H. Shepherd, dropped it into the river.

This strike was a prime example of the discipline and the expertise which strike groups had gained in conducting multiple "Alfa" strikes.

Approaching Haiphong with 24 planes, the strike group evaded a covey of SAMs and maintained their flight integrity. Nearing Haiphong proper, intense 37-mm., 57-mm., and 85-mm. fire was encountered, but the strike group pressed on. Execution was such that every bomb detonated within a period of 10 to 12 seconds. When the smoke cleared, three of the four bridge spans had disappeared. As the strike group retired, it strafed barge traffic in the nearby canals and rivers.

In a matter of weeks, all the main bridges around the two cities were made unserviceable for varying lengths of time. For example, TF 77 hit Haiphong's four major bridges in September. The North Vietnamese made intense efforts to repair them and by the next month they were in service again. Then TF 77 hit all four of them again.

The dredges necessary to keep Haiphong isolated were another prime target, for the harbor was subject to heavy silting from the entire Red River Valley, and constant dredging was necessary. In addition, Haiphong's tides—nine, and occasionally 12, feet—also silted the harbor. By mid-summer 1966, in fact, the depth of the dredged channel through the outer bar was only 14 feet, six feet below normal. This forced deeper-draft ships to anchor in the outer channel and discharge their cargo into lighters, which then became prime targets. (Later, Soviet and Bloc shipping companies were asked to send only ships with drafts of 22 feet or less to Haiphong.) The pilots from the *Bon Homme Richard* got the first dredge on 6 July 1967. Heavily bombed, the camouflaged vessel rolled over on her side, caught fire, and sank. To save its largest suction dredge, Hanoi ordered her towed to Red China.

The enemy responded to the isolation effort in several ways. Increasingly, shipments were made into Sihanoukville, Cambodia, whence by truck, barge, and sampan, war supplies were surreptitiously moved into the sanctuaries along the border with South Vietnam.

The Soviets increased their deliveries. During the first six months of 1967, almost 400,000 tons were delivered into Haiphong, despite the delays in unloading. This was a 38% increase over the corresponding period in 1966.

The enemy also responded by building numerous bypasses. Truck and supply boat activity increased. Boats were moored near foreign ships in order to lessen the chance of their being attacked. The number of boats on the waterways from Haiphong to Hanoi doubled in the last half of September, and tripled by the middle of October. Large open storage

areas near the Haiphong docks and throughout the city multiplied as the full weight of the campaign became evident.

It was during this period that Haiphong ran out of missiles and low on AAA ammunition. On the fifth successive day of striking targets in the Haiphong area, for example, Navy pilots were amazed to arrive over Haiphong without being greeted by the usual SAMs and intense AAA. The electronic signals were there to spoof aircrews, but no SAMs rose from the sites and only sporadic 37-mm. antiaircraft fire was observed, and then only at relatively low level. One flak suppression section circled over Haiphong for 15 minutes looking for an active AAA site and finally dropped their flak suppression weapons on the primary target. This phenomenon lasted for two days, when heavy rain and clouds from the tail end of a typhoon terminated all "Alfa" strike activity over North Vietnam for the next three days.

When the weather cleared and strike groups again returned to Haiphong, the enemy's defenses had been restored and there were many SAMs and heavy AA fire. As always, North Vietnam had resourcefully used the respite to replenish depleted stocks.

The almost continuous attacks on Haiphong began to have other effects. On 25 August, for example, an evacuation order was issued. All civilians except those vital to the defense of Hanoi and Haiphong and to the subsistence of those who defended it were ordered to leave. Women, children, and the elderly assembled, with their suitcases, at collection points where buses, trucks, and pedicabs picked them up. Workshops, offices, and institutions near military targets were moved out of the two city areas.

It was also in August that there began to appear unconfirmed reports that Hanoi was considering an agreement to negotiate as a device to stop the bombing and relieve pressure on its forces.

The American journalist, David Schoenbrun, made a trip to Hanoi in August and was given a lengthy interview with the Premier, a handshake by Ho Chi Minh, and a tour of the countryside. During these discussions, Schoenbrun was told that peace talks could begin rapidly once the bombing raids had stopped. The Premier was pessimistic about an early end to the war, described the peace offers as "false," and stated that he distrusted both secret negotiations and the U. S. government. Schoenbrun described Ho Chi Minh as a feeble old man with stooped shoulders. However, he was also impressed with the steadfast determination, organization, and morale of the North Vietnamese. To him, they seemed determined to achieve victory on their terms.

The First Walleye Attacks

In March 1967, a new Navy weapon called Walleye—a TV-guided air-to-surface glide bomb—was introduced into combat. This weapon represented a long stride forward in the accurate delivery of air-dropped ordnance, since Walleye could be locked on to its target by the pilot prior to drop, and after release, its TV eye would continue to direct the bomb toward the pre-selected aiming point without further help from the pilot, who could then devote his full attention to avoiding missiles and gunfire.

The first Walleye attacks were conducted under the supervision of Rear Admiral Thomas J. Walker, Commander Carrier Division Three, who was charged with their combat introduction. Rear Admiral Walker carefully selected six targets. Attack Squadron 212, commanded by Commander Homer Smith aboard the *Bon Homme Richard*, made the first attacks.

The first launch went against a large military barracks complex at Sam Son on 11 March 1967. Commander Smith launched the weapon, and he and the accompanying pilots watched the TV bomb fly straight and true into

a window of the barracks, exploding within—exactly like the brochure said it would.

The second attack went against the Phu Dien Chau highway bridge, and the third and fourth against other parts of the Sam Son barracks complex. The next day three more Walleyes were dropped against the Thanh Hoa bridge. Again, all were direct hits but damage to the bridge was assessed as minor.

"For the first time in the history of naval warfare," said Rear Admiral Walker, "a combat commander could launch one aircraft carrying one weapon with a high degree of confidence that significant damage could be inflicted on a selected target."

It was the beginning of a new era in aerial warfare and the first use of what soon became known as "smart bombs."

The Interdiction Effort Peak—1967

During the better weather months of May through October 1967, the interdiction campaign reached its peak of intensity—with the Iron Triangle receiving the maximum attention. An unprecedented barrage of major "Alfa" strikes was directed against this region. With a sufficient supply of Walleye weapons now available, several major strikes were directed against the Ngoc Kuyet railroad siding, a nearby bridge, and a bypass between Hanoi and Haiphong. One of the most important attacks went against the Hanoi Thermal Power Plant, which early in May was released as a target, for Walleye only. This indicated the high degree of confidence that Washington had gained in the new "smart bomb," for the reason that collateral damage in downtown Hanoi could be avoided.

"Bonnie Dick" was called out of Subic Bay with orders to hit the Hanoi Thermal Power Plant with Walleye as soon as possible. The weather cleared, and on 19 May 1967 the first attack was made. Once again, Commander Homer Smith led the strike, with Lieutenant

Mike Cater as his only wingman. Six F-8Es from VF-24 were flak suppressors. Air Wing 11 aboard the *Kitty Hawk* was scheduled to strike the Van Dien Truck Park located five miles southwest of the city simultaneously. The two air wings rendezvoused at sea and went "feet dry" (i.e., overland) well to the south. Some MiG-17 fighters were observed attempting to intercept the flight southwest of the city and Lieutenant Phil Wood of VF-24 shot one down at this time. The Walleye attack group maintained integrity and dropped down to a lower altitude to dash the last ten miles, over flat country, to the city. The MiGs were outdistanced at this time but the flight encountered a severe barrage of SAMs and AAA. The two Walleye A-4s pitched up to roll-in from west to east over the lake and delivered their weapon directly on target in the thermal power plant. Gunfire and SAMs continued to lace the sky as evidenced by Japanese news film taken from within the city and later shown on U. S. television. During this attack, two F-8s were shot down—one en route to target and the second during the attack.

The remainder of the flight retired at low level back toward the mountains to the southwest. At this point, the MiG-17s joined in earnest, attempting to get to the two A-4s. A major dog fight erupted just southwest of the city between the remaining F-8s and ten MiG aircraft. The fight ranged from treetop level up to 4,000 feet. Commander Paul Speer, Commanding Officer of VF-211, bagged a MiG-17 in a turning encounter behind the A-4s, followed a few seconds later by Lieutenant (j.g.) Joe Shea, his wingman, who bagged a second MiG-17. The fight continued moving southwest and Lieutenant Bob Lee of VF-24 got another one. With the A-4s safely over the mountains the engagement broke off and thus ended the Navy's largest jet air battle so far. Four MiGs were accounted for in this brief, furious encounter.

As TF 77's efforts intensified between May and October, the enemy's AAA fire was especially heavy. July, in fact, was a record month, with 233 SAMs being launched at TF 77 aircraft and, while 19 planes were lost, most of them were lost to antiaircraft fire.

The search for SAMs continued. On 19 July, the *Constellation's* Reconnaissance Squadron 12 brought home pictures of a SAM site in a most unusual place; inside a soccer stadium between Haiphong and Hanoi. During the day several attacks on the SAM missile battery, the missiles, the vans, transporters, and the stadium itself were made. Commander Robin McGlohn, Commanding Officer, VF-142, and Commander Robert Dunn, Commanding Officer, VA-146, led the first attack. They damged three missiles on their launchers and watched orange smoke rise out of the stadium. Later in the day, Commander Gene Tissot, Commander Carrier Wing 14, led a second strike that totally demolished the installation.

On 21 July 1967, a fierce seven-minute engagement occurred as the airplanes from the "Bonnie Dick's" Carrier Wing 21 approached for an attack on the petroleum storage area at Ta Xa. Eight MiG-17s attacked the F-8E/C fighter cover provided by VF-211 and VF-24 and the Shrike-armed "Iron Hand" A-4s of VA-76 and VA-212. One MiG was destroyed by a Sidewinder fired by Commander Marion H. Isaacks; a second was downed by the 20-mm. fire of Lieutenant Commander Robert L. Kirkwood; a third was destroyed by an air-to-ground Zuni rocket and 20-mm. guns fired by Lieutenant Commander Ray Hubbard, Jr.; and a "probable" fourth was damaged by another Sidewinder launched by Lieutenant (j.g.) Philip W. Dempewolf which hit but never exploded. Two other MiGs were damaged. Commander Isaacks and Lieutenant Commander Kirkwood's F-8s were damaged, but both got home safely.

During the Phy Ly railroad yard attack on

16 July, an F-8E from the *Oriskany* (Lieutenant Commander Demetrio A. Verich of VF-162) was hit by a SAM after dodging two others. Verich "punched out" and reached the ground safely in a karst area, a steep hillside covered with brush, tangled trees, and vines.[28] It was only an hour before dark, however, and too late for a rescue effort to be started. So Verich laid low, covered himself with branches and sweated out the long night, hearing voices of a nearby searching party. He was 30 miles south of Hanoi and about 50 miles from the coast. Early the next day a Big Mother helo flown by Lieutenant Neil R. Sparks and Lieutenant (j.g.) Robin Springer, with crewmen ADJ1 Masengale and AE3 Ray, made the extremely hazardous trip. The SH-3 spent two hours and 23 minutes over North Vietnam under continuous attack before snatching Verich from the clutches of the nearby North Vietnamese searching party. Sparks won the Navy Cross for his heroic rescue.

Such rescues deep within North Vietnam and close to villages and cities were becoming increasingly difficult and risky. Not far from the incident just described, two A-4Es from the *Oriskany*'s VA-164 were shot down on 18 July. Lieutenant (j.g.) Larrie J. Duthie was saved by a U. S. Air Force "Jolly Green Giant" helicopter in another hazardous rescue. But the attempt to rescue the second pilot was not successful. In this instance, the Big Mother SAR helo from the *Hornet* (CVS-12) was hit by ground fire as it approached the scene, killing one crewman. A second Clementine helo, flown from the *Worden* (DLG-18), was also hit by the heavy automatic weapons fire, which damaged the main rotor, cut six inches off one blade of the tail rotor, and hit in the fuselage. Later in the day, in a third attempt, an SH-3 helicopter was shot down and four crewmen were killed. In addition, during the intensive SAR effort, still another A-4E (Lieutenant Barry T. Wood, VA-164) from the *Oriskany* was struck by antiaircraft fire over the scene. Low on fuel, Wood managed to reach the ocean, where he ejected and was rescued by a boat from the *Richard B. Anderson* (DD-786).

Obviously the North Vietnamese were rushing antiaircraft guns into any rescue area, perhaps even allowing downed pilots to remain free while they set up flak traps. In many cases they used captured radios to send false messages.

The furious pace continued. In August 1967, 16 naval aircraft were shot down, six of them by SAMs. This was the highest loss to missiles in a single month. Two hundred and forty-nine SAMs were counted by the pilots, exceeding the previous high reached in July. During the single day of 21 August, 80 missiles were fired by the enemy, a record for the war.

Despite several days of bad weather early in August, TF 77 struck harder than ever before. For one thing, as we noted earlier, Washington had relaxed target restrictions along the Chinese border, and certain targets as close as eight miles to Red China, a minute's flying time, could be attacked. The Port Wallut naval base, the Lang Son railroad bridges, and the Na Phuco railroad yard, were now cleared for attack by aircraft from TF 77.

An example of one day's heavy work occurred on 21 August 1967, the day the 80 missiles were fired. The *Constellation*, *Intrepid*, and *Oriskany* were at Yankee Station, and the weather over North Vietnam was excellent.

Air Wing Ten on the *Intrepid* sent two major "Alfa" strikes against Port Wallut, 23 aircraft on the first attack, 21 three hours later on the second. A third Alfa strike by the *Intrepid*'s aircraft also struck the Van Dien army supply depot. Pilots saw at least seven secondary explosions and watched balls of black smoke rising to 1,000 feet. Eight buildings and warehouses were destroyed, seven others were damaged, the marine railway was lightly damaged, and one span of the bridge was knocked down. Fourteen SAMs were fired, but no aircraft were hit.

The *Constellation*'s Air Wing 14, meanwhile, was attacking two major targets, the Duc Noi railroad yard and Kep airfield. Both antiaircraft and SAMs were very heavy, and three A-6s of VA-196 were lost. At Kep airfield, one revetted Colt (transport aircraft) was destroyed, another damaged, the runway was cratered, and heavy damage was inflicted on three barracks. The pilots from the *Constellation* counted 51 SAMs fired at their aircraft.

Commander Bryan W. Compton, Commanding Officer of VA-163 aboard the *Oriskany*, led an attack on the Hanoi thermal power plant, the same one that had been battered on 19 and 21 May. With typical determination, the enemy had made repairs, and recently smoke was seen issuing from the generator plant. In anticipation of further attacks, the enemy had brought in several additional 85-mm. and 57-mm. guns to protect it.

Once again, Walleye weapons were used. On this occasion, five Walleyes were fired and five bullseyes resulted, three striking the generator hall and two the boiler house. Dense black and white smoke from the entire complex rose high in the air. Thirty SAMs were fired at the strike aircraft. The 85-mm., 57-mm., and small arms flak was the heaviest seen to date, but no planes were lost. Two were badly damaged. One, flown by Lieutenant Commander Dean A. Cramer, returned with 53 holes in it, while the second, flown by Lieutenant Commander James B. Busey, landed aboard with 127 holes, a fire in the starboard wing, the end of the starboard horizontal stabilizer gone, and all of the starboard elevator shot off.

In addition to hitting targets in North Vietnam, TF 77 pilots got a rare opportunity late in July and early in August to hit something besides interdiction targets: PT boats of the North Vietnamese Navy. On 28 July, Lieutenant Commander J. O. Harmon and Lieutenant (j.g.) R. L. Lindsay of VA-152 set fire to one PT boat near Haiphong. On 1 August, pilots from the *Oriskany* left a second one smouldering. And on 4 August, two A-4E pilots from attack squadron 164 on board the *Oriskany* (Lieutenant Russell H. Decker and Lieutenant David Hodges) sighted another P4 hidden against a small island. Attacking with Zuni rockets and 20-mm. cannon, they set her on fire. Lieutenant Decker called for help when he was out of ordnance and low on fuel. Two A-1 rescue combat air patrol pilots from the USS *Oriskany*'s VA-152, Lieutenant Commander J. O. Harmon and Lieutenant (j.g.) Ashton Langlinais, were vectored in to complete the kill. They fired Zuni rockets and 20-mm. cannon and, before they departed, the enemy boat had sunk.[29]

As the weather began to turn sour in October 1967, the A-6 Intruders once again came into their own as they had done during the 1966 northeast monsoon season, for at night and in bad weather they were the only aircraft in the American inventory able to find, strike, and destroy point targets in the heavily defended northeast quadrant. The Intruders became the scourge of the Iron Triangle.

On 27 October, six A-6s executed individual night time attacks on the Hanoi ferry slips, each successive aircraft encountering increasing opposition.

On the night of 30 October 1967, a single A-6A Intruder launched from the deck of *Constellation* successfully completed one of the most difficult single-plane strikes in the history of air warfare. Once again, the purpose of the strike was to drop eighteen 500-pound bombs on the all-important Hanoi railroad ferry slip, and to keep it inoperative. The A-6 mission was flown by Lieutenant Commander Charles B. Hunter with Lieutenant Lyle F. Bull, bombardier navigator, from VA-196. This mission will be described in some detail since it is typical of the capability of the A-6 and of the courage, tenacity, and airmanship of the A-6 Intruder crews.

By late 1967, Hanoi had become the most heavily defended city against air attack in the history of warfare. It was defended by fifteen "hot" or occupied SAM sites, at least 560 known antiaircraft guns of various calibers, and some MiG-17s or -21s at nearby airfields. The mission called for making a low-level, instrument approach across the rugged karst mountains surrounding the Red River Valley. It would then be necessary to drop a string of eighteen 500-pound bombs along an impact line of 2,800 feet. By using maximum concealment and by flying at low level, it was hoped that the plane could remain below the effective SAM envelope. However, this approach would require Lieutenant Commander Hunter to maintain a constant bombing course and altitude for several seconds during a highly vulnerable period of the attack.

The mission was routine until Hunter was about 18 miles from Hanoi, still navigating by radar between and over the karsts. At this point, his instruments and earphones indicated that the enemy's missile search radar had detected his presence. He immediately descended to hide himself below the radar horizon. Shortly thereafter Lieutenant Bull acquired the "IP" (initial point—a recognizable location) on his radar and immediately commenced to make his bombing solution on the aircraft's computer and bombing equipment. While he was doing so, Hunter's instruments and earphones indicated that a second SAM battery was preparing to fire at him, so he descended once again. To those who have not flown a plane, it is difficult to describe the courage and skill required to fly a heavily loaded aircraft at 460 knots, on instruments, at night, above unfamiliar terrain, while maintaining a very low altitude.

It was now time to turn to the bombing heading. As he did so, Hunter caught sight of the first of 16 SAMs that would be fired at him. "When I first saw it, it was dead ahead and above me," he said, "and it appeared that it would pass overhead. However, just as it got overhead, I could see it turn directly downward and head for us. To me, the rocket exhaust looked like a doughnut." At this point, he might have jettisoned his bombs, aborted the mission, and headed for home. Instead, with 9,000 pounds of bombs under his wings, he executed a high "G" barrel-roll to port from a very low altitude—an exceedingly dangerous maneuver. The SAM exploded within 200 feet, shaking the aircraft violently. Hunter's roll took him to 2,000 feet, inverted, but he continued rolling and leveled out again, flying low within a few degrees of the desired inbound heading. By keeping on course to target while making this violent maneuver, he was able to maintain Lieutenant Bull's accurate work on the computer so that the radar cursors could continue tracking the target and making the bombing solution.

The actual bombing run on the Hanoi ferry slip now began. "At this time," said Hunter, "the AAA fire was so heavy that it lit up the countryside and I could see details on the ground pretty well." As the sky lit up with flak, Bull spotted two SAMs approaching at 2 o'clock (to the right of his nose) and Hunter saw three more SAMs between 10 and 11 o'clock (to the left of his nose). At least five missiles were now airborne and aimed at the Intruder.

There was no chance to avoid them, if the attack was to be pressed. So, for the last seven miles, the aircraft was flown at deck level on the radar altimeter in the hope that during the on-the-deck approach the SAMs would be unable to guide on the fast-moving Intruder. As each successive SAM exploded directly overhead, approximately 400 feet above the canopy, it filled the cockpit with an orange glow and made the aircraft shudder. "During the run-in to target a continuous barrage of flak lit the sky around the aircraft as if it were daylight," said Hunter. Numerous searchlights also illuminated the aircraft for the benefit of small arms and automatic weapons sites.

Despite all the flak, SAMs, and searchlights, the A-6 bored in and released its bombs whereupon Hunter made a seven-"G" turn to starboard. During this turn, four additional SAM explosions were experienced aft and above the aircraft. In the amply flak-lit sky, it was easy to see the intended target clearly visible next to the Red River and to watch the string of bombs fall on the assigned target. Hunter rolled out, heading southeast at various altitudes, some of them high, and commenced heavy jinking to cope with a cockpit indication that a MiG-21 was on his tail. Sporadic flak was encountered until the coast was reached.

It was missions like this, night after night over Haiphong and Hanoi, which caused Vice Admiral William F. Bringle, Commander Seventh Fleet, to say, "The low-level night missions flown by the A-6 over Hanoi and Haiphong were the most demanding missions we have ever asked our aircrews to fly. Fortunately, there is an abundance of talent, courage, and aggressive leadership in these A-6 squadrons."

Attacks on Shipyards and Railroads

While the A-6s continued their nocturnal, single-plane raids, and the attempt to isolate Haiphong by multi-plane day attack was maintained, a new target system was struck: shipyards and barge-building yards. On 12 October 1967, the *Oriskany*'s pilots, led by Commander Elbert Lighter (Executive Officer, VA-163), conducted an Alfa strike on the Haiphong Shipyard, with excellent results. A power boat and five barges (one of which was in the graving dock) were sunk, and all support buildings within the yard were destroyed. A few minutes later, pilots from the *Intrepid* attacked the boat yard at Lach Tray and heavily damaged it. One A-4C sustained four 6-inch holes in its wing, but the pilot was able to return safely to the "Fighting I." The third yard, Haiphong West, was rendered completely unserviceable by the *Intrepid*. All support buildings, the fabrication shops, and the two marine railways were destroyed, and seven shipways were heavily damaged.

In November 1967, other shipyards were struck. On 7 November, the *Constellation*'s Air Wing 14 scored numerous direct hits on the Ninh Ngoai boat works and the An Ninh Noi boat yard. Three A-6s from the "Connie" made visual runs on the Yen Cuong boat repair yard, dropping fifty-four 500-pound bombs. Five vessels were destroyed, the building ways interdicted, and four barges under construction heavily damaged. Simultaneously, the *Intrepid*'s pilots attacked the Uong Bi barge yard and reported that their bombs produced several large fireballs. On 13 November, the *Intrepid*'s air wing attacked the Phui Nighai Thuong boat yard and the Uong Bi barge yard, while on the 16th, airplanes from the *Coral Sea* (CVA-43) attacked Haiphong shipyard number two. Photography showed excellent results—severe damage to one graving dock, the slipway destroyed, ten support buildings demolished, and six others damaged. Flak was heavy, and the *Coral Sea* pilots counted 8 SAMs during the attack. On 17 November 1967, the aircraft of *Intrepid*'s Air Wing 10 heavily damaged the Hanoi barge yard. The strike consisted of 26 aircraft, led by Commander Richard A. Wigent, Commanding Officer of VA-34. "There were many SAMs in the air," he said, "the most I've ever seen." One of them demolished a Skyhawk; the pilot ejected from his burning aircraft and was immediately captured.

LCdr. Charles B. Hunter on board the Constellation.

No attempt was made by the North Vietnamese to repair these damaged shipyards. Instead, the enemy took advantage of the sanctuaries of Haiphong and Hanoi. Photographs taken in January 1968 revealed four new barge construction sites in Haiphong, two along the streets and plazas, and two in heavily inhabited areas where attacks were forbidden. Thus, the Communists maintained their double standard, putting military targets in known sanctuaries, pulling every propaganda stop to call for a bombing cease-fire, and at the same time waging an unceasing campaign of assassination and terror against the civilian populace of the South. All this was suffered to pass with little criticism from the world community.

In December 1967, whenever the monsoon weather abated, the northeast quadrant was struck and the cordon around Haiphong was kept taut. The major rail lines of the Iron Triangle received particular attention. The

Oriskany's pilots caught a 40-car train southeast of Phy Ly on 14 December and destroyed eight cars and damaged eight more. Pilots from the *Ranger* (CVA-61) located and struck a 30-car train south of Hanoi and wrecked the engine and several cars.

The *Ranger* had arrived on station on 3 December, bringing two new aircraft, the A-7A Corsair II, flown by Attack Squadron 147, and the EKA-3B Tacos. The A-7A Corsair, a single place, light attack jet aircraft, featured advanced radar, navigation, and weapons systems, and could carry a 15,000-pound bomb load. The EKA-3B Tacos was a much-modified model of the A-3 Skywarrior, rebuilt especially for the electronic warfare environment of North Vietnam.

As the year closed and the holidays approached, the aerial mining of the coastal and inland waterways was intensified, for previous experience had shown that the Communists would make a maximum effort to move supplies during the holiday standdowns.

In 1966, in fact, the Joint Chiefs of Staff had taken a position of strong opposition to any cessation of military operations during the Christmas and Tet holiday seasons. But, if a cease-fire had to be made, the Joint Chiefs said, it should be limited to a maximum of 48 hours in order to minimize the military advantages given the enemy. In every previous case of a Tet or other holiday standdown, the enemy had conducted major resupply operations and had replenished his forces, all of which cost the United States greater casualties. For example, between 8 and 12 February 1966, aerial reconnaissance revealed significant logistic movement of material by water, truck, and rail transport—between 22,300 and 25,100 tons of supplies were moved from the north into the area below 19 degrees North latitude.

Prior to the 24-hour Christmas and 36-hour New Year standdowns in 1967, there were many indications that the enemy planned once more to take full advantage of these periods. Later events proved that he conducted a massive and well-organized resupply of his forces. Almost 1,300 trucks were noted in the Panhandle by pilots and photo-interpreters during Christmas and about 1,800 during the slightly longer New Year standdown. This compared with a daily average of only 170 for the other days between 22 December 1967 and 4 January 1968. Pilots of the *Kitty Hawk* flying over the coastal highway during the Christmas standdown counted 560 trucks bumper to bumper over a seven-mile section of road. During the New Year's standdown, more than 1,000 trucks were counted moving south. Pilots reported that the coastal road looked "like the New Jersey turnpike."

By October 1967, some 200,000 tons of goods imported by sea had piled up and were stacked in mountainous piles in open storage areas near the Haiphong docks. There was some uncertainty whether the enemy considered these stockpiles "safe" by our own self-imposed restrictions forbidding attack on them, or whether they were jammed up because the supplies could not be moved south. In any event, authority was never granted to attack these huge stockpiles or the Haiphong docks and warehouses.

On the positive side, early in November intelligence indicated that the frequent night and day air alerts were slowing work on the Haiphong docks as workers took shelter. Absenteeism among stevedores increased because of the dangers of coming to work. It was also reported that dock workers suffered from hunger and weariness. Ship unloading times increased from 13 days to 42 days. A shortage of trucks and lighters slowed down the unloading of ships and the clearing of cargo from the port. The mere presence of U. S. aircraft in the area reduced effective dredging of the approaches to Haiphong, and foreign merchant ships were unable to take advantage of their full load capacity.

The key rail line running south from Hanoi and Haiphong to Thanh Hoa was kept cut in several places along its 100-mile length. These frequent cuts often provided opportunities for attacks on trains trapped between cuts—58 cars were destroyed in the Ninh Binh railroad siding in November. Also, with bridges along the key rail line down, the enemy was forced to offload at every crossing, ferry the cars and supplies across (usually at night), and reload them on the other side. Aircraft from the *Coral Sea* and the *Intrepid* caught another train at a river crossing in November and destroyed 25 rail cars.

Although Secretary McNamara in late August 1967 had testified voluminously before Senator Stennis' Preparedness Committee against expanding the bombing, the first public expression of doubt that the bombing wasn't accomplishing what was expected reached the pilots in combat on 10 October 1967 when the Secretary voiced disappointment.

"I do not think [the bombing] has in any significant way affected their war making capability," he said. ". . . the North Vietnamese still retain the capability to support activities in South Vietnam and Laos at present or increased combat levels and force structure.

"All of the evidence is so far that we have not been able to destroy a sufficient quantity [of war material in North Vietnam] to limit the activity in the South below the present level, and I do not know we can in the future."

This post-strike photo of Phuong Dinh railroad bypass bridge, 6 miles north of Thanh Hoa, North Vietnam, shows spans of the bridge dropped into the water after an attack by A-4 Skyhawks from the Oriskany *on September 10, 1967.*

To the pilots who were risking their lives daily under the restrictive targeting system and flight rules imposed by Secretary McNamara, who were not allowed to destroy the supplies where they could be seen, it was a disheartening judgment.

Despite the bad weather, the missiles, the MiGs, and the flak, and despite all the bombing restrictions, the 1967 accomplishments of Task Force 77 *were* impressive. Thirty SAM sites and 187 AAA/AW gun batteries had been destroyed. Nine hundred fifty-five bridges were destroyed and 1,586 others were damaged. Seven hundred thirty-four motor vehicles, 410 locomotives and rail cars, and 3,185 watercraft had been destroyed.

During the year, eleven carriers had participated in operations as part of Task Force 77— the *Bon Homme Richard, Constellation, Coral Sea, Enterprise, Forrestal, Hancock, Intrepid, Kitty Hawk, Oriskany, Ranger,* and *Ticonderoga.* Many thousands of attack sorties had been flown over North Vietnam. Fourteen MiG aircraft had been destroyed in the air, 32 others on the ground. One hundred thirty-three aircraft had been lost in combat. This was a 9% increase over losses in 1966. Approximately one-third of the crews of aircraft shot down by the North Vietnamese had been recovered by the courageous and resourceful rescue units.

Admiral Roy Johnson, CinCPacFlt, made a cogent judgment. "There can be no doubt," he said, "that the effort of TF 77 in the North had saved many American lives in the land campaigns in the South."

Five hundred thousand civilians in North Vietnam were engaged in air defense or repair activities on the lines of communication. This diversion of manpower from other pursuits, particularly agriculture, had raised the cost and difficulty of the war for Hanoi.

As 1967 closed, and the northeast monsoon intensified, it was apparent that the war in Southeast Asia had become very much a war of determination, Communist determination to conduct and support aggression in the South versus the determination of the Free World to halt that aggression through the application of controlled air power.

1968

The final three months' effort before the 31 March bombing halt was drastically curtailed owing to the northeast monsoon. During January, February, and March, the weather was even worse than predicted. In the Iron Triangle, there was an average of only three days per month during which visual strikes could be accomplished. The weather in February 1968, in fact, was the poorest experienced during any month since the beginning of air interdiction, with only three per cent of the days having flying weather. In March, it was 6 per cent.

Thus, the A-6 Intruder, with its all-weather tactical bombing system, bore the brunt of the bombing, averaging a dozen sorties per day, hitting four airfields, four power plants, and two new targets, the Hanoi radio station and the Hanoi port facility.

The campaign against lines of communication around Haiphong forced the North Vietnamese to adopt extraordinary efforts to maintain a flow of material over existing lines. Distribution problems for Hanoi were further aggravated by the arrival of a near-record number of foreign ships in Haiphong: over 40 in January, and a similar number in March. The port of Hon Gai was pressed into service by the Communists as a discharge point in an effort to reduce the pressure on Haiphong. Normally this port served only the nearby coalmining area and did not contribute significantly to the flow of imports into the country.

Expansion of the road networks continued as North Vietnam sought to gain flexibility by adding bypasses and constructing new segments of road. Of particular significance was the route being built to connect Red China with the Haiphong region, a development which would make it possible to add 1,000 metric tons of supplies to the quantity entering North Vietnam each day. Repair efforts elsewhere in the country were vigorously pursued. The Paul Doumer bridge, located immediately north of Hanoi, was the object of numerous air attacks by the U. S. Air Force and suffered heavy damage. Along with repairs to that bridge, several bridge bypasses and ferry landings were built near the bridge, a testimony to the importance of the route to the enemy, who used it to move material coming from both Communist China and Haiphong.

1968 STANDDOWNS

There were two brief standdown periods in January—New Year's and Tet. As they had always done before, the North Vietnamese took full advantage of the ceasefire to move a great amount of supplies as far south as possible. In Route Package II alone, 378 trucks were seen and photographed, 337 of them moving south, and it was estimated that 9,000 tons of war materials had been moved in these vehicles. Reconnaissance sorties flown during the 36-hour New Year's standdown located a total of 800 trucks, 130 boats, and 159 railroad cars, 90% of which were headed south. Air strikes against these targets during the 24 hours immediately following New Year's accounted for 24 trucks destroyed and 13 damaged, 28 boats destroyed and 47 damaged, and 41 railroad cars destroyed and 47 damaged.

It was during these attacks that F-8 pilots from the *Oriskany* bagged two locomotives with their heat-seeking Sidewinder missiles. Commander Charles A. L. Swanson, Commanding Officer of VF-162, got one on 2 January, when he got a lock-on and a direct hit in the firebox, which resulted in a tremendous explosion. Later the stalled 45-car train was badly damaged. On 6 January, Lieutenant Commander John S. Hellman of VF-162 got the

second engine kill. His Sidewinder locked on and hit the locomotive boiler aft of the stack, with the boiler erupting in a geyser of steam and water.

The second January cease-fire, for Tet, was also scheduled for 36 hours (1800 on 29 January to 0600 on 31 January). But on the first day of the cease-fire, 29 January, the North Vietnamese launched their powerful Tet offensive against selected military installations and provincial capitals throughout South Vietnam. The most spectacular of these took place in and around Saigon, where the enemy attacked the President's Palace, the U. S. Embassy, and Tan Son Nhut Air Base, but were unsuccessful in their attempts to capture or destroy any of these. The main purpose of the attacks was psychological rather than political, to show that the Communists still had effective combat capabilities, that South Vietnam had not been made secure by the presence of more than a half million Americans, and that the bombing effort against North Vietnam was a failure.

As a result of the Communist offensive, the Tet cease-fire was cancelled and all forces resumed intensified operations. Moreover, U. S. forces were permitted to use armed reconnaissance aircraft south of Vinh which forced the North Vietnamese to use fewer and smaller truck convoys. Aircraft of Task Force 77 saw only 300 trucks in the Tet period, less than one-third of those sighted during the New Year's standdown period.

The Thanh Hoa Railroad and Highway Bridge

On 28 January, during a break in the northeast monsoon, several major Alfa strikes were directed against North Vietnam. One of the targets was the seemingly indestructible Thanh Hoa railroad and highway bridge. For three years, U. S. Navy, Air Force, and Marine aircraft attacked this steel bridge which carries both highway 1A and the main east coast rail line. In 1965, 277 sorties had struck it; 135 in 1966; 204 in 1967. More than 1,250 tons of all types of heavy ordnance had been dropped on this bridge, and eight aircraft had been lost in the nearly 700 attack sorties, but the rugged, heavily trussed stone bridge, built into an outcropping of solid rock, while often damaged, was still intact and is still in use.

"The enemy had long since built several bypasses around the Thanh Hoa bridge," said Rear Admiral David C. Richardson, the Commander of Task Force 77, "and it had lost a great deal of its importance in the interdiction effort."

"For this reason, I placed the bridge off-limits and would only occasionally approve attacks on it. To the pilots of TF 77, the psychological importance of that bridge far exceeded its tactical importance. Every air wing out in WestPac wanted the honor of knocking it down and it gave the pilots a real boost to occasionally go after it."

In November, on the last strike of their 1966 deployment aboard the *Constellation*, CVW-15 received approval from Rear Admiral Richardson for a final try at the Thanh Hoa bridge before returning home. Hopes ran high and the first post-strike reports of smoke, vapor, and dust obscuring the target kept open the possibility that this symbol of the North Vietnam transportation network was at last destroyed. In fact, the carrier's skipper, Captain Bill Houser, rushed the optimistic pilot reports to Rear Admiral Richardson. "We got it, we got it!" he exclaimed. Unfortunately, subsequent photography confirmed the fact that this narrow horizontal steel birdcage had once again withstood Yankee attack.

Five more strikes by the Navy and Air Force went against the heavily defended bridge in January 1968. Carrier Air Wing 15, including attack squadrons VA-153 and VA-155, this time aboard the *Coral Sea*, made attacks on 28 January. Direct hits were achieved on the span with 2,000-pound bombs, two holes were punched in the bridge decking, the truss structure at the eastern end of the bridge was damaged, and the western approach was closed. But, once again, the bridge did not go down, and by 8 February it was again in service.

Captain W. B. Muncie reported one theory for the seeming indestructibility of the bridge that the earth was composed of two giant elliptical hemispheres, spring hinged somewhere beneath the South Atlantic Ocean and clamped firmly shut on the other side by the Thanh Hoa bridge. This theory had it that if the Thanh Hoa bridge were ever destroyed, the world would snap open, flipping man and beast hither and yon, and upsetting the gravitational balance of the universe.

It was the one target in North Vietnam that nobody could destroy.

TF 77 PROVIDES RELIEF TO KHE SANH

During January 1968, TF 77 flew 811 attack sorties in support of the U. S. Marines at Khe Sanh, striking at enemy troop concentrations, artillery and rocket positions, and storage areas. On 31 January, TF 77 was requested to provide 1,000 sorties per day to help the embattled Marines in Operation Niagara. In February, almost 1,500 attack sorties were flown in support of the Marine base. Another 1,600 attack sorties were flown in March, attacking weapon sites, troop concentrations, rocket positions, base camps, tanks, and trucks. In many instances, TF 77 pilots dropped ordnance on enemy trenches within 100 meters of the defending Marines.

In February 1968, with Washington calling for increased bombing pressure against Hanoi to coerce the North Vietnamese to the conference table, and in the face of the monsoon season's worst weather, the burden fell again on the A-6 Intruders. The *Kitty Hawk*'s VA-75, commanded by Commander Jerrold Zacharias, led the way. On 1, 2, 5, 9, 10, 13, 14, 16, and 18 February, A-6s attacked a variety of targets in the Iron Triangle: airfields, power plants, the Hanoi-Haiphong bridge, barge construction facilities, the Hanoi radio communication facility, and railroad yards.

The A-6 mission flown on 24 February against the Hanoi port facility deserves mention. This was a newly authorized target on the southeast corner of the city, lying along the Red River and immediately south of Gia Lam airfield. Three aircraft were launched, with Commander Zacharias and his B/N, Lieutenant Commander M. R. Hall, leading the way.

"There was no moon," said Commander Zacharias, "and we used our terrain avoidance radar to fly at 400 to 500 feet above the peaks. When I knew we were clear of the mountains, I descended to the deck so the SAM radars couldn't pick us up. With no moonlight, I was strictly 'on the gauges' although I could just discern some ground texture at this altitude. After about a minute in the flat lands, we saw a SAM launch at twelve o'clock. The bottom of the overcast was 1,000 feet and the light from the SAM booster rocket reflected off the bottom of the overcast and from every rice paddy between the missile and the aircraft, providing a very nice horizon. The missile was about 10 miles away and had been fired directly toward us. I descended somewhat, but overshot a little and Mike called level at 40 feet. That was too low and so I went back up a way. A few seconds later we saw the second SAM headed our way—it was off our nose to the right, so I made a slight course change to the right to place the missile on the left side of the aircraft where I could see it at all times. About five seconds later, I saw the missile make a course change to compensate for our alteration of heading and it resumed its course toward us. I waited until I thought it was the right time and then changed both our course and altitude. The first missile exploded under us, right where we had been, and buffeted the aircraft quite a bit. On our inbound run they fired no more missiles, perhaps because they were afraid one would land in the city. At about six miles, every gun in town opened up and they were really awake by now. Mike picked up the target. As we got near it, I popped up and delivered 24 bombs. Although Hanoi was completely blacked out by the time we got there, there was enough light from all the flak so that I could see the river banks and determine that we were on our target. At bomb release I broke down and left and crossed the downtown part of Hanoi at 530 knots just to wake up the heavy sleepers. We then altered course frequently to avoid the many flak sites which were really hosing the sky. I could see it all going up and could pick the holes where it looked the lightest to go between."

After 60 days on the line, the *Kitty Hawk* welcomed the arrival of the *Enterprise* at Yankee Station. On board was VA-35, commanded by Commander Glenn E. Kollman. It would be their task to carry on the outstanding efforts of VA-75.

"During this period," Rear Admiral John P. Weinel commented, "the effort of the A-6 Intruders of VA-35 was magnificent."

Conclusions

On the night of 31 March 1968, President Johnson made his dramatic announcement of a bombing halt north of latitude 20 degrees North, and revealed his decision not to run again for the presidency:

"Tonight I have ordered our aircraft and our naval vessels to make no attacks on North Vietnam, except in the area north of the demilitarized zone where the continuing enemy buildup directly threatens Allied forward positions and where the movements of their troops and supplies are clearly related to that threat."

Seven months later, the President would order cessation of *all* attacks on North Vietnam.

The pullback from the war in Southeast Asia had begun.

The 37-month effort had cost Task Force 77 over 300 airplanes destroyed in combat over North Vietnam, 1,000 others damaged, 83 pilots and crewmen killed, 200 captured and missing. What had it accomplished?

The damage to the enemy had certainly been heavy. His transportation system, roads, rail lines, and bridges, had been wrecked. His above-ground fuel system had been destroyed. His war-making industry had been levelled. His other main industries had been severely damaged. All major electric power generating plants had been severely damaged. His airfields and his air force had been rendered ineffective. His military complexes had been devastated. In those 37 months, the enemy had not won a major ground battle. He had certainly not succeeded in subjugating South Vietnam by force.

On the other hand, we had not forced him to halt his aggression. We had forced him to the peace table, but we had not forced him to make peace.

Looking back on the campaign involving Task Force 77, several political, psychological, military, and technical insights into the experiences of the aerial bombing campaign deserve discussion.

POLITICAL

The air bombing campaign against North Vietnam was undertaken on three assumptions: that a vigorous, non-restrictive war against North Vietnam might involve the U. S. directly with Russia, or Red China, or both, and so must be avoided; that a restrained and gradually escalating bombing effort would

convince Hanoi that its goals in South Vietnam could not be achieved; and that American military involvement would be of relatively short duration and modest cost. With the benefit of hindsight, these assumptions now appear to have been questionable.

As a result of the third assumption, there were, at home, no restrictions on wages and prices, no increased taxes, no rationing, and no censorship. The ordinary citizen was not greatly affected, nor was he involved in the war in a personal sense. True, anyone could see it on TV and read about it in his newspaper, but the war was half a world away.

Similarly, despite repeated recommendations by military leaders that this be done, there was no call-up of reserves until 26 January 1968, following the seizure of the USS *Pueblo* (AGER-2) by the North Koreans. Thus shielded from the war's impact, there was no unifying action to bring the individual and the nation together in a common cause.

PSYCHOLOGICAL

There was also a major psychological miscalculation—that American determination and patience would exceed that of North Vietnam. President Johnson had said in his Baltimore speech in April 1965, "We will not grow tired." The early purpose of Rolling Thunder, as stated by Washington, "was to drive home to the North Vietnamese leaders that our staying power was superior to their own." Evidently, the "signal" never reached Hanoi, whose leaders proved to be not on our wave length.

It was a major miscalculation—that *we* would outlast *them*. Indeed, the North Vietnamese assumed just the opposite—that *they* would outlast *us*. Hanoi believed its own morale, tenacity, and patience would be stronger than that of the United States. From the beginning, they publicly stated their opinion that enormous costs and casualties would eventually persuade the United States to negotiate on their terms.

MILITARY

There were five major military lessons of the air war in South Vietnam.

First, there was a major miscalculation concerning the air bombing effort—that interdiction could succeed in snuffing out the war. Indeed, interdiction *might* have succeeded—had the restrictions and ground rules been different, had the recommendations for prompt and vigorous military action been accepted, and had the military pressure on Hanoi been steady rather than spasmodic. In fact, the interdiction campaign almost succeeded despite the rules. If Haiphong had been mined and closed, if military leaders had been given the flexibility needed to fight the war successfully, and if the full weight of American effort assembled in the Western Pacific had been applied properly, early, forcefully, and steadily, interdiction *might* have prevented "the enemy's use of an area or route."

A subtle distinction must be made here. As the war intensified in 1965, interdiction was not, per se, the objective of the bombing effort. The purpose of interdiction in the spring of 1965 was political, not military—to make the enemy stop the war and march to the peace table. Hence, the gradual release of targets and the carefully detailed military control of the war from Washington, a procedure which was never relaxed.

When, after a year, the war was getting bigger and more expensive, and the enemy had not given a single hint of either stopping the war or making a peace, the air war became one of dual purposes—to choke off the aggression in South Vietnam and also to persuade Hanoi to seek peace.

In *this* context, given the constraints, delays, and restrictions imposed, it was a false assumption that interdiction could succeed.

The second military lesson of the air war concerned the closure of Haiphong. In the opinion of most naval and military experts, the single military action which would have hurt North Vietnam most would have been the closing of Haiphong. The vast majority (at least 85 per cent) of the enemy's military strength—missiles, ammunition, trucks, fuel, and so on—came into Haiphong by sea. Hanoi and Haiphong were off limits in the early part of the war, so no mining was done then. Later, when the repeated proposals by the military to mine Haiphong were finally considered, studies were conducted which "proved" that mining was either impossible, infeasible, or would be ineffective. Two other reasons were given for not mining that port. First, that it would escalate the war and risk confrontation either with Russia or Red China or both; second, even if closing Haiphong with mines was accomplished, North Vietnam would be able to sustain itself by increased rail shipments from Russia and China, or even by flying the war materials into North Vietnam's air fields.

The third military lesson of the air interdiction campaign was that we should make use of what we have learned from previous wars. We learned in the Korean War that true air interdiction—the denial of areas and use of transportation systems—cannot be achieved against a determined enemy until night and all-weather bombing can be done with as much accuracy, sustained pressure, and efficiency as by daylight. And after Korea we concluded that never again would we give sanctuaries to an enemy; never again would we fight on the enemy's terms; never again would we handcuff ourselves.

The fourth, and perhaps the most curious military lesson of the interdiction campaign was one which did not surface until 1970. For five years in the Gulf of Tonkin (1965–1970) and for three years in the Sea of Japan (1950–1953), aircraft carriers had been employed as floating airfields—tied to a geographic station, less than a 100 miles from the enemy's coast, sending aircraft against targets deep in the enemy's land. This type of employment had become so habitual and predominant that, in the minds of many, it was assumed to be the primary purpose of attack carriers: sea-based tactical air augmenting (in the minds of some, competing with) land-based tactical air. Attack carriers can indeed be so employed—as Korea and Vietnam amply proved. This employment notwithstanding, the main mission for attack aircraft carriers is to assist in carrying out the Navy's prime mission, control of the seas. Supporting the land battle is strictly a secondary and collateral task.

The employment of carriers in the style of the Sea of Japan and the Gulf of Tonkin made no use of a prime advantage of carriers—their mobility—but this should not become a practice elsewhere.

Admiral Roy L. Johnson, CinCPacFlt, stated, "Had we faced a serious air threat or submarine threat in the Gulf of Tonkin, we might have gotten in serious trouble by operating near a fixed point. . . . Task Force 77 could have achieved the same approximate effort against North Vietnam by not operating in the Gulf of Tonkin, but by roaming up and down the coast."

The fifth, and most important, military lesson of the war in Southeast Asia was that it is not possible to conclude a conflict successfully if those who direct it are convinced it cannot or should not be done.

Two of the many other important military lessons of the war have to do with the policy of "gradualism" and targeting.

The policy of gradualism found its birth in a series of Pentagon papers in March 1964. The JCS, in a 2 March memorandum to Secretary McNamara, presented two ways of terminating the conflict in Southeast Asia without involving the United States with Red China. The first would be small-scale, cross-the-border operations by South Vietnamese forces against the Ho Chi Minh trail. The second way would be pressure against North Vietnam itself, especially air operations. These could be sudden or heavy air attacks to demonstrate U. S. determination to halt Hanoi's aggression, or they could be gradual attacks, at first by the South Vietnamese Air Force, on an accelerating line of severity. Secretary McNamara, in mid-March, recommended to the President a gradual campaign of overt naval and military pressure against Hanoi. The President approved this recommendation 17 March 1964, but called for prior approval by the United States' allies.

From the vantage point of hindsight, the policy of applying military pressure in small doses proved to be a mistake. It turned out to be more expensive in lives, weapons, treasure, and time than had the traditional system of choosing a political goal, adopting a strategy, and then granting authority and responsibility to the military to reach that goal.

The close control of targets, including tactical details, was excessive. Because of the unpredictability of the weather and the need for flexibility to meet rapidly changing tactical conditions, the interdiction effort was severely hampered by the remote-control system of targeting that developed. Recommendations by commanders in the field were not followed. In addition, the centralized control of the war from afar, which in the early months of the war specified the kind, size, and number of bombs to be dropped, and the number and type of aircraft to carry them, gave the leaders on the scene difficult and unwieldy problems.

TECHNICAL

One of the major technical accomplishments of TF 77 was the development of a tremendous capability to operate attack carriers around the clock, despite weather or darkness. For days and weeks on end, the carriers at Yankee Station operated without pause in a sustained manner which was unknown and, indeed unattainable, in either Korea or World War II. The replenishment process, of bringing ammunition, fuel, and supplies to the Fleet, was perfected, allowing the carriers to fly around the clock without interruption.

The 1965–68 war in Southeast Asia saw two major areas of warfare rise to prominence—electronic warfare and missile warfare. In every area—land, sea, and air—electronic countermeasures began to play a prominent role, and especially so in the air. Planes had to have electronic devices to warn of an approaching missile and devices to divert or "spoof" it. To attack the missile sites, other electronic devices were needed to point the location (or at least the direction) on the ground whence the missile radar signals came. Special weapons were developed to seek out and destroy enemy missile and radar sites by homing in on their radiations. The Shrike and Standard ARM were such weapons. Electronics were also the heart of another weapon, the Walleye, the flying TV bomb.

The simple and effective SAMs gave the enemy's defense a giant step forward, and forced pilots either to go low and face a deadly barrage of gunfire, or to go high and bomb with far less accuracy.

In terms of new airplanes, there was never a period in the history of naval aviation when so many new aircraft, weapons, and ideas came to fruition. Propeller aircraft, unable to survive in the high-threat areas of North Vietnam, disappeared from naval air's attack inventory. To take the place of the venerable A-1 Spads came the highly effective new attack bomber, the A-7 Corsair II. The A-6 Intruder, perhaps the best tactical military airplane ever developed, also came. And behind these two attack aircraft were several others—the RA-5C multi-sensor reconnaissance airplane, and the first built-from-the-ground-up ECM aircraft, the EA-6A (flown only by the Marines, but used on many occasions to support naval air missions in the north). Finally, there were the E-2A Hawkeye early warning aircraft and its cargo variant, the C-2 Greyhound.

In the field of weapons, the parade of progress was equally impressive: Walleye, Sparrow, Sidewinder, Snakeye, Shrike, Standard ARM, Focus, Rockeye, cluster bomblet ordnance, and the land-mine.

In the field of aerial tactics, the development of night visual bombing attacks on pinpoint targets (bridges, trucks, check points) was another important accomplishment.

CIVILIAN CONTROL OF THE MILITARY

If ever there was an American war where civilian control over the military was exercised during actual combat operations, the war in Southeast Asia certainly was it. Civilian control was complete, unquestioned, ubiquitous, and detailed, not merely at the higher levels of strategy and political decisions, but also—very importantly—at the lower levels of operations and tactics. This analysis of Task Force 77 operations has given only a few of the many details and numerous examples of the extensive nature of this control.

It is also evident that, at every level, the military was conscientiously obedient, subservient, and responsive to this civilian control. The record shows clearly that naval pilots obeyed the orders to bomb none other than authorized targets. Not once did a responsible commander exceed his authority or disobey his orders. Not once did any naval airman succumb to the temptation of dropping a string of bombs on a loaded merchant ship, or fire into the huge stockpile of oil drums and war materials stacked on the Haiphong piers.

In this war, civilian control was complete and total.

Summary

What would have happened to Southeast Asia if the United States had not intervened? Where would we be today if we had abandoned Indochina in 1965? What if the bombing effort had not been undertaken?

There can be little doubt that South Vietnam would now be lost, and in short order, Laos, Cambodia, and perhaps Thailand would have fallen. The Communist domination of the whole of Southeast Asia, including Indonesia, Malaysia, and Burma, would by now be far advanced or would already have taken place. Japan, South Korea, and the Philippines would have come under new and powerful influences.

But the firm stand of the United States in South Vietnam in the period 1965 to 1968 succeeded in preserving South Vietnam. It held the Communists at bay in Laos. It strengthened Thailand, and it bought time in Cambodia. When these facts are combined with the defeat of a Communist coup in Indonesia and the internal turmoil in Red China, it is a fair conclusion that U. S. involvement in Vietnam delayed indefinitely the Communist march across Asia and the Western Pacific. So, while there was no military victory, neither was there defeat. And while air interdiction did not strangle the war, it did force the opening of discussions for a political settlement, discussions which still continue.

Vice Admiral Ralph W. Cousins, Commander Task Force 77 during the height of the interdiction effort, summed up in his farewell speech perhaps the major lesson of the war:

"In these years," he told the Fleet on his departure, "we have seen Task Force 77 take the war to the enemy—into the very heart of North Vietnam—'downtown' Hanoi and Haiphong, as the pilots say—into an area where by general consensus the flak and the surface-to-air missiles presented our aircrewmen with the most hostile environment in the history of warfare. In late 1967, in a single day, as many as 80 SAMs were fired at our air wings over Haiphong. We lost aircraft and aircrewmen—and several hundred of the finest men in the world are now in prison in Hanoi.

"But in all that time, the morale of our aircrewmen never wavered. There was never any doubt in anyone's mind but that we could continue to dish it out—and take it—as long as necessary.

"If there were ever a force—a fleet that came to stay—this is it.

"The fact is that we hit North Vietnam so hard during the fall of 1967—and during the first few months of 1968 with A-6s—that Hanoi decided they had better go to the conference at Paris and see what relief—and concessions—they could win by negotiation.

"I am certain that the United States has never fought a war in which our young men have been as courageous—as competent—as they have in this one."

(*Naval Review*, 1972)

Notes

1. In July 1950 the *Maddox* was among the ships screening the carriers which made the first naval air strike in the Korean War.

2. It is an interesting but futile exercise to speculate what the American public reaction might have been if one of these torpedoes had hit. Would another Pearl Harbor reaction have resulted?

3. Actually, a few A-1s had been launched, but they were circling over the carriers. The majority of the strike aircraft were still in the process of getting ready to take off.

4. On 7 August, Secretary McNamara issued a press release which explained why the President's announcement was made before the actual attack

began. He said that he recommended that the President's talk be given at 11:40 P.M. Washington time (approximately 45 minutes prior to take-off). "By that time," (about 1315 Tonkin Gulf time), he said, "U. S. naval aircraft had been in the air on their way to the targets about one hour." He further explained that the North Vietnamese, by means of long-range radar, "had then received indications of the attack. The time remaining (from announcement to attack) before the aircraft arrived over their targets would not permit the North Vietnamese to move their boats to sea or to alert their forces." Unfortunately, Mr. McNamara's explanation was in error.

5. CVW-5 had also been the first air wing to see action in the Korean War.

6. One A-4E from the *Coral Sea*, piloted by Lieutenant E. G. Hiebert of VA-155, diverted to Da Nang because of hung ordnance. Making a wheels-up landing, some of the hung ordnance fell off and started burning. Lieutenant Hiebert managed to clear the burning aircraft safely and uninjured, but the main runway was closed for a few hours because of the damage.

7. It is believed that this name was chosen since it lay off *northern* South Vietnam, and because of an earlier joint operation with the Air Force known as Operation Yankee Team which, as early as 1964, had conducted reconnaissance flights over Communist infiltration routes into South Vietnam.

8. Late in 1964 and early in 1965, the *Ranger* spent 117 days out of 125 under way, with one stretch of 70 days continuously at sea. In 1965, the *Coral Sea* spent eight of ten and one-half months at Yankee Station.

9. This name was originated by Captain A. B. Grimes, U. S. Navy, then on duty in Reconnaissance Center, Pentagon.

10. A revealing article in the Hanoi Newspaper, *Nham San*, appeared on 24 July 1966 describing how the SAM batteries moved: "With our small roads and narrow bridges," the article said, "our heavy [missile] equipment must be handled with utmost care. A loose radio tube or an open wire is enough to make our missiles inaccurate . . . our engineering troops have stayed up many nights on end to build bridges across rivers for the missile sites to move. The local people have helped by collecting bamboo and straw that they spread out on the roads in order to ease the transportation of the equipment and not disturb the machinery."

11. In his book, *Confirm or Deny* (Harper & Row, 1970), Phil G. Goulding states on page 178 that the

37-day bombing pause was initiated by Secretary McNamara.

12. The record number of combat missions for the war in Southeast Asia was 306, flown by Commander Samuel R. Chessman, XO and later CO of VA-195. On one of the early Alfa strikes in the Iron Triangle, Commander Chessman ripped the slats off his A-4 in a negative "G" maneuver to avoid one of 20 SAMS fired at CVW-19 that day.

The second highest was 304, flown by Commander Charles E. Hathaway. Commander Hathaway was shot down on his 281st combat mission but managed to reach the safety of the Gulf of Tonkin before ejecting.

13. The A-6 strike discussed on these pages brought many a chuckle to the stateside Intruder community. The 20 April Radio Hanoi newscasts carried a tirade against "U. S. Escalation" claiming that the U. S. Air Force was now sending B-52 strikes into the north. As "proof" of this, the North Vietnamese cited the "stratofortress" attack against the Uong Bi thermal power plant on 18 April, a raid that was, in fact, executed by these two A-6 Intruders.

14. April also saw a change in location of Yankee Station. It was moved deeper into the Gulf of Tonkin, thereby providing shorter runs to targets in North Vietnam.

15. Commander Thomas was later killed on Black Friday, 13 August 1965, during the SAM hunt described on page 25.

16. Commander Leue became Commanding Officer of VA-153 in July 1966 aboard the *Constellation*. Flying the relatively short range and short endurance A-4Cs, Commander Leue's squadron as a routine practice took on additional fuel in the air at night in order to be able to spend more time in high fuel consumption, low altitude, operations hunting trucks under flares.

17. "Fast as a bastard."

18. Rear Admiral Richardson credits the development of this plan to his Operations Officer, Captain Robert F. Hunt.

19. Early in 1966, photography of Thanh Hoa and its nearby railroad yard showed that both spur and through tracks were built through the city, along streets and under the shelter of trees, to take advantage of the sanctuary provided by being in an inhabited town area.

20. As a matter of fact, in 1965 both CinCPac and CinCPacFlt had repeatedly recommended an anti-POL campaign.

21. Commander Foster later received a prosthetic arm and, after a long administrative battle, was continued on active duty.

22. The North Vietnamese Navy also reacted to the POL attacks near Haiphong. On the afternoon of July 1st, three P-6 type PT boats ventured out to attack the *Coontz* (DLG-9) and *Rogers* (DD-876) at North SAR station, some 55 miles southeast of Haiphong. The PTs were sighted at 1610 by two F-4s from the *Constellation* (flown by Lieutenant Commander Sven Nelson and Lieutenant Fred Miller, Lieutenant (j.g.) Gerry Goerlitz and Lieutenant (j.g.) Bob Robinson). They were picked up by the *Coontz'* radar five minutes later. By 1637 they were taken under attack by two A-6s from the *Constellation* flown by Lieutenant Commander Nels Gillette. Pilots from VA-153, VA-155, VF-151, and VF-161 also attacked. One boat sank and, at the ridiculous range of 12 miles, the remaining two launched their torpedoes and headed for home. Thirteen minutes later, planes from the *Hancock* and *Constellation* sank them both. The *Coontz*, *Rogers*, and *King* (DLG-10) picked up the first North Vietnamese Navy prisoners of the war, nineteen in all, including one of the commanding officers.

23. A review of the American press reports of the early months of the war reveals a great amount of speculation about American hesitation to go after the North Vietnam POL system. "It is my personal opinion," said Vice Admiral Edwin B. Hooper, "that this discussion by the press contributed to the prolonged warning the North Vietnamese received during which they dispersed and protected their POL supplies."

24. At the beginning of 1967, there were 104 important military targets in the northeast, but only 20 of these had been hit in 1966. By October 1967, 242 fixed targets in North Vietnam had been designated, but only 159 of these had been authorized and attacked.

25. On pages 174–177 of *Confirm or Deny*, Mr. Phil G. Goulding reveals that long before this July 1967 briefing—in fact, as early as September 1966—Secretary McNamara expressed the belief that the air bombing of North Vietnam could not stop the flow of men and material or break their will. In the spring and summer of 1967 (just prior to the briefing described above) Goulding says that Secretary McNamara had decided to recommend deescalation and restricting the bombing to the southern part of North Vietnam. It should be noted, however, that the bombing cutback did not come until 31 March 1968, eight months later.

26. For further details, see Goulding's *Confirm or Deny*, pp. 139–150.

27. Referenced in reports and dispatches by the acronym WBLC, while the pilots soon began to speak of them as "Wiblicks."

28. This was Lieutenant Commander Verich's second time to be shot down. A year earlier flying from the *Oriskany* he had also been bagged by the enemy.

29. A year earlier, a sharp-eyed photo interpreter aboard the *Constellation* had spotted several cleverly concealed patrol boats while reviewing reconnaissance films. The torpedo craft were moored alongside the "karst" islands between Hon Gai and Cam Pha, hidden under camouflage netting. On 7 July 1966, two strike groups were launched in search of these boats. Commander David E. Leue, CO of VA-153, and leader of the A-4 attack element, discovered four of the hidden boats. Despite heavy AAA fire, Commander Leue scored a direct bomb hit on one of the boats and proceeded to vector the other element of attack aircraft into the area. Two of the boats were sunk and two others damaged. These losses effectively took the stomach out of the North Vietnamese for attempting any more sneak raids on the U. S. Navy in the Gulf of Tonkin.

Half an Amphibious Force at War: The Marines in I Corps

In war, navies have three main jobs: to ensure that friendly sea traffic can flow and that enemy sea traffic cannot, and to land armies on hostile territory.

Except in the river approaches to Saigon and some other ports, during the war in Vietnam, the enemy did not threaten our sea traffic. At the same time the President decided that the United States would neither halt enemy sea traffic nor land any army on North Vietnam's long coastline. We have already seen that aerial bombardment, which was permitted—even ordered—by the President, was the only means left to most of the fleet to help out during the war.

In 1965 General William Westmoreland, who commanded the U. S. forces in Vietnam, ordered the Marines to defend the northernmost part of South Vietnam.[1] This part the South Vietnamese called I Corps Tactical Zone, or I Corps. (Later they renamed it I Military Region.) There, for over six years the Marines fought a strategically static war. One result of this was that the other half of the nation's amphibious power, the Navy's numerous landing ships and craft, was never used to anything near its full potential. Indeed, after several years in which the Marines and the Navy fought essentially separate wars, there were those in both services who questioned the further usefulness of the amphibious mission and the resources given over to it. It was not a new question in the Navy. It was in the Marine Corps.

When a battalion of the 9th Marines went ashore at Da Nang in March 1965, it was not the first combat unit of that service to arrive. Not only had two batteries of Hawk antiaircraft missiles been there for a month, but beginning nearly three years beforehand, a succession of helicopter squadrons had flown out of Da Nang's airfield, carrying South Vietnamese troops to and from the scene of battle.

Given the conditions of that war, some people believed that the Marines might have been used more effectively in the watery Mekong Delta than in the I Corps Tactical Zone. In the Delta, so it was reasoned, the long partnership of the Navy and the Marines might have been put to use quickly, with the one providing the mobility and gunfire support while the other provided the assault force. But the Delta is small and cramped, with little room for ground forces beyond those of the South Vietnamese army already present and none at all for jet combat aircraft. In fact, when U. S. ground combat forces did enter the Delta in 1967,[2] they only went in brigade strength and they stayed but two years. In the Delta the Marines would have been overpresent and underemployed.

In any event, Marine planners had long foreseen that if Marines could not be put to best use through the means of the amphibious assault, the next best place for them was in I Corps. The main reasons for this were that the area is physically, culturally, and historically separated from the rest of South Vietnam; that the important places to be defended were on or near the coast, thus taking advantage of the Marines' strong over-the-beach logistical capabilities without exposing their weak ability to support penetrations deep inland; that at Da Nang there was an airfield suitable for jet aircraft; and that at the same city there was a harbor which, if neither safe nor developed, was spacious and suitable for improvement.[3]

The first good-sized U. S. unit to engage the enemy was the Army's 173d Airborne Brigade, in June 1965 near Saigon. But the first substantial U. S. victory belonged to the 7th Marines at Van Tuong Peninsula just south of Chu Lai that August. With part of his force going overland, part heliborne, and the rest landed from the sea, Colonel Oscar Peatross engaged the Viet Cong's 1st Regiment, some 2,000 strong. In two or three days of fierce fighting in tropical heat, the Marines routed the foe, killed about half of them, and took possession of the ground on which the battle had been fought.

Alas! They could not and did not hold that ground. Just as the defeated Viet Cong slunk off in one direction, the victorious Marines sailed, flew, or walked away in another. Though it was a success, the battle had been nothing but a raid into enemy territory motivated by concern over a possible enemy attack on the Marines' new air base at Chu Lai. Foreshadowing the long war that was to follow, while tactically the Marines had been on the offensive, operationally they had been on the defensive. When, the following January, a visitor arrived at Colonel Peatross's field headquarters near Chu Lai, a request to visit the battlefield yielded the information that the enemy, uncontested, had long since regained possession.

And so the war went. The Marines and the Army, and sometimes, the South Vietnamese Army too, won victory after victory. But the enemy never went away for long. Partly this was for reasons already discussed, and partly it was because the Saigon government, on whose behalf those American and South Vietnamese troops fought, lacked strength, skill, belief in the rightness of its cause, and the respect of the populace, while the enemy had all those things. Eventually, as a result of the outrage produced by the enemy's Tet Offensive in January 1968, the Saigon government gained in many of those qualities, but at the same time the government in Washington lost much more than Saigon gained.

During most of the first two years of the Marines' commitment to Vietnam (that is, during the period covered in the following essay by General Simmons), the center of gravity of their operations was in the southern half of the five-province I Corps Tactical Zone, below Da Nang. But by the end of that period it had begun to shift northward, toward the Demilitarized Zone between North and South Vietnam, to meet the overt, though never admitted, invasion of South Vietnam by the North Vietnamese army across the DMZ.

Unlike that of the U. S. Army, or any other major army, a substantial part of the Marine Corps's fighting power consists of first-class fixed-wing combat aircraft. As long as the only important American combat elements in I Corps were Marines, problems over control of air operations did not arise. But when the enemy strengthened his forces there, U. S. Army and Air Force units had to follow. They brought with them the issue of who would have operational control of the Marines' fixed-wing aircraft. Would it be the Marines or the Air Force? This had been a troublesome matter in the Korean War, and the Marines found the solution on that occasion, which handed over control of their close air support to another service, to be unsatisfactory. In Vietnam a better solution was worked out, as the late General McCutcheon demonstrates. Whether that solution has the staying power to work in other places, with other air forces, and under other conditions, is yet to be seen. One thing is certain: sooner or later it will be tested.

The Marines stayed in Vietnam a long time; the last combat elements did not leave until mid-1971. Their work was well covered in successive issues of the *Naval Review*. The three essays republished here are fewer than half of those that originally appeared. The others, four in number, are General Simmons's "Marine Corps Operations in Vietnam, 1967" (published in *Naval Review 1969*), "Marine Corps Operations in Vietnam, 1968" (published in 1970), "Marine Corps Operations in Vietnam, 1969–1972" (published in 1973); and Colonel James B. Soper's "A View from FMF Pac of Logistics in the Western Pacific, 1965–1971," published in *Naval Review 1972*. All but the first of these issues did double duty, for beginning in 1970 they were also the May issue of the U. S. Naval Institute *Proceedings*.

Notes

1. Westmoreland, William C., *A Soldier Reports*. (Garden City, N.Y.: Doubleday, 1976), p. 124.
2. The naval portion of this experience is described later in this book by Captain Wade C. Wells.
3. Westmoreland, *op.cit*. See also the essays following.

Marine Aviation in Vietnam, 1962–1970

Lieutenant General Keith B. McCutcheon,
U. S. Marine Corps

The Beginning

Marine Corps aviation involvement in Vietnam began on Palm Sunday 1962, when a squadron of UH-34 helicopters landed at Soc Trang in the Delta. The squadron was Marine Medium Helicopter Squadron 362 (HMM-362), commanded by Lieutenant Colonel Archie J. Clapp.

Three U. S. Army helicopter companies were already in Vietnam, and the Secretary of Defense had approved deployment of one more unit to Vietnam. The Marine Corps seized this opportunity to fly toward the sound of the drums and offered to send a squadron. They recommended Da Nang as the area of operations, since it was that area to which Marines were committed in various contingency plans. The Commander, United States Military Assistance Command, Vietnam (ComUSMACV), decreed, however, that the need at the moment was in the Delta since that Vietnamese Army corps area was the only one of the four corps areas in Vietnam that did not have any helicopter support.

Colonel John F. Carey was the commanding officer of the Marine task unit of which HMM 362 was a part. He arrived at Soc Trang on 9 April, and over the ensuing five days an element of Marine Air Base Squadron 16 (MABS-16) arrived aboard Marine KC-130 aircraft from the Marine Corps Air Facility at Futema, Okinawa. Squadron HMM-362, augmented by three O-1 observation aircraft, embarked in the *USS Princeton* (LPH-5) at Okinawa and arrived off the Mekong Delta at dawn on Palm Sunday, 15 April. The squadron's helicopters completed unloading the unit's equipment and were ashore by late afternoon. The Marine task unit, which was to be known as "Shufly," was established ashore.

The mission of this unit was to provide helicopter troop and cargo lift for Vietnamese Army units, and its first operation was one week later, on Easter Sunday. The squadron continued to operate until August when it was relieved by HMM-163, commanded by Lieutenant Colonel Robert L. Rathbun.

In September 1962, the Marines were ordered by ComUSMACV to move to Da Nang, the high-threat area, an area with which Marine planners had become well acquainted in contingency plans, war games, and advanced base problems. Some had been there before. In April 1954, Lieutenant Colonel Julius W. Ireland had landed at Da Nang airfield with Marine Attack Squadron 324 (VMA-324) and turned over twenty-five A-1 propeller-driven dive bombers to the hard-pressed French. Now he was back as a colonel.

A Marine F-4B Phantom drops a 500-pound bomb on Viet Cong trenches concealed in a tree line south of Da Nang. Close air support missions, which Marine Corps pilots were performing before and during World War II; "vertical envelopment," which Marine Corps helicopter pilots perfected during the Korean Conflict; and the SATS—short airfield for tactical support—concept, which the Corps pioneered after Korea, were three of the major contributions to the defense of I Corps made by Marine aviation during its service in Vietnam.

He had replaced Colonel Carey as the commander of "Shufly."

The Marines initially occupied two areas on the air base. The helicopter maintenance and parking area was southeast of the runway. The billeting area was across the base on the western side, about two miles away. In those days there was not much traffic at Da Nang, so the Marines got into the habit of driving across the runway as the shortest route to commute back and forth. Four years later, this would be one of the two or three busiest airfields in the world.

In late 1964, the runway was extended to 10,000 feet, and a perimeter road, half surfaced and half dirt, was built around the base.

THE LAND AND THE WEATHER

Da Nang is the second largest city in Vietnam and the largest in the Vietnamese Army's I Corps Tactical Zone, commonly called I Corps and abbreviated as ICTZ. By 1970 Da Nang would have a population of approximately 400,000. An exact count is impossible because of the influx of war victims and refugees. ICTZ consists of the northernmost five provinces of Vietnam: Quang Tri, Thua Thien, Quang Nam, Quang Tin, and Quang Ngai.[1] The length of ICTZ is about 225 miles, and its width varies from 40 to 75 miles. Da Nang is approximately in the center of the north-south dimension and is on the coast. Hue, the next largest city, with a population of about 200,000, is roughly halfway between the Demilitarized Zone (DMZ) and Da Nang. Hue, the old capital of Annam, is inland a few miles on the Perfume River. About halfway between Da Nang and the southern boundary of I Corps is a sandy area on the littoral of the South China Sea that came to be known as Chu Lai.

Called Tourane by the French, Da Nang sits on a fairly large bay which provides a roomy, if not particularly safe, deep-water harbor and anchorage, although in 1965 it had few facilities to unload ships in any numbers. To the north of the bay are the Hai Van Mountains, called "Col des Nuages" by the French, which stretch eastward from the Annamite Mountain chain to the sea. These mountains are an important factor in I Corps weather and, in fact, form a barrier which can cause one side to be under instrument flight rule conditions and the other side under visual flight rule conditions.

East of Da Nang, across the Song Han River, is the Tien Sha Peninsula that juts past the city to provide a large breakwater for the bay. At the end of the peninsula is a massive 2,000-foot hill known as Monkey Mountain.

The terrain in I Corps rises as you move inland from the coast. In general, there are three broad regions: the coastal lowlands where rice paddies abound, and there 85 per cent of the three million people live; the piedmont area of slightly higher ground which permits cultivation of other crops, and which is home for most of the remainder of the people; and the hill country, or Annamite chain. These mountains go up to 5,000 feet and higher, some rather precipitously. For the most part they are heavily forested and in places there is a triple canopy which makes observation of the ground impossible.

Running generally from west to east, from the high ground to the sea, is a series of rivers and streams that follow the valleys and natural drainage routes. They are generally unnavigable except for small, oar-propelled, shallow-draft boats, but they do offer routes from Laos to the provinces.

The northeast monsoon begins in October and ends in March. September and April are more or less transition months. Rainfall increases in September and October, and by November the northeast monsoon is well established over ICTZ. Weak cold fronts periodically move southward, and usually there is an increase in the intensity of low-level winds (rising sometimes 20 to 50 knots). This is called a "surge." The "surge" causes ceilings of 1,000 to 1,500 feet with rain, drizzle, and fog restricting visibility to one or two miles. Occasionally the ceiling drops to 200 feet and the visibility to half a mile. After the initial "surge" has passed, the winds begin to decrease, and the weather will stabilize with ceilings of 1,500 to 2,000 feet prevailing. Visibility will fluctuate from seven miles or more to three miles or less owing to intermittent periods of fog or precipitation. Cloud tops are seldom above 10,000 feet.

The kind of weather just described was called "crachin" by the French. It can prevail for a few days at a time early in the monsoon season or for several weeks during the high-intensity months. As winds decrease, the weather generally improves. When the lower-level winds decrease to less than ten knots, or if the wind shifts from the northeast to a northwest or a southerly direction, a break in the weather is usually experienced. Such a break will result in scattered to broken clouds with bases at 2,000 to 3,000 feet and unrestricted visibility and may persist for a week before another "surge" develops.

During December, the monsoon strengthens, and in January, when the Siberian high-pressure cell reaches its maximum intensity, the northeast monsoon also develops to its greatest extent. Little change can be expected over ICTZ in February, although "surges" are generally weaker and more shallow than in January. By mid-March the flow pattern is poorly defined and the monsoon becomes weak. During April, traces of the southwest monsoon begin to appear and there is a noticeable decrease in cloudiness over the area. From then through August, the weather in ICTZ is hot and humid, with little rainfall.

The northeast monsoon had a direct impact on all military operations in ICTZ and especially on air operations. Because they can operate with lower ceilings and visibility minimums than fixed-wing aircraft, the helicopters would often perform their missions when the fixed-wing could not, at least along the flat coastal region. Inland, however, the hills and mountains made even helicopter flying hazardous at best. The pilots all developed a healthy respect for the northeast monsoon.

EARLY DAYS AT DA NANG

HMM-163 was relieved by HMM-162 in January 1963. Over the next two years other HMMs followed: 261, 361, 364, 162 for a second time, 365, and, finally, 163 for its second tour. Half the Corps' UH-34 squadrons had received invaluable combat experience before the commitment of the Marine Corps air-ground team of division-wing size.

In April 1963, an infantry platoon from the 3d Marine Division (3dMarDiv) was airlifted from Okinawa to join "Shufly." Its mission was to provide increased security for the base. In a modest way, the air-ground team was in being in Vietnam.

Brigadier General Raymond G. Davis, Commanding General of the 9th Marine Expeditionary Brigade (9thMEB), flew to Da Nang in August 1964, shortly after the Tonkin Gulf affair, and completed plans to reinforce the Marines based there in the event of an emergency. He then joined his command afloat with the Amphibious Ready Group of the Seventh Fleet. This Group was to be on and off various alert conditions for some months to come.

Early in December 1964, "Shufly" received a new title by direction of Lieutenant General Victor H. Krulak, Commanding General of the Fleet Marine Force, Pacific (FMFPac). It was now called Marine Unit Vietnam, or MUV for short.

Another aviation unit began arriving at Da Nang on 8 February 1965. This was the 1st Light Anti-Aircraft Missile (LAAM) Battalion, commanded by Lieutenant Colonel Bertram E. Cook, Jr. The battalion was equipped with Hawk surface-to-air missiles. Battery "A," commanded by Captain Leon E. Obenhaus, arrived by air and was established on the base just to the west of the runway. Within twenty-four hours it was ready for operation. The remainder of the battalion came by ship from Okinawa, arriving at Da Nang later in the month. This battalion had been sent to Okinawa in December 1964 from its base in California, as a result of ComUSMACV's request for missiles for air defense. The decision was made to retain the unit on Okinawa instead of sending it to Vietnam, but when the Viet Cong attacked Pleiku on 7 February, the United States retaliated with an air strike in North Vietnam. An order to deploy the Hawks to Da Nang was made at the same time. As in the case of Cuba in 1962, when a crisis situation developed, Marine missile units were among the first to be deployed.

By this time MUV was pretty well established on the west side of the Da Nang air base in an old French army compound. Colonel John H. King, Jr., was in command. The helicopters were moved from their first maintenance and parking area and were now located on the southwest corner of the field. A rather large sheet-metal lean-to had been made available by the Vietnamese Air Force (VNAF) to serve as a hangar. The parking apron was blacktop and was adequate for about two squadrons of UH-34s.

BUILDUP

Late in February 1965, President Johnson made a decision to commit a Marine brigade to protect the air base at Da Nang from Communist attack. On 8 March, the 9thMEB, including the 3d Battalion, 9th Marines, was ordered to land. They had been afloat and ready for such an operation for several months. Brigadier General Frederick C. Karch was then the commander of the brigade.

The 1st Battalion, 3d Marines, meanwhile had been alerted on Okinawa for a possible airlift. It, too, was ordered to Da Nang on 8

March. Because of the congestion which developed on the airfield, ComUSMACV ordered a temporary cessation to the lift. It was resumed on the 11th and the battalion arrived in Da Nang on the 12th.

Squadron HMM-365, commanded by Lieutenant Colonel Joseph Koler, Jr., was embarked in the *Princeton*. Koler's UH-34s were flown to the airfield at Da Nang, but the crews reembarked in the *Princeton* for the voyage to Okinawa. Aircrews and squadron personnel of Lieutenant Colonel Oliver W. Curtis's HMM-162 were airlifted by KC-130 from Okinawa to Da Nang to take over the UH-34s left by HMM-365.

Brigadier General Karch took operational control of the Marine aviation units that were already ashore. He also established an MEB command post in the same old French compound where Colonel King was set up. Colonel King had had the foresight to contact General Thi, who commanded I Corps and the ICTZ, to get permission to use some additional buildings.

The air component of the 9thMEB now included two HMMs and one LAAM battalion. Colonel King remained in command of the air units. He also received some service support elements from Marine Aircraft Group 16 (MAG-16) based at Futema, Okinawa, and since his command was now integrated into the MEB, the MUV was deactivated and MAG-16(−) took its place.[2] A rear echelon of MAG-16 remained at Futema, Okinawa.

Requests for additional military forces were submitted by ComUSMACV. One 15-plane Marine Fighter/Attack Squadron (VMFA) was authorized to deploy to Da Nang. VMFA-531, based at Atsugi, Japan, and commanded by Lieutenant Colonel William C. McGraw, Jr., received the order on 10 April. By dusk on the 11th, the aircraft and most of the men were in Da Nang, having flown there directly, refueling in the air from Marine KC-130 tankers as

they went. On 13 April, McGraw led twelve of his F-4Bs on their first combat mission in South Vietnam, in support of U. S. Marine ground troops. The F-4 was an aircraft that would perform either air-to-air missions against hostile aircraft or air-to-ground strikes in support of friendly troops.

As the tempo of retaliatory strikes against North Vietnam by the Navy and Air Force increased, the enemy air defense began to include greater numbers of radar-controlled weapon systems. The sole source of tactical electronic warfare aircraft readily available to counter the new enemy defense was Marine Composite Reconnaissance Squadron One (VMCJ-1) at Iwakuni, Japan. On 10 April 1965, the Commander-in-Chief Pacific (CinCPac), ordered the deployment of an EF-10B detachment to Vietnam. The detachment, led by Lieutenant Colonel Otis W. Corman, arrived in Da Nang the same day. The electronic warfare aircraft (EF-10Bs and later EA-6As) began to provide support to Marine, Navy, and Air Force strike aircraft. The photo-reconnaissance aircraft (RF-8s and RF-4s) arrived later and performed primarily in support of Marine units, but they also supported Army units in I Corps and flew bomb-damage assessment missions north of the DMZ.

Southeast Asia was an area familiar to the pilots of VMCJ-1. Detachments of RF-8As, the photographic aircraft of the squadron, had been aboard various carriers in the Gulf of Tonkin continually since May 1964, when CinCPac initiated the Yankee Team operations to conduct photo reconnaissance over Laos. Detachment pilots were also on hand to participate in the Navy's first air strikes against North Vietnam, and they continued photographic reconnaissance activities as part of carrier air wings until the detachment rejoined the parent unit at Da Nang in December 1965.

Colonel King now had an air group that

contained elements of two jet squadrons, two helicopter squadrons, a Hawk missile battalion, and air-control facilities so he could operate a Direct Air Support Center (DASC) and an Air Support Radar Team (ASRT). He also had the support of a detachment of KC-130 transports that were based in Japan.

The month of May was one of further growth and change. Several additional infantry battalions arrived and elements of MAG-12 landed at Chu Lai to the south of Da Nang. Major General William R. Collins, Commanding General, 3dMarDiv, arrived on 3 May from Okinawa. He set up an advance division command post, and on 6 May he established the Third Marine Expeditionary Force (III MEF); the 9thMEB was deactivated. Within a few days the title of III MEF was changed to Third Marine Amphibious Force (III MAF). The term "expeditionary" seemed to conjure up unhappy memories of the earlier ill-fated French expeditionary corps. And some believed "amphibious" was more appropriate for a Marine command in any event.

On 11 May, Major General Paul J. Fontana opened an advance command post of the 1st Marine Aircraft Wing (1stMAW) in the same compound. On 24 May, Brigadier General Keith B. McCutcheon, assistant wing commander, arrived to relieve General Fontana in the advance command post, and on 5 June he relieved him as Commanding General of the 1stMAW. The day before, Major General Lewis W. Walt relieved Collins as Commanding General, 3dMarDiv and III MAF. McCutcheon became Deputy Commander, III MAF, and Tactical Air Commander.

The Marine Air-Ground Team was in place. The 1stMAW now had elements of a headquarters group and two aircraft groups in Vietnam. Additional units were waiting to deploy and still others were requested. It was but the beginning of a steady Marine buildup in I Corps. It was summer and the weather was hot and dry. The heavy rains were not due to start until September.

Resources

BASES

The major constraint to receiving any more air units was the lack of adequate bases.

Da Nang Air Base was one of only three jet-capable airfields in all of Vietnam, and the only one in I Corps; the others were Bien Hoa and Tan Son Nhut, both near Saigon. In 1965, Da Nang had one 10,000-foot paved runway with a parallel taxiway. Less than half the length of the runway on the eastern side of the field had associated ramp space for parking aircraft. On the western side there was a black-top parking apron that could accommodate about two squadrons of helicopters.

A military construction board was formed in III MAF, and a list of requirements was prepared and submitted to higher authority. A second runway and taxiway had already been approved at the end of March for Da Nang as well as adequate hardstand and maintenance areas on the western side of the field. This would eventually accommodate one Marine Aircraft Group, a Support Group, and a Navy unit (Fleet Air Support Unit, Da Nang) which arrived in April 1968, in order to carry out various functions for the Seventh Fleet. The eastern side of the field would then be released to the U. S. Air Force and the Vietnamese Air Force. Before this construction could be undertaken, however, a base had to be made available for the helicopters then at Da Nang. And still another base was required for a second jet group.

There were several restrictions confronting III MAF as far as construction was concerned. First was the problem of obtaining real estate. This was a laborious and time-consuming administrative process. Second was the need to relocate the Vietnamese families living on the desired site. Equally important to the Vietnamese was the relocation of their ancestral grave sites. Third, there was inadequate engineering help available in Vietnam to build everything required, so priorities had to be established. And finally, security forces had to be provided, and any unit assigned to this task meant fewer troops for other tactical operations.

SATS AND CHU LAI

A second jet base was essential. Through the foresight of Lieutenant General Krulak, a likely site had been picked out about fifty miles south of Da Nang for a Short Airfield for Tactical Support (SATS). General Krulak had recommended it almost a year before to Admiral Sharp, who was CinCPac. Admiral Sharp and General Westmoreland had been discussing the need for another jet base somewhere in South Vietnam. General Krulak's main concern was to have a jet airfield in I Corps, where his Marines were to be committed if the contingency plans were implemented. Finally, on 30 March 1965, Secretary McNamara approved installation of a SATS at Chu Lai. Chu Lai was not a recognized name on Vietnamese maps at that time and the rumor is that Krulak gave it that name when he chose the place. Chu Lai reportedly is part of his name in Chinese.

By virtue of their experience in naval aviation, Marine aviators had long recognized the advantage of being able to approximate a carrier deck sort of operation on the beach. They realized that many areas of the world did not have adequate airfields, and that normal construction methods took too long. Something that approached an "instant airfield" was required.

In the mid-fifties, the Marine Corps Development Center at Quantico, Virginia, intensified development of both the concept and the hardware to realize this project. They visualized a 2,000-foot airstrip that could handle a Marine Aircraft Group of two or three aircraft

squadrons. The essential components of such a base would include a suitable surface for the runway, taxiways, and hardstands; a means of arresting the aircraft on landing similar to that on a carrier deck; a catapult or other means to assist in launching the aircraft; provisions for refueling, rearming, and maintenance; air-control facilities; and, of course, all the necessities for housekeeping. The installation time was to be from 72 to 96 hours.

Various projects were already under way that could provide solutions to some of these problems. Others had to be started. Furthermore, the entire concept had to be pulled together into a single system. Naturally, a name for the system was required and a name was found—SATS—Short Airfield for Tactical Support.

The kind of surface material to use was one of the harder problems to solve. Fabrics, plastics, soil stabilizers, and many other ideas were tried, but none was able to cope with the impact and static loads of aircraft operations and the temperature of jet exhaust. Finally, attention was directed to metals, and eventually a solid aluminum plank was developed which promised to do the job. It was known as AM-2. A single piece of this mat measures two feet by 12 feet and weighs 140 pounds. The individual pieces arc capable of being interconnected and locked in place, thus providing a smooth, flat surface that is both strong and durable.

The arrested-landing problem was already in hand with the use of modified shipboard arresting gear. Development of improved equipment was initiated, nevertheless, and the M-21 was the result. This is a dry-friction, energy-absorbing device using a tape drive with a wire pendant stretching across the runway. This arresting gear is now standard in the Corps.

Launching in a short space was a bigger problem. JATO (Jet Assisted Take-Off) bottles were available, but these could be a logistical burden over a long period of time. A catapult was desired. Development and testing were not complete in early 1965, but progress was promising.

The refueling problem was solved by adapting the Amphibious Assault Bulk Fuel Handling System (AABFHS) to the airfield environment. The result was the Tactical Airfield Fuel Dispensing System, or TAFDS. This system used the same 10,000-gallon collapsible tanks, hoses, pumps, and water separators as the AABFHS, but it added special nozzles for refueling aircraft: they were single-point refueling nozzles for jets, and filling-station gooseneck types for helos and light aircraft.

In a similar manner, all of the other requirements were analyzed and action was taken to find a solution. In May 1965, all were available except the catapult, but JATO was on hand, and Marine A-4s were modified to use it.

The concept of SATS visualized seizing an old World War II airstrip or some similar and reasonably flat surface that required a minimum amount of earth moving, and installing a 2,000-foot SATS thereon in about 72 to 96 hours. This would permit flight operations to commence, while improvements and expansion could be conducted simultaneously.

Chu Lai did not meet all the requirements visualized by SATS planners. It was not a World War II abandoned airfield. The soil wasn't even dirt. It was sand. And there was lots of it.[3]

But Chu Lai was on the sea, it had a semi-protected body of water behind a peninsula that could be developed into an LST port, it could be defended, and there were few hamlets in the area that would have to be relocated. All things considered, Chu Lai was the most likely site on which to build a new air base.

On 7 May 1965, Naval Mobile Construction Battalion 10 (NMCB-10), under Commander J. M. Bannister, crossed the deep sandy beach at Chu Lai along with the 4th Marine Regiment and elements of MAG-12. The Seabees went to work on 9 May, constructing the first SATS ever installed in a combat environment.

The landing force commander at Chu Lai was Brigadier General Marion E. Carl, one of the Corps' most famous aviators. He had brought his 1st Marine Brigade from Hawaii to the Western Pacific in March, and although that Brigade was disbanded, Carl had become Commanding General of the 3dMEB. As there were no stakes to mark the previously chosen site, he had a hand in picking the exact spot where the runway should go.

The sand proved to be a formidable enemy. Unloading from the ships was hampered, as driving vehicles through the sand was most difficult. Tracked vehicles were essential to move the rubber-tired ones. It required a superhuman effort to get the job done.

The general construction scheme was to excavate some locally available soil, called laterite, and use it as a sub-base between the sand and aluminum matting. Before that could be done, a road had to be built from the site of the airfield to the laterite deposit. This was done, but the combination of temperatures around the hundred mark and the effect of sand on automotive and engineering equipment slowed the progress of construction. Both men and mechanical equipment grew tired quickly in this hostile environment. Needless to say, no one expected to finish in four days. Even thirty looked totally unrealistic, but that was the goal. In spite of the problems and obstacles, Lieutenant General Krulak bet Major General Richard G. Stilwell, Chief of Staff of MACV, that a squadron would be operating there within 30 days.

By Memorial Day, approximately four thousand feet of mat and several hundred feet of taxiway were in place. Chu Lai was ready to receive aircraft, but tropical storms prevented the planes from flying from the Philippines to

Vietnam until 1 June. Shortly after 0800 on that date, Colonel John D. Noble, Commanding Officer of MAG-12, landed an A-4 into the mobile arresting gear on the aluminum runway. He was followed by three others, and, later in the day, four more arrived. About 1300, the first combat mission was launched using JATO with Lieutenant Colonel Robert W. Baker, Commanding Officer of VMA-225, leading.

General Krulak paid off his bet of a case of Scotch to Stilwell on the basis that a full squadron was not operating there in the forecast time, only half of one.

But construction continued and, as additional taxiway was built, more planes came in. Meanwhile operations continued on a daily basis.

The laterite, however, simply wasn't doing the job, so when 8,000 feet of runway was installed, it was decided to operate from the southern 4,000 feet and to re-lay the northern 4,000 feet, which were the first to go down. As it turned out, after the northern half was redone, the other half had to have the same treatment, and then the cycle was repeated still another time when, at last, the right sub-base combination was found. Various techniques were tried, including watering and packing the sand down without any other material, shooting the sand with a light layer of asphalt, and finally a combination of the latter and using a thin plastic membrane under the matting to keep rain from settling into the soil and undermining the runway surface.

Drainage was essential, of course, as any standing water under the mat set up a pumping action as aircraft rolled over the mat, which was particularly noticeable when a transport like a KC-130 landed and rolled out.

During these periods of 4,000-foot operations, JATO was used when high temperatures and heavy bomb loads required it. In addition, a Marine KC-130 tanker was kept available to top off A-4s after take-off, by inflight refueling.

A catapult was installed in April 1966, so all SATS components were then in place. The catapult was tested and evaluated under combat conditions but was not actually required on that date because of the length of the runway. It was used, but not on a sustained basis.

The SATS concept was proven under combat conditions at Chu Lai. The AM-2 mat became a hot item, and production of it was increased markedly in the United States, as all services sought it. It was used for non-SATS airfields and helicopter pads, and became as commonplace in Southeast Asia as was the pierced steel plank (PSP) in the Southwest Pacific in World War II. Likewise, TAFDS components became a common sight, and their flexible fuel lines could be seen almost anywhere.

The original "tinfoil strip," as it came to be called, was still in operation late in 1970, more than five years after it was laid down. Not even the planners back in Quantico in 1955 ever envisioned that someone would install a short airfield for tactical support on sand and leave it there for five years. But this is exactly what was done at Chu Lai.

KY HA AND MARBLE MOUNTAIN

The small civilian airfield at Phu Bai, South of Hue, could accommodate one helicopter squadron, which was required in that area to support an infantry battalion that was assigned to secure the region in 1965. But in addition, two major helo bases were required in relatively short order: first, to take care of MAG-36, which had been alerted to deploy from Santa Ana, California; and second, to free Da Nang of its rotary wing aircraft, so that construction of the parallel runway there could be started.

The peninsula to the northeast of Chu Lai provided a likely site for a helo group as well as an air control squadron. The Seabees began preparation of a flat area and laid down several kinds of metal matting, but they had no time to do anything else in the way of preparing for MAG-36's arrival. The group departed from the West Coast in August 1965, and arrived off Chu Lai early in September. They unloaded, moved ashore, and set about building their own camp. At night they also established their own perimeter defense as there was no infantry to do it for them. And, almost as soon as they landed, the rains began. Whereas at Chu Lai it was sand, at Ky Ha it was pure, unadulterated mud. The base was named Ky Ha after the village nearest the site.

For MAG-16, a site had been chosen east of Da Nang just north of Marble Mountain. There was a beautiful stretch of sandy beach along the South China Sea and just inland was a fine expanse of land covered with coniferous trees ten to twenty feet high. Unfortunately, as soon as word got out that Marines were going to construct an air base there, the local Vietnamese came onto the land in droves and removed all the trees including the roots, instead of the few that had to be removed to build the runway and parking areas. Thus, the troops and other inhabitants lost the protection these trees would have afforded against sun, wind, and erosion.

The civilian construction combine in Vietnam, Raymond, Morrison, Knudson-Brown, Root, and Jones (RMK-BRJ), received the job of building the helicopter facility at Marble Mountain. It was sufficiently advanced by late August 1965 to allow MAG-16 to move from Da Nang and operate at the new facility.

All during the summer, the question of whether or not another SATS-type airfield should be constructed in ICTZ was under serious consideration. There were four likely sites: from north to south, Phu Bai, Marble Mountain Air Facility, Tam Ky, and Quang Ngai. After much study and many messages, the idea was abandoned when it became clear that Da Nang plus Chu Lai would be adequate.

On the night of 27 October 1965, the enemy executed a coordinated sapper attack against Da Nang, Marble Mountain, and Chu Lai. The attack on Da Nang was thwarted by artillery fire against one column to the west, and by an alert ambush against a second force to the south.

At midnight, three sapper teams hit Marble Mountain Air Facility. The team from the north was met by aviation specialists standing guard duty and every attacker was killed. The southern team was driven off. But the one from the west managed to get on to the parking area and several of the enemy raced from helo to helo throwing charges into each. In short order, the place was a mass of burning aircraft. Over twenty were damaged beyond repair, and an equal number required varying degrees of repair.

At Chu Lai only a handful of sappers made it to the flight line, and half of them were killed. A few A-4s were damaged, two beyond repair.

Air bases were to become prime targets. They required close-in defense in depth to make sapper infiltration unprofitable, and they required an outer mobile defense by infantry to ward off rockets and mortars. The ground units did a superb job in keeping the enemy off balance, so that only a few rockets and mortars found profitable targets. Further, aviation and ground personnel tightened their perimeter defense, so never again was there an infiltration which equalled the success of the October attack.

DA NANG

Once MAG-16 had vacated the west side of Da Nang, construction could begin on the parallel runway and taxiway. Plans were made to construct the northern and southern concrete touchdown pads and connecting runways to the east runway first, the MAG operating and maintenance area on the northwest corner of the base second, the remainder of the runway third, and the parallel taxiway last. The two touchdown pads were required first because there was an urgent requirement to move VMCJ-1 from the parking apron on the east side of the field. Furthermore, an F-8 squadron was authorized for Da Nang, but there was no ramp space. The northern touchdown pad would provide ramp space for these two jet squadrons. The southern pad would provide a place to operate the KC-130s and C-117s.

The 1stMAW did not desire to have the entire runway completed before the MAG operating area was, because if it had been, it would have been used as a runway and not for ramp space. This priority was given to the completion of jobs because the engineer work-force was not adequate to undertake them all simultaneously. Although another runway was sorely needed, parking space was the more urgent requirement. Why wasn't a SATS built so a runway would be available at the same time parking space was? Because what was needed was a long runway for the long haul that would accommodate Marine, Navy, Air Force, commercial, and miscellaneous aircraft of all sizes.

MAG-11 moved into Da Nang from its base at Atsugi, Japan, in July 1965, and took command of the jet squadrons which up to that time had been under control of MAG-16. Colonel Robert F. Conley commanded MAG-11. The F-8 squadron, Marine All-Weather Fighter Squadron 312 (VMF[AW]-312), commanded by Lieutenant Colonel Richard B. Newport, arrived at Da Nang in December 1965 and occupied the completed northern touchdown pad along with VMCJ-1, which had moved over from the east side of the base.

The MAG operating area for MAG-11 and the west runway were completed late in 1966, and the last Marine flight operations were then moved from the east side of the base to the west side.

CHU LAI WEST

A 10,000-foot conventional concrete runway and associated taxiways, high-speed turnoffs, and ramp space for two MAGs was begun at Chu Lai, to the west of the SATS strip, early in 1966 and completed that October. Marine Air Group 13 arrived from Iwakuni, Japan, and occupied the new base. This Air Group had been stationed at Kaneohe, Hawaii, as part of the 1st Marine Brigade. It deployed to the Western Pacific with the Brigade and Brigadier General Carl in March, but bided its time in Okinawa and later in Japan, until a base was available for it in Vietnam. Beginning in the fall of 1967, both MAGs 12 and 13 operated from the concrete runway, and the SATS strip was made available to the Army for helos and light aircraft.

An AM-2 runway, complete with catapult and arresting gear, was constructed to connect the northern ends of the concrete and "tinfoil" runways. This provided for a cross-wind runway, about 4,800 feet in length, as well as an interconnection of the two fields for aircraft movement on the ground.

HELO BASES IN NORTHERN ICTZ

As the center of gravity of Marine operations moved north, the helos followed. Late in 1967, Phu Bai was expanded to accommodate a full helicopter group, and MAG-36 moved there from Ky Ha, which was taken over by the Americal Division. Later a base was established at Dong Ha to support the 3dMarDiv's operations below the DMZ. This proved to be a particularly hot area, as it came under fire with some regularity from enemy artillery north of the DMZ. In October 1967, the Quang Tri helicopter base, nine nautical miles south of Dong Ha and beyond the range of enemy artillery firing from the DMZ, was completed in a record 24 days. The helicopters were sent

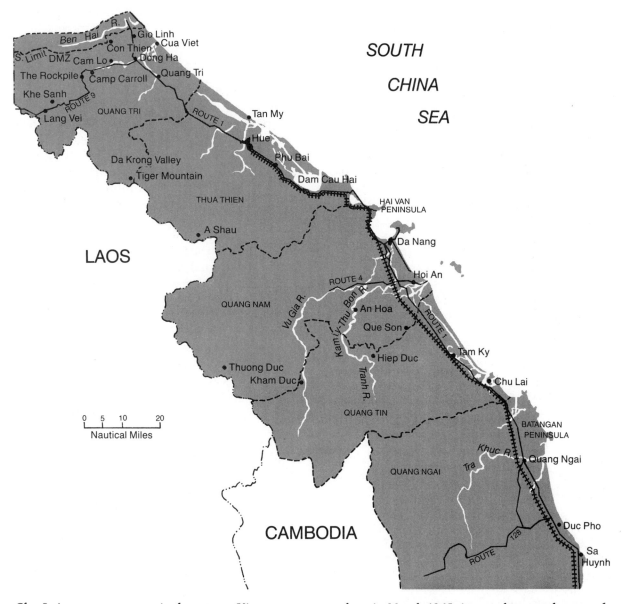

Chu Lai was not a recognized name on Vietnamese maps when, in March 1965, it was chosen to become the second (after Da Nang) jet base in I Corps; yet, in five years, the SATS concept was proven under combat conditions here.

there from Dong Ha and operations were begun immediately. In April 1968, a provisional air group, MAG-39, was established out of 1stMAW resources in order to provide better command and control over the helicopter squadrons based at Quang Tri to better support the 3dMarDiv.

MONKEY MOUNTAIN

Another formidable construction project was the emplacement of a Hawk missile battery on Monkey Mountain just east of Da Nang. The site selected was over two thousand feet above sea level and about one mile east of the Air Force radar site known as Panama. Naval Mobile Construction Battalion 9, led by Commander Richard Anderson, was given this task. A road had to be built first of all, and then the mountain peak had to be leveled in order to provide a sufficiently flat area to emplace the battery. On 1 September 1965, the site was sufficiently cleared to receive the equipment, and Captain Charles R. Keith's "B" Battery, 1st LAAM Battalion, was emplaced. As in the case of airfields, development of the site continued concurrently with operations. Late in 1966, a similar but less extensive construction effort was undertaken just to the east of Hai Van Pass, so that the LAAM Battery, which was still on Da Nang Air Base, could be moved to a better tactical location.

OTHER OPERATING AREAS

In addition to these permanent bases, many outlying fields and expeditionary operating areas were established as the military requirement dictated. Airfields suitable for KC-130s and helos were built or improved at Khe Sanh, An Hoa, Landing Zone Baldy, Tam Ky, and Quang Ngai; and the 1stMAW at one time or another had detachments stationed at these installations to provide for air traffic control, refueling, rearming, and other esential tasks. ("Suitable for KC-130s" means about 3,000 feet of runway with some sort of hard surface.) The 1stMAW had the capability to move where the action was. Its expeditionary character was well suited to this kind of campaign.

Men, Units, and Aircraft

From the time it established its command post (CP) at Da Nang in June 1965 until April 1966, the 1stMAW maintained a rear echelon under its command at Iwakuni, Japan. During this period the 1stMAW had cognizance over all Marine Corps aviation units deployed to the Western Pacific. It rotated jet units between Japan and Vietnam and helo squadrons between Okinawa, the Special Landing Force (SLF) afloat in the Seventh Fleet, and Vietnam. It also reassigned men.

In Vietnam the wing had a Headquarters Group and four aircraft MAGs: MAG-11 and MAG-12, with jets at Da Nang and Chu Lai respectively; MAG-16 at Marble Mountain and Phu Bai with helos; and MAG-36 at Ky Ha with helos. A Service Group, stationed in Japan as part of the rear echelon, did not arrive in Vietnam until 1966, when facilities became available. The Headquarters Group and the Service Group were both reorganized in 1967 by Headquarters Marine Corps into three groups instead of two: a Headquarters Group, an Air Control Group, and a Support Group. This reflected a realignment of functions to provide better management of resources, based on experience gained in the recent move of the 1stMAW from Japan and Okinawa to Vietnam.

The first aircraft squadrons to arrive in Vietnam were from 1stMAW units in Japan and Okinawa. These were "rotational" squadrons. Each had been trained in the United States and deployed as a team to serve a 13-month tour together in WestPac. At the expiration of that tour, another squadron was scheduled to arrive to replace the old squadron on station.

Because all members of the squadron arrived at the same time, it meant they all had to be sent back to the United States at the same time. Likewise, all the men in squadrons that arrived in Vietnam from Hawaii and the United States, whether their units were rotational squadrons or not, would also have to be replaced at the same time.

The Corps could no longer support unit rotation on that scale, so it was forced to go to a system of replacement by individuals rather than by units, except in special cases. This problem arose because the Stateside training establishment became saturated with training individuals as individuals and had no time to devote to team or unit training, except for those units which were reforming with new aircraft. In the latter case, unit rotation was necessary. In order to preclude all of a unit being replaced in one month, the 1stMAW went through a reassignment program in late 1965 in an effort to smooth out the rotation dates of men's tours. All like squadrons, for example all HMMs, had their men interchanged to take advantage of different squadron arrival times in WestPac so that their losses through rotation would be spread over several months rather than one. Short-touring a few men helped further to spread the losses. This program was called "Operation Mixmaster." It was a difficult one to administer, but it accomplished its objective.

In April 1966, the aviation units in Japan and Okinawa were removed from the 1stMAW and established as a separate command reporting directly to FMFPac. The rotation of aircraft, men, and units in and out of Vietnam then became the direct responsibility of FMFPac in lieu of the 1stMAW. The principal reasons for this were that the 1stMAW was increasing in size to the point that the staff could not manage men and equipment spread all over the Western Pacific, and the units in Japan and Okinawa were under the operational control of the Seventh Fleet rather than under General Westmoreland in Vietnam, who

did have the operational control of 1stMAW. So this realignment logically transferred administrative control to FMFPac.

When the war began in 1965, the Marine Corps was authorized 54 deployable aircraft squadrons in the Fleet Marine Forces: 30 jet, 3 propeller transport, 18 helicopter transport, and 3 observation.

After initial deployments to Vietnam in 1965, action was initiated on a priority basis to expand the Corps. Another Marine division, the 5th; one deployable helicopter group consisting of two medium helicopter squadrons; and two observation squadrons were authorized for the duration of the Southeast Asia conflict. The 5thMarDiv was organized, trained, and equipped, and elements of it were deployed to Vietnam. The helicopter group never did become fully organized or equipped. Only one of its helo squadrons was formed. Additionally, two fixed wing and two helicopter training groups, all non-deployable, were authorized for the permanent force structure, but they were not fully equipped until 1970.

The reasons why these aviation units were not completely organized and equipped were primarily time and money. All of the essential resources were long-lead-time items: pilots, technical men, and aircraft. All of them are expensive.

The Reserves could have provided trained personnel, but they were not called up in the case of the Marine Corps. The Reserve 4th Marine Aircraft Wing was not equipped with modern aircraft equivalent to the three regular wings, and it did not have anywhere near its allowance of helicopters, so even if the men had been left behind, it would not have been much help as far as aircraft were concerned.

Two years later the Department of Defense authorized the Marine Corps to reorganize its three permanent and two temporary observation squadrons into three observation and three light transport helicopter squadrons.

The net result of these authorizations was that the Marine Corps added one medium and three light transport helicopter squadrons, giving a total of 58 deployable squadrons.[4]

THE ARRIVAL OF NEW AIRCRAFT

Aviation is a dynamic profession. The rate of obsolescence of equipment is high, and new aircraft have to be placed in the inventory periodically in order to stay abreast of the requirements of modern war. In 1965, the Corps was entering a period that would see the majority of its aircraft replaced within four years.

The A-6A all-weather attack aircraft was coming into the FMF to replace six of twelve A-4 squadrons. (The Marine Corps could neither afford nor did it need to acquire a 100 per cent all-weather capabililty.) The squadrons retaining A-4s would get a newer and more capable series of A-4. Two-seat TA-4Fs would also become available to replace the old F-9 series used by airborne tactical air coordinators.

The F-4B was well along in replacing the F-8 in the 15 fighter squadrons, and in two years, it was to be replaced in part with an even more capable F-4J.

The RF-4 photoreconnaissance aircraft was programmed to replace the RF-8.

The EA-6A electronic warfare aircraft was procured to replace the EF-10B, which was a Korean War vintage airframe.

The O-1 was scheduled to give way to the OV-10A.

The UH-34 medium transport helicopter and the CH-37 heavy transport were to be replaced by the CH-46 and the CH-53, respectively, in the 18 transport helicopter squadrons.

The UH-1E was just coming into inventory to replace the H-43. In a few years, the AH-1G Cobra would fill a complete void. It would provide the Corps with its first gunship designed for the mission. It did not replace, but rather augmented, the UH-1E. (The Marine Corps had no AC-47s, AC-117s, AC-119s, or AC-130s. Every C-47, 117, 119, and 130 the Corps had was required for its primary purpose, and none was available for modification to a gunship role.)

Only the KC-130 tanker-transport did not have a programmed replacement.

New models were accepted all through the war. As each was received, a training base had to be built, not only for aircrews but also for technicians. In order to introduce a new model into the 1stMAW, a full squadron had to be trained and equipped or, in the case of reconnaissance aircraft, a detachment equivalent to one-third or one-half a squadron. As a new unit arrived in Vietnam, a similar unit with older aircraft would return to the United States to undergo reforming with new aircraft. After several like squadrons had arrived in Vietnam, they would undergo a "mixmaster" process in order to spread the rotation tour dates of the men for the same reason as the first squadrons that entered the country.

In June 1965, nine of the fixed wing and five helicopter/observation squadrons were deployed to WestPac. By the following June, 12 fixed wing and 11 helo/observation squadrons were in WestPac. A year later the total was 14 and 13, respectively, and by June 1968 it had risen to 14 and 14, essentially half of the Marine Corps' deployable squadrons. Except for one or two jet squadrons that would be located in Japan, at any one time all of these squadrons were stationed either in Vietnam or with the Special Landing Force of the Seventh Fleet operating off the coast of Vietnam.

More squadrons could not be deployed because all of the remaining squadrons in the United States were required to train replacements, either for the individual replacement program or for the limited unit rotation program to deploy new aircraft. Other commitments were drastically curtailed or eliminated. For example, no helicopters accompanied the infantry battalions to the Mediterranean. The capabilities of FMFPac and FMFLant to engage in other operations were substantially reduced.

Command, Control, and Coordination

1965–1968

The Marine Corps is proud of the fact that it is a force of combined arms, and it jealously guards the integrity of its air-ground team. Retention of operational control of its air arm is important to the Corps's air-ground team, as air constitutes a significant part of its offensive fire power. Ever since the Korean War, when the 1stMarDiv was under operational control of the Eighth Army and the 1stMAW was under the Fifth Air Force, the Corps has been especially alert to avoid such a split again. It is even more important now because of the increased reliance on helicopters and close air support.

Long before a Marine MEB landed in Vietnam, CinCPac was also concerned about how tactical air operations would be coordinated in the event of a war. Admiral H. D. Felt, who was CinCPac in the early sixties, had studied the lessons of the Korean War and concluded that we needed to do better. And since there was no doctrine upon which all the services were agreed on that score, he decided to form a board to look into the matter.

Brigadier General McCutcheon was then the assistant chief of staff for operations at CinCPac, and Admiral Felt appointed him to head a twelve-man board with representatives from the CinCPac staff and the three service component commands. All four services concerned were represented. The board convened in September 1963 and deliberated for three months. It looked at the full spectrum of tactical air support, which includes five principal functions:

a. Control. The allocation and management of resources (aircraft and missiles) to achieve maximum effectiveness.

b. Antiair warfare. The destruction of the enemy's air capability in the air and on the ground.

c. Offensive air support. The use of air-to-ground ordnance and other weapon systems in direct and close support of ground troops and in the interdiction of the enemy's rear areas.

d. Reconnaissance. The use of visual, photographic, electronic, and other airborne sensors to acquire information about the enemy and the battlefield environment.

e. Transport. The transportation of men, equipment, and supplies to and from and within the battle area.

The written report of the board contained a number of conclusions. One was that all services possessed aircraft and that all services required them in order to carry out their tactical missions. Another was that a joint force commander should appoint one of his service component commanders to be the coordinating authority for tactical air operations within the area of operations of the joint command.[5]

Admiral Felt neither approved nor disapproved of the board report in its entirety. Nor did his successor, Admiral U. S. Grant Sharp, who relieved him on 1 July 1964. But various recommendations of the report were put into effect by CinCPac in his exercise of overall operational command and management of tactical air resources within the Pacific Command. For example, when photoreconnaissance missions were initiated over Laos in 1964, CinCPac used the coordinating authority technique to coordinate Navy and Air Force reconnaissance efforts. Later on, CinCPac used coordinating authority when air activity was undertaken in Laos and in North Vietnam.

When plans were being made early in 1965

to land Marines at Da Nang, CinCPac informed ComUSMACV that:

a. The Commanding General (CG) of the MEB would report to ComUSMACV as Naval Component Commander.[6]

b. ComUSMACV would exercise operational control of the MEB through the CG of the MEB.

c. Commander, 2d Air Division, in his capacity as Air Force Component Commander of MACV would act as coordinating authority for matters pertaining to tactical air support and air traffic control in MACV's area of responsibility.

ComUSMACV replied to CinCPac that the Marine jet squadron of the MEB would come under the operational control of his Air Force Component Commander and that such control would be exercised through the tactical air control system. Of course, he added, if the MEB became engaged, it was understood that Marine aircraft would be available for close air support.

The following day CinCPac reiterated his previous guidance to ComUSMACV, namely, that operational control of the squadron would be exercised through the MEB and not the 2d Air Division.

In April 1965, CinCPac promulgated a directive on conduct and control of close air support for the entire Pacific Command, but with emphasis on Vietnam. CinCPac clearly stated that the priority mission in Vietnam was close air support, and the first priority was in support of forces actually engaged with the enemy. The directive went on to say that close air support aircraft would be subject to direct call by the supported ground unit through the medium of the related close air support agency. Among other things, the directive also said that nothing therein vitiated the prior CinCPac position that ComUSMACV's Air Force Com-

ponent Commander should act as coordinating authority in matters pertaining to tactical air support and air traffic control.

In June 1965, ComUSMACV initiated a revision of his air support directive, and he drew heavily from the CinCPac Tactical Air Support Board report. The directive was published later that year and revised slightly in 1966, but the pertinent provisions were unchanged.

The MACV directive designated Commander, Seventh Air Force (formerly 2d Air Division), in his capacity as Air Force Component Commander, to act as the coordinating authority for all U. S. and Free World Military Air Force air operations and Vietnamese Air Force activities in the MACV area of operation. Commander, Seventh Air Force, was further given responsibility to establish, in conjunction with U. S. and Vietnamese agencies, an air traffic control system to provide normal processing and flight following.[7] He was also charged to prepare joint instructions, in conjunction with Commanding General, III MAF, and appropriate Army and Navy commanders, to insure integrated and coordinated air operations.

In the same directive, the Commanding General of III MAF was directed to exercise operational control over all Marine Corps aviation resources except in the event of a major emergency or disaster when ComUSMACV might direct Commander, Seventh Air Force, to assume operational control. Commanding General, III MAF, was further enjoined to conduct offensive and defensive tactical air operations to include close air support, interdiction, reconnaissance, maintenance of air superiority, air transport, search and rescue, and other supplemental air support as required. He was also directed to identify to Commander, Seventh Air Force, those resources in excess of current requirements so that such resources could be allocated to support other forces or missions. Finally, he was charged to prepare in conjunction with Commander, Seventh Air Force, joint operating instructions to insure a coordinated and integrated effort.

Concurrently with the revising of the MACV directive, the Commander, Seventh Air Force, Lieutenant General Joseph H. Moore, and the Deputy Commander of III MAF for Air, Brigadier General McCutcheon, were engaged in discussions relative to the degree of control that the Seventh Air Force should have over Marine air assets, particularly with regard to air defense operations. The Air Force desired to have operational control, but the Marines pointed out that the F-4 aircraft was a dual-purpose aircraft and that the Marine tactical air control system was used to control all Marine aviation functions, not just air defense.[8] To relinquish operational control would deprive the MAF commander of authoritative direction over one of his major supporting arms.

Nevertheless, the Marines recognized the necessity of having one commander directly responsible for air defense so, after several joint meetings, it was decided to prepare a Memorandum of Agreement which would disseminate basic policies, procedures, and responsibilities. The Air Force was to have overall air defense responsibility and designate an air defense commander. The Commanding General, 1stMAW, was to designate those forces under his command that would participate in air defense, and he agreed that the Air Force would exercise certain authority over those designated resources to include scramble of alert aircraft, designation of targets, declaration of Hawk missile control status, and firing orders. This agreement was signed by the two commanders in August 1965. Overall operational control of Marine air resources was retained under III MAF, but requisite authority for purposes of air defense was passed to the Air Force.

These two documents provided the basic policy for command, control, and coordination of Marine aviation in Vietnam until early 1968, and they were entirely adequate as far as III MAF was concerned.

SINGLE MANAGEMENT (1968–1970)

Late in 1967, the buildup began for the Battle of Khe Sanh. General Westmoreland had directed massive air support for the garrison there, and both the 1stMAW and Seventh Air Force responded in full. Both General Westmoreland and General William W. Momyer, Commander, Seventh Air Force, believed more effective use could be made of MACV's total air resources if they were managed by a single commander and staff. Early in 1968, a directive was prepared to implement the concept.

The proposed directive required the Commanding General, III MAF, to make available to the Deputy ComUSMACV for Air (who was also Commander, Seventh Air Force) for mission direction all of his strike and reconnaissance aircraft and his tactical air control system as required. The term "mission direction" was not defined. Deputy ComUSMACV for Air was to be responsible for fragging and operational direction of these resources. "Operational direction" was not defined either. "Fragging" is a common aviation term which means to issue a fragmentary order to cover details of a single mission, that is, what is required, where, and when.

The Marines, both in Vietnam and in Washington, objected to the proposed directive on two counts: first, the system as proposed would increase the response time for air support; and second, they reasoned it wasn't necessary.

With regard to the first point, MACV modified the proposed system to improve the response time so that for Marines it wouldn't be any longer than it had been formerly, and for the Army units it would be better. On the second count, MACV remained convinced that it was necessary.

The directive was approved by CinCPac and went into effect in March 1968. The system required the 1stMAW to identify its total sortie capability to Seventh Air Force daily on the basis of a 1.0 sortie rate, that is, one sortie per day for each jet aircraft possessed. Previously the 1stMAW had fragged its aircraft against air support requests received from the Marine ground units, and then identified daily to Seventh Air Force the excess sorties that would be available. These were then fragged by Seventh Air Force on either out-of-country missions or in-country in support of forces other than Marine units. The majority of air support could be forecast and planned in advance except the requirements that might be generated by troops in contact with the enemy. These requirements could be met by extra sorties, scrambles from the hot pad, or by diverting aircraft in the air.

As time went on the participants in the single management system made changes in order to improve efficiency and effectiveness. One such change was the fragging of a portion of the air support on a weekly basis rather than daily. This permitted the more or less standard recurring flights to be handled with less paperwork, while the nonroutine requests could still be fragged on a daily basis. Seventh Air Force also fragged back to 1stMAW a set number of sorties to take care of unique Marine requirements such as helicopter escort and landing zone preparation which were tied closely to helo operations.

When single management was inaugurated, two new DASCs were added to I Corps. One was established at the III MAF Command Post at Camp Horn, in East Da Nang, and one at the XXIV Corps Command Post at Phu Bai. The one at III MAF was the senior DASC in I Corps and was given authority to scramble strike air-

craft without further reference to the Tactical Air Command Center (TACC) in Saigon. This scramble authority was not delegated to similar DASCs in other corps areas. I Corps was unique in that it was the only corps area that had both Marine and Air Force tactical air squadrons and both Marine and Army divisions.

Since the 1stMAW generally exceeded the 1.0 sortie rate, all sorties generated in excess of 1.0 could be scrambled by Horn DASC. These excess sorties, plus those fragged back to meet unique Marine requirements, amounted to a sizeable percentage of the 1stMAW's effort, and so, for all practical purposes, the system worked around to just about where it was in the pre-single management days as far as identification or fragging of Marine sorties was concerned.

There is no doubt about whether single management was an overall improvement as far as MACV as a whole was concerned. It was. And there is no denying the fact that, when three Army divisions were assigned to I Corps and interspersed between the two Marine divisions, a higher order of coordination and cooperation was required than previously.

The system worked. Both the Air Force and the Marines saw to that. But the way it was made to work evolved over a period of time, and a lot of it was due to gentlemen's agreements between the on-the-scene commanders. A detailed order explaining the procedures was never published subsequent to the initial directive. The basic MACV directive on air support, however, was revised in 1970 to take into account the advent of single management.

The revised MACV directive defined the term "mission direction" or "operational direction" which had been used in the basic single management directive but not defined. "Mission direction" was stated to be the authority delegated to one commander (i.e., Deputy ComUSMACV for Air) to assign specific air tasks to another commander (i.e., CG III MAF) on a periodic basis as implementation of a basic mission previously assigned by a superior commander (ComUSMACV). In other words, ComUSMACV assigned CG III MAF a basic mission to conduct offensive air support, and ComUSMACV delegated to his Deputy for Air the authority to task CG III MAF for specific missions on a daily and weekly basis in frag orders in order that III MAF assets could support the force as a whole.

Although single management never took operational control of his air resources away from CG III MAF, the Marines were worried that that might be the next step. If so it would be a threat to the air-ground team, and it would recreate the Korean War situation all over again. The new MACV directive allayed their fears on this score. Not only did the definition of "mission direction" spell out the extent of control to be exercised, but the directive clearly stated that CG III MAF would exercise operational control over all his air resources, and that he would conduct offensive and defensive air support missions to include the full spectrum of tactical air support.

In short, the Marines did not relinquish operational control of their resources, MACV as a whole received more effective air support, and III MAF continued to receive responsive air support from its own units. Within the system, III MAF had first claim on its own assets, so most Marine air missions were in support of Marine ground units and the majority of air support received by Marine ground units was provided by Marine air.

Control

Marine Corps doctrine prescribes that the commander of an air-ground team will have operational control of all his weapon systems and employ them in concert as a force of combined arms to accomplish his mission. The Marine commander exercises this operational control through his normal staff planning process and by means of the Marine Air Command and Control System.

The senior agency in this system is the Tactical Air Command Center (TACC). Because the Seventh Air Force had a TACC in Saigon, the 1stMAW center was called a TADC (Tactical Air Direction Center) as provided for in doctrine. This center was established in June 1965 in the wing compound at Da Nang and it functioned there throughout the war. Continuous improvements were made in its physical appearance, but the tasks performed remained essentially the same. The TADC monitored the employment of all Marine aircraft and allocated the resources to specific missions.

There were two principal agencies subordinate to the TADC. These were the Tactical Air Operations Center (TAOC) and Direct Air Support Centers (DASCs).

The TAOC is the hub of activity for air surveillance and air defense. It is provided for by a Marine Air Control Squadron (MACS).

On a Saturday night in May 1965, Marine Air Control Squadron 9 (MACS-9), based at Atsugi, Japan, and commanded by Lieutenant Colonel Charles T. Westcott, received a telephoned order to have an early warning radar and team ready to deploy by air to Vietnam the next day. Three KC-130s from VMGR-152 were loaded on Sunday and flown to Phu Bai where the team set up and began operating as a northern radar site for the Air Force radar station Panama on Monkey Mountain.

The remainder of the squadron deployed to Chu Lai in the summer and established a manual TAOC. The information from the various radars was plotted by hand on vertical display boards just as had been done during World War II and the Korean War. MACS-7 relieved MACS-9 in place in September 1965.

In June 1967, MACS-4 arrived in Vietnam and replaced the manual system with a modern semi-automated, computer-oriented

TAOC which had been developed as part of the Marine Tactical Data System, or MTDS. This system had been under development since the late fifties and was compatible with two similar developments by the Navy: the Navy Tactical Data System (NTDS) for surface operations and the Navy Airborne Tactical Data System (ATDS) for airborne control centers.

In order to make most effective use of this equipment it was decided to emplace it on Monkey Mountain where one of the Hawk missile batteries was located. This required more construction effort to enlarge the site to accommodate both MACS-4 and the Hawks. A considerable area was required for the radars and their antennae and for the sixteen helicopter-transportable huts that comprised the TAOC and the four huts that made up the Tactical Data Communications Central (TDCC).

The TAOC gave the 1stMAW a capability to handle 250 aircraft tracks, friendly and hostile, at one time. In addition, from an air defense point of view, the controllers could handle more than 25 air intercepts simultaneously and the TAOC had a built-in missile data link capability.

A team from the Joint Chiefs of Staff visited Southeast Asia and recommended that steps be taken to link the various services' air control systems together in that theater. A joint task group was established to work out the technical details.

The TAOC was already operating with the NTDS and ATDS units of the Seventh Fleet in the Gulf of Tonkin. The interface between MTDS and these two systems was the Marine TDCC on Monkey Mountain. The TDCC was the logical candidate, therefore, to become the interface with the Air Force system. One more shelter was required. This provided a special data terminal, or "modem," to convert from computer mode to communications mode. In addition, a new program had to be written for the Marine computer. In layman's terms, the result produced a TDCC which was the equivalent of a language translator in three languages.[9] It could receive either Navy, Marine, or Air Force messages and translate the one received into the other two and pass the translation to the respective centers where they could be displayed. The net result was that air defense and air control data could be passed from Thailand to Da Nang to naval ships in the Tonkin Gulf and vice versa. This interface became fully operational in August 1969 and marked a significant step forward in joint operations.

Whereas the TAOC is the main control center for anti-air warfare and air traffic control, the DASC is the main center for direct support of the ground troops. Each Marine division initially had a DASC located together with its organic Fire Support Coordination Center (FSCC). As the 3dMarDiv assumed responsibility for the very sizeable Northern I Corps area, it was necessary to establish a DASC at Phu Bai with the Division Headquarters and one at Dong Ha with Division (Forward). Requests for air support, both fixed and rotary wing, were requested and controlled through these agencies. During certain peak periods a Helicopter Direction Center (HDC) was established with the Regimental Headquarters at Camp Evans, midway between Hue and Quang Tri, and a mini-DASC at Khe Sanh. Information was provided by these facilities to aircraft, on request, relative to artillery fires in progress and major air strikes to enable planes to navigate safely between areas. This information was particularly helpful to helicopters. The wing also had the capability to install an HDC on short notice in a KC-130 to provide an airborne DASC if required. This was done on several operations. An airborne DASC was used whenever a ground operation was launched at such a distance from Da Nang that ordinary ground-to-air communication would be unreliable. The need for airborne DASCs decreased as bases were built throughout I Corps.

The Marine Air Support Squadron (MASS), which is the parent squadron for the DASC, also contains three mobile Air Support Radar Teams (ASRTs). Each team is equipped with the TPQ-10 radar course directing central which provides the capability to control aircraft in direct air support under conditions of low visibility. MASS-2 arrived in Vietnam in April 1965 from Okinawa, and MASS-3 arrived in October from California. The TPQs were up and operating early in the war.

During the summer of 1965, one TPQ-10 was set up for about six weeks near Pleiku in II Corps to provide air support for Army units operating in that area. Both Marine and Air Force aircraft were directed by it. Within I Corps the TPQs were moved as required to provide optimum coverage, and eventually they were deployed from near the DMZ to Chu Lai.

Lieutenant General Moore of the Seventh Air Force visited 1stMAW and was especially interested in this gear since the Air Force had nothing comparable. Subsequently, the Air Force took some radar bomb-scoring equipment and developed it into a ground-controlled radar bombing device. It became known as Skyspot. Compared to TPQ-10, it had longer range but less mobility.

The A-4, A-6, and F-4 were all equipped with beacons, and the TPQ radar could track them to almost fifty miles under the best conditions. Knowing the radar-aircraft and the radar-target sides of the triangle, the computer could solve the aircraft-target problem for the particular ordnance to be delivered and the operator could instruct the pilot when to drop. The A-4 was also equipped with a link to the auto pilot which could permit automatic control and drop by the TPQ with the pilot flying hands off. Aircraft without a beacon could be tracked by radar to a distance of about thirty-five miles.

The TPQ-10 was a development based on the MPQ-14 used by the Marines in Korea. Replacement for the TPQ-10, making use of recent technology, is currently under development in a joint venture with the Air Force.

Although not part of the tactical air control system, the Marine Air Traffic Control Units (MATCUs) played a vital role in the control of air traffic. Their mission was terminal traffic control around an air base. They provided approach control, ground-controlled approach, and tower facilities. The Corps is authorized one MATCU per jet group and, because of their dispersed operations, two per helo group. In Vietnam, the wing operated MATCUs at Chu Lai and Marble Mountain throughout the war and at Phu Bai, Quang Tri, Dong Ha, Khe Sanh, An Hoa, and Baldy as long as Marine units were operating at those bases. Without those units, air operations during the monsoon season would have been next to impossible.

The TAOC and MATCUs were linked together with communications so that enroute traffic handled by the former could be handed off to the latter for approach and landing clearance.

All of this command and control equipment—TACC/TADC, TAOC, DASC, ASRT, MATCU—is completely mobile and expeditionary by design. It can all be withdrawn from Vietnam (or wherever) and used elsewhere.

AIR-GROUND COORDINATION

The CG of the 1stMAW was designated as Deputy CG III MAG (Air) and as such he was the Tactical Air Commander for III MAF.

In Vietnam, from March 1966 when the 1stMarDiv entered the country, until November 1969 when the 3dMarDiv redeployed to Okinawa, there were two Marine divisions in III MAF. The Marine Corps could not deploy another wing for reasons pointed out earlier, but the 1stMAW was reinforced to the limit of the Corps's resources so it could support two reinforced divisions. Two LAAM battalions and two helicopter MAGs were deployed plus one air support squadron for each division.

The wing was short two or three transport helicopter squadrons, but no additional squadrons were available. The available squadrons were managed centrally by the wing in order to get the most out of them.

Although an air support squadron was placed with each division, it became evident that more authority was required at the DASC. This point was made abundantly clear when the two Marine divisions became geographically separated with one or two Army divisions employed between them. When the 3dMarDiv was operating in Northern ICTZ, it was well removed from the 1stMAW Command Post and TADC at Da Nang. The communications were not fast enough to permit command decisions to be made about aviation problems. The 1stMAW solved this problem by assigning an Assistant Wing Commander and a few staff officers to the DASC at the 3dMarDiv Command Post and empowering him to make decisions in the name of the Wing Commander regarding air support. Later, when it wasn't always feasible to have a brigadier general present, a colonel was assigned to each of the division DASCs and they had the same command authority. This arrangement worked well and provided a one-for-one relationship, air-to-ground, particularly in the vital area of helicopter support. Coordination was vastly improved.

Employment

ANTI-AIR WARFARE OPERATIONS

Vietnam, at least as far as the war in the south was concerned, was not a fighter pilot's war. There were no air-to-air engagements for Marine squadrons. No aces.

But there was a possible threat. So there had to be an air defense system and capability, and it was exercised under the terms of the agreement signed by Generals Moore and McCutcheon. The Marines provided two battalions of Hawk surface-to-air missiles for close-in defense at Da Nang and Chu Lai, F-4 Phantoms on hot pad alert, and an early warning and control capability through its air control squadron.

The Marine LAAM battalion is part of the overall anti-air warfare function. Its principal role is in close-in air defense. The battalion is normally a subordinate unit of the Marine Air Control Group, because in actual operations it is linked to the TAOC which provides information on friendly and enemy air traffic. The TAOC also normally gives "commence" and "cease" fire orders to the missiles.

One LAAM battery arrived in Vietnam in February 1965 and took position on the airfield at Da Nang. Subsequently it moved to Hill 327 west of the field. The two other firing batteries of the battalion eventually were placed on Monkey Mountain east of Da Nang, and in the Hai Van Pass to the north. Part of one of the batteries, known as an assault fire unit, was emplaced on Hill 55 eight miles south of the Da Nang vital area. The best defense of the installations at Da Nang would call for five battery sites, but adequate real estate did not become available until months later.

The 2d LAAM Battalion landed at Chu Lai in September 1965, and set up its firing batteries north and south of the SATS airfield. There were no elevated positions, but this posed a problem for any potential attacker as well.

Although neither battalion fired in anger, they did conduct live practice firings annually in order to keep their state of training high. In addition to firing at radio controlled drones, they fired at targets towed by manned fighter planes.

OFFENSIVE AIR SUPPORT OPERATIONS

The main employment of Marine jets was in the delivery of air-to-ground ordnance in direct and close support of ground troops.

In this connection there were some local rules of engagement which had developed over the years, influencing the tactics and techniques to be employed. With very few exceptions, all air strikes had to be controlled by an airborne controller, and most had to have a political as well as a tactical clearance. There was good reason for this. The population was spread out over a considerable area along the coastal region, and the U. S. and Vietnamese ground units were operating mainly in the same area. This led to the employment of Forward Air Controllers (Airborne) (FAC[A]). Thus, in a departure from prewar practice, the role of the FAC on the ground was minimized as far as control of air strikes was concerned. However, he had other useful employment.

The O-1 aircraft was used initially for this purpose. The Marine O-1s that were brought into Vietnam were rapidly approaching the end of their service lives, however, and on 1 September 1965, the Marine Corps stopped using them. The OV-10A, which was scheduled to replace them, did not become available until July 1968. To partially alleviate this situation, Headquarters Marine Corps and the Naval Air Systems Command managed to locate about a dozen old O-1s and had them overhauled and airlifted to Vietnam. These were too few, however, so the Marines had to rely on Army observation aircraft and Air Force FAC(A)s for those tactical air control missions demanding an airborne controller. The Air Force used the O-1 initially and later the OV-10A and the Cessna O-2. The latter is a small twin-engine, light aircraft with the engines in line. The one in front drives a tractor propeller and the one in the rear a pusher prop.

In addition to FAC(A)s, the Marine Corps employed Tactical Air Coordinators (Airborne) or TAC(A)s. Whereas FAC(A)s flew low performance aircraft and operated over friendly terrain and within range of artillery support, the TAC(A)s flew high performance jets and operated over territory controlled by the enemy. Their mission was to coordinate various strike aircraft and to ensure they hit the correct targets. In this role the Marines first used the two-seat F-9, but beginning in late 1967 they employed the two-seat TA-4F. These aircraft provided two sets of "eyeballs" rather than one and gave the TAC(A) an increased visual observation capability. The jet performance added a higher degree of survivability to the mission.

The Corps removed one of the two FACs it had in each infantry battalion because of the few opportunities offered them to control strikes and because their aeronautical talent could better be used elsewhere. The one remaining FAC plus the Air Liaison Officer, both aviation officers, continued to carry out their other responsibilities, which included advising their battalion commander on the employment of air support, requesting such support, and controlling helo operations and helo landing zones. This became big business in Vietnam. When the opportunity presented itself, the FAC did control air strikes from the ground.

The arrival of the A-6 aircraft in Vietnam introduced an advanced avionics weapon system. This system was further improved, as far as close air support is concerned, when the Marines deployed small radar beacons for use with their ground FACs. With this beacon, known as RABFAC, a FAC's precise position on the ground could be displayed on the radar scope in an A-6. The FAC could provide the bearing and distance of the target from the beacon, plus the elevation difference between the two, and the bombardier-navigator in the A-6 could enter this data into the weapon system computer, and bomb the target in bad weather or at night with accuracies approaching that of A-4s in clear, daylight deliveries.

The A-6 aircraft displayed great versatility and lived up to the expectations of those who pushed its development after the Korean War. It is the only operational aircraft that has a self-contained all-weather bombing capability including a moving target indicator mode. In this role it was used rather extensively in the monsoon season, not only in South Vietnam but also in Laos and over the heavily defended area of North Vietnam. The usual bomb load was 14,000 pounds.

Both the A-4 and F-4 were used in offensive air support with great success. The average bomb load for the A-4 was about 3,000 pounds, and for the F-4 about 5,000 pounds. These aircraft were generally fragged against planned missions, but they could also be scrambled from the alert pad, or they could be diverted in flight to higher priority targets.

The F-8 was also used during the period December 1965 through May 1968. It was in the process of being replaced in the Marine inventory by the F-4, but while it was in Vietnam it did a fine job in air-to-ground missions.

The F-8 was also the only Marine strike aircraft to be based on board a carrier of the Seventh Fleet during the Vietnam War. Marine All-Weather Fighter Squadron 212 (VMF[AW]-212), commanded by Lieutenant Colonel Charles H. Ludden, was embarked in the attack carrier USS *Oriskany* (CVA-34) in 1965 when she was operating off Vietnam. The squadron pilots were trained as fighter pilots but, when the carrier arrived in the Gulf of Tonkin, the urgent need was for attack aircraft which could deliver bombs. The primary mission of VMF(AW)-212 became the attack of ground targets, and the squadron flew strikes in North and South Vietnam. Both the Navy and Marine Corps would have liked to have had more Marine squadrons afloat, but if they had been afloat, they wouldn't have been ashore and the Corps couldn't do both. Now

that we have cut force levels in Vietnam, the Marine Corps has once again deployed aviation units aboard carriers.

During 1965, and into the early part of 1966, there was a shortage of aviation ordnance. Time was required to set up production lines in the United States and get the pipeline filled all the way to Vietnam. In the meantime, the 1stMAW used what was available in contingency stocks, and this included a great number of old high-drag "fat" bombs. The old bombs had a much larger cross section than the new ones, hence they added drag to the aircraft and reduced its speed and radius of action. Again because of their cross section, fewer of the old bombs could be loaded on multiple bomb racks. The wing never lost a sortie because of ordnance, but it did have to substitute items on occasion because the preferred store was not available. In order to husband its resources, the wing commander issued a message directing that if ordnance could not be dropped on a worthwhile target, it would be brought back to base, not jettisoned.

By late 1966, a wide range of ordnance was available, including 250, 500, 1,000, and 2,000-pound bombs; 2.75 inch and five-inch rockets; napalm; 20mm. cannon; smoke; and certain other stores for special targets. There is still a requirement, however, for better aviation weapons. We need to get better first-pass accuracy to reduce the number of passes over the target. One promising way to improve effectiveness appears to be offered by lasers.

Up to April 1966, ComUSMACV was not involved in the air war in North Vietnam. That war was conducted by the Commander-in-Chief, Pacific Fleet (CinCPacFlt), and the Commander-in-Chief, Pacific Air Force (CinCPacAF). 1stMAW electronic EF-10Bs flew missions in the north before this, but they did so in support of the Seventh Fleet or the Seventh Air Force as subordinates of PacFlt and PacAF. On 1 April 1966, ComUSMACV was authorized by CinCPac to conduct air strikes in, and to the north of, the DMZ in what was known as Route Package One. By summer, Marine aircraft were assigned to strike there against artillery and rocket sites as well as other military targets.

With the addition of the A-6A to its inventory, the 1stMAW had the finest all-weather bombing aircraft in the world. Late in 1966, A-6s began striking targets as far north as Hanoi and Haiphong and carried on until the bombing halt in 1968, striking mostly at night. North Vietnam was, of course, heavily defended with antiaircraft artillery and surface-to-air missiles. EA-6As provided electronic jamming in support of the strike birds, and Marine F-4Bs flew cover for them to keep MiGs off their backs. Additionally, the two Marine A-6 squadrons flew strikes in other route packages as directed.

RECONNAISSANCE OPERATIONS

As noted earlier, VMCJ-1 was one of the first fixed-wing squadrons to deploy to Vietnam. In more than five years of continuous operations from Da Nang, the squadron made major contributions in the field of electronic warfare and imagery reconnaissance.

During the opening phases of the air war against North Vietnam, the EF-10Bs of VMCJ-1 were the only jet tactical electronic warfare aircraft available to provide support for U. S. Air Force and Navy strikes. To meet the requirements levied on the squadron, active electronic countermeasures were emphasized. Electronic reconnaissance was conducted enroute to and from the target. In the target area, jamming occupied most of the electronic countermeasure operators' attention. In July 1965, U. S. Air Force aircraft conducted the first strikes in history against surface-to-air missile (SAM) sites. Six EF-10Bs from VMCJ-1 supported the strike. There was no loss of aircraft to radar-controlled weapons. The Navy also had an electronic warfare capability, but its EKA-3 was a combination tanker-electronic

warfare aircraft and was limited to standoff jamming as opposed to close-in jamming in company with the strike aircraft. The Navy also had some EA-1s, but these were propeller-driven aircraft and were not able to keep up with the jets, hence, they too were used in a standoff role. The Air Force effort in electronic warfare was devoted almost exclusively to larger aircraft and in a "strategic," rather than a tactical, role. After the war in Vietnam got under way, they did modify some B-66 aircraft to the electronic mission.

In November 1966, the EA-6A made its debut in the theater. The quantum increase in electronic warfare capability represented by the EA-6A came in the nick of time. The cancerous spread of SAMs throughout North Vietnam made an eventual confrontation between Marine attack aircraft and SAMs inevitable. In April 1967, a Marine A-4 was shot down by a SAM from a site located in the DMZ. In response to the new threat, EF-10Bs began a continual patrol along the DMZ during hours of darkness when the SAMs were prone to fire. The more sophisticated EA-6As provided electronic warfare support for missions against targets located in the high threat areas of the north. Because of the need for electronic warfare aircraft, it was not until 1969 that the old EF-10Bs were at last able to leave Vietnam. As of this writing the EA-6A is the only tactical electronic warfare aircraft in any service that can accompany strike aircraft to the target and maneuver with them.

In the relatively new art of electronic warfare, aircraft from VMCJ-1 performed in every role: escort for B-52s, support for tactical air strikes, and as intelligence collectors. Lessons learned were documented, tactics became more sophisticated, and hardware was evolved to increase the effectiveness of the electronic warfare capability.

The other side of the VMCJ-1 house, imagery reconnaissance, was equally engaged. Collection of imagery intelligence in the fight against the hard-to-locate enemy of the south varied to a great degree from flights over relatively well defined targets in the north. In the south, the usual imagery reconnaissance mission produced evidence of enemy activity, but the enemy was seldom pinpointed. To determine enemy intentions, reconnaissance flights over the same areas were conducted periodically. Interpreters then looked for telltale indications of change or deviations from the norm that had been established by previous flights. With the RF-8A, the imagery coverage of large areas required by this type of intelligence determination was confined to periods of daylight hours and relatively good weather. Replacement of the RF-8A with multi-sensor RF-4B aircraft, beginning in October 1966, provided VMCJ-1 with a round-the-clock collection capacity. As experience was gained with the new systems, night infrared reconnaissance played an ever-increasing role in the overall intelligence collection effort.

TA-4Fs flew hundreds of missions in the Route Package One area of North Vietnam, performing in the visual reconnaissance as well as in the TAC(A) role. They located SAM sites, truck parks, supply dumps, and other targets, and then controlled other strike aircraft against them. They also spotted and controlled naval gunfire for the USS *New Jersey* (BB-62) and other ships that participated in bombarding the north.

Visual reconnaissance by low-performance aircraft is still an absolute necessity. Maneuverable, fixed-wing aircraft still have a place in this role, and the OV-10A performed better than expected. However, there is a requirement for a quieter aircraft that can overfly targets without being detected. Had such an aircraft been available, it could have been used very profitably to patrol the rocket belt around the vital area of Da Nang. There is a prototype aircraft designated the YO-3 that gives promise of this capability, but the Marine Corps does not have any.

FIXED-WING TRANSPORT OPERATIONS

Marine transports and helos were not included under single management. The Marines had two models of fixed-wing transports in Vietnam, the venerable C-117 and the workhorse KC-130. The former was assigned only in small numbers, one per group, and was used for organic logistic support. It became apparent in 1965, however, that there were some voids in the Marine capability as far as aircraft were concerned, so the C-117s were rapidly drafted to fill some of these. Examples were flare drops, radio relay, and use as an airborne control center. Later on, US-2Bs and C-1As were assigned to the wing, and sometimes they were also used for some of these tasks.

Marine Refueler Transport Squadron 152 (VMGR-152) was based in Japan when the war began, but it moved to Okinawa late in 1965. It kept a four- (or more) plane detachment at Da Nang. This little detachment did everything imaginable as far as air transport was concerned. It hauled men and equipment between major bases in Vietnam and to outposts such as Khe Sanh that had suitable airstrips, and it air-dropped to those that did not. It provided aerial refueler service for Marine jets, particularly those that operated up north. In 1965, whenever the strip at Chu Lai was less than eight thousand feet and A-4s were required to take off with reduced fuel loads, there was a KC-130 tanker in orbit to tank them after climb-out. These Hercules also served as airborne direct air support centers and as flareships. They were a reliable and versatile transport.

The KC-130 is getting on in years, however, and in spite of the fact that it was retrofitted with larger engines, the aircraft is only marginally capable of refueling a loaded A-6 or F-4 in flight.[10] Furthermore, a considerable number of them are required to provide refueling service for a fighter squadron ferrying across the Pacific. Because they can't get to the same altitude as the jets, the jets have to descend to receive fuel. This requires blocking off a lot of airspace and frequently this is a constraint on a long trans-oceanic ferrying operation since it interferes with commercial flights.

What the Corps needs is a transport like the C-141, modified to be similar in capability to the KC-130.

The Corps also needs a replacement for the obsolete C-117s and those C-54s still on hand. It is willing to accept a smaller number of more modern aircraft to carry out the missions that are not applicable for the KC-130 or 141. A combination of T-39s and something like the Fairchild-Hiller F-227 would give the Corps a modern high-speed passenger and cargo hauling capability.

HELICOPTER OPERATIONS

Vietnam was certainly a helicopter war for U. S. forces. It is difficult to envisage how we would have fought there without them.

After years of study and development, the Marine Corps pioneered the use of helicopters in ground warfare in Korea. In the following years it planned to build up its force, and simultaneously it pursued the development of more capable aircraft. The Corps's basic requirement was for adequate helicopter lift to execute the ship-to-shore movement in an amphibious operation. To do this two basic transport helicopters were decided on, one for medium lift and one for heavy lift.

Although the Corps was authorized eighteen permanent transport helicopter squadrons and two temporary ones for Southeast Asia, it only deployed ten to the Western Pacific. The remaining nine (one temporary one was never formed because of lack of resources) were required to remain in the United States to train replacement pilots for the overseas pipeline. Additional squadrons could not be deployed because they could not be supported. The deployment of even one more would have upset the delicate balance of replacement training versus overseas requirements.

As part of the planning, programming, and budgeting cycle that takes place annually in Washington in each of the services and in the Office of the Secretary of Defense, the Marine Corps accepted a change in its transport helicopter mix, from fifteen medium and three heavy to twelve medium and six heavy.[11] With the one temporary squadron added, this gave thirteen and six. Eventually seven of the mediums and three of the heavies were stationed overseas.

The transition from the UH-34 and CH-37 to the CH-46 and CH-53, respectively, represented a major increase in capability, but at the same time, there were problems involving acceptance of the new models, shaking them down, training pilots and maintenance personnel, developing techniques and procedures, and establishing an adequate supply posture.

Squadrons equipped with the twelve-year-old UH-34 bore the brunt of helo operations in 1965 and for well over a year thereafter. CH-46s began to arrive in Vietnam in March 1966, when Lieutenant Colonel Warren C. Watson's HMM-164 flew to Marble Mountain from the USS *Valley Forge* (LPH-8). It was not until 1969 that all UH-34s were withdrawn. On 18 August, the blades of the last UH-34 were folded, thus marking the end of an era for Marine Corps helicopters in Vietnam. The UH-34 had performed for over seven years there in an outstanding manner.

A detachment of obsolescent CH-37s arrived from Santa Ana, California, in the summer of 1965 and did yeoman service pending arrival of the CH-53 in January 1967, when Major William R. Beeler brought in a four-plane detachment from HMH-463. By the end of the year there were two full squadrons of CH-53s in Vietnam.

In Vietnam there were several technical problems that had an impact on helicopter employment. First of all, the tropical environment reduced payload because of characteristically high temperatures and humidity. Second, the sandy and dusty landing zones created extensive maintenance problems, particularly for engines. Filters had to be developed for all helos to reduce the amount of foreign particles that were being ingested into the air inlets. These filters increased aircraft weight and lowered engine thrust by a few per cent. Third, there was a requirement to install additional armor in all helos to protect their vital parts against the ever-increasing enemy antiaircraft fire. Finally, the addition of armament and gunners naturally reduced proportionately what could be carried.

As a matter of necessity the transports were armed with door guns. The H-34s could only take the 7.62-mm. machine gun, and two of these with a gunner (the crew chief manned one gun) reduced the troop carrying capacity by two men. The CH-46 and -53 helos were able to carry .50-caliber machine guns, one on each side, and although their loads were reduced too, the reduction, particularly in the case of the CH-53, was not so noticeable.

During the period October 1966 through October 1967, the CH-46 experienced a series of catastrophic accidents which caused the Corps and the Naval Air Systems Command to take a hard look at the design of the aircraft. These accidents occurred in the United States as well as in Vietnam and in most cases involved failure of the aircraft's rear pylon. A program was initiated to strengthen that section of the airframe, and it was accomplished in two phases. The first improvement was incorporated in Okinawa for Vietnam-based aircraft. The second phase was performed later at overhaul. The modification program had an impact on helo operations in Vietnam because fewer were available for combat operations. To partially offset this shortage, some UH-34s were airlifted to Da Nang from Cherry Point, North Carolina, in Military Airlift Command

transports. Following the modification program, the CH-46 performed in an outstanding manner.

The Marine Corps experimented with armed helicopters as early as 1950, but it did not pursue an active program for several reasons. The transport helicopters in the inventory before the war began in Vietnam were limited in payload to begin with, and the Corps chose to devote their full-load capacity to carrying men and equipment, while relying on attack aircraft to escort the helicopters. At the same time, it sought to procure a light helicopter which could perform a myriad of tasks, including the role of a gunship. This program was a long time in materializing, but it finally resulted in the UH-1E. The Army, on the other hand, with no fixed-wing attack aircraft, depended heavily on "gun birds."

One gunship version of the Marine UH-1E was armed with a nose turret which could be elevated, depressed, and swung left and right. In addition, weight permitting, it could mount left and right fixed, forward-firing machine guns, or 2.75-inch rocket pods. A .30-caliber machine gun could also be installed in each of the two side doors.

The helo gunship proved to be indispensable. It was more immediately available than jets, more maneuverable, and it could work close-in with transport helicopters.

The UH-1E has been used by the Marines since 1965 to perform many tasks. They include serving as gunships; as command and control craft for MAF, division, wing, regimental, and occasionally battalion commanders; for liaison, courier, and administrative runs; for visual reconnaissance and observation; as aerial searchlights when special equipment was installed; as platforms for various kinds of sensors; as transportation for VIPs (and this was no small order); for medical evacuation of casualties; and for miscellaneous roles.

In 1965, the Corps was authorized 12 light

helos per wing, and these were included in each of the three VMO squadrons. Two additional VMOs were authorized for the war in Southeast Asia, and in 1968 the Department of Defense authorized the Marine Corps to convert them to three light helicopter transport squadrons (HML), giving the Corps three VMOs and three HMLs. The VMOs were to have 18 OV-10As and 12 light helos each, and the HMLs were to have 24 light helos. Two of each kind of squadron were on hand in the 1stMAW by the latter part of 1968. This provided 72 light helos (including gunships) to support two reinforced divisions, but it still was not enough to meet all of the requirements. If there is any lesson that has been learned in Vietnam, it is that the Corps needs more light helicopters. The statistics accumulated over the past several years indicate that on the basis of hours of use there is a requirement for these aircraft nearly equal to the combined total of medium and heavy helicopters.

The AH-1G Cobra was not available for Marine use until April 1969. The gunship was accepted with enthusiasm by the pilots, performed well in a fire suppression role, and was maintained at a rather high rate of availability. Organizationally, they might be in a VMO or an HML. Ideally, 24 of them would form an HMA, one in each wing.

The Corps has under procurement twin-engine versions of both the UH-1 and the AH-1, and these should be major improvements over the current single-engine configurations. The benefits will be increased payload capability under a wider range of temperatures and altitudes, and the added reliability provided by having a second power plant. The twin Cobra was due to enter the force in 1970, and the twin UH-1 in 1971.

The first UH-34 squadrons were employed in much the same way as they had been during the "Shufly" years. They lifted troops and cargo on either tactical or administrative mis-

sions and performed the usual spectrum of miscellaneous tasks. They conducted the first night assault in Vietnam in August 1965. The 2d battalion, 3d Marines, was lifted into Elephant Valley, northwest of Da Nang.

By the end of 1965, Marine transport helos were lifting an average of 40,000 passengers and over 2,000 tons of cargo a month while operating from their main bases at Ky Ha and Marble Mountain.

In 1968, the helicopters carried an average of over 50,000 men and over 6,000 tons of cargo a month. This increase in capacity was due mainly to the substitution of CH-46 helos for UH-34s between 1966 and 1968. The increase in the requirement came mainly because of heavy assault operations against North Vietnamese Army divisions which had invaded the I Corps Tactical Zone. And in the first half of 1970, even after redeployment had commenced, they were lifting more than 70,000 passengers and 5,000 tons of cargo in a month. Part of this increase can be attributed to the increased use of the CH-53 in troop lifts.

Even back in "Shufly" days, Marine helicopter pilots learned to expect all sorts of strange cargo on the manifest. They often had to move Vietnamese units, and this included dependents and possessions, cows and pigs included.

As larger transports entered service, larger loads were carried. And this of course included larger animals. HMH-463 with its CH-53s was tasked to move a remotely located Vietnamese camp. Included in the lift requirement were two elephants. Not big ones, but nevertheless elephants. These pachyderms were tranquilized and carried externally with no problem. The crews named them "Ev" and "Charlie," which proves that they had found some time to read the newspapers sent out from home.

With the CH-53, the 1stMAW could retrieve battle damaged UH-1s, UH-34s, and CH-46s that might otherwise have been destroyed. The CH-53 could not lift another 53, however, under operating conditions in Vietnam. There is a need for a small number of heavy-lift helicopters that can retrieve all helicopters and all tactical fixed-wing aircraft except transports. Such a heavy-lift helicopter would also be useful in lifting heavy engineering equipment and other loads beyond the capability of the CH-53. The Army's CH-54 Skycrane's lifting capability is not sufficiently greater to make it a really attractive choice. A payload of at least 18 tons is required. Furthermore, the helicopter should be compatible with shipboard operations, and it should be capable of being disassembled and transported in C-5A or C-141 cargo planes.

One of the most hazardous helicopter missions was the evacuation of casualties at night or in poor weather. The problem was twofold: finding the correct zone, and getting in and out without getting shot up. Since most medevacs were called in by troops in contact with the enemy, the available landing zones had no landing aides to help the pilot, and so he had to rely on an accurate designation and visual identification or confirmation. At night a flare aircraft was often required to orbit the area and illuminate the zone so it could be positively identified. Gunships or jets would provide fire suppression, if required, and the evacuation helo would make a fast approach and retirement, making maximum use of whatever natural concealment might be available.

There is no doubt about it, the helicopter saved countless lives in Vietnam. If the casualty could be evacuated to a medical facility in short order, his chances of survival were very good.[12]

Although a small number of helos were fragged each day specifically for medical evacuation, any helicopter in the air was available for such a mission, if required, and many evacs were made by on-the-scene aircraft. These helicopters of course did not carry hospital corpsmen as did those specifically fragged for the mission, but they offered the advantage of being closer, and thus quicker to respond.

The number of medevac missions flown by Marine helicopters is large indeed—in the peak year of 1968, nearly 67,000 people were evacuated in just short of 42,000 sorties—and a great many of the helos sustained hits and casualties themselves in the process of flying these missions. As a group, helicopter crews were awarded a very high percentage of Purple Hearts for wounds received in combat. They were and are very courageous men.

MULTI-FUNCTION OPERATIONS

The majority of operations conducted by III MAF required some degree of air support, and in most cases the support involved two or more tactical air functions. A complete recounting of all these operations is beyond the scope of this article. However, some representative examples are in order so that the reader may appreciate the role of Marine air in MAF operations.[13]

As the MAF units began to undertake offensive operations, helicopters were essential for troop transport and logistic resupply, and jets were equally important for close air support. Operation Double Eagle in late January and early February 1966 illustrates several techniques and tactics that were used quite frequently in later operations. This was a multi-battalion force commanded by the Assistant Division Commander of the 3dMarDiv, Brigadier General Jonas M. Platt. The operational area was southern I Corps. Coordination was required with Vietnamese Army units in I Corps and with U. S. Army units in II Corps, specifically the 1st Air Cavalry Division. One Marine battalion and helo squadron belonged to the SLF and were embarked in the USS *Valley Forge* and other ships of the Amphibious Ready Group. MAG-36 was placed in direct support of Platt's Task Force Delta. Colonel

William G. Johnson, Commanding Officer of MAG-36, located his command post adjacent to Platt's. He also established a helicopter operating area with limited maintenance support. This became known as "Johnson City." Logistic support was added: fuel, ammunition, supplies, and a medical aid station. This was in effect a Logistic Support Area (LSA), and it was essential to establish one in order to support mobile ground operations such as those in which General Platt was engaged. As the war progressed, these LSAs would become strategically located thoughout the Corps area and close to main roads so that the bulk of supplies could be brought in by truck convoys. If an airfield were near, fixed-wing transport could be used. MAG-36 and Task Force Delta had a mini-DASC located at "Johnson City" through which they could control aircraft assigned to them. Helicopters were immediately available through Colonel Johnson. Jets had to be requested, but the route was direct to the TADC which could scramble A-4s from Chu Lai or F-4s from Da Nang.

Major General McCutcheon was relieved as CG 1stMAW by Major General Louis B. Robertshaw on 15 May 1966. The Struggle Movement within South Vietnam which led to the establishment of the Ky government in Saigon was still unresolved at this point, and an upsurge of political activity forced the cancellation of the planned change-of-command ceremonies. A small impromptu one was held outside III MAF Headquarters.

During General Robertshaw's tenure, the center of action tended to shift north, both on the ground and in the air. In July and August 1966, Operation Hastings produced the highest number of enemy killed to date. The Prairie series of operations, which began shortly thereafter, took place in the same locale, just south of the DMZ. Names like Dong Ha, the "Rockpile," and Con Thien came into prominence. But there was another name which was

destined to become even more prominent, Khe Sanh. Late in April 1967, a Marine company made solid contact with North Vietnamese regulars northwest of Khe Sanh. On the 25th, the 3d Battalion of the 3d Marines was helolifted into Khe Sanh, and the next day the SLF battalion (2d Battalion, 3d Marines) was heloed into Phu Bai and thence lifted by KC-130 to Khe Sanh.[14] Both battalions took the offensive and attacked the enemy on Hills 881 South and North. In two weeks of bitter fighting, the 1stMAW flew over one thousand sorties in around-the-clock close and direct air support of Marine infantry in the area. Here was an example of the integrated employment of fixed- and rotary-wing transports, close air support, and air control.

Major General Norman J. Anderson relieved Robertshaw on 2 June 1967. His tour was marked with a further buildup of North Vietnamese forces in Northern I Corps and the introduction of single management. The enemy's Tet offensive of 1968, the battle of Hue, and the campaign of Khe Sanh all occurred on his watch. During the Khe Sanh campaign, the entire spectrum of tactical air support was called into play—not only Marine, but also Air Force, Navy, and Vietnamese Air Force. And SAC's B-52s dropped their heavy loads upon the enemy in the surrounding hills.

One example of how all Marine tactical air functions could be coordinated into a single operational mission was the "Super Gaggle." This was a technique developed by the 1stMAW to resupply the hill outposts in the vicinity of Khe Sanh. These hills were surrounded with heavy concentrations of enemy antiaircraft weapons, and every flight by a helo into one of the outposts was an extremely hazardous mission. Additionally, the weather in February was typically monsoon, and flying was often done on instruments. The "Super Gaggle" was a flight of transport helos escorted by A-4 jets and UH-1E gunships, all

under the control of a TAC(A) in a TA-4F. The
key was to take advantage of any break in the
weather and to have all aircraft rendezvous
over the designated point at the same time.

The operation was usually scrambled at the
request of the mini-DASC at Khe Sanh on the
basis that a break in the weather was expected
shortly. The TAC(A) and KC-130 tankers took
off from Da Nang, the A-4s from Chu Lai, UH-
1E gunships from Quang Tri and CH-46s from
Dong Ha. All aircraft rendezvoused over Khe
Sanh within a 30-minute period under control
of the TAC(A). Instrument climb-outs were
often required due to weather. Even the CH-
46s with external loads would climb out on a
tacan bearing until they were on top. Under
direction of the TAC(A), and taking advantage
of the break in the clouds if it did develop, the
area was worked over with napalm, rockets,
20-mm., and smoke. The CH-46s let down in a
spiral column and deposited their loads on
Khe Sanh and the hill outposts in less than five
minutes and then spiralled back on top and
returned to their bases. The jets also climbed
back on top, plugged in to the KC-130 tankers
for refueling, and headed back to Da Nang and
Chu Lai.[15]

The fourth commander of the 1stMAW was
Major General Charles J. Quilter. He relieved
Anderson on 19 June 1968. His tour saw a reversal of the trend that started in General
Robertshaw's era. The enemy withdrew after
taking severe beatings at Khe Sanh, Hue, and
elsewhere in ICTZ. The enemy gave up conventional large-scale operations and reverted to
the strategy of small unit actions and harassment.

III MAF forces underwent an operational
change too. Once the 3dMarDiv was relieved of
the requirement for a static defense along the
strong-point barrier, they were free to undertake a mobile offensive in Northern ICTZ and
strike at the enemy in the western reaches. One
of the finest examples of air-ground teamwork

took place during the period of January
through March 1969. The code name of the
operation was Dewey Canyon. The locale was
the upper A Shau Valley and southern Da
Krong Valley. This was a multi-battalion operation involving the 9th Marine Regiment,
commanded by Colonel Robert H. Barrow, and
two battalions of the 1st Vietnamese Army Division.

During the last week of the pre-Dewey Canyon period, Marine attack and fighter-attack
aircraft from MAGS 11, 12, and 13 flew 266
sorties over the objective area, dropping over
730 tons of ordnance.

On 21 January, D-1, a "Zippo" team, was
formed of representatives of the 1stMAW and
3dMarDiv. Infantry, engineer, helicopter, and
observation aircraft specialists were included.
This team was responsible to the overall
ground commander for landing zone and fire
support; base selection and preparation; and
coordination of the helicopter assault.

Early on D-Day the initial landing zones
(LZ) were prepared by fixed-wing air strikes
(made suitable for helo landings by bombing
and strafing to reduce threat of opposition to a
minimum), and elements of the 2d Battalion,
9th Marines, landed at 0800. In the rapid buildup that followed, CH-46s, under the control of
the division DASC and under the protective
umbrella of gunships and observation aircraft,
brought 1,544 Marines and 46 tons of cargo
into two LZs. By the evening of 24 January, a
battery of 105-mm. howitzers from the 2d
Battalion, 12th Marines, and the Command
Post of the 9th Marines were in place on one of
these landing zones, which became known as
Razor.

The following day, three companies of the
3d Battalion were helo-lifted on to a ridgeline
farther forward, known as Co Ka Va. It would
soon be developed into Fire Support Base
(FSB) Cunningham, named for the first Marine
aviator. In a few more days, elements of the 2d

Beginning in 1965, the UH-1E served as a gunship, a command and control craft, a liaison, courier, and administrative support craft, a platform for aerial searchlights and sensors, and a means of transportation for VIPs. But, perhaps its finest hours were served as, almost without regard to weather, it helped to evacuate casualties such as this Marine (center) wounded near Dong Ha in December 1967.

Battalion from FSB Riley pushed down the ridgeline to establish another FSB, Dallas, to guard the western approach to the area from Laos. To the east, the two Vietnamese battalions were lifted into two other bases. They would secure the left flank and cut off the enemy escape route to the east.

About the 1st of February, the "Crachin" season really began to make itself felt. This is a period when low clouds and drizzle cover the mountain tops in Northern I Corps and obscure visibility in the valleys.

On 4 February, a company of the 3d Battalion moved into and occupied what was to be-

come the last FSB for the coming infantry advance. Erskine was to be its name.

Marine helicopters continually worked out of FSB Vandegrift carrying essential supplies of ammunition, rations, and water to the various bases.[16] On the return trips they carried wounded back to aid stations. Often the weather precluded access to the area except by flying on instruments. Under such conditions, over 40 pallets of critically needed supplies were dropped by KC-130s and CH-46s under control of the TPQ-10 at Vandegrift.

When artillery was in place on both Cunningham and Erskine, the 9th Marines began

OPERATION DEWEY CANYON AIR OPERATIONS
STATISTICS, 22 JANUARY–14 MARCH 1969

Helicopter Support	Fixed Wing
14,893 Sorties	1,617 Sorties
5,050 Flight Hours	1,973 Flight Hours
3,515 Tons of Cargo	3,679 Tons of Cargo
21,841 Troops Lifted	390 TPQ Missions
611 Medevacs	

moving on foot from their bases into the Da Krong Valley with battalions on line. Their objective was Tiger Mountain and the ridgeline that ran west from it. As they advanced, landing zones were carved out of the jungle with 2,000-pound bombs or, as a minimum, sufficient space was created so that a medevac could be performed by helo hoist, or an external load could be dropped to the troops on the ground.

On 17 February, Marine helicopter resupply during instrument conditions received its biggest boost. Instrument departure and return corridors were established to permit loaded helos to operate out of Quang Tri in support of the operation. The technique was the same as that employed during Khe Sanh operations. During the next month of corridor operation, over 2,000 Marine aircraft were funneled in and out of this highway in the sky to keep Dewey Canyon alive.

Other elements of the air component continued to seek out the enemy and to attack him. O-1, RF-4, EA-6, A-4, F-4, and A-6 aircraft all participated. And when emergency missions arose during darkness, OV-10A, C-117, or KC-130 aircraft were called in to provide illumination by dropping flares.

The 22nd of February saw the lead element of the 3d Battalion gain the crest of Tiger Mountain. In a few days it became FSB Turnage.

The 24th found the 1st Battalion in possession of the enemy's headquarters at Tam Boi.

The 2d Battalion took control of the ridgeline overlooking Route 922, where it crosses from Vietnam into Laos.

The 27th marked the first time a TPQ-10 had ever been emplaced and operated from an FSB. One was placed on Cunningham and remained there for 17 days, controlling 72 air strikes, ten A-6 beacon drops, and three emergency paradrops.

The days that followed turned up masses of enemy equipment and stores, and the quantity accumulated and sent back to our bases was easily the largest amount yet discovered during the war.

The 18th of March marked the final day of operation of Dewey Canyon. On this day virtually the entire resources of the 1stMAW were committed. Over 350 tons of cargo and 1,400 Marines were helo-lifted out of Turnage and Tam Boi without a casualty. These were the last two bases to be vacated. Gunships and jets flew close cover and close air support.

Perhaps the most notable accomplishment of the operation was that only one helicopter was lost in spite of the adverse weather and terrain and the efforts of a stubborn, well-trained, and professional enemy to counter the operation. Lieutenant General Richard G. Stilwell, U. S. Army, commander of all U. S. ground forces in Northern I Corps under CG III MAF, summed it up in a few words when he said, "Dewey Canyon deserves some space in American military history by sole reason of audacity, guts, and team play. I cannot applaud too highly the airmen of the 1stMAW in a variety of roles."

General Quilter was relieved by Major General William G. Thrash on 7 July 1969. Thrash took command when the wing was at its maximum strength and operating a peak number of facilities. The wing was supporting two Army divisions, two ARVN divisions (splitting the helo load with Army helicopters), and the Korean Marine Brigade, in addition to

OPERATION DEWEY CANYON RESULTS

Enemy Personnel Losses	Ammunition Captured	Vehicles Captured
1,617 KIA	7,287 122-mm. Art'y Rounds	66 Trucks
4 POW	779 122-mm. Rockets	6 Truck Prime Movers
14 Detainees	187 140-mm. Rockets	14 Bulldozers
	4,983 120-mm. Mortar Rounds	3 APCs
Weapons Captured	210 85-mm. Art'y Rounds	1 Front Loader
	23,171 82-mm. Mortar Rounds	1 Air Compressor
1,212 Individual Weapons	994 75-mm. RR Rounds	108 Bicycles
215 Crew Served Weapons	33,509 60-mm. Mortar Rounds	
12 122-mm. Guns	2,004 57-mm. RR Rounds	Rations Captured
4 85-mm. Guns	13,521 B 40 Rockets	
13 82-mm. Mortars	23,730 37 mm. AA Rounds	110 Tons of Rice
12 60-mm. Mortars	4,500 23 mm. AA Rounds	2 Tons of Salt
24 57-mm. Recoilless Rifles	98,526 12.7 mm. AA Rounds	
4 37/40-mm. AA Guns	50,193 Grenades	Installations Seized
4 23-mm. AA Guns	9,576 Rifle Grenades	
39 12.7-mm. AA Guns	1,621 AT Mines	2 Major Headquarters
20 7.62-mm. AA Guns	855 AP Mines	1 Base Hospital
	444 Claymore Mines	2 Major Vehicle Maintenance
	553,000 Small Arms Rounds	Repair Shops
		1 Major Communication Center

the two Marine divisions.[17] It also flew out-of-country missions. Air-ground team performance reached a new high.

Several techniques that had been in use for several years were further improved during General Thrash's period of command. One of the most interesting was the insertion and extraction of reconnaissance teams. By their very nature, these teams operated well in advance of friendly lines and in enemy-controlled territory. Most of the terrain there was high and forested, and there were few landing zones that permitted helos to land. Teams frequently used long ropes and rappelled in.

Getting out was something else. If it was an emergency situation due to enemy contact, it was not feasible to use a one-man hoist. So flexible ladders were employed. These were as long as 120 feet, and 6 feet wide. They were dropped from the rear ramp of a CH-46, and the pilot would hover at a height so that 20 or 30 feet would lie on the ground. The recon team would hook-on individually to the ladder and

the pilot would then execute a vertical climb-out. The team would ride back to base hanging on the end of the ladder, 80 to 100 feet below the chopper and 1,500 to 2,000 feet or more above the ground.

During the extraction, a TAC(A) in an OV-10A would coordinate the air effort. Helo gunships would be directed to provide close-in fires to protect the reconnaissance team on the ground. A-4s and F-4s were available with larger ordnance if more authoritative action was required.

As soon as the CH-46 pilot cleared the pick-up zone, he would turn away from a planned artillery-landing zone line and call in artillery fire to the zone he had just left. This technique became well known to the enemy, so they did not always come too close. If they did not close, the Cobra gunships would work them over while the actual extraction was in process.

Another operation that was continually improved upon as the war progressed was the Sparrow Hawk or Kingfisher, or, as it later became known, the Pacifier. In any case, the basic idea was the same: find the enemy and preempt his move. A package of aircraft was married up to a rifle platoon: CH-46s to provide troop lift, gunships for close-in support, an OV-10A for visual reconnaissance, and a UH-1E for observation and command and control. The OV-10A and gunships would scout out the target area and attempt to find the enemy, and then the CH-46s would insert the reaction force to cordon off the area and fix the enemy. If heavier air support was needed, the command and control helo could request a scramble. This technique proved to be very profitable, and it was often used to seek out the enemy in areas which fired at Marine aircraft, particularly helicopters. Prompt retaliatory action was one of the best measures to reduce this enemy harassment.

Phase Down

The first Marine aviation unit to come into Vietnam after "Shufly" was a LAAM Battalion. The first aviation unit to redeploy without replacement was also a LAAM Battalion. The 2d LAAM Battalion departed in October 1968 for Twentynine Palms, California. The 1st LAAM Battalion followed in August 1969. Even though they had never fired a missile at an enemy aircraft, they had served their purpose.

On 8 June 1969, the President announced his intention to withdraw 25,000 U. S. servicemen from Vietnam. This increment became known as Keystone Eagle. One HMM departed

You're a "Recon" Marine and you and your team have made your reconnaissance in enemy-controlled territory. It's time to go home, and a hovering Sea Knight has dropped its 120-foot sky-hook, and you and your buddies climb on and hang on for the ride back to the base. You don't have a worry in the world; you don't know who the pilot of the helicopter is, and you couldn't care less. He's a Marine and getting you back safely is now his problem.

from the 1stMAW for Futema, Okinawa, and one VMFA departed for Iwakuni, Japan. The 1st LAAM Battalion was part of this increment.

Three months later, on 17 September, another incremental withdrawal was announced, this time 40,500 men from all of the services—nickname, Keystone Cardinal. The 3dMarDiv was the major unit to leave Vietnam in this increment, and it went to Okinawa. This division plus the 1stMAW (Rear) with headquarters at Iwakuni constituted I MAF. It is to be noted that the 1stMAW (Rear) was not associated organizationally in any way with the 1st MAW in Vietnam. It was simply a temporary title conferred on those aviation units outside of Vietnam that were deployed in WestPac as a component of the Seventh Fleet.

MAG-36 was the largest aviation unit to accompany the division. It deployed to Futema and became the parent group for all Marine helicopter squadrons in 1st MAW (Rear). One HMH, one HMM, and one VMO went to Futema as part of MAG-36. Another HMM returned to Santa Ana, California, to become part of the 3d MAW. One VMA(AW) with 12 A-6 aircraft deployed to Iwakuni and was attached to MAG-15 located there. These moves were all completed by Christmas 1969.

The President announced, on 16 December 1969, his intention to withdraw another 50,000 men. This increment was called Keystone Bluejay. MAG-12 from Chu Lai was the major Marine air unit to leave in this increment. It went to Iwakuni and joined the 1st MAW (Rear). One VMA accompanied it. Another VMA and one VMFA redeployed to El Toro, California, home station of the 3dMAW. One HMH also went to the 3d MAW. It was then stationed at Santa Ana. Keystone Bluejay ended on 15 April.

Before completing Keystone Bluejay, III MAF underwent a change in organization. Lieutenant General Herman Nickerson, Jr.,

turned over command, on 9 March 1970, to Lieutenant General Keith B. McCutcheon. At the same time General Nickerson was relieved as the senior U. S. Commander in ICTZ by Lieutenant General Melvin Zais, U. S. Army, Commanding General of XXIV Corps. After nearly five years, III MAF relinquished its position as the senior U. S. command in the area. The XXIV Corps headquarters took possession of Camp Horn, on Tien Sha Peninsula across from the city of Da Nang, and III MAF established a new command post at Camp Haskins on Red Beach, very close to where the 3d Battalion, 9th Marines, had come ashore on 8 March five years earlier. Camp Haskins was a Seabee cantonment, where the 32nd Naval Construction Regiment was headquartered.

On 20 April 1970, the President announced the largest withdrawal yet, with 150,000 to leave by 1 May 1971. On 3 June it was announced that 50,000 of these would be out by 15 October 1970. Keystone Robin was the nickname for this undertaking.

Another MAG was included in this increment. MAG-13, along with one VMFA and one VMA(AW), deployed to El Toro. Another VMFA deployed to MCAS Kaneohe, Hawaii, and joined MAG-24 stationed there. These three jet squadrons flew across the Pacific refueling from KC-130s and following the general route, Cubi Point in the Philippines, Guam, Wake, Midway, Kaneohe, and finally El Toro. Jet squadrons in previous increments had followed the same route.

The departure of MAG-13 marked the end of an era at Chu Lai. The last Marine jet flew off the concrete west runway on 11 September and headed east. The air base at Chu Lai was taken over by the U. S. Army's Americal Division.

VMCJ-1 also departed Vietnam and returned to Iwakuni, where it had been stationed prior to its arrival in Vietnam in 1965.

The other major aviation units included in

MARINE CORPS DEPLOYABLE SQUADRONS

Type of Marine Squadron	Abbrev	Number of Sqdns End FY		Model Acft in Sqdn End FY	
		1965	1970	1965	1970
All-Weather Fighter	VMF (AW)	8	—	F-8	—
Fighter Attack	VMFA	7	13*	F-4B	F-4B F-4J
Light Attack	VMA	10	7*	A-4C/E	A-4E/F
All-Weather Attack	VMA (AW)	2	6	A-6A	A-6A
Composite Reconnaissance	VMCJ	3	3	RF-8A EF-10B	RF-4B EA-6A
Refueler Transport	VMGR	3	3	KC-130	KC-130
Observation	VMO	3	3	O-1 UH-1E	OV-10A AH-1G
Light Helo Transport	HML	0	3		UH-1E
Medium Helo Transport	HMM	15	12	13 UH-34 2 CH-46	CH-46
Heavy Helo Transport	HMH	2	6	CH-37	CH-53
Total		53	56		

*One Squadron given up in order to retain three HMLs in Force Structure. VMFA-513 redesignated VMA-513 and placed in cadre status 30 Jun 1970; will become a Harrier squadron in last half FY71.

this package were one HMM, which departed for Santa Ana, and Marine Wing Support Group 17, which was relocated at Iwakuni.

The deployments of units in these four increments reduced the 1stMAW from a wing of six aircraft groups and three supporting groups[18] to a wing of two aircraft groups and two supporting groups.[19] The number of aircraft squadrons was now 10, compared to a peak of 26 in 1968 and 1969.

Shortly after the initiation of Keystone Robin, on 1 July 1970, Major General Thrash stepped down as CG of 1stMAW, and Major General Alan J. Armstrong took command. It was to be his lot to continue the reduction of Marine aviation units in Vietnam and probably take the 1stMAW headquarters out of that country.*

*The Wing left in April 1971, but without General Armstrong, who stayed behind as CG 3rd Marine Amphibious Brigade. (Editor.)

Retrospect

Marine Corps aviation was in Vietnam in strength for over five years. It was ready when the order was issued to go. The years since Korea had been used to good advantage. New techniques and new equipments were operational. The overall performance from 1965 to 1970 was outstanding.

It was a dynamic period. The Marines deployed to Vietnam in 1965 with UH-34, UH-1, and CH-37 helicopters; A-4, F-8, F-4B, RF-8, and EF-10B jets; and O-1, C-117, and KC-130 propeller aircraft. They added the CH-46, CH-53, AH-1G, A-6, F-9, TA-4F, F-4J, RF-4B, EA-6A, OV-10A, US-2B, and C-1A. From 1966 on they stopped using the UH-34, CH-47, F-8, F-9, RF-8, EF-10B, and O-1. Only the UH-1, A-4, F-4B, C-117, and KC-130 participated in operations from beginning to end.

Dynamism is one characteristic of a strong

and viable air arm. Technical advances continually present the planners with decision points. Marine and Navy planners had done well in the fifties, and that is one reason why so many new aircraft were under development in time to enter the Vietnam War. It is also interesting to note that A-1, A-4, A-7, F-4, F-8, and OV-10A aircraft in use by other services, U. S. and foreign, were the products of the naval aeronautical organization, as were such air weapons as Sidewinder, Sparrow, Shrike, Snakeye, Bullpup, and Walleye.

The Marine Corps takes pride in the fact that it has always put a great deal of emphasis on planning and looking ahead. Before World War II, it pioneered the fundamentals of close air support, and during that war it perfected the techniques that are still basic. After that war it entered into the evaluation and application of helicopters to ground combat. When the Korean War began, it was ready to test the concept in a combat environment. Following Korea, it accelerated the development of its concept of a short airfield for tactical support. All three of these major contributions to the state-of-the-art in tactical air warfare were used in Vietnam, not just by the Marines, but by the other services too. There were other Marine Corps contributions which included the MTDS, TPQ-10, RABFAC beacon, and tactical electronic warfare.

Even while the war in Vietnam was being fought, the Marines were still looking ahead to the future. As was discussed earlier, the lack of suitable air bases in Vietnam was one major constraint on the buildup of tactical airpower. There are still only two airfields capable of handling jets in ICTZ, and there is still not one south of Saigon. But there are airfields capable of taking light aircraft, KC-130, and Caribou transports and helicopters. And many of these fields could take the Harrier.

The Harrier is a jet vertical take-off and landing strike aircraft developed in England with the help of U. S. dollars, and it is operational now in the Royal Air Force. The Marine Corps saw in the Harrier an aircraft of great potential and initiated procurement action in the FY69 budget for twelve of them. It gave up some F-4 aircraft to get them, and they are coming aboard now. By the end of FY71, the Marines will have their first squadron.

The Harrier will not only permit operations from more sites; it will improve response time in close air support by reducing the time taken to request support (there will be fewer centers and echelons of command to go through), and it can be staged closer to the action, thus cutting flight time. The fact that it can operate from more sites should reduce its vulnerability on the ground, and because it can land vertically there should be a reduction in its accident rate (more landing areas available in an emergency).

The year 1965 was one of buildup. Bases had to be obtained and developed, supply pipelines filled, and initial operating difficulties overcome. The sortie rate for jet aircraft gradually climbed to over 1.0, which was the magic figure used by planners to compute sorties. That means one sortie per day per aircraft assigned. In 1966, the rate went well beyond that, and for the entire period the Marines averaged more than 1.0. When the occasion demanded it, they surged to 1.3, 1.4, or even 1.5 for days at a time. The 1st Wing was a consumer-oriented tactical air support command. If the customer had the demand, the wing would supply the sorties.

Twelve of the Corps's total of 27 fighter-attack squadrons were deployed most of the time and 10 or 11 of these were in Vietnam. Fourteen of its 25 helicopter squadrons were deployed—well over fifty per cent. The same airpower was diminished by the following losses in aircraft in all of Southeast Asia in the period starting 25 August 1962 and ending 10 October 1970.

USMC Aircraft Losses in Southeast Asia

Helicopter combat losses	252
Fixed-wing combat losses	173
Helicopter operational losses	172
Fixed wing operational losses	81

Marine Corps aviation surged for over five years in order to sustain the maximum possible strength overseas. The units overseas in turn exceeded all planning factors in terms of output and productivity, under less than ideal conditions.

Marine Corps aviation will leave Vietnam with a sense of accomplishment. It performed its mission for nearly six years and carried out every function in the tactical air book. The innovations and developments it had worked on over the years were proven in combat. The new environment created new challenges for men in Marine aviation, and these were met head-on and solved. The war was the longest, and in many ways the most difficult, one in which Marines have had to participate. The restraints and constraints placed upon the use of air power, and the demanding management reports of all aspects of aviation required by higher authority, imposed additional requirements on staffs with no increase in resources, in most cases, to perform the tasks. In spite of these difficulties, Marine aviation performed in an outstanding manner. An analysis of sorties flown compared to assets on hand will prove that no one outflew the United States Marines.

(Naval Review, 1971)

Notes

1. The Corps Tactical zones were redesigned as Military Regions in July 1970. ICTZ became MR1.

2. Marine terminology often describes units as plus or minus to make clear that a unit is missing a capability normally included in the composition of the unit, or it has been given an additional capability not normally part of the given unit.

3. The sand and dust were problems, but the biggest problem in the early days was a lack of facilities in which to conduct maintenance. Maintenance was performed on the line under strictly expeditionary conditions. As time went by, facilities were built. Structures that could accommodate two A-4s were erected as line hangars, shops were constructed, and electric power was installed. The problems were different at Da Nang. Da Nang at least had some hangar space, even if it was old and in poor repair. Eventually, some of the facilities built at both Da Nang and Chu Lai were probably better than those we have at air stations in the United States. But the Marine Corps does not expect to find these conditions at the outset of any operation. That is why the Corps has placed so much emphasis on the expeditionary aspects of its operations.

4. The following table lists the normal planning figures for each kind of aviation unit. Due to operational factors, not all squadrons were equipped with normal complements. Main deviations were VMO, VMCJ, and HML.

Type Squadron	No. Aircraft	Model Aircraft
VMA	20	A-4
VMA(AW)	12	A-6
VMFA	15	F-4
VMCJ	9	EA-6A
	9	RF-4
VMGR	12	KC-130
VMO	18	OV-10A
	12	AH-1
HML	24	UH-1
HMM	21	CH-46
HMH	18	CH-53

5. "Coordinating Authority" is defined in the *Dictionary of United States Military Terms for Joint Usage* as a commander or individual assigned responsibility for coordinating specific functions or activities involving forces of two or more services, or two or more forces of the same service. He has the authority to require consultation between the agencies involved, but does not have the authority to compel agreement. In the event he is unable to

obtain essential agreement, he shall refer the matter to the appointing authority.

6. CG III MAF also became Naval Component Commander, until 1 April 1966 when a new billet was created and designated Commander, U. S. Naval Forces, Vietnam. This officer then took charge of all U. S. naval activities in Vietnam including the Naval Advisory Group, the naval construction battalions, the naval support activities, the coastal patrol task force, the mobile riverine force, and the river patrol task force. Thereafter, III MAF consisted of one service reporting directly to ComUSMACV until U. S. Army units were assigned to ICTZ and placed under the operational control of III MAF.

7. Flight following is a service performed on request by a radar installation for an aircraft. It is usually used when flying conditions prohibit the pilot from maintaining a visual outlook. The radar site will follow his flight and advise him of any traffic that may interfere or create a potential hazard.

8. The Marines had no F-8s in Vietnam at the time these discussions took place. The first F-8s arrived in December 1965 and they too had a dual capability.

9. This was necessary because the three services used different data rates and message formats within their own systems. For example, suppose the NTDS plotted an aircraft track in the Gulf of Tonkin. The NTDS would send the essential data via radio to the TDCC on Monkey Mountain. The TDCC would translate this data or change it into two additional forms. One would then enter the MTDS and subsequently the track would be displayed on Marine operators' scopes. Another would enter the Air Force system and the track would appear on Air Force operators' scopes. The reverse process was also applicable.

10. A jet heavily laden with bombs or other external stores has to use power or fly faster to maintain a given altitude than one not so loaded. A KC-130 is much slower than a jet and cannot climb to normal jet operating altitude, so fueling is at less than the best altitudes and speeds for the jets, and the jet pilot can have a difficult time making his plug-in and holding formation.

11. The Corps did not request a change in helo mix. It had just completed a study that essentially reaffirmed the 5 to 1 mix of medium to heavy helos, but it also recommended an increase in total numbers to meet the Marine Corps's total operational requirement. The Office of the Secretary of Defense directed the change in mix from 5 to 1 to 2 to 1. One probable reason was that an increase in the percentage of heavies would increase the total lift capability of the fleet so that additional squadrons would not have to be approved. The Marine Corps did not appeal the mix decision. At the time it was made, the CH-46 tail problem was under serious study and it appeared desirable to have a greater percentage of CH-53s on that score alone.

12. See "Doctors and Dentists, Nurses and Corpsmen in Vietnam" by Commander F. O. McClendon, Jr., MSC, further on in this book. The patient's chances were about 99 per cent once admitted to a Navy field hospital or hospital ship.

13. For more details on Marine operations in Vietnam, see Brigadier General Simmons' excellent essays, the first of which is republished in this book.

14. Before the Seabees improved the strip with AM-2 matting, in the summer of 1966, there was a short strip at Khe Sanh made of pierced steel planking. When the base was closed in 1968, the AM-2 was removed.

15. Distance to Khe Sanh from

Dong Ha	23 nautical miles
Quang Tri	27 nautical miles
Da Nang	94 nautical miles
Chu Lai	136 nautical miles

16. Distances to Vandegrift from

Dong Ha	15 nautical miles
Riley	16 nautical miles
Razor	18 nautical miles
Dallas	19 nautical miles
Cunningham	20 nautical miles
Erskine	23 nautical miles
Tiger Mountain	26 nautical miles

17. The VNAF had two helicopter squadrons, but these were not enough for the ARVN's needs. The Army and ARVN received jet support from Marine, Air Force, Navy, and VNAF aircraft. The same general system of air support was used by all services. The language barrier was overcome by the fact that many Vietnamese and Koreans understood English.

18. MAGs 11, 12, 13, 16, 36, ProvMAG-39; Marine Wing Headquarters Group 1; Marine Wing Service Group 17, Marine Air Control Group 18.

19. MAGs 11 and 16; Marine Wing Headquarters Group 1 and Marine Air Control Group 18.

Marine Corps Operations in Vietnam, 1965–1966

Edwin H. Simmons, Brigadier General,
U. S. Marine Corps

On 6 March 1965, the Pentagon announced that two battalions of Marines, some 3,500 men, were being sent to South Vietnam at the request of the government in Saigon, and that they would have the limited mission of strengthening security at Da Nang. The next day, Secretary of State Dean Rusk told a national television and radio audience that the Marines would shoot back if shot at, but that their mission was to put a tight security ring around the Da Nang air base, thus freeing South Vietnamese forces for combat.

These Marines were the first U. S. ground combat forces to be committed to the war. The 23,500 American servicemen already in Vietnam were called "advisers"—although many of them were actually serving in combat support units, such as Marine and Army helicopter elements—but two reinforced Marine infantry battalions, despite restraints placed on their employment, could only be viewed as "participants." It was obvious that there had been a major change in policy. How had it come about?

In February 1965 our aircraft had begun to attack military targets in North Vietnam, not in tit-for-tat response to specific provocations, as in the past, but on a sustained basis. Many of the U. S. Air Force and South Vietnamese fighter-bombers making those attacks were based at Da Nang, whose airfield was vulnerable to retaliation—to the kind of raid, perhaps, that had been made on Bien Hoa on 1 November 1964, when four Americans were killed, and 27 aircraft were destroyed or damaged; or on Pleiku on 7 February 1965, when eight Americans were killed, 80 wounded, and 20 aircraft were destroyed or damaged. The Viet Cong were credited with the capability of doing this and more to Da Nang. Intelligence reports showed 12 battalions—6,000 men, more or less—within striking distance of the air base. Not until the threat to Da Nang was unmistakable did Secretary of Defense Robert S. McNamara recommend to the President that the Marines be landed.

On 7 March, the day Secretary Rusk made his broadcast, the Viet Cong probed the garrison town of Mieu Dong, three miles south of the Da Nang airfield. In Da Nang itself, all was quiet, but there was something of a feeling of being under siege. At sea, the 9th Marine Expeditionary Brigade waited for orders to go in.

Da Nang Landing

The northern arm of the Bay of Da Nang is formed by the Hai Van Mountains, a spur of the Annamite chain that comes out of the west, then drops precipitously from 1,192 meters down to the water's edge. The southern arm of

Da Nang, March 1965. Elements of the 9th Marine Expeditionary Brigade prepare to come ashore at Red Beach Two, beginning the commitment of U.S. ground combat forces in South Vietnam. Small craft, such as the LCU-1476, were hard-worked, thereafter, chiefly in logistic support of the ground and air forces ashore.

the bay ends in a bulbous fist made by the 621-meter Mon Ky (or Monkey) Mountain, once an island perhaps, but now an extension of the mainland, connected by a neck of sand. Except during the northeast monsoon, the bay is a good harbor—one of the few protected, deep-water anchorages on the Vietnamese coast—and, even in normal times, Da Nang was second only to Saigon in tonnage handled. It is the old French colonial city of Tourane, and from a distance looks colorful and exotic, but at closer range, you see that it is war-worn, shabby, and swollen with refugees and other newcomers who have doubled its population in the last five years to its present estimated 200,000.

For some years, Marine Corps contingency plans had taken into account the possibility of Marines being used in this area, but contingency plans are prepared for many places and usually are closely held: not much is heard about them at the junior officer and troop level. However, there was reason for much more broadly based familiarity with Da Nang, for it was the objective area in Marine Corps Schools' Amphibious Warfare Study XVI. Prescience or coincidence? Perhaps both. Before World War II, from 1936 to 1940, Advanced Base Problems III, VI, and VII had used Palau, Guam, and Saipan as target areas.

The Nam O bridge carries Highway One, which is the old Mandarin Road, and the Trans-Vietnam Railway northwards across the Song Ca De. As recently as the summer of 1964, one could travel by rail, albeit dangerously and with a certain amount of forbearance on the part of the Viet Cong, 380 miles south from Da Nang to Saigon. But by March 1965, the railroad had been badly cut and, southwards from just below Da Nang, all the major bridges were down, and much of the track had been removed. It was still possible, although at some hazard, to go 50 miles north by rail: after crossing the Nam O bridge (which the Viet Cong did not destroy until April 1967), the line goes past the Esso terminal at Lien Chieu, hugs the front of the Hai Van promontory, burrows through many tunnels, comes out on the north side, then hurries across the open flatlands to the imperial city of Hue.

Highway One roughly parallels the railroad, but chooses to zig-zag up over the Hai Van Mountains, through the pass the French called, with reason, "Col des Nuages" (Pass of the Clouds). At Da Nang, the monsoon season is the reverse of what it is in the rest of South Vietnam: the summer is hot and fairly dry; the winter is warm and wet. By March, the drenching rains have passed, but the prevailing wind is still from the northeast, coming down from China across the South China Sea. There is an

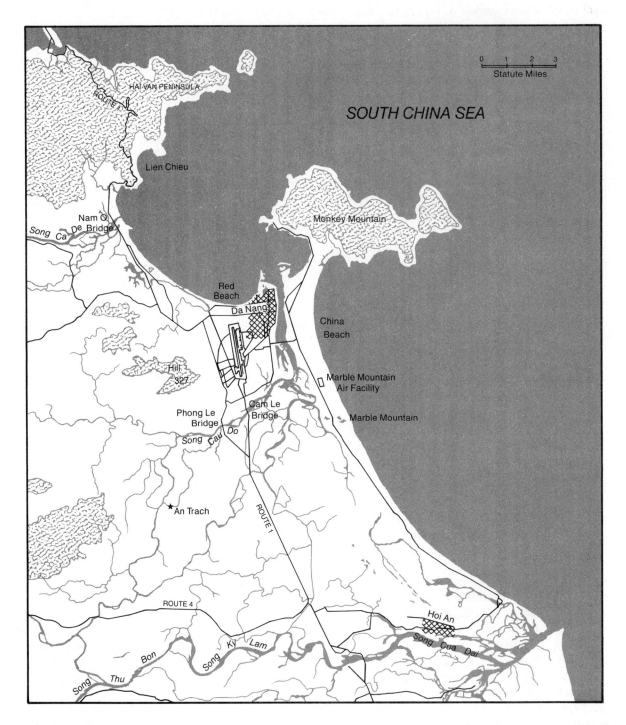

0 1 2 3
Statute Miles

SOUTH CHINA SEA

HAI-VAN PENINSULA

ROUTE 1

Lien Chieu

Monkey Mountain

Song Ca

Nam O
De Bridge

Red
Beach

Da Nang

China
Beach

Hill
327

Marble Mountain
Air Facility

Phong Le
Bridge

Cam Le
Bridge

Marble Mountain

Song Cau Do

An Trach

ROUTE 1

ROUTE 4

Hoi An

Song Ky Lam

Song Cua Dai

Song Bon

Song Thu

The coast and operating area, Da Nang to Hoi An. The coastal area south of Monkey Mountain is low, and sandy areas alternate with rice paddies. Roads were unimpressive. For example, below Marble Mountain the road paralleling the coast was a rutted dirt passage, degenerating at times into sand.

endemic condition in the spring months called "le crachin," when the clouds pile up on the mountains and the lowlands are filled with a drizzling mist.

ACROSS THE BEACH

On the morning of 8 March 1965, the 9th Marine Expeditionary Brigade (Brigadier General Frederick J. Karch) had been at sea for two months. Early that day, Commodore Henry Suerstedt, Commander Task Group 76.7, brought his three ships—USS *Union* (AKA-106), USS *Vancouver* (LPD-2), and USS *Henrico* (APA-45)—into Da Nang Bay. The ships took station 4,000 yards off Red Beach Two. Commander Amphibious Task Force and CTF 76, Rear Admiral Don W. Wulzen, was on hand in the USS *Mount McKinley* (AGC-7). The beach is a fine, curving strip of sand the color and feel of raw sugar, just north of Da Nang and south of the Nam O bridge. The skies were gray and sullen, and a stiff wind from the northeast was roughening the water. Sea conditions were such that H-hour, scheduled for 0800 local time, had to be delayed an hour.

The surf was still running five feet or more when the first wave of Battalion Landing Team 3/9 (Lieutenant Colonel Charles E. McPartlin, Jr.) crossed the beach at 0902. By 0918, all scheduled waves were ashore, and general unloading began. The area had been thoroughly swept by two Vietnamese battalions, and there was air cover. While 3d Battalion, 9th Marines, did not expect the beach to be defended, neither did they expect quite the reception they received: an elaborate official welcome, including a group of giggling Vietnamese girls who proceeded to decorate the leading edge of the landing force, including General Karch, with garlands of red and yellow flowers.

Battalion Landing Team 3/9 had been the Special Landing Force of the Seventh Fleet. The other BLT of the 9th Marine Expeditionary Brigade, BLT 1/3 (Lieutenant Colonel Her-

bert J. Bain), was airlifted to Da Nang from Okinawa in Marine KC-130s, and began arriving at 1100 local time. When 60 per cent of the airlifted troops and 25 percent of their vehicles and equipment had arrived, the field was glutted; it could not accommodate the in-rush of Marines and, at the same time, conduct normal flight operations. ComUSMACV put a 48-hour hold on the rest of the BLT. The airlift began again on 10 March, and was completed by 1800 on 12 March. In all, the lift went well, without incident except for a little VC small-arms fire while the aircraft were in the approach, and a couple of inconsequential hits on one KC-130.

Marine helicopters had been operating from Da Nang since September 1962. Some weeks before the landings, HMM-163 (Lieutenant Colonel Norman G. Ewers) had relieved HMM-365 and was the squadron in place when BLT 3/9 arrived. HMM-365, now aboard the USS *Princeton* (LPH-5), flew in its Sikorsky UH-34Ds and turned them over to HMM-162 (Lieutenant Colonel Oliver W. Curtis), whose officers and men were arriving from Okinawa by airlift.

Also already on the crowded airfield were two Hawk batteries of the 1st Light Anti-Aircraft Missile Battalion (Lieutenant Colonel Bertram E. Cook, Jr.), which had been ordered forward from Okinawa on 7 February. Now, with enough Marine infantry ashore to provide security, better positions for the missiles could be found in the surrounding hills.

DEFENSE OF THE AIRFIELD

General Westmoreland, ComUSMACV, was emphatic that the overall responsibility for the defense of the Da Nang area should remain with the Vietnamese. The specific mission assigned to 9th MEB was to reinforce the defenses of Da Nang air base and of such other installations agreed upon with General Nguyen Chanh Thi, Commanding General I

Corps and I Corps Tactical Zone. (General Thi's rank at this time was actually brigadier general. In the Vietnamese service this carried the insignia of two stars, there being another one-star rank, that of sub-brigadier general. Later Thi was promoted to major general with three stars. Finally, in the winter of 1965 the Vietnamese government brought the titles into consonance with the stars—and U. S. practise—and Thi became a lieutenant general.)

Besides its shared responsibility for the close-in security of the airfield, 9th MEB was given the task of defending about eight thinly populated square miles of high ground just west of the field, and the 3d Battalion, 9th Marines, moved toward that area early on 10 March. Company I climbed Hill 327 (327 meters or about 1,073 feet), the dominant terrain feature, named it "the hungry i" after themselves and a San Francisco night club, and began to dig in. Company K took over Hill 268, which was lower and farther to the north, while, behind them, the engineers began cutting a road. As soon as the road was ready, a Hawk battery was to move up from the airfield to a better firing position.

These moves put the 3d Battalion, 9th Marines, in classic position for defense of the airfield against an attack by a conventional enemy but, unfortunately, contributed little to its defense against the usual Viet Cong pattern of guerrilla action: mortar attack, infiltration, and demolitions. The 1st Battalion, 3d Marines, remained on the airfield to secure it against those forms of attack.

SECURITY

In a few years, the field had grown from a provincial airport to a major air base, a heterogeneous collection of activities—some military, some civilian, some Vietnamese, some American—clustered around a single 10,000-foot concrete runway, oriented just a little west of due north and south. On the east side of the field were Vietnamese and U. S. Air Force operations, most of the hangars and shops, the terminal of Air Vietnam, and the Vietnamese dependents' housing, which blurred into the city of Da Nang. Off the north end of the runway there was a narrow stretch of paddy, then the beach and the bay. On the west side were the Marine helicopter units, headquartered and billeted in a complex of crumbling old French barracks. Mixed in with them were a South Vietnamese armored outfit and bits and pieces of other Army of the Republic of Vietnam (ARVN) units. Just beyond the wire on the west side, where Highway One and the railroad run north and south, there had mushroomed what the Americans called "Dog Patch"—an aggregation of bars, laundries, tailors, photographers, and souvenir shops.

South of the field was the more rural Hoa Vang district, about a mile of it, and then the Song Cau Do River which flows from southwest to northeast. The Phong Le bridge carried the tracks of the railroad and alternate Route One across this river. A mile farther downstream was the Cam Le bridge. Except for a narrow strip along Highway One, the territory south of the river was pure Viet Cong, and aircraft approaching Da Nang had to run a spiteful gauntlet of fire from Viet Cong small arms.

The perimeter enclosing the air base had grown since the time of the French. It consisted of a ring of dilapidated, concrete blockhouses, interspersed with spidery, steel watchtowers, a perimeter lighting system of unreliable performance, and belts of rusting barbed wire hung, here and there, with triangular tin signs marking minefields left by some previous defender. Pressing close to the wire was a rabbit warren of Vietnamese dwellings, some substantial but most made of tin, thatch, and cardboard. Just before the Marines arrived, it was decreed that this warren must be cleared out to a depth of 400 meters, so that a kind of *cordon sanitaire* could be established around the base, but this involved relocating some 7,000 persons and would take months to do.

From this confused, congested field, virtually every kind of tactical and transport aircraft in the U. S. inventory was being operated. With all these tempting, soft-skinned targets available to the VC, it was chilling to the Marine defenders to realize that just beyond the wire and within mortar range, there lived some 250,000 Vietnamese of varying political inclinations.

I Corps Tactical Zone

Beyond Da Nang, there was the larger problem of the I Corps Tactical Zone, which is both a military zone and a political region. I Corps is the northernmost of the four Vietnamese corps areas and it includes five provinces—Quang Tri, Thua Thien, Quang Nam, Quang Tin, and Quang Ngai. Its northern boundary is the frontier with North Vietnam; the demarcation line, usually given as the 17th parallel, is actually a river, the Song Ben Hai, as far as the hamlet of Bo Ho Su, then, a straight line running west to where the boundaries of Laos, North Vietnam, and South Vietnam come together. The western border, shared with Laos, is the ridgeline of the Annamite Mountains. These mountains run some 750 miles southeastward out of China and average, along this stretch, 5,000 feet, but there are peaks that go up at least 8,500 feet (and some say 10,500 feet). It is these mountains that cause the reversal of the monsoon seasons. To the south, a spur of the Annamites runs down to the sea near Sa Huynh and forms the southern boundary of the I Corps area. From Sa Huynh north to the mouth of the Song Ben Hai is some 225 miles. The country is very slender here, varying from at most 70 miles in width to as

little as 30. There are about 10,000 square miles in the I Corps Tactical Zone, something less than one-sixth the total area of South Vietnam.

The coastline is a series of promontories, sandy beaches, and minor deltas formed by the rivers that have their beginnings in the Annamites. The roads leading to the interior follow the valleys of these rivers, and the most notable are Route 9, which moves west from Dong Ha in the north across into Laos, and Route 14, which appears on maps in this book and in those of the Army Engineers as Route 4. Route 14, which begins at Hoi An, below Da Nang, bends west into the mountains, then drops south to Kontum, Pleiku, and beyond.

Not only is the I Corps area physically separated from the rest of South Vietnam, it is also culturally and historically somewhat different. Southwest of the Annamites is old Cochin China. The I Corps area is part of the Central Lowlands and old Annam.

In 1965 it was estimated that 2.6 million persons lived in the I Corps area (as compared to 16.5 million for all of South Vietnam). Up in the hills, there was a scattering of montagnards subsisting mainly on hunting, fishing, and slash farming, and in the towns and cities there were some Chinese, Indians, and others—mostly shopkeepers—but at least 85 per cent of the population was ethnically Vietnamese. Most of them lived along the coast and in the little alluvial valleys tucked between the knuckles of the mountains. The rural Vietnamese tend to cluster together in hamlets—isolated houses are few, as are large towns—and most of them are either commercial fishermen or rice farmers. Nearly half a million tons of rice are produced annually in the five northern provinces.

Hamlets are the basic community unit. The next larger political unit is the village. (The term "village" is somewhat misleading; it is applied to a community more comparable to a township than to what we think of as a village.) Traditionally, the hamlets and villages have had a large degree of self-government and an old proverb says that the Emperor's law stops at the village gate. The villages are combined into districts, which are comparable to U. S. counties and are about the first level where the central government makes itself felt; districts, in turn, are the major divisions of the provinces.

I Corps's military boundaries followed the political boundaries. The tactical area of the 1st Division consisted of the two northern provinces of Quang Tri and Thua Thien. Its commander was Brigadier General Nguyen Van Chuan, an able and professional soldier, whose headquarters were at Hue. Although these two provinces are closest to the North Vietnamese border, conditions were measurably better in them than in the rest of I Corps area.

The tactical area of the 2d Division consisted of the two southern provinces of Quang Tin and Quang Ngai. This division was commanded by Brigadier General Hoang Xuan Lam, whose headquarters were at Quang Ngai city, and who was to outlast both Thi and Chuan.

By an arrangement formalized in September 1965, Quang Nam, the center province, was treated as a special sector and garrisoned by the 51st Regiment, under the command of diminutive, dependable Lieutenant Colonel Nguyen Tho Lap, and by a number of separate battalions. Government troops controlled the city of Da Nang, Hoi An, the capital of Quang Nam Province, and very little else except for beleaguered district headquarters, whose garrisons were immobilized because the VC were roaming almost at will throughout the province.

Corps headquarters occupied a handsome French colonial compound just east of the airfield at Da Nang. It took no great imagination to hear the ghostly bugles of the French Expeditionary Corps sounding through the galleried, two-story buildings, freshly painted yellow with red-brown trim.

Besides commanding the I Corps, General Thi, controversial even then, was government representative, that is to say, military governor of the region. In Saigon, they called Thi the "Warlord of the North." Native to the region, having been born near Hue, he was then 42 years old. He had fought for the French in World War II, had been captured by the Japanese, and had escaped. Under Ngo Dinh Diem he had commanded the Airborne Brigade, and his favorite uniform was still the red beret and the purple-and-green camouflaged utilities of the paratroops. A ringleader in the 1960 attempted coup against Diem, he had gotten away to Cambodia, where he remained three years in exile. After Diem's demise he returned eventually to become commanding general of the 1st Division. General Nguyen Khanh was then CG I Corps. After Khanh became premier, Thi moved up to corps commander and, later, was one of the leaders who combined to force Khanh out of the government.

I Corps was authorized about 30,000 ARVN troops—regulars—of whom about 25,000 were present for duty, and 18,500 of the Regional Forces, of whom about 12,000 were present for duty. The latter were lightly armed provincial troops, and, at this time, they had no formation larger than a company. Also on the rolls were some 23,000 of an authorized 29,000 Popular Forces—the local militia, used in squad- and platoon-sized security forces for the hamlets and villages.

Two chains of command extended down from General Thi, one military, the other political. The military chain, of course, passed through his division and special sector commanders. The political chain passed through the provincial chiefs, who were appointed by Saigon, presumably on the recommendation and with the concurrence of Thi. It was not easy to find civilians qualified and willing to serve as chiefs of the provinces; hence, most of the chiefs were military, generally in the rank of lieutenant colonel. Next below the province chiefs were the district chiefs and they, perhaps without exception, were Army officers, usually in the grade of captain, sometimes of lieutenant.

Typically, the district headquarters was the remnant of an old French fort, surrounded by mud and bamboo breastworks, usually triangular or square in outline with a bastion at each corner, reminiscent of Vauban and the seventeenth century. These little forts were garrisoned with, perhaps, a company of Regional Forces, a platoon or so of Popular Forces, and, if they were very fortunate, a section of 105-mm. howitzers with regular ARVN gunners. Dozens of these outposts were scattered throughout I Corps. Most often each controlled the ground within rifle shot of its fort, but very little more.

Move to Phu Bai

The landing of the 9th MEB had brought the strength of the Marines in the Da Nang area up to about 5,000 men. On 11 April, BLT 2/3 (Lieutenant Colonel David A. Clement), which had been on Jungle Drum III, a combined counterinsurgency exercise in Thailand, offloaded across Red Beach Two under a blazing sun, in contrast to the conditions when 3/9 had landed the month before.

The next day, a reinforced company from 2d Battalion, 3d Marines, was sent by helo 42 miles north to Phu Bai where, seven miles southeast of Hue, there was an airport and an important communications facility. On 14 April, after BLT 3/4 (Lieutenant Colonel Donald R. Jones) had arrived from Hawaii, the Marines moved into the Hue/Phu Bai area in strength.

Hue, halfway between Da Nang and the demarcation line, has a population of about 100,000, which makes it South Vietnam's third largest city. It is on the River of Perfumes, picturesquely named, but not suitable for oceangoing shipping. It has no industry to speak of, but it has other values. For two centuries Hue was the imperial capital; there are the royal palace, the ancient tombs, the old citadel built by the French. Even the Viet Cong view the city with respect, and it has been remarkably free from physical depredations. There is, however, a mutual antipathy between Hue and Saigon. Hue is Annam, and Saigon is Cochin China. Hue remembers that when it was at the height of its imperial splendor, Saigon was still a fishing village. The militant Buddhists are strong in Hue, which is also the seat of the University, and in recent years the city has often been the starting point for political disaffection.

Meanwhile, on 10 April, VMFA-531 (Lieutenant Colonel William C. McGraw, Jr.) began arriving at Da Nang. Its F-4Bs (McDonnell "Phantom IIs") were the first fixed-wing Marine tactical aircraft to be shore-based in Vietnam.

Activation of III MAF

On 3 May, Major General William R. Collins, CG, 3d Marine Division, arrived at Da Nang with a small advance party. Three days after his arrival, 9th MEB was deactivated and the III Marine Expeditionary Force was established, along with 3d Marine Division (Forward). Ground elements were under 3d Marines (Colonel Edwin B. Wheeler); aviation elements under Marine Aircraft Group 16 (Colonel John H. King, Jr.).

The next day, 7 May, the designation III Marine *Expeditionary* Force was changed to III Marine *Amphibious* Force (III MAF). The change came about in this way: there had been one or two back-page news stories, datelined Saigon, pointing out that the word "Expeditionary" in 9th Marine Expeditionary Brigade was not apt to be popular with the Vietnamese, as it might call up memories of the French Expeditionary Corps. ComUSMACV asked the Joint Chiefs of Staff to give the III Marine Expeditionary Force a more neutral name. The JCS agreed, but noted that designation of units was a service prerogative. Accordingly, General Wallace M. Greene, Jr., Commandant of the Marine Corps, looked over a list of possible designations. "III Marine Amphibious Corps" was a popular contender because of its famous World War II antecedents, but it was pointed out that, even though the Vietnamese used the word "Corps" to designate their own units, they might find it offensive as a U. S. designation. Thus, "III Marine Amphibious Force" was chosen.

Meanwhile, the 3d Marine Expeditionary Brigade, which equally suddenly had its designation changed to 3d Marine Amphibious Brigade, was approaching the coast of South Vietnam.

CHU LAI LANDING

On 10 March, the 6,000-man 1st Marine Brigade, based at Kaneohe and commanded by the Marine Corps's first air ace, Brigadier General Marion E. Carl, began loading out at Pearl Harbor aboard shipping that had arrived in February to lift the Brigade to California where it was to take part in Exercise Silver Lance. The Brigade's participation in the exercise was cancelled and the shipping held over: its destination was not California but Okinawa.

The Brigade, which included the 4th Marines (Colonel Edward P. Dupras, Jr.) and

Marine Aircraft Group 13 (Colonel Ralph H. Spanjer), represented about one-third of the 3d Marine Division plus supporting aviation from 1st Marine Aircraft Wing. First elements sailed on 11 March, arriving at Okinawa on 19 March. Meanwhile, on 14 March, the 3d MEB, General Carl commanding, was activated.

At 0800 local time on 7 May, 3d MEB made an unopposed landing at Chu Lai, a bare stretch of beach 55 miles southeast of Da Nang. The amphibious task force was again under Rear Admiral Wulzen, and the troop list included RLT-4 with BLTs 1/4 and 2/4, and HMM-161 (Lieutenant Colonel Gene W. Morrison). Other air support was provided by MAG-16 based at Da Nang. The troops of the 1st Battalion (Lieutenant Colonel Harold D. Fredericks) and of the 2d Battalion (Lieutenant Colonel Joseph R. Fisher) noted that the sand and pine trees were markedly similar to those on the beaches of North Carolina, but even the August heat of Camp Lejeune's pine barrens could not match the May temperatures of Chu Lai.

On 12 May, a third BLT, built around 3d Battalion, 3d Marines (Lieutenant Colonel William D. Hall) came ashore. This ended the amphibious operation: the 3d Marine Amphibious Brigade was dissolved and its parts were absorbed into III Marine Amphibious Force.

The immediate purpose of the landing was to secure the ground needed for an expeditionary airfield which could relieve some of the congestion at Da Nang. Seabees of NMCB-10 and Marine engineers went to work on the airfield site on 9 May. The deadline for the beginning of flight operations was 1 June. Some, but not all, of the difficulties in putting in a strip at Chu Lai had been foreseen. It was no surprise that the sand was bottomless, but the locally available laterite (a red clay made up of aluminum and iron oxides) did not live up to expectations as a stabilizer.

Nevertheless, the deadline was met. The

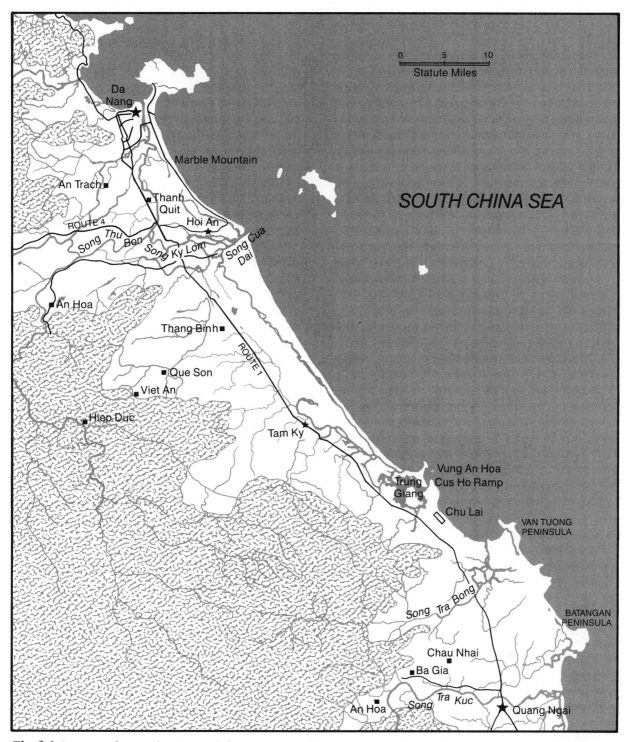

The fighting area during the Marines' first two years, from just north of Da Nang to just south of Quang Ngai. Route 4 on the maps in this book, and Route 14, discussed by General Simmons, are identical.

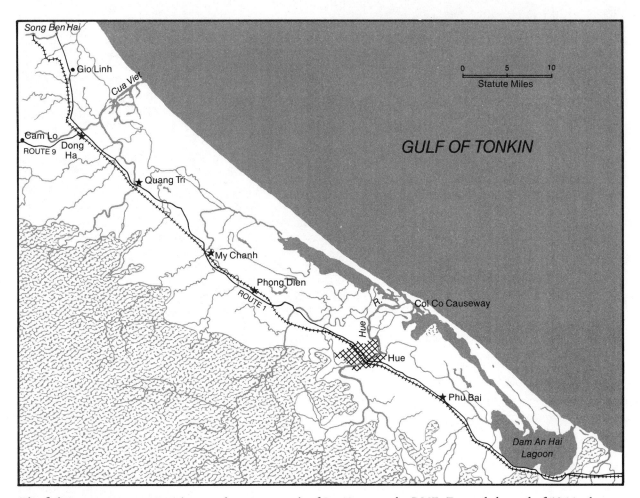

The fighting area in 1965 and 1966, from just north of Da Nang to the DMZ. Toward the end of 1966, the center of gravity of the fighting in I Corps Tactical Zone moved into this section, and thereafter the fighting there was fierce.

field was officially opened at 0800 on 1 June when eight A-4 "Skyhawks" arrived from Cubi Point in the Philippines. The first plane was piloted by Colonel John D. Noble, commander of MAG-12, which was to operate from the field. The "Skyhawks" were from VMA-223 (Lieutenant Colonel Robert W. Baker) and VMA-311 (Lieutenant Colonel Bernard J. Stender). At 1329 on the same day, the first combat strike was flown when four A-4s were launched

in support of the ARVN against targets seven miles southwest of Chu Lai. A third attack squadron, VMA-214 (Lieutenant Colonel Keith O'Keefe) arrived shortly thereafter.

New Commanders

General Westmoreland visited III MAF on 8 May and, besides seeing what the Marines were doing, he gave Major General Collins his concept of future operations: for the time being, the Marines were to continue with their defensive mission, consolidating and developing their base areas, which were now three—Da Nang, Hue/Phu Bai, and Chu Lai; then, when authorized, III MAF would be permitted to undertake limited offensive operations directly related to the defense of their bases; finally, it could be expected that a stage would be reached where III MAF would engage in more extensive offensive operations, if CG I Corps requested it to do so.

On 11 May Major General Paul J. Fontana arrived from Iwakuni, and established the headquarters of 1st Marine Aircraft Wing (Advanced) at Da Nang.

Something else that happened on 11 May was to have lasting consequences. Three companies of 2d Battalion, 3d Marines, searched and cleared Le My hamlet complex, eight miles northwest of Da Nang air base. Four hundred civilians were liberated from Viet Cong control, and a pilot model civic action program was begun.

Both General Fontana and General Collins were completing their Far East tours. On 24 May Brigadier General Keith B. McCutcheon assumed command of 1st Marine Aircraft Wing (Advanced), and on 30 May Major General Lewis W. Walt arrived to be the new Commanding General, III MAF, and CG, 3d Marine Division. General Collins was relieved officially at 0900, 4 June. Having been promoted on 10 May, just before he left Washington for Vietnam, Walt was the junior major general in the Corps. For the three years immediately before this assignment he had been the Director, Landing Force Development Center, Quantico.

As CG III MAF, General Walt was both a commander of a subordinate command and a component commander. As ComUSMACV, General Westmoreland exercised operational command over all forces assigned or attached to MACV, including III MAF. MACV, in turn, was a subordinate unified command under CinCPac. The commanding general of III MAF was also Naval Component Commander by virtue of *United Actions Armed Forces* (UNAAF), which says: "the Senior officer of each service assigned to a unified command and qualified for command by the regulations of his own service is the commander of the component of his service unless another officer is so designated by competent authority."

In this dual capacity, General Walt's position was comparable to those of General Westmoreland and Lieutenant General Joseph H. Moore. In addition to being ComUSMACV, Westmoreland was the Army Component Commander (Commanding General, U. S. Army Vietnam), while Moore was Commander, 2d Air Division, and Air Force Component Commander.

Naval Component Command functions in support of MACV were under the direction of CinCPacFlt. Of greatest pertinence at this time was the responsibility of the Navy to provide logistic support to U. S. forces operating north of Quang Ngai, that is, in I Corps Tactical Zone. At first, the tasks of operating port facilities, unloading and moving cargo, and operating supply depots were performed by provisional elements of the Seventh Fleet and by III MAF. On 21 July 1965, Naval Support Activity, Da Nang, was established to discharge these responsibilities. Naval construction effort had earlier been consolidated under the 30th Naval Construction Regiment.

(General Walt remained Naval Component Commander until 1 April 1966 when Rear Admiral Norvell G. Ward, until then Chief of the Naval Advisory Group, MACV, was named Commander, U. S. Naval Forces, Vietnam. This expanded responsibility for Admiral Ward represented a consolidation of all Navy activities in Vietnam, including the Naval Advisory Group, Naval Support Activity, 30th Naval Construction Regiment, and Task Forces 115 (coastal patrol) and 116 (river patrol). The III MAF, however, was specifically exempted from the command of U. S. Naval Forces, Vietnam.)

The III Marine Amphibious Force was, of course, a part of the Fleet Marine Force, Pacific; hence military command, other than operational control, remained with CG FMFPac.

General Moore, in addition to being Commander, 2d Air Division (later Seventh Air Force), was also Deputy ComUSMACV for air operations. There was, therefore, a special relationship between General Moore and General McCutcheon, who as CG 1st Marine Aircraft Wing, was also Tactical Air Commander and Deputy CG III MAF.

Two separate air wars were being fought in Vietnam. The "in-country" war, or that limited to South Vietnam, was being directed by General Moore. The Tactical Air Control System (TACS) was almost identical with that used in Korea, except that greater use was being made of airborne Forward Air Controllers (FACS). The system included a joint operations center (JOC) and a joint tactical air control center (TACC), manned by both Americans and Vietnamese, in Saigon, and direct air support centers (DASCs) in each of the Corps areas.

Allowance was made for the fact that III MAF operated its own integrated system in support of Marine ground operations, which had first priority. Marine aircraft not needed for these missions were made available for support of other forces and were fitted into the country-wide control system in exactly the same manner as U. S. Air Force aircraft.

Marine aircraft were also made available for the "out-of-country" war. These operations were not controlled by General Westmoreland or General Moore—although they might suggest targets—but by Admiral U. S. Grant Sharp, CinCPac.

Expanding Missions

On 30 May, with III MAF barely established, I Corps got its worst beating of the year. It happened along Route 5 which goes west from Quang Ngai parallel to the Song Tra Kuc. The 1st Battalion, 51st ARVN Regiment, was ambushed by the Viet Cong in a little hamlet a short distance from its base at Ba Gia. Of the 400 men in the battalion, only the three U. S. advisers and 65 South Vietnamese soldiers broke through. General Thi committed his last available reserves: one Ranger and one Vietnamese Marine battalion. In the confused fighting that followed, the 39th Rangers lost 108 men. General Thi, estimating his adversaries at five battalions, asked Saigon for two Vietnamese airborne battalions and the help of a U. S. Marine battalion. He got neither of those, but he did get Marine helolift and extensive close air support from VMFA-531. The fighting subsided, and friendly losses were counted at 392 killed and missing; 446 rifles and carbines, 90 crew-served weapons lost: it was claimed that 556 Viet Cong were killed and 20 weapons captured. A disaster had been averted, but the question had been raised: under what circumstances would U. S. combat troops go to the aid of the South Vietnamese?

By this time, the first week in June, after three months of defensive operations, the Marines had suffered nearly 200 casualties, including 18 killed in action. It had become increasingly apparent that they (and farther south, at Bien Hoa, near Saigon, the newly-arrived 173d Airborne Brigade) were engaged in more than static defense. As early as 28 April, during a visit to Da Nang, the Commandant of the Marine Corps had told the press that the Marines were not in Vietnam "to sit on their ditty boxes," they were there to "kill Viet Cong."

In Washington, the press asked the State

Department to redefine the U. S. military role in Vietnam. On 5 June, Robert J. McCloskey, speaking for the State Department, and indicating his statement had the approval of highest departmental officials, said:

"As you know, American troops have been sent to South Vietnam recently with the mission of protecting key installations there. In establishing and patrolling their defense perimeters, they come into contact with the Viet Cong and at times are fired upon. Our troops naturally return the fire.

"It should come as no surprise therefore that our troops engage in combat in these and similar circumstances. But let me emphasize that the Vietnamese Government forces are carrying the brunt of combat operations. Those United States forces assigned as advisers to the armed forces of Vietnam remain in that capacity."

At that time, of the 51,000 American servicemen in Vietnam, some 16,500 Marines and 3,500 Army Airborne troopers had "defensive" missions; the rest might be said to be in an "advisory capacity."

Meanwhile, Ambassador Maxwell D. Taylor was in Washington for consultations. His resignation and replacement by Ambassador Henry Cabot Lodge were in prospect, but had not as yet been announced. President Johnson met with Taylor and his top political and military advisers. A meeting of the National Security Council, in itself a rare event, was held. It was obvious that neither the air war, nor the ground war, nor the political war was going well. The original hope, that with Americans securing the major bases, the South Vietnamese could successfully carry the fight to the Viet Cong, was fast fading. With the coming of the summer monsoon (not in I Corps, but on the other side of the Annamites), various advantages would accrue to the Viet Cong. There was great concern over the Pleiku-

Kontum area in the Central Highlands, where there were as yet no U. S. combat troops. There was talk now of the eventual commitment of 300,000, even 500,000, U. S. troops to Vietnam.

On 8 June the State Department issued a statement which was widely construed to mean that, in recent weeks, President Johnson had given General Westmoreland authority to order U. S. ground forces into offensive combat. On 9 June the White House came out with a statement which partially contradicted and partially confirmed the previous day's release. It said in part:

"There has been no change in the mission of United States ground combat units in Vietnam in recent days or weeks. The President has issued no order of any kind in this regard to General Westmoreland recently or at any other time. The primary mission of these troops is to secure and safeguard important military installations like the air base at Da Nang. They have the associated mission of . . . patrolling and securing actions in and near the areas thus safeguarded.

"If help is requested by the appropriate Vietnamese commander, General Westmoreland also has authority within the assigned mission to employ these troops in support of Vietnamese forces faced with aggressive attack when other effective reserves are not available and when, in his judgment, the general military situation urgently requires it."

The above statement was, of course, consistent with the instructions given by General Westmoreland to General Collins, and later repeated to General Walt.

"ARMY" VERSUS "MARINE" STRATEGY

By this time, two supposedly conflicting "strategies" were being debated in the press. One strategy emphasized mobile operations: not only should U. S. troops go to the rescue of beleaguered SVN forces, but there should also be U. S. "search and destroy" operations, actively and aggressively seeking out the Viet Cong. The other, labeled the "ink-blot" strategy, held that U. S. forces should establish secure "coastal enclaves," such as Da Nang, and from these gradually reach out, in carefully conducted "clear and hold" operations.

The first strategy became known as the "Army" strategy, and the second as the "Marine" strategy. Each had its vociferous advocates who failed to see that the two strategies were not necessarily mutually exclusive. There were some critics who said that the Marines had become cautious and defensive-minded. It is true that at this time General Walt regarded the defense of Da Nang air base as his first and most important mission since the orders he had received so stated.

On 17 June, 1st Battalion, 9th Marines (Lieutenant Colonel Verle E. Ludwig) landed at Da Nang and assumed responsibility for the close-in security of the air base, relieving 3d Battalion, 9th Marines. Now at the end of its Western Pacific tour under the "transplacement" system then in effect, BLT 3/9 sailed for Okinawa, where its colors and unit designation would be transferred to a new BLT arriving from the States.

Just before dawn on 1 July the almost inevitable happened. A Viet Cong demolitions squad got through the barbed wire and onto the flight line on the east side of the runway and hit the south end of the field with mortar fire. Explosives and 57-mm. recoilless rifle fire destroyed two C-130s and one F-102, and damaged one C-130 and two F-102s. One U. S. Air Force airman was killed, and three Marines wounded.

The raiders had made their approach through the thickly populated area south and east of the field, an area where the ARVN was responsible for security. Up to the time of the 1 July attack, General Thi had been reluctant to

permit Marines to operate in heavily populated areas. After it, however, and at least partly as a result of it, it was agreed that the Marine area of responsibility should be expanded southward and eastward. The headquarters of the 9th Marines (Colonel Frank E. Garretson) and 2d Battalion, 9th Marines (Lieutenant Colonel George R. Scharnberg) landed at Da Nang on 6 July and moved immediately to the south of the airfield, giving some depth to the defenses.

In July a Provisional Base Defense Battalion (Lieutenant Colonel William H. Clark) was formed by drawing on the personnel of the support and service units. Admittedly, this was a short-term measure which, if extended too long, would work to the detriment of the parent units, but it did provide manpower for the airfield perimeter. These measures helped, but did not solve all the problems of close-in security for the field.

LANDING AT QUI NHON

In II Corps Tactical Zone, the military situation remained tenuous. About the middle of June General Westmoreland had asked General Walt to be prepared to deploy two Marine battalions to the Pleiku-Kontum area, if required, but the port of Qui Nhon presented a more immediate problem. There was an airfield there, and a substantial start had been made on creating an Army logistics base. Furthermore, at Qui Nhon, Route 19 strikes off at right angles from Route 1 and goes up through An Khe to Pleiku. Qui Nhon had to be held secure until Army troops could arrive.

On 1 July, the Seventh Fleet's Special Landing Force, then BLT 3/7 (Lieutenant Colonel Charles H. Bodley), supported by HMM-163, went ashore at Qui Nhon. On 7 July, BLT 2/7 (Lieutenant Colonel Leon N. Utter) landed and relieved BLT 3/7 which, the next day, went back aboard its shipping and reconstituted the SLF. Thus, 175 miles south of Da Nang and in

II Corps area, a fourth Marine "coastal enclave" was created.

Fact-Finding and Presidential Decisions

On 8 July President Johnson formally nominated Henry Cabot Lodge to resume his post as Ambassador to Vietnam in place of Maxwell D. Taylor, who had submitted his letter of resignation. Defense Secretary McNamara announced that he and Lodge would leave shortly for Vietnam to meet with Ambassador Taylor and to bring their impressions up to date. This would be McNamara's sixth fact-finding trip to Vietnam. They arrived in Saigon on 16 July, and on 18 July visited I Corps and III MAF. The party included Ambassador Taylor, Deputy Ambassador U. Alexis Johnson, General Earle G. Wheeler, General Westmoreland, Assistant Defense Secretaries John T. McNaughton and Arthur Sylvester, and others of almost equal rank.

"The over-all situation continues to be serious," said McNamara in Saigon before he left for Washington. "In many respects it has deteriorated since 15 months ago, when I was last here."

Six hours after McNamara's return to Washington on 21 July, President Johnson and his chief advisers began a series of discussions designed to hammer out major decisions about U. S. military, political, and economic involvement in Vietnam.

After eight days of intensive review, President Johnson on 28 July outlined his decisions in a nationally televised press conference. U. S. military strength in Vietnam would be increased from 75,000 to 125,000 "almost immediately." (The 1st Cavalry Division (Airmobile) was then in process of loading out from Gulf Coast and southern East Coast ports.) The reserves would not be called up. Instead, the draft would be doubled from 17,000 to 35,000 each month, and voluntary enlistment pro-

grams would be intensified. After the build-up reached 125,000, additional forces would be sent to Vietnam as required.

MARINE MANPOWER

Up to this point, the Marine Corps had supported the deployment of 25,000 Marines to Vietnam without increasing its authorized strength. The Corps had begun fiscal year 1965 with 190,000 Marines authorized, and as a step toward a pre-Vietnam goal of 206,000, an increase of 3,100 had been programmed and approved. So, at the time of the President's decisions, its authorized strength was 193,100.

Activation of the Organized Reserve would have given the Marine Corps an almost completely manned and trained 4th Marine Division and 4th Marine Aircraft Wing. But the Reserves were not to be called up. (As Secretary McNamara explained to the House Armed Services Committee, the call-up of the Reserves had been considered but rejected, because it was anticipated that operations in Vietnam would be drawn out and the Reserves would be a wasting asset if called up on a short-term basis under the President's emergency authority.) Further complications were that involuntary extensions of enlistment were limited to four months (and were to be terminated entirely by October 1966), and that most of the junior officers were Reserves who, on completing their obligated service, went home.

In peacetime, replacements to the Western Pacific were built around a "transplacement" system. This was essentially a rotation, on a 13-month cycle, of infantry battalions and aircraft squadrons between the West Coast and the Western Pacific. It was decided that the transplacement of infantry battalions would cease after the deployment of 3rd Battalion, 5th Marines, in September 1965. Rotation of aircraft squadrons would be limited in the future to squadrons introducing new types of aircraft and the return of squadrons with older aircraft.

Cancelling transplacement made it necessary to "homogenize" the carefully "stabilized" battalions and squadrons. Otherwise, everyone in a unit having the same rotation date would have resulted in unacceptable peaks and valleys of experience. This smoothing-out process, nicknamed Operation Mixmaster, which involved the inter-unit transfer of thousands of Marines, took place over the next several months.

While there would be no more rotation of units between the West Coast and the Western Pacific, there would be a limited rotation of units between Vietnam and the Western Pacific reserve based on Okinawa (and some air units in Japan), and it would be possible to maintain the 13-month tour for individual Marines.

In August 1965, as a direct consequence of the President's decisions, an increase of 30,000 Marines (to 223,100) was authorized. This would provide three new battalions (communications, engineer, and military police) and two helicopter training squadrons. It was hoped that it would also permit the manning levels of deployed units to be brought up to full strength, and a bit to be added to the training base and personnel pipeline. Also authorized were an additional 2,500 spaces for the Organized Reserve (to a total of 48,000).

Four Regiments

On 14 August the headquarters of the 7th Marines (Colonel Oscar F. Peatross) and BLT 1/7 (Lieutenant Colonel James P. Kelly) came ashore at Chu Lai. The 7th Marines, a 1st Marine Division regiment which had departed Camp Pendleton on 24 May, was now fully committed to Vietnam. Other 1st Marine Division units were on the way. Battalion Landing Team 2/1 was scheduled to become the SLF. In

the middle of July, BLT 1/5 had moved to Kaneohe, where it had become the major ground element of the reconstituted 1st Marine Brigade. On 16 August the headquarters of the 1st Marine Division left Camp Pendleton, and on 24 August Major General Lewis J. Fields, the division commanding general, opened his forward command post at Camp Courtney, Okinawa, assuming also the responsibilities of Commander Task Force 79.

The posture of III MAF's infantry regiments, which would remain essentially unchanged from mid-August until the end of the year, was as follows:

—3d Marines, with its 1st and 2d Battalions, was west and north of Da Nang air base. 3d Marines also had under its operational and administrative command the 3d Battalion, 4th Marines, stationed at Phu Bai.

—9th Marines, with its 2d Battalion, was south of Da Nang, as was part of the 1st Battalion. The rest of the 1st Battalion was on the airfield itself. A new BLT 3/9 (Lieutenant Colonel Robert J. Tunnell), one of the last "transplaced" battalions, arrived at Da Nang on 15 August.

—4th Marines, with its 1st and 2d Battalions, and 3d Battalion, 3d Marines, was at Chu Lai.

—7th Marines, with its 1st Battalion, was also at Chu Lai. Its 2d Battalion was at Qui Nhon (now under operational control of Army's Task Force Alpha) and the 3d Battalion was at sea as the SLF.

Four Marine Aircraft Groups

MAG-16, the veteran helicopter group, was at Da Nang air base, getting ready to move across the Tourane River to the new helicopter and light plane facility, originally called Da Nang East but later renamed, more solemnly, Marble Mountain Air Facility. One medium squadron was kept at Phu Bai in support of 3d Battalion, 4th Marines.

MAG-11 had come into country on 7 July and had taken over the fighter-bomber squadrons operating from Da Nang.

MAG-12 with its attack squadrons was at Chu Lai.

MAG-36, another helicopter group, was scheduled to come into Chu Lai on 1 September. One squadron was with 2d Battalion, 7th Marines, in Qui Nhon.

Coordinating with I Corps

On 30 July General Westmoreland paid General Walt a visit of more than routine interest. CG III MAF, said ComUSMACV, was to have operational control of all U. S. ground elements in the I Corps Tactical Zone; most notably, he would have operational control of the I Corps Advisory Group. This would provide an effective bridge between U. S. combat forces and the advisory effort. General Westmoreland also told General Walt that he had a "free hand" in the conduct of operations in ICTZ, and he expected Walt, in coordination with General Thi, to undertake larger offensive operations at greater distances from base areas.

General Walt reminded ComUSMACV that III MAF was still bound by the letter of instruction issued early in May; that the restraints were such that operations beyond base areas were essentially limited to "reserve/reaction" forces, a kind of rescue operation to be conducted if and when South Vietnamese forces were in serious trouble. General Westmoreland said these restraints were no longer realistic, and invited General Walt to rewrite the instructions, working into them the authority he thought he needed, and promised his approval.

On 3 August, General Walt, by formal message, advised General Westmoreland that III

MAF stood ready to undertake offensive operations. On 6 August, ComUSMACV granted authority for such undertakings, and designated General Walt as Senior Adviser, I Corps.

Colonel Howard B. St. Clair, U. S. Army, was redesignated Deputy Senior Adviser and continued as Commanding Officer, I Corps Advisory Group. This group was essentially a U. S. Army unit, although there were some 60 U. S. Marines and about an equal number of Australians serving as advisers.

Guidelines provided by General Westmoreland emphasized integration of Vietnamese and U. S. effort. A prime problem, however, was that there was no jointure of U. S. and Vietnamese command at any level. Without some kind of unity of command, how could two separate, distinct military structures, each of corps size, operate in the same corps area? Part of the answer was the designation of Tactical Areas of Responsibility (TAOR). In these TAORs, which radiated out from Marine bases, III MAF had primary (but not absolute) tactical responsibility and could conduct operations with a minimum of coordination with I Corps.

Various factors affected extension of these TAORs:

First, General Thi and I Corps had to permit the expansion. Initially, as mentioned earlier, he had been reluctant to allow Marines to operate in populated areas. This had been overcome, but still each increase in the size of a TAOR had to be carefully negotiated so as to be of greatest mutual benefit.

Second, growth of the TAORs was limited by the strength of III MAF; as the Force grew so could TAORs be expanded.

Third, the limits of a TAOR could not be the forward edge of the Marine positions. There had to be adequate room out front for reconnaissance, maneuver, and the use of supporting arms. (This requirement sometimes caused

problems. Uninformed observers tended to regard everything enclosed by a TAOR as being
under firm Marine control, which often was far
from the case.)

Fourth, there had to be a judgment as to the
capability of the Vietnamese to fill in behind
the advancing Marines, and to pacify what had
been cleared.

In August the 4th Marines (Colonel James F.
McClanahan), in company with elements of
the 2d ARVN Division, tried a number of
small-scale offensive operations west of Chu
Lai. As field exercises against negligible resistance, they were moderately successful, but
they showed conclusively that, without unity
of command, operations could best be described as "coordinated," not as "combined."
Several things could be done to help make this
coordination work.

First, the problems of coordination could be
simplified by giving the Americans and the
Vietnamese separate and distinct zones of action for their maneuver elements.

Second, fire support had to be coordinated
by a single agency, so there was agreement on a
single Fire Support Coordination Center.

Third, American advisers with Vietnamese
units had to act not only as advisers but also as
III MAF combat liaison officers.

OPERATIONS STARLITE AND PIRANHA

For some time there had been reports of an
enemy concentration south of Chu Lai. On 15
August, III MAF developed hard intelligence
indicating that the 1st Viet Cong Regiment,
some 2,000 strong, had moved into prepared
positions on Van Tuong Peninsula, 15 miles
south of Chu Lai airstrip. This information,
plus the fortuitous circumstance that RLT-7
with its 1st Battalion had just arrived at Chu
Lai, and the Special Landing Force (BLT 3/7)
was close by, made possible Operation Starlite, the first regimental-sized U. S. battle since
the Korean War. On 17 August, 2d Battalion,
4th Marines (Lieutenant Colonel Joseph R.

Fisher) and 3d Battalion, 3d Marines (Lieutenant Colonel Joseph E. Muir) were assigned to
RLT-7.

On 18 August Operation Starlite was
launched. It was a converging movement, using a river crossing in LVTs from the north, a
helicopter-borne assault on the west or inland
side, and an amphibious landing with lift provided by Task Force 76 on the southeast beach
of the Van Tuong Peninsula. By 24 August, at
least 964 VC had been killed, an attack against
Chu Lai had probably been frustrated, and the
1st Viet Cong Regiment had been rendered
combat ineffective. A more lasting result was
that the Viet Cong were disabused of any illu-
sion that they could defeat the Marines in a
stand-up battle. Moreover, this and later
amphibious operations by the Marines forced
the Viet Cong away from the coastal peninsulas where they had previously found sanctuary
from their enemies.

Operation Piranha came close on the heels
of Starlite—it began on 7 September. This
time the target was Batangan Peninsula, eight
miles southeast of Van Tuong, where a buildup, possibly remnants of the 1st VC Regiment,
was reported to be taking place, and which was
reputed to be a place of entry for the seaborne
infiltration of supplies for the Viet Cong. Operation Piranha was a coordinated operation;
sizable elements of the 2d ARVN Division and
some Vietnamese Marines participated. It took
longer to plan than did Starlite; the intelligence was not quite so good; results not so
spectacular. Nevertheless, in the three-day
fight the Marines—RLT-7 again—counted 183
Viet Cong killed in action, 66 of them in a
single cave. The South Vietnamese scored an
additional 66 VC kills.

BASE DEFENSE COORDINATION

While these heartening battles were going
on south of Chu Lai, progress of sorts was also
being made in the defense of Da Nang.

There had been another setback on 5 August

when the VC raided the Esso storage terminal at Lien Chieu, destroyed two JP-4 storage tanks and damaged three other tanks, resulting in a loss of nearly two million gallons of fuel. Lien Chieu is inside Da Nang Harbor, on the south shore of Hai Van Peninsula. There are good hydrographic reasons for the terminal being there, but at this time it was outside the Marine TAOR, and its defense had been entrusted to two understrength Regional Force companies. To protect it adequately, it would have been necessary to bring the entire Hai Van promontory into the Marine TAOR. This would have taken at least a reinforced rifle company, and that many men could not be spared at the time. However, subsequent to the attack, a Marine platoon was moved to the Nam O bridge, which crossed the Song Ca De about one mile down the road from Lien Chieu. The five-span steel structure was a much threatened target of the Viet Cong.

On the Da Nang airfield there were the Provisional Base Defense Battalion and part of the 1st Battalion, 9th Marines. About half of the 1st Battalion had been siphoned off by the increased involvement of the 9th Marines south of the Song Cau Do. On 16 August the newly arrived 3d Battalion, 9th Marines, relieved the 1st Battalion on the airfield.

Lack of unity of command continued to be a major barrier to effective security. As early as 29 May, ComUSMACV had named CG III MAF as the Special Area Coordinator for Da Nang. This assignment included responsibility for coordinating physical security, but the terms of reference were geared to an earlier situation: advisory and noncombatant. If General Walt was expected to carry out his mission of defending the airfield, he needed clear-cut authority over not only his own forces but, as far as security was concerned, over the other tenants. However, as base commander, Lieutenant Colonel Hung, Commanding Officer, 41st Tactical Wing, VNAF, had over-all responsibility for defense of the field and he could not

have relinquished it, even if he were so inclined.

Once again, "coordination" had to be substituted for "command." Lieutenant Colonel Clark, who commanded the Provisional Base Defense Battalion that was formed in July, was named Base Defense Coordinator, and was later relieved by Colonel George W. Carrington, Jr. Defense of the airfield was divided into two parts: III MAF assumed responsibility for tactical defense of the field, which involved the continued assignment of an infantry battalion to man perimeter positions and to patrol outwards: the other part of the defense was internal security, and in accordance with accepted military practice, each tenant unit was charged with its own internal security. A Joint Defense Communication Center was established to keep the tenants in contact with one another.

This new arrangement got its first testing as soon as it was activated. There was a series of minor probings the night of 17 August. The system seemed to work, for the VC did not get through the wire.

On 21 August operational control of 3d Battalion, 9th Marines, as Air Base Defense Battalion, was passed directly to III MAF, and on the 22nd, the Provisional Base Defense Battalion was dissolved and its members returned to parent units. From then until the following spring, battalions of the 9th Marines were rotated to serve six-week or two-month tours as Air Base Defense Battalion—an assignment that was less dangerous, but in many ways more tedious and exacting, than combing the rice paddies south of the river.

RAID ON MARBLE MOUNTAIN AND CHU LAI

China Beach, across the Tourane River and east of Da Nang proper, curves in a gentle arc from Monkey Mountain seven miles south to Marble Mountain. The 1st Battalion, 9th Marines, was operating in the vicinity of the latter eminence, an authentic monolith of black-veined, gray marble. (A moribund tourist trade revived with the arrival of the Marines and a brisk traffic in marble ash trays ensued.) Between Marble Mountain and Monkey Mountain, China Beach was filling up with support facilities: Seabee battalion camps, the Naval Hospital, and the Marble Mountain Air Facility, now occupied by MAG-16 (Colonel Thomas J. O'Connor) and its helicopter squadrons.

On the night of 27 October, a Viet Cong raiding force quietly assembled in a village northwest of MAG-16 and adjacent to a Seabee camp. Apparently, it came by boat, although whether downstream along the river or south across Da Nang Bay is not clear. Under cover of 60-mm. mortar fire which engaged the Seabees heavily, at least four demolitions teams moved out to attack the airfield and the hospital. Forty-one VC were killed, but six armed with bangalore torpedoes and bundles of grenades got onto the MAG-16 parking mat, where they destroyed 24 helicopters and damaged 23. Raiders also got into the nearly completed hospital across the road and did considerable damage. Three Americans were killed, and 91 wounded; fortunately, most of the wounds were minor.

The same night, about 15 raiders slipped through the lines onto Chu Lai airstrip. Most of them were killed or captured before they reached MAG-12's flight line, but two VC did get to the A-4s with satchel charges, destroying two and damaging six before they were cut down.

It was a bad night at Marble Mountain and at Chu Lai but, when morning came, it appeared that a larger attack against Da Nang itself had been averted. During the night a Viet Cong battalion 18 kilometers west of Da Nang was brought under artillery fire and dispersed. About the same time, eight miles south of Da Nang, near Thanh Quit, a VC company stumbled into a Marine squad-sized ambush, ran

into a sheet of fire, and fell back, leaving 15 dead on the trail.

Monsoon

Expected to begin in September in I Corps, the monsoon season did not come on in force until October. By November the rain was averaging an inch a day. The largest problems were logistic. The roads, optimistically surfaced with laterite, dissolved into thin red soup. Storage areas flooded. The northeast winds roughened the sea and made unloading at Da Nang and Chu Lai increasingly difficult. Construction schedules fell behind as engineers and Seabees were forced to switch to repair and maintenance.

The Korean Division had arrived at Qui Nhon. Amphibious shipping was going to lift BLT 2/7 out of Qui Nhon in the first week of November; the battalion was to be released from army control and taken to Chu Lai to rejoin its parent regiment. Then it was planned to move 3d Battalion, 3d Marines, to Da Nang in the same shipping.

BLUE MARLIN

It seemed logical to combine the above moves into a two-phase amphibious operation. Thus, Operation Blue Marlin got under way on 7 November, when BLT 2/7 loaded out at Qui Nhon in the shipping of Task Group 76.3 (Captain William J. Maddocks). At Chu Lai, TG 76.3 took aboard the 3d Battalion, Vietnamese Marine Brigade, then proceeded north. On 10 November, the Marine Corps's birthday, they landed northeast of Tam Ky, about 18 miles north of Chu Lai and a third of the way between Chu Lai and Da Nang. Sea conditions were marginal. Both the *Paul Revere* (APA-248) and the *Windham County* (LST-1170) parted their anchor chains. The Marines went ashore in LVTs and LCMs. The surf was rough, but there was no opposition other than the elements. Moving inland, the force turned southward astride Highway One, and joined a motorized column sent up to Tam Ky from Chu Lai. Resistance was negligible, but the coastal area from the water's edge west to Highway One and from Tam Ky, capital of Quang Tin province, south to Chu Lai at least had had the benefit of a thorough sweep.

Phase I of Operation Blue Marlin achieved an historic first: the Vietnamese Marines participated in their first combined amphibious landing with the U. S. Marines. Along with the Vietnamese Airborne Brigade, the Marine Brigade was classed as having the best fighting battalions in the South Vietnamese service. It had been much used as a mobile strategic reserve, so much so, in fact, that its amphibious potential had not been fully developed. The Vietnamese Marines were formed after the departure of the French in 1954, with the advice and assistance of the U. S. Marines. Originally a river-type landing force, it had grown to a brigade of five infantry battalions, an artillery battalion, and an amphibious support battalion.

Phase II of Blue Marlin began with the loading-out of 3d Battalion, 3d Marines (Lieutenant Colonel William H. Lanagan, Jr.) from Chu Lai. They landed on 16 November south of Hoi An, 25 miles below Da Nang, and were joined by two Ranger battalions and two special ARVN "strike" companies. This area, south of the Song Gua Dai, mostly fishing villages, was known to be heavily infested by the Viet Cong and to be the source of much harassment against Hoi An, capital of Quang Nam province (and site of ancient Fai Fo, where the Portuguese in the 16th century had established a trading station). In the three-day operation that ensued 25 VC were killed, 15 captured.

Hiep Duc

On the night of 16/17 November, while Blue Marlin was in progress, the Viet Cong attacked and overran Hiep Duc, a district capital, 25 miles west of Tam Ky. Hiep Duc is in the valley of the Song Tranh: to the north, Nui Chom Mountain goes up to 944 meters, to the south, Nui Da Cao goes to 670 meters. The monsoon fills the valley with rain, and even when Da Nang and Chu Lai are fairly clear, the clouds driven in from the sea hang on the mountains. There were no good radio contacts with the survivors of Hiep Duc, but there were reports that the attackers were from the 1st Viet Cong Regiment, that this regiment after Starlite had withdrawn to the mountains of western Quang Tin province, had refilled its ranks, and was emerging under cover of the monsoon to do battle once again.

I Corps counterattacked with two battalions of the 5th ARVN Regiment, which were helilifted into the area in one of the most difficult of such operations yet attempted. The weather was bad and the enemy were using heavy antiaircraft machine guns—the first time these had been encountered in any numbers. On 17 November MAG-16 and MAG-36 lifted in 788 ARVN troops. Twenty of the participating 30 helicopters were hit by ground fire. Covering air support flown by MAG-11's F-4s and MAG-12's A-4s dropped 14 tons of bombs and fired 512 rockets and 1,532 rounds of 20-mm. The next day, 463 more ARVN troopers were lifted in.

Hiep Duc was retaken, but there was a sad and all-too-frequent epilogue. General Thi estimated that a garrison of at least a battalion would be needed to hold the town. He could not spare it. The 5th Regiment was returned to Quang Ngai. Hiep Duc was abandoned.

Throughout I Corps, other garrisons and outposts were being hit. Some held and some did not. The outlines of the VC monsoon strategy were clear. Against the South Vietnamese forces, that strategy was to concentrate on the destruction of isolated outposts: to strike with locally superior forces, holding out a reserve with which to ambush would-be rescuers. Outlying district headquarters, with their Popular Force and Regional Force garrisons, were to be eaten up, one by one, and then perhaps a move would be made against the provincial capitals. The aim was not to seize and hold terrain, but to inflict as much damage and embarrassment as possible; to wear down the ARVN as they marched in a dozen directions to counter VC moves.

Against the Americans, the VC strategy was to avoid the risk of a stand-up battle. There would be no large-scale attacks against major bases, but if small units—fire teams, squads, even platoons and companies—were unwary, they would be surprised and struck. And to show that the American defenses were not impervious, carefully prepared and skillfully executed commando raids would be made against rewarding targets—raids such as those already executed against Lien Chieu, Marble Mountain, and Chu Lai.

Thach Tru

On 22 November the triangular fort at Thach Tru, on Highway One, 29 kilometers south of Quang Ngai, was hit. This time, however, the enemy overstepped himself. The fort was not manned by an underarmed Popular Force or Regional Force contingent. The headquarters and one company of a Ranger battalion were in the fort itself, another company was on a nearby commanding hill, and a third company was in the village. In a brutal fight that began in the last hours of darkness and lasted until mid-morning, the enemy succeeded in getting through the belts of barbed wire and over the palisade into the fort.

Fortunately, the USS *O'Brien* (DD-725) (Commander Charles S. Christensen) was within range when the firefight started and, at noon, she was joined by the USS *Bache* (DD-470) (Commander Arthur R. Hasler, Jr.). The battalion commander of the Rangers credited naval gunfire with breaking the back of the

attack. (In 26 hours, the *O'Brien* fired 48 tons of ammunition, a total of 1,392 rounds of 5-inch at an average rate of one round every 66 seconds.)

Marine air came on station in the morning, and, in spite of abysmal flying weather, hammered at the enemy, who had taken up defenses in the hills west of Thach Tru. The 3d Battalion, 7th Marines, which had been standing by, ready to go into Hiep Duc, if necessary, began arriving by helo in mid-afternoon, while the 2d ARVN Division started a mechanized column down the road from Quang Ngai. The Seventh Fleet moved the Special Landing Force into position offshore, ready to land on two hours' notice. At nightfall, the USS *Fletcher* (DD-445) (Commander Robert L. Morgan) relieved the *Bache*.

Seventy-one of the defenders of Thach Tru were killed, 74 wounded, and 2 missing. But the attackers paid a much higher price: 175 dead, 3 prisoners, and an unusually large bag of weapons—5 75-mm. recoilless rifles, 9 machine guns, 6 60-mm. mortars, 2 submachine guns, and 114 rifles.

Next morning, 23 November, 3d Battalion, 7th Marines, attacked to the west, driving a holding force out of the first line of hills, killing three, for sure, and capturing eight weapons including a machine gun. From captured weapons and prisoners, it became evident that the force attacked was not Viet Cong, but a PAVN formation from North Vietnam. Later, it was decided that it was the 95th Regiment of the 325th Alpha Division.

Reassessment by McNamara

On the afternoon of 28 November, Defense Secretary McNamara arrived once again in Saigon. With him, as before, were the JCS Chairman, General Wheeler, and Assistant Secretaries McNaughton and Sylvester. At a brief news conference, McNamara told the press that accelerating infiltration by North Vietnamese regulars would clearly require counteraction. He then had a five-hour meeting with Admiral Sharp, General Westmoreland, and MACV's principal staff officers and subordinate commanders, including General Walt. The core of the discussion was the entrance of PAVN formations into overt combat, the rate of infiltration of these units from the north, and the corresponding increase in U. S. forces which would be required to counter it. It was accepted that there were seven PAVN regiments in the country; the presence of an eighth was considered "probable," and of a ninth "possible."

The fight at Thach Tru had solidly established the presence of elements of the 325th Alpha Division in lower Quang Ngai province. With less certainty, it was believed that there was at least one PAVN regiment operating south of the DMZ in Quang Tri province, and, perhaps, elements west of Hue in Thua Thien province.

The next day, 29 November, McNamara spent some two hours in further discussion, then he and his party made a quick tour of Vo Dat, An Khe (this was shortly after the Cavalry's first big victory at Iadrang Valley), and Camranh Bay, before departing for Guam and an inspection of the B-52s based there.

FIVE TASKS FOR III MAF

General Walt had recommended to ComUSMACV that the number of Marine infantry battalions be increased from 12 to at least 18, and the supporting fighter-attack squadrons to eight. He based these recommendations not so much on the threat of North Vietnamese formations, as on estimates of what was required to pursue effectively a balanced strategy in I Corps. As III MAF saw it, this strategy involved five fundamental tasks:

First, to defend and continue to develop secure base areas.

Second, to support the operations of the Vietnamese I Corps.

Third, to conduct offensive operations against the Viet Cong.

Fourth, to be prepared to provide forces to support contingencies elsewhere in South Vietnam.

The fifth task, less military, but every bit as important, involved what, for the moment, was being called "rural construction." Successive euphemisms have served as formal substitutes for the word "pacification." "Revolutionary development" succeeded "rural construction." Informally, many Vietnamese and Americans continued to use "pacification."

If there was a fundamental difference at this time between Army and Marine thinking on how the war should be prosecuted, it lay probably in differences of opinion as to just how large a role U. S. forces should play in pacification. The Marine Corps was more sanguine about the chances of American success in this role; it had gotten off to an earlier start, and had developed a number of procedures and techniques that showed promise.

(It should be remembered that up to this time, most of the Army's combat operations had been in the thinly populated highlands against Main Force and North Vietnamese formations. Later, when the Army operated in more heavily populated areas their methods pretty much paralleled those of the Marines. Conversely, as will be shown later, when the North Vietnamese crossed the DMZ into I Corps in strength, an increasing percentage of Marine forces had to be deployed against them, to the detriment of the pacification effort.)

PACIFICATION, MARINE STYLE

Some of III MAF's optimism stemmed from early successes at Le My. On 19 June 1965, for example, some 350 rice farmers from farther up the Song Ca De Valley had voluntarily come into the protected hamlet. Le My rapidly developed into a modest showplace. On their tour of Le My, visitors to Da Nang (and there were many; everyone—political, military, theatrical, journalistic, business, and international personages—found reason to visit Da Nang) got a sand-table orientation, met the village officials, saw the dispensary, the school, and the new market place.

For a while, pacification appeared remarkably simple: you liberated a hamlet or village from VC domination, provided it with a shield of security, and nurtured and encouraged the renascence of governmental control and institutions with a sincere and carefully thought-out program of civic action. While this seemed to work well in the thinly populated, generally pro-government area west of Da Nang, which was the 3d Marines' zone of action, it did not work so well, or at least the results were not so dramatically apparent, south of Da Nang in the 9th Marines' zone of action. The spinal cord of the latter zone was Highway One running south. Fifteen miles below Da Nang, it crosses the Cua Dia (or Thu Bon or Ky Lam, the river changes its name every few kilometers). There, Route 14, which starts at Hoi An, runs along the north bank of the river, intersects Highway One, and then continues inland. A thin belt of territory along the highway and the eastern section of Route 14 was under government control; all the rest of the zone—rich ricelands, where two crops a year are harvested—was dominated by the Viet Cong. The area, eventually assigned to the 9th Marines, is heavily populated, having some quarter of a million people.

GOLDEN FLEECE

From 1 September until mid-October, when the rains began in earnest, the 9th Marines conducted Operation Golden Fleece, designed to save the rice harvest from the exactions of the Viet Cong. Golden Fleece consisted of high-density, small-unit patrolling, many night ambushes, and cordons of Marines to protect the rice harvesters. A sizable part of the harvest was saved from deflection to the enemy. The term "Golden Fleece" became a generic one; it was applied to subsequent operations by III MAF for protection of the rice harvest.

By October, the 9th Marines had cleared one-third of the way to Hoi An—the half of Hoa Vang district that lay south of the Song Cau Do, nine villages in all. Then came the real test: the pacification of that area.

By the end of the month, the chief of Quang Nam province—at that time, the vigorous and brilliant Lieutenant Colonel Tung—had completed his planning for the two-phase Ngu Hanh Son program (also called the Five Mountain program, or the Nine Village program). A trained government cadre of 350 men, enough for five villages, was available. Phase I, which was to be completed by the first of the year, would be the pacification of the five villages west of Highway One. Phase II would be the pacification of the four villages east of the highway. Popular Forces would be recruited, trained, and organized for the security of the district. In accordance with the formula of one squad for each hamlet and one platoon for each village, nearly 1,000 men would be required; less than 100 were available. Until the Popular Forces were ready, security would be provided by the 59th Regional Force Battalion, specially formed of five companies, one for each of the villages of Phase I. The program began on 1 November 1965.

As III MAF saw it, the Marines' job was to provide the environment, the circumstances, the outer shield of tactical defense, and some of the material resources needed to make the program work.

STAFF REORGANIZATION

To improve its coordination of civic action efforts, III MAF underwent a fairly radical revision of staff responsibilities. By doctrine, "civil affairs" were the responsibility of G-1; "psychological operations," the responsibility of G-3. But in Vietnam, four-fifths of "psychological operations" were concerned with relations with the populace, not with tactical operations, and "civic action" meant a much more direct contact with the local people than did the traditional "civil affairs."

Therefore, III MAF created a new general staff section, G-5, to coordinate all civic action programs, except medical assistance, which remained the province of the Force Surgeon. The 3d Marine Division followed suit and established a Division G-5, and the regiments and battalions, whose civil affairs and psychological warfare functions had been assigned to officers as additional duties, moved toward having full-time S-5s. Several young platoon leaders, having completed their Vietnam tours, voluntarily extended to fill these challenging civic action billets.

To improve coordination with other U. S. agencies supporting pacification in I Corps, the Joint Coordinating Council had been formed on 30 August. Among the members were the Deputy Senior Adviser, I Corps; the Regional Director, USOM; the Refugee Representative, USOM; the Senior Field Representative, JUSPAO; and the G-5, III MAF. On 28 October, General Thi appointed a personal representative to sit with the Council. Later, General McCutcheon, as Deputy CG III MAF, was named permanent chairman. In addition to the parent council, there were a number of supporting committees: Public Health, Public Safety, Agriculture and Fisheries, Education, and so on, with both U. S. and Vietnamese membership.

SECURITY OF THE HAMLETS

It was recognized that, in spite of all these arrangements, pacification would not work without adequate security; the Viet Cong would see that it did not, by assassinating and kidnapping village and hamlet officials, burning schools, and tearing down, both psychologically and physically, whatever the government of South Vietnam, with the help of the Americans, attempted to build.

The III MAF had recognized early that the key to the kind of security that was needed was an effective, grass-roots gendarmerie—self-defense at the hamlet and village level. This was no great revelation. Established doctrine for the Popular Forces was sound. So was the rule-of-thumb formula: a squad of PF for each hamlet, a platoon for each village. The difficulty was that the PF program wasn't working out the way it was intended.

At the root of that failure was the fact that the Popular Forces were at the bottom of the priorities list in the Vietnamese armed forces. For example, no one who was eligible for service in the Army of Vietnam could enroll in the Popular Forces. Furthermore, pay was low— 1,200 piasters or less than ten dollars a month; weapons were scarce, usually limited to carbines and grenades; uniforms were often promised, but seldom delivered. (Many of the Popular Forces had the dismaying but unavoidable habit of wearing the peasant's traditional black pajamas, the uniform usually worn by the Viet Cong. Recognition of the PF under these conditions was sometimes fatally difficult. In desperation, officers sometimes briefed patrol leaders and pilots in words to this effect: "If you can see them, they are Popular Forces; if you can't see them, they are Viet Cong.")

Under these circumstances, it is no wonder that the Popular Forces tended to become urbanized rather than rural—it was much safer and more comfortable in Da Nang; that many of the units became the personal bodyguards of the village or district chiefs, and offered little or no protection to the constituents; and that some units and individuals existed on the pay rolls but could not be found on the ground.

The surprising thing was that certain Popular Force units were as good as they were. Throughout the summer and fall they had shown that, properly trained and properly led, they could fight well and bravely. Their combat losses attested to this.

COMBINED ACTION COMPANIES

At Phu Bai, the base from which 3d Battalion, 4th Marines (Lieutenant Colonel William W. Taylor), was operating, an effective rapport with the surrounding hamlets had been established. During the summer, a "Joint Action Company" was established (later the name was changed to the more accurate "Combined Action Company" or "CAC"). A provisional platoon of hand-picked Marine volunteers, under Lieutenant Paul R. Ek, who spoke Vietnamese, was formed and given intensive training, not only in advanced counterinsurgency techniques, but also in Vietnamese language, history, customs, and military and governmental organization. One Marine squad, with a Navy corpsman attached, was then assigned to each of five Popular Force platoons.

These Marines entered into the life of the village where they were assigned, and became an integral part of its defenses. To the Popular Force platoons they could offer training in weaponry and tactics, and effective communications—vital for supporting fires or reinforcements; and to the communities involved, they offered a very real Marine-to-the-people civic action program, including medical aid.

At Phu Bai the Combined Action Company worked because the circumstances there were right for it, and General Chuan, CG of the 1st ARVN Division, gave it his interested and active support.

While informal reciprocal arrangements were being worked out elsewhere, the first full-fledged expansion of the Combined Action Company concept took place at Da Nang in January 1966. The 3d Battalion, 9th Marines, now commanded by Lieutenant Colonel Taylor, who had been transferred from Phu Bai, was the Air Base Defense Battalion. Drawing on his Phu Bai experience, Taylor organized a second Combined Action Company. This new company paired off a Marine squad with each of seven Popular Force platoons located in the area roughly surrounding the air base. The quality of patrolling out to the limits of mortar range around the airfield improved immediately.

HARVEST MOON

After the Vietnamese government forces withdrew from Hiep Duc in late November, the Viet Cong moved eastward into the Phuoc Valley, and the government garrisons at Viet An and Que Son came under pressure. To remove this pressure and, hopefully, to entrap the enemy, suspected of being the 1st Viet Cong Regiment reinforced with North Vietnamese heavy weapons units, a coordinated operation, Harvest Moon, was planned.

The scheme of maneuver was for an ARVN column to move into the Phuoc Valley from Thang Binh, a town on Highway One, about midway between Da Nang and Chu Lai. A lateral road going along the valley floor and linking Thang Binh, Que Son, Viet An, and Hiep Duc was to be the axis of advance. After the ARVN had developed a contact, two U. S. Marine battalions would be helilifted to the rear of the enemy. A third Marine battalion would be held in reserve.

Headquarters of the 5th ARVN Regiment, with its own 1st Battalion on the left of the road, and the 11th Ranger Battalion on the right, moved out on the morning of 8 December, and marched six kilometers without incident. There was a halt for lunch; the march was resumed; and at about 1330, the 11th

Rangers found themselves semi-encircled and under heavy, close-in attack. The battalion commander went down, badly wounded, and was hit a second time as he was carried out on the back of the American adviser. In half-an-hour, the 11th Rangers were out of action and moving to the rear. The 1st Battalion, 5th ARVN, did a right face but could not get across the road. At 1434 Marine helicopters lifted 1st Battalion, 6th ARVN, into the Rangers' position, and the Viet Cong broke contact.

Next morning, 1st Battalion, 5th ARVN, south of the road, was hit hard by the VC; the regimental commander, who, the previous month, had bravely fought his way back into Hiep Duc, was killed, and the battalion was driven south and east.

At this point, the Marine battalions entered the battle. The 2d Battalion, 7th Marines (Lieutenant Colonel Leon N. Utter), landed seven kilometers west of the line of contact, and the 3d Battalion, 3d Marines (Lieutenant Colonel Joshua W. Dorsey, III), was helilifted southeast of the original battle area to take the pressure off 1st Battalion, 5th ARVN. Next day, 10 December, 2d Battalion, 1st Marines (Lieutenant Colonel Robert T. Hanifin, Jr.)—which was the Special Landing Force—came in by helicopter against heavy resistance, and landed about midway between the two Marine battalions already committed.

Control headquarters for the operation was Task Force Delta (commanded, first, by Brigadier General Melvin D. Henderson, and later by Brigadier General Jonas M. Platt), which had set up its command post, along with a bobtailed artillery battalion, at Que Son. General Lam, CG of the 2d ARVN Division, a figure familiar to the Marines in his black beret with silver badges, tanker's jacket, and swagger stick, first established his field headquarters at Thang Binh, but later moved in side-by-side with General Platt.

The Marines started moving against the southern rim of the valley, while the ARVN moved to the northern rim. Between the 12th and 14th of December, B-52s made four strikes, the first in direct support of Marine operations, and the Marines were much impressed by the precision of the bombing patterns and their neutralizing effect.

By 16 December, VC resistance had faded away, and the 3d Battalion, 3d Marines, started marching out to the northeast. By 18 December, it was out of the valley. The 2d Battalion, 1st Marines, followed in trace, and was out by 19 December. Meanwhile, 2d Battalion, 7th Marines, a Chu Lai battalion, marched 23 miles to the east and at Ky Phu, west of Tam Ky, ran into an attempted ambush. The VC got the worst of it, with 105 counted dead. The Chu Lai Marines continued on and were also out on Highway One by 19 December. At dusk, the Viet Cong tried a small ambush, were promptly eliminated, and the operation was over. The tally was 407 VC dead, and 13 crew-served weapons, 95 individual weapons, and many stores (including an amazing amount of paper and uniform cloth) taken from a base area uncovered on the reverse slope of the ridge south of Que Son.

The Special Landing Force (2d Battalion, 1st Marines, and Medium Helicopter Squadron 261) reembarked. It had had three busy months. Before being landed in Harvest Moon, it had made amphibious raids against the coast at Vung Mu, Ben Goi, Tam Quan, Lang Ke Ga, and Phu Thu. On 20 December, the force went on up to Phu Bai and relieved 3d Battalion, 4th Marines, which rotated back to Okinawa.

New Year

Harvest Moon was over before the Christmas holiday. The Viet Cong said they would observe a 12-hour truce from 1900 Christmas Eve until 0700 Christmas Day. The United States and South Vietnam improved on this;

they said they would observe a 30-hour truce from 1800 on the 24th until midnight on the 25th. The Marines were unenthusiastic about the truce and distrustful of Viet Cong observance. There were three small-scale attacks in the Da Nang and Chu Lai TAORs, and it wasn't clear whether or not the VC were observing the longer truce period. The Marines had hoped to signal the end of the truce with a maximum artillery barrage at 0001, 26 December. In this they were disappointed; the barrage had to be cancelled because, at the last minute, the truce was extended, for reasons not clear to the Marines, until later on the morning of the 26th.

As 1965 ended, there were 180,000 U. S. troops in South Vietnam, and 38,000 of them were Marines.

There was another truce in January, at the time of the lunar New Year—"Tet" as it is called in Vietnam—a holiday to be taken more seriously than Christian Christmas. This time the Viet Cong said they would undertake no offensive operations from midnight 19 January until midnight 23 January. Saigon's counterproposal was for a truce from noon 20 January until 1800 on 23 January. The Year of the Snake was ending and the Year of the Horse was beginning, by tradition a good year for martial enterprise. An old man, asked for his thoughts on the subject, stroked his beard and said, "There will be a lot of fighting and killing."

Better observed than the Christmas truce, the Tet truce was not seriously violated in I Corps, but close on the heels of the holiday, shortly after midnight on 25 January, there was a shelling of Da Nang air base and Marble Mountain Air Facility by 81-mm. and 120-mm. mortars. No aircraft were hit, but two Americans and two Vietnamese were killed and a number wounded. The disturbing thing was the use of 120-mm. mortar. This caliber of weapon had been encountered in I Corps only

once before, in an attack against Khe Sanh Special Forces camp, near the Laotian border.

FIRST MARINE DIVISION

As a result of Secretary McNamara's November visit and subsequent, more detailed conferences held at CinCPac in January, the introduction of the 1st Marine Division into Vietnam was approved. The 7th Marines were already there, as were the 1st and 2d Battalions, 1st Marines. The remainder of the 1st Regiment and the 5th Marines were scheduled to arrive at the rate of about one BLT per month through June.

In March, with two-thirds of the 1st Marine Division in place, Major General Lewis J. Fields would move his flag forward to Chu Lai. The zone of action assigned to the 1st Marine Division coincided with that of the 2d ARVN Division: the southern two provinces of I Corps, Quang Tin and Quang Ngai.

DOUBLE EAGLE

Another Task Force Delta operation began on 28 January 1966. This was Double Eagle, the most ambitious yet tried, and coordinated not only with I Corps but with II Corps and the U. S. Army's Field Force Victor. The target was the 325A PAVN Division, believed to be straddling the border between the provinces of Quang Ngai and Binh Dinh.

The 3d Battalion, 1st Marines (Lieutenant Colonel James R. Young), and 2d Battalion, 4th Marines (Lieutenant Colonel Rodolpho L. Trevina), came across the beach, 20 miles south of the town of Quang Ngai and close to Thach Tru, scene of the November fight with the PAVN, in the largest amphibious operation of the war up to that time. Commodore Maddocks was Commander, Amphibious Task Force. His flagship was the USS *Paul Revere* (APA-248), and there were two other attack transports, an attack cargo ship, three LSTs, two LSDs, an LPH, a cruiser, a destroyer, and two auxiliaries.

The Special Landing Force—now 2d Battalion, 3d Marines (Lieutenant Colonel William K. Horn), and HMM-363 (Lieutenant Colonel James Aldworth)—was in floating reserve, aboard the USS *Valley Forge* (LPH-8), the *Monticello* (LSD-35), and the *Montrose* (APA-212). On D plus One, 2d Battalion, 3d Marines, was helilifted from the Amphibious Ready Group to an objective area five miles west of the landing beaches.

On D plus Four, 2d Battalion, 9th Marines (Lieutenant Colonel William F. Donahue, Jr.), moved from a ready position at Quang Ngai airstrip into the mountains northwest of the beach, in exploitation of the first of three B-52 strikes.

It was a hopscotch kind of battle; contacts were intermittent and seldom solid. It soon became apparent that most of the North Vietnamese had moved south into Binh Dinh province. There—in an operation known first as Masher and, later, to sound less bellicose, as Operation White Wing—the 1st Air Cavalry Division and II Corps troops fought a larger battle north of Bong Son and on into An Lao Valley.

There were reports that the enemy was concentrating west of Tam Ky, north of Chu Lai. Phase I of Double Eagle ended (VC body count 312) on 19 February, and Task Force Delta moved by helicopter and truck to the new battle area to begin Phase II, which lasted until 1 March; the body count was 125 VC.

Honolulu Conference

The Honolulu Conference, the meeting between President Johnson and Premier Ky, held from 6 to 8 February 1966, ended with a declaration which emphasized winning the war through a combination of military action and expanded civic reforms. The joint communique issued at the end of the conference included the statement:

"The leaders of the two governments received comprehensive reports on the intensified program of rural construction. The Government of Vietnam set forth a plan for efforts of particular strength and intensity in areas of high priority, and the President gave directions to insure full and prompt support by all agencies of the U. S. Government."

Two of the points agreed upon as essential for rapid progress were:

"Continued emphasis by both Vietnamese and all forces on the effort to build democracy in the rural areas—an effort as important as the military battle itself."

"Concentration of resources—both Vietnamese and American—in selected priority areas which are properly related to military plans so that the work of rural construction can be protected against disruption by the enemy."

NGU HANH SON PROGRAM

Hoa Vang district, south of Da Nang, was a "selected priority area," and the Ngu Hanh Son program planned in October was consistent with the principles enunciated in the Declaration of Honolulu. But a combination of factors had made progress in the first five villages disappointingly slow: the original schedule was over-ambitious; the government cadre was undertrained; there was dissension and a rapid turnover among the Vietnamese leaders charged with the program; liaison between Vietnamese security elements and surrounding Marine units was imperfect; and, finally—perhaps most important of all—there was the concentrated effort of the Viet Cong to make the plan fail.

In late February and early March, the program began to pick up momentum. One reason for that was that Lieutenant Colonel Lap, commander of the 51st ARVN Regiment, was placed in over-all charge of both the security and rural construction aspects of the program. A compassionate man, brought up in the classical Confucian ethic, Lap had an affinity with the people and a maturity of judgment which previously had been lacking.

A second reason was that the 9th Marines, charged with supporting the program, had evolved a number of new techniques. The most useful technique, and the one which eventually attracted the greatest attention, was the one called County Fair. The first County Fair, a kind of dress rehearsal, was held from 24 to 25 February in Phong Bac hamlet, just northwest of where the Phong Le bridge crosses the Song Cau Do. Many such operations followed. Just as "Golden Fleece" became associated with the protection of the rice harvest, so "County Fair" became a generic term and was used throughout III MAF's area. U. S. Army units operating in II and III Corps subsequently developed a similar operation, and called it "Hamlet Festival."

County Fair

A "County Fair" was essentially a fairly elaborate cordon and search effort combining U. S. and Vietnamese military and government elements. The objective was to break down the infrastructure of the Viet Cong, the local force cells of five to ten guerrillas who, when main forces left or were driven from an area, remained behind and continued to dominate the life of the hamlets. Before an area could be considered "pacified," or ready for "rural construction," there had to be a scrubbing action to get rid of these hamlet guerrillas. The procedure for a County Fair went something like this:

During darkness, Marines, or sometimes Marines and Vietnamese regulars, would surround the target hamlet, in order to seal it off:

to prevent any Viet Cong in the hamlet from slipping out, and at the same time, to prevent their being reinforced from the outside. At dawn, the inhabitants were informed by loudspeaker and leaflets that the hamlet was to be searched, and that all residents must leave their homes and move temporarily to an assembly area.

Things were made as pleasant as possible at the assembly area. District and village officials met with the people (sometimes for the first time), and explained to them what was taking place. Other officials checked identity cards and conducted or verified the hamlet census. The first rule of population control is to know who is living where. In Vietnam, this is the sort of thing that can best be done by Vietnamese. It is almost impossible for Americans to do it effectively.

A temporary dispensary would be set up to give the villagers medical and dental help, and they were assured that such aid would be continued. Something of a picnic atmosphere was sought: a community kitchen was established, candy and soda pop were distributed to the children, and entertainment was provided—movies, live entertainers, often either a Marine band or drum and bugle corps.

The villagers were held in the assembly area at least overnight. Meanwhile, the hamlet was being given a thorough going-over by the search party. This was another thing that could best be done by the Vietnamese. In almost every case, arms caches, propaganda materials, or the Viet Cong themselves were found. Most often, the VC were found underground and were pulled out or blasted out by the search party. If they elected to run, or tried to escape, as they sometimes did, they had to contend with the cordon.

Hard Fighting

In February and March, there was a series of hard-fought, violent actions.

Operation New York was a crisply executed response to an I Corps request for help. It began about 2000 on 27 February, when 2d Battalion, 1st Marines, was alerted that 1st Battalion, 3d ARVN Regiment, was being hard-pressed by the 810th Main Force Battalion of the Viet Cong northeast of Phu Bai. The first wave of a night helicopter assault was off the ground at Phu Bai at 2320; by 0200 three companies were in the objective area. The Marines attacked in line across the Phu Thu Peninsula; the VC positions were well-prepared and in depth, and the operation continued with intermittent contact until 3 March. Final count was 122 Viet Cong killed in action; 6 crew-served weapons and 63 individual weapons captured.

On the evening of 3 March, CG Task Force Delta, Brigadier General Platt, was told that elements of the 2d ARVN Division had made a successful contact a few miles northwest of Quang Ngai city, and prisoners they had taken reported the 36th (also called the 21st) PAVN Regiment in the vicinity of Chau Nhai village. Next morning, Operation Utah began when Marine helicopters covered by Marine close-air support took the ARVN 1st Airborne Battalion to a point southwest of Chau Nhai (3) (hamlets within the same village often bear the same name and are numbered for convenience). The landing zone was hot with automatic fire, a Marine F-4 was lost, but the Vietnamese battalion landed and went into the attack in good order. It was followed in mid-morning by 2d Battalion, 7th Marines (Lieutenant Colonel Leon N. Utter), which moved into the fight on the right flank of the 1st Airborne.

In mid-afternoon, 3d Battalion, 1st Marines (Lieutenant Colonel James R. Young), was landed north of the action. The 2d ARVN Division was also putting in additional battalions, and the last opening in the ring was closed on the morning of 5 March when 2d Battalion, 4th Marines (Lieutenant Colonel Paul X. Kelley), landed to the south. In mid-afternoon of that day, the Task Force reserve—the headquarters of 1st Battalion, 7th Marines (Lieutenant Colonel James P. Kelly), a company from 2d Battalion, 7th Marines, and a company of ARVN scouts—took up blocking positions six kilometers southwest of Binh Son. Most of the action was over by dawn on 6 March. It had been a short, hard fight. The Marines claimed 358 killed, the ARVN 228; in all, about a third of the 36th PAVN Regiment's original strength was destroyed.

On the night of 9 March the Special Forces camp at A Shau, near the Laotian border, garrisoned by 17 Green Berets and about 400 various Vietnamese, came under heavy attack by, perhaps, three North Vietnamese battalions. ("Special Forces" camps were garrisoned by CIDG—Civilian Irregular Defense Group—citizen militia recruited for the most part from local Montagnard tribes. The Vietnamese camp commander was advised by detachments from both U. S. and Vietnamese Special Forces.)

It turned out to be an ugly business. Many of the irregulars wouldn't fight. Worse, some went over to the enemy, and turned their guns on the defenders. The brunt of the attack was borne by the Americans and some native troops flown in the day before as reinforcements.

The fight went on for two days; the defenders were backed into a corner of their camp. In marginal flying weather typical of the tail end of the monsoon season, Marine air and the Air Force went all out; close air support, resupply, medical evacuation. The Marines lost three UH-34s and one A-4C. There was no saving the camp. On 11 March evacuation began. There was panic among the irregulars. Some tried to rush the helicopters, had to be cut down by U. S. Green Berets and Marine crewmen. Evacuation continued on 12 March: in all, 12

Green Berets and 172 Vietnamese were located and lifted out.

Another call for assistance from the Vietnamese triggered Operation Texas. An Hoa, an outpost 30 kilometers northwest of Quang Ngai, garrisoned with a Regional Force company, came under heavy attack on 19 March. On the morning of 20 March, 3d Battalion, 7th Marines, and the 5th ARVN Airborne Battalion landed within a kilometer of the fort, while 2d Battalion, 4th Marines, landed seven kilometers farther south. The enemy, who appeared to be Chu Lai's old adversary, the 1st Viet Cong Regiment, was sandwiched in between; in four days of fierce fighting 405 VC died.

Operation Indiana was a repetition of the pattern. On 28 March, the 3d Battalion, 5th ARVN Regiment, was heavily engaged in almost the same location as the Utah battleground. General Lam asked for help. The 1st Battalion, 7th Marines, landed to the rear of the enemy; 69 VC were killed, 19 weapons were captured.

The Struggle Movement

General Walt had left Da Nang on 10 February for a month's temporary additional duty in Washington—including consultations with the Joint Chiefs of Staff and others, and the happy surprise of being nominated to the rank of lieutenant general by the President. When he returned to his command in Da Nang in mid-March, he found his counterpart, General Thi, in serious trouble.

On 10 March, there was a meeting of the National Leadership Committee, the military junta which had ruled since the previous June with Ky as premier. Thi, a member of the committee, was present. The other nine generals present voted to oust Thi on grounds of insubordination. Nguyen Van Chuan, the able commanding general of the 1st ARVN Division, was named I Corps commander.

Pro-Thi, anti-government demonstrations began to bubble up in Saigon, Da Nang, and Hue. On 13 March most of the shops in Da Nang closed down for half a day in protest at the dismissal of Thi. Longshoremen did not report for work. Students at the university in Hue went out on strike, and high-school students in Hue and Da Nang copied them. The leaders of the agitation began to call themselves the Military and Civilian Struggle Committee, shortened later to "Struggle Force." On the 15th, a general strike virtually shut down Da Nang.

On 1 April, Lieutenant General Pham Xuan Chieu, third ranking member of the government hierarchy, was detained by Buddhist students in Hue. He was quickly released, but his detention was accepted as a signal that the Saigon government no longer prevailed in I Corps. Two days later, 3,000 members of the 1st ARVN Division marched through the streets of Hue, behind their Division band, demanding the overthrow of the Saigon government.

In Saigon, Ky announced that he would use loyal troops to "liberate" Da Nang and Hue. On the night of 4–5 April he airlifted three Vietnamese Marine battalions—distinctive in their green- and black-striped utility uniforms—to Da Nang. The exact temper and inclination of the I Corps regular troops was not certain. The 1st ARVN Division seemed entirely in the Buddhist camp. The 51st Regiment and the Ranger battalions in and around Da Nang were divided. The troops in Hoi An were strongly pro-Struggle Force. Quang Ngai and the 2d ARVN Division were relatively quiet.

On 9 April, American noncombatants were evacuated from Hue and Da Nang. This was done smartly, some 750 being moved out by Marine helicopters under protection of U. S. Marine ground elements.

The same day, a mechanized column of Struggle Force adherents started up toward Da Nang from Hoi An. The column was cut in half at Thanh Quit bridge, some nine miles below Da Nang, by Company F, 9th Marines, who contrived to have a truck break down and block the bridge. There were similar, smaller confrontations between the U. S. Marines and both sides of the Vietnamese struggle. The mission of the Marines was simply to provide insulation, to do what could be done to prevent unnecessary bloodshed by either side.

This same day, 9 April, the reserved Major General Chuan resigned as Corps commander and was replaced by the more flamboyant Lieutenant General Ton That Dinh. The crisis seemed to be subsiding. One of the Vietnamese Marine battalions left Da Nang for Quang Ngai. The other two battalions returned to Saigon on 12 April.

But it soon became obvious that Dinh's sympathies were on the Buddhist side. On 15 May, Ky airlifted two battalions of Vietnamese Marines and two battalions of Airborne troops into Da Nang air base. I Corps headquarters was surrounded, Dinh was deposed and replaced by Brigadier General Huynh Van Cao. There followed a week of confused, nasty fighting in and around Da Nang.

On 17 May, anti-Ky ARVN forces took up positions on the east side of the Tourane River bridge. Vietnamese Marines took positions on the west side, then crossed the bridge. General Walt prevailed upon General Cao to withdraw the Vietnamese Marines. The anti-government forces then promptly moved forward and mined the bridge. General Walt now negotiated in turn with the Struggle Force, got them to remove the demolition charges, and got both sides to agree to turn the security of the bridge over to a company of U. S. Marines.

On 21 May, a government plan to attack an ammunition dump in east Da Nang, almost across the road from III MAF headquarters, brought a counterthreat from the Struggle Force that they would blow up the dump (and possibly a good part of east Da Nang with it) if the attack was not called off. Again General Walt negotiated, and after a two-day parley,

U. S. Marines moved in and took over security of the dump.

Meanwhile, the Struggle Force still held the center of the city. Cao was not moving fast enough to suit Ky, and he was replaced by Brigadier General Du Quoc Dong. The hard spots of Buddhist resistance were the three principal pagodas, and when they were taken, about 23 May, active resistance in Da Nang collapsed.

Attention shifted to Hue. For the second time, American noncombatants were evacuated. On 31 May, rioters sacked and burned the U. S. Consulate. The highway south of Hue was strewn with curious barriers: family altars were hauled out into the road to halt the northward march of Ky's tanks and personnel carriers. The road blocks were more picturesque than effective. Government troops moved north and into Hue. They had it under control by 19 June. Three days later Vietnamese Marines and paratroopers marched into Quang Tri, northernmost city of significance in I Corps. Resistance by the Struggle Force was virtually at an end.

It was probably the pacification effort that suffered most from the unrest. An obvious target of the Viet Cong was the Ngu Hanh Son program in Hoa Vang district. The district chief, never enthusiastic over the program, was one of those who had gone over to the Struggle Force. Not only had the VC reinfiltrated the hamlet cadres, but by a wave of terrorist acts, they had renewed their impact on the populace. There were also open Viet Cong attacks aimed at getting around or behind the Marines. Two companies of VC got as far as An Trach, four miles south of Da Nang air base and something of a civic action showplace, before they were intercepted and destroyed by 1st Battalion, 9th Marines (Lieutenant Colonel William F. Doehler).

The 3d Battalion, 1st Marines, was brought up from Chu Lai and put into the five-village area to help repair the damage. The Battalion moved in side by side with the badly shaken 59th Regional Force Battalion. Soon there was combined patrolling—the high-low silhouette of tall Marines and short RF troopers could be seen along the paddy dikes—and the security of the area improved dramatically.

Ky Lam Campaign

In March, when General Walt returned from Washington, Major General Wood B. Kyle also arrived and took command of the 3d Marine Division. A careful tactician, with a strong background in infantry operations and command, General Kyle wanted to clear up (in a literal sense) the situation south of Da Nang. This desire coincided with the long-term ambition of the 9th Marines to make a careful, thorough advance to Hoi An and the line of the Thu Bon–Ky Lam River. There followed a series of operations:

Kings, which moved the forward edge of the regiment to Route 14.

Georgia, which put 3d Battalion, 9th Marines, into An Hoa (another An Hoa, there are many in Vietnam), 20 air miles southwest of Da Nang, and important because a hydroelectric and chemical complex which had been begun there, became isolated when the Viet Cong cut off rail and highway communications, in late 1964.

Liberty, which broadened the front, by bringing the 3d Marines in on the 9th Regiment's right flank, and the 1st Marines on its left.

On Da Nang air base, the 1st Military Police Battalion (activated December 1965, one of the new formations made possible when 30,000 additional Marines were authorized in August 1965) relieved 3d Battalion, 3d Marines, as Air Base Defense Battalion. The 3d Battalion, 3d Marines, had served in Vietnam with the 4th Marines, 7th Marines, and 9th Marines, but never with the 3d Marines. When relieved from the air base, it returned to its parent regiment.

Operation Jay, conducted about 20 kilometers northwest of Hue, began 25 June and lasted nine days. The 2d Battalion, 4th Marines, landed north of the 812th Main Force Battalion, and 2d Battalion, 1st Marines, landed south. Caught in between, the enemy lost 54 dead the first day, and 28 more in the next eight.

South of Da Nang, the engineers, who had closely followed the advance—and sometimes preceded it—celebrated the Fourth of July by opening "Liberty Road" as far as Route 14. Before the end of August, the road was open as far as An Hoa, and once again there was land communication with the hydroelectric and chemical complex.

The Fourth of July also saw the beginning of Operation Macon. The principal adversary of the 9th Marines had been the Doc Lap Battalion, a Main Force battalion of great tenacity and skill, particularly adept at ambushes, mine warfare, and sudden, sharp ripostes against unwary units up to company size. The Doc Lap Battalion was now north of An Hoa and south of the Thu Bon River. Operation Macon was an open-ended operation that went on for three months. At one time or another, five Marine battalions had a crack at it, and at the end 507 dead VC had been counted.

Infiltration across the DMZ

A larger, more violent action was being fought in the north. During the first week of July there were intelligence indications that a North Vietnamese division, probably the 324th Bravo, had moved across the DMZ into northern Quang Tri province. The 2d Battalion, 1st Marines (Lieutenant Colonel Jack D. Spaulding), and a reconnaissance element were sent to investigate. What followed involved some 8,000 Marines and 3,000 South Vietnamese, and was the most savage battle of the war, up to that point.

Task Force Delta, this time commanded by

Brigadier General Lowell E. English, launched Operation Hastings on 15 July. To begin with, three battalions were engaged: 2d Battalion, 1st Marines; 2d Battalion, 4th Marines (Lieutenant Colonel Arnold E. Bench); and 3d Battalion, 4th Marines (Lieutenant Colonel Sumner A. Vale). The airstrip at Dong Ha, 38 miles north of Hue, provided a convenient staging base. Contact was made in the vicinity of Cam Lo on Route 9, seven miles west of Dong Ha, near a 700-foot hill, the "Rock Pile," which is a cork to the valleys leading down from the north and west. The SLF, then 3d Battalion, 5th Marines (Lieutenant Colonel Edward J. Bronars), landed at Pho Hai, and joined up with Task Force Delta two days later. The 1st Battalion, 1st Marines (Lieutenant Colonel Van D. Bell, Jr.), was committed on 20 July; 1st Battalion, 3d Marines (Lieutenant Colonel Robert R. Dickey, III), on 22 July. Five Vietnamese battalions also entered the fight, and B-52s bombed the DMZ for the first time.

Hastings ended on 3 August, by which time 824 of the enemy had been killed, and 214 of his weapons captured. In Hastings, the Marines met a new kind of enemy—fresh North Vietnamese troops, fighting with their backs to their homeland. They found the well-trained light infantry tough and well-equipped with Chinese assault rifles, automatic weapons, and mortars. There was a savage satisfaction in meeting an enemy who stood and fought.

But why had the 324B Division crossed the DMZ?

There is no way of knowing for certain, but two reasons suggest themselves.

First, perhaps the North Vietnamese were testing the short route into South Vietnam, to see if they could avoid the long, debilitating march through Laos.

Second, it might have been an almost desperate response to Marine successes in the Hue, Da Nang, and Chu Lai TAORs. Main force VC units had been badly mauled in engage-

ments in the spring and early summer. Local force guerrillas were also hurting as the pacification effort and accompanying security operations regained the momentum they had lost during the Buddhist troubles.

OPERATION PRAIRIE

When Hastings ended, three battalions stayed north to guard against a reentry by the North Vietnamese. Almost immediately, the 324B Division struck again. The new operation was called Prairie; the battleground was the same as for Hastings.

By the end of August, 110 more of the enemy had been killed, 60 more weapons captured. A fourth battalion was added to the operation in September. On 15 September, in a related operation, Deck House IV, the SLF (now the 1st Battalion, 26th Marines, and HMM-363) went ashore north of Dong Ha. On 25 September, having added 254 more enemy to the lengthening list of the killed, the SLF reembarked. As September ended, the total killed in Prairie was 943. The operation lasted until 31 January 1967. At one time, seven Marine battalions and three ARVN battalions were involved, and the total of enemy killed went to 1,397.

FIFTH MARINE DIVISION

The 1st Battalion, 26th Marines, was the first element of the 5th Marine Division to reach the theater. Reactivation of the 5th Marine Division had been announced by the Secretary of Defense on 1 March 1966. The Division's principal base was Camp Pendleton, where it filled in facilities left vacant by the departed 1st Marine Division. Regimental Landing Team-26—the 26th Marine Regiment with accompanying slices of Division troops, including a battalion of the 13th Marines, the 5th Marine Division's artillery regiment—was activated first. The 27th Marines and 28th Marines followed in sequence.

First to command the reactivated 5th Divi-

Men of H. Company, 2/4, use a jungle stream for a road as they move forward to meet the North Vietnamese 324B Division below the DMZ in July 1966.

sion was Major General Robert E. Cushman, who was also the Commanding General, Marine Corps Base, Camp Pendleton, and, since 7 February, Commanding General, 4th Marine Division. This last assignment resulted from the creation of a headquarters nucleus (29 officers, 69 enlisted men) to do mobilization planning for the 4th Marine Division which had not, of course, been called to active duty.

Manpower for the 5th Marine Division came out of an additional 55,000 spaces authorized for the Marine Corps late in 1965. The Marine Corps was building toward a goal of 278,184 by 1 July 1967. Its peak during the Korean War had been 261,343, and its all-time high of 485,113 had been reached during World War II. In fiscal year 1966 the Marine Corps took in 80,000 volunteers and nearly 19,000 draftees.

Manila Conference and Pacification

In Vietnam, the national election to choose members of the Constituent Assembly, who in turn would draft a new constitution, a step along the way to a return to civilian government, was held as scheduled on 11 September 1966. Experts guessed that perhaps 60 per cent of the 5,288,512 registered voters would go to South Vietnam's 5,238 polling places. If as many as 70 per cent voted it would be considered a clear-cut victory for the Ky government. No one expected 80.8 per cent of the voters to turn out, which is what happened, despite VC terrorism (on election day alone, the VC killed 19, wounded 120) and Buddhist threats to boycott the election. In Hue, stronghold of the Buddhists, a surprising 84 per cent of the registered electorate cast ballots.

A month later, when he was in Australia and on his way to the Manila Conference, President Johnson, thinking perhaps of a growing list of military successes and of more political stability in South Vietnam, said, "I believe there is a light at the end of what has been a long and lonely tunnel."

Certainly, a part of the light at the end of the tunnel had been provided by III MAF operations. A balance sheet struck in mid-October 1966 would have shown:

—an 18-month build-up to close to 60,000 Marines.

—a growth in Marine areas of responsibility from eight square miles and a population of 1,930 to nearly 1,800 square miles and almost 1,000,000 people.

—more than 150 regimental- and battalion-sized operations that accounted for a total of 7,300 of the enemy killed.

—more than 200,000 patrols, ambushes, and other small-unit actions that killed an additional 4,000 guerrillas.

—a cost to the Marine Corps and to the nation of 1,700 Marines dead and more than 9,000 wounded. (Over 80 per cent of the wounded returned to duty).

In October, General Greene said III MAF had "solid control of three separate coastal combat bases which we will eventually expand into one." Joining the three bases would give control of 2,700 square miles and nearly 2,000,000 people.

One of the efforts foremost in President Johnson's mind at Manila was pacification. A major change in policy was implicit in the low-key language of the communique issued at the end of the conference:

"The Vietnamese leaders stated their intent to train and assign a substantial share of the armed forces to clear-and-hold actions in order to provide a shield behind which a new society can be built."

This represented agreement by Premier Ky that Popular Force and Regional Force units would not be the only ones assigned security missions; as many as half of the 120 regular ARVN maneuver battalions would be retrained for this kind of duty. (In August 1967 Ky announced the number would be 53.) Major General Nguyen Duc Thang, Minister of Revolutionary Development, enthusiastically endorsed the new policy. A two-week orientation course was convened 2 November in Saigon, and each ARVN Division sent a 12-man team headed by a colonel or lieutenant colonel. The four corps headquarters and the elite General Reserve units—the Marine and Airborne Brigades—also sent representatives. Instruction was given by both Vietnamese and American officials.

At first it was envisaged that one battalion would be redeployed to each of the provinces in the respective ARVN divisions' zones of responsibility. Their job would be much like that performed by the 59th Regional Force Battalion and elements of the 51st ARVN Regiment in the Ngu Hanh Son program—primarily security for the work of the government cadres. In I Corps, 14 battalions would be so assigned.

When 1966 began there were about 15,000 trained cadres. During the year another 10,000 were graduated from the training center at Vung Tau. The total number was scheduled to go up to 60,000 in 1967. They were employed in 59-man teams, each of which, by rule of thumb, was supposed to be able to pacify two hamlets a year. Pacification entails eradication of the last vestiges of VC control, and the substitution of government control and services. When self-government and self-defense have been achieved, the team can move on to another hamlet. There are various indices by which a hamlet is judged "secure" or "pacified": one of the most pragmatic and useful is whether or not the chief sleeps in his hamlet at night. There are 11,000 hamlets in South Vietnam; 4,500 were considered to be under government control as 1966 ended, 3,000 contested, and 3,500 under Viet Cong domination.

On 23 November 1966 a directive placed all U. S. non-military agencies supporting revolutionary development under an Office of Civil Operations headed by Deputy Ambassador William J. Porter, number two man in the U. S. Embassy in Saigon. A few days later it was announced that regional directors were being named for each of the four Corps areas. These regional directors would have under them all related civilian efforts; AID's program, JUSPAO's psychological operations and information services, CIA's pacification activities. Assigned to I Corps was Assistant Deputy Ambassador Henry L. T. Koren, 55, a career diplomat and number three man in the Embassy.

Heart of the Matter

Over-all strategy had come around to recognizing what the Marines had insisted upon from the beginning: the overriding importance of the pacification effort. It was also beyond argument that, despite its special problems and setbacks—including the Buddhist Revolt and the North Vietnamese push across the DMZ—I Corps had made greater progress than the other Corps areas in coordinating Vietnamese and American approaches to pacification. The Joint Coordinating Council, the Golden Fleece and County Fair operations, and the Combined Action Companies could be cited as early experiments in cooperation that had worked.

By the end of 1966, for example, there were 58 Combined Action Platoons in being. In November one of these platoons got a rugged testing when An Trach, south of Da Nang, was hit by a North Vietnamese force guided by local guerrillas. The raiders got into the perimeter with small arms, rockets, grenades, and demolition charges. The defending platoon was battered but it held, and after a 40-minute firefight the attackers were driven off.

Near the end of 1966, Ambassador Henry Cabot Lodge said: "In this war, when we have beaten the army of North Vietnam and the main force battalions of the Viet Cong, we have simply won the opportunity to get at the heart of the matter, which is more than 150,000 terrorist guerrillas highly organized throughout the country and looking exactly like civilians."

General Walt said much the same. The battles against the North Vietnamese and the Viet Cong main force battalions were only a prelude. "Our most important job is eliminating the guerrilla." The ultimate solution lies in pacification. "I believe in all my heart that we are on the right track . . . but there are no dramatic changes in this war. It is slow because you are changing minds. That takes time."

(Naval Review, 1968)

Application of Doctrine: Victory at Van Tuong Village

O. F. Peatross, Brigadier General, U. S. Marine Corps

In order to build and protect a base for the use of attack aircraft in the Republic of Vietnam, U. S. Marines and Seabees landed across a sandy beach about 40 miles south of Da Nang on 7 May 1965. They named the area where they established the base Chu Lai. Shortly thereafter, Viet Cong regulars began to move into Van Tuong village, to the south and within easy striking distance of the base at Chu Lai. By mid-August, not only was the base flanked by enemy regular forces, but it was encircled by scattered guerrilla units, some of company size. The threat had grown to the point where these forces, totaling at least five battalions—perhaps as many as eight—might have been able to overrun the three Marine battalions, 1/4, 2/4, and 3/3, defending Chu Lai and its installations.

Fortunately, the Marines had an abundance of attack aircraft, artillery, tanks, anti-tanks, engineers, Seabees, and other combat support units. Even so, the situation looked bleak to the III Marine Amphibious Force/Naval Component Commander (III MAF/NCC), Major General L. W. Walt, U. S. Marine Corps. General Walt was responsible for the defense of all U. S. installations in the I Corps area, that is, the northern part of South Vietnam, and his infantry battalions were thinly stretched over three bases: Hue-Phu Bai, Da Nang, and Chu Lai. In

all three places there were installations vital to U. S. interests and to the security of South Vietnam, and their defenders could not be spared for other purposes. Small forces could be shifted from one area around a base to another and, occasionally, from one base to another, but there was no force available to conduct even battalion-sized operations outside the bases.

When Regimental Landing Team Seven (RLT-7) arrived in Okinawa in June, its 3rd Battalion Landing Team (BLT 3/7) and helicopter squadron HMM-361 re-formed the SLF that had been kept afloat for several years to cope with emergencies but had been committed ashore in Vietnam in late spring. These forces were embarked in the attack transport *Talladega* (APA-208), the amphibious assault ship *Iwo Jima* (LPH-2), and the dock landing ship *Point Defiance* (LSD-31). Early in July, BLT 2/7 had been committed to Qui Nhon, midway down the South Vietnamese coast, where an Army logistics base had to be defended. This is the seaward end of Route 19, which runs inland to An Khe and Pleiku in the central highlands of the II Corps area.

From the moment in May 1965 when RLT-7, then stationed at Camp Pendleton, California, was alerted for movement to a restricted area, it was given daily intelligence briefings on the situation in Vietnam, with special emphasis on the Marine bases. These briefings were continued while the landing team sailed across the Pacific during late May and early June. In July, when the RLT was in Okinawa, its commander and his staff, along with his logistics support group commander, visited all Marine areas in Vietnam. That tour gave the command a first-hand appreciation of logistics problems and, together with the continuing intelligence briefings, was invaluable in enabling it to prepare for commitment in Vietnam in any capacity.

Now consisting of RLT Headquarters, BLT 1/7, and the just-attached BLT 3/9, RLT-7(−) (Rein) embarked at Okinawa on 8 August in ships of Amphibious Squadron Seven for movement to Chu Lai, and arrived there on the 14th. Training of the RLT had been based on established doctrine, principles, tactics, and techniques, so it was well prepared for the operation it was soon to launch. Its naval and aerial counterparts in the amphibious ships, the naval gunfire support ships, and the Marine air support squadrons, were similarly well prepared. Training in the Marine Corps' tactical doctrine on the employment of the helicopter-borne forces was particularly important, as helicopter-borne attack had not yet been tested in combat. Every step of the operation was based on the training that had been given.

While RLT-7 was en route to Chu Lai, two days prior to its arrival, its composition changed a second time, when BLT 3/9 was detached to serve at Da Nang. Consequently, when RLT-7 landed within the security of the perimeter at Chu Lai on 14 August, it consisted of its Headquarters Company and its First Battalion only.

Discovery of the Enemy

The next evening, it was learned that a force of professional VC soldiers, estimated to be 2,000 strong (this later proved a remarkably accurate estimate), was in the Van Tuong village complex, 14 miles southeast of the base at Chu Lai, and General Walt was so advised early on the 16th. As was soon to be proved by captured documents, the VC were planning to attack the Marines at Chu Lai. They were well situated for the execution of their plans: they were near Chu Lai, they controlled the Song Tra Bong, the river between the Van Tuong area and the Chu Lai complex, and they had access to many sampans and basket boats in which they could cross the river when they were ready; guerrilla units elsewhere outside the perimeter of the base were to hold its Marine defenders in place by fire or attack, thereby preventing them from reinforcing those Marines being pressed by the main attack.

It was believed that the 1st Viet Cong Regiment, composed of the 60th and 80th Battalions, and a heavy weapons company, later identified as part of the 45th Heavy Weapons Battalion, comprised the main enemy force. The heavy weapons company was armed with 82-mm. mortars, 57- and 75-mm. recoilless rifles, and antiaircraft machine guns, and was split up to support the battalions. The battalions had an assortment of Chinese-made copies of U. S. rifles, light machine guns, hand grenades, and 60- and 81-mm. mortars. They also had some U. S.-made weapons of those types and some bolt-action rifles. At first, it was not certain that the 80th Battalion, also known as the 40th—a confusing but common situation in VC and PAVN units—was in the Van Tuong area. The 90th VC Battalion was believed to be in the area, but proved not to be. Some elements of the 52nd VC Company, a local guerrilla organization, were in the vicinity.

The Commanding General, III MAF, had to decide whether to keep his forces around the base and defend it against the anticipated assault, or to move them out and attack the main enemy before he could move. To take forces away from any of his bases in order to attack, would leave the installations from which they were taken in a precarious position. On the other hand, to allow the enemy time to build up his logistic support and to concentrate his forces might be fatal to the defense of Chu Lai.

General Walt flew to Chu Lai and assembled the key officers concerned: Brigadier General F. J. Karch, Assistant 3rd Marine Division Commander; Colonel J. F. McClanahan, Commanding Officer, 4th Marine Regiment; and Colonel O. F. Peatross, Commanding Officer, 7th Marine Regimental Landing Team. (The difference between a regiment and a regimental landing team is that the latter is a regiment reinforced by engineers, artillery, tanks, communications units, LVT units, and other specialized forces needed to make an amphibious landing. The 7th Marines at this time had such reinforcement, the 4th Marines did not.)

After a discussion of the advantages and disadvantages of the two courses of action available to him, General Walt directed that an attack be launched immediately against the 1st VC Regiment. The designated landing force commander, Colonel Peatross, decided on a dual amphibious and heliborne attack, and General Walt provided the means to make it. One reason for settling on the dual assault was that, even had there been enough helicopters available to land two battalions simultaneously (there were not), amphibious shipping would be needed to land heavy weapons and equipment, such as tanks, Ontos, and LVTs, as well as the logistic support needed to keep the assault rolling. Another reason was the tactical advantage gained by assaulting the enemy from both the sea and the air.

An overland assault, rather than an amphibious assault, might conceivably have been attempted. But against that was the fact that ships were available and ground transportation was not. Nor were there the troops necessary to make secure the only supply route, which would have had to be Highway 1, a route that goes through and beyond the perimeter. Nowhere does Highway 1 come closer than 12,000 meters to the Van Tuong village complex, and the combat supporting equipment and supplies would have had to travel those 12,000 meters by minor roads and trails. By attacking from the sea, all these difficulties would be avoided: the supply routes would be secure; so would the supplies themselves, as they waited offshore readily available to the landing force. And the seaborne assault provided something else that a ground attack would have lacked—the element of surprise.

The Plan

For tactical reasons, battalions were juggled once again, to make RLT-7 consist of BLTs 3/3, 2/4, RLT-7 Headquarters, and the necessary specialized reinforcements, totaling 3,000 officers and men.

On the evening of 16 August, the participating units were alerted for a combined amphibious and vertical assault on the 1st VC Regiment at the Van Tuong village complex. The assault was called Operation Starlite. The newly landed 1/7, under Lieutenant Colonel James B. Kelly, relieved Lieutenant Colonel Joseph Muir's 3/3 of its defensive chores around the base and, until Starlite was nearly over, the defense of Chu Lai depended mainly on that battalion and on 1/4.

Lieutenant Colonel Charles H. Bodley's Battalion Landing Team 3/7, with 1,550 officers and men, in the *Talladega*, *Iwo Jima*, and *Point Defiance*, was alerted to rendezvous in the Amphibious Objective Area and to assume the mission as RLT reserve. The *Iwo Jima*, with BLT 3/7 Headquarters and Companies I and L embarked, was at Subic Bay, 700 nautical miles to the east. She sailed at once. The *Talladega*, with Companies K and M embarked, was at sea not far from Subic Bay. She changed course immediately and steamed at her best speed toward Vietnam. The *Point Defiance*, with the remainder of the Battalion Landing Team aboard, was engaged in the salvage of the destroyer *Frank Knox*, which had run aground on Pratas Reef, 600 miles to the northeast. She, too, headed for the waters off the Van Tuong village complex.

The RLT-7 Headquarters had been loaded to land tactically in case it had to do so before it reached Chu Lai; but such was not the case, and it had landed administratively only two days before—on 14 August—and typewriters, communication sets, and so forth, had not yet been sorted out. While that sorting was being done, 4th Marine Headquarters provided men and facilities to help with the planning. On the 16th, the RLT and BLT staffs, representatives of the supporting arms, officers from the amphibious task force, and naval gunfire liaison officers assembled, and planning went on all night. By the morning of the 17th, operation, administration, and embarkation orders were completed and distributed.

While plans for the landing force were being drawn up, Amphibious Squadron Seven (PhibRon-7), commanded by Captain William R. McKinney, U. S. Navy, was alerted for the operation, and Commodore McKinney was designated Commander of the Amphibious Task Force. PhibRon-7's ships had been unloading RLT-7 at Chu Lai and 3/9 at Da Nang so, fortunately, they were either at one of those two places, which were only 50 miles apart, or they were steaming from Chu Lai to Da Nang.

Also fortunate was the fact that RLT-7 and PhibRon-7 had operated together in Exercise Silver Lance at Camp Pendleton in February and March 1965, and had recently moved together from Okinawa. Thus, their commanders and staffs had worked closely together before. Moreover, BLT 3/7, the SLF force with the helilift capability, had also been the helilifted unit in Silver Lance. Such happy circumstances as those cannot be counted on to recur.

On the morning of 17 August, a tent was hastily erected on the beach at Chu Lai for another briefing of the staff of PhibRon-7, the staff of RLT-7, and representatives of supporting arms. At this meeting, the many last-minute details of the planning and coordination were smoothed out. The concept of the operation, to land one BLT and RLT Headquarters from the sea and to land the other BLT by helicopters, was intended to lead to the isolation of the battlefield and entrapment of the 1st VC Regiment between the Marines and the South China Sea. The SLF, which could land by helicopters and by landing craft, and could resupply itself by either means from SLF shipping, was to be prepared to operate anywhere in the Amphibious Objective Area.

The beaches in the area had been surveyed by an underwater demolition team both before and after the Marines landed at Chu Lai the previous May, so that task, which must be done before plans can be made firm, did not have to be done again. Two of the beaches in the Amphibious Objective Area appeared suitable for landings. They are 4,000 meters apart, and both have sandy bottoms and foreshores but, beyond the high-water mark, they differ.

When selection of the landing area was being discussed, the Commanding General, III MAF, loaned his helicopter so that the commanders concerned could reconnoiter the two beaches and the terrain from the air. They observed that the proposed battleground was mostly rolling country, about three-quarters cultivated, and elsewhere there was thick scrub from three to six feet high. Hedgerows, ranging in height from six to 100 feet, notched the area, and there were a few rice paddies. The beaches were sandy, with dunes in some places as far inland as 200 yards.

After flying over the area, the commanders

returned to Chu Lai and discussed the characteristics of each beach—gradients, width, shelter afforded, tides, terrain inland, and so forth. Finally, both the Landing Force Commander and the Amphibious Task Force Commander chose the more southerly, at An Cuong (1) because, from there, the enemy could be driven toward Chu Lai and into an area where a blocking position could easily be established by an overland march from Chu Lai. The selected area was named Green Beach. The rejected beach was at Phuoc Thuan (3), situated midway between two headlands about a mile apart. Rise and fall of the tide, surf conditions, and beach gradient at An Cuong (1) would be satisfactory at any time of the day.

Next on the agenda was selection of the helicopter landing zones (HLZ), of which there were to be three, called Red, White, and Blue. In theory, it is desirable to land in the rear of the enemy front line, but in Vietnam there seldom is such a line. The VC defend the entire perimeter of whatever they occupy, and there are usually trees and houses within the defended area. The landing zones would have to be on open ground so that the aircraft could land, and far enough inland so that the VC forces could be isolated from other Viet Cong, between the helilanded forces and the South China Sea. They would also have to be far enough inland to permit the BLT landing over Green Beach to use supporting arms as it advanced inland to its link-up with the helilanded BLT. They would have to be away from populated areas because naval gunfire and air strikes would be used to prepare them. And, for the same reason, they could not be too close to one another. The center of each HLZ was to be about 2,000 meters from the center of the next.

The landing zones must be kept secure in all directions as long as they are in use. Then, as attacking companies move out, headquarters must either advance, too, under protection of one of the rifle companies, or if it stays in the rear, provide its own security. Though the VC hardly ever attack during the day, at night great attention must be paid toward protecting the rear, and a rifle company is often deployed for that purpose.

To ensure isolation of the enemy, all components of the RLT, those landing in the helizones and those landing over the beach, would have to link up during the early afternoon of D-day. That would leave the enemy with only one escape route, to the north, and that route could be blocked by a reinforced rifle company. Therefore, it was decided that such a company would march overland and be in a blocking position before H-hour on D-day. Then, with the landing beach, helizones, and blocking positions selected, the scheme of maneuver and plans for supporting arms were quickly prepared. H-hour was determined by light, and sunrise on the 18th would be at 0629. The ships were directed to be anchored 2,000 meters offshore at first light.

Concurrently with the over-all planning, the organizations chosen to take part in Starlite were assigned their tasks so that each could make its own plans. Because Lieutenant Colonel Muir's BLT 3/3 was nearest to the beach, it was selected to be the surface-landed BLT. By the same token, Lieutenant Colonel Joseph Fisher's command, BLT 2/4, located near the center of the base area, was selected to be helilifted.

Each unit began to make embarkation and landing plans. Just as did the amphibious task force and landing force commanders, they based their plans on *Doctrine for Amphibious Operations*, a publication called by the Navy NWP 22(a), by the Marine Corps LFM-01, and by the Army FM 31-11. Having been advised of the general area where the helicopter landing zones were desired, BLT 2/4 selected the specific areas, assigned one company to each zone, and held one in reserve. Plans were completed as quickly as they were because the forces involved were well trained in doctrine. Had there not been such a set of guidelines, or had the forces not been trained in them, the VC would have had time to strike at Chu Lai long before the Marines were ready with their attack.

Equipment and supplies were staged on the beach for the ship movement, and at Chu Lai airstrip for the helilifted unit. At 1400 on 17 August (D minus 1) men and their supplies and equipment began embarking in the ships of PhibRon-7 which had been chosen for the operation. Headquarters of RLT-7 embarked in the amphibious force commander's flagship, the USS *Bayfield* (APA-33); BLT 3/3 Headquarters, plus Companies I and L, in the USS *Cabildo* (LSD-16); and Company K in the USS *Vernon County* (LST-1161). The tank and well decks of the ships were loaded to capacity with tracked vehicles, their troop spaces were full, and their cargo spaces were almost full. Staffs at all levels conducted parallel planning in detail into the early hours of D-day.

At one point during the planning, the withdrawal of the landing force upon completion of the operation was mentioned, but the subject was dropped because there was not time to discuss it, and because the commanders of the forces involved were confident that the withdrawal could be planned and carried out on very short notice. As it turned out, the planning for the withdrawal was done aboard the *Bayfield* between 0100 and 0300 on the sixth and next-to-last day of the action. The smoothness of that operation also bore testimony to the soundness of doctrine.

The commodore got under way at 2200, well after dark, and in order to deceive any of the many sampans and junks in the area that might be VC reconnaissance craft, sailed his ships on an easterly heading, then turned back in time to make H-hour.

The Assault

Operation Starlite actually began unobtrusively at 1000 on D minus 1, 17 August, when Company M of BLT 3/3 left Chu Lai in LVTs, moved out into the South China Sea, and went inland on the northwestern face of the Trung Phan peninsula. From there, they proceeded on foot in a southeasterly direction to occupy a blocking position in the northern sector of the Amphibious Objective Area. Despite the presence of a hostile regiment, sending a single company of Marines involved little risk so long as they were in defensible terrain and were covered by naval gunfire, artillery, and aircraft. In point of fact, on several previous occasions, 3/3 had sent patrols down to this position and had experienced no difficulties. Indeed, up to the time of this writing, the VC have never moved a battalion or larger force during daylight in order to attack a Marine unit of company size or larger.

At 0600 on D-day, the 18th, two helicopter squadrons, HMM-261 and HMM-163, with 36 UH-34 aircraft, and BLT 2/4, less Company F, which remained behind as battalion reserve and also as part of the Chu Lai defenses, were staged at the Chu Lai airstrip.

Considering the short space of time in which this operation was planned and executed, we were fortunate to have three ships to lend gunfire support. The three were the USS *Galveston* (CLG-3), with six 6-inch and six 5-inch guns, and the USS *Orleck* (DD-886) and USS *Prichett* (DD-561), each with four 5-inch guns. Just before H-hour, the first two steamed into the Amphibious Objective Area and took their stations. The captains of these ships did not attend the pre-landing conferences, but this is normal. If the captains of the gunfire support ships are familiar with the doctrine on amphibious operations and their gunnery officers have detailed knowledge of the naval gunfire support role, it will be sufficient—as it was in this case—for the gunfire support officer of the amphibious task force to be present at planning conferences.

At H-hour, 0630, 1st Marine Aircraft Wing squadrons VMA-214 and 225, flying the A-4, VMFA-311, 513, and 542, flying the F-4, and VMO-2, flying the UH-1E, began to prepare the helicopter landing zones. These aircraft could make about 20 air attacks in one hour. Throughout the first and second days, four jets and from two to six armed UH-1Es were constantly on station, and more airplanes were standing by. Throughout the operation, Marine close air support was all that could be desired in quality and effectiveness and, in most areas, in quantity. Two Army aviation platoons and part of a third, whose pilots and observers had been operating in this area in support of the 2d ARVN Division and were more familiar with the area than the Marines were, took part in the operation, providing seven UH-1E gunships and some Cessna OE light observation planes, a type no longer used by the Marines. On 20 August, the third day of Starlite, the 2d ARVN Division began operations against the VC to the south and west of the Marines, the closest point of the division's approach to the Marines being about 4,000 meters.

As preparation of the helicopter landing zones began, at 0630, Companies I and K of BLT 3/3, coming out of the sea in armored LVTs, landed abreast over Green Beach, I on the left, K on the right. The beach and selected areas just inland had been strafed from the air before the landing, but no bombing was done because there were a lot of houses near the beach.

After bombardment by aircraft and naval gunfire had made ready the helicopter zones, BLT 2/4 began to land. The first wave of Company G landed in zone Red at L-hour, 0645. The

second wave of that company landed 25 minutes later, the third at L plus 50, and the final wave at L plus 60, 0745. All told, 220 Marines had been landed. Meanwhile, Company E began landing in zone White at 0730 and Company H in zone Blue at 0745. Half an hour later, the Command Group (Headquarters 2/4) landed in zone White. The troop-laden UH-34 helicopters were escorted, ahead, astern, and on both flanks, by armed UH-1E helos. Just before the former landed, UH-1Es flew over the landing zones, ready to attack targets that had not been destroyed by the fixed-wing aircraft. More armed helicopters could have been used, had they been available, to attack both "close-close" and small, fleeting targets, as well as to provide observation over the zone of action and the general environment for our small units, such as squad, platoon, and company.

In temperatures up to 110 degrees Fahrenheit, normal load for the UH-34 for distances up to about 20 miles is seven men. Their average weight, including armored vest, is figured at 240 pounds each. When mortars, ammunition, and other heavy items are carried, the number of passengers must, naturally, be reduced. Turn-around distances must be figured closely, because, again naturally, the more passengers and cargo are carried, the less fuel can be carried. A choice must be made between keeping the fuel load low in order to carry more men and cargo per flight, and carrying more fuel at the expense of men and cargo. In the latter case, time will not have to be spent refueling the airplane at the end of each round trip.

As quickly as possible after the lead helicopters have landed, the landing zone must be secured against small-arms fire. In an attack such as Starlite, the assault rifle platoons will land on the side nearest the enemy and in the direction of attack, and will be followed by the reserve platoon. It will be noted that L-hour was set 15 minutes later than H-hour. This was done in order to permit maximum support to be devoted first to the beach and, then, to the helicopter landing zones, and thus avoid having to split the support between the two areas. Further, it was desirable that the stronger force—the one that came over the beach —should be established before the other one was landed. The beach-landed force was the stronger because heavy weapons could be landed with it, and because there was an uninterrupted flow of combat support and combat service support between the ships and the beach. Battalion Landing Team 2/4 had to land without tanks or artillery, because the helicopters available could not lift such heavy, bulky items. However, two tanks and three Ontos belonging to that BLT were brought in by ship, landed over the beach, and moved inland with BLT 3/3, until the link-up with 2/4 was made. Company I, 3/3, on the left flank of Green Beach, linked up with the heliborne force at about 1000 on D-day. No problem arose over linking the units and despite the separation of his companies, the commander of BLT 2/4, Lieutenant Colonel Fisher, was continually able to maintain control over them.

Company H of BLT 2/4 encountered moderate resistance as it landed in helicopter landing zone Blue, on the southern flank. That is to say, the company was opposed by the enemy but was not held up or prevented from maneuvering. The landing in zone Red, on the northern flank, was unopposed. Sporadic small-arms fire was the only opposition to the landings in zone White, and that was eliminated by UH-1Es and attack aircraft. No friendly casualties were sustained during the landing. However, as the forces from zone Blue advanced northwards, they met strong enemy resistance and had to have help from supporting fires.

At 0730, the tactical control elements of RLT-7 Headquarters landed on Green Beach. At 1200, when the RLT Command Post was established 1,000 meters inland from the beach, command and control shifted from the Amphibious Task Force Commander, Commodore McKinney, to the Landing Force Commander, Colonel Peatross. Headquarters of the RLT could have gone in by air with 2/4, but had it done so, the commander would have had to land without his tracked command landing vehicle (LVT(C)). This vehicle not only gave him mobility as soon as he was ashore, but also provided him with the communications he needed to control the battle. It is desirable— and, once again, in accordance with doctrine— for the commander to be where he can exert most influence on the battle. Being with the heavier of his two battalions and near his logistic support put him in the best possible spot for that purpose. As planned, by the end of the day, the Command Post complex was well established for the command, control, and administration of the operation. Logistic support was good throughout Starlite, and the flow of ammunition and supplies was sufficient to keep up the momentum of the assault.

Meanwhile, BLT 3/3's Company M, the blocking unit, opposed only by a few snipers, had advanced about two miles south during the night of 17–18 August. It established its blocking position, two miles directly north of zone Red, at about 0420, two hours before H-hour. At approximately 0930, helicopters delivered a battery of 107-mm. mortars of 3/12 into Company M's position.

By this time, the remainder of BLT 3/3 was advancing inland from Green Beach. At first, it met with only sporadic small-arms fire, but about 1000, as Company I neared landing zone Blue, where it was to link up with BLT 2/4, it took heavy mortar and automatic weapons fire from the hamlet of An Cuong (2), an area outside BLT 3/3's zone of action. Because the fire was preventing its advance, BLT 3/3 requested and obtained permission from RLT Headquarters for Company I to go into An Cuong (2) and secure it.

Besides other installations in the RLT Command Post complex, there was BLT 3/3's Command Post Rear, which was handling the battalion's logistics, an aid station, and five supply-laden LVTs. At the time, there was no armor on the beach, but nine M-48 tanks, two flame tanks, and eight Ontos were afloat in the assault ships. BLT 3/3 asked for the flame tanks and the loaded LVTs. The flame tanks were brought ashore, and they and the LVTs trundled off toward Company I. When they had gone about 400 meters to the north and west from the BLT Command Post Rear, and were moving between hedgerows where it was difficult to maneuver, they came under heavy fire from enemy 3.5-inch and 57-mm. recoilless weapons, mortars, and small arms. This was at 1225, and they were still 200 meters away from Company I. That chance encounter may have saved the Regimental Command Post complex from being overrun, for it seems likely that that is where the VC unit engaged was headed when it came upon the LVTs and flame tanks. Be that as it may, at 1305 when word of the encounter reached headquarters, Company I was ordered to the assistance of the vehicles. But it, too, came under heavy fire, and its progress was slow.

Meanwhile Company L, 3/3, the battalion reserve, landed across Green Beach from LCM-8s and an LCU. As it landed, it received heavy small-arms fire from just inland on the right flank of the beach, and was immediately committed to advance north, parallel to the beach, to attack this source of resistance. At 1305, when Company I was ordered to assist the LVTs, Company L was switched to the position formerly held by Company I, thus placing companies K and L abreast in the assault. These two companies advanced against light and

sporadic small-arms fire until 1525, when Company K became engaged in a fire fight. Preparatory fires were called down from a platoon of 155-mm. guns and a battery of howitzers located on the north side of the mouth of the Song Tra Bong, from Marine aircraft overhead, and from the ships. Both companies then assaulted and carried a hill about 1,500 meters north-northeast of the Command Post complex, where they established a perimeter defense for the night.

With both of his original battalions fully committed, these heated engagements resulted in the RLT Commander halting the attack temporarily and, at 1400, requesting that Lieutenant Colonel Bodley's BLT 3/7, most of which had arrived in the Amphibious Objective Area, be landed. True enough, the victory would have been won if the reserve had not been used—air, artillery, and naval gunfire would have seen to that—but it would have been even more "touch and go" than it was, and the VC would have been able to inflict heavier casualties than they did on our troops. At 1600 Company L of BLT 3/7 landed at the RLT-7 Command Post complex in HMM-361 helicopters from the *Iwo Jima*, which had steamed into the Amphibious Objective Area at 0930 that morning. The *Talladega* arrived at 1400 and the *Point Defiance*, with the armor of 3/7, followed shortly after midnight.

By nightfall on D-day, Company L of 3/7 was heavily engaged with the enemy at a point just short of landing zone Blue. This company relieved the enemy pressure to such an extent that one platoon of Company H, 2/4, which had had a hard day's fighting and had become separated from the rest of the company, could be taken out of the area. The relieved platoon was ordered to the Regimental Command Post complex where it joined Company I, 3/7, which had been helilifted in from the *Iwo Jima* about 1730. All units in the area of zone Blue engaged the enemy at close range until early morning.

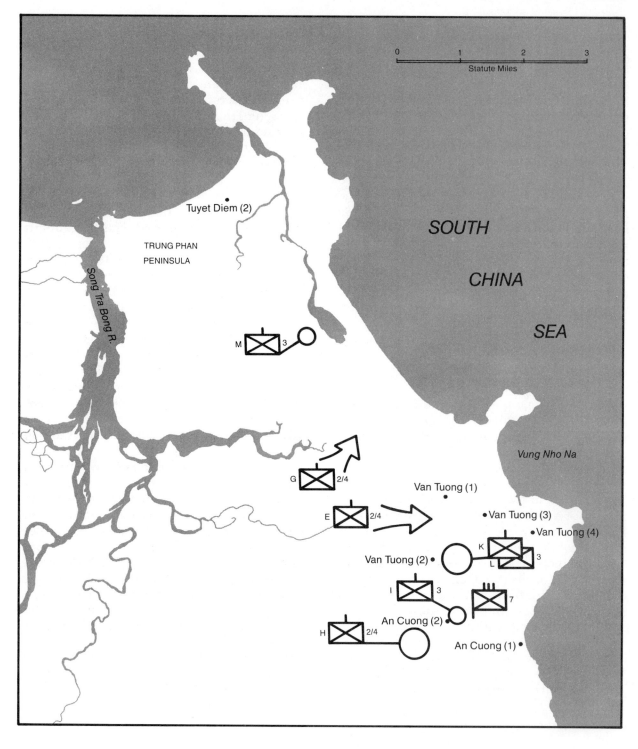

About midnight, LCMs and LCVPs from the *Talladega* landed Company M, 3/7, on Green Beach, and, in accordance with amphibious doctrine, that company provided security for the beach that night, while Company I, 3/7, and the platoon from H, 2/4, guarded the Command Post complex.

The Second Day's Fighting

The following morning, 19 August, BLT 3/7 was ordered to attack and to seize both the area about landing zone Blue and the area where the LVTs and flame tanks had been engaged. The latter had also been hotly contested during the night. At 0900, following preparatory fires, Companies I and M of BLT 3/7 attacked and by 1200 had destroyed organized resistance in the areas they had been ordered to seize. They spent the rest of the day disposing of pockets of resistance, and searching and destroying caves. Company L of BLT 3/7 had been detached temporarily to 3/3, and Company K was still being held in reserve afloat in the *Talladega*.

Meanwhile, at 0700 on the 19th, BLT 2/4 and BLT 3/3, supported by air, naval gunfire, and artillery, resumed their attacks, and encountered resistance varying from light to heavy. Some of the artillery support came from the big weapons at Chu Lai, and some from the 107-mm. mortars with Company M, 3/3, in the blocking position about 6,000 meters to the north-northwest. That was the only Marine artillery in the battle area supporting the operation but, afloat in the ships of the Special Landing Force, there was a battery of 107-mm. mortars and one of 105-mm. howitzers that

could be brought in, if needed. Tanks helped in the advance, as they had done since they were brought ashore on the first day, and were especially useful in attacking fortifications dug in open ground, but there were few such installations. When a helicopter was downed near landing zone Blue, three tanks and a squad of riflemen put up a successful defense until repairs were completed and the aircraft was able to lift off, having spent nearly four hours under fire.

Company H of 2/4, still hotly engaged near the site of its landing in HLZ Blue 24 hours earlier, shared the morning success of BLT 3/7's two companies. Companies G and E of 2/4, which had landed the day before in helicopter landing zones Red and White, respectively, had had an easier time of it. They met only sporadic fire, suffered some casualties, but were able to make substantial progress in their easterly push towards the sea. Company G advanced 2,000 meters on the first day, and had as far again to go to reach the sea. Company E, after taking its casualties within 800 meters of the landing zone, had advanced 2,500 meters towards the sea, and had another 2,500 meters to go.

Battalion Landing Team 3/3, with Company L on the right, K in the middle, and Company L, 3/7, on the left, jumped off from the perimeter it had established around the hill the night before. As these Marines drove north, they neared the hamlet of Phuoc Thuan (3) on the shore of a small bight, Vung Nho Na, the site of the rejected landing beach. Here, intense small-arms and mortar fire were encountered, but artillery and air were called in and lent

Tactical movements of Regimental Landing Team 7 on the afternoon and evening of D-day. The ships of Amphibious Squadron 7, an APA, an LSD, and an LST, were anchored 2,000 meters offshore. Later they were joined by those ships with the Special Landing Force—an APA, an LSD, and an LPH. Naval gunfire support was provided by a light cruiser and a pair of destroyers. The second day's fighting took place in much the same locations as the first day's. Thereafter, Marines moved north and south seeking remnants of the foe. The last elements of the landing force returned to Chu Lai on 24 August.

support until all fire from the enemy had ceased. That was the end of the heavy fighting.

What was believed to be the VC regimental headquarters was captured in Van Tuong village that day. Evidence that it was a headquarters was scanty: there was the fact that the defenses were structured to repel any attack on Van Tuong village; there was knowledge of the VC habit of locating a regimental headquarters wherever there are two battalions of that regiment; and, left behind, were a PRC-10 radio, a couple of field telephones, and some wire. This last was not much to go on—but, then, VC communications are never elaborate.

The End of the Battle

The next day, 20 August, BLT 2/4, whose mission was accomplished when it reached the South China Sea, was helilifted back into the base at Chu Lai. The same helicopters that brought 2/4 out of the action brought 1/7 in from the base to relieve 3/3, which, along with Company L, 3/7, returned to Green Beach. BLT 3/3 then resumed its old tactical area of responsibility on the perimeter of the base. There was not enough organized resistance left to justify three full battalions, so 2/4 was not replaced. The 20th was the last day on which tanks were used.

While all this was going on, the blocking force, Company M of 3/3, had been conducting patrols and setting up ambushes day and night, but it never directly encountered the enemy. Because it was established on high ground, it frequently saw small enemy units, but they were too far away to be reached by small-arms fire, and the company called down artillery, air, and naval gunfire. In the afternoon of the 20th, Company M was helilifted back to the base at Chu Lai, and the mortar battery went by helilift to the RLT Command Post complex. The whole movement was completed by 1925. Though it met no VC, Company M served its purpose, for its presence pre-

vented the enemy from escaping the battalions attacking from the south and west.

There was also great activity in the amphibious task force, whose ships were providing suport in the entire field of logistics: a surgical team and a fuel dump, for example, and, when the need for them was over, a place to evacuate all equipment, including wheeled and tracked vehicles.

Strains and stresses occurred in the logistic support, as demands for ammunition, water, or casualty evacuation, were made simultaneously by the engaged battalions. And there were times when elements of the logistic force could not be used for resupply as, for example, on the first day, when the five LVTs were tied up in the fire fight. But every critical demand was met. The teams that had been trained together demonstrated their desire to meet all challenges: the ships worked their crews day and night, and the surgical team used its skills around the clock for more than five consecutive days. Many instances of willing cooperation could be cited, but one will do: the USS *Cabildo* placed her people on critically reduced water rations for five days in a row, so that enough water could be sent ashore to the men directly engaged against the VC.

On the 20th and 21st, the last of the organized Viet Cong resistance was destroyed. However, there was still quite a sizable area to be cleared and searched, and heavy underground fortifications to be destroyed.

Most of the underground fortifications and caves in Vietnam are old, so their mere existence does not mean that the VC are in a given area. Some of the fortifications in Quang Ngai province, where Starlite took place, are over 20 years old, many others were built as long ago as 1954. The VC continually improve their installations, and it is not unusual for 300 to 5,000 people in a fairly small area to be working on them nightly for several weeks. Though they are well planned by VC engineers and approved by battalion or larger units, the majority of the fortifications are ill-equipped. Command posts of battalions and larger units are modestly supplied with chairs, desks, field telephones, lanterns, and candles. Most of the caves are used as stowage sites for rice, ammunition, and other items common to the Viet Cong military organizations.

The 22nd and 23rd of August were spent searching systematically for supply and weapons caches, and making sure that fortifications had been destroyed. These operations were conducted by BLT 3/7 in a series of ground sweeps to the south and southwest of the battle area. Beginning at the RLT Command Post, 3/7 advanced southwestward about 3,000 meters toward some sparsely inhabited high ground. Then, keeping to the high ground, where they found and killed a few Viet Cong, the force advanced south for another 3,000 meters before turning toward the sea, first in an easterly and then in a northeasterly direction, ending up at An Cuong (1) outside Green Beach. They captured about 80 Viet Cong and killed 13. Numerous fortifications and training sites, and quantities of equipment and weapons were destroyed. Three times during this operation, one company would be helilifted to a blocking position 500 to 1,000 meters in advance of the rest of the troops, and wait there until the latter arrived on foot. At 1400 on the 24th, when BLT 3/7 had completed its mission, it was directed to reembark before dark, and did so in the same way it landed—by LVTs, landing craft, and helicopters. It then resumed its mission as the Special Landing Force.

On the same days, BLT 1/7, which had relieved 3/3, killed and captured about as many Viet Cong as did BLT 3/7. BLT 3/3 had moved through the five Van Tuong hamlets tactically and therefore did not search or destroy any underground fortifications, but 1/7 did, using Ontos when necessary.

On the morning of 24 August, BLT 1/7 was ordered to march through the Trung Phan peninsula, capturing or destroying any enemy encountered. As the column marched, the *Galveston* and *Prichett*, ready to provide gunfire support, and the *Bayfield*, with her supporting arms coordination center in full operation, advanced at sea parallel with it. Also keeping pace were two LCUs loaded with tanks, which could be landed over any one of the many suitable beaches, if heavy enemy resistance suggested their use. Helicopters delivered water and rations to the advancing Marines, and evacuated the small number of casualties. That afternoon, at 1700, BLT 1/7 reached its pick-up point on the South China Sea, 600 meters west of the hamlet of Tuyet Diem (2), and met the LVTs that took the men back to Chu Lai. By 1800, BLT 1/7 was back inside the Chu Lai defenses.

Operation Starlite was completed at 2100 on 24 August, when the last elements of RLT-7 Headquarters, which had reembarked over Green Beach just before dark on the 23rd, landed at Chu Lai, and the Task Force was deactivated.

So ended the most successful operation conducted thus far in Vietnam. The threat to the base at Chu Lai had been wiped out. By body count, 645 enemy were killed. Later information, taken from prisoners of war, from villages, from captured documents, and in the course of other Marine operations, suggests a toll of just over a thousand enemy dead, or half the enemy's entire force. This does not count the wounded. Marine casualties were 45 dead and 203 wounded. Several helicopters and one observation plane were downed by enemy fire but, with the exception of one UH-34, all of them were repaired and returned to service.

Three factors contributed to the success of Starlite: accurate information, speedy reaction to the information, and the secrecy under which the operation was conducted. But, important as those factors are, the credit really belongs to the doctrine, tactics, techniques, and training of the amphibious forces; and especially to the Navy and Marine Corps schools which trained their officers and men to execute their various roles in amphibious operations.

The landing of troops on a hostile beach within 72 hours of the discovery of the enemy's presence, set a record for speed of reaction, and speaks well for the ability of our people to apply basic principles to a specific situation.

(*Naval Review*, 1967)

A Novel Role: The Logistic Support of a Major Campaign Ashore

Whether their weapons have been solid shot, shells, torpedoes, or aerial bombs, whether their ships have been driven by the wind, by burning coal, by burning oil, or by nuclear power, one of the most common acts by American naval leaders in wartime has been to establish advanced bases as close as possible to where the enemy might be met.

In the Vietnamese war, the main fleet already had its advanced base at Subic Bay in the Philippines, established well before the war began. It was from that base, carved out from the shore of an otherwise unused harbor on Luzon's west coast 700 miles to the east of the Tonkin Gulf, that the ships of Task Force 77 were fed, fueled, armed, and equipped. It was to Subic Bay that they went for rest and repair.[1]

And, as we shall see in the next section, all up and down the South Vietnamese coast, and far inland on every navigable river, the Navy established bases for its fighting boats as near as possible to the enemy.

At Da Nang, however, and before long at every inlet and usable river in I Corps Tactical Zone, the Navy did something entirely new. This was to create and operate the logistical springboard from which a large and seemingly endless ground campaign was conducted.

In 1965 the Marines were prepared to carry out a brief, but if necessary violent, struggle no great distance from the sea. They had few of the resources necessary to sustain themselves either far inland or for any great length of time. The Army was different. To soldiers, serious war only begins after they are well established ashore. So they are prepared to support themselves logistically as far inland as the struggle might take them. They also have organizations that can use seaports, can improve them as necessary, and can connect the ports to the fighting units. Unfortunately, in 1965 most of these were Reserve units, and in the Vietnamese war, Reserve units were not called up.

This meant that the Army was hard-pressed to meet its own needs in the primitive conditions of the II and III Corps Tactical Zones in Vietnam. There were no Army logistical units available to support the Marines in I Corps.

Who was left? Only the Navy, who, to begin with, had put the Marines on the beach. Like the Marines, the Navy was prepared for a brief encounter with the foe after which someone else would deal, among other things, with the problems of providing safe harbors, deep channels, suitable piers, appropriate storage spaces, adequate roads, responsive medical assistance, and effective perimeter defense of installations ashore.

As Captain Huff and Commander Collins make plain, Da Nang was far from being an ideal harbor through which to support a vast military endeavor. But, because for hundreds of miles there was no other harbor, it had to be used.

Moreover, while Da Nang was in South Vietnam, it was only nominally in friendly territory. The coastal railroad, which might have carried heavy shipments from Da Nang to staging points near the main fighting units, had been put out of business by the enemy long before the Americans arrived. And the roads, which sometimes were little more than dirt tracks, were so dangerous as to be unusable even for distances as short as those in I Corps. Long after the Americans were on the ground in force, the enemy showed whose territory it was. Captain Merdinger tells us that one bridge near Da Nang had to be rebuilt six times. Toward the end of 1967, the Seabee brigade command reported that "during one period 22 bridges were built while 21 were destroyed by sabotage." The VC and their North Vietnamese allies proved their belief in Alfred Thayer Mahan's observation that "communications dominate war."

When there are sufficient aircraft of the right types and adequate fields at both ends, local aerial logistical support can be quite effective, as General McCutcheon's essay shows. But in addition to suitable aircraft and fields, the distances have to be right and so must the number of people and things to be moved. Even so, in aerial supply, things can quickly get out of proportion. For example, moving people and things the 40 miles between Da Nang and Chu Lai by twin-engined C-123s and four-engined C-130s, is an extraordinarily inefficient use of resources. Moreover, if a person or a shipment had to wait, say, five hours for a flight to his, or its, destination, that was a speed of advance of only 8 miles per hour. Was there no better way?

If there was water, as in I Corps, there surely was. But that did not come for nothing either. There was a river near the DMZ, another ran right through Hué and on to the sea, and Chu Lai was next to an inlet. But all of these were narrow, shallow, uncharted, unmarked, and bordered by hostile shores. All could be widened, deepened, surveyed, and buoyed. Ramps and piers could be built, fuel lines could be laid (and laid again and again after the monsoon seas tore and mangled them), and roads and warehouses could be provided. Captains Huff and Merdinger and Commander Collins tell us about these achievements. And, in the next section, Commander Swarztrauber will discuss some of the actions taken to combat enemy efforts to sink our supply boats and craft (or, to use the bloated terminology employed by our aviators over North Vietnam, "to interdict" our "waterborne logistical craft.")

As it turned out, the campaign ashore appears to have turned on our possession of such mundane ships and craft (their names give them away) as coastal tankers, LSTs, LCUs, YFUs, LCM-8s, and LARCs. The last-named were small Army supply boats which, when they touched the beach, could crawl up and continue their progress ashore on wheels. The LCM-8s could carry a tank, but usually they bore less interesting cargoes, though not often for any great distance. LCUs were able to make independent voyages along the I Corps coast in good weather. YFUs were superannuated LCUs and had much the same qualities. LSTs deserve a bit more comment. Almost all those used in logistical support in Vietnam were built in World War II. They were good-sized seagoing ships 328 feet long and capable of carrying several thousand tons of cargo right to the beach. They were simply built, cheap, versatile, and shallow-draft ships that reasonably could be risked when "better" ships might not be. None of these old LSTs now exist in the U. S. Navy, though in an emergency a few might be found overseas. The price to acquire them might be thought wildly unfair, but in any "Third World" war, and certainly for any "First World" war, there would be occasions when they would be far more valuable than many a newer and more "sophisticated" ship. As Captain Huff and, in a farsighted essay not here republished (because it was more prescriptive than descriptive), Commander Willard F. Searle, make plain,[2] the 205-foot World War II LSM, or some reasonable successor, "would have been excellent."

Without people, sensors do not notice, weapons do not fire, ships do not sail, and airplanes do not fly. But in the best of times people get sick and injured. In war more people become sick or get injured than in peace. And in war the enemy kills as many as he can. Usually he fails to kill them. But in any event, in his efforts to kill them, he wounds far more than he kills. There is nothing more valuable a combat force can do—at least one that wishes to continue being such a force—than to care for its sick, its injured, and its wounded. Toward the end of his brief essay, Commander McClendon makes it clear that the Navy skimps this part of its task—or at least it did 20 years ago. Still, when the war began, the Navy sent its doctors and dentists, its nurses and corpsmen, to where the fighting was; the rest of the Navy and Marine Corps made do as best they could. In addition, the Navy recommissioned first one and then a second hospital ship. Neither ship was new, neither was ideal. But as is usually the case, something is better than nothing; the people of the old *Repose* and *Sanctuary* proved they were very good indeed. In contrast to pre-Vietnam defense theory, it is now recognized that hospital ships have an important place in war. Recently two large commercial tankers have been converted into modern seagoing hospitals, with one ready for deployment from the East Coast and the other ready from the West Coast.

The new hospital ships show that we have learned at least one of Vietnam's many logistical lessons. The problem in many other cases is to separate those lessons likely to be useful in the future from the others, and then to assure that those most likely to be useful are acted upon effectively. How well we have done these things remains to be seen.

Notes

1. For a brief discussion, see Edwin B. Hooper, "The Service Force, Pacific Fleet, in Action" in *Naval Review 1968*, pp. 114–127. Rear Admiral Hooper commanded that force at the time of his writing. Most of his article dealt with subjects covered in greater detail by the authors in this book.

2. See Willard F. Searle, Jr., "The Case for Inshore Warfare" in *Naval Review 1966*, pp. 2–23. That issue was published late in 1965. Commander Searle's essay was written six months or a year beforehand.

Building the Advanced Base at Da Nang

K. P. Huff, Captain, U. S. Naval Reserve

In March 1965, a Marine force, soon to become the Third Marine Amphibious Force, or III MAF, landed in Da Nang to defend the local air base against the Viet Cong. Building the advanced base at Da Nang for the logistic support of the Marines and others, presented the U. S. Navy with a challenge in a field in which it had invested little, if any, thought, training, or money in recent years. Not since World War II had the U. S. Navy been required to develop an advanced base for combat logistical support, either for itself or for troops and air forces ashore.

Da Nang

Called Tourane by the French, Da Nang is on the South China Sea and, because of its harbor, is the natural gateway to northern South Vietnam. It is also the second largest city in South Vietnam, half its population of about 200,000 being refugees from war.

Da Nang's harbor and port are beautiful but, when the Americans arrived, bringing with them a large appetite to have things moved through that port, the facilities were antiquated. The harbor is the only natural one in the I Corps Tactical Zone—the northern quarter of the country—capable of anchoring scores of ships. However, its entrance is wide open to the winds and swells of the northeast monsoons, which last from September or October until January or February, and often make it impossible to unload ships. Only three of its deep-draft anchorages are protected at all from the monsoons. There were no mooring buoys and, under the influence of high winds, ships could drag their anchors in the sand and silt bottom. The depth of the anchorages at lowest low water varies from 32 to 52 feet.

During the monsoon, winds are often 20 knots, gusting to 35, and occasionally they are 30 or 35 knots, gusting to 60. They raise swells seldom smaller than 3 feet and sometimes as large as 12 or 14 feet, whereas in non-monsoon weather, the swells run from 3 to 6 feet in height. With the winds and the swells comes the rain, all together resulting in ships offloading at anchor losing 20 to 25 per cent of their time. Ships moored to piers lose, perhaps, 8 or 10 per cent. During the hot season, which lasts from May through September, more rest periods are needed, and this means that more men must be available to stevedore gangs. Men in night crews average more work than those working in the daytime, but their problem is that they have difficulty sleeping in the intense heat of the day. Although the harbor is large and deep, the channel in the Da Nang River (known also as the Tourane River and the Han River) is only 15 feet deep, which makes Da

Four ships, an LSD, two VC-2 freighters, and an R2B refrigerator ship, at the new deep-draft piers on 28 February 1967. Da Nang is in right background. The 15-foot channel lies to the left of the long breakwater leading up-river. In the left background loom the peaks of Marble Mountain. (Frank Uhlig, Jr.)

Nang a lighterage port for most ships, and restricts cargo discharge at the piers along the river bank to coasters, junks, and sampans.

Da Nang lived on revenues from freight and storage operations, but it didn't do as well as it might for it was tied to such customs as a minimum of 25 per cent female stevedores, two-hour siesta periods, and poor stevedore pay. There was no sense of urgency. The port captain and his assistant were capable, but they were hampered by inept management at the port director level.

On the west bank of the Da Nang River, the port had the 350-meter Commercial Pier, a 30-meter T pier, and a 60-meter T pier, two LST ramps, and a stone quay wall along Bach Dang Street. The quay wall was ravaged by flood in 1964, but sampans and small junks were still using it as a pier. In March 1965, an LST belonging to the Military Sea Transportation Service (MSTS) was damaged by a floating mine while she was at the Commercial Pier. On the east side, there was Tien Sha ramp, which could accommodate three or four LST and four

LCU. Most transient storing had to be done in the street, as did most staging. The exception, in the case of staging, was Commercial Pier where there were about 30 meters of space between the edge of the pier and some warehouses, whose doors were too narrow for forklift traffic.

Because of a preference for the old methods, Commercial Pier rarely used its one crane (a 10-ton crawler) or its pair of forklifts. It was the site of back-breaking individual labor. Unavoidably, the main supply route, which cleared the port, ran through the heart of downtown Da Nang, whose narrow streets were choked by a multitude of children, dogs, bicycles, and cyclos, still moving at the pace of colonial days.

Most of III MAF, the port's major customer, was on the west side of the Da Nang River, which divides the city, whereas most of the ramp sites and terminals were on the east side. When the Marines arrived in Da Nang, there was only one bridge across the river—a temporary, single-lane span with an 11-ton limit.

To alleviate that bottleneck, III MAF operated an expeditionary pontoon ferry to transport heavy lifts across the river. These inadequate means of moving cargo to where most of it had to go put heavy constraints on port clearance. The Air Force and the Army, both also on the west side of the river, were much smaller customers. Naval Support Activity (NSA) berthing and hospital and some Marines were on the east side. While NSA Da Nang was supporting the local U. S. military and naval forces, U. S. civilian operations and Vietnamese military forces were supported by their own freighters. Although NSA's operation was huge, its effect on civilian traffic in and out of Da Nang was insignificant, because it was not in competition for their stevedores, barges, or tugs.

Chu Lai

Chu Lai, some 50 miles to the south of Da Nang, is where the U. S. Marines and Seabees landed in May 1965 to establish a SATS airfield for support of III MAF ground operations. At that time, Chu Lai—a sandy waste of searing heat facing the South China Sea—was not to be found on any map or chart. Access to Chu Lai by road from Da Nang was impossible because of Viet Cong activity. There was a railroad, but it was seldom in operation. Logistic support, therefore, had to be waterborne or airborne. One might wonder why, since it had no harbor, road, or rail, Chu Lai was chosen. The answer probably is that it was suitable tactically, and no other place in the area would have been any better logistically.

An eight-sectioned amphibious pontoon causeway and a bottom lay amphibious fuel line, put in place in May 1965, linked the shore with the South China Sea. Four officers and 40 men of the WestPac detachment of Naval Beach Group One operated and maintained the causeway and the fuel line, and the Marine Shore Party handled the offloading.

Hue and Phu Bai

The third area of logistical support for the I Corps Tactical Zone, or ICTZ, was Hue/Phu Bai, 45 miles north of Da Nang, which was established by the Marines in April 1965. There were Marines at Phu Bai, but the only Americans at Hue were Army and Air Force advisers. Four avenues of resupply from Da Nang were available—water, rail, road, and air. Shallow water restricted resupply by that means to LCU and smaller craft. Further, even under the best conditions, negotiating the entrance to the Hue River was tricky, for a sand bar had built up and made it necessary for the last leg of approach to be parallel to the surf. Craft could land at the Col Co Causeway, near the mouth of the Hue (also known as the Perfume) River, or, in June 1965, they could sail 12 miles up the river to an offloading site at Hue City Park. The river was reasonably secure but, because there were no navigation markers, shipping stopped at dark. From Hue, supplies for Phu Bai had to go 12 miles south, by truck. Early in July 1965, however, the water level in the river dropped too low for LCU and LCM to make passage, and the entrance to Col Co was navigable only at high water and, even then, boats had to churn through the mud. Consequently, in the summer of 1965, there was very little seaborne resupply of Hue and Phu Bai.

Rail service between Da Nang, Hue, and Phu Bai was spasmodic, for the Viet Cong could cut the rails and blow the bridges at will. Vietnamese civilian trucking firms used the road, and Esso trucks carrying POL and other trucks carrying routine cargoes used it extensively and consistently. The Army of the Republic of Vietnam (ARVN) ran convoys on the road, whose switchbacks and hairpin turns over the Hai Van Pass made tractor-trailer operations impossible and restricted truck size to about 7 tons. Air was the only reliable means of delivering vital war goods to Phu Bai and, except for POL, which was delivered by Esso, Marine and Air Force C-130s and helicopters did the job. This grim situation would have been hopeless, had it not been for the fact that, at the time, the forces to be supported were relatively small.

Task Group 76.4

Onto this stage, filled with constraints caused by nature and peopled by a tough enemy familiar with the terrain, came the U. S. Navy with the mission of providing seaborne logistic support for the U. S. and Free World forces in the I Corps Tactical Zone. The Commander-in-Chief U. S. Pacific Fleet assigned the responsibility for the mission to Commander U. S. Seventh Fleet, and command of the task force, whose job it was to carry it out, fell to Commander Amphibious Forces U. S. Seventh Fleet.

Task Group 76.4, the amphibious logistic support group, was formed in June 1965 and given the mission of delivering cargo to the water's edge. It was not responsible for shoreside offloading or for delivery to terminal and transient staging areas. In order to keep all the work at Da Nang under one hat, the defense of the harbor was assigned to TG 76.4, making it an operational, as well as a logistical, task group.

Ships and shore units of the Seventh Fleet, Atlantic Fleet, MinPac, ServPac, and many individuals on temporary additional duty made up TG 76.4. To begin with, the *Merrick* (AKA-97) was the flagship, but she was relieved by the *Navarro* (APA-215), and the latter, in turn, was replaced by another APA. There was always a destroyer on hand, the first one being the USS *Prichett* (DD-561), and an LSD. The first LSD was the *Belle Grove* (LSD-2), with the men and boats of Assault Craft Division 11 (six LCU and seven LCM-8). The boat crews of ACD-11 were augmented by crews from ACD-12, making 18 in all. There were also 50 men from

the Naval Beach Group; a Mobile Inshore Underwater Warfare (MIUW) unit (relieved early in 1966 by a non-mobile group); Cargo Handling Battalions One and Two; a skeleton staff from Landing Ship Flotilla One (including the author, who was Task Group Commander); a UDT element; an EOD element; a nucleus port crew (from the Third Naval District); and individual sailors from Fleet commands (principally PhibPac) to provide the men required for stevedoring, security, and operations. At the end of June, there were 775 officers and men in TG 76.4, not counting ships' companies of the APA and LSD. A nucleus port crew consists of officers and men on shore duty who train periodically on a collateral duty basis, and are supposed to run an organized port, not to be amphibious, or to run a primitive port such as Da Nang. Nucleus port crews on the West Coast are called on to meet Atlantic emergencies, East Coast crews to meet Pacific emergencies.

The organization of the task group was parallel to that for an unopposed amphibious assault at the "commence general offloading" phase. Command relationships differed, of course, from those for an amphibious assault, but from the water's edge seaward they were virtually the same. Consequently, this assortment of skills, people, and units was organized into task elements with titles descriptive of their missions:

Title	Composition	Senior Officer
Amphibious Logistic Support Group	CLSF1, NPC	CLSF1
Flagship Element	1 APA	CO APA
Support Element	1 APA, 1 LSD	CO APA
Lighterage Element	LCU and LCM	Senior ACDiv Officer

Title	Composition	Senior Officer
Service Craft Element	YTL, YFNR, etc.	OinC Mobile Support Unit
Freight Terminal Element	CHB1, CHB2, Assorted Individuals	CO CHB1
Harbor Defense Element	1 DD	CO DD
Harbor Security Element	MIUW, UDT, and EOD	OinC MIUW Detachment
Chu Lai Element	NBG1 WestPac Detachment	Senior NBG Officer

Communications facilities were provided by the flagship, which had been supplied with half a dozen extra radiomen to meet the need, and were satisfactory for long-range communications. It will be seen that there were serious gaps in our ability to communicate locally.

At this time, command relations in Vietnam were sometimes difficult and often strange, but it must be remembered that a big build-up of U. S. forces was just starting, and the Americans were in the process of shifting from an advisory status to combat operation. The Navy had few resources "in country" under the direct operational control of ComUSMACV, and the Naval Component Commander (NCC) under ComUSMACV was the CG III MAF, Major General L. W. Walt. General Walt was responsible for component commander functions in the ICTZ—functions which were administrative in nature and were concerned chiefly with the development of bases. The senior naval officer in Vietnam was the Chief, Naval Advisory Group, in Saigon. Both he and CG III MAF reported directly to General William C. Westmoreland.

Colonel Robert Boyd, U. S. Marine Corps, was CG III MAF/NCC's Deputy Chief of Staff for NCC matters and, with a small staff, he directed and coordinated the flow of cargo from the ramps and piers. He was CTG 76.4's opposite number on the beach. Colonel Boyd and his staff were located in the White Elephant, an old warehouse and office building on Bach Dang Street in downtown Da Nang, facing the river. At this time, III MAF was located near the air base, west of the city but, later, it moved to Da Nang East, directly across the river from the White Elephant. For closer liaison with the NCC, TG 76.4 established an office, consisting of one room, one telephone, two desks, and a couple of filing cabinets, in the White Elephant.

Thus was born a partnership that worked toward a common goal, regardless of hardships, problems, or personal desires.

In order to fill the communications gap and to be flexible and responsive to the customers' needs, the two principals held a daily meeting at the White Elephant. This meeting, chaired by an NCC staff officer, was attended by representatives of the Marine Shore Party and Motor Transport Battalion, III MAF G.4, USAF, ARVN, First Area Logistic Command adviser, MSTS, Vietnamese stevedores, and TG 76.4 operations, freight terminal, and lighterage elements. At this meeting, priorities were set for ships awaiting offloading, lighterage and stevedore facilities were assigned to ships, offloading points for various cargoes were selected, and trucks (mainly the property of the Marines) were assigned for the following 24-hour period—0800 to 0800. Decisions made at these meetings were, in effect, set in concrete because of our inability to communicate rapidly with pier and ramp sites, cargo ships, lighters, tugs, and headquarters itself. Furthermore, because both boats and vehicles were scarce, supervisory personnel were tremendously hampered in getting about to

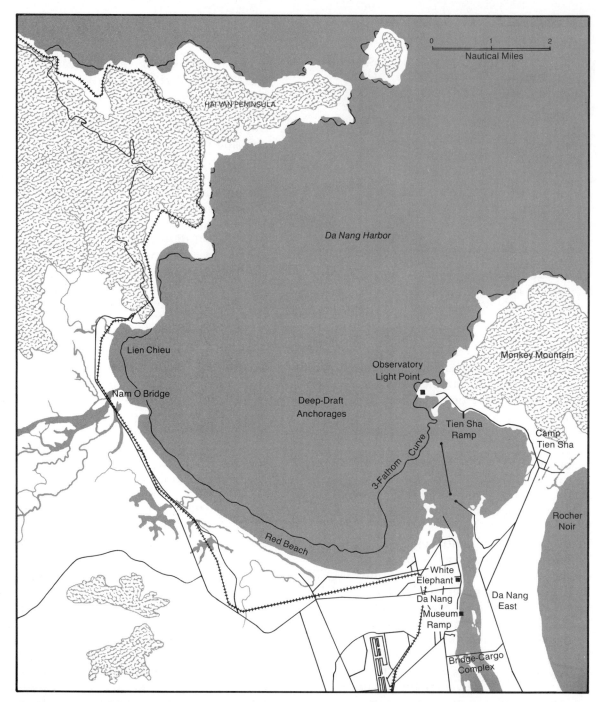

Da Nang, second largest city in South Vietnam, with a jet airfield and the only harbor of consequence in the I Corps Tactical Zone. The old LSTs could go upstream as far as the bridge-cargo complex. But until the lagoon behind Observation Light Point was filled in and the deep-draft piers built, larger ships had to be offloaded from anchorages exposed to the northeast monsoon.

assess and correct problems before the next daily meeting.

As mentioned above, Vietnamese stevedores attended the daily meetings, but only in the early days, when local lighters and stevedores had to be used. But, since civilian port operations took priority over military ones, as soon as TG 76.4 was able to do all its own work, the use of Vietnamese port assets was discontinued. Besides having our own sailors serve as stevedores, TG 76.4 used U. S. Navy LCU, LCM-8, LCM-6, YC barges, and YTL tugs, and Army LARCs.

Working hours were established on the basis of 12 hours on and 12 off, seven days a week. As it turned out, those who actually kept such hours were the fortunate few—the remainder were lucky if they were off the job six hours a day.

I can only agree with those critics who have described the Navy's logistic terminal operations in the I Corps Tactical Zone as reactive and not responsive. Through July of 1965, TG 76.4 did react as cargo arrived, rather than anticipate arrivals and requirements. However, considering the conditions that prevailed at the time, that was not strange. Tasks must be accomplished by reaction, while the ability to respond is being developed.

Naval Support Activity Da Nang

Late in July, we at Da Nang received information that it had been decided to expand the U. S. Navy's logistic role in ICTZ. The author received BuPers message orders on 25 July, and was relieved immediately as ComLanShipFlot One. He was to report to ComServPac as CO Naval Support Activity (NSA) Da Nang, continue as CTG 76.4 as directed by ComSeventhFlt, and report to the Naval Component Commander for additional duty.

The official OpNav notice established NSA Da Nang on 21 July 1965, and the responsibilities and mission were provided by CinCPacFlt

to ComServPac later that month. As first promulgated, the mission was divisible into seven parts; the eighth listed below was added in August 1965:

1. To provide common-item support for U. S. and Free World forces in the ICTZ and to operate such terminals as may be required.

2. To operate such ports and beaches between Quang Ngai and the Demilitarized Zone as might be directed.

3. To conduct offloading operations and delivery to terminals operated by NSA and to provide in-transit storage.

4. To consolidate POL requirements, receive, store, and issue bulk and packaged POL to all U. S. armed forces. (From their facilities ashore, Shell and Esso provided bulk POL to NSA Da Nang. Tankers chartered by MSTS supplied bulk POL to U. S. installations by means of fuel lines in the harbor. Late in 1966, RMK-BRJ completed a sea line for Shell from the South China Sea to Da Nang East. The ARVN had their own POL storage on the west side of the river, south of the Museum.)

5. To receive, store, maintain, and issue ammunition. (This task was changed in August 1965: To offload ammunition ships and deliver ammunition to customer at the water's edge.)

6. To operate subdepots at such places as may be required by CinCPacFlt.

7. To provide harbor defense.

8. To operate a station hospital.

It was fairly simple to establish the organization of NSA, in that there obviously would have to be departments for administration, operations, supply, public works, medicine, and dentistry. Until there were enough men on board to set up a separate department, the operations department was responsible for engineering and repair. Certain areas of responsibility were not immediately clearly defined: camp administration, and security from the land side of the waterfront, of the warehouse areas, of the POL dumps, and of other sites belonging to NSA Da Nang. These situations were resolved by the naming of an OinC of the camp at Da Nang—Camp Tien Sha—and by creating a First Lieutenant's department, which was responsible for all shoreside security. Both the OinC and the First Lieutenant were department heads.

Thus, in July 1965, NSA was established and TG 76.4 ceased to exist. But, until 15 October, the date set by CinCPacFlt for NSA to assume its tasks under command of ComServPac, it existed in name only. It had a force of 800 officers and men, all TAD from other commands, and the mission of conducting all the operations of the Da Nang terminal, but it had no assets of its own, no personnel allowance, no facilities on the ground, and no funds for military construction. Hence, while all planning was focused on 15 October, support from the Seventh Fleet, the type commands, and other naval units, continued to operate under the task group organization.

By 15 October, most men aboard were new arrivals, assigned to NSA, and their TAD predecessors had returned to their parent commands. Notable exceptions were the MIUW and CHB 2. Naval Support Activity started out with 12 LCU, 18 LCM-8, 16 LCM-6, 10 LARC, 5 YC, and 4 YTL. The APA, the LSD, and the LSTs that had supported the task group remained with NSA, but were never under its operational control.

Experts to advise, assist, and expedite the forming of NSA with the assemblage of men, equipment, and facilities it needed, came from the office of the CNO, the then-bureaus of the Department of the Navy (notably BuDocks), the Fleet Commander-in-Chief, ServPac, and other type commanders, Seventh Fleet, MACV, and III MAF. Worthy of special mention is the Advanced Base Division that Rear Admiral Edwin B. Hooper, ComServPac, established within his staff. It must also be said that without the cooperation, leadership, and example of Major General Walt, CG III MAF, the infant NSA would have been hard-pressed.

Planning for Port Operation

Basic planning for port and terminal operations, and for advanced bases, may be likened to an equilateral triangle—I like to call it the Triangular Concept of Terminal and Depot Operations—whose three sides are: facilities, equipment, and men. Together, those three elements yield "throughput," or the tonnage of cargo passed through the port each day.

There can be no substantial increase of throughput without each side of the triangle being increased proportionately. Tonnage moved cannot be increased appreciably by providing more men unless we also provide more facilities and equipment. Similarly, it's not much use having lighters to handle more cargo than the offloading facilities and trucks can handle. The story of building the advanced base at Da Nang is the story of the simultaneous growth of each side of the triangle, and each will be discussed in detail.

First, one has to compute how many tons will have to be passed through the port every day. This was done by taking projected force levels in ICTZ, allowing a ratio of one ton per man per day and, on that basis, computing what the total effort per month would have to be.

Add-ons to this figure are the construction equipment and material needed by the Seabees and civilian builders for base development. This is not to be confused with combat engineer equipment and material, which is included in the ton/man/day computation. I stress this, for that was an area in which planning figures were, at best, conjecture. In ICTZ, USAID and Republic of Vietnam Armed Forces had their own facilities at that time, so we did not have to consider their tonnages in planning personnel and equipment. In planning our facilities, however, we did have to consider their use of our limited offload sites so that they and the U. S. armed forces should not be competing for facilities. Although, in general, we found it best when we stayed out of their way and they stayed out of ours, arrangements were made for the joint use of some facilities— Tien Sha ramp, for instance, which the ARVN also used—and they worked satisfactorily. Joint use of that facility was taken into consideration when the amount of U. S. tonnage that this facility could clear was computed.

Being the only deep-water harbor in ICTZ, Da Nang obviously had to redistribute most of the requirements at Hue/Phu Bai, and approximately 50 per cent of those at Chu Lai. Chu Lai received most of its ammunition directly by LST from either Sasebo or Subic Bay.

When the proper factoring was done for weather, roads, staging and transient storage limitations, impaired availability of new facilities due to concurrent construction, and the sharing of facilities with other agencies, *Unified Action Armed Forces* (JCS Pub 2) was found to be the most accurate guide for computing offloading capabilities.

Despite the amount of work to be done and the haste necessary, it was plain that unless we kept accurate records, we would not be able to keep a continuous check on our capabilities and to refine our factoring technique to reflect experience. Such records were kept, albeit in simple form. One officer was continually busy on this project. A graph showing daily backlog, offload, throughput, and estimated tonnages is a great help in planning and analyzing, and is also a pictorial history of performance. For example, weather factors can be quite accurately analyzed, the consequences of too many ships to offload and of poor cargo mix can be determined, and the effects of adding cargo handlers and equipment are portrayed. The port operator cannot control the cargo mix of the ships in the harbor but, by judicious offloading, the shoreside facilities can be worked to maximum to avoid "feast or famine" situations. When warehousing is scarce, the fluctuating and suddenly changing needs of the customer can have a very big and disruptive effect: a ship with low-priority cargo might have to wait idle for a long time, while newcomers with more urgently needed cargo are worked. Hardship can be worked on customers in other places if, for example, a ship has low-priority cargo for one port stowed over high-priority cargo for another port.

FACILITIES

For many reasons, the base of the triangle— facilities—upon which all else is supported proved to be the most difficult to provide on time. None of the basic ingredients of a facility—real estate on which to build, money for construction costs, materials and equipment to build with, advanced base functional components (ABFCs), construction talent to deliver the finished product—were readily available.

The selection of facilities to be built was based on an estimate of the tonnage to be handled, and that, in turn, was based on a projection of force strength. The tonnage had to be broken down into the stages in which it might be at any time: offload, storage, redistribution from Da Nang to other places in the ICTZ, and methods of moving cargo, i.e., by truck from deep-draft piers, by LST and LCU for further distribution, by sea, air, pipe, or truck from POL locations, and so on. Geography played a large part in our choice of sites for facilities, for the real estate had to be not only available, but accessible. Although local politics were unsettled during much of late 1965 and early 1966, they did not affect our decisions on facility planning. Whoever happened to be in office as mayor of Da Nang was cooperative and helpful. The tactical situation also played a part in determining what was to be built and when and where.

Real Estate

Acquiring real estate was the ultimate in frustration. No one disagrees with the basic rules that U. S. monies cannot be used either to buy land or to build on land leased from private owners, that RVN-controlled land must be processed through the RVN central government in Saigon, and that cultural and religious customs regarding graves must be honored. But, compliance with all three rules when time was of the essence did, indeed, cause nail-biting. To illustrate how frustrating the situation was: a parcel of land in Da Nang East was selected for the first depot operation. It was to provide 10 acres of open storage, over 500,000 square feet of covered storage, 300,000 cubic feet of refrigerator storage, and the space required for an efficient flow of transportation. After locating the land, the first step was to determine the ownership of the property by searching Da Nang city records. Although the city engineer was a most efficient and cooperative individual, one did not just go to his office and check out city plans: for final determination of ownership, the NSA real estate officer had to walk over the land with city officials and the village or district chief. This called for making appointments at times mutually agreeable—more loss of valuable time, for city officials the world over are not easily hurried.

After establishing that the land was publicly owned, that is, the owner was the Republic of Vietnam, a letter, complete with annotated chart, had to be written to the NCC requesting use of the land for NSA facilities. If the NCC real estate officer determined that the land in question had not been requested by another U. S. agency, and that neither the Vietnamese armed forces nor the mayor of Da Nang had any plans to use it, the request for use was submitted to the ComUSMACV real estate officer for U. S. approval. At this stage, the graves entered the picture, for the request to ComUSMACV had to include a complete list-

ing of every grave, the family involved, and the cost of relocation. Every vacant piece of land in Vietnam in or near every city, village, or hamlet has graves—marked and unmarked—and the piece in question had more than 4,000. But, one does not move remains and grave sites at will: a religious ceremony is involved. Therefore, the NSA real estate officer had to contact the village chief and, with him or his assistant, identify the families of the deceased, tabulate their names, and call on them to arrange the amount of indemnification fees. This took time and patience—for if one appeared to be in a hurry, a myriad of obstacles could crop up. In this particular case, we had to level ground for a new cemetery and agree to transport the remains and their markers. The tabulated list accompanied ComUSMACV's request to the central government.

After granting the "right to use" the real estate, the government of Vietnam then had to provide piasters for grave removal indemnification. Since U. S. agencies were not allowed to pay indemnities directly to the families, these monies were sent to the city of Da Nang, which turned them over to the village chief for distribution. One does not have to read between too many lines to see the difficulties that could arise before a family got the hard, cold cash that permitted it to move the remains and grave, in accordance with tradition and with religious customs.

This time-consuming work, which in a counterinsurgency environment was delicate, was carried out by Lieutenant Harold Higgins, CEC, U. S. Navy. His charm, easy manner, and obvious honesty, coupled with hard work, determination, and strong will, enabled NSA to procure the real estate it needed, despite almost insurmountable odds.

Construction Money

There could be no facilities without money, and this money had to come from Military Construction (Milcon) funds. Naturally, before the engineers could develop cost estimates, we had to decide what facilities were needed for either reprogramming or inclusion in fiscal year 1965 add-ons or fiscal year 1966 funding. In this area, too, the assistance and guidance of the Pacific Fleet and of Service Force, Pacific Fleet, were invaluable. Particularly noteworthy were the advice and assistance given by Captain Custer F. Krickenberger, Jr., CEC, U. S. Navy, and others on the staff of the Pacific Fleet.

Studies were made and engineering effort expended to provide the NCC with a coordinated package covering Milcon requirements for the whole of the I Corps Tactical Zone for submission to CinCPacFlt and ComUSMACV. These two commanders could then, in turn, prepare all "in-country" Milcon requirements in a single package within assigned priorities. Things moved rapidly, and many projects were developed, costed, and submitted on the basis of where future operations might take place, and of what forces and support facilities might be required. This sensible approach allowed early consideration of most conceivable contingencies and development of a support package complete with estimated cost. Thus, when the NCC Base Development Board, which existed even before TG 76.4 was created in June, met, all ICTZ requirements were discussed and priorities were assigned on the basis of current and future operational concepts.

The second senior officer in III MAF, Major General Keith McCutcheon, was senior member of the Board, on which U. S. commands in Da Nang were represented. The Base Development Section, headed by a U. S. Navy Civil Engineering captain, continued to expand. The captain and his staff were reassigned to Naval Forces Vietnam on 1 April 1966 when that command came into being and its head, Rear Admiral Norvell G. Ward, became Naval Component Commander.

Concepts that had no hope of immediate implementation were not ignored. For example, our project for a subdepot at Quang Ngai would acquire a high priority, should operations and forces in that area be increased substantially. In the meantime, it was given such a low priority that it could not be funded. However, the plan had been made, engineered, and costed, and was ready to be put into operation if the tactical situation changed.

In this way, immediate needs were provided for and a solid base was laid for possible future requirements. Further, this system ensured that funds would be used to build the facilities best able to fulfill the mission assigned. The choice of the Da Nang deep-water piers, rather than "Scheme X," is an example of how this worked: the two deep-water piers, plus a De Long pier, which can be moved, if necessary, lie at the edge of about 10 acres of dredged land behind Observatory Light Point, on the east side of the harbor and butting against Monkey Mountain. Rock for construction was hard to come by, and there was only one road from this site to anywhere else. As mentioned earlier, most of the ramp sites and terminals were on the east side of the Da Nang River, and the only accesses to the west side were an 11-ton one-lane bridge and a cargo ferry service. However, a new bridge was to be built alongside the old one.

Scheme X called for the construction of a "small Port Hueneme" at Red Beach, on the west side, where the Marines had landed in March. This was to be done by dredging a channel in from the harbor, and dredging out a basin with marginal piers for four deep-water ships. Engineering estimates of littoral sand drift and of the dredging that would be required to keep the channel open were weighed against the limited natural protection offered the deep-water pier sites. The balance favored the latter, and it was decided to place the deep-water piers in high priority and to hold Scheme X in abeyance but available if substantially higher force levels should increase throughput requirements, in which case a package would be ready for funding. Real estate has been selected and programmed for future use and valuable months in the future have already been "saved."

We familiarized ourselves with the sea coast of ICTZ, and developed support packages for every location where facilities might conceivably be needed. These "paper packages" included dredging, roads, piers, ramps, and depot buildings for specific force levels. Thus, we were readying ourselves to move as operations dictated within funds allotted. This meant that we could have a project submitted for a support base at Hue, for instance, even though the engineers had not completed their testing of the Dam An Hai lagoon to determine whether that would be a better site for facilities than the Col Co at the mouth of the Hue River.

Advanced Base Functional Components

The fact that, at the time, NSA was permitted to order ABFCs for assembly and shipment without citing Milcon funds, probably contributed more than any other single factor to the rapidity of the buildup of facilities in Da Nang and Chu Lai. The ABFC catalogue was invaluable to those responsible for planning and operating advanced bases. Entire components, down to the paper clips, were catalogued, so that even though we had no real estate and no funds, we were able to plan and order the entire shoreside complex, except the deep-water piers, on the basis of projected total throughput and other missions. Delivery was made by sea from the United States. If ever a concept was proved, the ABFC was at Da Nang. This is not to say that the system had no defects: lack of updating of many components was one; and failure to preposition parts of the components overseas was a second.

Construction Talent

In the summer of 1965, four of the Navy's 10 Seabee battalions were in Vietnam, three in Da Nang—a detachment of one of these battalions was in Phu Bai—and one in Chu Lai. Seabee battalions in 1965 did not compare with the Seabee image created between 1943 and 1945. In 1945 Seabee battalions consisted of 1,000 men, whose average age was 35, whereas our Seabee battalions had only 450 men, with an age average of 23, and suffered by comparison in both construction capability and productive effort. The one ingredient found in both, however, is the spirit of Can Do, and the 1965 Seabees need take a back seat to no one in their contribution to the effort in Vietnam.

Raymond, Morrison, Knudsen, enlarged to RMK-BRJ when Brown & Root and B. A. Jones Co. joined them, were the joint-venture civilian contractors under the Officer in Charge of Construction (OICC). Because the civilian contractor had to be able to cite Milcon funds before he could mobilize his construction effort, and because there were no Milcon funds at the beginning, Seabee projects began first.

One Seabee project, the bridge cargo complex, had a 300-foot wooden pier (ABFC) with an LST ramp on either side, and two other ramps that could each take two LCU at a time. Additionally, there were 1,400 feet of marginal wharf which was dredged to only 10 feet, due to the length of sheet steel piling used. Twenty-five acres of staging area were built from dredging spoil but, because the spoil was silty and did not compact well, it was a long time before the area could be used. In fact, it was not usable for staging as late as April 1967. The dredge fill at the pier site, however, was perfect and compacted rapidly.

Construction contracts within certain monetary limitations could be awarded to Vietnamese contractors, and this was done. These were instrumental in rehabilitating the White Elephant, the first rehabilitation of Camp Tien Sha (which was an ARVN facility), and other projects whose cost fell within the limits allowed.

EQUIPMENT

The second side of the triangle—equipment—includes as many and as varied types as can be imagined. Equipment for use both afloat and ashore came from most of the systems commands and type commanders. Because it had no deep-water piers, Da Nang needed lighters, and because even shallow-water piers were scarce, they had to be lighters that could beach and offload through the ramp.

A study of the "Beneficial Occupancy Dates" of port development projects (deep-water piers, bridge cargo facility, piers and ramps, Museum Ramp, ferry pier and ramp) showed clearly that the craft and equipment we would need eventually were different from those we needed initially. But the latter were required right away, if the job was to be done.

Landing craft—LCU and LCM-6—were provided immediately from PhibPac. That command also supplied some LCM-3 and some LCVP, but the latter proved impractical and were replaced by 50-foot motor launches for personnel transportation. The LCM-8 and YFU were taken out of mothballs.

Tugs and barges—the traditional lighterage port equipment—were also needed, and again the assets of a type commander, this time ServPac, were pressed into service. The first to arrive were the 350- and 500-ton YC barges (open lighters) and YTL, which came under tow by either ATF or commercial seagoing tugs from the United States. The YTL were the craft available when tugs were needed, but they were really too small, and had trouble in seas over 8 feet and especially in winds over 30 knots. Of the various types of boat, the LCU and LCM-8 were the most valuable. Had any existed, LSM would have been excellent for the redistribution runs to Chu Lai, Hue, and the Cua Viet. The YC barges carried a great deal, needed few men per ton of cargo moved, and little maintenance. But, unlike the landing

craft, they did need piers. Except as a workboat for riggers and so forth, the LCM-6 was impractical and needed too many men for the tonnage carried. Some LARC-5s, originally Army-owned and -operated, carried USAF ammunition direct from ship to dump, thus reducing handling. BARCs were too big for the roads at Da Nang.

It is interesting to note that while the YC and LCM-6 had to be secured from operations when the monsoon swells reached 5 feet, the LCM-8 and LCU were able to stay alongside in seas up to about 8 feet.

The use of LCU and YTL with their "live-aboard" crews brought other requirements—water and fuel. Accordingly, a YOG and YW were requested. The latter got her water from a stream on the northwest side of Monkey Mountain, collecting it through hoses leading from the stream to a buoy in the shadow of the mountain. A second YW was sent to Da Nang in mid-1966. To service these lighters and yard craft, an LSD from the Seventh Fleet was stationed in Da Nang. However, the priority assigned to the building of a service craft repair facility ashore was so low that an afloat repair capability would be required for many months. Therefore, in order to allow the LSD, one of the most valuable and versatile of all ships, to be returned to the Seventh Fleet, Da Nang requested a floating dry dock with an accompanying carpenter barge, and a YR with an accompanying parts barge. One reefer barge (YFRN) had been sent to Da Nang before the formation of TG 76.4, but because refrigerated storage ashore would not be available until well into 1966, two more such barges were requested. After their arrival in the fall of 1965, we had about three days' supply during normal operations. This was still not enough, and an MSTS reefer ship was assigned to Da Nang. The YFRNs were shuttled by tug between the reefer ship and the pier space, which was a pontoon causeway used as marginal wharf, and situated across the street from the White

An LST backs away from the ramp at the bridge-cargo complex in February 1967. Later a new bridge was built parallel to the old one-lane structure visible at left, making simultaneous two-way traffic possible. The bridge-cargo complex was built by U.S. Navy construction battalions. In the background, the peaks of Marble Mountain thrust up from the lowlands by the sea.

Elephant. Da Nang's open fish market was moved from its site opposite the White Elephant, so that YFRN could be brought alongside the quay wall and unloaded into trucks on the street. Anyone familiar with Vietnamese fish markets in 100-degree heat will appreciate how welcome a change that was for the people who worked in the White Elephant. After June 1966 the reefer barges were shuttled, not to the space opposite the White Elephant, but to the new bridge cargo complex up the river.

Many of the merchant ships that entered Da Nang were not self-sufficient, and it soon became apparent that we needed a heavy-lift floating crane to unload them. A 100-ton float-

ing crane, a most valuable asset in port operations, arrived in November 1965, but it soon became a casualty and had to be replaced.

By September 1966, when deep-draft piers, augmented by non-self-propelled lighters and tugs, were about to replace self-propelled lighterage for most of the work in the harbor, Da Nang's waterborne assets were in balance with its shoreside facilities. Some tugs belonged to the Navy, others to U. S. towing companies. The self-propelled lighters would be used increasingly for the resupply of the outports, particularly as operations in Thua Thien and Quang Tri provinces to the north were being stepped up. The LCM-6 could not be used in such work, and the LCM-8 was not ideal. The

LCU, YFU, and LST did nearly all the resupplying. The YFU is the World War II version of the LCU and, when new, was called LCT. There being no piers at the outports, tugs and barges (except fuel barges) could not be used in outport resupply.

Communications equipment excepted, most of the ground equipment came under the purview of the Bureau of Yards and Docks. Warehouse forklifts and related equipment were under the Bureau of Supplies and Accounts. Planning teams, with the experience and know-how to determine the kinds and numbers of rough-terrain forklifts, cranes, trucks, and so forth, that would be required, were sent to Da Nang. Planned increases in the scope of operations were taken into account, and the occupancy dates of facilities were carefully checked against the availability of equipment, so that the sides of the triangle would grow simultaneously.

Great emphasis was placed on the rough-terrain forklift. This vehicle, with its huge rubberized wheels, each-wheel drive, and high ground clearance, is the lifesaver of cargo-handlers in primitive expeditionary conditions, for it is the only forklift that can negotiate the ramp on a beached landing craft. For each such craft, there should be three rough-terrain forklifts working, not counting those in maintenance. These vehicles should be programmed for the first 14 months of every cargo-handling operation considered and, as hard stand becomes available, should be replaced in open-storage operations by heavy-duty warehouse forks. The forklift that can position its forks horizontally as well as vertically is by far the best. Planners should see to it at least 1,000 hours' worth of spare parts, arrive *with* the equipment, and should program enough of the vehicles to allow for 50 per cent of them being down for overhaul and/or routine preventive maintenance. The hours lost trying to find a replacement for an equipment casualty

can never be regained, and when an offload site ashore is clogged, the bottleneck extends all the way to the ship being offloaded, and tonnages offloaded are consequently decreased.

A brief word on cranes: attention should be given to the mix of crawlers and mobile, or wheeled, cranes. A general rule is to use mobile cranes for emergency replacements, and for open storage of lifts weighing less than 15 tons; use crawlers for heavy-lift near the capacity of the crane, for stable on-site work at piers, marginal wharfs, quay walls, and ramps (for palletized cargo). However, it should be remembered that offloading through a lighter's ramps is the most time-consuming method of removing palletized and loose cargo.

By September 1966, NSA Da Nang had more than 60 rough-terrain forklifts, about the same number of warehouse forklifts, and about 18 cranes.

MEN

The third side of our equilateral triangle was men. Planning for increased personnel requirements and inputs timed to match the growth of the other two sides was difficult. We used several ground rules—all crews were scheduled for 12 hours on the job and 12 off, and no free time was allowed for. In order for self-sustaining craft, such as the LCU and YOG, to operate 24 hours per day, their crews were to be slightly larger than normal—they had living spaces to permit this, though it meant a little more crowding; non-sustaining craft were to have two crews each. Offloading sites were allotted two gangs per space, e.g., at Commercial Pier, which was 60 meters long and could handle two LCU at a time, we allotted four gangs. The size of a gang depended on how hot the day was, the kind of cargo being handled, and the size of the pier on which it was working. Normally, it was between 8 and 15 men. Hatch teams for merchant ships were planned at 14 men per gang per hatch. Harbor security forces were watch and watch, and their numbers were programmed to keep pace with the delivery of harbor security craft. The latter were: 50-foot picket boats; LCPL, Mark 4; and 16-foot Boston Whalers. The 50-footer was outstanding: fast enough, comfortable enough, and a good platform for .50-caliber machine guns. The LCPL was uncomfortable, but was suitable for checkpoint work. The Boston Whaler, or "skimmer," driven by a 75-horsepower outboard engine, was fast and surprisingly good in seas up to 8 feet. It was, of course, also good for shallow-water work.

The Public Works Department had a difficult programming task, for repair facilities were marginal and it was difficult to estimate the arrival of transportation assets. Programming of people to operate the warehouses and terminals was tied directly to the readiness of the facilities, and when the latter slipped—which didn't happen very often—personnel arrangements had to be adjusted. As more men were assigned, there had to be a corresponding increase in the support ratings, such as YN, PN, and CS. ComServPac was the "type commander" for NSA Da Nang. A new section of that command, the advanced base staff, working with EpdoPac and BuPers, worked miracles in providing both the numbers and the quality of men needed.

Future planners should profit from our mistakes, and the biggest mistakes in personnel planning were made in the planning for internal security, where the need was grossly underestimated in the beginning. Several factors were responsible for this—primarily lack of appreciation of the situation, and failure to realize that, though the tactical forces could clear the area of organized enemy units, each cantonment, terminal, and depot would require a sentry force to repel attacks by individuals and small groups. The original "fire watch" concept obviously did not provide for enough men. Moreover, in the early stages, before our real estate acquisitions were settled, we did not realize how spread out our facilities would be, with each isolated facility requiring security. Early in the planning stage, we foresaw using dogs, but, suffice it to say it was a long while before any dogs arrived. Future planners of advanced bases should be aware of the following limitations and abilities of sentry dogs: they cannot work more than one 6-hour shift per day, and they are not very effective in a noisy, busy environment. On the other hand, they are very effective on perimeter patrol, day or night, and they are a decided deterrent to sneak thieves, because nobody wants to tangle with 90 pounds of fighting dog. Again I say to those charged with planning personnel in the future: look critically at security requirements.

One of the most worrisome aspects of the personnel situation was housing. At the outset, in June, except for the few men who lived ashore, all hands were billeted on the APA. This arrangement kept us going for many months, but although the APA had 1,500 bunks because of inadequate locker space, she could handle only 900 or 1,000 men for any length of time. Therefore, she obviously did not provide the long-range solution. Three APL, which could billet 650 men each, were ordered as housing for seaside operations, and shoreside housing was to be built for the majority of the men. Again, construction of facilities required funding, and this was still in the future. Fate did smile on us, though, and through the efforts of the NCC's Colonel Boyd, we were able to take possession of the ARVN 2nd Division cantonment on Tien Sha Peninsula. This was an old French camp, most of whose buildings were hollow shells without lighting, plumbing, or other conveniences. Camp Tien Sha consisted of land, trees, some walls, and some roofs. We started reclaiming one building at a time, using local contractors—a slow process but some progress was better than none. The first men to move into Camp Tien Sha ate C rations, drank water from canteens, showered when it rained, and used the slit trench for other functions. The camp was planned to accommodate 4,000 men, and with the 3 APL (1,950 men, total), the self-sustaining craft (500 men), the station hospital (550), and the few billets in the city of Da Nang (about 200), we would be able to berth and mess approximately 7,200 officers and men, which appeared to be sufficient. However, construction priorities delayed the completion of Camp Tien Sha until March 1967, and the APA was the lifesaver in providing interim berthing and messing.

This discussion of our personnel problems would be incomplete without words of appreciation for the Marines. Had they not filled the gap at Tien Sha ramp, at Cus Ho ramp in Chu Lai, and elsewhere, until NSA could take over, the progress of NSA in other areas would have been much less rapid than it was.

Keeping Chu Lai Operational

Chu Lai, the second largest III MAF base in Vietnam and a vital airfield used for close air and helicopter support of combat troops, was accessible from Da Nang by air and sea only. Its open roadstead lies in a straight path from the Bashi Channel, and receives the full force of the northeast monsoons. Chu Lai had a pontoon causeway leading into the South China Sea, and a 1,000-foot-long, four-inch, bottom-lay amphibious fuel line terminating in 30 feet of water, enough to accommodate a T-1 tanker only. U. S. Navy AOGs, MSTS T-1s, and small, chartered commercial tankers were all used to shuttle from the station tanker at Da Nang. We planned to install a permanent line, 4,000 feet long ending in 45 feet of water, so that large tankers could offload directly. Ships' pumps are used to force the oil through the pipe. Force levels projected for Chu Lai in July 1965 and the amount of ammunition that the aircraft

would need, indicated that the incoming tonnage would be too great for one causeway to handle, even in a mill pond. And we would not be operating in a mill pond. That summer, we attempted to unload the SS *Iberville*, as she lay at anchor in the open roads, by using LCU and LCM-8 as lighters. But the swell made it impossible. Even under the best of conditions, such an open-sea operation would be highly impractical.

Thus, in July of 1965, not only did we have a serious resupply problem needing immediate solution, but we came to the shocking realization that, in two or three months when the monsoons arrived, we would be "in extremis." Just north of the airstrip at Chu Lai there is a peninsula and a river—the Truong—emptying into a small bay, the Vung An Hoa. On a big island across the river was a Vietnamese Navy junk base, which in late July or early August was overrun by the Viet Cong, and two Americans, an officer and a petty officer—half of the advisers there—were killed. After that attack, the base was re-established alongside the big Marine encampment, which could give it some protection. As is the case with all the rivers in the I Corps area, there is good water near the mouth of the Truong, but across the mouth where the current and tide lose their maximum carrying ability, a sand bar has formed, and the sand and silt settle out.

Nevertheless, the Truong was the only place we could hope to use for offloading, so a combat UDT surveyed Vung An Hoa and the river up to a point near An Hai village. The survey indicated a bar with only 8 feet of clearance at mean low water (which occurs several times a month), but inside the peninsular neck, sufficient water for LST approaches and landings on the sandy beach. Early in August, the author and several members of his staff went to Chu Lai to see what the situation was, and to decide whether to ask for Seabees to build an LST ramp to do foreshore work and, also,

The Cus Ho ramp at Chu Lai during the monsoon rains in October 1965. The men walking through red mud belong to Naval Beach Group One. The LST is the Cam Ranh of the South Vietnamese Navy. The bar is out of the picture at right. Upstream there is a small Vietnamese Navy junk base. (Ken Bumpus, PHC, U.S. Navy)

whether to request dredging of the sand bar at the earliest possible time. To get to Cus Ho ramp in August 1965, one had to travel over a road that LVT had cut through scrub and tapioca fields, and one had to be escorted by a Marine fire team. We decided to go ahead with building the ramp, but prospects for getting immediate dredging were grim, because the U. S. Navy does not own any dredges. Perhaps it should. It is difficult to describe our anxiety when, in mid-August, heavy weather, a forerunner of what was to come, demolished the causeway, and we knew we were faced with using Cus Ho or nothing. The Seabees dumped laterite and stone over the soft sand and, by mid-September, had the ramp sufficiently stable for us to offload an LCU without trouble.

At that time, we were still hoping for a dredge to level the sand bar and, consequently, had not tried to bring an LST in to the ramp.

But, by late September, when it became obvious that no dredge would be forthcoming and that, even if we had one, it would not be able to work in the surf over the bar during the monsoon, we decided that our only hope was to try getting an LST over the bar. Accordingly, about 21 September, with Lieutenant William Therriault, who in August had brought the first LCU into Cus Ho and knew the water better than anyone else, and Lieutenant (j.g.) Charles Burke, MSTS representative in the ICTZ, we went to Chu Lai to attempt to bring in an LST, loaded with 400 tons of cargo, and drawing 10 feet 6 inches aft. If we could have brought her in drawing 12 feet, we could have more than doubled her cargo, to 900 tons, but it was to be a long time before that was possible. We selected a day when the high water was in daylight and was more than 4 feet, yielding a depth of 10 feet over the bar. Since there were only one high tide and one low tide a day, the times when they occurred were most important.

A party including the MSTS master and navigator came into Cus Ho first on an LCU, and as we proceeded in, the navigator took soundings from the lowered ramp. After the party had beached, its anxious query, "Will you bring her in, skipper?" brought an unemotional, "Ah so." The LST slid over the bar but, as the master turned almost 90 degrees to make his beaching run, the 16-knot wind came right on his beam, and he started to sail broadside down the river beyond the surveyed area into what, we did not know. With a tremendous display of seamanship, the master turned his ship almost 360 degrees and came up again for a beaching run. This time he made it and, minutes after the ramp was dropped, the Marine shore party had the first pallet offloaded. It had been proved possible to bring an LST into Cus Ho, and a tremendous sigh of relief came from all hands. Many acts of courage and seamanship were displayed in the transiting of the channel to Cus Ho before it was dredged. Notable in that respect was Lieutenant Barney O'Rourke, commanding officer of the *Henry County* (LST-824), who made the first night transit without any navigation aids. He was also the first to put an LST on the ramp when two others were already there. War materials were kept flowing by men who surf-boarded their LSTs through the 10- and 15-foot breakers into the mouth of the river.

As a sidelight and a point to be considered seriously by those responsible for new ship construction, it is worth noting that the LST-542 class is the only class of LST that could have kept the Chu Lai operation going. The old LSM would have been fine, but there were none available. One wonders if the new 20-knot LST, which not only has beaching restrictions but is too big to go everywhere a 542 class

can go, should not be complemented by a replacement for the 542 design—many of us who relied so heavily on the latter believe so.

After the channel was dredged, early in 1966, one of the much bigger LST-1156 class went into Chu Lai.

With the knowledge that Chu Lai could be resupplied, we went ahead with plans for a subdepot there. As at Da Nang, planning was done on a triangular basis, and LCUs supplemented LSTs for carrying high-priority cargo from Da Nang to Chu Lai. Soon after the first LST beached at Cus Ho, the Marine shore party was relieved by the Naval Beach Group Detachment. These naval officers and men lived and worked for a long time ashore under the most primitive of conditions, but their performance was anything but primitive.

When one considers that, during the monsoon torrential rains, a man could sink up to his hips in red mud as he crossed the main supply route ashore, it is obvious that nothing about the Chu Lai operation was easy. But, it would have been even more difficult without the experience we had gained in Da Nang. The geography was such that, except for POL, a complete operation could be contained within one compound. But relying on a thin and tenuous supply line while waiting for plans to become realities was a test of nerves and sinews.

In December 1965, the bottom-laid fuel line failed during the height of the monsoon, and our UDT men dove time and again in the rough water to find the 4-inch steel line, which was wrapped into a 30-foot circle. Working in the heavy surf to rig and maintain a buoyant system, also 4 inches in diameter, was a task that called for raw courage. But our people did it in a few days, and although we came near to the point where close air support sorties would have to be stopped, we did not reach it. Credit for seamanship and tenacity must also be given to the Navy AOG skippers and the civilian T-1 masters, who hung on to the sea end of the fuel line in swells of 14 feet and more.

Keeping Phu Bai Operational

The third separate base of the III MAF was Phu Bai, some 12 miles to the south of the ancient capital city of Hue, and about 40 miles north of Da Nang. In the summer of 1965, the operation at Phu Bai was only battalion-sized and was defensive in nature. It was supported tactically by part of a Marine helicopter squadron. The force levels and tonnage estimates were too small to cause any great concern. Accordingly, top priorities in construction, funds, and men were assigned to Da Nang and Chu Lai.

We did, however, plan for what would be required if Hue/Phu Bai were to become the terminal point for the support of larger forces in the two northern provinces of Quang Tri and Thua Thien. Two different areas of approach from the sea were studied; both of them required a considerable amount of construction and security precautions. From the standpoint of moving material from the staging area to a Phu Bai terminal, the more attractive approach was the Dam An Hai lagoon, 13 miles to the south, on Route 1, a good road, in open country. On the other hand, the six-mile road from the Col Co Causeway to Hue, is narrow, occasionally flooded, and was insecure at night. When traveling it even in daylight, one had to wear body armor. Then, after passing through the crowded city of Hue, there are still 12 miles to go before reaching Phu Bai.

However, for purposes of resupplying Quang Tri province to the north, the Hue River mouth and Col Co Causeway had several advantages, one of which was quite simply that Col Co is farther north than Dam An Hai. A combat UDT surveyed Dam An Hai, but only partially, for one did not linger in this VC-infested area. But the Marines provided security while an engineering study was made, and

the results of that study settled the issue. The average depth of water at Dam An Hai was about four feet, and the bottom consisted of extremely fine silt. The lagoon could be dredged, but the silt would flow so freely back into the channel that the latter would have to be made too wide for the project to be practical. Accordingly, in spite of the advantages offered by the Dam An Hai approach, planning proceeded with "port" development at the Col Co Causeway at the mouth of the Hue River.

As pointed out previously, the development of a port must include clearance to the terminal and on to the customer. The six-mile road from Col Co to Hue was secure only in daylight, was marginal for trucks of more than five tons, and parts of it were under water during the monsoons. The streets of Hue are wider than those of Da Nang, but still are not suitable for constant use by U. S. military logistic traffic. Accordingly, a whole new route had to be surveyed, engineered, and costed, and the real estate officer had to start obtaining land on which to build it. Most of the route selected ran through rice paddies, and the nearest rock that could be used to build the road was about 14 miles distant from Phu Bai, fortunately, in country that was reasonably secure, but still the task facing the constructors was obviously not a simple one. Although no significant construction or dredging could be done until the monsoons were over early in 1967, planning continued.

When operations near the DMZ began, the suitability of Hue as the site for a terminal was open to question. Perhaps it would be better for work on the Cua Viet River, in Quang Tri province, to take precedence, for by August 1966 NSA was using LCU and LARC to deliver direct to Dong Ha via the Cua Viet, despite two large sand bars in the river. The LCUs made the 70 sea miles and 8 river miles to Dong Ha under their own power, except during the northeast monsoons when some of them went as far as the mouth of the Cua Viet River in an LSD. When the LCUs could not get over the sand bars, they carried loaded LARCs, which shuttled the cargo over the sand bars to Dong Ha. It is worth noting this further proof that, though it is tempting to try to blow underwater sand bars with ordinary demolition, it does not work—the sand settles right back in again. In good weather and good light, it is not difficult to enter the Cua Viet.

Supplies of POL went overland in trucks from Esso's Lien Chieu terminal, near Da Nang, to Dong Ha.

Bitter Days

The rapid buildup of forces in Vietnam in 1965 naturally generated tremendous logistic support requirements, 98 per cent of which were delivered by sea from the United States. The tonnage created a tremendous surge, as it crashed into the ports of embarkation.

This surge reached Da Nang in October and November 1965, a time that could not have been worse. There were no new facilities for offloading, the permanent personnel had just begun to relieve those cargo handlers TAD from the Fleet, and the equipment was moving at a trickle. Moreover, the surge of ship arrivals coincided with the arrival of the northeast monsoon. At times, the winds, seas, and never-ending heavy rains caused cargo operations to be shut down completely. Our U. S. sailors handled endless tons of cargo and struggled with weak packages that disintegrated in the rain, strewing their contents into the mud underfoot—mud that was anywhere from six inches to two feet deep. Boat crews worked endless hours in heavy weather alongside ships, and transited the channel at night in blinding rain with almost no navigation aids. Coupled with all that nature could throw against them, the threat of the Viet Cong hung over the men as they worked. They had seen the Esso POL terminal at Lien Chieu burn in

August 1965, they knew that toward the end of October our new hospital had been one-third destroyed by satchel charges, and they worked at night under flares intended to illuminate ground action not far away.

Basically, our problem was that there was too much tonnage for an undeveloped port to handle in bad weather. But two of the other factors that had a lot to do with creating the bottleneck that existed in November 1965 were multiple-port shipments and inadequate packaging.

At first, cargo bound for Vietnam was sent on the first available ship, and multiple-port discharges for a single ship were common. The desire to get cargo moving from the United States was understandable, but because of the lack of facilities in Vietnam, offloading took a long time, and a backlog of shipping developed and grew at every port. Cargo near the top of hatches had to be discharged first; therefore, a ship had to go first to the port for which her top cargo was intended. There, she would have to wait for offloading to begin. When her top cargo for that port finally was removed, she could go on to the port for which her second layer of cargo was destined, and there, again, she would wait to be offloaded. Multiple-port shipments might have to go through this procedure at five or six ports. Except for those carrying top-priority cargo, which was offloaded as soon as the ship came in, ships were normally offloaded in order of arrival. Thus, ships with multiple-port cargoes went to the back of the line five or six times, before they were completely offloaded. Often, too, high-priority cargo for one port was overstowed by low-priority cargo for another port. When that happened, either the port desiring the high-priority items had a long wait before it got them, or, if the ship was sent to that port first, the low-priority cargo had to be offloaded, staged, and reloaded before it reached its destination. Either procedure was wasteful. Single-port loading was by far the most efficient method, even if it meant that the material waited longer in the marshalling area at home. Single-port discharge in Vietnam is tied to single-port staging and embarkation in the United States. Shiploads for specified ports should be assembled at one port of embarkation under one command. For example, all cargo destined for the I Corps Tactical Zone might be loaded at the Naval Supply Center, Oakland, California, under the direction of the commander of that supply center.

During the first six months of our operations, inadequate, flimsy packaging and palletizing was the greatest obstacle to efficient cargo handling, and was the greatest cause of waste and loss. Cargo that came to us neither packaged nor palletized was equally bad, but less common. We thought we had learned these lessons in World War II, but evidently we didn't learn them well enough. Desire to expedite shipment was partly responsible for the misloading, but mostly responsible was a lack of understanding of the conditions under which offloading, distribution, and terminal storage had to be done in Vietnam. Aluminum barrels of asphalt sealed at either end with pop-out plugs so flexible that regular barrel chines, combined with the 125-degree heat of a ship's hold, or the brilliant tropic sun on the beach, would exert enough pressure to pop them out, provided a few unforgettable instances. When such barrels were unloaded, asphalt was everywhere. One ship was fully loaded this way, and the loss was fantastic. Another unhappy practice was the double loading of commercial pallets (96 cases to a pallet rather than the normal 48) with inadequate "cap and strap" procedures: the flimsy commercial pallets could not stand the weight and the handling—consequently pallets broke and we suffered loss and injury.

Cement packaging was not consistent. Seabee cement from Port Hueneme was beautifully packaged in polyethylene wrapping inside

wooden boxes—expensive, undoubtedly, but worth it, for in Vietnam the Seabees could use 100 percent of what was shipped. Cement from other American ports was shipped in open bags on flimsy pallets: the bags soon gave way in the monsoon rains, and the percentage of loss was high. Corrugated aluminum culvert half sections are invaluable in a land of rice paddies and monsoon rains. But when they were loaded loose in a ship's hold in bundles of six, handling them was a terribly slow and cumbersome process. More care in packing and loading at home would have paid dividends at the other end of the supply line. Packing articles that are highly susceptible to pilferage—cigarettes and PX supplies, for instance—in cartons, with content description clearly marked on the outside, was an open invitation for theft and diversion. Fortunately, this never became a major problem at Da Nang.

Much improvement in the packaging of cargo came after the first six or seven months, but there is still much that could be done. This discussion of packaging should not be taken to mean that the author is advocating containerization as the cure for all packaging problems. It is extremely useful, but only if there are port facilities geared to handle containers, and in an expeditionary background sophistication of that kind cannot compete for construction materials and talent with such mandatory projects as combat airfields and main supply routes. It was estimated that there would have to be 40 acres of hard stand at the port of Da Nang in order for container-ships to be efficiently handled there. Until June 1966, there were none, but in that month two acres of open storage became available. Fourteen more acres became available early in 1967, and another 25 were still awaited at that time.

Containers come in various sizes: we liked the 20' × 8' × 8' size best. Thus industry, supply, and procurement activities must specify and can require the use of standard-size sturdy pallets; materials must be boxed and water-proof-covered, then capped, and strapped with materials strong enough to withstand at least 10 different handlings in torrential rains. This type of packaging is essential until port facilities can be made ready for container-ship operations. The above comment is not a disparagement of the Army's 8.5-foot-square Conex boxes which, when used properly, assist tremendously in the efficient movement of cargo. In fact, all easily pilferable items consigned to advanced bases should be packed in Conex boxes. Unfortunately, the fact that the boxes make excellent dry shelters and "goodie lockers," resulted in a small return flow of them, and that, in turn, reduced their usefulness.

One more thought on packaging: a fortune—and the eternal gratitude of all cargo handlers—awaits the individual who invents a method of packaging reinforcing rod so that it can be handled efficiently. What miserable material that is to handle!

The Supplemental Offload Plan

In case all else failed, we had what was originally called "the Monsoon Plan." This was a plan to be used if it proved true that, during the worst of the monsoons, deep-draft ships could be worked only 50 per cent of the time. The Supplemental Offload Plan—to give it its formal name—was based on use of the LST, which could find several sheltered offloading spaces in Da Nang: the Tien Sha, Museum, and Commercial ramps. These ships would shuttle between Da Nang and Subic Bay, where deep-draft ships could offload under more sheltered conditions than Da Nang could offer. At Subic Bay, the cargo would be sorted and staged, and according to priority, loaded into the LSTs for the journey to Da Nang.

This plan highlighted the shortage of LSTs but, fortunately, it had to be used only to expedite some high-priority cargo during the most

serious part of the jam that occurred in November 1965. It also highlighted the need to plan on having advanced staging areas that could serve as logistical surge tanks when there was to be a rapid buildup in an area of undeveloped ports and facilities. Such areas will at least keep the bullets and beans, if not all the desired items, flowing during periods of construction, in bad weather, or when other obstacles prevent deep-draft ships from the United States going directly to their destinations. It was a mistake not to have Okinawa ready to play that role.

Early in January 1966, we could see the beginning of the end of our bitter days. The first surge of ships sent to Vietnam had created a vacuum on the U. S. end of the pipeline, so that we could expect fewer ships to arrive at Da Nang in January. Our messages about poor packaging and multiple-port loadings were being read and acted on in the United States, while at Da Nang the weather turned fine. The personnel and equipment sides of the through-put triangle were growing, but not the facilities side. However, through the efforts of the port captain and of the mayor of Da Nang, we had been able in August 1965 to lease 60 lineal meters of the Commercial Pier and a 30-meter T pier on the river in Da Nang West. The street had to serve as the staging area for the T pier, and the mayor permitted us to keep two city blocks closed to commercial traffic. All these areas were returned to the city in May 1966.

Finally, in February 1966, the time arrived when for 36 hours there was not one single ton of cargo in Da Nang Harbor waiting to be offloaded. It was a weary but jubilant group of men who had their first day off.

Before concluding the story of the expanding triangle that began in June 1965 and, in 12 months, transformed Da Nang from a port able to handle only a few thousand tons into one capable of moving over a hundred thousand tons, and two hundred thousand tons in October 1966, we should examine some specific, though somewhat unrelated, aspects of the advanced base operations: POL, the station hospital, ammunition, short-range communications, and Public Works.

POL

So far as POL was concerned, NSA's mission was to consolidate requirements, and to receive, store, and issue four different kinds of fuel: avgas, JP4, mogas, and diesel fuel, in either bulk or packaged form. The need for POL was immediate and to meet it the following facilities were used initially:

1. Amphibious bottom-lay systems at Da Nang and Chu Lai.
2. Marine Corps bladders for shoreside storage.
3. Esso railroad tank cars and tank trucks.
4. Shell tank trucks.
5. An above-ground rubber line to the U. S. Air Force at the Da Nang air base.

The Shell terminal, just north of the bridge cargo complex on the west side of the Da Nang River, the Esso terminal at Lien Chieu in Da Nang Harbor, the 4-inch amphibious bottom-lay lines at Red Beach and at Chu Lai, and a buoyant line from the South China Sea to the Marble Mountain Air Facility at Da Nang East, could be serviced only by T-1 or smaller tankers. Therefore, continuous shuttle service between the T-3 and T-4 tankers anchored in the deep water of Da Nang Harbor had to be supplied. Shuttling went on around the clock, interrupted only by the severest of weather and by events such as the Viet Cong attack on Esso's Lien Chieu terminal. Despite this concerted effort, we scarcely ever had more than a few days' supply of oil in the bladders.

Outlying areas, such as Tam Ky, Dong Ha, Hue, and Phu Bai, were supplied from Da Nang by air and by commercial tank trucks—Quang Ngai was supplied by air from Chu Lai. That commercial trucks could deliver over roads controlled by the Viet Cong is odd, but true, nevertheless.

Triangular planning provided the guide for the permanent installations, and the ABFC again came into the picture with bolted, steel tank assemblies. Storage areas were selected and underground piping systems (which also can be part of an ABFC) planned to allow maximum flexibility and continuity in case of enemy attack or sabotage. Deciding factors were the types of aircraft to be supported, both those on hand and those expected, since they would cause changes in the balance of avgas versus JP4 requirements. Also, some sea lines that Shell intended to lay at Rocher Noir (Da Nang East) were incorporated into the overall planning. Those lines are now in existence, and underground pipe ties them in with the various fuel depots. Amphibious buoyant systems played an important part in providing rapid response to increased needs at Chu Lai, Da Nang (both East and West), and seaside near the mouth of the Hue River. However, over the long haul, a bottom-lay pipe is better than buoyant hose. It should be noted that the buoyant systems belonged to a type commander—ComPhibPac—another example of the responsiveness of the Fleet. So that the amphibious forces should not be required to lend their assets to a permanent installation, it might be well for buoyant hose to be in the ABFC inventory.

Station Hospital

In August 1965, the U. S. Naval Hospital, Da Nang, then under construction, became Station Hospital, NSA, and its CO became senior medical officer. It was to be a 400-bed package, made up of four 100-bed units. These units came from the ABFC and again proved both the soundness of that program and the mistake of not updating equipment. As an example of the latter, the laundry's oil-fired dryers did not work at all, and since the manufacturer had not produced the model for some years and no spare parts were available, the machines never could be used.

It was because the Seabees built the hospital unit by unit, and used the ABFC concept, that the hospital was able to recoup rapidly when the Viet Cong attacked it with satchel charges on 28 October 1965 and demolished one unit. Another ABFC unit was ordered immediately, and the opening of the hospital was delayed only about one month. An example of the imbalances that can occur when the triangular concept is not employed from the beginning is to be found in the planning for the hospital: doctors and corpsmen arrived months before it was completed and had to be sent TAD to various commands. The leadership of Dr. Bruce Canaga, Captain, Medical Corps, U. S. Navy, was largely responsible for the success of this mission in the face of such difficulties.

Ammunition

Originally, NSA's mission was to receive, store, maintain, and issue ammunition, but it was soon changed and NSA was required only to unload ammunition ships and deliver their cargoes to the water's edge. The change meant that the customers had to do the trucking from the pier or ramp to their own ammunition points, and to do their own storing and issuing, thus relieving NSA of most of the ammunition problems. However, a comment must be made about the offloading of ammunition ships. Under the Air Force's "special express" system, fortunately no longer in use, ammunition ships were, in effect, floating dumps, from which required ammunition had to be offloaded on a selective basis, whereas ships carrying ammunition for the Marines were unloaded hatch by hatch from top to bottom. Especially in a wet environment, such as Vietnam, selective offloading is lengthy, dangerous, and costly. A much better practice is to keep ammunition ships steaming off the coast until the port is ready to apply its shoreside facilities to working as many hatches as possible, 24 hours a day. The staging of hundreds of tons of ammunition on the street by T pier until trucks were available to move it out will go down in the author's memory as the greatest risk he ever took. Happily, there was not one single accident.

Short-Range Communications

As we have seen, poor local communications were one of the severest handicaps we suffered during the first nine months of operations at Da Nang. If any lesson should be printed indelibly on the minds of advanced base planners of the future, it is that they must have ready plenty of unsophisticated short-range (1 to 20 miles) radio and telephone communications. When limited facilities are dispersed over a large area and connected only by poor roads, it is essential to have a control center where decisions that will keep cargo flowing evenly at all facilities can be made instantly. Moreover, rapid response, which can be achieved only with good communications, is vital in the saving of lives and in reacting to enemy attacks. A short-range communication package should be part of an updated and prepositioned ABFC.

There was a telephone switchboard with phones and wires in the ABFC inventory, but stringing wires was not an easy job at Da Nang, where the river and the downtown area had to be crossed. Our wires went in front of the Buddhist pagoda that was a key center of the resistance group, and in May 1966 they were all shot away. Short-range, high-reliability radio is essential to the rapid development of an advanced base.

Public Works

Public Works is the most humdrum part of the most unglamorous aspect of logistics in support of military operations. Nevertheless, even the most efficient stevedoring and lighterage services will bog down if forklifts, cranes, and trucks are not working steadily to clear the

---

offload sites and keep the cargo flowing to the terminal and the customer. This equipment must be kept on the line, and the construction mechanic who services and maintains it is as vital to an advanced base—whose success is measured in terms of port clearance—as is a boatswain's mate to the unloading of a ship.

There was nothing in the TG 76.4 organization that remotely resembled a shoreside Public Works Department, so that when permanent Public Works personnel arrived to take over from the Marines' Force Logistic Group, they had to start from scratch. Adding to the difficulties was the fact that when the Construction Battalions were expanded, most of the Group VIII ratings in the Navy were used up. Consequently, most of NSA's allowances for construction mechanics were originally filled with aircraft mechanic ratings. These men did a fine job, but their skills were being misused.

We have discussed real estate problems, but not the engineering effort that was put into the preparation and justification of sound Milcon requirements. This is a tremendous job for even an established Public Works Department. When normal problems are complicated by a shortage of manpower, temporary office space with virtually no equipment, and the long, hazardous job of site survey in a combat zone, the challenge becomes formidable. The pace of the action required is illustrated by the fact that, when the first Public Works officer to be sent to Da Nang, Commander Archibald Floyd, arrived in September 1965, he left the next day to attend a military construction conference in Hawaii.

Establishing a contract section to solicit bids and award contracts to local construction companies is not without intricacies. And when those negotiations were completed, Public Works still had to supervise the implementation of the work being done.

In August 1965 Lieutenant Timothy Goodwin, CEC, U. S. Navy, took over a motor pool area, which consisted of nothing more than an office and parts building and a garage. There was no electricity, the office and parts building was only a shell, and the prior tenant of the garage had removed the corrugated metal roof and siding, leaving only the bare sticks. Lieutenant Goodwin built from scratch a large well-equipped garage in Da Nang East, and manned it mostly with Korean mechanics under a Philco contract. Meanwhile, the original garage in Da Nang proper was given a new roof and siding, and became as efficient as any the world over. BuDocks and PacDocks helped plan and expedite procurements and were enormously important to our efforts in Da Nang.

Public Works planning was not limited to Da Nang: it included Chu Lai, Hue, Phu Bai and the other important U. S. bases in ICTZ. As time went on, it became evident that the scope of Public Works had to expand to meet the situation. That is, Public Works would have to provide the maintenance required for facilities, utilities, and lines of communication that did not fall within the missions of either the combat engineers or the Mobile Construction Battalions. The mission of Construction Battalion Maintenance Units (CBMU), a World War II institution, had been taken over in peacetime by the Public Works Department. Accordingly, at NSA, Public Works was made responsible for maintenance of the non-expeditionary facilities in Da Nang, Chu Lai, and Phu Bai. A recommendation that the CBMU be reformed for the purpose of maintaining small Marine airfields and facilities, such as those at An Hoa and Dong Ha, was approved. The force at Public Works consisted of Vietnamese civilians, third-country nationals, and U. S. sailors, with U. S. Navy supervision at most levels. This aspect of our operations called for a large effort, and it is one that planners for future counterinsurgency operations similar to those in Vietnam should take into account.

February to October 1966

During the above period, our plans for Da Nang became actualities. NSA had grown large enough to require a flag officer at its head, and in February Rear Admiral Thomas R. Weschler assumed command. The sides of the triangle lengthened equally, as planned, making it possible for the projected through-put to be handled and cleared. By October 1966, staging areas, roads, facilities for repairing small craft, and POL facilities remained to be finished, but we could use the three deep-draft piers; the two 300-foot wooden piers (one at the bridge cargo complex, the other at the Da Nang East ferry pier); the bridge cargo complex itself, with more than 1,600 feet of marginal wharf for lighters; the 500,000 square feet of covered storage; the 300,000 cubic feet of refrigerated storage; and some hard stand. The two wooden piers had been acquired simply by cutting a 600-foot ABFC pier in half, so that we could serve a lot of small ships rather than a few large ones. Manpower was available on schedule, and the equipment and its maintenance facilities were on hand.

In Chu Lai, the POL storage was progressing; the sub-depot was almost ready for use, and the people to operate it were either there or soon would be. The 800-foot marginal wharf was not completed, and the intensity of the monsoons would have to be faced shortly; but compared to the situation in 1965, Chu Lai was in good shape.

In the northern provinces, however, there had been no progress in the development of Hue and Phu Bai, and little had been done to make the Cua Viet River to Dong Ha usable for the support of the operations in Quang Tri province. So, clearly, many tasks lay ahead to test the sinew of NSA.

One never does reach a static situation when forces are building, scenes of operations are shifting, and the scope of operational commit-ments has not been specifically delineated. However, by October of 1966, NSA had reached a plateau and was ready to progress evenly as operations and the other demands of war dictated.

In conclusion, it is to be hoped that all phases involved in the establishment of the advanced base in Da Nang will be used by the U. S. Navy as a guide to the planning and positioning of ABFCs, so that they will be ready for instant deployment to any area where an advanced base may be required.

Modern equipment must constantly replace the obsolete or worn out. Further, research funds must be allocated so that new systems of cargo handling, new ways to distribute material to field forces in an undeveloped country, new methods of instant port development, including ready-made breakwaters, deep-water piers, and marginal wharfs, and techniques for more rapid dredging, can all be incorporated into the ABFC concept.

These responsibilities can be assigned to the Service Force or to some other type command. But whatever command has the responsibilities should be required to maintain the necessary skills by establishing advanced bases during regular Fleet exercises. For the next ten years, the Navy will have officers and men experienced in this kind of work, but unless the above measures are taken, who knows what will happen if the experience is dissipated and the skills are lost? True, there are Advanced Base Units in the Naval Reserve. But, just as we did in Vietnam, we may have to work without them if a similar crisis develops in the future.

However much may be said about the things involved in building the advanced base at Da Nang, all remain in the shadow of the performance of the men. Their dedication to duty under the severest of conditions has earned for them a place in the history of the Navy that ought not to be forgotten.

(*Naval Review*, 1968)

Maritime Support of the Campaign in I Corps

Commander Frank C. Collins, Jr., U. S. Navy

The opinion, "From a logistics standpoint, this is by far the *best* and *most* managed war in which we have ever been involved," voiced by one of our leading flag officers involved in logistics, may not be shared by everyone. But it is not likely to be disputed by any of the some one thousand officers and forty thousand bluejackets who have served in the largest Navy overseas shore command, the Naval Support Activity, Da Nang.

The establishment and functioning of the Naval Support Activity, Da Nang, is a unique chapter in the U. S. Navy's proud history. The origin of NavSuppAct (or NSA), Da Nang, is well treated in Captain K. P. Huff's article, published in the 1968 issue of the *Naval Review.*[1] I shall not attempt to improve on that portion of NSA's history; rather, this article will attempt to highlight the accomplishments and events which make this logistic effort worth remembering. NSA Da Nang could well serve as a model for navy logisticians in future wars fought in terrain where shallow waterways are the preeminent lines of communication.

Administrative Relationships

During its five-year history, NSA Da Nang was commanded by one captain and five flag officers. The command relationship under which these officers operated was complex, dictated by the rather intricate command structure under which the war in Vietnam was prosecuted. Since Commander Naval Forces Vietnam was the naval component commander in Vietnam, ComNavSuppAct, Da Nang, reported to him as an operational subordinate. ComNavForV was also ComNavSuppAct, Da Nang's, link in the chain of command with the Commander, U. S. Military Advisory Command, Vietnam.

In turn, the Da Nang support activity commander served as the NavForV representative for real estate matters in I Corps. Because ComNavSuppAct, Da Nang, was created to support the Third Marine Amphibious Force (III MAF), there was perforce a close relationship with the Commanding General, III MAF.

A good working relationship with the Vietnamese Joint General Staff in I Corps was also maintained though, except in real estate matters, the Admiral normally worked through III MAF headquarters when dealing with the Vietnamese I Corps commander. During 1969 with the implementation of the Accelerated Turnover To Vietnam (ACTOV) program, and as Vietnamization of the war began in earnest, this command relationship grew even more important.

In the I corps area, the Marine Corps continued to depend on its natural element—their legendary Captain Jimmie Bones said it best: ". . . water settles everything, and that's what our name means"—as, with road and railroads blocked, logistic support had to come by sea. In the picture, the old YFU-61 begins the return voyage down the Perfume River from Hue to Tan My and back to Da Nang, as several other YFUs and LCUs off-load at the ramp on the far side of the river.

A contemporary twist on the Golden Rule stipulates that "He who has the gold, *rules*." This brings into focus the final link in the rather extensive command relationship: the Commander of the Service Force, U. S. Pacific Fleet. As the Commander-in-Chief, U. S. Pacific Fleet's principal logistic agent, ComServPac controlled NSA Da Nang's purse strings. Considering the size of Da Nang's budget, it is easy to understand that the relationship with ServPac was an important one.

INTERNAL ORGANIZATION

If NavSuppAct's external command relationships appear complex, its infrastructure was no simpler. Beginning with an amphib-

ious command, Captain Huff's Landing Ship Flotilla One staff (Task Group 76.4) was augmented as necessary and given the job of managing logistic support for the Marines at Da Nang. This forerunner of NavSuppAct, Da Nang, was basically developed along the standard naval staff organization. However, rather than having the normal five or six divisions, plus special assistants, Rear Admiral Thomas Weschler, the first flag officer to command Da Nang, found it necessary to expand this to eleven divisions and special assistants. These department heads included public works, administration, operations and plans, medical, dental, communications, supply and fiscal, industrial relations (a civilian), enlisted personnel (commanding officer, Camp Tien Sha), first lieutenant (under whom came physical security and the fire marshal), and repair.

Special assistants included the legal officer, chaplain, public affairs officer, and civic action officer. In 1966, when Chu Lai was established, an additional link was added to the already broad scope of management control. The Officer-in-Charge Naval Support Activity Department (or NSAD) Chu Lai, was not a department head per se as he reported directly to the assistant chief-of-staff for operations and plans. But essentially he acted with the same powers since he had direct access to the Chief of Staff. Reporting to Admiral Weschler, when the Admiral was acting as Naval Forces Vietnam Representative (NavForVRep), was the base development officer, a senior captain of the Civil Engineer Corps. Since little organizational precedent existed for this particular mission, staff organization was an ad hoc affair in the beginning.

By 1968, tasks had sorted themselves out well enough to enable the Commander to create a more conventional Navy shore staff organization. Department heads were redesignated assistant chiefs of staff. The staff consisted of ACOS for administration, security and intelligence, operations, supply and fiscal, communications, public works, and plans. Special assistants included the repair officer, industrial relations officer, senior medical officer, dental officer, commanding officer enlisted personnel, base development officer, staff judge advocate, and the officers in charge of Chu Lai, Phu Bai-Hue, Tan My, Dong Ha-Cua Viet, and Sa Huynh.

DYNAMIC GROWTH

From its modest beginning on 24 April 1965, until Rear Admiral R. E. (Rojo) Adamson hauled down his flag on 30 June 1970, the Naval Support Activity, Da Nang, was a con-

tinuing example of dynamic growth and accomplishment. Established by the Navy of necessity rather than by choice, after the U. S. Army Pacific (USARPAC) confirmed it lacked the resources needed to operate in Da Nang, in addition to all the other ports and beaches in South Vietnam, NavSuppAct Da Nang began with a Marine landing over Red Beach in Da Nang harbor in 1965. It developed into a highly complex port with cargo clearance and storage facilities in Da Nang, and thriving cargo operations in Chu Lai, Hue-Tan My, Cua Viet-Dong Ha, Sa Huynh, and Quang Tri; additionally, it gave limited assistance in a logistics over the shore (LOTS) operation at Duc Pho. It grew from the handful of officers and men who began the original effort under Captain Huff's able command, to approximately 450 officers and 10,000 bluejackets under Rear Admiral E. P. Bonner in 1969. Add to these figures a civilian work force of 69 U. S. and 5,888 local nationals, and then consider the civilian contractors, employees who, in November 1969, amounted to 725 local nationals and 513 third country nationals (mostly Korean) in the Korean Express cargo handling contract, and 1,251 local and 2,905 third country nationals plus 123 U. S. civilians in the Philco-Ford maintenance contract, and you get some idea of the scope of this mammoth Navy industrial complex.

The number of Support Activity people grew with support requirements. From its modest beginning at Red Beach in Da Nang, support facilities grew to what was then an unimagined extent. Da Nang's early seaside facilities have been comprehensively described in Captain Huff's article, so only the "outports" which substantially came into their own after he left will be considered here.

Sixty miles to the south, the Naval Support Activity Detachment at Chu Lai became a microcosm of the Da Nang operation. While never able to accommodate deep draft vessels,

Chu Lai's LST ramps became well developed and were expanded to accommodate six of the 542 or 1156 classes of LST. Navigational aids in the form of buoys and ranges were considerably improved, as was the depth of the channel which initially afforded only marginal conditions to LST skippers. The hard-topped ramps made it easier for vehicles to unload cargo and the all-weather road complex allowed rapid port clearance. With the major portion of Marine Air Wing One stationed at Chu Lai, fuel was a most important consideration. Compared with the initial "assault bulk stowage" in 10,000-gallon neoprene bladders, by early 1967 Chu Lai boasted a modern and commodious rigid-wall storage tank farm which was umbilically connected to its seaborne source by bottom-laid sea load lines. While these lines were inoperative a significant portion of the time during the monsoon season, NSA Da Nang managed to keep up with fuel requirements, though at times it was touch and go, and required innovations such as sending a partially loaded T-2 tanker or one of Da Nang's YOGs into Cus Ho Ramp to pump cargo directly into Marine refuelers for shuttle to the flight line.

HUE-TAN MY FACILITIES

The NSAD at Hue-Tan My, 30 miles north of Da Nang, began with an LCU ramp near the University of Hue in the downtown area and a bladder fuel farm at the coastal Vietnamese recreation area of Tan My, near the Col Co causeway, in late spring 1966. Initially all cargo had to be cleared as soon as discharged at Hue, since there were no facilities for staging or security. Fuel was delivered to the assault stowage containers by way of a four-inch amphibious assault hose, but this regularly parted or became tangled in its marker buoy moorings. All these shortcomings were overcome by the building of the LST facility (four LST ramps) at Tan My, the installation of the

overland six-inch pipeline from Tan My to Phu Bai and Quang Tri, and completion of rigid stowage tank facilities with a combined capacity of 5.7 million gallons.

DONG HA FACILITY CREATED

Operations Hastings and Prairie in the summer of 1966 marked the beginning of major operations by the U. S. Marines in Northern I Corps Tactical Zone (ICTZ). From battalion to regimental to divisional size, tactical activity in this area adjacent to the Demilitarized Zone (DMZ) grew steadily, requiring complementary growth in support from Da Nang. At first, tactical headquarters for this new offensive was centered in Dong Ha, where the Marine combat base was established. Dong Ha differed from Da Nang in that it was located inland. It differed from Chu Lai because of its lack of a sufficiently large waterway to accommodate an LST, and from Tan My because of its significant distance from Da Nang. It was about 90 miles by open sea from Da Nang to the mouth of the Cua Viet River,[2] which was destined to become the lifeline for the Dong Ha combat bases. Discovering that an LCU could penetrate the twisting, silt-filled waterway, NSA committed itself to relieve the overworked C-130s which skillful Marine pilots had flown in endless succession to keep Operation Hastings supported.

Occasionally LCM-8s were pressed into service on the open sea convoy leg of this supply run, though they were inadequate to cope with the seas when the monsoon season set in. The ramp at Dong Ha, adjacent to the concrete bridge which continues the Vietnamese Route One north across the Cua Viet River, was about three-fourths of a mile from the sprawling base and airfield, from which the Third Marine Division operated. Originally graded to serve as a climb-out ramp for LARCs, which were used to unload anchored LCUs or YFUs,[3] the ramp was eventually widened to accommodate up to six

LCUs and boasted a sizeable hard surfaced area which was illuminated at night.

CUA VIET LST RAMP CONCEIVED

During the fall of 1966, it became apparent that the LCU chain from Da Nang was going to be inadequate to keep the Marines at Dong Ha supplied. The transit, which took the older boats from 10 to 12 hours in good weather in convoy, lengthened to 24 or even 36 hours when the northeast monsoon created 10–16 foot swells. There just weren't enough LCUs in Da Nang to do the job. Pressed by Lieutenant General L. E. Walt, Commanding General of III MAF, Rear Admiral Weschler decided that if ammo by the LCU load was not enough to feed the Marines' guns, the Navy would have to move it in LSTs. LSTs could not navigate the Song Thach Han and Song Hieu Giang (collectively referred to as the Cua Viet), but it appeared feasible to dredge the bar at the mouth of the Cua Viet to permit the entry of LSTs. The latter then could discharge their cargo for transhipment up the final seven miles to the Dong Ha ramp by LCU or LCM-8. The U. S. Army Corps of Engineers' civilian-manned hopper dredge *Hyde* was brought up from the Delta to finish the 15-foot-deep channel[4] which was started by the small Canadian suction dredge *Helbar* and her predecessor, a drag line run from a DeLong pier. Between them, the *Helbar* and the drag line succeeded in scratching out a channel through the bar to permit entry of the hopper dredge. Opened 15 March 1967, NSAD Cua Viet grew to a sizeable organization which, when the occasion demanded, worked around the clock unloading the beached LSTs. River operations, because of hostile fire and lack of navigational aids, ceased at dusk. Air cover was effective during the day so that vessels could sail up to Dong Ha in comparative safety. A four-inch assault line was replaced by a six-inch sea load line, and eventually, when this line became inoperative because of weather,[5] the AOGs which furnished the fuel flow would steam into the Cua Viet estuary, where there was some protection from the weather, and pump directly to the beach bladder.

As action in northern ICTZ became more intensive, the Song Thach Han was reconnoitered by Commander Hal Barker, plans officer for Rear Admiral Paul Lacy, who had succeeded Admiral Weschler. The establishment of a supply line to Quang Tri appeared feasible, and in 1968 it became a reality.

SA HUYNH ESTABLISHED

Late in 1966, U. S. MACV became concerned by the relative sanctuary which the Viet Cong and North Vietnamese forces enjoyed in the southern portion of ICTZ. The First and Third Marine divisions were stretched as thin as they could be and still permit them to accomplish their mission to the north, so it was decided to bring in a provisional Army division from one of the southern Corps areas. Duc Pho, in Quang Ngai Province approximately 100 miles south of Da Nang, was chosen as the center of this new area of operations. Logistic requirements to the north initially precluded NSA from supporting this operation other than by providing facilities to land cargo over the beach. A pontoon causeway, reefer barge, and assault pipeline were installed to assist the Army to become established. Later, in 1967–68, as the Army presence in southern I Corps became more extensive, NSA Da Nang established Naval Support Activity Detachment, Sa Huynh. Since Sa Huynh was at the southern boundary of ICTZ, about 65 miles south of Chu Lai, the Navy could now boast detachments from border to border of I Corps.

A lesser known, but nevertheless important, operation by NSA was the operation of the Liberty Road Ferry. This consisted of an LCM-8, which operated as a ferry across the Song Thu Bon to the south of Da Nang keeping the important Da Nang to An Hoa overland line of communication (LOC) open. Getting the LCM-8-860 up the shallow Song Thu Bon from the South China Sea in mid-1966 was a hazardous and exciting transit protected by the Marines in the area. In February 1967 the Seabees completed a bridge and the ferry was no longer needed.

I Corps Military Expansion

From the small force of Marines which landed in the spring of 1965, the U. S. military population grew to more than 205 thousand men in August 1968. These troops depended on the Naval Support Activity for everything from ordnance to soft drinks and beer, from concertina wire and sand bags to skivvies and boot daubing.

If the NSA's achievements were measured throughout its five-year history, there would probably be as many different views of the priority of accomplishment as there were people making the evaluation. Nevertheless, few would deny that the movement of cargo comes at the top of the list. Following close behind would be the development of ports and of land lines of communication; the construction and maintenance of facilities; and the development of a fuel network sufficient to provide fuel for jet aircraft, for trucks and equipment, and for the hundreds of propeller aircraft which supported the forces in ICTZ. Finally, the building of medical facilities, the salvage of ships and craft, and the conducting of civic action programs rank as important activities.

Facilities in Da Nang continued to expand and improve as the stateside pipeline began to respond to requirements. The deep-draft Thong Nhat piers (sometimes called the Allied piers) resembled a busy stateside port, as staging areas were enlarged and additional port clearance equipment became available. Increased LST tonnage was handled at the Tien Sha, Bridge, Museum, and Ferry ramp cargo

facilities. Ashore, in addition to the accomplishments so well described in Captain Charles J. Merdinger's comprehensive article on the Seabees' phenomenal work,[6] the scope of NSA logistics widened to include a milk plant operated by Foremost Dairy Products, which in addition to milk, provided all U. S. servicemen in I Corps with cottage cheese and ice cream. Common User Land Transportation (CULT) plus vehicle and machinery maintenance, utility provision, construction, and road building functions kept the Navy and contractors well occupied. Bulk storage, covered storage, and refrigerated storage were expanded from a few thousand square feet to acres.

Perhaps a better feeling for the magnitude of the expansion can be achieved when one considers that in Da Nang the supply depot space increased from approximately 33 thousand square feet of covered storage in 1965 to over 900 thousand square feet in 1969, from none to over 500 thousand cubic feet of refrigerated storage, and from very little to over two million, seven hundred thousand square feet of open storage. Package and bulk fuel storage expanded from about 40 thousand gallons to accommodate more than 50 million gallons of JP-4, aviation, diesel, and motor vehicle fuel.

Another clue to the scope of industrial activity is the size of the budget, which grew from approximately 41 million dollars in FY 1967 to 102 million dollars in FY 1969. Over half of this operating and maintenance budget was used in the mammoth public works program sponsored by NSA Da Nang.

Never did a single Navy industrial complex operate as many boats and craft as did NSA Da Nang. Starting in December of 1965, with 12 LCUs or YFUs, 16 LCM-8s, 10 LCM-6s, 2 LCM-3s, and 8 YCs, all of which, save the YCs, were amphibious force assets, the Da Nang navy grew to number over two hundred and fifty craft, which included not only the types mentioned above, but also floating cranes, self-propelled water barges, reefer barges, YTLs, YTMs (pulled out of the mothball fleet in mid-1966), YTBs, AFDLs, YRs, LARCs (acquired from the Army), LCPLs, and finally, the new Skilaks (Eskimo for "strange craft"), a commercial coastal cargo vessel designed for the Alaska trade. The Skilaks represented a significant improvement over the LCUs.

By December of 1968, the self-propelled lighterage inventory alone had increased from that enumerated above to 11 Skilaks (each estimated as being worth two and a half LCUs or YFUs), 42 LCUs or YFUs, 46 LCM-8s, and 36 LCM-6s and LCM-3s. It is easy to understand why the Support Activity required the highest density of qualified boat masters of any activity in the Navy during this period. The allotment of cargo hauling and handling machinery also kept pace with the increased transfer of goods. Material handling equipment and especially the rough-terrain forklifts which Captain Huff spoke of as being difficult to keep in operation owing to an inadequate supply of spare parts, finally achieved an acceptable maintenance level.

Moving Cargo

Captain Huff's group, during the period prior to NSA Da Nang's formal establishment in October of 1965, moved cargo in an amount sufficient to keep the 3rd Marine Expeditionary Force (as it was originally identified) supported. The 35 thousand measurement tons handled at Da Nang in July of 1965 seems modest indeed when compared to nearly 471 thousand measurement tons handled in September of 1969. During the same September, Dong Ha reported over 47 thousand MT, Chu Lai had 86,195 MT, Hue and Tan My received 54,423 MT, and Sa Huynh reported 3,088 MT. The progressive growth of Da Nang's cargo handling capacity can be observed in the following average monthly

figures: 135,500 short tons in 1966, 198,300 ST in 1967, 333,300 ST in 1968, followed by a decline in 1969, as the withdrawal began, to 320,400 ST.[7]

The very early calculation of the contemporary need to move a ton of cargo per man per day (if considered in the context of freight terminal men) was significantly exceeded during the last six months of Rear Admiral Adamson's tour in 1970, at which time the average amount of cargo moved per man per day was 3.25 ST.

Initially, all-Navy cargo handling teams were used, because of the scarcity of Vietnamese stevedores. Commander NSA Da Nang had a tight rope to walk in forestalling any accusation of pirating from the inadequate local labor pool. Yet he had to acquire the stevedores to cope with the ever-expanding flow of cargo through the military port of Da Nang. The shortage of labor was met by the twelve-hour workday which each American sailor worked for seven days a week. Two round-the-clock shifts kept cargo moving ashore prior to the formal dedication of the Thong Nhat piers on 15 October 1966 (which was, coincidentally, the first anniversary of NSA Da Nang).

Working ships at the pier, which reduced the double handling that lighterage demanded, was an inestimable boost in cargo handling. Soon many Vietnamese who were not employed by the local commercial port were hired, and their training was accomplished in record time. While the Vietnamese were unable to work the same long day as their American counterparts, their ten-hour day helped the Navy effort at a time when increasing pressure was being brought to bear to reduce, where possible, the manpower drain which NSA Da Nang made on Fleet resources.

To add more manpower, in mid-1966 the Commander of the Naval Support Activity, Da Nang, entered into a contract with the Korean Express Stevedoring Company (KEKN). On 19

August 1966, Korean Express unloaded its first ship. The realization of the terms of their contract, which called for them to unload a minimum of 70 thousand MT monthly took some time, while the hard-working Koreans were getting sufficiently organized. During Rear Admiral Lacy's tour (February 1967 to February 1968), 25 fifteen-man Vietnamese hatch crews had been engaged to augment the handling of the increased tonnage.

DEVELOPING THE PORT OF DA NANG

Before the Navy was assigned to give logistic support in I Corps, Da Nang (or Tourane as it was called by the French) had had little to offer in the way of port facilities. The small commercial port which Da Nang boasted was limited in both size and depth of channel. Storage and modern material handling equipment were also very limited. When the build up in ICTZ began, it was obvious that port facilities would have to expand rapidly.

Many who lived through the first monsoon season, after the Thong Nhat piers were put into commission, cursed the location. As operations officer in the year 1966–67, I was among the cursers. The harbor is a very large natural roadstead, but unfortunately its entrance from the South China Sea is to the northeast, and of course Da Nang's location, above the bend of Vietnam, causes it to be most susceptible to the northeast monsoon. As the winds began to blow, normally in October, the piers stood completely exposed to the rigors of the high swells which came in at heights which belied belief. Ships lying at their berths would be picked up and banged against the piers, doing damage to both ship and pier. The vertical movement of the ship caused by the swells during these storms normally prevented the hatch teams from working the ships. It was then necessary to get a pilot aboard quickly, and shift the ship to an anchorage before damage occurred.

Nevertheless, those who made the decision on the location of these piers had very little choice. From the standpoint of port clearance, Thong Nhat was the most suitable spot, for it was accessible by road and had adequate room for staging and expansion. Two 600-foot steel-framed and steel-jacketed piers, as well as one DeLong pier, furnished sufficient space to accommodate the deep-draft ships. Ironically, the DeLong pier, which had been towed in from Thailand to accelerate deep-draft pier availability for Da Nang cargo operations, was not ready for cargo handling until several months after the conventional piers were being worked. The contractor was delayed in finishing the pier because the materials needed were slow in arriving.

Roads between NSA's covered storage and that of the Marines' Force Logistic Command (FLC) were widened and hard surfaced to accommodate the heavy trucks and "semis" with which NSA's freight terminal division accomplished port clearance.

Since heavy reliance for moving goods in-country was placed on small ships and boats, LST ramps were established at these points in Da Nang: the Ferry Landing across from the Da Nang Hotel, the Museum Ramp, adjacent to the Cham Museum on the same side of the river as the NSA headquarters building (the White Elephant), and at the Bridge-Cargo complex, which could accommodate LSTs, as well as LCUs or YFUs and barges. In addition, there were ramps for LSTs, LCUs, or YFUs on the Tien Sha Peninsula, just southeast of the deep water piers. The last named were the best located with relation to NSA's vast covered storage complex because trucks were not obliged to pass through the heavy traffic in the city.

Harbor Improvements

The channel in the Da Nang River (Song Han) from the harbor to the Bridge-Cargo com-

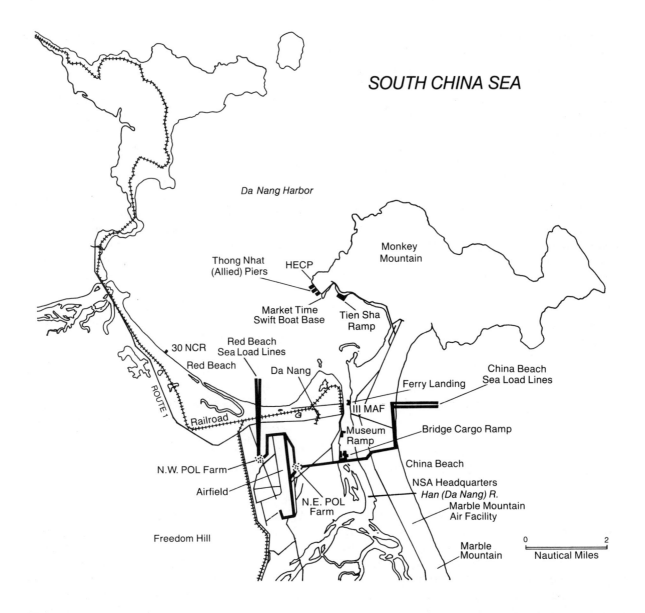

SOUTH CHINA SEA

Da Nang Harbor

Monkey Mountain

Thong Nhat (Allied) Piers

HECP

Market Time Swift Boat Base

Tien Sha Ramp

30 NCR

Red Beach Sea Load Lines

Red Beach

Da Nang

Ferry Landing

China Beach Sea Load Lines

III MAF

Museum Ramp

Bridge Cargo Ramp

N.W. POL Farm

Airfield

N.E. POL Farm

China Beach

NSA Headquarters
Han (Da Nang) R.
Marble Mountain Air Facility

Freedom Hill

ROUTE 1

Railroad

Marble Mountain

0   2
Nautical Miles

plex was dredged to about 18 feet to permit the passage of 1156 class LSTs at any tidal stage. A channel was also dredged eastward from the northernmost end of the main breakwater to Tien Sha cove to permit passage of YOs, YWs, YTBs, and even LSTs to the Small Craft Repair Facility (SCRF). This facility was established in 1967 to take care of the many ship and craft repairs associated with Da Nang's large fleet. Navigational buoys were installed to replace the makeshift oil-drum buoys for which the Vietnamese had such a penchant. Lighted ranges on the river made it possible for LSTs to sail at night.

By 1967, Red Beach, where the 3rd Marine Expeditionary Force (III MEF) had landed in 1965, boasted a ten-section causeway with a special, seven-can-wide "T"-shaped turn-around section on the seaward end. Since this causeway provided a convenient transfer point for bulky and oddsized construction material, such as pipe, pilings, and lumber, destined for either the 30th Naval Construction Regiment Yard or the Marine FLC dump, in good weather LSTs were normally assigned the Red Beach Causeway for loading. The "T"-shaped turn-around sections on the end of the causeway permitted trucks to drive out on the causeway instead of backing out, and then turn around to back into the LSTs for their loads. This saved much time and anxiety, particularly with green drivers. Unfortunately, the causeway could not be used during the northeast monsoon season.

Sea Load Lines

Ten- and twelve-inch sea load fuel lines were extended both in Da Nang Harbor and seaward off China Beach. Since there were no tanker piers in any of the I Corps ports, these bottom-lay lines made the difference in being able to supply the needed fuel which, in December 1968, amounted to 1,700 thousand gallons per day.

Land Communication

A look at the means of land transportation in I Corps explains why sea lines of communication played such a very important part in the logistic effort. With the exception of South Vietnam's main north-south artery, Route 1, Bernard Fall's "Street Without Joy," roads adequate for logistic support of a military operation of the scope of the Marine effort in I Corps do not exist. Why was the railroad, which so closely parallels Route One, not used? Partly because it was only a narrow-gauge railroad. More importantly, it was hard

to keep open. One has but to look at the terrain to appreciate the vulnerability of both the highway and the railroad. Together, Route One and the railroad probably include more trestles and bridges per road mile than any other roadbed in the world. Keeping either in commission continuously taxed both the Seabees and the Marine Corps Engineer companies. Nonetheless, the railroad, which had been essentially abandoned to the Viet Cong since the French threw in the towel in Vietnam, was a project which early in its existence NSA planned to press back into service. Japanese-manufactured freight, flat, and gondola cars arrived in country in the spring of 1967, but the railroad was not opened even for limited use until Rear Admiral E. P. Bonner's tour (December 1968–December 1969), when it was opened between Da Nang, Phu Bai, and Hue, with the first logistically significant load being a cargo of drummed fuel delivered to Phu Bai. By this time the railroad had little military significance, however, since the water lines of communication had been well established. It never offered much assistance in cargo movement. Its primary employment was to carry civilian passengers and goods.

THE DEVELOPMENT OF THE "OUTPORTS"

Chu Lai, the second most important port in I Corps by virtue of population and the lack of an alternative supply route, also went through a massive growth program. By the spring of 1967, the Chu Lai channel was dredged to the extent that YOGs and even coastal freighters could get into the harbor, although until the quaywall was completed later that year, they could do nothing more than anchor in the tiny Truong Giang estuary. Tides and currents were very strong at Chu Lai, so that, except in an emergency, ships entered and exited only with the favorable tides.

Port and industrial activity at Chu Lai resembled a mini-Da Nang, and the small ex-

peditionary force which opened the operation in the spring of 1966 grew to over 1,000 naval officers and men. The buoyant four-inch assault hose, which first supplied fuel for all the machinery, was replaced with eight- and twelve-inch sea load lines. Because they were exposed to the northeast monsoon, the pipelines were often inoperative during the stormy season. Most commonly, the flex hoses, which made the hook-up to the tanker, were torn up by bad weather. If the line stopped functioning, YOGs would come right into the Truong Giang estuary at Chu Lai during the period 1966–67 and pump directly to marine refuelers.

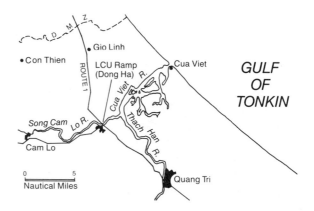

NSAD Cua Viet Established

In the spring of 1967, after the long and eventful dredging experiences at Cua Viet (which included two explosions in the small Canadian dredge *Helbar* and the loss of the chartered tug *Saun Maru*, which was used to shift the DeLong pier dredging platforms around), the river entrance basin was opened to LSTs. The first two to enter, on 15 March 1967, were the USS *Caroline County* (LST-525) and the USS *Snohomish County* (LST-1126). The ramp could accommodate two of the large amphibious vessels, though for security reasons two were not normally scheduled on the ramp at any one time. Within range of North Vietnamese artillery and rockets, it was not good business to place that many eggs in one basket. The ramp area at Cua Viet, first covered by Marston matting, was given a soil cement hardpan in mid-1967. A steel pile bulkhead was driven adjacent to the LST ramp to accommodate the rock barges which made frequent trips from Da Nang. Cua Viet was transformed from a beautiful, white, unoccupied, sandy beach into an ugly, but thriving, cantonment of plywood huts and mess halls, a small boat repair facility, and a sizeable bladder fuel farm. The last was at first supplied by a four-inch bottom-lay line from a buoy offshore and later by a rigid six-inch sea load line.

For two years, boats transferring goods to Dong Ha or Quang Tri from Cua Viet, were able to use that river practically unmolested. But after NSAD Cua Viet was finished, "Charlie" and the North Vietnamese Army came to life and began to harass our riverine logistic forces. The enemy made navigation of the river at night impossible, and in 1968 and 1969 he attacked the supply vessels in daylight.

Sufficient staging areas to accommodate an LST's load of cargo were available at the Cua Viet Ramp. Since this was a transhipping point only, cargo stayed in the staging area only long enough to be loaded into a smaller craft for the seven-mile trip up river to Dong Ha. Normally forklifts moved cargo directly

(Left) *Some of the variety of small craft that supported the Marines along the DMZ are seen in this trio of photographs taken at Cua Viet. The left-hand LCM, converted to a floating dry dock, is flooded* (upper photograph) *to repair a PBR. A 1600-class LCU* (center) *passes the LST ramp near the river's mouth on her way out to sea. In the bottom photo, an LCU, a YFU—notice the open bow ramps—and smaller craft, pass one another near the mouth of the Cua Viet.*

from LSTs to river lighters when the latter were available.

Fuel was transported up the river to Dong Ha in bladder boats (LCM-8s equipped with 10 thousand-gallon bladders) and then when adequate numbers of Ammi pontoons became available, in those infinitely safer containers. The half-submerged sections were propelled by warping tug power units.

Fuel delivered to Dong Ha ramp was pumped overland for the remaining mile to the local Combat Base tank farm through four-inch hoses. At first the Marine Shore Party handled the unloading at the Dong Ha ramp, working from dawn to dusk. As Dong Ha and Cua Viet were expanded, and an increased Navy personnel allowance was approved, NSA Da Nang relieved the Marines of port clearance and began round-the-clock operations when they were required to remove any backlog remaining at the end of the day.

Tan My

Tan My was the potential site of a super-logistic complex which never quite materialized. It served as NSA's control point for river traffic dispatched to Hue or Phu Bai and consisted of a bladder fuel farm manned by Marines, a security unit, and the small NSA detachment cadre which ran the communications van providing liaison between NSA Da Nang and the Hue city ramp. By mid-1967 the detachment had two separate ports groups, one an augmented unit at Tan My which took over all logistic support for the Marine security and fuel farm personnel, and the other a stevedoring group at the new Hue city ramp. The latter were berthed with the Seabee detachment at Phu Bai. Fuel, which heretofore had come to Phu Bai via Hue by tank truck over the narrow and tenuously controlled road from Col Co causeway at Tan My, was eventually delivered by six-inch pipeline laid above ground from Tan My to Phu Bai.

Because dredges were scarce in Vietnam, dredging on the LST port at Tan My could not be started until completion of the Cua Viet channel to the north. But by 1968 it was a reality. Dredging at Tan My consisted of cutting a channel which ran parallel to the surf line inside an offshore sandbar, then digging out a turning basin inside the natural lagoon which served as a runoff area for the Huong, or Perfume, River. The obviously undesirable orientation of the channel was dictated by the lagoon's opening to the sea.

Dam Sam Plan Abandoned

Early in 1967 plans for a large logistic complex on the Dam Sam were made. This included a deep-water port and a combined tactical and logistic airfield with complete warehousing facilities and access roads, which would perforce be carved through rice paddies and swamp. Mui San, which represents the apex of the land extending into Dam Sam, was to be the depot site. A new deep-water channel was to be cut through the narrow strip of land southeast of the NSAD, Tan My, cantonment. The high cost estimate for this undertaking caused its abandonment, and the alternate Col Co development plan was implemented.

Duc Pho

In the spring of 1967, when the Army proposed plans to insert troops in the Duc Pho district of Quang Ngai Province, approximately 60 miles south of Chu Lai, the Naval Support Activity at Da Nang made known to the Army many misgivings about the logistic feasibility of such a move. The operation could not be supported overland from Da Nang because of the very poor roads. Sea support in a straight Logistics over the Shore (LOTS) operation was feasible during the non-monsoon season; however, it appeared out of the question once the October-March monsoon storms began because the beach was completely unsheltered.

NSA operations personnel, which included UDT men, reconnoitered candidate coves up and down the coast between Chu Lai and Sa Huynh. The only site that appeared suitable for development into a port was Sa Huynh, almost on the southern border of ICTZ. A natural lagoon with the odoriferous name of Dam Nuoc Man (Nuoc Man is the name of a strongly scented condiment made of fermented fish juice) had an opening to the south. While the lagoon was shallow and surveys indicated that LCUs would have a narrow channel to thread to get into the lagoon from the South China Sea, it appeared that a little dredging would make it suitable as an "outport." The shallow water in the lagoon created tidal flats, which made this a natural salt farm, and the VC had long before staked their claim to it. Nonetheless, it appeared that the small island of Sa Huynh could be developed sufficiently to support the southern I Corps operation.

Tight dredge resources, and the deceptive ease with which the Army was able to support itself logistically directly over the beach with MSTS-manned LSTs, during summer when weather was not a factor, combined to defer establishing Sa Huynh during 1967. However, the monsoon season in 1967 removed all doubt that only with development of a port at Sa Huynh would the Quang Ngai Province operation be successful on a year-round basis. And so, Sa Huynh was established as NSA Da Nang's southernmost activity. It had LCU ramps and roads from the sea terminus to the Army area of operations. A four-inch sea load line was installed at Duc Pho and an assault fuel farm was built to store the fuel. As can be readily imagined, the sea in Duc Pho's open roadstead played havoc with this line during the monsoon.

Storing and Delivering Fuel

Fuel in I Corps was delivered ashore by pipes from the sea. The development phase in

such a system normally was carried out by men from an amphibious construction battalion who would float ashore a buoyant four-inch system. These lines, temporary installations at best, take both skill and effort to install. Their main drawback is that they are easily damaged by boats and by surf; their advantage is that they can be streamed from LCMs and so installed very quickly.

The buoyant lines were replaced as rapidly as possible by rigid steel pipe lines on the sea bottom which were pulled out from the beach by an LCU equipped with an "A" frame, designated an LCU(F). The seaward end would be anchored with substantial concrete clumps; a flexible "pigtail" completed the rig. A mooring buoy was anchored at the end of it to serve both as a marker for the seaward end of the line and to provide the AOG, which was used to fuel all the outports except Chu Lai,[8] a place to moor and thus avoid inadvertent anchoring on, and consequent pulling up of, the pipe when getting under way. These rigs worked well during the calm seas of the summer months, but failed from time to time after the start of the monsoon season. The ten- and

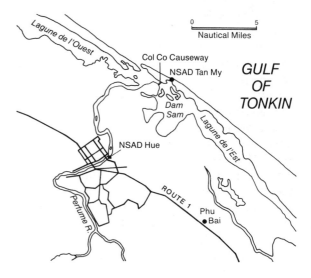

twelve-inch lines installed at Chu Lai and Da Nang withstood the storms somewhat better than the eight-inch lines first used, though their sea ends also fell victim to the high winds and sea, which prevailed from October through March.

At Phu Bai, which supported the intensive campaign north of Da Nang and was the head-quarters of the 3rd Marine Division, the fuel situation became critical enough to warrant the installation of a "Swivel-Top" or Mono Buoy. This was an extremely large buoy measuring 30 feet in diameter and 13 feet in depth. Securely moored off Tan My by eight 12,000 pound "Stato anchors,"[9] it had the sea ends of two eight-inch sea load lines coming up through the buoy and terminating in a swivel-ing goose-neck connection on top. Two eight-inch flexible hoses were attached to the goose neck to complete the hook up rig for an oiler to pump its product ashore. The hoses were equipped with flotation rings which kept them afloat when not in use to prevent their tangling in the mooring chains. Unfortunately, this flotation gear was not monsoon-proof and the answer to keeping them afloat was eventually found in the use of buoyant hoses. The cost, ($300 thousand each) precluded initial in-stallation of these buoys in Da Nang and Chu Lai, but when the Marine action shifted north of Da Nang, the buoy's value was reconsidered. In September 1969, one was installed at Tan My. In retrospect, considering the men and equipment which were tied up in repair of the line after a monsoon storm, the buoy would doubtlessly have been an excellent investment at Chu Lai also. And, of course, one must add to these costs the Commander's anxiety over the possibility of being unable to support the fuel requirements for the Chu Lai area. Never dur-ing the length of his tour, Rear Admiral Lacy asserted, did he feel completely comfortable about the future fuel supply in I Corps.

SHIP SALVAGE

Monsoon storms exacted their toll from the Navy support effort not only in fuel lines but also in ships. Probably one of the least-publicized aspects of NSA's work was that done in the salvage of vessels. NSA had no salvage tugs or salvage divers in its organiza-tion. Harbor Clearance Unit One, which assisted in clearing a hulk near Museum ramp and in the attempted salvage and ultimate clearance of the USS *Mahnomen County* (LST-912) at Chu Lai, belonged to ComNavForV. But the weather did not pay attention to our orga-nization and each year it demanded, and got, a considerable salvage effort from us. Christmas week of 1966 was an example.

On Christmas Eve morning, Da Nang re-ceived the word from the detachment at Dong Ha that its warping tug, which had been sent up to salvage the four-inch bottom lay line, had gone aground just north of the channel leading into the Cua Viet. Thus far local salvage efforts had failed. The Luzon Stevedoring Company's diesel tug *Tiburon*, under charter to NSA, was ordered to proceed to Cua Viet to salvage the warping tug. The Filipino skipper and crew, with the placid resignation which mariners develop about such things, headed north from Da Nang. The following morning, Captain Jim Linville, Assistant Chief of Staff, Operations and Plans, for NSA Da Nang, flew up to Dong Ha to see how our bluejackets were faring dur-ing their first Christmas under the shadow of the DMZ. As he flew north from Tan My, he noted what appeared to be a vessel in distress. He directed the pilot of NSA's "gooney bird" to make a sweep over the vessel. Sure enough, it was the *Tiburon*, in trouble. En route north, the *Tiburon* had grounded in the coastal shallows and the wind and sea had done the rest. Con-tinuing his flight to Dong Ha, the Captain re-layed the news of the tug's trouble to Da Nang.

The word was passed to the Coast Guard, which sent an 82-foot WPB from Market Time Operations nearby. An LCU was also dispatched to the scene. A line was passed to the stricken vessel. Unfortunately, a monsoon storm developed at the same time. Lines parted and waves became too high for the two small rescue vessels to continue their work. Under the merciless pounding of the waves, the *Tiburon* was driven into the beach and finally rolled over on her side. Grabbing the ship's log and any personal belongings they could stuff into their clothing, the captain and crew abandoned their ship and swam into the beach through the surf. Shivering from the cold, they were plucked from the unfriendly beach by a Marine helicopter sent from Phu Bai. The following day I flew up to Phu Bai and thence to the beach about 10 miles north of Tan My where the Pacific fleet salvage officer and I swam out to the *Tiburon*, which, by this time, had been turned by the swells so that her bow pointed seaward. She still lay flat on her starboard side, as she was when abandoned by the crew. Her position made salvage attempts impractical. The company accepted the Navy's recommendation and abandoned the tug. For at least the following year, she served as a reminder to all who flew north from Da Nang to Cua Viet of the fury and uncertainty of the sea. Ironically, the warping tug, which the *Tiburon* had been sent to rescue, was pulled off the shoal by an LCU the next day.

Two days later Da Nang had a bit of a blow. The Harbor Entrance Control Post advised ships anchored in the southeastern part of the harbor to check their position carefully to guard against dragging. One ship in particular, the *Coastal Trader*, on a General Agency Agreement charter, appeared to be getting set down toward the beach by the wind and swells. The following morning the Master sent out word that he was aground in a soft mud bank. The one NSA YTB, several pusher boats, and a couple of YTLs were all sent to pull the freighter out. After much tugging and twisting, the stranded merchantman floated free and was pulled to a safe anchorage. The next day word was received that the *LCU-1493* had gone aground about ten miles south of the Cua Viet. A LARC and a YFU from Dong Ha were dispatched to assist the stricken vessel. Two days of skillful efforts finally freed this craft, permitting her to resume her trip north. The rescue was not without its cost, however. The LARC, then under tow by the LCU because of engine failure, slowly filled with water and sank.

The Loss of the USS Mahnomen County

The climax to this turbulent week occurred on New Year's Day during the midwatch, when the USS *Mahnomen County* (LST-912) parted with her anchor off Chu Lai while waiting for better weather so she could enter and discharge her one-thousand-ton cargo of cement. Before the main engines could be brought on the line, a combination of high winds, mounting seas, and a uniquely high tide picked the hapless LST up and deposited her on a rock shelf adjacent to the MAG-36 helo pad. Salvage efforts were begun the next morning with the discharge of the cement over the stricken T's side. Elements of HCU One were flown down to Chu Lai to begin the salvage. The best efforts of three ATFs and an ASR pulling in concert were unable to dislodge her. It was puzzling, as well as disheartening, to witness all the effort exerted to dislodge the ship from her perch, and yet to see no evidence of movement. Later, when the seas calmed down sufficiently, divers were able to discover the reason for the failure in their salvage scheme. The LST had settled down on three rock pinnacles which had penetrated her bottom and sealed her fate. Efforts were made to cut the hull in two and tow the ship off as a bow and stern section. Salvage efforts were finally determined to be futile and the ship was cut down to the second deck. The first reason was to remove any hazard to aircraft, but the strongest motive was to make less conspicuous a U. S. naval vessel wrecked on the coast of South Vietnam.

The Dredge Hyde *Mining Incident*

The *Hyde* was one of the operational anomalies of the logistic organization in I Corps. The Army at sea working for the Navy on land. The U. S. Army Corps of Engineers dredge *Hyde* was the first vessel working for NSA to fall casualty to enemy action. Steadily engaged in dredging the Cua Viet bar to permit the entrance of LSTs in this most northerly NSA outpost, the *Hyde* was the victim of two limpet mines placed on the starboard bow and port quarter, respectively, on 9 May 1967. The bow mine exploded first at about 0400 on 9 May 1967, whereupon the quick-thinking mate on watch cooly dumped his hopper of sand and headed the dredge into the south bank, where he beached the sturdily constructed vessel. Two hours later, the second charge detonated. Fortunately, the dredge, with sand dumped, had lost three feet of draft and the charge blew a hole about the size of a grapefruit in the ship's counter now above the water. Minor damage was done to the after steering machinery room. The hole in the bow was a different matter. It was seven feet long by four feet high and allowed the flooding of a ballast tank, the bosun locker, paint locker, carpenter shop, and sail locker. A cofferdam was placed over the hole into the working spaces, and a layer of cement was laid over the hole in the paint locker deck. A piece of quarter-inch boiler plate was welded over the skin of the ship to serve as a fairwater, and, within thirty-six hours, the intrepid dredge and her undaunted Master, Captain James Bartell, were resuming their slow but steady assault on the sand which formed the river entrance bar.

The USS *Coconino County* (LST-603) was the first major naval ship to suffer from the hands of enemy swimmers in the I Corps Tactical Zone. Mined while on the ramp at Cua Viet on 29 June 1967, the "lucky Coco" was towed back to Da Nang for patching by the Small Craft Repair Facility, before being towed to Guam for final repairs.

CIVIC ACTION

Although not specifically charged with Civic Action in its original charter, NSA assigned men to that job with the necessary equipment. It was a good investment in the country of South Vietnam, especially when one considers the stark destruction of war. The first big effort was in the establishment of Civic Action Teams, or CATS. CATS were composed of skilled petty officers who volunteered to live in the hamlets with the Vietnamese and assist them in myriad projects ranging from building schools and digging wells to just plain instruction in sanitation and hygienic improvements. The accomplishments of these dedicated men were most impressive.[10] By living with the people they sought to help, they helped to dispel the suspicion, distrust, and resentful feeling among the villagers that they were charity cases, which are not uncommon to people of less-developed areas. When the rocket and mortar attacks occurred, NSA CATS took their lumps with the villagers, and then were the first out of the shelters to begin the rebuilding.

The work of the CATS or VATS (Village Action Teams) had a strong appeal to NSA officers and sailors, and more and more of them succeeded in contributing to the program on their own time. Volunteer sick calls, city beautification projects, clothing distribution, and the like sprang up as a result of the generosity which lies in the hearts of all Americans when faced with the plight of the less fortunate. During July 1967, some 273 projects were completed by CATS involving the building of 60 classrooms, 19 hamlet offices, and 275 houses.

The training of Vietnamese civilians in basic skills became a very valuable adjunct to the work of the CATS. Auto repair and sewing were two of the most popular and productive classes. These and many other vocational training opportunities assisted the local people to aspire to personal improvement. Sanitary conditions at Da Nang were greatly enhanced by the garbage disposal system organized by NSA. Streets and alleys, once rife with garbage, were once again negotiable without the former stench. Fire protection was another mutually benefitting civic action provided by the Support Activity.

In 1969, when the Accelerated Turnover to Vietnamese (ACTOV) began in earnest, the training program, begun as a matter of Civic Action, was converted into a Navy training program to equip the Vietnamese to operate the marine craft, vehicles, and electronic equipment which were being transferred to Vietnamese military personnel.

SMALL CRAFT REPAIR FACILITY

No account of the achievements of the Support Activity at Da Nang would be complete without describing the work of the Small Craft Repair Facility (SCRF). At first the SCRF was a branch of the operations department, but by mid-1966 it was accorded department status. The engineering and repair division, forerunner of the SCRF, was organized in January of 1966 and consisted of two officers and 22 men, one LCM work boat, and three sections of pontoon causeway. By that April, the repair section expanded to include a YR, an AFDL, and a YFND.[11] These craft were originally positioned in the southeastern section of Da Nang Harbor.

But this was exposed to the sea and therefore dredging, including a 20-foot channel, was begun in the eastern-most section of Tien Sha cove. This would not only permit the entry of craft to be repaired, but would also permit the floating drydock to submerge for pickup of the vessels to be drydocked. Soon another YR was received, as was another YFND. These were moored near the Vietnamese Naval Base behind Monkey Mountain and were designated to handle maintenance work on the boats assigned to Market Time.

The skill and ingenuity of the officers and men who manned the Small Craft Repair Facility cannot be praised too highly. To give the reader some idea of the tempo of operations during the month of March 1968, 68 small craft were drydocked. The engine shops in the YR worked around the clock overhauling the propulsion units for the essential lighters.

In the early days of the Support Activity, regular overhaul of lighterage, from LCM-3 to LCU or YFU-size, was done in Subic Bay or Japan. The YWs,[12] YOs, and YOGs, together with the tugs of various sizes, also had to make the long journey, either in an LSD or by sailing escorted, to receive their regular overhauls. It was the dream of the Repair Officer, Commander Ray Pierce, that SCRF would some day be able to save these long transit times and accomplish the overhauls in Da Nang. In February of 1967 this dream was realized when the overhaul of the first YFU in ICTZ was completed. Routine maintenance of the vast armada of service and lighterage craft[13] precluded overhauling all the vessels. However, the two months consumed by an overhaul outside Vietnam became unnecessary for a significant number of the craft.

Perhaps the most impressive of SCRF's many talents lay in their versatility. They never protested that because they lacked facilities, special tools, or specially trained men, they couldn't do a job. Whether it was changing one of the dredge *Hyde*'s large screws, placing a patch on the *Coconino County*'s ruptured bottom, replacing the bottom and major portion of the hull of a YFU damaged by a mine, changing gas turbine engines in the gunboat *Asheville* (PG-84), or drydocking the Alaska Barge and Tug Company's tug *Makah*, SCRF could do it. In addition, the attached Navy divers were active during the monsoon season in keeping the sea load fuel lines in commission, as well as in aiding successful salvage work from one end of I Corps to the other. A small repair detachment was maintained in Chu Lai, which was adequate for performing maintenance and emergency repairs on their support craft. When the Cua Viet ramp was put into commission in March of 1967, a small detachment of repairmen was assigned to keep the many lighters operational. They were the same men who that May were to have the *Hyde* back in operation within 36 hours of the time she fell casualty to the mine.

The move to Tien Sha Cove by the SCRF greatly enhanced its value. It permitted the expansion of facilities on the beach. A finger pier, replacing pontoon causeways, was built alongside for mooring craft in need of repairs.

THE NSA HOSPITAL

Just as the SCRF cared for sick craft, the NSA Hospital served the sick and wounded men in I Corps.[14] Construction of the 400-bed hospital began in July of 1965. By early 1966 it could accommodate 165 patients and consisted of 18 buildings which ranged from laboratories and an X-ray room to an optical shop. By June of that same year, it had grown to 330 beds and included air-conditioned operating rooms and wards. By the end of August, the goal of 404 beds had been reached. This capacity, added to the almost 800 beds in the hospital ship *Repose*, greatly assisted in the

rapid and excellent medical attention which has become one of the remarkable accomplishments of the Vietnam war. In the spring of 1967, the USS *Sanctuary* (AH-17) joined the USS *Repose* (AH-16) and added 780 hospital beds. Eventually Da Nang Hospital increased to 600 beds.

Each person who has served in Vietnam probably has his favorite example of the outstanding medical service available in country. My favorite example of cool courage combined with remarkable professional skill involves the removal of a live 60 mm. mortar round from the chest of Private First Class Nguyen Luong, ARVN. This daring operation was accomplished by Navy Medical Corps Captain H. H. Dinsmore with the assistance of Chief Engineman J. J. (Shorty) Lyons, Navy explosive ordnance demolition expert. The pair, working in an area surrounded by sandbags to protect the rest of the operating room staff should the mortar round detonate, calmly made the incision and then gently lifted out the round with its detonating plunger just millimeters away from contact with the explosive squib. True to the Navy practice of awarding honorary memberships, Dr. Dinsmore was appointed an honorary member of the EOD fraternity, while Chief Engineman Lyons was made an honorary corpsman. Captain Dinsmore also received the Navy Cross for his intrepidity.

During the four years the hospital was operated under Navy management, a total of 66,007 patients, 21,523 of whom had combat related injuries, were treated. In addition, nearly a million persons received outpatient care (958,051 to be precise).

NEW EQUIPMENT ENHANCES CAPABILITY

New concepts and equipment were identified and used in an ever urgent attempt to keep the "customer happy." One of the early techniques used to keep supplies flowing into Northern I Corps was the use of LSDs to carry

LCUs and YFUs "piggyback" during the monsoon season. As has been previously indicated, when the great northeast monsoon swells built up, transit time for the old YFUs was doubled, often tripled, or more. In an attempt to keep the Third Marine Division supplied, YFUs or LCUs filled with cargo were loaded into the well deck of an LSD, which then steamed north at three to four times the old lighters' speed. Arriving off Cua Viet in the morning, the LSD would disgorge her boats and then pick up a load of empties for the trip back south. Frequently AKAs were also used to assist in clearing cargo backlogs, or to assist in rotating Marine units out of Vietnam. In each of these cases, the Support Activity supplemented the AKA's own boats to speed loading and unloading.

INTRODUCING THE CONTAINERSHIP AND THE ROLL-ON ROLL-OFF

Containership operations in Vietnam were started in ICTZ on 1 August 1967, when the steamship *Bienville* arrived in Da Nang with 228 35-foot-long trailer truck size containers, 55 of which were refrigerated vans. Within 18 hours the *Bienville* was unloaded and her cargo, still in its containers, was on its way to the customer. The vans, lifted out of the ship's holds by her own cranes, were moved to the side of the ship and lowered carefully to the waiting wheeled frames and tractors parked on the pier below. Customers were pleased with this new method of packaging and delivery. The time saved in handling by NSA Da Nang was substantial. Since the vans were locked, pilfering was reduced, and critical pier space was saved by the rapid movement of vans from the unloading area. The vans also afforded a convenient container for retrograde cargoes, such as empty brass.

Refrigerated vans were particularly valuable. Lettuce picked in the Salinas Valley of California was packed in the refrigerated container in the field and, without further handling, traveled to Da Nang in an ordinary containership. In this way spoilage was drastically reduced in all refrigerated items. The reefer vans also offered critically needed temporary refrigerated storage space. Finally, the vans eliminated the need to handle and stage cargo at ocean terminals. Despite the early concern that the monsoon weather might make the unloading of containers unfeasible, it was discovered that there was no appreciable effect on the operation during most of the monsoon season. The use of Skycrane helicopters for unloading containers was experimented with in Da Nang, but was never adopted.

The introduction of Roll-On Roll-Off (Ro Ro) shipping, however, which in Vietnam was begun at Cam Ranh Bay, in II Corps, also proved quite advantageous in the movement of rolling stock to and within I Corps. In November 1967, the steamer *Transglobe*, under MSTS charter, began a Ro Ro service between Da Nang and Okinawa. On the first occasion, 44 trailers and 15 miscellaneous vehicles were discharged in a five-hour period. The Ro Ro concept allows a vehicle to be driven both aboard and off the ship. The ship to be unloaded is moored alongside a pier in the normal manner. When alongside, she is gently eased back until her stern ramp is within reach of the causeway or barge located astern on to which her cargo is driven. The causeway or barge is connected to the land so that the vehicles are easily driven ashore. This system was used not only at Da Nang, but also at Cua Viet, and was a welcome improvement in the logistic movement of vehicles, especially in the handling of trailers and semi-trailers.

THE "SKILAK"

So far as local seaborne lines of communication are concerned, the greatest improvement coming out of the war was the introduction to the Navy of the "Skilak." The old YFU, and its newer version, the 1400-class LCU, did a yeoman job of handling the unique shuttle of cargo from Da Nang to the many ancillary ports served. They sailed when all the rules of prudent seamanship dictated that they should stay in port. They lost their way because their primitive navigational equipment was never designed for such open sea voyages. In spite of the efforts of a group of hard-working electronic technicians, their radars and communication gear were out of order about as often as they operated. Yet they continued to sail north and south from Da Nang with their hundred-ton loads of cargo. The intrepid crews who manned these "U boats" were undaunted in carrying out their arduous and often monotonous routine, which, beginning in 1967, became hazardous as well. Sometimes the "U's" were stranded on unfriendly shores and on occasion sailed past the DMZ only to have the North Vietnamese garrison on Tiger Island fire at them, giving them their first clue that they had passed their destination.

Then, in late 1967, the first of the new breed of cargo carrier came into the picture. The "Skilak" was designed in San Francisco for the Alaska trade. When NSA examined the new craft concept, it was apparent that its greater capacity made the "Skilak" perfect for logistic operations in I Corps. When the first one of them arrived in Vietnam in the well deck of an LSD, the NSA lighterage operators were convinced. Here was a craft that could carry 360 ST of dry cargo for harbor operations and 260 ST for coastal operations (the lighter load gave a greater amount of freeboard and allowed for greater safety). The "Skilak's" draft and speed was about the same as the 1400-class LCU. The living quarters were better than quarters on either the YFU or LCU, being roomy and air-conditioned. Engineering spaces were roomy and accessible compared with the YFU wherein the engineer was forced to walk in a crouch through his main engine room. About the only

disadvantage was that the main well deck was not strengthened to carry tanks, and in a purely logistical role, this really wasn't a drawback. One favored use was in the movement of ammunition. The "Skilak" was loaded alongside ammunition ships and then proceeded to her destination at Tan My or Dong Ha without any further handling.

In addition to her improved dry cargo capacity, the "Skilak" had a very impressive liquid cargo storage capacity. In December of 1969, with the sea load line at Cua Viet not operational because of monsoon storm damage, "Skilaks" delivered 130,000 gallons of diesel oil to Dong Ha. Designed as they were for the rough weather of the Alaskan trade, they had few problems in the monsoon weather.

THE VERSATILE AMMI

Another new design to come out of the war in Vietnam was the Ammi Pontoon. This versatile piece of equipment, which measured 90 × 28 × 5 feet, offered answers to a wide range of requirements associated with forward area logistic operations.

Designed to accommodate 22-inch steel spuds at each corner, the Ammi could become a quick reaction mini-DeLong pier. These same spuds served as guides when the Ammi was flooded and used as a forward area small craft drydock. With the craft positioned over it, the water was removed with compressed air and up came Ammi with up to 200 tons of small craft high and dry. Equipped with large warping tug "outboards," it became a self-propelled fuel barge with a capacity for 58 thousand gallons of different kinds of fuel in its six tanks. When further equipped with a transfer system, the Ammi was used to fuel lighters in Da Nang harbor and relieve the overworked YOGs and YOs. Eventually it relieved the LCM-8 bladder-equipped boat on the Cua Viet fuel shuttle to Dong Ha. In November of 1969, when the *YOG-76* was mined in the Cua Viet, the reliable

Ammi played a role in helping to refloat that valuable fuel carrier. Both Ammi and "Skilak" have earned a well-deserved spot in the history of Navy logistic support operations in Vietnam.

Operational Obstacles

Certainly, a logistic operation the size of NSA faced obstacles, as the reader has come to learn. Obsolescence of equipment, absence of clearing port staging areas, shortage of spare parts, disagreeable geography, unknown hydrography, enemy action, and difficult weather were the major problems which provided daily challenges to the Commander and his staff.

Obsolete equipment represented a definite obstacle to a smooth, efficient operation of NSA. Twenty-year-old service craft posed problems in maintenance and reliability. They continued to function only because of the masterful efforts of their dedicated crews, and the ingenious repair department people, who never let anything deter them from meeting a craft's sailing schedule. Tired engines, worn out transmissions, and poor preservation made most of these relics of another war candidates for a scrap yard. In fact, before the war began two of the YFUs had been sunk at Yokosuka to serve as improvised harbor breakwaters. Pumped out and refloated, they were overhauled and sent to Da Nang to join the coastal shuttle which kept the Marines in business in I Corps.

Clearing cargo staging areas was initially a problem of some magnitude. There simply were not enough trucks to keep the cargo cleared on its way to the customer or to storage. The roads, few in number and bad in quality, contributed to this problem.

Worth its weight in gold when it worked, and yet a millstone around the freight terminal officer's neck when it needed repairs, was the rough terrain fork lift. It was ideal for working cargo on the unimproved terrain and it was able to move itself about the confines and obstacles which an LST ramp and tank deck presented; but the lack of repair parts kept many inoperable during the first two years. The shortage of these versatile vehicles had a definite deleterious impact on cargo movement.

Geography and hydrography of the area also posed substantial obstacles to logistic operations. Waterways were shallow and filled with sandbars, which made voyages at all tidal stages difficult. The labyrinth of waterways which crisscrossed the countryside made travel ashore difficult because of the enemy's land mines, booby traps, and sabotage of bridges. There is just no easy way to move cargo in the land of rice paddies and coolie hats.

ENEMY INTERFERENCE

As one might expect, enemy action provided some obstacles to NSA operations. A few examples will suffice:

On 12 June 1967, NSAD Cua Viet received 200 rounds of rocket and artillery fire. Three 10,000-gallon bladders and their contents were destroyed.

In February 1968 the Officer-in-Charge of NSAD Hue was killed during the Tet offensive.

In September 1968, three LCM-8s were damaged by mining in Dam Nuoc Man at Sa Huynh.

On 16 January 1969, *YFU-62* was mined while transiting Cua Viet. The craft sank. Eight were killed, three wounded.

On 27 February 1969, a rocket and mortar attack on the Bridge Cargo Facility at Da Nang sank the *LCU-1600* and *YFU-78*, killing 13 in the one and 6 in the other. Both craft were loaded with ammunition.

That more NSA bluejackets and officers were not killed can be credited more to a kindly and protective Providence than to any invulnerability which their craft, armament, or cargo offered.

WEATHER

Weather complicated the job of the logistician in I Corps. We can give weather full credit for keeping two, and sometimes three, dredges on duty in I Corps waterways—and there were times when these busy craft did not prove adequate to keep the channels open after a typhoon, such as Doris in September of 1969. We can credit weather with making life miserable for salvage and UDT divers who had to get out and check to see if the sea load lines were intact after each northeast monsoon. Many a young lieutenant (junior grade) was thwarted in his job as YFU convoy commodore by 14-foot waves which caused him to postpone sailing his vital cargo until the storm had abated. For further confirmation of the weather's role, ask any of the skippers of the craft whose hulks litter the foreshores of northern I Corps.

OVERCOMING THE OBSTACLES

Among the lighters, obsolescence was slowly overcome by introducing the new "Skilak," while as soon as reasonable data on parts usage could be compiled for the rough terrain fork lift, the spare parts problem for this equipment disappeared. The geography was changed by ambitious and skilled Seabees to accommodate land transportation, and the hydrography was altered to support river operations by the courageous crews of the dredges. Enemy action could be controlled by Marines pushing the perimeter out and maintaining good air cover and tight security support. But the weather was, as Mark Twain said, "something everybody talked about, but nobody ever did anything about." While improvements have occurred in the realm of all other obstacles mentioned, the weather, for all the talk, has not improved one whit. It was the principal item on an NSA commander's list of worries.

Additional Contributions

Not surprisingly, there were many miscellaneous support functions provided by NSA, such as the rescue of two Marine Corps pilots by the *LCU-1615* and *LCU-1619* off the Cua Viet River on 26 and 29 September 1967, or the tactical support provided by NSA's LCUs and YFUs as they redeployed tanks and heavy equipment in support of ground operations throughout I Corps. While NSA was chartered to support only U. S. and Free World forces in I Corps, its people never failed to provide visiting ships of the Fleet with water, diesel oil, or provisions to the limit of their ability. For instance, during January 1967, NSA supplied ships from the Fleet with 793,912 gallons of diesel oil and over a million gallons of fresh water. On the 17th through the 22nd of May in 1967, when the DMZ sterile zone was being created, the *YFU-55* and *YFU-57* evacuated the Vietnamese population north of the Cua Viet. Two NSA LCM-8s were responsible for towing to Chu Lai the North Vietnamese trawler which had been forced ashore by Market Time forces 15 miles south of Chu Lai in July of 1967.

NSA harbor security forces cooperated periodically with the Vietnamese harbor police in pulling periodic surprise junk identification checks in Da Nang Harbor. NSA operations department men also represented the commander in the joint port coordinating committee which worked with the Vietnamese Army and civilian port directors in improving aids to navigation and port facilities. Disposing of defective ordnance and supporting USAID (the foreign aid agency) were two more of the many activities engaged in by the Support Activity. The excellent communications department, in addition to providing support for the commander, also assisted from time to time in supporting the Fleet broadcasts.

NSA had come into existence for the special purpose of supplying the Third Marine Amphibious Force in I Corps when the Army said it was unable to assume the logistic task. As it became apparent that the U. S. must reduce its presence in Vietnam and look to Vietnamization of the war, the need for continued Navy support in I Corps lessened. It was determined that the Army should properly relieve the Marines of the ground action and the Navy of the support effort. The Commanding General XXIV Corps relieved the Commanding General III MAF as I Corps Commander in March of 1970. The phasing out of the Naval Support Activity, Da Nang, began in earnest in December 1969. The ACTOV, or Accelerated Turn-Over to the Vietnamese program, saw *YOG-71, YG-51, YFRN-997, YFR-888,* four LCUs or YFUs, three LCM-8s, and other miscellaneous small craft turned over to the Vietnamese. NSA people assisted in the training of their new operators.

Since by then the sea communications were replaced by land supply routes, on 15 February 1970, NSA Da Nang closed its detachments at Dong Ha-Cua Viet, and Sa Huynh. On 15 March, Tan My was turned over to the Army. By 26 March, all fuel supply operations in ICTZ were being run by the Army. NSAD Phu Bai was turned over on 10 April; the support organization at Chu Lai came under Army operation on 1 June. The NSA Hospital became an Army cantonment after its patients were sent in mid-May to the USS *Sanctuary,* the Marine's 1st Medical Battalion hospital, or the Army's 95th Base hospital. On 30 June 1970, just three and a half months short of five years from the date of its original commissioning, Rear Admiral R. E. Adamson, Jr., transferred all remaining logistic support functions to the U. S. Army in Vietnam. From NSA Da Nang's impressive force of over 400 officers and over 10,000 men, whose domain stretched from the DMZ to the southern boundary of Quang Ngai Province, came the Naval Support Facility, Da Nang, which, on 15 September 1970, consisted of 2,500 to 3,000 persons of the U. S. and Vietnamese navies and Vietnamese civilians. NSF

Da Nang is now the second largest naval industrial establishment in Vietnam.

NSF's New Role

When Rear Admiral Adamson decommissioned NSA Da Nang, his chief of staff became Commanding Officer of the new facility, which consists principally of the SCRF and Camp Tien Sha. Here U. S. Navymen teach their counterparts in the Vietnamese Navy the skills of repair and maintenance of patrol and logistic craft which have been turned over in the ACTOV program. This will culminate in the turnover of the Small Craft Repair Facility complex.

The organization was combined in October 1970 as a joint U. S. and Vietnamese naval base, with a Vietnamese executive officer and assistant department heads, the commanding officer and department heads being U. S. officers. In a concluding memo to the U. S. Navymen remaining at NSF Da Nang, Rear Admiral Adamson stated, "Those of you remaining here will carry out the tremendously important job of preparing the Vietnamese Navy to take over responsibility for prosecuting the war effort. Training is the key to success of this undertaking, and this is where each of you becomes very important. The degree of success you have in communicating your experience and knowledge of the job to your counterpart will dictate just how soon the Vietnamese Navy will no longer require your presence."

Training is divided into three phases, the first of which is classroom instruction lasting about 12 weeks. The second phase involves on-the-job training, the Vietnamese working alongside their U. S. Navy counterparts. Phase three begins with the Vietnamese actually relieving our men. The entire process has all the earmarks of being an orderly and effective Vietnamization of the war with no Irish pennants left over to mar the splendid record built by the Navy's I Corps support activity.

Significant to any operation of this magnitude upon its completion are the lessons learned. A Joint Logistics Review Board, consisting of very senior officers from all services, convened in 1969 and completed its review of the logistics effort in Vietnam in June of 1970. This paper does not presume to guess what the JLRB will have concluded; however, certain points appear obvious.

Lessons Learned

The first of these is that the lack of logistic tradition may well have been the key to the Navy's success in ICTZ. The Army logistic Table of Organization and Equipment (TO & E) spells out the support requirements for various Army forces. There is no guesswork and consequently little flexibility in this system. The Army operates a "push" logistic pipe line. Conversely the Navy, lacking all but the most rudimentary guidelines and having few experienced people (most of whom were to be found in a very small number of Cargo Handling Battalions), started with a small support force, extracted the maximum effort (12 hours per day, seven days a week) and then expanded as necessary to keep the troops supported. The Navy pipeline was a "pull" effort, the Naval Support Activity Commander and his staff being expected to keep the supplying logistic agent advised of their needs. While this method did not afford the admiral and his department heads a feeling of complacency, the fact that details were not spelled out in a book back on the mainland did afford them an exciting challenge. It provided motivation and stimulated ingenuity at every level of the support organization, and the job was done well. It was a manifestation of the old Navy "Can Do" spirit honed down to its finest edge. There was no fat in the NSA organization. Documentation of this effort will provide the Navy with guidelines on the minimum requirements to perform a maximum effort in any future opera-

tion of this type. In addition, it allowed the seagoing Navy to remain at maximum strength at a time when our commitments on, under, and above the surface of the seas were most demanding.

The second lesson was a revalidation of the efficacy of an arm of the Navy which earned its place on the Navy-Marine Corps team during World War II, the Seabees. The construction requirements in all of Vietnam were unbelievable in scope. Captain Merdinger described the Seabee impact on the war effort in his excellent article in last year's *Review*.* Little could be added here to describe the courageous and professional job that they did as construction men and fighters. They proved themselves capable of following the Marines ashore and building airfields, cantonments, utility plants, landing ramps, piers, and even an ice cream factory.

Brown Water Logistics

NSA wrote a new chapter in the book of warfare on shallow water resupply. Assault craft found new uses as draught wagons using the waterways which criss-crossed Vietnam. New craft such as "Skilak" were pressed into service to increase the efficiency of the logistic effort. As long as there are waterways and small craft available to ply them, lack of organized land lines of communication should never again cause logistic support to falter.

Weaknesses in assault fueling techniques were discovered and corrected; this knowledge will serve us in good stead in future operations. It was reaffirmed that sheltered piers, large enough to accommodate seagoing tankers, were not necessary to support the prodigious fuel requirements of modern warfare. The Mono-buoy appears to have answered a great many questions on how to keep the seaward

---

*And which appears next in this book. (Editor)

end of bottom lay lines functioning during the severe storms such as those which plagued I Corps during the monsoon seasons.

ULTIMATE LESSON

Of all the lessons learned, one stands out above all others—Man is still the ultimate answer in logistic support of large armies. For men sailed the battered YFUs to their destinations deep in the heart of hostile territory; men unloaded ships in 120-degree tropical heat during long twelve-hour shifts; men built the airstrips and carved out the roads and dredged the silt-filled sand bars from the waterways; men dived in murky and turbulent waters to locate the elusive ends of the 12-inch flexible hoses which wrapped themselves about the chains of mooring clumps; men guarded the cargo operations from the enemy and from the thieves. It was the U. S. bluejacket who gave credence to the Naval Support Activity, Da Nang motto—"They Shall Not Want."

(*Naval Review*, 1971)

Notes

1. "Building the Advanced Base at Da Nang" by Captain K. P. Huff, U. S. Naval Reserve, in *Naval Review 1968.*
2. In Vietnam the Cua Viet River is called the Hieu Giang, while the American version derives its use from the name of the river mouth (Cua Viet), literally South Mouth.
3. An LCU and a YFU are basically the same craft with two different designations for two uses. The former stands for Landing Craft Utility, the latter stands for Harbor Utility Craft. In general, LCUs, when old, become YFUs. LARC is the Army acronym for Amphibious Resupply Cargo Lighter, which comes in 5- and 15-ton sizes. The Army owns most of the LARCs in the U. S. inventory.
4. Now 18 to 20 feet deep.
5. These fuel lines frequently broke during the northeast monsoon. Wave and surf action tangled hoses with buoy moorings and ripped them apart.
6. "Civil Engineers, Seabees, and Bases in Vietnam" by Captain Charles J. Merdinger, Civil Engineer Corps, U. S. Navy, which follows.
7. *Measurement tons.* 1 MT = 40 cubic feet. This volumetric measurement is best used for low density cargo such as vehicles and boats.

Short tons. 1 ST = 2,000 pounds. This measurement is best used for high density cargoes such as cement, ammunition, and construction steel.
8. Where the larger T-2 tanker was used.
9. Modified Danforth anchors.
10. Described in detail by Captain C. E. Merdinger, CEC, U. S. Navy, in his article, "Civil Engineers, Seabees, and Bases in Vietnam," which follows.
11. A YR is an internal combustion engine repair barge. It is not self-propelled, but is covered. An AFDL is a small floating drydock used to support amphibious action. A YFND is a covered barge used as a shop stores vessel. The last two types are non-self-propelled.
12. These craft provided water to ships calling at Da Nang, obtaining their cargo from a stream running down the side of Monkey Mountain.
13. On 1 January 1969 NSA Da Nang had 53 LCUs or YFUs, 36 LCM-6s or LCM-3s, and 46 LCM-8s.
14. See "Doctors and Dentists, Nurses and Corpsmen in Vietnam," by Commander F. D. McClendon, Jr., MSC, U. S. Navy, further on in this book.

Civil Engineers, Seabees, and Bases in Vietnam

Captain Charles J. Merdinger,
Civil Engineer Corps, U. S. Navy

Unplanned, unwanted, undeclared, and un-popular, the Vietnam War in most American eyes just happened. And few people were quite sure how it had happened. The newspapers from time to time carried the unhappy stories of the French and their troubles in Indo-China in the turbulent years following World War II. After Dien Bien Phu came an uneasy period of truce between North and South Vietnam punc-tuated by reports of terrorism and assassina-tion and an unstable government in Saigon. Slowly, Americans began to fill the vacuum left by the French. American advisors pene-trated the jungles, American warships cruised the Tonkin Gulf, and then it was March 1965 and American Marines landed at Da Nang. United States combat troops were now com-mitted to the mainland of Asia.

This proved to be no mere show of the flag in a banana republic. These Marines were the vanguard of an American force which was to expand steadily beyond half a million troops. They were there to win the hearts and the minds of the people of South Vietnam, to free these people from the terror of the Viet Cong, and to help them to get on their feet politically, economically, and militarily. Halfway around the world they were to engage in a frustrating and perplexing war with an elusive foe, where there were no fixed battle lines, yet where there

were absolute lines of containment as far as United States forces were concerned, which were self-imposed by political decisions in Washington. The war that seemed to many to have just happened, turned out to be several wars in one; it was, among other things, a guer-rilla war, an air war, a political war, and an engineering war. A major portion of that en-gineering war was waged by the U. S. Navy.

How did the U. S. Navy get landlocked in such a place anyway? Like the war itself, Navy involvement was piecemeal and gradual, planned almost on the spur of the moment. Certainly the top deep-water sailors of the Navy had no intention of committing large numbers of Navy men ashore in a place like Vietnam. Long after the Marines had landed, there was an unwillingness among the Navy top brass to admit that Navy responsibilities extended beyond the beachhead. Now that the Marines were ashore—apparently for a pro-tracted period—they would need support of engineers. They, and the Army and the Air Force units soon to follow, would need ports and roads and airfields to get a foothold in this undeveloped land. In World War II in General MacArthur's island-hopping campaign, en-gineer troops comprised 18 per cent of the total troop strength committed. Where were the en-gineers to come from now? The Army, hard

Here's how to move concrete in South Vietnam when the monsoon rains turn the earth into mud.

pressed to take care of itself, wasn't prepared to supply them to the Marines, and the Marines didn't have the capability either. Fortuitously, the Navy's Bureau of Yards and Docks under the command of Rear Admiral Peter Corradi, CEC, United States Navy, already had a large, responsible U. S. contractor at work in Vietnam. The Navy's Seabees, though small in number, were mobile and capable of deploying quickly. Expediency prevailed—the Navy Civil Engineers, who guided both the Bureau and the Seabees, were handed the job.

The job would not be easy. Hurdles of a political and an administrative nature in Washington, too complicated to relate here, were enormous. Suffice it to say that Pentagon rivalries, lack of understanding in some quarters as to the requirements and importance of the engineer effort, and reluctance to relinquish decision-making which was better made in the field (an attitude which also prevailed at Pearl Harbor initially) only served to complicate this overwhelming task. To develop the ports, to start a pipeline of materials across the Pacific, to determine the what, where, and when of facilities to be constructed, involved countless decisions that could not wait. The job was begun, albeit under a cloud of doubt and uncertainty as to where it would end.

Fortunately for the U. S., the threat of what the enemy could do was not matched by what he actually did, and the contractor was thus able to mobilize and build with a minimum of harassment in the early days. Similarly, many military construction troop units were able to work under relatively peaceful conditions. General William C. Westmoreland, while still commanding in Vietnam in 1968, stated that the Viet Cong got their rockets too late, that with Soviet weapons they could have neutralized Saigon in 1966. By the time the Viet Cong and North Vietnamese did move in strength, the fundamental facilities from which to move American troops, planes, and ships were in place. The construction effort generated was impressive by any standard. Let us now take a look at the Navy's contribution—made up of disparate elements but brought together under the aegis of the Civil Engineer Corps.

Before 1965

"Without the Seabees we could not do it! This is more evident on each of my trips to Vietnam." With this salute to the Navy's construction men, the Commandant of the Marine Corps, General Wallace M. Greene, Jr., continued the accolades which stretched back a quarter of a century to World War II when General MacArthur complained to their boss, Admiral Ben Moreell, ". . . the only trouble with your Seabees is that I don't have enough of them."

If paucity of numbers produced a complaint during World War II when the Seabees reached a strength exceeding a quarter of a million, surely one can sympathize with involved operational commanders on the eve of the Vietnam adventure when Seabee (Group VIII) strength world-wide totaled only 8,500 men. Their officers—Civil Engineer Corps— who had reached a high of 10,000 during the war now numbered less than 1,700. The one hundred and fifty battalions of World War II had dwindled to two shortly thereafter, were rebuilt to eleven during the Korean War, and returned to ten from that point until the Vietnam build-up in 1965. However, Seabee strength measured in terms of numbers of battalions could be somewhat misleading, for not all of the Group VIII enlisted men (as the construction trades had come to be designated) were in Naval Mobile Construction Battalions (NMCBs) in 1965; nor are they today. Almost half of them were assigned to such diverse activities as the State Department Naval Support Unit, the Antarctic Support Activity, Nuclear Power program, two Amphibious Construction Battalions (ACBs), and

Public Works Departments scattered all over the world. Furthermore, battalion strengths differed. Those in the Pacific Fleet, home-ported at Port Hueneme, California, and deployed at various times in unit or sub-unit strength to Guam, Okinawa, Midway, Adak, and Sangley Point, were five in number, each of 525 men. Home-ported at Davisville, Rhode Island, and similarly deployed to Argentia, Bermuda, Morocco, Spain, Roosevelt Roads, and Guantanamo Bay, were the five battalions of the Atlantic Fleet; three with an allowance of 400 men and two with an allowance of 200. Parenthetically, it should be noted that while everyone attached to one of these battalions was a Seabee, not all were Group VIIIs. The cooks, yeomen, medical corpsmen, and other men in essential support roles generally comprised about 15 to 20 per cent of a battalion's complement. Similarly, though the battalions were led and predominantly staffed by Civil Engineer Corps (CEC) officers (17 of the 24), also included were officers of the Line and Supply (two each), and one each from the Medical, Dental, and Chaplain Corps—Seabees all.

The decision to place large numbers of Marines ashore in Vietnam in 1965 signaled a change, not only in the number, size, and deployment of Seabee battalions, but in the Group VIII family, the Civil Engineer Corps, and their parent headquarters, the Bureau of Yards and Docks (now the Naval Facilities Engineering Command) in Washington.

Of course, Vietnam was not entirely new to Navy men. Back in May of 1845 at Tourane (now Da Nang), Captain John Percival, commanding the USS *Constitution*, saw fit to seize as hostages some three Mandarins to force, unsuccessfully, as it turned out, the release of a French bishop at Hue. Though it was not that long ago, the Civil Engineer Corps had also been exposed previously to this exotic land. In August and September 1954, elements of ACB-

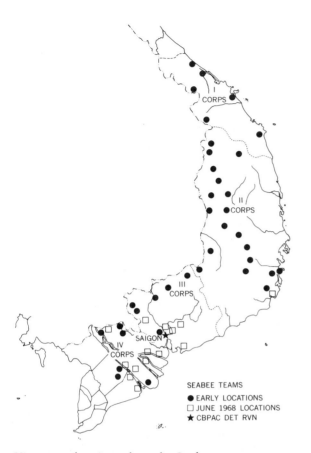

Vietnam, showing where the Seabee teams were. Originally they were deployed mainly in the Central Highlands, but later were concentrated in the Delta. All Seabee battalions worked in I Corps, chiefly in support of the Marines.

1 under Commander L. N. Saunders participated in Operation "Passage to Freedom," a massive evacuation of people and equipment from the Tonkin Delta region of French Indo-China to the south. Because of the truce agreement, these Seabees were not allowed ashore at Haiphong, their original destination, but they did some work at Tourane and, after removing all American military identification from their clothing and equipment, they disembarked at Cap St. Jacques and provided significant assistance in the construction of a

15,000-man refugee camp. Seabees returned again in 1956 when a group of five officers and six men from NMCB-10, led by Commander W. M. Brown, surveyed some 105 tortuous miles of jungle, the toughest link in a master survey involving 1,800 miles of existing and proposed roads in South Vietnam.

Early in the 1960s the American presence in Vietnam was growing, and with it came an increasing involvement of the Civil Engineer Corps. Members of the U. S. Military Assistance Group (MAAG), predominantly Army, came into the country along with civilian organizations and soon found themselves in need of more extensive logistic support than they could provide for themselves. Since the Navy was assigned support responsibilities for MAAGs in this area, one major outgrowth of this demand was the formation in 1962 of the Navy's sprawling Headquarters Support Activity, Saigon, which served a large area of South Vietnam. The Support Activity's Public Works Department, during Captain S. C. Gill's tenure as PWO, ultimately numbered well over 2,000 people, of whom nearly 200 were Seabees. This was the first appreciable number of Seabees in one unit committed to Vietnam on a continuing basis. The majority of the remaining 1,800 were Vietnamese. Their responsibilities were those normally associated with Navy public works operations, namely design and construction of facilities, acquisition of real estate, maintenance of facilities, and operation of utilities and ground transportation. Though the bulk of their work was in the Saigon area, public works forces operated country-wide. For example, roving one- and two-man Seabee automotive and generator repair teams rendered service to Special Forces, MACV Advisors, and U. S. Government civilian agencies located in remote provinces. Seabee inspectors ranged from Phu Quoc Island in the south to Dong Ha and Lang Vei in the north, overseeing Vietnamese civilian construction contracts for

MACV. HSA Saigon was phased out in May 1966 and replaced by the Army's First Logistics Command. The smaller Naval Support Activity, Saigon, immediately came into being to take care of those scattered Navy elements in the southern sectors (II, III, and IV Corps) which the Army found difficult to support.[1]

The Seabees in the Saigon area departed with the demise of HSA, but in June 1966 some one hundred of them were back again, on "loan" from the newly formed Public Works Department at Naval Support Activity, Da Nang.

Seabee Teams

In the meantime, other Seabees in small units, originally known as Seabee Technical Assistance Teams (STATS), later shortened to "Seabee Teams," became a part of the Vietnamese scene, commencing in January 1963 when the first two organized teams, 0501 and 0502, under Lieutenant (j.g.) R. L. Ferriter and Lieutenant C. V. M. Popowich arrived at Dam Pau in the central part of the country and Tri Ton in the southwest for the construction of civic action and tactical support projects. Forerunners of the teams, detachments from regular battalions, had served in Ecuador from 1959 to 1962, in Chile from 1961 to 1963, and in Haiti from 1962 to 1963. Subsequently, Seabee Teams were to see duty in the Dominican Republic, Upper Volta, Costa Rica, the Central African Republic, Liberia, and Thailand.

The teams were designed to be small, mobile, and cross-skilled. Consisting of a junior Civil Engineer Corps officer-in-charge, a hospital corpsman, and eleven men in the ratings of construction equipment operator and mechanic, builder, steel worker, construction electrician, utilities man, and engineering aid, these teams were normally given some months of intensive language and technical unit training at one of the three Naval Construction Battalion Centers—Port Hueneme, California,

Davisville, Rhode Island, or Gulfport, Mississippi (starting in 1968), prior to being sent on a mission.

Initially, to counter Viet Cong political influence in the villages, their missions in Vietnam were of two basic types: to construct small fortified camps and support facilities for U. S. Army Special Forces (Green Berets), and to assist Vietnamese civilians in civic action projects in relatively secure rural areas. Approximately 30 per cent of initial financial support was provided by the U.S. Military Assistance Command, Vietnam (MACV), for teams supporting the Special Forces. The first two teams in the country in 1963 were in this category. Then, two teams designated for the rural development program were deployed in the latter part of 1963, and from October of that year, the United States Operations Mission (USOM), whose functions were later replaced by the State Department's U. S. Agency for International Development (USAID), sponsored and financially supported these two teams. The average annual cost to the sponsor was $88,000 per team for materials, transportation, and so on, plus $200,000 to the Navy for initial outfitting, training, and personnel costs. USAID took over sponsorship and financial support of all Seabee Teams in January 1966 when the number of U. S. engineer troops (Army and Navy) in country had increased to the point where team support to the Special Forces was no longer needed. Early in 1968, responsibility for all rural development and allied civic action type programs was vested in a newly created MACV/U. S. Embassy organization entitled Civil Operations and Revolutionary Development Support (CORDS), and the subsequent placing of Seabee Teams came under its jurisdiction.

During the early years, ten teams (four teams at any given time), on six to seven month tours, supported the Special Forces, and two others had split responsibilities between military and rural development programs. The Special Forces, who were advising and training Vietnamese Strike Forces and Civilian Irregular Defense Groups in anti-guerrilla fighting and defense tactics, were usually located in remote forward areas, and fortified camps able to withstand ground and mortar attack were essential to their survival. In addition to constructing these camps complete with utilities systems, bunkers, and earthen parapets, the Seabees were called upon to construct access roads and tactical airstrips, 1,500 feet long at a minimum, to accept the Army's twin-engine STOL Caribou planes which delivered camp supplies. Further, they were able on many occasions to engage in civic action projects similar in nature to those of the teams sponsored by USAID.

While they were primarily builders, these Seabees were in some instances directly involved in battle. The most significant action occurred on June 9–11, 1965, at Dong Xoai, 55 miles northeast of Saigon, where 2,000 Viet Cong troops overran a Special Forces camp containing 400 South Vietnamese and allied Asian troops, 11 Green Berets, and nine Seabees of Seabee Team 1104. Seven of the Seabees were wounded and two of them killed. One of the dead was Marvin G. Shields (CMA-3), who was posthumously awarded the Congressional Medal of Honor for conspicuous gallantry in carrying a critically wounded man to safety and in destroying a Viet Cong machine gun emplacement at the cost of his life. He was the first Seabee to win the nation's highest award and the first Navy man to be so decorated for action in Vietnam.

From 1963 through 1966, there were normally four Seabee Teams working in Vietnam at any given time, and from 1966 on all were devoted to civic action projects exclusively. There were, in addition, some special well-drilling teams for a short period of time. Their success in the villages where they acted as teacher-builders, working alongside the local people, speaking their language, and providing a measure of elementary medical care the people had never known before, prompted the State Department to request more and more of these "military Peace Corps" units. The number of teams in country was upped to eight in 1967 and by July 1968 their number had grown to fifteen. By that time some 56 teams had served in Vietnam, and every one of the four corps areas had felt their presence.

Statistics have, of course, changed rapidly, but some idea of the contribution of the teams may be gained from these figures gathered at Seabee headquarters in Hawaii (ComCBPac) in mid-1968: "Pioneered or upgraded to all-weather standards over three hundred and fifty miles of provincial roads and highways; planned and built four 'New Life Hamlets'; planned and laid out six Refugee Villages; built three provincial and four local district market places; built sixteen Special Forces Camps; constructed thirty hospitals and dispensaries; added sixty school houses to the Vietnamese educational system; placed over 286,000 cubic yards of fill; provided on-the-job training to more than five thousand Vietnamese refugees, villagers, public works personnel, and 'Chieu Hoi' returnees (ex-Viet Cong) (more than half of these in 1967 alone); built over 4,000 feet of bridges (12 to 400 feet in length) and laid over two hundred culverts; constructed over eight miles of airfields; added 865 one-family housing units to various refugee villages; placed over fifty fresh water wells; and, constructed 168 civic and public buildings for the Vietnamese Government." One other statistic is also worthy of note; at the time of this report team hospital corpsmen had treated well over 150,000 Vietnamese at sick call.

One of the most significant factors concerning the teams was that they were—from 1966 on—embarked solely on missions essentially nonmilitary in character, even though the war continued to rage all about them. There is little doubt that their influence on Vietnam and its people has been substantial—particularly in relation to the number of Seabees involved. Vice President Hubert Humphrey in addressing the Senate of the United States put it this way:

"The Seabee Team has been called the military peace corps and the reasons for that comparison are obvious. Like the Peace Corps, the Seabee Teams put something into the country: They develop human resources. Such a contribution is valuable indeed.

"Dollar for dollar, the Seabee Team program has been called one of our best overseas investments. These teams have earned praise from high officials of every country involved, even though the program as a whole is still relatively young.

"Although this Seabee Team program is not widely known, I believe it is encouraging to learn of this down-to-earth attempt to assist our friends in Southeast Asia to build better communities for themselves and their families."

OICC and RMK-BRJ

Yet another element of the Civil Engineer Corps was in Vietnam long before the 1965 buildup. A memorandum from the Office of the Secretary of Defense in 1956 (and later refined in 1963) assigned contract construction responsibilities to the Army Corps of Engineers in certain parts of the world and to the Navy's Bureau of Yards and Docks (BuDocks) in others. Southeast Asia became Navy responsibility. In that same year BuDocks established its Officer in Charge of Construction (OICC) office under a CEC Captain, G. M. Inscoe, at Bangkok. It was responsible for administering contract construction, including design, in Cambodia, Laos, Thailand, and Vietnam. An offshoot of that office, the Resident Officer in Charge of Construction (ROICC) for Vietnam was established in Saigon in the spring of 1961. Its first project was to administer an architectural and engineering contract for the layout of a runway at Bien Hoa. It might be noted that the OICC office had some capability for doing its own design in house with a small number of U. S. civil servants and third country nationals, but the bulk of its design work was carried out by architectural and engineering firms located in Southeast Asia.

Before the end of the year the foundations were laid for one of the greatest construction ventures in history. In December 1961 a letter contract with a joint venture of two U. S. firms, Raymond International of New York and Morrison-Knudsen of Asia, Inc.—based in Boise, Idaho—was executed by the Bureau of Yards and Docks for the construction of "Airfields and Communication Facilities" in the Republic of Vietnam. This was converted to a cost-plus-fixed-fee contract in January 1962 in the amount of some $15 million, plus government-furnished materials and equipment which brought the total to more than $22 million. The sites involved were Pleiku, Bien Hoa, Tan Son Nhut (Saigon), and Da Nang. Coincidentally, in January 1962 the Saigon ROICC office was expanded to eight officers and 72 civilians and upgraded under a more senior officer. Its head, also a CEC Captain, now carried the title of Deputy, though the Saigon office became increasingly independent of the main office in Bangkok. In mid-1965 the break was completed when OICC Republic of Vietnam was formally established as a separate entity with 135 people, including 20 officers. The remaining 115 were U. S. civil servants, Vietnamese, and civilians from other countries. Subsequently, under the direction of a Civil Engineer Corps Rear Admiral—the first being William M. Heaman—the staff grew to over 1,000, including 100 officers and a small number of enlisted men.

Up until 1965 the contractor was engaged largely in building facilities for the armed forces of Vietnam under the Mutual Assistance Program. The original $22 million worth of work had grown to a total of more than $150 million over the three years. When it became evident that a U.S. troop build-up was in the offing, BuDocks hastened to enlarge the contractor's construction capability to include support of U.S. forces. Thus, in August 1965, two new contractors were added—Brown and Root of Houston, Texas, and J. A. Jones of Charlotte, North Carolina. This became the final consortium of the four contracting companies which were to carry out the bulk of the construction effort in Vietnam under the banner of RMK-BRJ; Raymond-Morrison-Knudsen-Brown-Root-Jones.

Under their resident boss in Saigon, M-K's Bertram L. Perkins, RMK-BRJ rapidly increased their labor force of 15,000 in mid-1965 to over 51,000 men within a year. Specially significant in this achievement is the fact that the American contingent was always less than ten per cent of the total work force. Included in their numbers were some 4,200 Americans, 41,800 Vietnamese, and 5,700 "free-world journeymen," mostly Filipinos and Koreans. This peak number was short-lived, however, for it looked as though military construction troops would take over and finish the job. By late 1967, the contract force had dwindled to less than 16,000. Plans were revised again shortly after the Tet offensive in January and February 1968 when the decision was made at a Commander in Chief Pacific conference to rebuild RMK-BRJ to 25,000 men for the indefinite future.

The Americans and free-world employees signed on for 18 months. A number lasted only a short while, but, conversely, many—some 40 per cent of the Americans, for instance—returned for at least one additional tour. One interesting statistic shows that by mid-1969 the hiring office at San Bruno, California, had screened over 385,000 U. S. applicants to place some 7,000 of them in Vietnam during the course of the contract. As the contract effort went down, most of the non-Vietnamese left the country. Information on the released Vietnamese workers is sparse, but many carried their newly developed skills into the Vietnamese Army, Vietnamese enterprises of various sorts, and the growing maintenance organizations supporting the U. S. forces. Some became skilled, even by our standards, as a result of working with RMK, Public Works, or Seabee Teams.

Monitoring the RMK-BRJ contract was a major part of the OICC's responsibilities. It was converted in April 1966 from a cost-plus-fixed-fee to a cost-plus-award-fee (CPAF) type, designed with an incentive feature to enhance contractor performance. But this was not the OICC's sole job. As construction agent for the Department of Defense in Vietnam, the OICC was concerned with a large design effort, both in house and by contract, and he let numerous lump sum contracts to smaller construction contractors (largely Vietnamese or Korean) for the U. S. Army, Navy, Air Force, and State Department. Until 1966 each service, upon receipt of its military construction funds, placed its requirements directly on the OICC for design and contract accomplishment.

As the troop build-up mounted in 1965, the conflicting demands and changing priorities of the various services demonstrated the need for a new regulatory body on the staff of the U. S. Commander in Vietnam. In February 1966 the Directorate of Construction, U. S. Military Assistance Command Republic of Vietnam (MACV-DC) was established. Headed by an Army engineer, Brigadier General C. H. Dunn, and staffed with officers from all the services, this office became responsible for setting construction standards (i.e., number of square feet per man in barracks), authorizing and setting

236 CIVIL ENGINEERS, SEABEES, AND BASES IN VIETNAM

priorities of construction by contract or troop labor, and coordinating the acquisition of real estate. The formation of MACV-DC did not alter the basic design, construction, and financial responsibilities of the OICC office which still reported back through its own chain to the Naval Facilities Engineering Command. In addition to setting construction standards which were binding on all services, another major function of MACV-DC was to receive the requirements which the various services had heretofore placed on the OICC, sort out relative priorities among the services, and then assign construction responsibility to the OICC or troops.

An ofttimes frustrating feature of the preconstruction process was that, despite the wartime environment, they were handled to a large degree on a peacetime basis. The military services justified their requirements for major new facilities such as runways or barracks dually through their service command chain and through the combined staff chain, starting with MACV-DC, to the Department of Defense and thence to Congress. After apportionment to the services in Washington the funds were then returned through the Naval Facilities Engineering Command (NAVFAC-formerly BuDocks) chain to the OICC-RVN who acted as banker, before and after the formation of MACV-DC, for all major military construction funds in Vietnam. Individual projects under $25,000 financed by "Maintenance" rather than "Construction" funds and tactical support construction projects were not subject to this process but were handled by the separate services who used troops, in-house civilians, or contractors, as convenient. Each of the services in Vietnam had its own engineering planning groups who concentrated on defining their own requirements such as siting, number of units, and the like. In addition, they also turned out final designs and let small construction contracts. However, most of the design

work for the larger facilities was done under the direction of the OICC, in consultation with the engineers of the affected service and the users, regardless of whether MACV-DC assigned the construction to the contractor or to the troops.

One of the biggest problem areas was real estate. Property was not automatically available for our bases but had to be bargained for, haggled over, rented, bought, or condemned as the situation demanded. Relocation of graves from construction sites with appropriate ceremony and compensation was a problem of unbelievable proportions.[2] Our bases were not necessarily shaped by military or economic reasons but rather by the efficacy of our real estate negotiations.

Just as with many other facets of this complicated war, there was no sharp dividing line between work assigned to the contractor and that assigned to troops. In general it may be stated that the contractor took the larger, more complicated jobs in relatively secure areas while the troops concentrated on lighter jobs in the more forward areas. In late 1967 and early 1968, in I Corps particularly, there were a number of instances where RMK-BRJ men worked next to Seabees on similar jobs. As a matter of fact, as the contractor's force was reduced, it turned a number of its jobs over to the troops for accomplishment. Conversely, as the Seabees were called upon for more tactical support, work originally assigned them was shifted to the contractor.

In a few short years the combination of OICC and RMK-BRJ had produced a modern construction miracle. Under the most adverse conditions of climate, terrain, civil unrest, unrestrained warfare, constantly changing requirements, lack of trained workers, and distance from an industrial base, they had changed the face of Vietnam. Building airfields, ports, roads, cities, and almost every kind of facility imaginable, they had by early

1969 placed nearly $1.5 billion worth of new construction.

Other Construction Organizations

As more units moved into Vietnam, it became impractical for the OICC to preside over every bit of construction, even that accomplished by contract. By early 1969 nearly half of all the military construction in Vietnam had been undertaken by some force other than RMK-BRJ. There were, of course, numerous small contractors, some of whom worked for the OICC and some who did not, who were employed by engineer elements of each of the services and by USAID. Collectively these local contractors had accounted for some $75 million worth of construction by the fall of 1966.

Also significant were a few large U. S. contractors who did not belong to the RMK-BRJ combine. Despite a long-standing Pentagon policy which confined major military construction administration to the Army and Navy engineers—and another policy which made the Navy the DOD construction agent in Vietnam—the Air Force managed to build under their own direction an air base at Tuy Hoa. In May 1966 they awarded a cost-plus-incentive-fee "Turn-Key" contract (a complete package, including design and construction) to Walter Kidde Constructors, a subsidiary of Electric Bond and Share Company, at an estimated cost of $52 million. The contractor did not accomplish the work completely on his own, however; he was given a lot of help by Air Force construction troops and airlift. Air Force arguments to gain permission from Secretary of Defense McNamara for this departure from policy included the charge that RMK-BRJ lacked sufficient capacity to meet the requirements of all the services in Vietnam and that the U. S. Command in Saigon had short-changed the Air Force in the assignment of construction priorities. Though completed, this project was unique. No further project similar to this one in size and scope came to fruition outside the established construction policies.

Another contract of importance, valued at $10 million, was negotiated by the Army in June 1966 with the Vinnell Corporation for the construction of power plants and utility lines at various sites. Even more significant were the combined cost-plus-fixed-fee contracts for repair and utility functions at Army facilities negotiated between the Army and Pacific Architects and Engineers, Inc. Starting in May 1963, and negotiated on a yearly basis, these contracts grew steadily, exceeding an annual cost of $100 million in less than five years. While P.A. & E.'s primary job was one of maintenance and operation, its forces did contribute materially in the construction of troop housing, administrative areas, and related facilities. Some observers have attempted to compare the Army's P.A. & E. contract with that between the Navy and Philco-Ford, but comparisons are difficult. In the case of P.A. & E. the Army essentially turned over the entire responsibility for repair and utilities to the contractor. The Navy, on the other hand, used Philco-Ford primarily to furnish Korean artisans who were integrated into a combined Seabee-civilian Public Works Department at Da Nang run by CEC officers.

By far the greatest construction effort outside of the RMK-BRJ joint venture came from the U. S. construction troops. And, of course, there was a significant amount of "self-help" construction by non-engineer troops who were furnished materials and plans and left largely to their own devices. Operating for the most part in the central and southern areas of the Republic of Vietnam (II, III, and IV Corps areas), the Army engineer battalions carried the largest load of the services. Smallest of the military contingents were those of the Air Force, Civil Engineering Squadrons (Heavy Repair), which operated at selected Air Force sites. And in I Corps, supporting the Marines, were the Seabees.

Seabee Battalions in I Corps

The encounter between North Vietnamese and U. S. warships in August 1964, soon to be known as the Tonkin Gulf Incident, touched off a series of actions which culminated in the landing of U. S. Marines in Da Nang in March 1965. U.S. combat troops, not "advisors," were now committed to the land war in Asia which so many had hoped to avoid. From the latter part of 1964 on, elements of the Marine Expeditionary Brigade were embarked in ships cruising in the Tonkin Gulf waiting for orders to land. In company with the Marines were Seabees of Amphibious Construction Battalion One, deployed from Yokosuka, Japan. ACB-1 Seabees had been ashore in Da Nang in April 1964 to place in operation a 200-ton drydock for small, fast boats being turned over by the U. S. to the Vietnamese Navy. Now ACB-1 was standing by with its full assault teams in the amphibious ships, ready with piers, fuel systems, and appurtenances to support the landing when and if it came.

Conditions ashore were such that the Seabees were not needed to make the landings at Da Nang. They did, however, in the next month, install a number of fuel systems, provide causeways for off-loading LSTs, and establish camp support ashore in Da Nang.

When the Marines next landed, at Chu Lai, some 50 miles south of Da Nang, during the period 7–10 May 1965, elements of ACB-1, under Lieutenant Commander R. T. Field, went ashore with the third assault wave. Their placing of two eight-section causeway piers from the open sea was described by Major General Collins, Commanding General of the 3rd Marine Division, as ". . . the one single function that made the entire operation possible." Following placement of the causeways, another group of Seabees, Naval Mobile Con-

struction Battalion Ten, under the command of Commander J. M. Bannister, came ashore to build an expeditionary airfield with AM2 aluminum matting. This marked the first amphibious landing of a full Seabee Battalion since World War II. Fortunately, enemy harassment was minimal in this early period, but temperatures reaching 120°F. and a fine, almost completely uniform sand, which was hard to work in, make all vehicles useless except those with tracks. Despite the handicaps of weather and terrain, the "Men of Ten" had put enough of the airfield in place (3,500 feet) to enable Marine jet planes to operate from it 23 days after the initial landing.

NMCB-10 had been, prior to the Marine landings, the alert battalion on Okinawa, prepared to move en masse to any trouble spot on short notice. Accordingly, it was engaged on rough construction projects which could be dropped immediately when the call came. A semi-alert battalion was based at Guam, ready to move to help also should the alert battalion need assistance. Also on Okinawa, but deeply engaged in major construction primarily for the Marines, was a third battalion. The other two Pacific battalions were at their home port of Port Hueneme, taking leave and retraining, having recently returned from overseas assignments. Similarly, the five Atlantic battalions were in various stages of deployment off the East Coast of the U.S., in the Caribbean, in Europe, and in Africa.

In the initial months the Marines occupied three major enclaves at Da Nang, Chu Lai, and Hue-Phu Bai, with a primary objective of driving the main force Viet Cong units back into the hills and linking the enclaves. I Corps, comprising all five northernmost provinces of South Vietnam, from the DMZ southward over 200 miles, became the Marines' responsibility. The extent to which the Navy in general and the Seabees in particular would support the Marines once they got ashore was not clearly spelled out at the time of the landing at Da Nang, nor was it for some time thereafter. It soon became evident, however, that this was not to be a short hit-and-move-on amphibious operation but rather one in which the Marines, contrary to their normal doctrine, would settle in.

Their burgeoning requirements for ports, cantonments, utilities, aircraft support, supply areas, and other support facilities were well beyond Marine organic capabilities. Coincident with the RMK-BRJ build-up, Seabee help was now mobilized. In late May 1965, NMCB-3 deployed from Guam and the next month NMCB-9 left Port Hueneme; both reported to Da Nang. Two battalions were shifted from the Atlantic to the Pacific Fleet in 1965 and went immediately to Vietnam. In the fall of 1965, four new battalions were authorized and they were commissioned in February, March, July, and August of 1966. The old base at Gulfport, Mississippi, was raised from a totally industrial facility to become the third home port for the Seabees, along with Port Hueneme and Davisville. In the spring of 1966 three new regiments were formed, one at each Construction Battalion Center. Atlantic battalions, in the meantime, were recalled to Davisville, increased in strength, and then flown directly to Vietnam. Ultimately every Seabee unit went to Vietnam except CBU-201, which was a small force serving the Antarctic research program. NMCB-6, the last peacetime battalion to deploy to the war zone, arrived in May 1966. Subsequently, five more battalions were commissioned, and two reserve battalions, MCB-12 and -22, were recalled for just about a year of active duty in April 1968. This brought the total number of battalions in 1968–69 to twenty-one. The maximum number in Vietnam reached twelve early in 1968 and was reduced to ten before the end of that year. They were all assigned to I Corps, distributed in mid-1968 as follows: Five

battalions in Da Nang, two in Chu Lai, two in Phu Bai, one in Camp Evans north of Hue, one in Quang Tri, and one in Dong Ha.

The rapid build-up of the battalions brought organizational changes to the whole Seabee structure. During peacetime deployments in the Pacific areas the battalions had reported directly to Commander Naval Construction Battalions, U.S. Pacific Fleet (ComCBPac), in Hawaii, and he in turn, reported to Commander Service Force, U. S. Pacific Fleet (ComServPac), also located in Hawaii. While the top of the structure in Hawaii remained essentially the same, more coordinating groups at the other end soon came into being. First of these was the 30th Naval Construction Regiment, formed in Da Nang under Captain H. F. Liberty in early May 1965 to provide operational control over all Seabee battalions in Vietnam. This was a reactivation of the last Seabee Regiment to be decommissioned when the large Seabee construction effort at Cubi Point, Philippines, came to a close some ten years before. When CBPac planners had been working on contingency plans with the Marines on Okinawa they had visualized, under the direct chain of command of the Commanding General, the Commander of the 30th NCR (a CEC Captain), wearing a second hat as Commander of the Force Engineer Group (FEG). This would have given him the same command authority over Marine battalions with construction capability (division and force battalions oriented primarily toward tactical support) as he had over the Seabees. With the thought that he would be invaluable in coordinating the efforts of the Marine battalions, a Marine colonel was requested, and assigned, to serve as chief staff officer of the 30th NCR. However, the Commanding General of the 3rd Marine Amphibious Force, Lieutenant General L. W. Walt, as the commander in I Corps, in consonance with ComNavForV, made the decision not to place the FEG under the Seabee commander, and the combined use of all engineer elements never did take place. A few months later when it came time for the chief staff officer, Colonel W. R. Gould, to be relieved, he was replaced by a CEC officer.

The next significant change, the placing of all Seabee battalions under a Civil Engineer Corps Flag Officer in Vietnam, came with the formation of the 3rd Naval Construction Brigade under Rear Admiral R. R. Wooding, CEC, United States Navy, on June 1, 1966, at Saigon. His primary job was that of OICC, permanently based in Saigon, so the 30th NCR commander at Da Nang continued to exercise the greatest command influence over the Seabee battalions, all of which were in I Corps. With the projected assignment of a second CEC Flag Officer to Vietnam, the OICC shed his brigade responsibilities and the Regimental Commander in Da Nang, Captain A. R. Marschall, took command of the brigade as well, briefly during the summer of 1967. In the late summer when the new Brigade Commander, Rear Admiral J. V. Bartlett, CEC, United States Navy, arrived in Da Nang the 30th Naval Construction Regiment was split into two regiments, each under a Captain (C. W. Turner and J. M. Hill). The 30th Naval Construction Regiment continued in Da Nang, and the new 32nd Naval Construction Regiment established headquarters to the north in Phu Bai-Gia Le. Thus, after two years of experimentation and growth, the Seabee Command in Vietnam had developed into a 9,000-man, 12-battalion force of two regiments under one brigade. (However, it should be noted that *all* Seabees assigned to duty in Vietnam did not come under the command of 3rd Naval Construction Brigade. The Public Works and CBMU Seabees reported to the Naval Support Activity Commanders at Da Nang and Saigon, and the Amphibious Construction Battalion Seabees were part of the Amphibious Force.) Adminis-

tratively, the Pacific battalions still reported individually to ComCBPac and the Atlantic battalions to ComCBLant with the result that the brigade and regimental staffs could concentrate entirely on the operational business of getting on with the construction. Though the Brigade Commander reported to Commander Naval Forces Vietnam in Saigon, there was little question that on a day-to-day basis the Seabees were working for the senior officer in I Corps, the Commanding General III Marine Amphibious Force.

As the conflict escalated and command relationships evolved, the battalions themselves also underwent transition. During World War II the 1,080-man Seabee battalion had come into being, but its successor, which was developed in the following years of peace, was a more mobile highly compact unit with about half the number of men. At the start of the Vietnam conflict the authorized allowance of a battalion was 21 officers and 563 men. Special requirements in Vietnam—particularly in the area of road and airfield construction—raised the number by 125, primarily in the equipment operator and mechanics trades. Subsequently 50 more were added to provide perimeter security for base camps and job sites, bringing new authorized allowances to 24 officers and 738 enlisted men.

Parenthically, as a matter of comparison, it might be noted that the Army Engineers, who at their peak had 27 battalions in country, had two kinds of battalions—combat and construction. The former were involved in combat engineering functions such as minesweeping, demolition, and field fortification. The latter had responsibilities similar to the Seabees for more standard construction chores. These Army construction battalions were slightly larger, having 41 officers and 879 enlisted men. Generally speaking, they operated in II, III, and IV Corps, but when Army units moved into

A member of CBMU-301, top, *welds the final touches to the runway at Dong Ha early in 1969.* At lower left, *Seabees clean up the rubble after the Metropole Hotel in Saigon was bombed in December 1965. The Seabees,* at right, *made use of their weapons, helmets, and armored vests when they came under fire while on an isolated job in April 1966. (G. A. Miller, EAD2, U.S. Navy; L. F. Jones, PH1, U.S. Navy; and Veeder)*

I Corps to reinforce the Marines in 1967–68 four Army engineer battalions accompanied them. The Air Force also had a few heavy construction squadrons known as "Red Horse" (Rapid Engineer Deployment, Heavy Operational Repair Squadron) consisting of 12 officers and 388 enlisted men. For the most part, they tended to concentrate on work of a temporary or emergency nature at scattered Air Force sites. Like the Army, the Marines had two types of engineering units in the field—the Division Engineer Battalions (1st and 3rd) and Force Engineer Battalions (7th, 9th, and 11th), all of whom operated, of course, in I Corps. The former, consisting of 34 officers, 735 men (and a few naval medical personnel) per battalion, provided close combat support to the division. The latter, with 46 officers and 1,049 men per battalion, provided more general engineering support of a deliberate nature for the landing force (division and wing).

Even though the Army brought their own engineers with them to I Corps, during the build-up period about 25 per cent of the Seabee effort was devoted to support of the Army.

The first Seabee battalions to arrive in Vietnam came by ship from Okinawa, Guam, and Port Hueneme, but later personnel deployments in and out of the country were accomplished by air. Each battalion had about 10,000 measurement tons of tools, equipment, and supplies valued at $4.4 million. Included in the bulky items were some 250 pieces of tactical automotive and construction equipment such as bulldozers, tractors, and mobile cranes. About 9,000 tons remained in country with its successor when a battalion was relieved, and the other 1,000 tons, such as hand tools and weapons, shipped by sea or air, accompanied the battalion back and forth to insure that the battalion retained the capability to mount out for another contingency or to reinforce Vietnam on short notice if required.

Here it should be noted that the Seabee battalions rotated as complete units. This was contrary to the general policy among the armed forces in Vietnam wherein individuals and not units were rotated. There were many highly placed recommendations to stop the interchange of battalions, but experience with the huge Seabee construction effort at Cubi Point a decade before indicated that productivity and morale were enhanced by keeping the battalions intact. The cycle of eight months in country followed by six months back in the U. S. for leave, training, and regrouping cut to a minimum the number of individuals leaving the battalion during its deployment in Vietnam. Obviously there were many uncompleted projects when it came time for a battalion to leave for home, and there was some lost motion as the relieving battalion took over. This hiatus was cut to a minimum, however, by having advance parties from the new battalion get on site several weeks before the official change-over. As a result, loss of productive man days was not a significant factor. Moreover, personnel programs developed to complement the unit rotational concept, enabled the Navy to reduce total Seabee manpower requirements by about 2,000 men.

Productivity and the cost of doing work loomed large in the eyes of Pentagon analysts who sought to determine whether civilian contractors or troops should carry the burden of the construction effort. Though the two modes of construction were difficult to compare, the best evidence seemed to indicate that from the government's standpoint the ultimate costs were about the same. When charges against project funds were made, troop charges were about one-quarter those of the contractor; but the other three-quarters, though hidden, were real enough, for they were charged against other appropriations such as military pay, operations cost, and the like. A few 1968 figures may help to put Seabee costs in perspective. The first year total cost of a battalion was estimated to be $13,476,000 (including $3,184,000 for operating costs). One could expect to receive per battalion 19,000 man days of productive labor a month. Put another way, a battalion could be expected to place about $350,000 worth of new construction a month.

Another area of interest has been a comparison of skills between the civilians on the contractors' rolls and the Seabees. Once again, generalizations as to differences are difficult to make. RMK-BRJ had a relatively small cadre of highly trained American artisans, a slightly larger number of skilled Asians from outside of Vietnam, and a very high percentage of Vietnamese, most of whom possessed very little skill when they were first hired. While the Seabees also encompassed a wide spectrum of skills and competence within those skills, they had few, if any, who were capable only of common labor. Again, by and large, a standoff.

Though cost and skill comparisons tend to equate the contractor and military engineer capabilities, it is to be remembered that the primary purposes in maintaining engineer troops are to possess flexibility, to be able to provide rapid initial support to contingency operations, and to have the ability to work in a zone of intensive hostilities.

Insofar as construction equipment is concerned, there are varying opinions as to whether Vietnam put a tougher strain on equipment than might be expected elsewhere. During the dry season the sand and laterite dust caused problems, and there was more of the same from the soupy laterite during the wet season. Certainly, round-the-clock operations accelerated the breakdown of equipment, particularly where time out for adequate maintenance was hard to come by. Such was the case immediately after the initial landings at Chu Lai where MCB-10 experienced extremely high deadline percentages (up to 45 per cent of the equipment inoperable). It was only after they had the Marine jets flying that

they managed to give sufficient attention to the proper care and maintenance of their equipment. In time, procedures were developed which brought the deadline figure under five per cent for all battalions then in country. The availability of spare parts tends to be a perennial problem, but the Seabee forces after a period of shakedown did not find it an insurmountable one. Stocked at the Construction Battalion Centers at Port Hueneme and Davisville were repair parts for 1,800 construction hours (two 10-hour shifts for 90 days) for each piece of equipment. Air shipment to Vietnam of critical items could normally be accomplished within 30 days of ordering. Supply Corps officers and rates attached to the battalions working with the Seabee oriented Construction Battalion Center supply departments played a major role in accomplishing this support through various routes of the Navy supply system.

Experience ultimately showed that the life cycle of a piece of equipment committed to Vietnam averaged 45 months from the time it was received from the factory in a U. S. depot until it passed out of the system (a little better than half the life cycle in the U.S.). Further, from an economical and capability standpoint, this piece was good for only one depot overhaul. It was usual for a piece of equipment to be in country for about 16 months before it left for overhaul, and on its return it was used for another 16 months. RMK-BRJ took care of itself but did not appear to have the capability to overhaul Seabee equipment on top of its own work load, so pieces were sent for overhaul primarily to the U. S. but also to Japan, Okinawa, the Philippines, or Guam. It should be noted that this program did not deny battalions essential equipment because of the availability of an adequate backup pipeline. Throughout this period a pool of augmentation equipment was steadily building up under the control of 3rd NCB, a pool which early in

1969 totalled 1,000 pieces of specialized construction equipment not contained in the standard battalion allowance, valued at some $28,000,000.

Also assembled as material kits in a pool status in Da Nang and Port Hueneme were Seabee Tactical Support Functional Components (TSFC) available to support Navy and Marine tactical requirements. They included such assemblies as bridges, bunkers, medium lift airfields capable of handling the C-130, water distribution systems for 1,000-man cantonments, combat support hospitals, and a host of others. Not only were they packaged units, but their use was not subject to the normal budgetary snarl of the line-item oriented military construction program under which most of the permanent facilities were built. Release of the TSFCs could be authorized by Commander 3rd Naval Construction Brigade when the senior operational commander could certify that his need qualified under ten criteria, which boiled down to urgent, unforeseen, and needed for direct tactical support against the enemy.

The Advanced Base Functional Component system, an outgrowth of lessons from World War II, consists of definitive advanced base component designs and pre-stocked hardware which had been designed, refined, bought, sorted, and stored during the peaceful years. These components were invaluable in getting the Seabee construction effort under way even though some obsolescent equipment was in the system. One good example of a component was the 400-bed quonset hospital erected swiftly in Da Nang by one of the earliest battalions in country. It provided the needed medical facility in a hurry, but many pieces of its equipment such as galley stoves—though never used—were of such an age that the manufacturers no longer made spare parts for them or the manufacturers no longer existed. Obsolescence of this kind was more of a nuisance than a major problem, however, and upgrading of

equipment was a continuous process the longer a facility remained in existence.

Naturally, all Seabee materials were not in the stored components. Apart from sand, rock, and gravel which were available in Vietnam, most of their materials such as lumber, pipe, and fittings came from the U. S., largely by ship but some by air. A small amount of material found its way into Vietnam from other countries, but "gold flow" prohibitions by the U. S. precluded this source from becoming more than a trickle. While a number of the old stand-bys of World War II, the metal quonset huts in stock, were used, particularly during the early phase of the buildup, the majority of the structures erected were of wood. Where large spans were called for, or where metal buildings were more desirable than wooden ones, the box-like prefabricated Butler building was a popular choice.

In the course of their duties the Seabee construction forces were involved in just about every kind of job imaginable. They built cantonments for thousands of men, hospitals, roads and airfields, warehousing, POL storage, harbor facilities such as piers and ramps, utilities systems, recreation areas, and many other facilities which were essential to the military effort but which in themselves were not necessarily combat oriented. Many items they built did fall in this category, however: items such as bunkers, revetments, and sentry towers. They even became involved in building stable platforms from which the Army could fire their 155-mm guns into the DMZ. Many times they had to do a job over again. A particular bridge near the Hai Van Pass was destroyed six times. A 3rd NCB report of 1 December 1967 stated matter-of-factly:

"Progress to date: Approximately 29 bridges have been constructed utilizing timber construction primarily. Net progress has been minimal since during one period 22 bridges were built while 21 were destroyed by sabotage." Though this report referred essentially to timber bridges, the Seabees also used pre-cast concrete, steel substructure with timber decking, Bailey Deck Type, and the AMMI (a multi-purpose steel pontoon designed by NAVFAC's Chief Engineering Advisor, Dr. Arsham Amirikian). In one of their largest concerted efforts of the war, six Seabee battalions worked on the upgrading of Routes #1 (from south of Hue-Phu Bai through Quang Tri and Dong Ha to the DMZ) and #9 (from Dong Ha west through Khe Sanh to the border)—an effort which contained 133 bridges (30 per cent ranging in length from 50 to 2,100 feet) in 138 miles of road—nearly one bridge per mile!

Following the initial landings in 1965, the Seabee battalions spent about 18 months developing the enclaves at Da Nang and Chu Lai and later in Phu Bai. Here they were concerned, along with the contractor, with erecting buildings, installing pipe lines, grading roads—all phases of construction necessary to create these major logistics bases. They built for everyone—Marines, Navy, Air Force, Army, Free World Forces, the Vietnamese Armed Forces; but they worked primarily for the Marines. Da Nang was the keystone, the major deep water port and the major air base. Most of the materials coming in country came by ship to Da Nang where they were off-loaded and placed in shallow-draft vessels for further shipment south to Chu Lai and north to Tan My and Hue, servicing Phu Bai. As troop strength increased, another small port at the mouth of the Cua Viet, some four and one-half miles from the DMZ, was established in 1967 to provision the Marine combat base at Dong Ha and its satellites.

In the early days the Marines sent small parties out of the enclaves on village pacification and "search and destroy" missions. These gradually moved away from the coastal plain to the highlands and evolved into sweep operations of battalion size. Operations expanded in

the latter half of 1967 when a considerable build-up of Marine and Army troops took place in I Corps to meet the threat around the DMZ. Further escalation of combat operations was, of course, generated in January 1968 when the Tet offensive was touched off by the Communists. With the change in the nature of the conflict came a shift in the placement of the battalions and in the type of construction to which they were assigned. In June 1968 one-half of all Seabee battalion personnel were located north of the Hai Van Pass (just north of Da Nang), whereas a year previously only one-fifth of them had been so located. A steady shift to tactical support construction was also in evidence. The June 1968 report showed that two-thirds of the battalions' man-day effort now went into tactical support, just double that of the previous year; and by January 1969 the proportion had grown to three-fourths. But as the Seabees in the battalions moved more into the tactical end of the business, there were other Seabees in country who did not; these were Public Works and Construction Battalion Maintenance Unit (CBMU) Seabees attached to the Naval Support Activities headquartered in Da Nang and Saigon, but actually spread all over the country.

Formation of NSA Da Nang

When the Marine Expeditionary Brigade was ordered to land at Da Nang in March 1965, there was no naval activity ashore to support it and no indication in official files that the Navy would move to establish such an activity. The Navy's Headquarters Support Activity in Saigon was being phased out, being replaced by the Army's 1st Logistics Command, and the general assumption in Navy circles seemed to be that the Army would henceforth provide logistic support ashore throughout Vietnam. Although a CinCPac order in April 1965 stated that military logistics operations at ports and beaches at Da Nang and Chu Lai would be accomplished by the Navy, this was considered by the top command in the Navy as a temporary assignment at most. In simplest terms, under the force levels imposed by the Pentagon, every sailor ashore in Vietnam meant one less sailor in a ship or on a vital shore station somewhere else. As late as 28 May 1965, Chief of Naval Operations sent "do not concur to establishing NSA Da Nang" to CinCPacFlt. This brought an exchange of personal notes in late May and early June between the Commandant of the Marine Corps and the Vice Chief of Naval Operations. The former stated that the Marines did not have this support capability and suggested that naval assets outside of Pacific Fleet be tapped. The VCNO indicated that CinCPacFlt could do the job temporarily, that he would seek additional assets from the Secretary of Defense to do the job if the Army Logistics Command were not to be assigned long-range responsibility, and that the Navy would seek an authoritative interpretation of policy to determine "whose responsibility it is." It turned out to be the Navy's.

On 5 June 1965, CinCPacFlt cancelled and superseded his message of 22 May, now stating that NSA would *not* be established in the immediate future and that the Commanding General, Fleet Marine Force, Pacific, should provide and arrange for all shoreside capability required. One month later, on 17 July, a Secretary of the Navy Notice established NSA Da Nang.

So, NSA Da Nang came into being in mid-1965 as an activity desperately needed by the Marines, which they were not organized to provide for themselves and which no other service seemed ready to provide. Apparently roles and missions of the various forces had not been clarified to cover this contingency. While the Navy's responsibilities in this area were still being debated in Washington, however, efforts were made, primarily in ComServPac, to lay

down some general rules for the operation of NSA, should it become a reality. The concept at this time was that NSA Da Nang would concern itself with operating ports and beaches from Chu Lai to the DMZ and would operate a supply depot, shipping, and some ancillary services. Getting supplies over the beaches—with the Marines taking over from there—was to be the primary mission of NSA.

Public Works Da Nang and the CBMUs

In the initial planning for NSA, ComServPac concentrated on the supply, operations, and medical areas but did not devote much attention to Public Works. As a matter of fact, the term "Public Works" was not used in the original planning documents setting forth the tasks and missions of NSA. This is not to say that the omission was not of concern in some quarters. In June 1965 the Chief of Civil Engineers in a letter to Chief of Naval Operations noted that the current planning for NSA did not contain Public Works components. He pointed out that the Mobile Construction Battalions had construction missions and would not be available for maintenance. He therefore urged the inclusion of a Construction Battalion Maintenance Unit (none in commission at the time) and early action to determine the scope of public works functions at NSA. These suggestions went all but unheeded and there was, for all practical purposes, no Public Works Department as such included in the initial NSA organization as planned.

Upon activation of NSA in July 1965, however, a fledgling Public Works Department was formed under a CEC lieutenant (H. L. Higgins), soon replaced by a commander (A. E. Floyd), then a captain (R. D. Pinkerton). NSA, first under Captain K. P. Huff, U. S. Naval Reserve, then under Rear Admiral T. R. Weschler, U. S. Navy, and his successor, Rear Admiral P. L. Lacy, expanded rapidly. Along with NSA Da Nang, Public Works experienced phenomenal growth, and in less than two years became the largest public works organization the Navy had anywhere in the world. In June 1967 it included over 3,200 personnel, a year later 4,900, and by early 1969 the total approached 7,000. In the beginning the buildup was military, but then the Seabees in Public Works were augmented by direct-hire Vietnamese civilians and Koreans brought into the country through a contract with Philco-Ford. Additionally, design personnel, Americans, Filipinos, and Nationalist Chinese, were provided through a contract with Metcalf and Eddy. Much of the early public works effort was directed toward leasing living and working facilities for NSA in the city of Da Nang (est. pop. 250,000). Practically all of the public works activity in the early months was internal to NSA itself and was theoretically limited to the "secure" areas; but as the troop buildup continued, the demand for an expanded public works organization became more pressing. Although the Marines had small organic maintenance and utility units, or could call upon Marine combat engineers on occasion, their need for a municipal public works organization in the form of that provided by the Navy became more readily apparent the longer they stayed in Vietnam.

"Expanded" meant, at first, giving design, real estate, some transportation, minor construction and alteration, and maintenance and utility support to Marine facilities in the "secure" areas in Da Nang, Chu Lai, and Hue-Phu Bai. This was started officially in March 1967 for the First Marine Air Wing and soon spread to the other Marine units in the major enclaves. It was a short step from providing Public Works support in "secure" municipalities (which subsequently turned out to be something less than secure at times) to that in "nonsecure" areas, particularly Marine airfields. Maintenance of the air strips at Dong Ha, Khe Sanh, and An Hoa was stated as the proximate

cause for bringing in the first Construction Battalion Maintenance Unit, CBMU-301, some 300 strong (later more than 500), to Vietnam in May and June 1967. From the beginning the unit, although it belonged administratively to ComCBPac and maintained its integrity as a unit, acted as an extension of "Public Works North" and its Commanding Officer, Lieutenant Commander H. A. Holmes, took his basic instructions from the Public Works Officer at Da Nang. Initially, these were to maintain the airstrips at the three sites mentioned above and to render whatever other public works support the battalion was capable of. Later, the unit sent details to many different sites to maintain them or to repair battle damage. Personnel in public works and the CBMU were shifted as circumstances dictated. For instance, during one critical period of the extensive rebuilding of the runway at Khe Sanh there were more Seabees from Public Works Da Nang on the job than there were from the CBMU. On the other hand, CBMU-301 at times provided a number of supervisors and skilled hands for some of the main public works shops in Da Nang.

The concept of public works operating only in a "secure" municipality was to break down completely in 1967. The need for NSA to establish a base at Cua Viet, some four and one-half miles from the DMZ, to support Dong Ha in the late spring brought Public Works Seabees to construct and maintain the camp. In August of 1967 public works support of the I Corps MACV Advisors (mostly U. S. Army with all other services represented, including Australian Army) was started. This not only called for roving teams of automotive and generator mechanics, but also brought permanently assigned Seabees from Public Works to all of the major advisor compounds in I Corps—Quang Tri, Hue, Hoi An, Tam Ky, and Quang Ngai. Public Works Da Nang had not reached its required strength to support the Marines when it was directed by MACV to give repair and utilities support to all Army units in areas now served by public works, this service to commence 1 January 1968. Some selected Air Force sites were also included. For all practical purposes, it was now Public Works I Corps.

This international mixed military and civilian force, organized along Public Works Center lines, had grown with roughly equal proportions of Seabees, Vietnamese, and Koreans. Early in 1969 their numbers approximated 2,500 Seabees (of whom less than 500 were in the CBMU), 2,500 South Koreans, and 2,000 Vietnamese, led by fewer than 100 officers. Many of the crews were a mixture of all three nationalities, the aim being ultimately to train the Vietnamese to take over from the more skilled Koreans and Seabees. This transfer of expertise to the Vietnamese in the building trades—also accomplished under the RMK-BRJ contractors—gives promise of being in the long run the greatest legacy the U. S. will leave in Vietnam.

Though conceived primarily as a base maintenance and operations organization (including trucking operations incident to moving cargo from the Da Nang piers to supply depots), Public Works also found itself in the business of constructing cantonments, dams, utility lines, and, above all, reconstructing battle damage to every type of facility. Despite the size of RMK-BRJ and the Naval Mobile Construction Battalions, there was need for more construction capability than they could provide. On many occasions the regular construction forces, for reasons of lack of materials or changing priorities, left jobs "95 per cent complete"—and unusable. In other cases, under the stress of wartime planning, items might be left out of the drawings and the construction forces would move on before the occupant-to-be realized what was missing. Thus, for a variety of reasons, public works was also, in part, a construction force.

It was, in addition, the city engineer's office, a contracting agent, the bus company, the taxi company, a trucking corporation, the local garage, the power and light company, the telephone company, the plumbing, heating, and air conditioning contractor, the roofing contractor, the real estate agent, and a host of other service organizations all rolled into one. Spread out over 200 miles of war-torn country, operating in cities and hamlets, and catering to all the elements of the U. S. Armed Services as well as to those of other countries, it was the largest and most diverse public works organization the Navy had ever put together.

Support of Naval Installations in II, III, and IV Corps

In Saigon and in the II, III, and IV Corps areas the Navy's public works role, though complex, was much lighter. In these areas the Army had this responsibility for the U. S. Armed Forces, relying heavily on its contractor, P. A. & E., to furnish "Repair and Utility" support. Even in Saigon this appeared to be marginal in the early days (it later improved), with the result that the 100 or so Seabees loaned to NSA Saigon by Da Nang in 1966 were kept in the south until their individual tours were completed. Similarly, repair and utility support at the numerous small and scattered naval activities in these Corps areas left much to be desired. The Navy's answer to this problem was to import CBMU-302, a slightly smaller (200 and later 300 men) version of the CBMU which went to I Corps about the same time. These Seabees were broken up into various details, sent to different bases, primarily in support of Game Warden and Market Time operations in the II, III, and IV Corps areas, and assigned the usual public works responsibilities, which included construction and alteration and even extended to small boat repair. In this instance the CBMU played a much more dominant role than its counterpart in I Corps, supplying some two-thirds of the manpower involved in public works functions under the cognizance of NSA Saigon.

Essentially the Seabees of Public Works and the CBMUs attached to them had the same basic mission—to come in behind the construction forces and maintain and operate the bases already built. In theory the CBMUs were a little better trained to defend themselves as units, but there the difference ended. One year tours and rotation of individuals, not units as in the case of the NMCBs, was the case for both PW and CBMU officers and men. The fact that they were engaged primarily in maintenance and operations where a gradual turnover provided more continuity and less disruption made the individual rotation system preferable to the unit rotation.

Infantry Training

Regardless of their unit, be it a construction battalion, amphibious battalion, public works, maintenance unit, or some other, they were, as Seabees, not only trained as construction men but, in addition, were given infantry training by the Marines. In pre-Vietnam days some of the Seabees considered this something of an extra drill which interfered with their prime interest in construction work. After the Dong Xoai Seabee Team action, opinions began to change, and when MCB-9, working on the hospital in Da Nang in October 1965, was hit with mortars and infiltration gangs the lessons hit home. This military training was to stand many of them in good stead, for every different type of organization to which they were assigned was exposed to enemy action sometime in Vietnam (by mid-1968 the Seabees wounded in action totaled more than those in World War II and the killed-in-action rate per total men deployed was four times that of World War II). And it soon became clear in the early months of the conflict that every

able Seabee, sooner or later, would take his turn in Vietnam.

Personnel

The Vietnam conflict was to trigger the trebling of Seabee strength to a new total of some 26,000 men. First order of business was to bring the existing construction battalions up to wartime strength, and this was followed by the activating of new units. While a vigorous recruiting plan was instituted, the initial buildup of the battalions was accomplished by transferring Seabees out of shore stations all over the world—some to the battalions and some directly to Vietnam. In many places in the U.S., civil service and trade union restrictions had kept them from working in their trades, so they were employed in a variety of jobs (such as Shore Patrol, Master at Arms, Commissary) in which they could be replaced by other sailors. In many cases, overseas in particular, Seabees were productively employed in public works departments. Here, in some instances, they were replaced by civilians, in others by Fleet sailors, but in many spots there were no replacements at all, and a slow deterioration at these facilities began to set in. In like manner, whole battalions were pulled off jobs to go to Vietnam; in some places civilian contracting firms took over for them and in others the jobs just died.

To get young men into the Seabees simply to build up to the required numbers was not particularly difficult. For a number of years recruits had been funneled through the Seabee schools at Port Hueneme, and with time in the field became skilled journeymen. With the rapid buildup, there were not enough experienced petty officers on active duty to go around, and the voluntary recall of reservists yielded little more. To get the required experience level in uniform in a hurry, the Navy instituted in the spring of 1966 a Direct Procurement of Petty Officers program. In a meeting with 18 presidents of the AFL-CIO Building Trades, Navy officials made known their needs, and this word went out immediately to all the locals in the United States. Within six months 5,000 new petty officers had been recruited. In FY68 the program fell short when only 3,200 were enlisted, but in the following year the number returned again to the 5,000 mark.

The DPPO program was a great success in terms of the journeyman quality of the recruits. They were an outstanding group of young men, and without them the Seabee effort in Vietnam would have been severely curtailed. Unfortunately, from the Navy's standpoint, few of them chose to stay in the Navy, electing to return to civilian life after 30 months or less in the service. During this time it was possible for them to serve two eight-month deployments with a battalion, or a split tour with some time in a battalion or shore-based outfit and the rest with a public works or CBMU assignment of a year in Vietnam. This was in line with the standard policy which called for transferring a man to shore duty after he had served in Vietnam under the above conditions. The policy was not hard and fast, for a man could volunteer for more Vietnam duty and many did.

Few military units saw more duty in Vietnam than the Seabees. While the DPPOs should be considered in a special category, there is some small evidence that the relatively high exposure rate to Vietnam duty experienced by the Seabees affected all reenlistment rates adversely. Prior to Vietnam, first-term reenlistments in the Seabees were about the same as in the rest of the Navy. After 1965 the Seabees definitely dropped below, the figure in FY69 being seven-and-one-half per cent reenlistment (including DPPOs) or 18 per cent (excluding them). Among the career Seabees— second reenlistments and beyond—there was also a gradual dropping off, the reenlistment rates from FY66 through FY69 being 91 per cent, 86 per cent, 80 per cent, and 76 per cent.

In the years prior to FY69 the career Seabees had a slightly higher reenlistment rate than their contemporaries in the fleet, but FY69 marked the crossover point.

Despite their lack of enthusiasm for reenlisting, there was no lack of enthusiasm among the Seabees for their work in Vietnam. They worked 60- to 90-hour weeks with little complaint under the most adverse conditions. It is interesting to note the comparative age of the World War II Seabees, who averaged 35 years of age, whereas their successors during the Vietnam conflict averaged 23 years. Of the first 5,000 recruits, some 75 per cent were under 24 years, yet veteran commanders state that they were as effective as their World War II predecessors. Rear Admiral Edwin B. Hooper, U. S. Navy, Commander Service Force Pacific, in January 1968 stated: "An elite group within the Service Force. . . . When it comes to specific action contributions, the Seabees are second to none."

Their effectiveness was due in part, of course, to the officers who led them. The Civil Engineer Corps had always been relatively small, supervising predominantly civilian organizations. Although technically trained, the CEC officers tended to be more involved with policy making and overall supervision, while the civil service engineers were primarily concerned with more detailed technical aspects of the jobs. Vietnam brought an additional 500 officers to active duty, making the total 2,200. Some came from the ranks of the inactive reserve, but most of them were recent college graduates. Like the majority of regulars, they did not all have degrees in civil engineering; they entered the Corps with a wide variety of scientific, architectural, and engineering degrees as well. It might be noted that about four per cent of the Corps was composed of limited duty officers and another three per cent of warrant officers. These two groups were officers who had come up through the enlisted ranks and were top managers in their trades. Like the rest of the CEC they were scattered throughout the Navy—generally in shop management positions. At any given time, normally two of the seventeen CEC officers assigned to a construction battalion would be limited duty or warrant officers.

Since CEC officers can be assigned to a number of different billets in design, construction, education, research, contracts, public works, and others, there is no such thing as a permanent Seabee officer. In the course of a full career an officer will not normally have more than two two-year tours with the battalions. In one way or another every career CEC officer will have some duty with Seabees, and most officers tend to consider Seabee duty among the most rewarding they have experienced. This has been a general comment, not only concerning Seabee duty, but also about all duty connected with the Vietnam efforts, and most career CEC officers have served in Vietnam.

Summing Up

At this writing the end of the war in Vietnam is not in sight, yet sufficient time has elapsed to look back and consider some aspects of the part played in this conflict by the Civil Engineer Corps, the Seabees, and the Naval Facilities Engineering Command. Even though there were few contingency plans upon which to build, the Naval Facilities Engineering Command was able to muster practically overnight a tremendous and unprecedented design and construction capability which was so essential to place and maintain combat troops ashore in Vietnam. All the resources of the Command—its officers, civil servants, enlisted men, research facilities, design agencies, contracting offices—were pressed into service to meet this new demand. Industry was mobilized, construction and maintenance troops were organized, and vast logistics bases were created under the guidance, assistance, and advice of the Civil Engineer Corps.

It has been a strange war in many ways, but certain unique operations involving this group

are worthy of mention. One has been the vital, continuing involvement of civilian contractor employees in construction, in maintenance, and in operations while, practically speaking, on the battlefield, ill-defined though it may be. Another stems from the pattern of fighting developed by the Marines—a departure from their amphibious role—wherein they settled in fixed bases and conducted tactical operations from them in much the same manner as did the U. S. Army and ARVN. This called into being massive public works support and, further, marked the first time that Seabees were used in large numbers in forward areas in direct support of combat troops. At the same time we managed to generate an extensive military peace corps effort in and around the war. The idea of one-service support in an area was pushed by top command and began to make some headway. Prosecution of the war itself seemed to be marked by more political considerations than we had experienced in the past. What have we learned about those areas which are vital to our military posture, and which affect or are affected by the naval civil engineer?

In an address to the Naval War College in February 1968, Rear Admiral A. C. Husband, CEC, U. S. Navy, Chief of Civil Engineers and Commander of the Naval Facilities Engineering Command from 1965 to 1969, touched on the following points which continue to be valid and which are paraphrased below:

1. Assuming we need ports, airfields, etc., in some future Vietnam, we cannot expect to produce them instantly. We were fortunate to have a large contractor on site capable of rapid expansion. We may not have a contractor there next time. We should, therefore, maintain the Seabees at sufficient peacetime strength to meet the construction requirements of approved contingency plans.

2. Much greater emphasis on base development planning for contingency operations must be made. Navy and Marine forces were deployed in country for months before ade-

quate planning elements were developed. Witness the failure to even plan for the Public Works Department at Da Nang which became the largest in the Navy within two years.

3. Joint service planning factors and construction standards will have to be developed prior to a contingency. For example, at the same base a difference in construction standards for berthing facilities between the Army and Air Force caused unnecessary morale problems.

4. Joint service planning standards should lead to compatible systems among services, of what the Navy has called Advanced Base Functional Components. We learned of their value again in Vietnam, but it should be emphasized in many cases—in the hospitals, for instance—the hardware from World War II stocks had not been updated.[3]

5. If we are to use the ABFC system we must have adequate stocks of the components in our war reserve stocks. We frequently found in Vietnam that items were not in stock and long delays ensued in getting them. Sound contingency plans must be developed which encourage appropriations necessary to keep the stocks current.

6. It is important that officers of the line and the other staff corps develop an appreciation for the base development problem and that naval planning staffs in general pay more attention to it. The Navy cannot think only in terms of deep draft ships, the carriers and submarines, but also must deal with concepts such as support ashore for the Marines and riverine warfare. Navy planners should concern themselves with the full range of naval warfare, which includes the bases supporting the ships, aircraft, and Marines. Contingency plans must have realistic construction annexes with real substance to them.

7. Programming requirements by the line item (a barracks or aircraft parking apron, for example) through channels to Congress for authorization and funding has been standard procedure in developing the peacetime annual construction program. Programming construction requirements in Vietnam through a similar line item system proved cumbersome, time-consuming, and out of step with the tempo of events. A changing tactical situation precluded programming individual line items many months in advance of the availability of funds. Future programming must be on the broadest possible basis and must be more responsive to the operational commander's needs.

8. The Navy must become more involved in the development of terminal logistics systems. Heretofore we have assumed that the Army— or perhaps the Marines—would do it. Operations at NSA Da Nang have clearly demonstrated that we must be prepared to handle large amounts of cargo in underdeveloped ports in areas where the Navy will be required to support the Marine Corps.

The above are just some of the highlights; there have been, obviously, many other lessons to be learned from our involvement in Vietnam. It seems clear that our system, stock reserves planning, and procedures can be vastly improved. Certainly our equipment and materials have not reached their ultimate development. The degree to which we can improve on the men is another matter. It is hard to visualize that we could get more courage, stamina, ability, intelligence, and spirit than has been exhibited in Vietnam by the officers who led them, and by our "sailors in green," the Seabees.

(*Naval Review*, 1970)

Notes

1. See "Naval Logistic Support, Qui Nhon to Phu Quoc," by Captain Herbert T. King, U.S. Navy, further along in this book.

2. For more about this interesting situation see "Building the Advanced Base at Da Nang" by Captain K. P. Huff, U. S. Naval Reserve, in this book.

3. For further discussion on this point, please turn to Commander F. O. McClendon's essay "Doctors and Dentists, Nurses and Corpsmen in Vietnam" and to that of Captain K. P. Huff, USNR, "Building the Advanced Base at Da Nang."

Doctors and Dentists, Nurses and Corpsmen in Vietnam

Commander F. O. McClendon, Jr.,
Medical Service Corps, U. S. Navy

During the past five years much has been said and written about Vietnam by both political and military persons. But little has been published describing the health care and medical services committed in support of the American Armed Forces, allied military forces, and the Vietnamese population. This article is intended to describe briefly the evolution of the medical effort of the Navy in Vietnam and the medical resources, which include the manpower and facilities necessary to fulfill our commitments. It will describe casualty recovery rate, causative agents, and problems experienced in providing medical support in a prolonged counterinsurgency land conflict.

It is not well known that Navy Medical Department personnel were at work in Vietnam long before the enlargement of the American force commitment in 1965, though our contribution prior to 1959 was modest. After Headquarters Support Activity Saigon was established in 1962, medical service requirements increased with the buildup of U. S. forces, and a handful of Navy Medical Department people increased to the more than six thousand men currently committed to direct support of Vietnam action. Included are more than 400 medical officers, approximately 140 dentists, over 100 Medical Service Corps officers, 95 nurses, 5,000 hospital corpsmen,

and 300 dental technicians serving aboard two hospital ships, the *Repose* and *Sanctuary*, the Station Hospital, Da Nang, III MAF, the 1st and 3rd Marine Divisions, and other major operational units both ashore and afloat. By and large, they are concentrated in the I Corps area and assigned to facilities of three basic types: those organic to Marine Corps units; the Station Hospital, Naval Support Activity Da Nang; and offshore facilities.

Before discussing these facilities, their resources, and capabilities, one must examine the few medical facilities in Vietnam during the years 1960 to 1965, during which time U. S. forces increased from approximately 800 military members, including 60 officers and enlisted members assigned to the Navy section of the Military Assistance and Advisory Group, to more than 137,000. As escalation continued, medical support was eventually required for troop strengths in excess of 500,000, including approximately 38,000 Navy men and 85,000 Marines.

Navy Medical Department Activities

NAVY HOSPITAL—SAIGON

Medical care for the relatively small number of Navy and Marine personnel assigned to the Navy section of the Military Assistance and Advisory Group was initially provided by the

A volunteer dental team, on the way to work on civilian patients, passes through the outskirts of Saigon.

American Embassy Dispensary. This facility became inadequate to meet increased requirements, and in 1959 it was designated as "American Dispensary" and staffed by U. S. Army, Navy, and Air Force medical and dental servicemen. This was considered satisfactory until 1962 at which time Headquarters Support Activity Saigon was commissioned. Responsible for providing administrative and logistic services to all U. S. forces in Vietnam and distributing Military Assistance Program supplies to the Vietnamese, HSA Saigon subsequently became the Navy's largest single overseas command.

A corresponding increase in medical and dental requirements led to establishment of the Navy Station Hospital, Saigon, in 1963. This one-hundred-bed hospital consisted of a four-building apartment complex of five stories with an adjoining annex, and the Metropole Hotel across the street, which housed the outpatient clinics, record offices, pharmacy, laboratory, and X-ray department. The main hospital was leased on a no-cost basis from the Republic of Vietnam Government, and the outpatient clinic was leased through the real estate section of Headquarters Support Activity. Located at 263 Tran Hung Doa in downtown Saigon, it provided for the first time a full inpatient and outpatient capability for the supporting U. S. forces in South Vietnam's third and fourth corps area (which include Saigon and the Delta) and for treating people of the U. S. diplomatic and AID missions, and allied military personnel: Australians, New Zealanders, Filipinos, South Koreans, and also Vietnamese civilians when possible.

The dental clinic, which was established in the American Embassy Dispensary in 1956, was a separate department. It was initially staffed with one dental officer and one technician. The first treatment was recorded in August 1956. Sometime before Headquarters Support Activity Saigon was established in 1962, the clinic was moved to 100 Pham Ngu Lao, Saigon. It subsequently absorbed the American Dispensary and became an integral part of HSA Saigon. The allowance soon increased to five dentists and seven technicians. Within a short period of time it became a highly efficient, modern dental department. Dental procedures increased from an original report of 76 restorations to an average of 15,000 procedures a quarter. When their schedule permitted, the dental department donated their time to helping the Vietnamese people and, as a result, promoted the American image. All members of the department performed commendably and were recommended by the Vietnamese military for the Vietnamese Medal of Honor, and four similar medals were presented to dental personnel completing tours of duty. During late October 1965, the U. S. Army Logistical Command started the first phase of taking over the dental department, assuming full responsibility for its operation shortly thereafter.

The hospital staff eventually consisted of 10 medical officers, 2 medical service officers, 16 nurses, and approximately 90 hospital corpsmen. All were U. S. Navy with the exception of a Vietnamese civilian opthalmologist, three U. S. civilian nurses, and five Thai nurses. When their workload permitted, many taught in the Saigon medical school or practiced in the Saigon-Cholon medical community. Their responsiveness and overall performance in treating combat casualties brought directly from the battle zones, as well as mass casualties wounded as a result of terrorist activities in Saigon, exemplified the highest degree of professionalism and dedication. For example, during the early morning hours of 1 November 1964 the Bien Hoa Air Base was attacked. Casualties mounted throughout the action, and after the enemy broke contact, the problem of treating the wounded became one of primary importance. Initial treatment was done at the Air Base, but because of its limited capabilities, the more seriously wounded were transferred to the Navy hospital by helicopters which used a soccer field landing zone, five minutes from the hospital, where ambulances and attendants met arriving casualties and carried them immediately to the hospital.

After this attack, seventeen men were received, four of whom were considered either seriously or critically wounded. The hospital staff spent the next eleven hours treating these casualties and performing lifesaving surgery. As terrorist activities continued, the crowded Brink BOQ located in the heart of the city of Saigon was ripped by an explosion on Christmas Eve of 1964. Immediately following the blast, hospital ambulances and medical men

were at the scene rendering first aid and searching for casualties trapped in the debris. Approximately ninety casualties were received at the hospital, and although four nurses were injured in the explosion, they continued to work at the scene.

On 17 March 1965, the U. S. enlisted barracks at Pleiku, two hundred miles northeast of Saigon, came under attack, sustaining heavy casualties. Sixteen of the more seriously wounded were flown to the hospital in Saigon, and the operating room staff subsequently worked 17 continuous hours treating their wounds.

The next major scene of VC terrorism was the United States Embassy where a large explosive device was detonated at approximately 11 A.M., 30 March 1965. The explosion killed 19 people, and more than a hundred were injured. Since the Navy hospital was the closest military medical facility, almost all casualties, Vietnamese and American, were treated at the hospital. A seemingly never-ending stream of civilians, including women and children, bleeding and in shock, were treated in the first hour. During this incident a naval officer sustained a severed carotid artery and arrived at the hospital with a corpsman who had initially rendered aid and who undoubtedly was instrumental in saving his life.

The increase in troop strength and in the frequency and intensification of attacks including repeated attacks on Bien Hoa Air Base, mining of the My Canh restaurant twice in 1965, and other incidents, combined with the hospital's responsibility for treating casualties directly from the field, produced a workload far exceeding the concept of the hospital's original planners. However, in July 1965, the Army's Third Field Hospital occupied a vacant, new American school near Tan Son Nhut Airport, and was made ready to receive patients.

This greatly increased the number of hospital beds available to meet the rising casualty rate, and it enabled the Navy hospital staff to participate aggressively in the people-to-people program. The medical officers gave freely of their time to assist Vietnamese colleagues in diagnosing and treating patients, the nursing staff provided instruction and scheduled observation visits to the hospital for the Vietnamese nurses, and elective surgical procedures for correction of congenital abnormalities were performed. This program was highly successful, and with the assistance of religious organizations, provincial representatives, and Marine Corps personnel who arranged for admission of likely candidates for surgery, approximately fifty Vietnamese children underwent corrective surgical procedures in 1965 for harelips and cleft palates. They were afforded treatment which otherwise they may never have received.

By late 1965 many of the functions of HSA Saigon were being turned over to the Army, the predominant service in the area, and despite its many successes, during command reorganization the Navy hospital was transferred to the Army in March 1966. Navy medical staffs were redistributed, being sent to Da Nang, USS *Repose*, the Philippine Islands, Japan, or back to the U. S. They had done their job well during the short life-span of the hospital, and from the time the doors to the hospital were opened in 1963 to March 1966, more than six thousand patients had been hospitalized and in excess of 130,000 outpatient visits were recorded.

STATION HOSPITAL—NSA DA NANG

The landing of the first units of the Third Marine Expeditionary Force (shortly renamed Third Marine Amphibious Force) at Da Nang early in 1965, a prelude to troop buildup later to include the 1st and 3rd Divisions, 1st Marine Air Wing, and supporting combat units, combined with the attention being given to the role of Naval Support Activity, Da Nang, as a major logistic command, caused consternation in the medical service concerning the way in which medical support could be made available for troops in I Corps Tactical Zone (ICTZ). Existing facilities were not considered adequate, and in May 1965 the Chief of Naval Operations was requested by CinCPacFlt to activate the hospital ship *Repose* (AH-16) and to authorize an Advanced Base Functional Component G4 hospital at the Naval Support Activity, Da Nang. Response was immediate, and within 24 hours after receiving the request, the hospital component was assembled and shipped from Port Hueneme, California. Supplemental medical equipment and supplies for outfitting the hospital were subsequently shipped from Oakland, California. The request to reactivate the *Repose* was approved shortly thereafter and will be discussed separately.

Construction began on the hospital in July 1965 and the prospective senior medical officer and the medical administrative officer arrived 31 July 1965. By then the Seabees were well established and busily clearing the hospital site. Construction proceeded on schedule until 28 October 1965, at which time enemy forces overran the compound and inflicted major damage to the hospital with satchel charges and other explosives, including destruction of three receiving wards, a hut housing the central sterilization room, and X-ray and laboratory facilities. Rebuilding commenced immediately and on 10 January 1966 it was opened with sixty beds. It was officially dedicated 17 January 1966 by the Commander in Chief, U. S. Pacific Fleet, and by July 1966 the hospital was expanded to its initially planned peak of four hundred beds. Force buildup continued with a corresponding increase in medical requirements, and an additional two-hundred-bed component was completed in 1968. It continued to function with six hundred beds until mid-1969 when a temporary expansion to seven hundred beds was authorized because of increased malaria cases.

Organizationally, the hospital is a department of the U. S. Naval Support Activity (NSA) Da Nang. For the most part it consists of "quonset hut" buildings used in the Advanced Base Functional Component System. It is equipped with some of the most modern medical equipment, is normally staffed with approximately six hundred officers and men of the Medical Department, including 48 physicians, 20 medical service officers, 12 dentists, 34 nurses, and 485 hospital corpsmen, and has all the professional services of a general hospital plus a preventive medicine unit, a naval medical research unit, frozen blood bank, optical fabrication shop, armory, helo pad, and triage area. It is by far the largest casualty hospital in Vietnam and is responsible for providing both emergency and definitive hospital care (or total care involving care by specialists). The hospital is primarily for members of the Navy and Marine Corps in ICTZ; for furnishing medical services to patients with diseases and injuries involving specialties not available in medical elements organic to Marine units; and also to provide dispensary services for other eligible people, including American and third-country civilians, the latter being employees of the U. S. government from countries other than the U. S. or Vietnam, such as the five Thai nurses employed at HSA Saigon.

Since it is an acute casualty hospital, the surgical services occupy the greatest percentage of space. It has eleven operating rooms, an intensive care unit, recovery room, and five surgical wards, each of fifty to sixty beds. Because of the high incidence of malaria, parasitic diseases, and tropical fevers, the medical service is almost equally as extensive with five wards, each having a capacity of thirty to sixty beds.

Complementing the hospital is a research detachment of the Naval Medical Research Unit, Taipei, Taiwan, and a surgical research group. Among other duties, those assigned to these units conduct studies in the I Corps area involving: diarrhea, insect-borne, and exotic diseases, methods of improving diagnostic techniques to assist medical officers in Da Nang to diagnose and treat patients, and evaluation of treatment of shock from battle wounds. The surgical shock study group has been a major factor in establishing the high level of patient care and has published several papers on the valuable work which it has done. From a practical viewpoint the research unit has had charge of many of the most seriously wounded and has given them total care. Over a two-month period it received 23 very seriously wounded patients, usually double or triple amputees. All but one survived. Without the special, sophisticated, and meticulous care provided by this research group the mortality rate may have been higher. Of further importance, the work of the group will be of invaluable assistance to both the military and civilian medical communities in studying ways of improving the quality of patient care.

Since the doors to the Da Nang hospital were first opened in 1966, its workload has been phenomenal. During 1968, 23,437 patients were admitted to the hospital, accumulating in excess of 150,000 sick days. More than 2,500 were admitted during the May 1968 offensive, an all-time high for admissions in a single month. Of the total hospitalized, 51 per cent were treated for wounds or injuries, requiring more than 23,000 major surgical procedures. Despite this tremendously heavy workload, and repeated rocket and mortar attacks inflicting injuries to the hospital staff and damage to the hospital, the staff has consistently performed superbly. Major structural damage to clinics and wards occurred during an attack in 1968. The most recent attack occurred in August 1969 when the hospital took 10 mortar hits, sustaining 18 casualties (none of which were critical, fortunately), and damage to clinical spaces.

III Marine Amphibious Force Organic Medical Support

Medical support to the Marine Corps is provided by: integral elements, force-troop supporting elements, and by Navy hospital facilities ashore and afloat. For example, the Navy hospital at Da Nang, while under the command of Naval Support Activity, is responsible for any care to Marines which exceeds the capabilities of their own units. These medical units are manned by medical officers and hospital corpsmen of the Navy Medical Department. Prior to assignment to duty with the Marines, the officers and men are given a course of instruction in Marine Corps organization and tactics, field medical problems, sanitation, and such like, and physicians may receive additional instruction in tropical medicine, staff procedures, and exercise in the employment of field medical units. Generally, all corps codes (medical, dental, medical service, and nurses) receive instruction and training in organization, field medical problems, and other subjects mentioned. The training period varies from two to four weeks at the field medical service schools, Camp Lejeune, North Carolina, and Camp Pendleton, California, to ten months at the Command and Staff College, Quantico, Virginia. The latter course is limited to senior medical and medical service officers.

The Marine Division organic medical support consists of those medical elements at various headquarters and regiments, and the medical battalions. The medical battalion is a separate supporting battalion within a division. It consists of a headquarters and four collecting and clearing companies (C&C Companies). The headquarters contains the command element, the preventive medicine section, motor transport section, and the medical records section. Collecting and clearing companies consist of a company headquarters, two clearing platoons, and one collecting platoon. Each clearing platoon is staffed and equipped to establish and operate a thirty-bed clearing station. The textbook flow of patients is from the field to battalion aid station to collection and clearing company and to designated ships of an amphibious task force. However, with the advent of helicopters, battalion aid stations are being bypassed to a large degree.

Each headquarters within the division is provided a dispensary sufficient to furnish day-to-day medical care to the unit. When circumstances warrant, the Marine Corps may provide, from outside a division, a hospital company for support of casualties. This is a one-hundred-bed hospital designed and equipped to provide surgical and medical care for non-critical cases.

Basically, medical support is provided to Marines in I Corps by battalion aid stations, regimental aid stations, the 1st Medical Battalion, and 1st Hospital Company, 1st Marine Division, the 3rd Medical Battalion, 3rd Division, the 9th Marine Amphibious Brigade, and the 1st Marine Airwing.

The battalion aid stations have limited capabilities, mainly first aid, routine sick call, and a 48- to 72-hour holding capability. The regimental aid stations give the same kind of support for regimental headquarters.

The 1st Medical Battalion works in a hospital kind of facility and maintains the capability of deploying any of its four collection and clearing companies to the field in support of infantry regiments. It is currently in Da Nang and has 240 beds authorized. The 1st Hospital Company has 100 beds authorized and is also at Da Nang. The 3rd Medical Battalion, at

Quang Tri, has 218 beds. The 1st Marine Air-wing operates small dispensaries for each aircraft group. Such dispensaries were first in tents, but have progressively advanced to semi-permanent structures.

More than 1,500 Medical Department people are serving with the 1st Marine Division, and approximately 1,200 are assigned to the 3rd Division. Nearly 300 are serving with the 1st Marine Airwing.

Of the total Medical Department strength providing direct medical support to Vietnam activities, more than 3,200 personnel including approximately 200 medical officers, 70 dentists, 50 medical service officers, 150 dental technicians, and more than 2,700 hospital corpsmen are committed to the support of the 1st and 3rd Marine Divisions, 1st Marine Airwing, and combat supporting units in the I Corps Tactical Zone (ICTZ). Charged with the responsibility for rendering first aid, performing emergency surgery, collecting, temporary hospitalization and evacuation of casualties, these personnel are serving generally with the 1st and 3rd Medical Battalion, First Force Hospital Company, the 1st, 3rd, and 11th Dental Companies, and directly with combat elements.

Initial medical support to elements of the Third Marine Amphibious Force, which landed in Da Nang in March 1965, consisted of two medical officers and approximately fifty hospital corpsmen. As the buildup evolved, elements (collecting and clearing companies) were brought ashore and by 25 June 1965 the complete Medical Battalion was landed. The collecting and clearing companies which had been established at Da Nang, Chu Lai, and Phu Bai were later developed into field hospitals. Currently field hospitals are located at Da Nang, Quang Tri, and Dong Ha with a capacity of approximately 560 hospital beds, and as tactics dictate they may be shifted in the I Corps

Tactical Zone. During 1968 more than 24,000 men were hospitalized in these facilities accumulating more than 111,000 sick days. Of the total admissions, 43 per cent were returned to duty and approximately 56 per cent were transferred either to Da Nang, the *Repose,* or the *Sanctuary* for continued treatment and disposition. The mortality rate was less than one per cent.

MEDICAL SUPPORT IN II, III, AND IV CORPS TACTICAL ZONES

Assignment of unprecedented responsibilities to the Navy for logistic support of U.S. troops and Free World Military Assistance Forces in I Corps Tactical Zone caused the Army to be given responsibility for inpatient care in II, III, and IV Corps tactical zones while the Navy concentrated on medical support in ICTZ. The Navy continues to provide dispensary care to coast surveillance and land-based riverine forces at widely separated detachments. Normally hospitalization for patients too badly injured or too sick to be properly cared for at these detachments is provided by Army and Air Force units.

Navy medical support to the Mobile Riverine Force when it was active in the Delta in 1967–1969 was by and large provided by Navy hospital corpsmen assigned to the base ships (APBs). Army medical units organic to the force, consisting of doctors and corpsmen, supported their troops. The base ships of the force, USS *Benewah* (APB-35) and USS *Colleton* (APB-36), had limited facilities, and casualties from the force were therefore generally evacuated to the Army's Third Mobile Surgical Hospital at Dong Tam.

OFF-SHORE MEDICAL SUPPORT

Off-shore medical facilities consisting of two hospital ships, the *Repose* and *Sanctuary*, and surgical casualty evacuation teams on

LPHs were established to provide medical support during amphibious assaults and to back up land-based medical elements.

USS Repose (AH-16)

After eight months of extensive preparation, fitting out, and refresher training, the *Repose* arrived off the coast near Chu Lai on 16 February 1966. Her arrival marked the beginning of a major increase in medical facilities in the I Corps Tactical Zone (ICTZ). The hospital spaces were equipped with the most modern medical facilities available, including 560 hospital beds, which could be increased to 750 beds. This was accomplished by setting up or increasing the number of beds in wards or rooms designed for patients' beds. It represented the ultimate in casualty care. The hospital staff numbered more than 300 including 25 medical officers in all specialties, 7 medical service officers, 3 dentists, 29 nurses, 8 dental technicians, and more than 200 hospital corpsmen in all technical specialties.

Under the Seventh Fleet Command, *Repose* is responsible for providing direct hospital support to operating forces, including both emergency and definitive hospital care. Primarily service is rendered to Navy and Marine personnel in the ICTZ, and to forces engaged in amphibious operations in other tactical zones. Movements of both *Repose* and *Sanctuary* are coordinated with the Seventh Fleet by III MAF.

The ships are stationed near sites of heaviest action. Virtually all casualties are received aboard by helicopter. The *Repose* seldom leaves the combat zone and spends approximately eighty days of the quarter on the line. Ever-increasing demands for medical services made it difficult to gain relief for even brief upkeep periods. During December 1967, admissions and medical treatments continued to reach new highs as evidenced by reaching the five-thousandth helicopter landing that

month. This was followed by the six-thousandth landing 30 April 1968, and the seven-thousandth landing 22 June 1968. She marked the ten-thousandth safe helicopter landing in January 1969.

On 29 July 1967, the *Repose* was called upon to give emergency assistance to the USS *Forrestal* (CVA-59) which had suffered a major fire while on Yankee Station in the Gulf of Tonkin. It was later determined that 134 men had been killed and 162 were injured by the explosions and fire. The response of the *Repose* was immediate as she set course to meet the *Forrestal*. The two ships met at their rendezvous at 2230, 29 July 1967. By 0500 the next morning, 25 critically and seriously injured had been flown to the *Repose* and assistance was given in disposing of the remains of those killed in the fire. This emergency demonstrated the versatility of hospital ships. While the *Repose* was absent from line medical service support responsibility, the *Sanctuary* took over her duties.

By December 1968, nearly 17,000 casualties had been admitted to the *Repose*. Approximately 7,000 of those were hospitalized for treatment of wounds, and the remainder for treatment of disease and other injuries. In spite of the strenuous on-line commitment of more than eighty days a quarter, a high degree of professionalism prevails, and quality of service and morale have continued to be high.

USS Sanctuary (AH-17)

Demands for more beds continued along with a troop buildup in ICTZ, and in March 1966, only a week after the *Repose* anchored off Chu Lai, the USS *Sanctuary* was pulled from the Reserve Fleet to be overhauled and outfitted. Much was learned from the fitting out and the early days of the deployment of the *Repose*. These lessons were applied during the recommissioning of the *Sanctuary*, insuring improved use of hospital spaces. After installing the latest innovations for treating the sick, injured, and wounded, she arrived in Da Nang Harbor 10 April 1967. Her mission, like that of the *Repose*, was to provide direct hospital support to forces fighting in Vietnam. Her hospital staff (approximately 317) and bed capacity of 560 beds, essentially the same as the *Repose*, were employed immediately off the coast to support our forces in I Corps. For the remainder of 1967, more than 4,000 patients were admitted to the *Sanctuary*, and an average of 389 beds were occupied daily. As military activities increased in 1968, the *Sanctuary* experienced a comparable increase in her workload, while casualties sustained more devastating wounds. These wounds were a result of the increased tempo of operations in areas long occupied by enemy forces; use of more sophisticated weaponry by hostile forces such as plastic explosives, land mines, and booby traps. Admissions totaled 6,799 during 1968, including 2,360 patients hospitalized for treatment of wounds.

On 11 January 1969, the *Sanctuary* was ordered south to Cape Batangan to participate in Operation Bold Mariner, one of the largest amphibious operations of the Vietnam conflict. More than 120 casualties were received by the *Sanctuary* during this operation, including nine double and five single amputees, and one triple amputee. The *Sanctuary* subsequently reported that wounds encountered during this operation were unlike those previously treated and that land mines and other explosive devices had inflicted massive soft tissue defects of the extremities, buttocks, and abdomen, loss of limb and eye injuries from multiple fragments, and that it was not unusual to have three teams of surgeons working on a single casualty simultaneously. Shortly after supporting this operation, the *Sanctuary* entered the yard at Subic Bay after a record 116 consecutive days on the line. Generally both AHs are on line 85 days a quarter with a

5-day yard period for maintenance and upkeep. A combatant spends approximately 60 days a quarter on line.

Medical Support of Amphibious Ready Group/Special Landing Forces

As tactics dictate, amphibious assaults are mounted from special landing forces afloat. These amphibious groups are composed of several ships which include LPH class vessels. The supporting LPHs have an expanded medical capability and are augmented with a modified surgical team, casualty evacuation team, and a surgical team supply block. The additional teams, which generally remain on board the LPHs, consist of four medical officers, two male nurses, and twenty hospital corpsmen on each LPH and are capable of providing initial care for casualties sustained during an assault operation. For instance, in an operation in January 1969, 172 casualties were received aboard an LPH, 94 of which were treated for combat wounds. Depending on the area of assault operation, further evacuation of casualties may be made to either Navy or Army medical facilities.

Military Provincial Health Assistance Program

Vietnam is a land where the civilian population has more than twenty thousand people to each physician. Contrast this to the U. S. civilian/physician population ratio of eight hundred people to one physician. Early in the contingency, the importance of providing medical assistance to the Vietnamese was recognized by all branches of the U. S. Government in Vietnam, and the Agency for International Development, with the State Department, developed a team concept referred to as MILPHAP (recently renamed USMACV Field Advisory Elements JTD) to render assistance to the civilian medical services. The Department of Defense was asked to provide military personnel to staff these elements, and the Navy

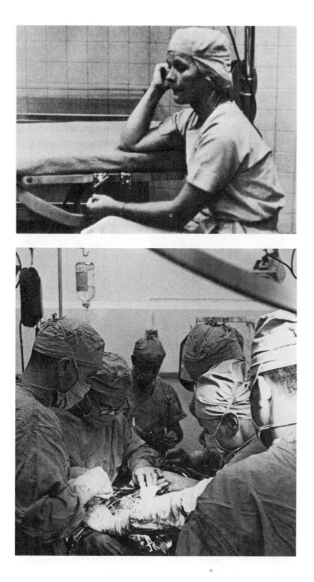

Helping others can be exhausting, as shown by Lieutenant Alvina Harrison, Nurse Corps, U.S. Navy, after a hard day in surgery at a civilian hospital in Saigon in 1966, and by Hospital Corpsman Leslie G. Osterman, caring for a heat-exhausted Marine while on patrol in I Corps in 1968. The other photograph shows surgeons at work in the Repose in April 1966. (Frank T. Peak, PH3, T. B. Davis, PH3, and J. E. Cote, PH1, U.S. Navy)

has currently assigned a quota of nine teams requiring a total of 24 medical officers, seven medical service officers, and 83 hospital corpsmen to assist the Ministry of Health at the Provincial and/or Prefecture hospital, district dispensaries, and maternity centers, or in public health, sanitation and preventive medicine programs at provincial or district levels. Five teams are located in I Corps (Quang Ngai, Quang Nam, Quang Tin, Quang Tri, and Thua Thien), and four are in IV Corps (Vinh Binh, Bac Lieu, Vinh Long, and Chau Doc). The teams report to USMACV in Saigon for command and coordination control. Reports document improvement in the American-Vietnamese relationship by this endeavor, and in the quality of patient care and advances made in paramedical areas, such as logistics and records.

Medical Civic Action Program

Unlike USMACV Field Advisory Elements JTD (MILPHAP) the Medical Civic Action Program is equipped and supplied by U. S. forces. This program has proven to be an effective means of reaching the people of the nation, and MEDCAP teams throughout I Corps are committing much time to improving the health and environment of the Vietnamese. The magnitude of the MEDCAP contribution can be envisioned from the number of patients and types of medical care rendered. During 1968, 1,273,238 medical and dental treatments were provided by medical elements in III MAF, 5,776 serious or critically ill evacuated, and 3,044 received medical-dental training. In that same year nearly six hundred Vietnamese civilians were hospitalized at the Naval Hospital, Naval Support Activity Da Nang, and an average of nine thousand outpatient visits were recorded monthly. More than two hundred thousand immunizations, mostly plague and cholera, were given, and many unrecorded days were spent in health and sanitation inspections and in instructing the Vietnamese in food service and public health practice. The medical needs of the Vietnamese people are great, and this undertaking not only has provided treatment to many who otherwise may have been neglected, but it has also created much good will between the teams and the Vietnamese.

Malaria

Fever of undetermined origin and malaria represent the major causes of temporary disability in Vietnam. During 1969, 3,352 members of the Navy and Marine Corps were hospitalized for treatment of malaria in the I Corps area, with an average patient stay of 31.5 days.

An interview of patients, the majority of whom had been with forces in the hills, suggested strongly that malaria discipline was lax and nearly 50 per cent reported they had not taken Chloraquine-Primaquine (C-P) tablets as instructed, nor had they followed other preventive measures. As a result of an increase in malaria cases in May and June 1969, additional people, including 2 medical officers, 2 nurses, and 18 hospital corpsmen, were temporarily assigned to the Da Nang hospital to assist with the increased workload, and in early July 1969 a study group from the U. S. entered I Corps to evaluate the malaria problem and to submit recommendations of possible control measures.

Casualty Recovery Rate and Causative Agents

The type of the military action being waged in Vietnam can be the cause of devastating wounds, and multiple wounds of a massive nature are not uncommon. The type of encounter is generally reflected by the nature of wounds seen at medical service facilities. Offensive deployment usually generates a high proportion of small arms and artillery wounds. On the other hand, multiple fragmentation wounds caused by mines, booby traps, and grenades are associated with search and destroy missions. Thus far, 65 per cent of the nonfatal injuries have occurred from fragments and represent some of the most serious wounds, requiring prolonged hospitalization. Conversely more than 41 percent of combat deaths have been due to small arms fire, a much higher rate than experienced in either World War II or Korea.

Since January 1965, more than 120,000 Navy and Marine Corps patients have been admitted to hospitals in Vietnam and supporting offshore medical facilities. The largest number of admissions during the period of 1965–1968 occurred in 1968 when the Navy and Marine Corps sustained more than 31,000 combat casualties, 60 percent of which required hospitalization.

Of the total hospitalized during this time, approximately 73,000 (69 per cent) were returned to duty after treatment in either hospitals in Vietnam or offshore medical facilities. More than 21,000 (18 per cent) were returned to duty by U. S. hospitals upon completion of treatment. Approximately 8,000 (7 per cent) required separation because of residual disability precluding performance of further useful military service. More than 5,000 (five per cent) remain under treatment. The mortality rate is less than 1 percent (.86) of those hospitalized, the lowest ever before achieved in any military action.

Summary

In summary, the missions of Navy and Marine Corps forces deployed in Southeast Asia are diverse and include large Marine combat units in the most northern sector of South Vietnam; small naval units engaged in riverine operations in the South and surveillance operations along the coast; and Marine and naval units involved in aerial and surface bombardment of targets in both North and South Vietnam. This diversity of missions dictates different requirements for medical support at various locations within the I, II, III, and IV Corps tactical zones. The Navy was the first of the services to provide a major inpatient and outpatient capability in the southern sector of South Vietnam, and approximately six thousand Medical Department servicemen, including more than one hundred assigned to give medical assistance to the Vietnamese under the AID Program, were eventually committed in direct support of forces involved in the conflict. With reorganization and a shift in tactical requirements employing a large Navy and Marine force in I Corps, most Navy medical forces were redeployed from the southern sector and concentrated in I Corps area. Included are major medical units organic to III Marine Amphibious Force, a 600-bed hospital at Da Nang, and the hospital ships *Repose* and *Sanctuary*, each of which have 560 beds. Navy medical support to land-based riverine and coastal surveillance forces is limited to dispensaries, and any required hospital support other than in I Corps area is generally provided by the Army. Additional medical teams on LPHs provide support for amphibious assaults, and depending on the area of operations, casualties may be evacuated to either Navy or Army medical facilities. Of those requiring hospitalization (approximately 120,000), 87 per cent were returned to duty, 7 per cent required separation because of residual disability, and 5 per cent remain under treatment. The mortality of those admitted to the hospital has been, as previously shown, less than 1 per cent.

Observations

Personnel

More than 13 per cent of the Medical Department is serving in Southeast Asia. Approximately 14 per cent of all Navy personnel in Vietnam are medical. There was an overall increase of 30 per cent in total Navy medical personnel strength during the Fiscal Years 1965–1969, while Navy-Marine strength increased by approximately 25 per cent. This major medical support of troops in Vietnam has not been without sacrifice in other areas. Because of austere peacetime staffing, a reduction in the U. S. facilities was necessary to insure that deploying units were fully staffed. While the staff of the Medical Department increased from approximately 36,000 to slightly more than 47,000 during the Fiscal Years 1965–1969 in support of a combined Navy-Marine strength of 1,094,000, manpower resources continue to be strained because of a 54 per cent overall increase in the daily average number of patients (from 11,000 to nearly 17,000) occupying hospital beds; the prolonged nature of the Vietnam conflict, requiring a large number of personnel in pipeline; and a relatively low staffing ratio of medical personnel to total Navy-Marine strength. Retention of Navy Medical Department personnel continues to be a problem, but the major deterrent in delivering medical services is a shortage of billets.

A recent comparative analysis of the staffing ratio of medical personnel in the Army, the Navy, and the Air Force to total strength revealed significantly lower staffing in the Navy Medical Department when compared to the other services. An additional 4,500 officers in all corps codes and nearly 8,000 enlisted members would be required to give the Navy a medical staffing level comparable to that in the Army and the Air Force.

Performance

The magnificent performance of medical officers and men in Vietnam is most noteworthy, especially the performance of the hospital corpsmen serving with combat forces. These young men have exhibited great courage and compassion in rendering medical assistance to the wounded, oftentimes at great personal risk. More than six hundred have earned personal decorations for valor including 90 Silver Stars, and in excess of four thousand have been awarded the Purple Heart for wounds received in action. Their high degree of competence and heroic performance have gained recognition and admiration throughout the naval service.

Hospital Ships

Upon deployment, the USS *Repose* (AH-16) and USS *Sanctuary* (AH-17) both were staffed with highly specialized personnel and were equipped with the most modern medical equipment, including special items such as an artificial heart enabling surgeons to bypass part or all of the heart; an artificial kidney; a recompression chamber for treatment of anaerobic infections (gas gangrene, tetanus, and the like), and ultrasonic diagnostic equipment for detecting foreign bodies in the brain. On the other hand, both the *Repose* and *Sanctuary* were converted to AHs during World War II, and their effectiveness is limited by obsolete hull configuration. Neither ship had a triage area until deployment to Vietnam. The last ship to be planned and constructed from the keel up as a hospital ship was the *Relief* (AH-1) in 1916. Again, the operating room space is not sufficient to meet heavy casualty requirements, the existing triage area for initial resuscitation of wounded is inadequate, and the helicopter platform limits the number of casualties that can be received simultaneously. This also represents a hazard because the larger, heavier helicopters now in service must land and be launched from a platform not adequate to their needs.

Yet there is no question that a hospital ship provides a vital mobile medical capability to the operating forces. Unfortunately, existing hospital ships were conceived for wars past, and experience has shown that placing such ships in the reserve fleet does not ensure ready availability of modern facilities. The ships operate differently today than either in Korea or World War II. More casualties bypass medical facilities ashore, which more often than not have limited capabilities, and casualties are flown directly to the hospital ships. This improved forward-looking management concept; larger helicopters; increased frequency of medical evacuation flights requiring larger and stronger landing platforms; expanded triage area for initial resuscitation of the wounded; a radiology area adjacent to triage; and increased operating room space; all require new design. This is not a question of reconfiguration or arrangement but rather one of obsolescence, and the obvious need is to provide replacement vessels developed and designed as hospital ships.

Facilities

For several years prior to the Vietnam commitment, the Navy Medical Department repeatedly recommended development of new advanced-base functional components, particularly the use of more modern structures for medical facilities. Though in-house studies had been done on this project, they had not reached a point where radical improvements could be made prior to the necessity of locating these facilities in support of Vietnam operations. Consequently, the field medical facilities deployed to Vietnam by the Navy and the various Marine elements were of the same general configuration as those used in World War II, and later in Korea. On the other hand, the Army introduced the "medical unit self-contained transportable" (MUST), a building unit which provides a modern controlled environment and ancillary facilities necessary for patient care. The Air Force later introduced modular components both for fixed and mobile medical installations. Components of two MUST units were subsequently bought by the Navy and are currently being tested in the field by the First Hospital Company at Da Nang and the Third Medical Battalion at Quang Tri. Both the Army and Air Force components, which can be set up quickly and which provide for a comfortable, air-conditioned, clean environment for patient care, are a great improvement over tents and quonset huts used by the Navy and Marines in Vietnam. They are symbolic of progress made by other services in providing improved facilities for treating casualties. Space requirements have repeatedly been documented by the Navy Medical Department. A civilian architectural and engineering firm is conducting on-site studies in Vietnam before redesigning medical and dental advanced base components. In the meantime, existing Navy medical facilities in Vietnam continue to be housed in obsolete structures because of the low priorities previously given this program.

Air Ambulances

Helicopter evacuation, which began in Korea and is used extensively in Vietnam for movement of casualties, has revolutionized combat medicine with the ability to pick up the wounded within minutes of injury. There is little question that this saves lives and often it is the only mode of transportation possible. The Army has a superb single-mission ambulance helo medical evacuation system with assigned medical crew members. On the other hand, neither the Navy nor the Marine Corps has air ambulances designed for movement of patients from combat medical support units to more sophisticated medical facilities in the rear. Though there is no significant statistical difference between the Marine/Navy mortality rate and that of other services, studies show that the present system using operational aircraft for movement of Navy/Marine casualties takes longer, is inefficient, and they often arrive without necessary equipment to move casualties. They frequently do not have medical personnel aboard. While the Marine Corps has flown more than 127,000 medical evacuation missions in Vietnam during the years 1966–1969, and has saved countless lives, the system as it currently exists cannot be favorably compared with the Army's. Perhaps if the Navy were to adopt a modified version of the Army's evacuation system, and designate specific Navy helicopters as air ambulances, this would represent an optimal step forward.

Conclusion

The record of the Navy Medical Department in Vietnam is good. It is good because of the high degree of professionalism exhibited by a group of ingenious individuals dedicated to meeting constantly changing conditions in Vietnam, because of the cooperation of sister services, and because of swift medical attention virtually assured by the use of helicopters as air ambulances. This should not be misunderstood to mean we were fully prepared for the contingency and that we experienced no medical or logistical problems generated by a heavy commitment of troops in Southeast Asia. It required more than eight months for the *Repose* to arrive on station after the decision was made for her outfitting and reactivation. And after nearly five months of construction, an advanced base hospital was virtually destroyed during an enemy attack, and an additional three months were required before it could be partially opened in January 1966.

The Navy has a good record because of the gradual nature of escalation in the conflict. Time was in our favor and assisted us when we had to meet increased demands. By the time our heaviest casualties were sustained, in February and May 1968, medical facilities had been expanded to serve the new needs.

The Navy's record in Vietnam is good because of the courage, competence, and integrity of Medical Department personnel in Vietnam. But, as vital as these qualities are in combat medicine, the material side cannot be disregarded. No improvement has been made in design of advanced base hospital components since World War II, and the hospital ships are of limited effectiveness because they are obsolete in hull design. However, in spite of the inherent deficiencies, they have demonstrated most commendably their versatility and mobility, and the mix of the hospital ship, land medical facilities, and a modern air ambulance evacuation system is considered essential to providing required medical support for either amphibious operations or for prolonged counterinsurgency land conflicts.

While the Navy has a good record in Vietnam, it remains to be seen if we will benefit from experience. The challenges and opportunities for satisfying both current and future medical requirements are great, and obviously they are not a task for the Medical Department alone. Will we reexamine priorities, establish an improved staffing ratio for medical personnel, fund and develop an air ambulance evacuation system, a modern hospital ship for the active Fleet, and new advanced base hospital components, or will we quickly put these lessons behind us when the fighting stops? Without both administrative and legislative action, we may well expect to be confronted by similar or greater deficiencies in meeting future medical demands when treating mass casualties either in the civilian or military sector. We may not be as fortunate next time—time may not be in our favor.

(*Naval Review*, 1970)

Fighting Where the Ground Was a Little Damp: The War on the Coast and in the Rivers

It was with small forces sailing in small places that the U. S. Navy soon found itself carrying out its main tasks of protecting the flow of friendly shipping, halting the flow of enemy shipping, and landing armies on hostile shores.

The places were the coastal waters, rivers, canals, and swamps of South Vietnam. The forces consisted of the same officers and men who, but for circumstance, might have spent hard, humdrum lives on Yankee Station in a carrier, a replenishment ship, or one of their escorts. They used old ships and craft returned to activity after years of seemingly terminal idleness, new boats adapted hastily from successful commercial prototypes, and aircraft discarded by those who had found better ones.

A century had passed since the Navy had last had to fight serious coastal and riverine campaigns. It was in 1863 that President Lincoln could say correctly of his naval officers and men that "at all the watery margins they have been present. Not only on the deep sea, the broad bay, and the rapid river, but also up the narrow muddy bayou, and wherever the ground was a little damp, they have been and made their tracks."[1] During that century the tradition of inshore and inland naval warfare had been lost—happily lost, for it had been born of a great civil war. But when the need for inshore and riverine naval forces arose in Vietnam, the seagoing services, the Navy and Coast Guard, responded rapidly, imaginatively, and well.

In I Corps, as we have seen in other parts of this book, the Marines on the DMZ, at Hue and Phu Bai, and elsewhere, depended on seaborne and river-borne supplies to keep them alive and fighting. Commander Swarztrauber tells us that when the enemy threatened their riverine lines of communication, the Marines called on the Navy's fighting boats in the Mekong Delta to come north to help protect the logistic shipping on those rivers. It is interesting that aircraft, riverbank patrols, and artillery were not enough to secure the safety of river transport. Fighting boats had to be there too. By themselves, of course, the boats would not have been enough, either. It was only by the combined efforts of all the forces available that the Americans, and not the North

Vietnamese and Viet Cong, gained and kept control of the essential rivers running inland from Da Nang north to the DMZ.

In "one of the most savage pieces of terrain in the world,"[2] the Rung Sat Special Zone, or "Forest of Assassins," there was another struggle for mastery of waters essential to our shipping. It was via a narrow twisting passage through that dense mangrove swamp that the oceangoing ships, laden both with the goods of war and those of peace, passed from the South China Sea to the quays and moorings of Saigon. Mines in the channel could put an end to that traffic. Even a short interruption while a sunken ship was raised and removed would be unendurable. This the enemy knew as well as we. He tried, chiefly with mines, but also with rockets and automatic weapons, to sink or at least to intimidate merchant ships passing through. He had some successes, but not many.

The enemy's main opponents here were the lightly armed and totally unarmored 57-foot wooden minesweeping boats which, at 8 knots, twice daily dragged grapnels down one side of the channel and then up the other. Their objective was to cut the wires with which the foe controlled his mines.

The minesweeping boats, of course, became prime objects of attack. They, in turn, were protected by gunboats, helicopter gunships, and the Air Force's now-long-reviled defoliant aircraft that spread Agent Orange along the banks of the Long Tau.

To wipe out the enemy in his lair, the Navy, first in combination with the Marines, and then with the Army, made amphibious attacks on his stronghold. Lieutenant Commander Mumford describes the first of these, "Jackstay," conducted in March and April 1966. During that operation landing craft sailed into the forbidding heart of the swamp, put their Marines ashore and, hours or days later, met them on the banks of entirely different streams. During that operation, and on many occasions afterwards, the enemy chose not to fight, fading, instead, into some farther fastness. Eventually, though, the Americans came to control the Rung Sat so well that they could use it as a training area for units just entering the war.

Clearly, even in so small an area as the approaches to Saigon, the protection of shipping called for a wide variety of naval and military skills and an equally wide variety of forces to employ those skills.

U. S. naval forces went on the offensive against the enemy's lines of communication both in the flat, canal-laced Mekong Delta and on South Vietnam's long coast. This was not nearly as good as going on the offensive off the enemy's coast and that of his Cambodian vassal, but it helped.

A suspicion that the enemy was using the sea to support the Viet Cong was tested in 1962, but no evidence could be found to support that suspicion. Shortly afterwards, however, the enemy must have chosen to use the sea, for as General Westmoreland reports, "Before 1965 the Viet Cong had received an estimated 70 per cent of their supplies by maritime infiltration," an infiltration not countered at all by the South Vietnamese army or navy.[3] Captain

Hodgman of the Coast Guard describes the conditions he and his men found when they arrived in the Gulf of Thailand in mid-1965 to set up the first American coastal interdiction force, and he tells what they did. Divided into small crews in small boats, Navy and Coast Guard seamen cruised months on end off the long, uninviting shores of South Vietnam, inspecting thousands of boats, examining tens of thousands of documents. Sometimes the work was dangerous, but as generally is characteristic of naval warfare, more often it was tedious. Yet, continues General Westmoreland, by the end of 1966 the direct seaborne share of Viet Cong supplies "had been reduced to a trickle of less than 10 per cent."[4]

For his logistical runs the enemy used steel trawlers of between 80 and 130 feet in length, each capable of carrying between 100 and 400 tons of cargo. Some sailed from Haiphong, others from ports on China's Hainan Island.[5] Captain Hodgman tells how, following a nighttime interception, his ships and boats sank one of those supply craft on the eastern shore of the Ca Mau Peninsula.

Eventually 17 such craft were sunk by U. S. or South Vietnamese forces. Others, frustrated in their attempt to reach their destinations, gave up and returned north. Confronted with this unsatisfactory situation, the North Vietnamese began their use of Sihanoukville in December 1966. That was a supply route the U. S. forces did not cut.

At first, the prime objective of Task Force 116, the 31-foot river patrol boats and their associated helicopters, was to halt the enemy's mobility in the Delta by denying him use of the rivers. However, the Viet Cong seldom traveled up or down stream. Instead, they went across the stream, which was difficult for our forces to control. Eventually, TF 116 had enough resources to extend the struggle from the broad rivers into the multitude of small canals. This became particularly important after the enemy began using Sihanoukville, for it was via the canal system that arms passed from that port to the Viet Cong. Commander Schreadley describes how the swift but unarmored patrol boats of TF 116 worked in those canals with the armored but slow craft of the River Assault Force, Task Force 117.[6] Commenting upon one of many operations in this effort, "Giant Slingshot," which was carried out late in 1968, Major General William B. Fulton, U. S. Army, wrote that "extremely large quantities of arms, munitions, and supplies were uncovered in caches buried along the river banks, proving beyond doubt that vital enemy infiltration lines had been cut."[7] But as long as Sihanoukville remained open to the enemy, there were more arms where those had come from.

Like the River Patrol Force, the River Assault Force was intended to go on the tactical offensive, though always in conjunction with the Army. As Captain Wells makes clear, the boats were to provide the advantages of mobility to a brigade of the Army's 9th Division when that brigade was introduced into the soggy, nearly roadless Delta. Combining the mobility of their heavily armed and armored fighting craft with that of their floating base, this Army-Navy team was able, especially when complemented by helicopter-borne forces, to catch the enemy unprepared time and again.

More might have been done by this force. Unfortunately, from the beginning it was undercut by interference on the part of that most unsuccessful of our defense secretaries, Robert McNamara, who, among other things, chose to delete most of the planned infantry berthing spaces in the afloat base. General Fulton who, as a colonel, had been the first to command the 2nd Brigade, 9th Division, and thus had been Captain Wells's opposite number, describes the situation this way: "The decision of Secretary of Defense McNamara in late 1966 to cut the requested number of self-propelled barracks ships by three eliminated berthing space for two of three infantry battalions. The Navy, however, resourcefully provided space for one of the two battalions by giving the force an APL—a barracks barge—and a larger LST of the 1152 class. The Secretary of Defense's decision could have been disastrous to the execution of the Mobile Afloat Force plan had these innovations by the Navy not been made."[8] The author goes on to point out that, even so, "the brigade was forced to operate without its third maneuver battalion. . . "

Despite the handicap imposed on them, the River Assault Force and the 2nd Brigade, 9th Division, collectively known as the Mobile Riverine Force, did well until long after the departure of Captain Wells and Colonel Fulton. Then the Army found new work for the 2nd Brigade, and the force faded away. Its craft were among the first to be turned over to the South Vietnamese.

No more than the Marines in I Corps could the coastal patrol, river patrol, or river assault force operate without people, bases, ammunition, food, fuel, spares, and transportation for all those. It was the task of Naval Support Activity Saigon to provide those people and things. As described by that activity's founding commanding officer, Captain King, his task was to support "one naval campaign in the Delta and another up and down the long coast, and nearly every base . . . was, in effect, on an island . . ."

Captain King's observation was not only accurate, but it could be applied to nearly the whole war, for in Vietnam the U. S. armed forces, whatever their nature, were all "in effect, on an island." The space between each base, as we saw in I Corps, and as illustrated by the authors in this section, was occupied by those who were indifferent or hostile both to their government and to our presence. In these circumstances the sea itself, always indifferent to human hopes and fears, was the least hostile of environments.

When events abroad suggest we again engage in war, it will be important before we commit forces that we are sure those we hope to help indeed want and have earned our help. Only then will our forces not be interlopers isolated on their islands, only then can they be sources of strength and hope to those who seek and deserve their help.

Notes

1. Lincoln to J. C. Conkling 26 August 1863. Quoted in Heinl, Robert Debs, Jr., *Dictionary of Military and Naval Quotations* (Annapolis, Md.: U. S. Naval Institute, 1966), p. 209.

2. Westmoreland, William C., *A Soldier Reports* (Garden City, N.Y.: Dell Publishing Co., 1976), p. 185.

3. Ibid., p. 184.

4. Ibid., p. 184.

5. Tho, Tran Dinh, *The Cambodian Incursion* (Washington, D.C., 1978), p. 22. This work is one of a series, "Indochina Monographs," published by the U. S. Army Center of Military History.

6. For descriptions of the craft the Navy and Coast Guard used in the coastal and river campaigns, see Miller, Richards T., "Fighting Boats of the United States" in *Naval Review 1968* (Annapolis, Md.: U.S. Naval Institute, 1967), pp. 296–329.

7. Fulton, William B., *Riverine Operations 1966–1969* (Washington, D.C., 1973), p. 182. This work is one of a series, "Vietnam Studies," published by the Department of the Army.

8. Ibid., p. 186.

The Naval War in Vietnam, 1950–1970

Commander R. L. Schreadley, U.S. Navy

Truck convoys valiantly crossed streams, mountains and forests; drivers spent scores of sleepless nights, in defiance of difficulties and dangers, to bring food and ammunition to the front, to permit the army to annihilate the enemy.

Thousands of bicycles from the towns also carried food and munitions to the front.

Hundreds of sampans of all sizes, hundreds of thousands of bamboo rafts crossed rapids and cascades to supply the front.

Day and night, hundreds of thousands of porters and young volunteers crossed passes and forded rivers in spite of enemy planes and delayed-action bombs.

Near the firing line, supply operations had to be carried out in the shortest possible time. Cooking, medical work, transport, and the like were carried on right in the trenches, under enemy bombing and crossfire.

Such was the situation at Dien Bien Phu. . .

General Vo Nguyen Giap,
People's War, People's Army.

Genesis of the U. S. Navy's Role in the War

As the quotation from General Giap so well affirms, the importance of logistics in war has not changed very much since Napoleon's famous dictum that an army travels on its stomach. The popular conception of the enemy in Vietnam is that he is an ephemeral figure who travels light, lives off the land, and at the moment of battle somehow always manages to supply himself with arms and munitions dug up from long-buried caches, or plucked magically from the hollow stumps of jungle trees. Such a conception is of course largely romantic. The Communist soldier in Vietnam travels and fights only to the extent permitted him by slender lines of supply connecting him to a secure rear area. Many of these lines of supply run through or across navigable water, and naval operations, dating back to the Indochina War, have endeavored to sever or disrupt them.

Control of the waterways of Vietnam also

The executive officer of River Assault Division 91 recorded the capture of enemy tax collectors when PBRs searched a family-sized sampan that had pulled out into the Mo Cay Canal from a suspected VC stronghold that was under attack by a combined force of Navy Seals and Mobile Riverine Force. He also photographed his division's three monitors conducting "beach softening" operations prior to a search-and-destroy operation in May 1968.

implies control of a large part of that country's population. Vast numbers of people live on or near the rivers, canals, and seacoasts. Waterborne transportation is relied upon almost exclusively in the rural areas for the movement of goods and crops to market, and for intervillage communications. Fish from the rivers and seas are an important staple in the Vietnamese diet. Wet-rice farming, the principal agricultural activity, requires an intricate system of irrigation dikes and canals. It was inevitable that a significant phase of the counterinsurgency war in Vietnam would be fought on water.

The first permanent United States naval presence in Vietnam was established in August 1950, soon after the outbreak of the Korean War, when the Navy Section of Military Assistance Advisory Group, Indochina, was formed in Saigon with Commander James B. Cannon, U. S. Navy, and seven officers and men.

In the fall of that year a joint State-Defense Survey Mission visited Vietnam. The senior military officer on this Mission was Major General Graves B. Erskine, U. S. Marine Corps, and the naval officers attached were Captain Mervin Halstead and Commander Ralph J. Michels. They recommended that, since there was no apparent threat to the French in Indochina from the sea, the American naval aid program should be concentrated on a buildup of river and coastal forces of employment against the Viet Minh insurgents.

Specific recommendations included: (1) the provision of modern, radar-equipped patrol aircraft; (2) the supply of a variety of small ships and craft for extending the offshore patrol into coastal waters, and for broadening the scope of river operations; and (3) the establishment of adequate repair and logistic facilities to maintain the new equipment to be provided. With little modification, these early recommendations shaped the broad direction of our naval program in Vietnam for the next fourteen years.

The outbreak of the Korean War had brought with it a change in our assessment of the war in Indochina, and we began to view it in certain respects as an extension of the struggle in Korea. American aid to the French in Indochina burgeoned, and part of this aid took the form of naval ships and craft, mostly small amphibious types, but including one aircraft carrier (the ex-USS *Belleau Wood*). The Navy section of MAAG Indochina was thus intimately concerned with the training and logistic support required to use the material we were then furnishing the French. The Vietnamese Navy itself was not formally established until 1954, and our early advisors worked almost exclusively with French counterparts.

By 1954, the strength of the French Navy

engaged in the Indochina War stood at more than 10,000 men, and the tiny Vietnamese Navy mustered an additional 1,500 officers and men. The two navies together operated more than 300 amphibious ships and craft, 75 patrol vessels and minesweepers, two cruisers, and two aircraft carriers.

Overall command of the navies was exercised by Commander French Naval Forces Far East, who was himself directly subordinate to the theater commander, Commander in Chief, Armed Forces Indochina. Under the senior naval commander was the officer actually responsible for naval operations in Indochina, Commander Naval Division Far East. His forces were divided into three area commands; North, Central, and South Vietnam. The area commands were in turn divided into river, coastal, and sea forces.

Despite an avowed intention late in the war to increase the combat role of the Vietnamese, particularly under the ill-starred Navarre Plan, the war ended with the Vietnamese Navy operating only one Infantry Landing Ship Large (LSIL), one LCU, and some thirty smaller amphibious craft. Further, the Vietnamese Navy was commanded by a French officer, and most other important posts and commands were held by Frenchmen.

The Indochina War lasted seven years, seven months, and two days, more than twice as long as the Korean War. French Union forces suffered more than 172,000 casualties, including 45,000 dead and 48,000 missing. After Dien Bien Phu there was simply no French stomach left to continue the struggle, and, on 20 July 1954, a cease-fire agreement was signed at Geneva.

Passage to Freedom

Under the terms of the Geneva agreement, a military demarcation line was established near the seventeenth parallel in Vietnam. A period of 300 days was set aside for the phased withdrawal of Viet Minh and French military forces to the north and south of that line respectively. During this same period, civilians residing in either zone were to be allowed complete freedom to move to the other zone.

In the North, warnings were scrawled on the walls of public buildings, urging the populace to flee in advance of the Viet Minh Army. The Roman Catholic Church advised its adherents to abandon ancestral homes and fields and seek sanctuary in the South. The streets of the two principal evacuation centers, Hanoi and Haiphong, were soon choked with masses of desperate people. Public services broke down in the crush. Personal possessions representing the savings of a lifetime were hawked fruitlessly from door to door.

The heaviest fighting of the war had occurred in the North, and consequently the bulk of the French Expeditionary Force and the great mass of its equipment were located there when the fighting ended. It was readily apparent that French transportation alone could never cope with the staggering demands placed upon it, and the assistance of the U. S. Government was requested. On 16 August 1954, the first U. S. Navy transport to be assigned to Operation Passage to Freedom loaded refugees in Haiphong.

Rear Admiral Lorenzo S. Sabin, U. S. Navy, Commander Amphibious Group Western Pacific, was assigned responsibility for aiding the exodus from the North. Operating initially with five APAs, two AKAs, two LSDs, two APDs, and four LSTs, his task force grew in the first three months of the operation to more than 100 Navy and MSTS ships and craft. When the operation ended on 18 May 1955, at the expiration of the 300-day regroupment period, more than 310,000 people, 8,000 vehicles, and 69,000 tons of cargo had been carried to the South by the U. S. Navy.

In all, more than 800,000 people are thought to have fled the North, while less than 100,000, including Viet Minh troops, opted to make the journey in the opposite direction. This "balloting by feet" was acutely embarrassing to the Communists, and during the latter part of the regroupment period the agreement on freedom of movement was openly violated and would-be refugees were prevented from leaving. The companion piece to this tragedy, often conveniently forgotten by later critics of the war and self-styled pacifists, was the liquidation of perhaps 50,000 "enemies of the people," by the Communists' own estimate, during the consolidation of Viet Minh rule in the North.

The Advisory Period

At Geneva, France pledged to remove its Expeditionary Force from all of Vietnam when and if requested to do so by "the Government of Vietnam." The nominal Chief of State in the South at that time was the Emperor Bao Dai, then in exile on the French Riviera. His long-time associate and premier, Ngo Dinh Diem, announced on 7 July 1955 that a referendum would be held in October to permit the people to choose between Bao Dai and himself. Shortly before the referendum, Diem informed the U. S. Government that he had decided to ask the French to withdraw the Expeditionary Force by March 1956, explaining that he considered the continued presence of French troops in the south to be "one of the principal Communist assets."

On 26 October 1955, Diem proclaimed the Republic of Vietnam with himself as President. The effects this development had on the U. S. Navy's role in Vietnam were extremely important and resulted in the eventual substitution of American for French influence in the shaping of the young Vietnamese Navy.

At about this same time, a personal friend and confidant of Diem, Lieutenant Commander Le Quang My, was appointed to the important post of Naval Deputy to the Vietnamese Armed Forces General Staff. One of this officer's very first acts was to remove French officers from the Vietnamese Navy and Marine Corps Headquarters.

For a time, U. S. and French naval advisors worked together in a combined training mission called TRIM, but for all practical purposes the U. S. Navy had assumed primary responsibility for advising the Vietnamese Navy in the fall of 1955. The last French naval advisors were those assigned to the Naval Academy at Nha Trang, and they left in May 1957.

At the beginning of the "American period," the Vietnamese Navy had a fleet of over 100 modified landing craft, two LSMs, two PCEs, and three MSCs, almost all of which had originally been transferred to the French through the American naval aid program during the Indochina War. The strength of the Vietnamese Navy at this time was about 1,900 officers and men.

Until 1960 the Vietnamese Navy experienced a period of modest growth and modernization, assisted by a Navy Section of the U. S. Military Assistance Advisory Group (MAAG), which, in July of that year, had increased to 60 officers and men.

There were then two major operational commands—the River Forces and the Sea Forces. The former had six River Assault Groups (RAGs) which were patterned after the old French Division Naval D'Assaut, but with two significant differences. The RAG was not provided with a permanently assigned landing force, and, for all practical purposes, operational control had been surrendered to regional Army commanders who employed the river craft almost exclusively in logistic support of encamped ground forces. In numbers of ships and craft assigned, the River Forces had not appreciably changed since 1955. Certain small increases had been made in the Sea Forces, however, and overall strength had grown to about 3,500 officers and men.

The effect of the U. S. naval advisory effort on the relatively static insurgency of the preceding five years was minimal. The increase in Vietnamese naval manpower, a modest sign of change at best, is a typical example of the handicaps suffered by the program. While some additional men were absorbed by the training program and by the Sea Forces, many names simply appeared on a padded payroll, or belonged to a disproportionately growing shore establishment.

The insurgency problem in South Vietnam began to assume serious proportions late in 1959, when it became apparent to many observers that increased U. S. military aid would be required if the independence of the South was to be preserved. In following months additional equipment was transferred to the Vietnamese Navy, primarily patrol craft, and accelerated training of both officers and enlisted men began; some of it in schools in the United States. In May 1961, President Kennedy announced an expansion of the Military Assistance Program for Vietnam, including large increases in the paramilitary Junk Force, which had been operating some 80 sailing junks on patrols near the seventeenth parallel, since about 1960.

In a series of graduated increases, the Junk Force was authorized an increase to 644 motorized junks less than two years later. All the older sailing junks were either converted to power, or discarded.

The Junk Force at this time was "paramilitary" rather than "military" because it was manned by civilian irregulars, and was but nominally officered and led by the Vietnamese Navy, which was charged with its operation and support.

At the urging of American advisors the Junk Force was absorbed into the Vietnamese Navy in 1965. It was hoped that this move would increase the morale and the performance of the force.

In June, 1961, Admiral Arleigh Burke, Chief of Naval Operations, cited an urgent need for the U. S. Navy to prepare to assume naval responsibilities in restricted waters and rivers.

In spite of greatly increased levels of military assistance, the situation in South Vietnam continued to deteriorate. Naval advisors complained that their advice was frequently not taken, that new equipment and military supplies were not being used effectively.

The feeble political position of the Vietnamese Navy in the General Staff organization made it almost totally subservient to Army control, and to commanders who were often ignorant of how to exploit Navy capabilities. River Assault Groups seldom went on combat missions. There was a general reluctance within the Sea Forces to maintain active patrols. Morale flagged.

At this time the Government of Vietnam commanded little support within its own structure. A sense of frustration and lack of incentive was part of the dry rot that had set in as early as 1956, paralyzing effective action and inducing a curious numbness in the operating forces. Furthermore, a large percentage of the Vietnamese Navy was recruited from relatively well-to-do city populations who preferred the smaller risks of that service to those offered by the Army of the Republic of Vietnam (ARVN). The Vietnamese Navy was thus handicapped by poor leadership, its inferior status compared to the Army, corruption, the disastrous political situation, inertia, and a well-developed sense of caution among some of its members.

In December 1961, U. S. air, sea, and ground forces began to play a limited operational role in Vietnam. In that month U. S. Navy Oceangoing Minesweepers (MSOs) joined Vietnamese Navy ships in barrier patrols near the seventeenth parallel. The MSOs were not themselves permitted to intercept suspect shipping, but used their radar to vector Viet-

namese naval units to suspicious contacts. Late in February 1962, similar operations began in the Gulf of Thailand, between Phu Quoc Island and the Ca Mau Peninsula, with U. S. Navy destroyer escorts participating. The results of these early patrols, which might be considered precursors of later Market Time operations, did not seem to indicate the existence of large-scale infiltration from the sea. U. S. Navy DEs were withdrawn from the Gulf of Thailand on 26 May 1962, and the MSO patrol was suspended on 1 August.

The advisory effort, meanwhile, grew rapidly. Advisors were assigned to the Sea, River, and Junk Forces, to the Naval Shipyard in Saigon, and to the Vietnamese Navy Headquarters. In recognition of the expanding U. S. role, Military Assistance Command Vietnam (MACV) was established in February 1962, and the Headquarters Support Activity was commissioned on 1 July.

In October 1962, the President's Special Military Advisor, General Maxwell Taylor, arrived in Vietnam to assess the situation. As a result of his visit, Project Beef-up was launched, which, in addition to more men, money, and supplies for the Vietnamese military, called for increased U. S. operational participation in the war. Despite Project Beef-up, 1963 did not bring a dramatic reversal of the situation, and South Vietnam continued to plunge into political chaos, culminating in the overthrow and murder of President Diem in November of that year.

As 1963 drew to a close there were 742 U. S. Navy officers and men in Vietnam. The Vietnamese Navy had grown to a force of 6,200 officers and men who operated 50 patrol ships and minecraft, and 208 amphibious and riverine craft.

Given the seriousness of the military situation, the performance of the Vietnamese Navy was far from satisfactory. The daily average employment of those Sea Force and River

Force units available for work at sea (and many were unavailable) was roughly 50 per cent. The Junk Force put only an average of 40 per cent of its available boats to sea on any given day. Advisors reported that even these statistics did not reflect the true situation, since units were frequently only "administratively" employed. "Combat patrols" often consisted of short trips to and from anchorages. The Junk Force was notorious for "gun-decking" its operational reports.

The Commander-in-Chief of the Vietnamese Navy in the last years of the Diem regime was Captain Ho Tan Quyen. When President Diem was overthrown, Captain Quyen, who was closely associated with the fallen President, and who had been instrumental in defeating several previously attempted coups, was himself murdered by a subordinate officer sympathetic to the incoming regime. This ushered in nearly three years of turmoil in the senior Vietnamese Navy leadership.

The Bucklew Report

The shift to "stage three" of the insurgency, with its attendant pitched battles involving large units, forced Hanoi to make an important decision concerning the continued supply of Communist forces in the South. Until 1964 the Viet Cong were not equipped with standardized weapons and fought with a large variety of French, Russian, Chinese, and captured American arms. The battlefield supply of ammunition for all of these assorted weapons was a difficult and vexing problem. It was decided, therefore, to shift to a standard family of small arms, using the same caliber of ammunition, and provide more modern supporting weapons. This in turn committed Hanoi to a sharp expansion of its infiltration effort.

The most economical and direct routes for supplying the Viet Cong were sea routes. Though the number of Vietnamese Navy ships

available for coastal patrol increased to 28 during the year, detection remained low.

The Junk Force was seriously undermanned, with some Coastal Groups reduced to little more than 50 per cent of authorized strength. At the end of 1963, the Junk Force consisted of 632 junks, 400 VNN officers and men, and 3,700 civilian irregulars. The causes of the undermanning in the Junk Force centered upon poor pay and living conditions, widespread desertion, and to an extent, the pay list manipulations referred to above.

The irregulars were ordinarily recruited from the population in the vicinity of each coastal group. Frequently, these were individuals who by reason of age or infirmity were ineligible for service in the uniformed services. It is probably correct to state that few, if any, of those recruited desired to serve in the Junk Force. Some were levied through direct or indirect pressures on families or villages, others had very little but starvation as an alternative when the war ruined their farms or turned their traditional fishing grounds into restricted areas.

The Junk Force was officered by the Vietnamese Navy, but it was a frequent complaint of U. S. Navy advisors that seldom, if ever, did a Vietnamese naval officer actually accompany the junks on patrol.

In January 1964, a team of eight naval officers, headed by Captain Phillip H. Bucklew, met in Saigon to study the infiltration problem. Its conclusions were that infiltrations from the North existed on a scale sufficient to support the expanded level of operations by the enemy in South Vietnam, and that only nominal resistance to that infiltration was being made.

The Bucklew Report was critical of the sea patrol then in effect, and recommended augmenting it with U. S. forces. It pointed out, however, the essential futility of a sea quarantine in the absence of an accompanying effort to block inland infiltration routes. It recommended the development of a mobile patrol force along the Cambodian and Laotian borders. Finally, the Report indicated that U. S. Navy forces might have to be deployed in the Delta rivers to stop Communist infiltration, thus anticipating later Game Warden operations.

The year 1964 was one of rapid change in the posture of U. S. Navy activity in Vietnam. In May, Military Assistance Advisory Group Vietnam was absorbed by Military Assistance Command Vietnam (MACV), and Navy Section MAAG became the Naval Advisory Group, MACV. Tests were completed on a 36-foot river patrol craft (RPC), and 34 of them were ordered. Huge construction projects were started at Cam Ranh Bay, Da Nang, and elsewhere.

The attack on the U. S. destroyer *Maddox* in the Tonkin Gulf in early August signaled a new and dramatically different phase of the war in Vietnam. On 7 August, a Joint Resolution of the Congress affirmed that the United States would continue to support the Republic of Vietnam and "take all necessary measures to repel any armed attack against the forces of the United States." By the end of the year, the U. S. military strength in Vietnam numbered about 23,000 officers and men.

THE VUNG RO INCIDENT

At 1030 on 16 February 1965, Lieutenant James S. Bowers, U. S. Army, while piloting a UH-1B helicopter on a medical rescue mission from Qui Nhon, sighted a camouflaged ship lying in Vung Ro Bay on South Vietnam's central coast. Lieutenant Bowers promptly notified the Second Coastal Zone Senior Advisor, Lieutenant Commander Harvey P. Rodgers, U. S. Navy, in Nha Trang. The "Vung Ro Incident," as it came to be called, led directly to

Market Time, the U. S. Navy's first large-scale operational participation in the Vietnam War.

Lieutenant Commander Rodgers reported the sighting to his counterpart, Lieutenant Commander Thoai, Vietnamese Navy, the Second Coastal Zone Commander, and arranged for an aircraft to investigate. The ship was observed to be of the trawler type, about 130 feet long and displacing perhaps 100 tons. Air strikes were called in, and after the third strike the ship was awash in shallow water, resting on her port side. A fourth strike was directed at a nearby area on the beach where crates were stacked and from which small arms fire had been received.

Lieutenant Commander Thoai then arranged for a company of Vietnamese troops from the 23rd Division at nearby Tuy Hoa to be lifted into the area by the Vietnamese Navy's Landing Ship, *LSM 405*. Units from Vietnamese Naval Coastal Group 24 were also ordered to assist, and requests were sent out for a Vietnamese Navy SEAL Team (LDNN) to provide divers for an attempted salvage of the sunken trawler.

That night (16–17 February) the requested air strikes and illumination failed to materialize. An observation plane reported lights and activity near the stricken ship, and on the adjacent beach.

The following morning *LSM 405* arrived at Tuy Hoa to embark the company of troops, but the Province Chief refused to provide them, asserting that the area surrounding Vung Ro Bay and the Cap Varella peninsula was too strongly held by the Viet Cong. At 1430 on the 17th, *LSM 405* arrived off Vung Ro without troops. Preceded by air strikes, two attempts were made to enter the harbor, but both were stopped in the face of small arms and automatic weapons fire. The LSM anchored offshore for the night, and the requested air services again mysteriously failed to appear.

The next day, 18 February, a conference was held in Nha Trang with Brigadier General William E. DePuy, U. S. Army, of the Military Assistance Command Vietnam J-3 staff, presiding. Also attending were representatives from the Vietnamese Army's 23rd Division, the Vietnamese Special Forces, the Vietnamese Navy, and the U. S. Navy. An action plan was devised which called for a two-battalion blocking force to take position inland along Route 1, while one company advanced along the coast from the nearby Deo Ca outpost. A company of Vietnamese Special Forces, meanwhile, would be lifted by helicopter to Dai Lanh, south of Vung Ro, where they would board *LSM 405* for an amphibious landing near the sunken trawler.

While the conference was progressing, *LSM 405* was joined at Vung Ro by the Vietnamese *PCE 08*. Lieutenant Commander Thoai, apparently to effect the further destruction of the trawler, ordered both units to proceed into the harbor. No opposing fire was experienced and after extensively shooting up the area, the ships withdrew. *LSM 405* then departed for Dai Lanh, returning in the early evening with the company of Special Forces. At this time a message was received, its origin unclear, which postponed the scheduled landing.

The same night the Vietnamese *PC 04* with 15 LDNN and the U. S. SEAL Advisor, Lieutenant Franklin W. Anderson, aboard, arrived to join the growing forces at Vung Ro. In the morning, shortly after 0800, all three ships moved into Vung Ro Bay, preceded by heavy air strikes and naval gunfire support. PC 04 and LSM 405 immediately began a run to the beach, but at a range of about 500 yards encountered small arms and automatic weapons fire. Engines were backed just before beaching and the landing was aborted. A second attempt was made several hours later, moderate opposition was again experienced, and the ships once more withdrew. Finally, at 1100, on

the third attempt, the Special Forces company was put ashore. Light sniper fire was taken, but by mid-afternoon the immediate area near the sunken trawler was secured and the LDNN began salvage operations.

Not far from the landing area, the Special Forces uncovered a large cache of about 4,000 assorted rifles, submachine guns, BAR type weapons, several thousand cases of ammunition, and very large quantities of medical supplies. *LSM 405* landed a company of Vietnamese Army troops at 1830 to assist with the handling of this material, but an hour later, in spite of heated argument by the American advisors, both companies were embarked in *LSM 405*, although large quantities of arms and munitions remained on the beach. The Special Forces company commander reported that he couldn't hold the beachhead overnight and that with "very little arms and ammunition remaining," it was not worthwhile to land again. Lieutenant Commander Thoai, supported by Lieutenant Commander Sang from the office of the Vietnamese Navy Chief of Staff, refused to order the troops back ashore. At 0215 the next morning, however, message orders were received to do so immediately.

Shortly before 0600 on 20 February, therefore, both companies were again landed. The Special Forces company commander displayed great reluctance to use his men to assist in moving the remaining cache material to the beach and refused to order an end to the looting of medical supplies, which took place on a large scale.

That afternoon, additional caches were uncovered. Area clearance and mopping-up operations continued until 24 February, plagued as before by continued foot dragging and intransigence. On the last full day of the operation a particularly large ammunition cache was destroyed.

The Vung Ro Incident confirmed what had long been suspected, but for which there had been no previous evidence.[1] The large amount of material discovered indicated that more than just a few shipments had been made. The simultaneous appearance in other coastal areas of the new 7.62 family of enemy weapons strongly suggested that other sites were being used to receive shipments by sea. Further, the disappointing performance of the Vietnamese armed forces at Vung Ro cast renewed doubt on the capacity and the willingness of the Vietnamese to stop such infiltration on their own.

On 21 February 1965, the Commander of the U. S. Military Assistance Command, Vietnam requested the Commander-in-Chief Pacific and the Commander-in-Chief Pacific Fleet to send representatives to Saigon to plan a combined U. S.-Vietnamese Navy patrol effort.

MARKET TIME

The conference requested by General Westmoreland met on 3 March 1965, and in the following week the basic concepts of the combined patrol operation were worked out. It was assumed that infiltration into South Vietnam by sea fell into two categories: (1) coastwise junk traffic mingling with the more than 50,000 registered civilian craft which plied the coastal waters of South Vietnam; and (2) vessels of trawler size or larger which approached the coast on a generally perpendicular line. These trawlers were believed to originate in North Vietnam and Communist China.

It was the opinion of the conference that "the best tactic to interdict coastal traffic infiltration would be to assist and inspire the Vietnamese Navy to increase the quality and quantity of its searches."

With regard to the second category of infiltration, it was recommended that a conventional patrol be established by U. S. Navy ships and aircraft. A defensive sea area was proposed which would extend 40 miles from the coast, and it was recommended that the Republic of Vietnam authorize U. S. naval

forces to "stop, board, search, and, if necessary, capture and/or destroy any hostile suspicious craft or vessel found within South Vietnam's territorial and contiguous zone waters."

The U. S. Joint Chiefs of Staff approved the proposed operating concept on 16 March, and on that very day the first U. S. Navy ships reported for duty, the destroyers *Higbee* (DD-806) and *Black* (DD-666). Daily coastal surveillance flights by SP-2 aircraft, operating from Tan Son Nhut, had begun shortly after the conference of 3 March 1965. The code name Market Time was assigned to the operation on 24 March.

In April the operation expanded rapidly. By the first week of the month, 28 U. S. Navy ships were participating, under the operational control of CTF 71 in the USS *Canberra* (CAG-2). In a departure from the planning conference recommendation of the preceding month, the decision was taken to introduce U. S. PCFs (Swifts) for close inshore patrolling. On 29 April it was announced that Coast Guard Squadron One, with seventeen 82-foot cutters (WPBs), would be lifted to Vietnam for Market Time operations.

On 30 April, Secretary of Defense Robert S. McNamara approved the eventual transfer of the operational control of Market Time to the Chief, Naval Advisory Group (CNAG), as the agent for ComUSMACV. Significantly, this marked the formal recognition of the Naval Advisory Group's new role as an operational as well as an advisory command. Concurrent with this announcement, Rear Admiral Norvell G. Ward, the first Navy flag officer to be assigned to Vietnam, was ordered to relieve Captain William H. Hardcastle, Jr., U. S. Navy, as Chief, Naval Advisory Group. The change of command took place on 10 May 1965.

On 11 May the Government of South Vietnam granted formal authorization for U. S. Navy Market Time units to stop, search, and

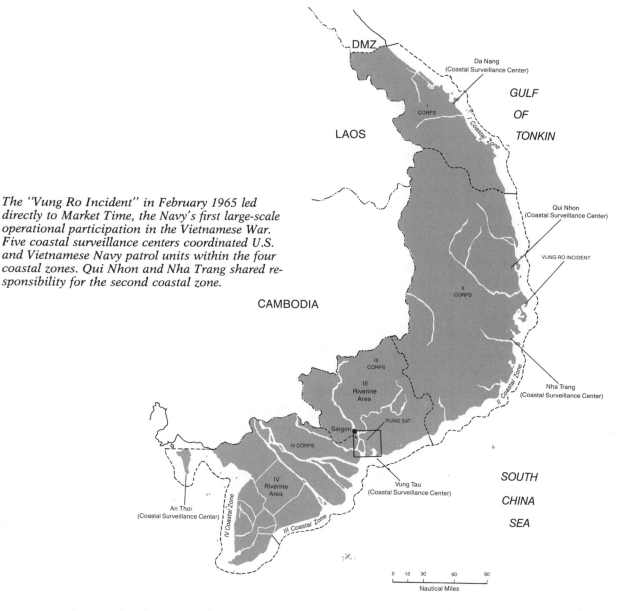

The "Vung Ro Incident" in February 1965 led directly to Market Time, the Navy's first large-scale operational participation in the Vietnamese War. Five coastal surveillance centers coordinated U.S. and Vietnamese Navy patrol units within the four coastal zones. Qui Nhon and Nha Trang shared responsibility for the second coastal zone.

seize vessels not clearly engaged in innocent passage, inside the three mile limit of the Republic of Vietnam's territorial waters. Vessels in the contiguous zone, extending 12 miles from the coast, suspected as infiltrators were also made subject to search and seizure. Beyond the contiguous zone, vessels thought to be of South Vietnamese registry could be searched. Compensation would be paid by the Government of South Vietnam if they proved to be foreign ships. The first capture of infiltrators by a U. S. Navy ship occurred late in May, when the USS *Buck* (DD-761) boarded a junk near the seventeenth parallel.

On 1 August 1965, operational responsibility for Market Time passed from the Commander-in-Chief, Pacific Fleet to General Westmoreland, and operational control from Commander Task Force 71, who had held this duty as a collateral function, to Commander Task Force 115, which was the new designation of the Commander of the Coastal Surveillance Force. At this time Admiral Ward was both CNAG and CTF 115.

Task Force 115 consisted of seven DERs, two MSOs, two LSTs originally used to provide radar coverage of the Mekong River entrances, five SP-2H patrol aircraft based at Tan Son Nhut Airfield at Saigon, and Coast Guard Squadron One with nine WPBs based at An Thoi and eight at Da Nang. Additional patrol aircraft were provided by the Commander of the Seventh Fleet.

Lockheed P3A Orions from Sangley Point in the Philippines patrolled north of Vung Tau to the seventeenth parallel. Martin P5 Marlin seaplanes, operating from tenders, and Lockheed P2V Neptunes flying from Tan Son Nhut and later from Cam Ranh Bay, carried out patrol missions across the river entrances south from Vung Tau to An Thoi. The Marlins were phased out of service by 1967.

By the time TF 115 was formed, Market Time operations were already in their twentieth week.

Almost no tangible results had been achieved to measure the effectiveness of the operation. In some respects, of course, the effectiveness of such an operation was probably not measurable, for like the tariff in international trade, Market Time may have discouraged certain Communist arms shipments from ever being attempted. Statistical studies, however, showed that detection probabilities at the level of forces then assigned were still quite low.

As a result of recommendations made to the Secretary of Defense during his July 1965 visit to Vietnam, additional Swift boats were ordered, bringing the approved total to 54 from the 36 originally planned. It was decided the boats would be based at Qui Nhon, Cam Ranh Bay, and Vung Tau. In the same month the Vietnamese Navy was finally persuaded to absorb the Junk Force into the regular Navy, a move long urged by advisors as one which might lead to increasing the effectiveness of coastal patrols.

The Junk Force was viewed by many Vietnamese naval officers with something akin to disdain. With few exceptions, the Coastal Groups (the Junk bases) are located in areas considered undesirable for duty.

There was, in addition, opposition within the Joint General Staff of the Vietnamese Armed Forces for any aggrandizement of the Vietnamese Navy, which has always been the political inferior of the ARVN. It took a great deal of persuasion and strong representations at the highest level, before the shotgun wedding was brought off.

While the Junk Force was concerned with inshore and Delta river traffic, the Vietnamese Navy Sea force ships assigned to Market Time patrol were ordinarily placed under the operational control of the Coastal Zone commanders. These in turn were tied in with the U. S. Task Force 115 operations through the various Coastal Surveillance Centers. It was the function of these centers to coordinate patrols of the two navies, but in practice some duplication occurred. This undoubtedly irritated those Vietnamese officers who felt their functions were being usurped by the Americans.

Task Force 115 operations at this time were divided into nine patrol areas, 30 to 40 miles deep and 80 to 120 miles long, stretching from the seventeenth parallel in the north along the coast to the Brevie Line[2] in the Gulf of Thailand. Normally, each patrol area was the responsibility of a DER or, if sufficient DERs were not available, an MSO. Coast Guard

Squadron One provided WPBs for barrier patrols along the seventeenth parallel and in the Gulf of Thailand. Five Coastal Surveillance Centers (Da Nang, Qui Nhon, Nha Trang, Vung Tau, and An Thoi) were responsible for coordinating U. S. Navy and Vietnamese Navy patrol units. Though there were five Coastal Surveillance Centers, there were only four Coastal Zones, Qui Nhon and Nha Trang sharing responsibility for the Second Coastal Zone. Overall Market Time operations were controlled from the Surveillance Operations Center located at the Naval Advisory Group Headquarters in Saigon. Ships were loaned to CTF 115 by the Seventh Fleet. The Commander-in-Chief Pacific Fleet, common superior of Commander Seventh Fleet and Chief, Naval Advisory Group, determined which units would be assigned.

The primary mission of Market Time at this period was "to conduct surveillance, gunfire support, visit and search, and other operations as directed along the coast of the Republic of Vietnam in order to assist the Republic of Vietnam in detection and prevention of Communist infiltration from the sea." An additional mission was "to improve the Vietnamese Navy's counter-insurgency capabilities and assist Vietnamese and U. S. Forces to secure the coastal regions and major rivers in order to defeat the Communist insurgency in Vietnam."

The chief naval advisor, Admiral Ward, foresaw the necessity for eventually returning responsibility for all naval operations in Vietnam to the Vietnamese Navy. His command and control decisions were shaped by the following principles: (1) U. S. Navy operations in Vietnam would be coordinated with Vietnamese operations, allowing integrated operations to be instituted as soon as practicable; (2) facilities required for U. S. naval operations would be located with Vietnamese naval installations so that support operations could be integrated, and later turnover of the facilities more practically achieved.

Late in September 1965, representatives of CNO, CinCPac, CinCPacFlt, ComUSMACV, and CNAG met in Saigon to review the progress of Market Time operations to that date.

There was a tendency on our part, based largely upon the observations of our naval advisors, to discount the effectiveness of VNN patrols, but force levels were not determined on the supposition that we would be doing the job alone. The military decisions that were taken at this time were not, nor could they be, based solely on our operational experience in the war. The situation inside South Vietnam was becoming critical, and a rapid buildup of our military strength seemed imperative to keep the Government from going under. The force levels decided upon in September 1965 were later increased, and thus it may be assumed they were not in themselves sufficient. At the conclusion of their meeting, recommendations were made to increase the number of off-shore patrol ships from 9 to 14, to double the patrol aircraft coverage, to increase the number of PCFs available for inshore work from 54 to 84 and the number of WPBs from 17 to 26. An additional LST was recommended for providing radar coverage of the mouths of the Mekong (three were already providing this service, but the normal needs of rest and maintenance meant that that number was insufficient to provide constant cover).

Finally, it was recommended that an extensive river patrol be established, with 120 river patrol craft operating from LSTs anchored off the mouths of the major rivers. It was proposed that these patrols extend upriver for a distance of 25 miles, the range thought practical for appropriate logistic support and for the objective of controlling the river mouths. The concept of the proposed river patrol operations was that they would not be a part of Market Time, but would be directed by the same officer, the Chief, Naval Advisory Group.

Naval Forces, Vietnam

By the fall of 1965, U. S. Navy units in Vietnam included: (1) the Marines in I Corps; (2) Navy support personnel under ComPhibPac's command at Da Nang and Chu Lai (on 1 October Naval Support Activity, Da Nang, was established under ComUSMACV's operational control and PhibPac support terminated); (3) Construction Battalions in I Corps and Seabee Teams throughout the country who also worked under the Military Assistance Command Vietnam; (4) the Officer in Charge of Construction and his organization; (5) the Naval Advisory Group; (6) the Headquarters Support Activity, Saigon (whose responsibilities were being phased out and taken over by the U. S. Army); (7) the Military Sea Transportation Service Office, Vietnam; and (8) numerous smaller activities. With Navy strength burgeoning and diversifying, the need for a formal Navy command structure was evident.

Although the Chief, Naval Advisory Group was the senior naval officer in Vietnam, he was not in actuality a commander. The Naval Advisory Group was a division of the MACV staff organization and Chief, Naval Advisory Group was therefore without command authority, including disciplinary authority, over any naval personnel in-country. All Navy personnel then being ordered to Vietnam reported to Military Assistance Command Vietnam for further assignment to the Naval Advisory Group, and Westmoreland delegated operational control of assigned naval forces to the Chief, Naval Advisory Group.

In September 1965, Rear Admiral Ward raised the question of naval command relationships in Vietnam with CNO and with

General Westmoreland. They agreed that a study should be conducted on the subject. What had been conceived and organized as an advisor's job, no longer fit the changing nature of growing operational command. The advisory role was taking second priority and receiving less command attention than the growing direct involvement of U. S. fighting units. On 1 January 1966, the following recommendations were submitted:

1. That a Naval Force, Vietnam (NavForV), Command be established as the Naval Component Command in Vietnam under the operational command of CinCPacFlt[3] and operational control of ComUSMACV.[4]

2. That NavForV be commanded by a naval officer, and that this naval officer have additional duty as Chief, Naval Advisory Group.

3. That NavForV not include III MAF, which would continue under the operational command of CinCPacFlt and operational control of ComUSMACV.

4. That all Navy commands, unless otherwise specified, be under the operational control of ComNavForV.

5. That ComNavForV be responsible to ComUSMACV for logistic support of all naval forces, including III MAF in I Corps.

6. That ComNavForV administer all naval construction in Vietnam.

These recommendations were approved by the Joint Chiefs of Staff, and on 1 April 1966 in ceremonies at Saigon, Rear Admiral Ward established Naval Forces, Vietnam and became the first Commander. On 16 April he relinquished his duties as CTF 115 to Captain Clifford L. Stewart, U. S. Navy, the new Commander of the Coastal Surveillance Force.

GAME WARDEN

In the meantime, TF 116, Game Warden, had been established (on 18 December 1965) with an assigned mission "to assist the Government of South Vietnam in denying the enemy the use of the major rivers of the Delta and the Rung Sat Special Zone." Rear Admiral Ward was assigned additional duty as CTF 116. In keeping with the recommendations of the September conference, it was planned that the task force would initially consist of 120 specially designed river patrol boats (PBRs), 20 LCPLs, an LSD, an LST, and 8 UH-1B helicopters. Ships and patrol craft would be manned by the U. S. Navy, and the U. S. Army would furnish helicopters and pilots. The Vietnamese Navy would assign liaison personnel to the PBRs and LCPLs.[5]

Under the original concept, the LSD and LST were to anchor off the mouths of the major rivers in the Delta and serve as operational bases, each supporting 30 PBRs. Four specially outfitted LSTs, scheduled to arrive by September 1966, would replace the original support ships.

In February 1966, the first Game Warden sailors reported for duty, and in March the first PBRs arrived. Interim Game Warden bases were established at Nha Be and at Cat Lo. In April, as the first Game Warden PBRs became operational, patrols were begun in the Rung Sat Special Zone, and in the following month operations were expanded into the Delta. On 18 May 1966, Captain B. B. Witham, U. S. Navy, relieved Rear Admiral Ward as CTF 116.

Meanwhile, to the despair of U. S. Navy advisors, the Vietnamese River Assault Groups frequently found themselves involved in logistic support and static defense roles assigned them by ARVN ground commanders. Attempts were made to coordinate their operations with TF 116 and TF 117 units with widely varying success depending upon the areas and personalities concerned.

In June the first operational test of the offshore support ship concept was initiated when the USS *Tortuga* (LSD-26), which had arrived in May, anchored near the mouths of

the Co Chien and Bassac Rivers. Embarked were 10 PBRs, a helicopter fire team, and two Patrol Air Cushion Vehicles (PACVs). Almost from the very beginning, the weather was an inhibiting factor. Monsoon winds and the long fetch over shallow water combined to produce frequent periods of unfavorable sea conditions for small boat operations. On 15 July, the Commander of River Patrol Section 512 reported that heavy seas and high winds were restricting PBR operations almost 50 per cent of the time. Similar conditions were experienced when the LSTs especially reconfigured for Game Warden arrived in Vietnam, and so gradually the offshore support concept was abandoned in favor of afloat and shore support bases in the rivers themselves.

Growing Pains in the Vietnamese Navy

The large buildup of U. S. Navy forces in Vietnam was accompanied by a rapid expansion of the Vietnamese Navy. American-furnished material doubled and redoubled the Vietnamese Navy inventory. By the fall of 1968, on the eve of the introduction of the U. S. naval command's Accelerated Turnover (ACTOV) Program, the personnel strength of the Vietnamese Navy was more than 17,500. This "hot-house" growth was the more notable because it was accomplished in conditions of near constant crisis in the senior Vietnamese Navy leadership.

The successor to the murdered Captain Quyen as Commander-in-Chief of the Vietnamese Navy was Captain Chung Tan Cang. He found himself the victim of a mutiny on 8 April 1965, when his Force Commanders and other senior officers rose against him, charging him with graft in the operation of a fleet of coastal freighters, which had been seized by the government at the time of the 1963 coup. Cang, who had been promoted to the rank of rear admiral in the interim, was relieved of his command, as were the mutineers pending

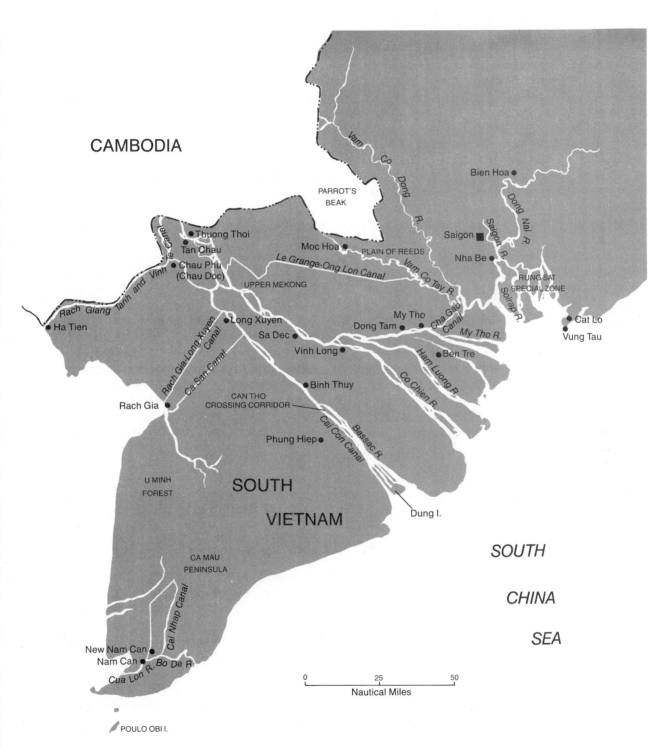

CAMBODIA

PARROT'S
BEAK

Bien Hoa

Thuong Thoi
Tan Chau
Moc Hoa
Chau Phu
(Chau Doc)
Le Grange-Ong Lon Canal
UPPER MEKONG
Rach Giang Tanh and Vinh Te Canal
Ha Tien
Long Xuyen
Sa Dec
Vinh Long
Binh Thuy
Rach Gia-Long Xuyen Canal
Ca San Canal
Rach Gia
CAN THO
CROSSING CORRIDOR
Phung Hiep
Cai Con Canal
PLAIN OF REEDS
Vam Co Dong R.
Vam Co Tay R.
Saigon
Nha Be
Dong Nai R.
Saigon R.
RUNG SAT
SPECIAL ZONE
Soirap R.
Cat Lo
Vung Tau
My Tho
Dong Tam
Cha Gao Canal
My Tho R.
Ben Tre
Ham Luong R.
Co Chien R.
Bassac R.
Dung I.

U MINH
FOREST
SOUTH

VIETNAM

CA MAU
PENINSULA

Cai Nhap Canal

New Nam Can
Nam Can
Cua Lon R. Bo De R.

POULO OBI I.

SOUTH

CHINA

SEA

0   25   50
Nautical Miles

completion of an investigation of the affair. Stripped of its top leadership, and its remaining officers in a state of high excitement and confusion, the Vietnamese Navy careened along an uncertain path. The Naval Advisory Group reported that "there were cases of failures to carry out orders and missed commitments, but not as many as might have been predicted."

On 26 April 1966, Captain Tran Van Phan, the former Chief of Staff to Admiral Cang, was designated Acting Commander-in-Chief, and in May all of the mutineers, with the exception of the River Force Commander, who was replaced, were returned to their original posts.

Captain Phan's command was marred by extreme factionalism within his navy, the exiling of many senior naval officers, and inept leadership. By the summer of 1966, nearly 50 per cent of the senior officers of the Navy were either out of the country or assigned to non-Navy duties in the country. The consequences of this bitter infighting for the operational effectiveness of the Vietnamese Navy, in this period, may well be imagined. It should be considered by those who criticize the U. S. Navy for "usurping" responsibilities rightfully belonging to the Vietnamese Navy at that particular stage of the war. In fact, many of those responsibilities fell on the U. S. Navy by default and, as has been shown, it was our policy at the highest levels to return responsibility for operations to the Vietnamese Navy as soon as that Navy was prepared to accept it.

In September 1966, Captain Phan was removed from his post, and command of the Navy passed to Lieutenant General Cao Van Vien of the Vietnamese Army. Most Navy officers interpreted this as a serious loss of face for the Vietnamese Navy, but a few actually thought that it might be a blessing in disguise, since the Navy would at last have a voice at meetings of the Joint General Staff.

This peculiar command structure was not destined to last, however. Captain (now Commodore) Tran Van Chon was named to the top Navy post on 31 October 1966, a move that took the Naval Advisory Group completely by surprise, since he had been "exiled" for so long (five years).

Captain Chon had served a previous tour as Commander-in-Chief in the period 1957–1959. In 1959–1960 he attended the U. S. Naval War College, and his most recent assignment prior to re-assuming command of the Vietnamese Navy was that of Commander, Regional Force Boat Group, a command which did not fall under the operational control of the Navy, and which obviously and providentially had afforded the new Commander-in-Chief some relief from the necessity of having to choose sides in the recent political machinations of the naval officer corps.

Captain Chon brought dynamic leadership, a new sense of purpose, and, perhaps most important, a period of much-needed command stability to the Vietnamese Navy. He practiced and preached the need for his officers to avoid the political involvements which had crippled the Navy for so long. Many long-standing deficiencies were corrected and the worst of the factionalism rapidly disappeared. Without the reforms introduced and enforced by this officer, the later "Vietnamization" of the naval war would have been virtually impossible.

THE MOBILE RIVERINE FORCE

In the summer and fall of 1966, the establishment of a "Mekong Delta Mobile Afloat Force" (MDMAF) was the subject of discussions between ComUSMACV and ComNavForV. In essence, the early planning envisioned a highly mobile force of river assault craft and embarked troops capable of sustained search-and-destroy missions in the Delta. The proposed force would have been quite similar, in fact, to the old French Division Naval d'Assaut generally known as Dinassaut. As planning progressed, the concept gradually evolved to provide a floating base, with accommodations for a full Army brigade and associated Navy support elements. U. S. Marines, traditionally the force trained and equipped for amphibious assault operations, were not available, already having been committed in maximum strength to the I Corps Tactical Zone.

Original plans called for four APBs, two ARLs, two LSTs, and two River Assault Squadrons (RAS) each consisting of 34 converted LCM-6 craft (26 ATCs, 5 Monitors, 2 CCBs, 1 Refueler), and 16 ASPBs which would be newly constructed.[6]

On 1 September 1966, the first administrative unit of the future Mobile Riverine Force, River Assault Flotilla One, was commissioned at the Naval Amphibious Base, Coronado, California, with Captain W. C. Wells, U. S. Navy, as its Commander. The first units of the new force arrived at Vung Tau on board the USS *Whitfield County* (LST-1169) on 7 January 1967 and began training with elements of the U. S. 9th Infantry Division. On 12 January the Commander-in-Chief, Pacific assigned the task force designator 117 and the descriptive title "Riverine Assault Force." On 28 February, TF 117 was officially activated under the operational control of ComNavForV and the administrative control of ComPhibPac.

Initial operations were confined to the Rung Sat Special Zone, where increased Viet Cong attacks on shipping and minesweepers were then being experienced.

The swampy Rung Sat controls the waterways connecting Saigon with the sea. Vigorous efforts had been made, beginning in 1966, to clear the area of the enemy to prevent the ambushing and mining of the ships in transit. This had been largely accomplished with river patrols, drastic defoliation, minesweeping, and by hunting the enemy on land.

Early effort notwithstanding, the Viet Cong

successfully mined one ship each in 1965 and 1966 (the SS *Eastern Mariner* and the SS *Baton Rouge Victory*, respectively). In 1964 an enemy mine sank an aircraft transport which was later raised at her berth in Saigon. However, no further successes were achieved by the enemy until the mining of the Panamanian freighter *Welfare* in July 1969. The military impact of harassing attacks on Long Tau shipping was virtually nil, but the Viet Cong derived great propaganda value from their efforts.

The arrival in March of elements of the second River Assault Squadron, RAS 11, permitted the deployment of the first units of RAS 9 to other parts of the Delta. These units at first operated from the Army base at Dong Tam on the My Tho River.

On 14 April 1967, the first of the permanent Riverine Assault Force support ships, the USS *Kemper County* (LST-854), arrived at Vung Tau. Later in the month the USS *Benewah* (APB-35) reported. With the arrival of the second APB, the USS *Colleton* (APB-36), in early May, plans were made to move all these units of the Mobile Riverine Base to Dong Tam. On 1 June the transit was made.

By the middle of June, Task Force 117 had received all 68 of its programmed converted LCMs. Now fully operational, the Riverine Assault Force began a long series of actions with the 9th Infantry Division embarked. River assault craft not only landed and extracted troops, but also provided close and accurate gunfire support, medical evacuation of the wounded, and the supply of ammunition.

The Mobile Riverine Force had its own floating artillery in the guns of the support ships, and the barge-mounted 105-mm howitzers of the 9th Division. The howitzers were towed along with the base, or positioned in advance of operations.

Helicopters and fixed wing aircraft supported the Mobile Riverine Force. More than 5,000 landings were recorded in the first year of operations from the single-spot helo deck of the USS *Benewah* alone.

There was literally nowhere in the Delta, given navigable water, that the Riverine Assault Force could not go. An extremely interesting and ingenious operation occurred on 22 February 1968, in the Phung Hiep district of the Delta. A span of the Phung Hiep bridge was raised early in the morning with the assistance of the Army Engineers, and two River Assault Divisions with troops embarked passed 14 miles up the supposedly "inaccessible" Cai Con Canal for an assault on Viet Cong positions. The commander of the task force could say with obvious pride that "Commanders involved in this unique operation felt that they had succeeded in gaining the most difficult of all military advantages in this war—surprise."

On 27 April 1967, just as the Mobile Riverine Force was getting started, Rear Admiral Ward was relieved as ComNavForV (and as CNAG) by Rear Admiral Kenneth L. Veth.

Tet—1968

The savage communist assault on the cities of South Vietnam during the great Tet Offensive of 1968 called forth the finest in performance from both the U. S. and the Vietnamese navies, and at the same time it underscored the prevailing strategic weakness of the overall interdiction effort to that time. It was unmistakably evident that great amounts of supplies for the Communists had been brought into Vietnam to support and fuel the offensive. Beyond question, much of that material had entered and traversed South Vietnam on navigable water, despite Market Time, Game Warden, and the Mobile Riverine Force. The best evidence seemed to point to the fact that what the Bucklew Report had warned would happen, had happened. As Market Time throttled infiltration from the sea, the communists simply shifted their principal supply lines to inland routes, which crossed the borders from

supposedly "neutral" Cambodia and Laos. The interdiction effort that had been directed against these routes was concentrated on the major rivers, and might be likened to an attempt to stem the flow of water through a sieve by the tactic of inserting a limited number of needles in selected openings in the sieve, effective locally, but virtually useless overall. The Communists merely moved to smaller waterways when they were forced off the large rivers.

Why had not the Bucklew Report's recommendations concerning a mobile patrol force along the Cambodian border been implemented? There were really two reasons. First, until late 1968 the operational and logistic capability to mount such a naval patrol did not exist. Second, there was (and to a degree there continues to be) a profound reluctance on the part of Vietnamese ground force commanders to commit their troops to the aggressive river bank patrols essential to the effectiveness and safety of naval operations on narrow and restricted waterways. Such patrols were considered tiresome, time consuming, and virtually devoid of the tangible results obtainable from "search-and-destroy" operations.

The fallacy of "the numbers game," the seeming preoccupation with body count, Communist "structures" destroyed, and even, in some quarters, with bomb and ammunition expenditure reports was driven home with a vengeance when the Communists unleashed their Tet offensive, for while it was true that the "cream" of the enemy's forces was destroyed in that offensive, it was also undeniable that the South Vietnamese people and the credibility of the U. S. and the Government of Vietnam's political and military effort in the war had suffered grievous setbacks, from which they were a long time recovering.

In the IV Corps Tactical Zone, the Mobile Riverine Force was the only friendly force that retained the ability to mount sustained and effective counteroffensive operations. It literally rebounded from battle to battle and was later credited by General Westmoreland with having "saved the Delta." The River Patrol Force and the Vietnamese Navy outdid themselves as they brought their highly mobile fire power and unquestioned courage to the defense of the besieged cities.

The Coastal Surveillance Force enjoyed its finest hour as it thwarted a desperate attempt by the Communists to resupply the offensive by the simultaneous infiltration of four steel-hulled vessels of the fishing trawler type laden with arms. Three were destroyed, and the fourth was forced to turn back before she entered the "contiguous" zone.

Task Force Clearwater

In the North, the intense and tragic struggle for Hue made it absolutely essential that water communication by way of the Perfume River remain open. It was the only uncut supply line of any consequence for allied military forces there. On 20 February 1968, Deputy Com-USMACV (Forward) requested that ComNav-ForV designate a senior naval officer to act as a task force commander whose mission would be "to coordinate overall activities concerning the movement and protection of LCUs and LCMs through inland waterways to Hue ramps." In response, ComNavForV designated Captain Gerald W. Smith, U. S. Navy, as Commander Task Force Clearwater. The task force was activated on 24 February with headquarters at Tan My, under the operational control of Commanding General, III MAF. On 25 February, an additional responsibility was assigned to maintain the lines of communication on the Cua Viet River, just south of the Demilitarized Zone.

Forces initially at the disposal of the Clearwater task force commander included TF 116 PBRs, helicopter gunships, attack aircraft, artillery, and ground security troops. The task force was organized into two groups, the Hue River Security Group and the Dong Ha River Security Group. On 2 March 1968, in recognition of the increasing importance the northern group was assuming, the commander of the Clearwater task force moved his headquarters to Cua Viet.

The facilities at Cua Viet were almost constantly subject to enemy artillery and rocket attack, and the pressures and rigors of life at this exposed forward base were extreme. During the long months of the northeast monsoon the climate is probably the country's worst, with cold, grey and rainy days following each other in seemingly endless succession. Outside the river mouth, there are restless shoals and a pounding surf. Some of the unsung heroes of this war are the captains who guided low-powered and frequently age-weakened ships and craft through the treacherous white water of the Cua Viet inlet, and other equally hazardous channels in northern I Corps. The LCUs usually had chiefs or petty officers first class as captains. The LSTs had lieutenants or lieutenant commanders.

The men at Cua Viet lived little better than moles in heavily bunkered huts burrowed down among the sand dunes. When the rain stopped falling, the sand, fine-grained and gritty, began to blow, accumulating in drifts before the huts, sifting through screens and under doors, finding its way into lockers and between sheets and even into the food the men ate.

In October 1968, a program was initiated to gradually rotate all Cua Viet personnel back to Da Nang or Tan My, to ensure that no one would be required to spend more than six months at the advanced base. It is a tribute to the splendid morale of our sailors, and their sense of sharing in what was in many ways a unique drama, that many volunteered to stay on and finish their tours at Cua Viet.

Vice Admiral Zumwalt and the New Strategy

There were only seven officers and men in Commander Cannon's first Navy Section of the Military Advisory Assistance Group, Indochina. However, on 30 September 1968, when Vice Admiral Elmo R. Zumwalt, Jr., the first naval officer of three-star rank to be assigned to Vietnam, relieved Rear Admiral Kenneth L. Veth as Commander Naval Forces, Vietnam, the personnel strength of the Navy command stood at 38,386.

There were four flag officers either on hand or with orders to Vietnam at the time of Vice Admiral Zumwalt's assumption of command—ComNavForV, Deputy ComNavForV, Commander U. S. Naval Support Activity, Da Nang, and the Officer in Charge of Construction.

The Naval Support Activity, Da Nang had grown to become the Navy's largest overseas shore command. The Naval Support Activity, Saigon, which was commissioned when the Headquarters Support Activity was disestablished in May 1966, supported naval operations in II, III, and IV Corps Tactical Zones through its many scattered detachments. The operational forces had undergone many changes in organization and strength. The Vietnamese Navy and the advisory effort had expanded sharply.

The Riverine Assault Force with its 3,717 officers and men operated 161 specialized river craft, and these included 103 ATCs, 31 ASPBs, 6 CCBs, 17 Monitors, and 4 Refuelers. The addition of 17 more craft in October brought the force very close to its authorized allowance of 182 boats. The River Patrol Force had 2,032 men assigned and 197 of its authorized 250 PBRs. In October the number of PBRs attached to the task force increased to 220. The Coastal Surveillance Force (it had moved its headquarters to Cam Ranh Bay in July 1967) employed 1,051 officers and men, exclusive of those attached to Seventh Fleet units temporarily assigned to the task force. In September 1968, it had 81 of its authorized 85 PCFs and 24 of an allowed 26 WPBs. There were 39 smaller craft assigned to support the harbor defense operation, which was code-named Stable Door, under CTF 115.

Vice Admiral Zumwalt decided to concentrate his efforts on three principal tasks. The first of these was to bring the naval forces under his command together in coordinated operations to stop enemy infiltration into the Delta and to further the cause of pacification. The second task was to wrest the initiative from the enemy in the Rung Sat Special Zone through aggressive military and psychological campaigns in order to secure the vital Long Tau shipping channel to Saigon.

The Rung Sat was the one area where the Navy had, so to speak, a piece of the ground war (responsibility for military operations there rested with the Vietnamese Navy), and as Senior Advisor to the Vietnamese Navy the Admiral considered his position to be somewhat analogous to that of a Senior Advisor to one of the Combat Tactical Zones.

The third and perhaps most important task was to develop and recommend a plan which, if approved, would make it possible to accelerate the scheduled turnover of U. S. Navy equipment to the Vietnamese.

SEA LORDS

The Southeast Asia Lake, Ocean, River, and Delta Strategy (Sea Lords) brought to fruition the long-considered plan to complement the Market Time blockade of the coast of South Vietnam by an inland naval patrol along the Cambodian border from the Gulf of Thailand to an area northeast of the "Parrot's Beak." Hard intelligence had repeatedly confirmed that the bulk of enemy war material for the III and IV Corps areas entered Cambodia from the sea, in Communist Chinese and Eastern Bloc ships, primarily through the port of Sihanoukville. It was transported overland to various staging areas just north of the border, and was then brought into South Vietnam by the enemy's well-organized network of Commo-Liaison and transportation people. Well-documented infiltration routes had been traced, and it was one of the three aims of Sea Lords to bar these where they crossed or followed navigable water. The second aim was to "pacify" certain vital trans-Delta waterways,[7] and the third was "to stir up the enemy and keep him off-balance" by Market Time raider incursions into the rivers of the Ca Mau peninsula.

A new task organization, TF 194, was created for Sea Lords, and assets were chopped to "First Sea Lord" for specific operations by the commanders of Market Time, Game Warden, and the Mobile Riverine Force. Captain R. S. Salzer, U. S. Navy, was the first officer to function as "First Sea Lord," and upon his detachment the post was assumed by Rear Admiral W. H. House, Deputy ComNavForV. In concept, it was planned that a Brown Water Navy Task Fleet would be formed from the heavy, armored riverine assault craft, and the speedy and highly maneuverable PCFs and PBRs. The Navy helicopter gunships, Seawolves, would provide support for Sea Lords in much the same way that they were supporting Game Warden and Mobile Riverine Force operations. The Navy's fixed wing OV-10 light attack aircraft (Black Ponies) would not arrive in Vietnam until the following April.

The Interdiction Barriers

Operation Search Turn was launched on 2 November 1968 and succeeded in establishing the first of the interdiction barriers, on the Rach Gia Long Xuyen and Ca San Canals in the upper Mekong Delta. Search Turn was followed, on 16 November, by Operation Foul Deck (later renamed Tran Hung Dao), which placed naval patrols on the Rach Giang Thanh and Vinh Te Canal at the Cambodian border itself, and by Operation Giant Slingshot on 6 December, which extended the barrier patrols to the Vam Co Dong and Vam Co Tay rivers on either side of the notorious Parrot's Beak. The final link in the chain of barriers was forged on 2 January 1969 when Operation Barrier Reef was established on the La Grange-Ong Lon Canal.

The impact these naval patrols had on the enemy infiltration effort was soon measured in terms of heavy fire-fight activity, the seizure of large arms caches, and reports of enemy war material backing up in the north. The long-term effects the interdiction barriers seemed to have on the infiltration problem were these:

1. Where in the past large shipments[8] had moved with virtual impunity across the border, shipments henceforth were made in two or three sampan lots and at great risk;

2. The enemy was unable to infiltrate and stockpile sufficient material in the Delta to sustain any significant offensive action, much less repeat the violence unleashed in the 1968 Tet offensive;

3. Enemy forces in the Delta were gradually starved for supplies and ammunition, and hard pressed to maintain themselves; and

4. Huge stockpiles accumulated just north of the border in Cambodia as the enemy waited for more propitious times to move them into South Vietnam.

The border interdiction barriers brought to the war, which the French had called *la guerre sans fronts*, a front of sorts. Properly supported by vigorous and aggressive bank patrols, it is possible that the barriers might have succeeded in virtually shutting off what they could only curtail in the absence of the required level of ground support. The problem of attracting adequate ground forces has already been addressed. In IV Corps Tactical Zone, this situation would plague Sea Lords operations from beginning to end.

Operation Sea Float

The pacification of vital trans-Delta waterways was the second of the Sea Lords objectives. Combined operations in November and December 1968 cleared the important Cho Gao Canal and swept through the Can Tho Crossing corridor and the Dung Island complex in the Bassac River. The most significant Navy pacification effort, however, grew out of the Market Time raider incursions into the Cua Lon and Bo De rivers in the Ca Mau peninsula.

The Nam Can district of An Xuyen Province is located on the southernmost tip of the Ca Mau peninsula, some 150 miles southwest of Saigon. A region of ragged forests, thick mangrove swamps, barren mud flats, and interlacing rivers and canals whose waters churn to vicious tidal currents, it is not readily apparent why anyone would choose to live there. It appears to be sparsely populated in comparison with the rest of the Delta, but an accurate census has never been taken. Estimates of the area's population have varied from 5,000 to 13,000.

Historically, woodcutting has been the principal economic activity of the Nam Can, with fishing ranking a distant second. As is true for much of the Delta, waterways are vital routes to and from markets, and roads are virtually nonexistent. Route 12, which once connected Old Nam Can City with Ca Mau City, has long since fallen into disuse, and has all but vanished in the swampy terrain. The war destroyed the old French cisterns and what few wells there were in the area. Until quite recently all fresh water had to be brought in by sampan from settlements in the north. The rivers of the Nam Can, being tidal, are heavily salted.

An industrious woodcutter and his family can earn a very decent living by Vietnamese standards from their labors in the forests of Nam Can. The wood they cut is called *cay go* or simply "tree wood." It is extremely hard and dense, and if dropped in the water it will ordinarily sink. Young trees are cut into long, straight poles, stripped of their bark, and sold for construction purposes. Heavier timbers are sawed into short lengths, split, and sold to the charcoal makers. It is hard and demanding work. Power saws and modern lumbering techniques have not yet been introduced in the Nam Can.

The fishermen in the Nam Can harvest several varieties of shrimp and small fish. These are netted in cleverly designed fish traps which are located strategically in the waterways to make best use of the currents and backwaters. The catch is salted and dried in the sun prior to shipment to market.

At one time charcoal preparation was an important source of the area's meager wealth. In the summer of 1969 a few charcoal kilns were still standing in the midst of the ruins of Old Nam Can. The city, a pathetic oasis of nominal Saigon control, in a region which had been a Communist sanctuary for many years, was finally overrun during the 1968 Tet offensive and later abandoned by the Government of Vietnam. Most of its people were removed to a site roughly ten miles to the north which was named "New Nam Can" to distinguish it from the old district capital. The old city was declared a free fire zone and became in effect a dumping ground for bombs and other air ordnance that could not be conveniently expended elsewhere in the Delta. Within a short time of its capture by the Viet Cong, Old Nam Can presented a scene of the utmost devastation, and it was literally true that scarcely two stones were left piled one upon the other, save for the brick heaps of the ruined charcoal kilns.

Prior to the establishment of Market Time operations, the Nam Can provided a terminus for many Communist arms shipments arriving from the sea. Enemy trawlers operated with virtual impunity along the coasts of the Ca Mau peninsula and in the mouths of its rivers. From Nam Can the communist supply chain ran northward into the remainder of the Delta and into III Corps. After Market Time broke the sea end of this chain, the logistics flow reversed itself and the local Viet Cong were supplied with necessary munitions infiltrated from the north. What could not be moved in was often manufactured in concealed munitions factories by using scrap and dud rounds, which were in plentiful supply. Food, clothing, and other necessities were of course obtainable locally through the levying of Viet Cong "taxes" on the region's inhabitants. These were normally collected by armed sampans which took up stations on the heavily traveled water routes. In addition to taxes in kind, it was estimated that the Viet Cong were able to extort several million piasters each year from this region to fuel their war effort in the lower Delta.

In October 1968, U. S. Navy Swift boats began regular raids into the rivers of the Nam Can, threatening the enemy's "sovereignty" in an area he had come to call his own. The objective of the raiders was "to stir up the enemy and keep him off-balance," but other dividends were soon realized in terms of enemy equipment destroyed, and in the increased commitments he was forced to make in defense of his well-entrenched position in the Nam Can. Numerous bunkers and fortifications were thrown up, and solidly constructed barricades appeared across the more important waterways in an all-out Viet Cong effort to end the Swift boat raids.

In December, an operation called Silver Mace, involving the first open sea transit of heavy riverine assault craft, struck at these barricades and in three days removed them.

Elements of Task Group 117.2, Captain J. G. Now commanding, made the transit from Rach Gia to the Song Cua Lon on 19 December 1968. The group included ATCs, Monitors, and ASPBs. They were accompanied by the USS *Mercer* (APB-39) and the USS *Satyr* (ARL-23). After the operation they returned to Rach Gia by the same coastal route. A great deal of attention was of course paid to weather forecasting, and the transit was accomplished in the Gulf of Thailand's "good weather" part of the year.

In the early months of 1969, pressure was increasingly applied on the enemy in the Nam Can. In addition to the Market Time raiders, the following forces were employed: SEALS, UDT/EOD teams, Mobile Strike Force and RF/PF troops, Coastal Group junks, tactical strike aircraft supplied as needed by the U. S. Army, Navy, or Air Force, and helicopter gunships. In April, Operation Silver Mace II was launched with combined U. S. Navy, U. S. Air Force, Vietnamese Army, Navy, and Marine Corps units. The mission of the two-week operation was "to seek and destroy all enemy units and their logistic support in the AO (area of operations)." Contact with a generally elusive enemy was established on seven occasions. The enemy suffered 21 casualties and the loss of 380 weapons.

These and subsequent operations in the Nam Can during the first half of 1969 relied heavily on offshore support ships (primarily LSTs and ARLs), which, because of very shallow water, had to anchor about five miles off the Ca Mau peninsula. The disadvantages of this support concept for continuing boat operations were the same as noted earlier for the offshore support of PBRs during early Game Warden operations. It was obvious that from an operational standpoint the establishment of a permanent base on the Cua Lon or Bo De Rivers, capable of supporting PCFs, junks, and river assault craft, was highly desirable. There were other reasons as well which argued strongly in that direction. It was not proposed that "Vietnamization" of the naval war would include the transfer of the large units which made offshore support of the Nam Can operations feasible, if less than desirable for the U. S. Navy. If the Vietnamese Navy were to continue effective operations in the area after the withdrawal of the U. S. Navy, some sort of an operational and support base would be required. A location on one of the two rivers mentioned above was considered ideal, since it would permit egress to the South China Sea in the east and to the Gulf of Thailand in the west. This was a factor of no small importance in an area affected by monsoon winds and seas. Further, it seemed important that in the wake of effective search-and-destroy operations a permanent Vietnamese Government presence be established in the Nam Can. Effective pacification would deny the enemy a strategic haven and source of material and financial support. Under Vietnamese protection this war-ravaged region might be coaxed back to life. A concerted and innovative psychological operation might succeed in winning the people to active support of the government of Vietnam, the majority of whom were judged to be apolitical.

The proposal to establish a permanent base in the Nam Can met with little enthusiasm in IV Corps Headquarters. Vietnamese ground commanders, and some of their American advisors, thought that such a base would be virtually indefensible. Looking at it from the north, across many miles of difficult and enemy controlled terrain, their view was quite naturally a different one from that enjoyed by the Navy, which eyed the proposal from the vantage point of the sea. Furthermore, ground commanders generally tended to discount the economic and strategic importance of the Nam Can. Efforts at population and resources control should concentrate, they argued, in areas where the population was heavier and the resources greater than they were in the uninviting barrens of the Nam Can. This, so it seemed to the Navy, ignored the potential of the region and the history of its use by the Viet Cong.

On 15 May 1969, therefore, CTF 115 proposed that a PCF Mobile Advance Tactical Support Base (MATSB) be built and positioned in the middle of the Cua Lon River near Old Nam Can. By drawing upon the lessons learned in the deployment of the Advance Tactical Support Bases (ATSBs) in the Giant Slingshot operation, such a base, using an array of Ammi pontoon barges, was considered both feasible and defensible.

The proposal was thoroughly discussed at ComNavForV headquarters. Eventually a plan was approved which called for a complex of nine Ammis (later increased to 13), including a helicopter landing platform. It was the Admiral's view at the time that "Vietnamese Navy participation is the key to the success of this operation." To underscore the importance of the cooperative aspects of the venture, a Vietnamese naval officer was assigned as second in command of the MATSB.

The Ammis were fitted out at Nha Be. The roofs of huts were strengthened for defense against mortar attack, and the sides were heavily sand-bagged to afford protection from small-arms fire. Numerous automatic weapons and mortars were emplaced, though the primary defense of the MATSB was considered to be the mobile firepower provided by the naval craft and the helicopter fire teams that would be supported there. When the work at Nha Be was completed, the Ammis were carried to the mouth of the Cua Lon River by Seventh Fleet LSDs.

The combined operation, called Sea Float by the U. S. Navy and Tran Hung Dao III by the Vietnamese, began with the towing of the first Ammis up the river to the vicinity of Old Nam Can on 25 June 1969 by U. S. Navy YFUs. The mooring of this large complex of Ammi barges in tidal currents, which frequently reached velocities of six to eight knots, proved to be a considerable feat in itself. A six-point fore and aft moor with 9,000-pound anchors and heavy concrete clumps was selected. The holding ground was good and the moor was successful.

The roaring current provided the best defenses from swimmer attack, and on nearby shore areas an array of electronic sensors was emplaced to provide early warning of enemy movement.

Enemy reaction to this unwanted presence in his midst took the form of increased mining and ambush of Swiftboat patrols, and a vigorous psychological warfare operation of his own. Viet Cong banners were raised along the waterways which read "Americans and Vietnamese Soldiers Who Come Here Will Die," and "We Kill Americans." English language leaflets were floated to the MATSB on tiny wooden rafts. They urged an end to the "U. S. aggressive war" and threatened to "blow the American Navy out of the water." A rumor, the authenticity of which could not be determined, circulated on Sea Float that "Hanoi Hannah" herself had taken note of the new operation and she had warned that the MATSB would be "at the bottom of Song Cua Lon by 17 July." An old Vietnamese woodcutter, captured and abused by the Viet Cong, escaped to tell Vietnamese interrogators that his captors had boasted that they would "visit" Sea Float some day.

The people of the Nam Can were warned by the Viet Cong to stay away from Sea Float. Gradually, however, as it became evident that the campaign was not going to be of short duration, visitors to the MATSB came in ever-increasing numbers. They were given hot meals, small gifts, and services which ran the gamut from sampan motor repair to the grinding of woodcutters' axes on a wheel specially acquired for that purpose in Nha Trang, and shipped to Sea Float by CTF 115. Simple medical treatment was also provided, and the scope of this expanded rapidly with the arrival of a Vietnamese hospital ship (LSM-H).

On 24 July, a Sea Float "Annex" began operations near the intersection of the Cua Lon River and the Cai Nhap Canal. This was an important communications artery some six miles east of Sea Float, through which passed virtually all north-south commercial traffic. At first, the Annex was composed of two PCFs, an LSIL, and the Vietnamese hospital ship. The PCFs and the LSIL inspected traffic on the river, and provided protection for the hospital ship while it conducted its civil action program. These units got under way each morning from Sea Float and returned each night. Almost immediately the Annex began to outstrip the main complex itself in the number of visitors it attracted. In time a new hamlet was established at the site.

With the eviction of Viet Cong "tax collectors" from the principal water routes, civilian traffic on the rivers noticeably increased. During the first five days of the Sea Float operation, an average of 102 sampans per day was sighted on the Cua Lon. By the middle of August the number had increased to 159 per day and the average size of the sampans was larger as heavier cargoes, mostly of wood, were moved to market. The markets were towns to the north, New Nam Can and Ca Mau primarily. By September the Nam Can population figures were growing at a rapid rate, doubling the number of people in the Sea Float area of operations every 25 days. By the middle of October 1969, it was estimated that more than 3,000 people were living under Vietnamese control in the Nam Can. The people came from all over the Delta to harvest the wood and fish of the area. Many came from the enemy-controlled region of the Nam Can.

Additional naval forces, U. S. and Vietnamese, were committed to the operation. Armored river assault craft were assigned to the Cai Nhap patrol and were joined by Coastal Group junks and a Vietnamese Navy reaction force. Maximum use was made of SEAL, EOD, and UDT men. The EOD and UDT teams were often used interchangeably to destroy the enemy's fortifications. SEALs were used on special warfare and intelligence missions. Most importantly, a favorable decision was taken on the establishment of a permanent Vietnamese naval base on the site of Old Nam Can. The nickname Solid Anchor was given this project on 24 October 1969. It was described as a combined U. S. and Vietnamese naval operation to construct a Coastal Group junk and PCF base at Old Nam Can.

The economy of the Nam Can grew dramatically, the population mushroomed, and the pace of the pacification effort was quickened to keep in step. Long lines of motorized cargo sampans moved north through the Cai Nhap[9] laden with wood and fish products. On their return from market they brought potable water, rice, cloth, beer, and other staples. In the newly settled hamlets of Tran Hung Dao One and Tran Hung Dao Two, lying along the north bank of the Cua Lon, between Sea Float and the Cai Nhap, small stores appeared, and a restaurant opened its doors for business. New fishtraps were hammered into the river beds and wired into place. Broad areas of the banks were soon taken over by the drying catch. Seemingly from nowhere, skilled masons appeared and began the painstaking reconstruction of the area's once ubiquitous beehive charcoal kilns. In December the first baby, a little girl, was born on Sea Float to the obvious delight of every sailor on board. The number of people then living under Vietnamese control in the area was estimated to be about 9,000.

Sea Float sailors constructed schools in each of the two newly settled hamlets. The children's desks were fashioned from ammunition boxes, as were the floors of the classrooms. Notebooks and pencils were secured and distributed. Teachers were found and hired.

Vietnamese flags fluttered from the tops of tall *cay go* poles in each hamlet, and from crude flagstaffs on virtually all water craft, and

from the fronts of most of the people's hootches or shelters. To what degree this public display reflected allegiance to the government in Saigon was difficult to determine, but that the people enjoyed a measure of safety and prosperity long denied them was indisputable. The river hamlets, for all their bogs and sloughs of mud, were alive with activity and sparkled with the laughter of children.

The Rung Sat

Drawn carefully on a map, the Rung Sat Special Zone looks curiously like a human brain, its convolutions etched by numberless rivers and streams. There is little good land in the area and it has value, as mentioned earlier, only because of the vital Long Tau shipping channel, and because of its nearness to the capital. The terrain of the Rung Sat is ideally suited to guerrilla warfare. Dense foliage and thick swamps make detection of soldiers from the air and pursuit on the ground extremely difficult.

Though broad strips on either side of the Long Tau had been defoliated and cleared, attacks on merchant ships proceeding to and from Saigon began to increase significantly in the first half of 1969. By the end of June, 51 such attacks had occurred, compared to 44 in all of 1968.

Minings in the Long Tau, with relatively few exceptions, involved either limpet mines attached to ships at anchor by swimmers or mines detonated under passing ships from observation points on the river bank. When the Navy became involved in port security (basically an Army responsibility), the incidence of minings at anchor fell off. Drastic defoliation of the banks of the Long Tau made the planting and the firing of command-detonated mines extremely hazardous for the enemy. He could no longer approach or withdraw from the river with his old assurance. Naturally, stand-off weapons, frequently command-fired from concealed positions well inland, became more attractive to the enemy.

Few of these attacks managed to score hits, much less cause serious damage, but the enemy probably reaped considerable propaganda benefit from them and in the world press was credited with more strength than he actually possessed. There was always the danger that one of his attacks might succeed in sinking a large ship in the deep-water channel, thereby disrupting the flow of supplies to Saigon.

Part of the increase in the number of attacks on shipping could be attributed to the longer-range weapons then coming into use. They permitted the enemy to fire from relatively safe positions, well back from the river bank. The Rocket Propelled Grenade (RPG-7), for example, had an effective range nearly three times that of the older RPG-2. Allied sweeps along the Long Tau in this period were also occasionally uncovering 107-mm. and 122-mm. rockets, some of which were wired for command firing from camouflaged spider holes many meters away from the banks.

The structure of the enemy force responsible for the attacks on Long Tau shipping was rather well known. A sapper group, Doan-10, had been identified. It was believed to consist of either nine or ten elements (Doi) of between 30 and 55 men each. Complicating the task of engaging and destroying Doan-10 was the fact that the unit enjoyed a relatively safe and untouched base camp area just north of the Rung Sat area of operations in the Nhon Trach District of Bien Hoa Province. Attacks on the Long Tau were ordinarily carried out by small groups of five or fewer men who, after firing their weapons, simply faded back into their haven in the north. In microcosm this was the sanctuary tactic employed by the enemy along the national borders with Cambodia, Laos, and North Vietnam. In this instance, however, the sanctuary lay wholly within the territory of

South Vietnam and scarcely 15 miles from the capital. This situation, spawned and tolerated by the fractured and at times intransigent Vietnamese command structure, had existed for a number of years.

The June attacks in the Long Tau made it imperative that effective and decisive action be taken against Doan-10. The Senior Advisor in the RSSZ at this time was Commander C. J. Wages, U. S. Navy, and in concert with his Vietnamese Navy counterpart, Commander Nguyen Van Tan, he proposed that the RSSZ area of operations be enlarged temporarily to permit sweeps against the enemy's "sanctuary" in the Nhon Trach. This proposal received strong backing from ComNavForV and from Commanding General, II Field Force Vietnam. Permission to conduct these operations was granted.

A battalion of either Vietnamese Marines, or the Mobile Strike Force was requested to augment the Rung Sat Commander's ground troops. Neither was available. Assistance was provided, however, by the First Australian Task Force and by the Royal Thai Army Volunteers. Thus, a truly international conglomerate of soldiers and sailors launched the combined operation against Doan-10 on 22 June 1969.

The operation achieved immediate and striking success in its objective of easing pressure on the Long Tau shipping channel. Whereas 19 attacks on merchant shipping occurred in June prior to the start of the operation, a high for the war, none at all occurred during the remainder of the month, and only two occurred in July.

As was proven time and time again in Brown Water Navy operations in Vietnam, cooperation with trained and aggressive ground forces was the real key to success. Without that cooperation a measure of initiative always remained with the enemy, who had the choice of when and where to dispute the control and ownership of a particular stretch of navigable water. In the absence of ground forces, the enemy could employ a further application of the strategy of sanctuary, for our boats could "pursue" only to the maximum effective range of their installed weapons. Air power, to be sure, could further that pursuit and proved invaluable in support of our boats when they were caught up in a fire fight, but a lesson that was learned in the Indochina War and which was re-learned in the Vietnam War, is that air power has only limited effectiveness in a counterinsurgency war and in the interdiction of enemy lines of communication through difficult and largely trackless terrain.

In August new combined operations were launched against the base camp areas in the Nhon Trach "sanctuary" area outside of the Rung Sat, which was a much harder area for the Viet Cong to hide in. These were given the nicknames Friendship and Platypus. In September, Operation Chuong Duong struck at the same area, and in October the first of a series of operations called Wolf Pack lashed out at Doan-10. All of these operations used U. S. Navy and Vietnamese Navy forces as a blocking force while a combination of Australian, Thai, and Vietnamese troops methodically swept the area around the guerrilla group's base camp.

The tactic of keeping the enemy constantly on the move, never surrendering the initiative, and denying him a secure base area completely changed the complexion of the war in the "Forest of Assassins." Pacification programs took hold, abandoned hamlets were resettled, and the economy improved. "Vietnamization" proceeded at a steady pace. By early February 1970 the Vietnamese Navy operated more than 50 per cent of the boats in the Rung Sat.

From an operation which at one time was thought to have been assigned to the Vietnamese Navy because no Vietnamese Army officer in his right mind could be found to

accept it, the Rung Sat Special Zone by early 1970 had become a model for what could be made of a seemingly hopeless situation, given leadership, singleness of purpose, and a spark of imagination.

ACCELERATED TURNOVER PLAN (ACTOV)

By the fall of 1968, "Vietnamization" of the war (although the term itself was not to be coined until the President-elect's speech on 31 December) had become a matter of the greatest political urgency and it seemed clear that it would remain so, regardless of the outcome of the November elections in the United States. In October, ComUSMACV directed that a program be developed for an accelerated turnover of U. S. equipment, while the war continued, in order to make the Republic of Vietnam Armed Forces (RVNAF) as self-sufficient as possible. This requirement was strongly re-emphasized later in the month when General Abrams returned from a visit to the United States. The decision had been made in Washington that Vietnamization was vital to continued home support of the war. Over all hung the specter of the French defeat, "in the streets of Paris rather than on the battlefields of Indochina."

At about this same time public statements by Secretary of Defense Clark Clifford signaled the changing U. S. policy on the war. There was a need for "an accelerated progress in improving Vietnamese capabilities in order that U. S. forces could, in fact, be withdrawn in significant numbers." In testimony before the Senate Armed Services Committee, the Secretary was further quoted as saying that "our orientation seems to have been more on operations than on assisting the South Vietnamese to acquire the means to defend themselves." While this may not have been intended as criticism of the past conduct of the war, it was unmistakable direction as to where future priorities were to be placed. In the light of these events, ComNavForV's Accelerated Turnover Plan (ACTOV) was approved.

Prior to his departure, Rear Admiral Veth had recommended to General Abrams and to the Chief of Naval Operations a plan to turn over two River Assault Squadrons (roughly the equivalent of six Vietnamese Navy River Assault Groups) by the end of the fiscal year 1969. Vice Admiral Zumwalt proposed to expand that plan so that virtually all U. S. Navy operational responsibilities in Vietnam with the equipment necessary for meeting them, would be turned over by 30 June 1970. He further proposed that all support functions and bases be transferred by the end of the fiscal year 1972.

The enormity of this undertaking could not be measured solely in terms of the numbers of the Vietnamese naval personnel it would be necessary to recruit and train. Significant improvement in the existing structure and performance of the Vietnamese Navy would also be required. The Vietnamese leadership, on which the ultimate success of the plan rested, was already heavily burdened.

The Vietnamese supply system seemingly could not or would not work, though many studies had demonstrated its theoretical excellence. The Naval Shipyard struggled along with barely 60 per cent of its authorized work force, and skilled labor could not be attracted or held because of wage scales that were chronically below the market level. Training activities ashore suffered from a lack of facilities and a lack of instructors. Training afloat depended almost entirely on the whims of individual commanding officers, because there was no effective system to ensure that standards set by higher authority were met. Administrative procedures were antiquated and incredibly complex. A most significant factor was the deplorable care, housing, and security of dependent families.

In the fall of 1968 our naval advisory effort in Vietnam was entering its nineteenth year. Over the years the finest officers and men our Navy could muster were sent to live, to work, and some, eventually, to die alongside their Vietnamese counterparts. Particularly in the years following 1964, enormous sums of money and huge quantities of material and equipment were transferred. It is a fair question to ask ourselves why, after such a great and prolonged effort, we had not succeeded in accomplishing more.

The heart of the problem was, of course, political and not peculiar to the Vietnamese Navy, nor for that matter to the Vietnamese armed forces as a whole. It spread its roots through virtually every sector of Vietnamese society. It is a bitter pill for a whole generation of American "nation builders" to swallow, but the brutal fact is that no Vietnamese Government until possibly the present one inspired in its people the loyalty, the unhesitating support, the patriotism and spirit of self-sacrifice essential to the welding of an effective defense force.

The situation in the fall of 1968 was not one for faint hearts. To carry out the politically necessary task of Vietnamizing the naval war, it was estimated that the Vietnamese Navy would require an additional ten thousand men on top of the seventeen and a half thousand it then had. Minimum training requirements for the buildup were estimated to be: (1) Recruit training increased by a factor of four; (2) The Vietnam Navy's advanced school capacity tripled; (3) A four-fold increase in offshore training; and (4) English language training expanded by almost thirty times.

Assistance, advice, and expertise in the formulation and implementation of the accelerated turnover program could be expected, within budgetary limitations, from the other Pacific commands and from the Navy in Washington. It was obvious, however, that what Naval Forces Vietnam and the Vietnamese Navy actually faced was a gigantic boot-strap operation which had to be carried out concurrently with the prosecution of the war.

The concept of sequential turnover was the keystone of the Navy's ACTOV plan, and it called for a gradual phasing in of Vietnamese personnel in all U. S. craft and facilities to be turned over. By "sequential" it was meant, for example, that a VNN sailor would be placed in the crew of one of our boats and trained in the duties of his American counterpart. When he was considered ready to take over, the American would leave and a second VNN sailor would be assigned to train in the duties of another American crew member until eventually the entire crew became Vietnamese. The American boat captain would be the last to leave, and control and ownership of the boat would remain with the U. S. as long as he was aboard.

Our operational boats would be the first to complete turnover. The training programs at logistic support bases would, of necessity, be much longer and would proceed at a much slower pace. As a final step in the ACTOV program, the advisory effort would be phased out.

In the plan, great reliance was placed on "on-the-job" training, and it was hoped that by living with, and operating with, our Brown Water sailors the VNN sailors would learn much by example. Prior to reporting to our boats Vietnamese sailors would be given at least a minimal English language training, but even so it was recognized that to a greater extent than perhaps desirable, "show and tell" instruction would really be "show and do." The motivation of the men concerned was expected to be high. There were no "spare" people on our boat crews. Each man assigned had to pull his share of the load. Thus, the American sailors who realized that a member of their "team" was going to be replaced in a short time could be expected to see to it that the new replacement really did know how to operate, for example, the after machine gun. Conversely, the Vietnamese sailors, seeing that the boats and the responsibility for operating them were soon going to be theirs, would be expected to redouble their efforts to prepare themselves.

There was a great deal of flexibility built into ACTOV. If the war, or domestic political considerations, made it necessary to turn over less American equipment, fractional Vietnamese crews could be collected from our boats and brought together to form crews for a lesser number of boats. If more time should become available, the acceleration could be slowed and the training cycles could be lengthened.

With relatively few exceptions, our sailors, American and Vietnamese, accepted the challenge and performed well in the months following the implementation of the plan.

THE FIGHT FOR DEPENDENTS' WELFARE

The deep-seated economic ills of the Republic of Vietnam, exemplified by a roaring inflation, drove the Vietnamese serviceman up against the wall. In mid-1970 cyclo drivers in Saigon were earning more than Vietnamese Navy lieutenants, and it was not at all uncommon to encounter beggars in uniform on the streets of the capital city.

The struggle to improve the living standards of the Vietnamese sailor proved to be one of the most critical tasks associated with the ACTOV program, for as the turnover progressed, and the day approached when sizable Vietnamese Navy populations would take up duties at scattered bases throughout the Republic, it was clear that the already intolerable situation of dependents' care and housing would grow immeasurably worse, unless firm action were taken at once.

ComNavForV directed all commands to

make a maximum effort to mobilize local construction equipment and to obtain excess materials in support of the Self-Help shelter program. The minimum requirement established was that pilot programs be under way and materials stockpiled to complete construction with the arrival of the first dependents at the ACTOV bases. Specific activities which were initiated included:

1. Development of plans for several standard shelters constructed from concrete block, some of which would use ferro-cement dome roofs.

2. Creation of a NavForV dependent shelter project team to coordinate allocation of materials and technical assistance.

3. Establishment of Seabee teams which were made available to instruct and provide technical assistance in construction of shelters.

4. Provision for systematic screening of materials declared excess by all military commands.

5. Construction of a block plant at Cam Ranh Bay.

6. The issuance of a personal appeal to the Navy League for donations of construction materials, which could be transported to Vietnam on deploying Navy ships.

7. Having the Naval Ships Systems Command provide bunks and mattresses, which might be available from Navy ships being decommissioned.

In all, it was estimated that the growing Vietnamese Navy would require 14,000 housing units. By the spring of 1970 it was believed that appropriated funds could be found to finance 10,500 of these. The remainder would have to be sought elsewhere.

As Vietnamese sailors replaced American sailors on the rivers, and as other American sailors became available from the gradual phasing out of Navy responsibilities in I Corps, Naval Construction Action Teams (NAVCATS)

were formed, and young and sometimes bewildered U. S. Navy sailors, under Seabee supervision, became laborers, hod carriers, masons, and carpenters in the dependents' shelter project. These sailors brought a high level of enthusiasm and dedication to their unconventional assignment, and as a result of their labors dozens of austere "Levittowns" sprang up at remote base sites throughout the country. The individual shelter units were by no means grand, but they were a vast improvement over the pitifully few shelters that had existed before.

The NavForV program did not stop with the construction of shelters. "Pigs and chickens" programs were initiated at most bases to provide the necessary protein that was often lacking in the diet of the Vietnamese dependents. If it seemed unusual for the U. S. Navy to go into the pigs and chickens business halfway around the world, it was. But it was a necessary business, and the Brown Water sailor attacked the job of getting it done with the same enthusiasm he had shown in seeking out the enemy on the rivers and canals of the Delta. Other parts of the U. S. Navy family came to his assistance. The Fleet Reserve Association pledged to raise $75,000 to support "Project Pay Dirt"—an expansion of the animal husbandry program. On 31 March 1970 a group of American businessmen in Saigon, including several ex-naval officers, established the "Operation Helping Hand Foundation" for the purpose of soliciting and accepting personal contributions to the Vietnamese Navy's welfare programs. In the United States, "Project Buddy Base" was launched to encourage U. S. Navy bases to provide equipment, material, encouragement and advice to Vietnamese Navy bases in the overall effort to raise the standard of living of VNN personnel and their dependents.

All of these programs hoped to bring about permanent and self-sustaining projects, which would survive the eventual conclusion of the Vietnamization process.

The Road to Turnover

Unquestionably, the Navy's ACTOV program was in the van of the general movement to Vietnamize the war. The first turnover of U. S. Navy boats and equipment occurred on schedule on 1 February 1969, when River Assault Division 91 of the Riverine Assault Force was dissolved and VNN River Assault and Interdiction Divisions 70 and 71 were formed.

The two Vietnamese RAIDs promptly began operations on the Giant Slingshot barrier. A year later there were virtually no U. S. Navy combat craft in Vietnam with wholly American crews. By 1 April 1970, 242 craft, worth more than $68 million, had been turned over under the ACTOV program.

With the craft went the responsibility for operations. The American sailors were gradually being sent home. By the spring of 1970, the personnel strength of Naval Forces, Vietnam had declined by almost 25 per cent since the start of the ACTOV program, and it was projected that by the following August another 25 per cent or more would possibly go home. In spite of changes in the turnover plans, which required the recruiting and training of nearly 10,000 additional Vietnamese Navymen and the transfer of a proportionately larger number of craft, five-sixths of all operational craft would be turned over by June 1970, and the rest by December of that year. Under the combined leadership of Vice Admiral Zumwalt and Commodore Chon a tremendous momentum had been built up. The men of both navies had adopted the Admiral's daily watchword and admonition to all concerned: "Go faster."

Conclusions

A rare application of sea power developed on the rivers and canals of the Delta, the water-ways of I Corps, and along the length of the Vietnamese coast. A new family of fighting craft appeared, newly built or adapted from older boats in our inventory. New basing and support concepts were created. New tactics were devised; new strategies tested. New task forces were put together to help fight a war that was in many respects a completely alien experience for the modern American sailor.

In the Vietnam War, sea power made possible one of history's longest supply lines. Though we live in what has frequently been termed the "air age" or even the "space age," the fact remains that fully 96 per cent of the immense quantities of material delivered to Vietnam to support the war came in ships. Many of those ships were tired relics of our great merchant fleet of World War II, soon to be consigned to the scrap heap. Our Navy itself was old and afflicted with bloc obsolescence. One of the hidden, but nevertheless real, costs of the war lies in the Fleet ships that, because our resources were diverted elsewhere, were not built as replacements for those long overdue for honorable retirement.

The river assault craft of the Brown Water Navy, with few exceptions, notably the ASPB, were modifications of World War II landing craft. The ships and barges that made up the floating support assets were also to a great extent pulled from our aging mothball fleet. They performed valuable service but, like our Victory and Liberty merchant ships, it is doubtful how much additional service life is left in them. Many of these vessels, of course, have been, and are being, transferred from our inventory to that of the Vietnamese Navy through the ACTOV program.

While many of our ships were old, and much of our equipment was, too, the Brown Water sailor exemplified youth. Young officers and petty officers were assigned staggering responsibilities in this war and they shouldered them well. The leadership of our Navy for many years to come will be drawn largely from the ranks of those whose courage and sense of responsibility were fire-hardened on the rivers of Vietnam.

The Great Green Fleet of the Delta, the brave PBRs, the Swift boats, and the Brown Water sailor himself will one day soon belong to the past. Ultimately, only the rivers and memories will remain.

(*Naval Review*, 1971)

Notes

1. The patrols along the seventeenth parallel, and near the Brevie Line in the Gulf of Thailand in late 1961 and 1962, in which U. S. Navy MSOs and DEs participated in a very limited way (using their radars to vector VNN ships to suspicious contacts), did not indicate large-scale infiltrations from the sea. In 1963, Vietnamese patrols searched a reported 135,911 junks and 388,725 people, of whom only 6 were determined to be infiltrators. In 1964, VNN Coastal patrols searched 211,121 junks and 880,335 people. Only 11 were confirmed Viet Cong. These statistics could of course be interpreted two ways; either there was little sea infiltration, or the counter-infiltration effort was remarkably ineffective. On the basis of the evidence—the 17 infiltrators identified in two years—there was little to support the claim of large-scale sea infiltration.

2. The Brevie Line is the geographic division in the Gulf of Thailand between Vietnam and Cambodia. Islands and territorial waters to the north of that line are Cambodian and, to the south, Vietnamese.

3. Operational Command is the authority to assign missions or forces.

4. Operational Control is the authority to direct forces assigned.

5. See "River Patrol Relearned" by Commander Sayre A. Swarztrauber, U. S. Navy, which follows.

6. APB self-propelled barracks ship, ARL Landing Craft Repair Ship, LCM Landing Craft Mechanized, ATC Armored Troop Carrier, MON Monitor, CCB Command and Control Boat, ASPB Assault Support Patrol Boat, LST Tank Landing Ship.

7. In this sense "pacify" means: establishing control over the people who live on the banks, ending Viet Cong tax extortion, denying the waterways to enemy use, while at the same time, restoring the use of the waterways to friendly civilian and military use.

8. A large shipment was considered to be 15–20 sampan lots.

9. This canal is 50 to 100 feet wide, 15 to 20 feet deep, and 10 to 12 miles long. The author estimates the sampans travel at about six to eight knots depending on the tide.

Market Time in the Gulf of Thailand

James A. Hodgman, Captain, U. S. Coast Guard

There is nothing new about the United States conducting naval operations with small ships in remote areas. The first extended deployment beyond our coasts was made in 1799 when Navy squadrons made up of small brigs and corvettes, and cutters of the Revenue Marine (forerunner of the Coast Guard) cruised the West Indies and, over a period of two years, laid by the heels more than 85 French privateers. Soon after, in 1803, Commodore Preble showed the world what a force of U. S. Navy small vessels could do when, with a fleet of schooners, brigs, ketches, and gunboats, he blockaded the Barbary Coast and even sailed into Tripoli Harbor to attack the enemy. His crews halted pirate raids on U. S. merchantmen and put an end to the payment of tribute to the four Barbary states. In spite of those early successes, the use of small naval ships in areas remote from established naval bases is an art that has been little practiced in recent years. However, the need for inshore naval forces today in counterinsurgency operations and limited war was recognized and documented by Commander W. F. Searle, Jr., U. S. Navy, in *Naval Review 1966* and by Commander Andrew G. Nelson, U. S. Navy, and Lieutenant Norman G. Mosher, U. S. Navy, in the June 1966 *U. S. Naval Institute Proceedings*.

This essay will show how ideas were con-verted into action in Vietnam through the development of a coastal surveillance force. In particular, it will deal with the naval operations in the Gulf of Thailand, where all the elements of a balanced force were first assembled. The first year of those operations, when the concept, plans, deployment, and operations were developed, will be discussed; results will be evaluated, and unsolved problems will be presented.

Although what the Navy has been doing in the Gulf of Thailand is not formal or extensive enough to qualify as a campaign, Coast Guard and Navy forces have been, and are, engaged on a small scale in a wide range of surface naval operations. Moreover, in cooperation with South Vietnam's own navy, similar forces are at work along the entire coast of South Vietnam.

Phase One—March 1965

U. S. coastal surveillance operations in Vietnam started in February 1965, when a U. S. helicopter on a medical rescue mission spotted a camouflaged trawler close ashore in Vung Ro Bay, about halfway up the east coast of Vietnam. Air strikes were called in, and the 130-foot trawler was sunk in shallow water. Over 100 tons of guns, ammunition, and other supplies were found on board the ship or

Fishermen hand over a plastic bag holding their boat's registration papers and their own identification cards to a Coast Guardsman leaning over the rail of the 82-foot cutter Point Comfort. *There were 26 such cutters operating from the DMZ to the Cambodian border, including nine in the Gulf of Thailand. The normally white Coast Guard vessels were painted deck gray in the fall of 1965.*

cached in the immediate area, and evidence recovered—markings, documents, and weapons—showed clearly that the trawler had come from North Vietnam.

This evidence was particularly significant because it was uncovered at a time when the complexion of the war was changing. Whereas earlier it had been possible to launch small-scale guerrilla operations with homemade and captured weapons and ammunition, in 1965 the Viet Cong needed guns and ammuni-

tion imported from outside South Vietnam in order to handle the major confrontations taking place. American and South Vietnamese pressure on the land lines of communication was making infiltration by those routes increasingly expensive, and a logical alternative for the Viet Cong was to use the sea. That they were doing so, was proved by the discovery at Vung Ro. The quantity of arms and ammunition recovered there could, at that time, have supplied the entire VC effort for some weeks.

Proof of infiltration from the sea led the Vietnamese naval forces to intensify their boarding and searching operations in territorial waters and in the contiguous zone out to 12 miles. Destroyers and destroyer escorts of the Seventh Fleet were deployed along the coast to detect and track all suspect vessels. They reported their findings to Vietnamese naval units, but they were not authorized to board. Vietnamese liaison personnel were assigned to U. S. ships. By mid-March, in order to improve the coordination of operations, joint Vietnamese Navy–U. S. Navy coastal surveillance centers were established at Da Nang, Qui Nhon, Nha Trang, and Vung Tau on the South China Sea, and at An Thoi in the Gulf of Thailand. The Vietnamese watchstanders acted as command representatives of the Vietnamese Navy Coastal Zone Commander; the American watchstanders collected and evaluated information and relayed it to U. S. Navy ships, to long-range Navy patrol aircraft assigned to complement the surface forces, and to the U. S. Navy Operations Center in Saigon. By the end of March 1965, the Vietnamese Patrol Force—Task Force 71—had been formally established under Commander Seventh Fleet, and the designation "Market Time" had been given to the U. S. effort to counter infiltration.

Late in April 1965, the government of the Republic of Vietnam declared that its territorial waters out to the three-mile limit constituted a Defensive Sea Area, and it listed car-

One of the larger Market Time ships, the USS Lowe *(DER 325) is shown on a windy, rainy day somewhere near the Demilitarized Zone between North and South Vietnam. (Chief Photographer's Mate Jerry L. Means, U.S. Navy)*

goes which would be considered suspect and would be subject to seizure unless their legitimate destination could be identified clearly. On that list were weapons, ammunition, communications equipment, explosives, chemicals with military uses, and medical supplies and foodstuffs of North Vietnamese, Chinese Communist, or Soviet-bloc origin. The government warned also that fiscal, immigration, and customs regulations would be enforced on all ships within the 12-mile contiguous zone. It further indicated that it intended to act beyond the 12-mile contiguous zone to prevent or punish infringements of laws by its own vessels and, where appropriate in the case of other vessels, to invoke the international doctrine of hot pursuit.

During this period the governments of South Vietnam and the United States were planning further integration of their naval operations. Minesweepers had joined the destroyers and destroyer escorts, procedures for

surface patrol had been formalized to some degree, and aerial barrier patrols, using P-2, P-3, and P-5 aircraft, had been developed. Procedures for naval gunfire support had been established, and such support, as well as psychological operations, had been assigned as the secondary task of Market Time units.

On 11 May 1965, the government of Vietnam authorized the forces of Market Time to stop and search vessels of any country found inside the territorial limits of Vietnam and not obviously engaged in innocent passage, and to seize such vessels when appropriate. Within the 12-mile contiguous zone, South Vietnamese vessels, or vessels believed so to be, were made similarly subject to U. S. search.

MARKET TIME PLANNING

As might be expected, deployment of U. S. forces to Market Time was limited, at first, by the resources available to Commander Seventh Fleet. Later, the situation was evaluated, and plans were developed on a long-term basis. Deployment was complicated by the shape of Vietnam. It is long and narrow, and its 1,000-mile coastline runs south from the 17th parallel, along the South China Sea to the tip of the Ca Mau Peninsula; then it doubles back north along the Gulf of Thailand to the Cambodian border. As one travels south along the coast from the 17th parallel, he finds that rice fields are soon replaced by the Annamite Mountains, which run down to the sea and create many bays and inlets. In the south, countless connected canals lace the rich rice paddies of the Mekong Delta. Tropical forests and dense mangrove swamps border the coast and, in many areas, the inland waterways. Offshore, some 50,000 junks and sampans fish and carry passengers and cargo.

Seagoing forces of the Vietnamese Navy were divided into a Sea Force and a Coastal Force. The Sea Force, whose mission was to conduct sea and inshore patrol operations and to counter infiltration and attack from the sea, consisted of 2 PC, 5 PCE, 12 PGM, 3 MSC, 5 LSIL, 3 LSSL, and several small logistic ships. These ships were based in Saigon, but when on patrol, they operated from bases located in the same places as were the coastal surveillance centers previously mentioned. Some 50 U. S. Navy advisers served as ship technical and staff advisers to the Sea Force.

The Coastal Force was made up of 28 groups, each with from 9 to 24 sail or motor junks, and more than 100 U. S. Navy advisers were to be assigned to it. Coastal groups were based at more than 20 locations, and were charged with preventing infiltration from the sea and with assisting customs, security, and fisheries patrols. However, they often had to remain close to their bases for fear that if they got far away, the Viet Cong would attack the bases. Their operations were further hampered by the low speed of their junks, lack of any capability for night detection, and problems attendant upon converting their organization from a paramilitary to a military force.

Thus, at the outset it was obvious to all con-

The USS Krishna *at her northeast monsoon anchorage in An Thoi Harbor, 4 February 1966. Alongside are the 82-foot* Point Banks *and two 50-foot Swift boats, the PCF 3 and PCF 4. During her long transpacific passage, the crew of the* Krishna *did a remarkable job of transforming her into a highly habitable and efficient command and repair ship. (Frank Uhlig, Jr.)*

APPROXIMATE CHARACTERISTICS AND CAPABILITIES OF MARKET TIME PATROL CRAFT

Type	Length	Speed	Full Load Draft	Full Load Displacement (tons)	Armament	Crew	Endurance at Moderate Speed
WPB (Coast Guard cutter)	82 feet	17 knots	6½ feet	70	1 81-mm. mortar 5 .50-caliber machine guns	2 officers 9 enlisted men	4 days
PCF (Navy craft procured from commercial sources and normally called "Swifts")	50 feet	22 knots	4½feet	22	1 81-mm. mortar 3 .50-caliber machine guns	1 officer 5 enlisted men	2 days

cerned that Vietnamese naval forces would require reinforcement if they were to prevent infiltration from the sea.

During Phase One, March–July 1965, the U. S. Navy maintained a total of nine warships—DD, DER, and MSO—along the coast, but that was not enough adequately to supplement Vietnamese naval forces. Also, there were many areas, particularly in the south, where the water was too shallow for them to work close inshore. Conferences held between the staffs of Chief Naval Advisory Group Vietnam, Commander Seventh Fleet, and Commander-in-Chief Pacific Fleet arrived at a preliminary definition of the requirements for small patrol craft to reinforce the larger units. Since there were no such craft in the U. S. Navy, the Coast Guard and commercial sources were investigated. The Coast Guard's 82-foot cutters, 95-foot cutters, and 40-foot utility boats were considered, as was a 50-foot, aluminum-hulled boat that was in commercial use in the Gulf of Mexico. Finally, it was decided that the 82-foot cutter and a 50-foot commercial boat, known as the "Swift," would fill the bill. Approximate characteristics and capabilities of both these craft are shown in the accompanying table.

Logistic, rather than operational, considerations made the 82-foot cutters preferable to the 95-footers. Maintenance and support would be simpler because they have only two engines, whereas the 95-footers have four; they require smaller personnel allowances; and, had the choice fallen on 95-footers, it would have been necessary to accept two models with differing machinery, in order to acquire the number of units needed. Furthermore, the 82-foot cutters provided a bonus in that they were air-conditioned.

The number of 82-footers to be deployed was arrived at on the basis of how many of them were available, rather than on how many were theoretically required. The Coast Guard reviewed its search-and-rescue requirements along the coasts of the United States and its possessions. After determining where minimal acceptable search-and-rescue coverage could be provided by placing other of its ships, shore stations, and aircraft on longer standby, and balancing this increased effort and smaller coverage against the requirement in Vietnam, the Coast Guard proposed deployment of 17 of the 82-foot patrol boats, which, on both coasts, numbered 44. When the proposal had been accepted by the Secretaries of the Treasury, the Navy, and Defense, President Johnson approved the deployment on 6 May 1965.

Coast Guard advice was against the use of its numerous 40-foot utility boats in the open seas off Vietnam, not only because they lack messing and berthing facilities, but also because, with their small size and open cockpit aft, they do not have the sea-keeping capabilities to operate continuously, particularly in unfavorable monsoons. Consequently, the Navy proceeded to procure 20 Swift boats to complement the cutters. The 82-foot cutters had full HF, VHF-FM, and UHF communication suits, reasonably shallow draft, moderate speed, relatively stable platforms for boarding and naval gunfire, facilities and crew sufficient to provide effective coordination with other forces, and they were the smallest ships that could mess and berth a crew on a continuing basis. Swift boats had five knots more speed than the cutters, and because they drew two feet less, could operate in shallower waters than the cutters. Their disadvantages were that they had less endurance and sea-keeping ability, less stable platforms, limited communications capability (a 100-watt single-sideband HF transceiver and a VHF-FM PRC-10), could spend less of their time under way, and their crews had to mess and berth ashore. Because the PRC-10 was almost useless, communications were, in practice, restricted to the SSB. This, in turn, lacked a pilothouse speaker and suffered from the noise of the engines. Some of those disadvantages have since been overcome.

Following the decision to deploy the 82-footers, planning proceeded along three parallel tracks. First, the Coast Guard selected the specific cutters and arranged for them to spend a short period in a shipyard while they awaited MSTS transportation to Subic Bay. Peacetime crews were augmented and sent to a four-week training course consisting of one week of counterinsurgency, one week of survival, evasion, resistance, and escape, one week of either 81-millimeter mortar and .50-caliber machine gun or firefighting and damage control, and a final week of operational readiness refresher training and processing. In their normal roles, the 82-footers are commanded by CPOs, but for their mission to Vietnam, they were to have officers and they, also, had to be selected. Thus was created Coast Guard Squadron One, and the author, then a commander, was given its command.

The cutters were fitted out forward with an over-and-under .50-caliber machine gun/81-mm. mortar combination in place of the 20-mm. gun formerly mounted on the forecastle, and aft with four .50-caliber machine guns mounted singly. Fortunately, the Coast Guard had developed the 81-mm. mortar and adapted it for use on small ships after the lack of a suitable weapon for this type of work was recognized during the Cuban crisis. An 81-mm. mortar can do three things that a 20-mm. gun cannot: illuminate, bombard shore targets, and inflict heavy damage on a large trawler or merchantman. Some of the qualities lost when the 20-mm. was removed were recovered when the .50-caliber was mounted atop the mortar. The only other appreciable change that was made before the cutters left the United States was that ready-service boxes and additional bunks and reefers were installed. Other modifications were to be made and equipment added at Subic Bay.

It was correctly anticipated that within six months of deployment the pipelines would be filled and supply for the cutters would be systematic. But, to ensure that there should be no gap, the Coast Guard called on all U. S. sources to come up with spare parts for all equipment sufficient to last the cutters for six months. The required parts were forthcoming and were either shipped with the cutters, sent via air freight or merchant ship to Subic Bay, or sent in the support ship.

Parallel to the Coast Guard preparations, the Navy selected the USS *Krishna* (ARL-38) as the support ship for the cutters. The *Krishna* had to cease her operations as a repair ship for PhibLant, make major alterations in her habitability, auxiliary power, and allocation of shop space, fit out, and sail for Southeast Asia, all in a period of three weeks—a monumental task for a rather small ship with a small crew.

The third parallel track involved determination of the most effective way of operating the cutters and Swift boats in Vietnam. Rear Admiral Norvell G. Ward, Chief Naval Advisory Group Vietnam, was selected to take over command of the surveillance forces from Commander Seventh Fleet. Admiral Ward's plan was to have the cutters form barriers along the border between South Vietnam and North Vietnam at the 17th parallel, and along the border between South Vietnam and Cambodia in the Gulf of Thailand. Also, so far as was practical, to have the patrol craft work back along the coasts toward the center of the country. The DDs were to phase out of Market Time, while the DERs and MSOs would patrol offshore along the entire coast. When the Swifts arrived, they would reinforce the craft already on scene.

During the first 10 days of June, representatives of CinCPacFlt, ComSeventhFlt, ComServPac, Commander Coastal Surveillance Force, ComSerGru Three, ComNavBase Subic, Chief Naval Advisory Group Vietnam, ComCortRon Five, and ComCoGardRon One met periodically to make detailed plans for the support of the cutters and general plans for future deployment of the 20 Swifts. They visited the two base support sites tentatively selected—

Da Nang Harbor in the north and, to the south, islands in the Gulf of Thailand—then spent three days in Saigon developing logistic requirements and evaluating in-country support capabilities. A two-day conference at Subic Bay, chaired by ComSerGru Three, concluded the planning.

Among the recommendations of the conference was the establishment of two organizations for the support of the cutters and Swifts—one in Da Nang Harbor and the other at An Thoi in the Gulf of Thailand. As far as possible, both were to be resupplied from U. S. depots in-country, and anything not available there was to be supplied by the Navy and Coast Guard, via Subic Bay and ComSerGru Three ships. During the early months of deployment, the in-country support was minimal: at Da Nang some support could be obtained from nearby Air Force and Marine units, but in the Gulf of Thailand there were no comparable sources. The DERs and MSOs were to be repaired at NavBase Subic and in their home ports, and, while on patrol, were to get underway replenishment from ComSerGru Three ships.

Support at Da Nang was to be provided by a repair barge, the YR-71, still in a state of preservation at Subic Bay, and this barge was to be supplemented either by a companion living barge or by a shore facility when the Swifts arrived some months later. In the Gulf of Thailand, the *Krishna* alone would provide support and, when the Swifts arrived, a companion barge and pontoon causeway would be added. Since permanent facilities would not be on scene by the time the cutters were deployed, LSTs were assigned as interim support ships. To reduce the underway replenishment responsibilities of ComSerGru Three, two AKLs were to be modified and assigned to carry provisions and general stores from Subic Bay and Saigon to the support facilities at Da Nang and An Thoi. These recommendations for logistic support were approved by ComSeventhFlt and CinCPacFlt, and planning proceeded accordingly.

PREPARING TO DEPLOY

By the time all these plans had been made in early June, an advance detail of Coast Guardsmen had arrived at Subic Bay. During the rest of that month, cutters and more men of Coast Guard Squadron One came in. The former, which displaced 70 tons, arrived as deck cargo on merchant ships sailing from various ports in the United States. This deployment was made under the control of MSTS, which proved most efficient. Immediately upon arrival, the cutters were put in availability status at the Naval Ship Repair Facility, where several minor modifications were made to lifelines, gun platforms, and living accommodations, and any necessary repairs were made. Sealed-beam deck lights were installed so that junks alongside could be illuminated, while the occupants of the junks could not observe activity on the cutter. Single-sideband radio transceivers were also installed, after considerable effort had been expended in tracking down the shipments of the equipment and in obtaining necessary installation materials. This experience pointed up a major lesson for the future: every effort should be made to make necessary modifications to the small craft before they are deployed to a forward area.

When the men arrived at Subic Bay, they were given more training for survival in the jungle environment of Southeast Asia. They stayed with the boats they had had at home; the officers, as mentioned earlier, were all new, and were assigned cutters.

While the cutters were being readied and the men were getting their extra training, the squadron staff, together with the boat crews, drew up lists of general stores, stock, and tools to be loaded in the LSTs which were to be the temporary mother ships. Squadron personnel

requisitioned a full three-month load-out, and sorted the material when it was received. At the same time, the six-month load-out of Coast Guard repair parts, which was arriving by air and merchant ship, was inventoried, and stored. Finally, Standard Operating Procedures were developed for the squadron, the cutters were given a four-day shakedown, and the temporary support ships, the *Snohomish County* (LST-1126) and *Floyd County* (LST-762), were loaded for deployment.

The events that took place in the 75 days between approval of the deployment and the squadron's arrival off Vietnam may seem routine, but those days drew more on the talents, time, and experience of the squadron staff and the supporting personnel from the Coast Guard, ServPac, and SerGru Three than did any other period of the deployment. It must be remembered that, in that brief space of 75 days, Coast Guard cutters on search-and-rescue duty along the coasts of the United States were transformed into an effective force operating off a hostile coast halfway around the world. No ships could have been deployed more expeditiously. As Commander Coast Guard Squadron One, I relied particularly on Lieutenant Commander Richard Knapp, U. S. Coast Guard, Squadron Chief Staff Officer, and Lieutenant Commander William Lehr, U. S. Coast Guard, Squadron Engineer Officer.

On 16 July 1965, while still at Subic Bay, Coast Guard Squadron One was split into two divisions. That day, the eight cutters that constituted Division 12, under the command of Lieutenant Commander Knapp, in company with the *Snohomish County*, set sail for Da Nang, where they were to provide the northern anchor of the Coastal Surveillance Force. Division 11, consisting of the other nine cutters, and under the command of the author, departed Subic Bay on 24 July in company with the *Floyd County*, to provide the southern anchor of the force.

After weeks of preparation, all hands were eager to get on with the job. The fitting-out and shakedown at Subic Bay had been satisfactory, but the divisions had not yet undergone the test of operating far from a base. The cutters had never operated at sea beyond their fuel endurance—three to four days—and planning for their use at home was based on a fire-engine concept: that is to say, they would have long periods of stand-by and limited periods at sea. Their seaworthiness had been proved, but what no one knew was for how long men in these small cutters could take a beating by the sea and still maintain an aggressive, effective patrol. For Division 11, the first test came on the 1,100-mile transit to An Thoi Harbor in the Gulf of Thailand.

While the cutters were at Subic Bay, a fueling-at-sea rig using the astern method had been developed and tested in calm water, but not in high seas. As was anticipated because of the time of year at which it was made, the passage to the Gulf of Thailand was marked by continuous head winds and seas—winds to 35 knots and seas to 15 feet. Fueling the small cutters under these conditions, with a jury rig and a crew with limited training, is tricky at best, as there is not much to hold on to when handling the fueling rig on deck. But, thanks to excellent seamanship aboard both the *Floyd County* and the cutters, the operation went very well, and provided a surprising lesson: that the most effective way of fueling was from a very short—approximately 75 feet—towline of 5-inch nylon. Running at slow speed to a taut hawser, the cutters rode well, for they were light and fine enough to be pulled through the seas with the stretch of the nylon line acting as a shock absorber. I must admit that the thought of nine small ships, out of fuel, drifting all over the South China Sea haunted all of us that day, and undoubtedly had something to do with the skillful handling of the situation. At the island of Con Son off the coast

of Vietnam the division again refueled, this time from the seaplane tender USS *Currituck* (AV-7), and was given operational briefings. We then proceeded around the hook of Vietnam and into the Gulf of Thailand. At about this time, Chief Naval Advisory Group Vietnam, Rear Admiral Ward, took over operational control of the Coastal Surveillance Force, which was redesignated Task Force 115.

THE GULF OF THAILAND

Although the Mekong River empties into the South China Sea, its silt deposits, which have been emerging for centuries from the shallow seabed, are the main constituents of the lands bordering the Gulf of Thailand. Just inland from the coast stretches the long U Minh Forest, or Forest of Darkness, which has been under Communist control since before the establishment of the Republic of Vietnam. A multitude of small interconnecting canals laces the coastline, and thick tropical vegetation is a common feature. Here and there, low peaks protrude from the flat lands. Off the coast, the Gulf is merely an extension of the land—a flat, submerged, alluvial plain. Near the border between Cambodia and Vietnam, it is pocked by numerous small, rather precipitous rocky islands, and, farther offshore, there is the larger island of Phu Quoc.

Phu Quoc is mainly a mixture of mountains and jungle, but it has some fertile plains and grasslands, which have a potential for considerable agricultural development. Prior to the present war, Phu Quoc had major cash crops of pepper and rubber, but the Viet Cong's domination of the countryside has choked off these resources. Fishing is the chief source of livilihood for the people who live on Phu Quoc and on the other offshore islands, as well as for many of those living along the mainland bordering the Gulf. The muddy waters of the Gulf yield a rich crop of the fish and shellfish natural to tropical waters.

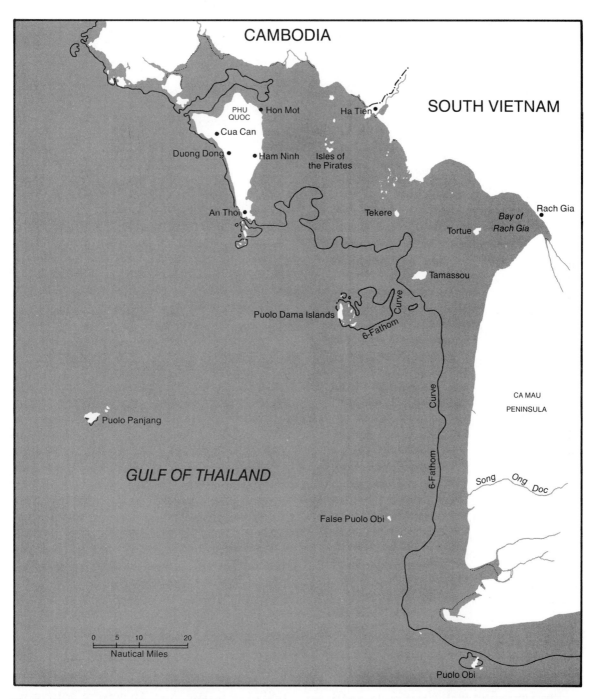

The Gulf of Thailand. The operating area ran from northeast of Puolo Obi to the Cambodian border.
The border extends from just north of Ha Tien, through the Isles of the Pirates, and then north and west
between Phu Quoc Island and the mainland.

From May to October, the southwest monsoons bring the rain, heavy winds, and squalls characteristic of a wet monsoon in Southeast Asia. From November through February, the northeast monsoon brings clear skies and winds that are also quite fresh. However, as the latter blow offshore, the seas close along the mainland are relatively calm. In February, the northeast monsoons begin to taper off into fairly calm weather, with afternoon squalls later in the period presaging the arrival of the southwest monsoons in May.

Contrary to expectation, the number of fishing vessels in the area did not vary markedly with changes of season. The several thousand fishing vessels in the area, which ranged from small sampans, perhaps as small as six feet in length, to 40-foot fishing junks, were never all at sea at one time. Except for a very few with sails, all junks in the Gulf were powered. Some sampans were powered, others rowed. This is not an area for the steel-hulled trawlers, and the only steel-hulled vessels ever seen inshore belonged to fish buyers from Singapore who, with government permission, occasionally operated off Song Ong Doc, on the Ca Mau Peninsula. Large, wooden cargo junks traveled continually between the major towns along the mainland and the offshore islands, carrying people, provisions, firewood, and fish.

Transportation in the delta area, whether inland on the canals or offshore in the Gulf itself, is primarily by boat. Trucks and buses run in convoy between the coastal towns of Ha Tien, Rach Gia, and Can Tho, an inland city on the Bassac River, although the road is often mined.

Most of the people living on the southern part of the mainland are of Vietnamese ethnic origin, but near the Cambodian border there is considerable ethnic mixing, as there is on the island of Phu Quoc. Cambodia has claimed this island as part of its territory, although it is generally recognized as being part of Vietnam. There has been some resettlement of refugees of both Vietnamese and Chinese extraction from North Vietnam to Phu Quoc and to the mainland south of Rach Gia.

Language difficulties and limited contact with Vietnamese, other than government civil and military officials, make it very difficult for U. S. operating forces to evaluate personally the feelings of the people. However, there appeared to be general satisfaction with the government, and acceptance of military control. Yet, on the island of Phu Quoc many of the families in the towns under government control had relatives with the Viet Cong in the hills. Though most of the people lived in flimsy tropical huts, they sent their children to primary school, and even the poorest appeared to have sufficient food. The main religious groups—Buddhist, Catholic, Cao Dai, and Hoa Hao—live together with no outward manifestations of dissent, but each apparently prefers to associate with its own.

Cambodian patrol craft were kept at sea in their waters north of Phu Quoc and between Phu Quoc and the mainland. There was almost no trade and no fraternization between Cambodian craft and Vietnamese craft, and the navies of the two countries worked to keep it that way.

Only seven enclaves along the 250-mile coastline of Phu Quoc and the mainland bordering the Gulf of Thailand were controlled by the government of Vietnam, although the government did control the many small outlying islands. The government enclaves were Duong Dong, An Thoi, Ham Ninh, and Cua Can on Phu Quoc and Ha Tien, Rach Gia, and Song Ong Doc on the mainland. Government forces, particularly those at Duong Dong, Rach Gia, and Ha Tien, were able to defend their perimeters and to deploy into the countryside pretty much at will. However, they were not strong enough to control the latter and were likely to encounter the Viet Cong. On the other hand, the Viet Cong did not have sufficient organized forces to provide continuous control over the entire hinterland or to take the large towns. Even if they took the small towns, they would not be able to hold them against the forces that the government could bring to bear. Nevertheless, they were free to roam the countryside and could, at their own choosing, concentrate a sizable force in any given area. Their military activity consisted of harassing the government enclaves, launching full attacks on the numerous outposts on the mainland, and ambushing government forces on patrol. A major activity of the Viet Cong was collecting taxes from peasants and fishermen to support further VC activity.

Vietnamese naval forces under Commander Fourth Coastal Zone consisted of three patrol craft—a mix of PGMs, PCEs, LSILs, LSSLs, or MSCs—deployed from Saigon, and seven coastal groups. Three of these groups were based on An Thoi, three at Rach Gia, and one at Puolo Obi. This last is a small, mountainous island near the tip of the Ca Mau Peninsula. Each coastal group consisted of approximately three motorized command junks and 17 smaller motorized junks. The junks ran from 37 to 54 feet in length, made speeds of between five and eight knots, carried small arms and, on the command junks, .30- or .50-caliber machine guns.

When Coast Guard Division 11 arrived in the Gulf on 30 July 1965, the only U. S. military personnel in the area were the U. S. Army advisers to the Vietnamese Army at Duong Dong, Ha Tien, and Rach Gia, and the U. S. Navy advisers to the Vietnamese Coastal Force at An Thoi, Rach Gia, and Puolo Obi. The only U. S. operational unit in the area was a DER or MSO on patrol offshore.

At this time, little was known about the extent of Viet Cong infiltration. Intelligence reports of varying reliability indicated that there was infiltration by junk and sampan, but the amount of ammunition and the number of arms and Viet Cong captured at sea in the preceding six months had been small. The DERs and MSOs patrolling offshore, generally outside the five-fathom curve, had had no success in contacting enemy forces since Market Time deployment began in March, but that might have been because, in many places, the water was too shallow for DERs and MSOs to enter.

Commander Coast Guard Squadron One/Division 11 was designated the permanent unit commander for surface patrol in the Gulf. Forces assigned included one DER or MSO from the Seventh Fleet on continuous patrol and the nine Coast Guard cutters of Division 11, a maximum number of which were to be kept on patrol. The main mission of the patrol unit was to conduct coastal surveillance and to prevent infiltration of hostile men and materials into the Republic of Vietnam. Secondary missions were to support movements of friendly troops, to conduct shore bombardment, and to participate in psychological operations.

Another hat given at this time to ComCoGardRon One was that of Commander Gulf of Thailand Support Group, and the *Floyd County* was assigned to provide support until the permanent repair ship, the *Krishna*, arrived. The mission of the Support Group was to maintain the cutters, provide logistic support, and insure their operational readiness. All of these missions were, of course, coordinated with the Vietnamese Navy. Liaison with that navy was maintained through the Senior Naval Adviser Fourth Coastal Zone and the joint U. S. Navy/Vietnamese Navy Coastal Surveillance Center located at the Vietnamese Naval Base at An Thoi.

OPERATIONAL PLANNING

Until the Coast Guard cutters arrived in the Gulf of Thailand, the commanding officer of

The first American loss during Market Time operations, the Swift boat PCF 4, *on a happier occasion. These little craft were fast and they drew little water, but even in a modest sea state they were hard riding, and the accommodations for their crews were sparse. For their size, they were heavily armed. (Jean C. Cote, PH1, U.S. Navy)*

the DER or MSO on patrol had served as U.S. naval patrol unit commander. This operational commander reported to a surface patrol group commander who, together with an air patrol commander, reported to the commander of Task Force 115. Under this system, the surface patrol unit commander in the Gulf of Thailand, or in any other area, would serve three weeks and, as his ship was relieved, would turn over command to his successor. This lack of continuity made it impossible for the commanders to obtain a good grasp of the tactical situation in time to use it. They could not familiarize themselves with the details of their area, especially when it was as complex as the Gulf of Thailand, with its many islands, shallow water, and varying traffic and fishing patterns. Furthermore, they had to work with several Vietnamese Army commands ashore, and continuing liaison with the Vietnamese Army and Navy commanders was particularly important.

Effective control in the Gulf of Thailand required an operation center manned by officers and men who were familiar with the physical peculiarities of the area, intelligence, communications, the operations and capabilities of friendly forces, and the habits of the local population. The local aspects of surveillance were so extensive that, from the very beginning, operational commanders had to supplement the Task Force commander's operations order with specific guidance on these subjects.

Designation of ComCoGardRon One/Division 11 as permanent unit commander for surface patrol in the Gulf marked the end of those procedures, and the Gulf of Thailand became an experimental area for the development of command and control procedures, and for the development of tactics and doctrine for the entire Market Time operation. Shipboard organization and routine were the responsibilities of the squadron and division commanders. The Coast Guard used the Standard Organization book for 82-footers, which had been amended to reflect conditions in Vietnam, and when the Swift boats came on the scene, Commander BoatRon One developed his own administrative and readiness procedures. Beginning in November 1965, the Gulf served also as an experimental area for the consolidation of operational and advisory commands, and for operation of the Swift boats, which spent months in the Gulf before being sent elsewhere. Immediately after its arrival in the Gulf, Division 11 devoted its time to familiarization, experimentation, accumulation of local knowledge, and development of operating tactics. Meanwhile, Division 12 at Da Nang was forming the barrier along the 17th parallel, according to Admiral Ward's plan, and providing naval gunfire support to Marines in the I Corps area. It was working under the old system of changing operational commanders every three weeks.

At first, control of Market Time forces in the Gulf was exercised through an operations center established on the USS *Floyd County*, a ship with marginal communications capability and lacking the space needed for the role she was playing. In mid-September, six weeks after operations began, she was relieved by the *Krishna*. While en route, the latter had constructed a very efficient operations center with provision for an evaluator and six voice radio operators, as well as necessary display boards. Patrol aircraft—P-2s from Tan Son Nhut airfield in Saigon, and P-5s from seadromes in the sheltered harbor at Con Son—were under the operational control of their own commanders, who reported directly to the task force commander in Saigon. However, they coordinated with the surface patrol unit commander through both the Market Time operations center in the *Krishna* and the joint Coastal Surveillance Center at the Vietnamese naval base at An Thoi.

A key factor in the planning that had been done in pre-deployment conferences was the assumption that the cutters could be maintained on patrol at sea two-thirds of the time. In the United States, Coast Guard cutters of this type spend no more than 25 per cent of their time at sea, although they spend long periods on standby. A broad search of Navy and Coast Guard records indicates that no ships less than 210 feet long operate continuously year in, year out, with more than 35 per cent of their time at sea. While deployed with the Seventh Fleet off Vietnam, major warships have spent upwards of 80 per cent of their time under way, thereby establishing remarkable records. However, they return to their home ports and undergo repairs at Subic Bay or at bases farther to the rear, which means that individual ships spend considerably less than 80 per cent of their time at sea on station off southeast Asia on a year-in, year-out basis. Yet the plan was for the cutters of Squadron One to spend two-thirds of their time on patrol for an indefinite period. In order to maintain this schedule and to allow periods of rest and recreation for the men, eleven complete crews were provided for the nine cutters. However, in practice, we found that the two spare crews had to be used not only as intended, but also to make up shortages in operating crews, to stand watch in the operations center, and to assist the maintenance force and other support details.

At sea, the cutters operated on the basis of a three-section watch: three men (OOD, helmsman, and radioman) on four-hour watch; a second section serving as boarding party; and a third off duty. Captain and cook, of course, stood no watches. An officer was on hand for all boarding, though not for all contacts. Most of the maintenance had to be done, and most rest obtained, between patrols. Navigation was mainly by radar, backed up by fathometer and seaman's eye. Charts for the northern Gulf were surprisingly accurate, but soundings were poor around the tip and east side of the Ca Mau Peninsula.

As already noted, in the early days of its operations, Division 11 got its food and fuel from the *Floyd County*. A 17-man Coast Guard maintenance detail attached to the division assisted the cutter crews with repairs and maintenance, and issued general stores and spare parts. In turn, the *Floyd County* and the maintenance detail got their support by underway or in-port replenishment from the ships of SerGru Three. When the *Krishna* arrived, her commanding officer, Lieutenant Commander Eugene E. Rueff, U. S. Navy, and Commander Coast Guard Squadron One agreed that the maintenance detail of Division 11 should be transferred to the *Krishna* and integrated into her crew. It then became the task of the *Krishna* to provide the cutters with all maintenance beyond the capability of their own crews, except for dry-docking. The ingenuity and foresight of Lieutenant Commander Rueff, who had been given only the most meager guidance the preceding May, were largely responsible for the fact that the *Krishna* had been provided not only with the modern operations center mentioned above, but with shops rearranged and altered to suit the ship's new mission, and with quarters for the three Coast Guard officers who comprised the Squadron One/Division 11 staff and for the spare boat crews. Because the division was understaffed, the four officers of the two spare boat crews had to add staff work to their normal duties until arrival of a trio of ensigns in November.

Phase Two—August 1965

At first, all patrol unit forces were controlled directly from the operations center afloat. The operating areas for the cutters were on the west side of Phu Quoc Island, the area between Phu Quoc and the mainland, and thence along the mainland to approximately 20 miles south of Rach Gia. The DER or MSO covered the southern part of the area. This allocation of forces was designed to create a barrier between Phu Quoc and the mainland along the Cambodian border, following Admiral Ward's plan, and to let the cutters operate in the shallow areas of the Gulf of Thailand, while the bigger ship operated in the deep water adjacent to ocean shipping lanes. At this time, patrols were made completely at random, and most attention was given to boarding and night operations. The DER or MSO assigned remained on station for three weeks, and then was replaced by another ship from the Seventh Fleet. The cutters patrolled for four days and then spent two days in transit and alongside for replenishment, repair, and rest.

A Vietnamese Navy liaison officer or petty officer was to be assigned to each cutter, but during the first year of operations, there were not enough available for every U. S. ship on patrol to have one. Those who were available were assigned to cutters patrolling in areas where there were a lot of junks. The areas where most junks were to be found varied, of course, according to season, fish, and weather, and therefore could be predicted with reasonable accuracy.

Not only did the liaison officers assist in inspections and boardings, but they explained to the local population the purpose of our operations. An inspection was a check of papers and a look into a junk or open sampan from the deck of a patrol boat. A boarding meant searching the boat: a sailor would crawl into the after cabin, if there was one, and drop down into the fish holds to see what was there.

Before Division 11 arrived, there had been almost no night boarding inshore, and our boarding program created some immediate problems. For instance, although 999 out of every 1,000, or perhaps 9,999 out of every 10,000, junks boarded contained innocent fishermen, the cutters had to be alert and ready for instantaneous action every time they approached a junk. A searchlight shining unexpectedly on a junk fishing at night, followed by a small warship with armed roundeyes coming alongside, terrified some of the poor fishermen, and that reaction was, naturally, disconcerting to the American sailor. With liaison officer assistance, the population came to realize that none but American warships would be conducting operations in the middle of the night, and local fishermen accepted, by and large, that it was necessary for us to do so. Our men learned that by giving cigarettes, candy, or a small, inexpensive article—along with a smile and some words of pidgin Vietnamese—to the crew of a junk, which often consisted of a family, they could create a friendly atmosphere. Also, they became expert at giving first aid and other minor medical attention to the local population. The doctor in the *Krishna* performed yeoman service in handling medical cases on the islands in the Gulf, particularly on Phu Quoc. Civil agencies—Joint U. S. Public Affairs Office and AID—helped us to gain the confidence of the people, as did the Vietnamese government. The importance of psychological operations cannot be overemphasized, for security around the Gulf of Thailand depends ultimately—as does that of the rest of Vietnam—on whether the Vietnamese people reject or accept their government.

I must mention a hazard that existed in the give-away program. When it started, it was appreciated by the Vietnamese and achieved its purpose. However, some boats made a point of giving something to every junk that was boarded, and there were fishermen who came

to expect, and almost to demand, such treatment. To counter this attitude, we enforced a standard procedure whereby gifts were distributed only when boarding caused inconvenience or hardship in the craft involved. This system proved to be a reasonable compromise between all or nothing at all. As our organization and support caught up with our operating forces, we were provided with small, psychological operations packages for distribution to the junks. This innovation was not only useful, but it took the financial burden off our men.

ANCHORAGE SELECTION

There were few anchorages suitable for the support ships. None of the harbors along the mainland coast of the Gulf were deep enough to take the support ships which, fully laden, drew about 14 feet, and the strong winds of both the southwest and northeast monsoon made it imperative to anchor in a lee. In the early weeks of deployment, we tested the harbor in the Puolo Dama Islands, about 20 miles south of An Thoi, and found it to be the best. It is relatively secure from strong winds and seas, holding ground is good, and, to the best of our knowledge, there were no Viet Cong in the fishing villages of the island group. However, being some 20 miles away from the Vietnamese naval base, from the U. S. Navy advisers, and from the joint Coastal Surveillance Center at An Thoi was very inconvenient. Every day, long, classified messages had to be carried by hand from the *Krishna* to the Coastal Surveillance Center. But, even more unacceptable was the lack of face-to-face liaison with U. S. Navy advisers and with the Vietnamese Navy area commander.

There were excellent lee anchorages close inshore on both the east and west coasts of Phu Quoc Island, but they were unacceptable because the Viet Cong controlled all of the adjacent coast, with the exception of An Thoi proper. An Thoi Harbor is fairly well protected from the northeast monsoons (which, around there, are almost easterly), but not from the south-west monsoons. It has a sandy bottom and the holding ground is fair to good. But, since the perimeter controlled by government forces extended only about 1,000 yards inland, any anchorage in the harbor proper would be within mortar range of the Viet Cong. This last point gave considerable concern, for I had not heard of any major U. S. Navy support ship being continuously at an anchorage within the range of enemy guns. This concern diminished when experiments with a darkened ship showed that the likelihood of a mortar hit at night was almost nil. During the daytime, the *Krishna*, with her anchor ready to slip, maintained standby status near extreme 81-mm. mortar range, and in case of need, mortar fire could be returned from the cutters and from the base. These factors lessened the risk, and An Thoi Harbor was reluctantly accepted as the most practical alternative to the Puolo Dama Islands. As further protection, an LCM patrolled around the *Krishna* at night to prevent local craft or swimmers from approaching her. The *Krishna* had to shift from one anchorage to another, according to the seasons. When the southwest monsoons were blowing, she was anchored close in the lee of the small islands to the south of An Thoi, while, when the northeast monsoons were blowing, she was anchored as close to An Thoi as possible.

Supporting the cutters from a repair ship in a relatively open roadstead presented a two-fold problem: it was easy for the cutters to get damaged when they were nested alongside the ship in heavy seas, and the crew suffered considerable loss of rest. On deployment, large, pneumatic fenders had been ordered to prevent hull damage to cutters while moored alongside, but it was some months before they caught up with us. In the meantime, we used all types of makeshift camels and fenders, none of which worked satisfactorily. Even

when we had the pneumatic fenders, it was occasionally necessary for the cutters to break off and anchor close in the lee of one of the small islands south of An Thoi to wait for a change in the weather.

BOARDING AND INSPECTING

Our operational and support people learned a lot during the first two months of deployment. The commanding officers of the cutters were encouraged to use their own initiative in development of patrol procedures and boarding techniques. Extensive briefings and debriefings were held after each patrol. Data concerning the reliability of charts, trade routes, fishing areas, types of fishing craft encountered, location of friendly forces, Viet Cong strongholds, tactics of Vietnamese Navy ships, means of communication with army and civil authority—all were documented and analyzed. For example, it became apparent that, other things being equal, patrols in square areas were more effective than patrols in long, narrow areas of the same size. One reason for this was that, as a rule, a patrol plane could vector a cutter to a suspect junk more rapidly in the square areas. Communications between the aircraft and the cutters were generally good, but the Swifts, limited as they were to SSB, had a more difficult time, especially as the aircraft crews preferred to use UHF/VHF; but in time, solutions began to appear. Communications between boats were acceptable. We had limited communication between the U. S. boats and our advisers in the Vietnamese junks, who might have a PRC-10 or -25, but these efforts had to be worked at.

Original calculations as to the number and type of forces required to provide a reasonable coastal surveillance effort were based on rough, statistical estimates of the probability of detecting infiltrators. Naturally, those estimates did not take into account all the factors just discussed. Therefore, we recommended to

First contact with the enemy. After failing to evade the Point Marone, *this junk attacked the cutter with gunfire and grenades, but lost the contest to the* Point Marone's *machine guns. She sank in shallow water and was raised the next day. The black dots are .50-caliber bullet holes.*

the task force commander that patrol areas within the Gulf be revised on the basis of the information that we had acquired in the first two months of operation. Our recommendations, which were approved, took into account the need for a tight patrol of the Cambodian border and the mainland coast because, whether infiltrators came from the coast or from offshore, they had to pass through the coastal area. The new plan called for cutters to patrol north of Phu Quoc and along the southern part of the Ca Mau Peninsula, inshore of the DERs and MSOs, thereby filling a large gap in our earlier surveillance. The new plan contained enough flexibility to allow the Swifts, when they arrived, to be integrated into the revised areas, and to permit redeployment of cutters if and when a random patrol or a concentrated one were needed elsewhere.

Boarding procedures also were analyzed in the light of our experience, but no drastic revisions were made. We tried different ways of bringing the junks and sampans alongside in varying seas, and made comparisons between bringing junks alongside and boarding from the Boston Whalers that served as the cutters' small boats. Various factors, such as risk from the enemy, risk of accident in different weather conditions, and speed of boarding were evaluated. The general conclusion of the skippers was that bringing junks and sampans alongside was preferable to using a small boat.

However, the Whalers were often used in special circumstances, such as when there were concentrations of junks and sampans.

Not many of the mechanical aids that were tested during the first few months of operation were found useful. A piece of quarter-inch round stock, six feet long and with a handle, was used as a probe to help determine whether arms and ammunition were hidden among the junks' fishnets and in holds full of ice and fish. A small net on a 10-foot pole was used to pass junk registration and personal ID cards from junk to patrol boat without risk of loss; occasionally, a rope was passed beneath junks to check for contraband hung from hulls, and canted mirrors on a handle were used as an aid in searching cramped areas in holds.

Mine detectors and other devices for detecting metal were tried, and some of them promise limited success with further refinement. The probe, the net, and the rope were continued in use, but nothing that was developed could take the place of a thorough, manual search. Most of the local craft in the Gulf of Thailand are 40 feet long or less, and some of the men who board them have to climb down into cramped holds, and spend between 10 and 30 minutes probing around among smelly fish, while others, including the liaison officer, check the identification papers of the crew. Sample identification papers helped to detect incorrect papers; however, even though the local authorities provided us with long lists of known or suspected Viet Cong, we are not aware of any instance where inspection of papers led to the capture of any Viet Cong during the entire first year of operations in the Gulf. In any event, a government supporter today may be a Viet Cong tomorrow, and in a guerrilla type of operation the use of a rather loose ID card system is of questionable value.

Coordination was of the utmost importance, not only to ensure effective operations, but also to ensure that U. S. naval forces did not, by mistake, attack friendly forces and that friendly forces in turn did not attack us. In the early months, this coordination was very difficult to achieve, and it always will demand the close attention of the operational commander. We had a squadron staff officer who spent much of his time visiting the several Vietnamese Army and Navy commands bordering the Gulf and associated U. S. advisory personnel in order to ensure coordination and proper identification of allied units. Different frequencies, codes, and languages all added to the difficulty of the task, but the need for success made continued effort imperative. One aspect of the problem is the establishment of recognition signals between U. S. and Vietnamese warships and junks: codes for that purpose were developed and tested, and every effort was made to train all units to use them properly.

One way to simplify surveillance patrols is to designate prohibited zones, from which all junks and sampans are barred. This was done by the Vietnamese authorities, and U. S. forces helped to enforce the prohibition. However, this tool did not prove universally effective because, in many cases, the best fishing grounds were in the prohibited areas. Also, fishermen who lived inshore of the prohibited zones could not, in theory, pass through them to get to sea. Junks had no navigational means of measuring accurately their distance off the coast, and their estimates usually favored the good fishing. There were cases where strict enforcement of the prohibited zones appeared to threaten the source of livelihood of the fishermen, which made the device unpopular with the local population—and often with the Vietnamese Navy, too. The regulation of zones was an internal responsibility of the Vietnamese government, but U. S. forces encouraged establishment of reasonable zones with strict enforcement by the Vietnamese. American assistance was tailored to the degree of effort shown by the Vietnamese authorities in enforcement.

Motivation is the last factor in patrol and boarding procedures that must be discussed, and it is at least as important as any of the others. Unfortunately, the primary yardstick by which higher authority could evaluate the effectiveness of patrols was the number of boardings, inspections, and sightings made. That yardstick is suspect. For example, it would be quite possible at any time to double those statistics by boarding hundreds of junks that do not go any farther than two or three miles from their home ports. True, such a procedure would greatly increase the number of junks boarded, but it would also greatly decrease the surveillance of the entire patrol area. Similarly, cursory searches would take less time and, thus, would allow more of them to be made and to appear in statistics. This situation is mentioned only to emphasize that the area patrol unit commander is the person best able to measure the effectiveness of his patrol units. If the areas to be patrolled are chosen on a sound basis; if the ships' skippers see to it that boarding is done aggressively, that searching is thorough, and they emphasize night operations; if they are careful not to let their operations fall into a pattern; if they have inquisitive minds and investigate everything out of the ordinary; if they are hungry to catch the Viet Cong, yet recognize the importance of maintaining friendly relations with the local population; then, it is far more likely that infiltration will be detected than it is if we merely have impressive statistics.

By repeated test and observation, we discovered that at some point between four and six days of patrol in rough waters, or of continuous boarding operations in smooth waters—or of some mix thereof—crews become fatigued and lose much of their efficiency.

When a cutter returns to the support ship, she spends an average of a day and a half alongside. During that time, her crew must replenish provisions and fuel, carry out routine maintenance, order parts, get haircuts, buy small stores and personal items, collect mail, be debriefed, be briefed again before going out, and on and on and on. The net result of that routine was that, in one turnaround, the men could count on having no more than three or four hours for relaxation. Patrols were scheduled to last four days, but they were often lengthened to six, to cover for cutters that were undergoing scheduled 6,000-hour overhaul alongside the *Krishna* or were out of the area for annual dry-docking. The fuel endurance of the cutters is three or four days, so a six-day patrol meant either a rendezvous with the nearest DER or MSO, or else a brief visit to the *Krishna*, for fuel. Dry-docking, which was needed only once a year, was done either at Saigon or in Thailand. All boats had been docked before leaving the United States. A floating dry dock of suitable size now exists at Camranh Bay, and there is another at Da Nang, but these were not used by Division 11.

After observing our men for some time, I concluded that in order to maintain the high motivation and the effective patrols it produced, it was essential for them to spend one week away from the division every three months. It was not easy to sell this concept. Comparisons were made with the staff in Saigon who were working seven days a week, with the Marines and soldiers in the foxholes, and with the men in the ships of the Seventh Fleet. I certainly know that life in a foxhole has its hardships, but I know also that operations in these small patrol craft are more exhausting physically and mentally than is sea service in large ships. Further, the large ships do, from time to time, get back into liberty ports, whether the time spent there is called R&R or not. Regardless of the validity of these comparisons, I am convinced that the man who gets time away from his patrol craft every three months will be a much more effective combatant sailor than one who puts in a full 12 months without any liberty. Rear Admiral Ward supported my contention, and as a result Division 11 and, later, the crews of the Swift boats, could count on an average of three periods of from five to seven days in Saigon, Vung Tau, or Bangkok during each one-year tour.

While on the subject of our people, I would like to emphasize the tremendous asset Division 11 had in its officers and men. Each commanding officer had had approximately two years' experience as the CO of a similar small cutter. The boatswain's mates and enginemen on the cutters had sailed in the same cutters back in the States. Time and again, when things got tough, I found that I could count on the judgment, skill, and devotion to duty of these professionals. When the ships operate Stateside they carry a crew of eight, headed by a chief boatswain's mate as officer-in-charge. In the extended operations off Vietnam, the allowance was one lieutenant (junior grade), one ensign, one BMC, one ENC, one BM1, one EN2, one ET3, one CS2, one GM2, one FN, and one SN.

If the men were well suited to the task at hand, so were the cutters. Less than five years old, they belonged to the third generation of their type to be designed since World War II, and well designed they were. Pilothouse control, an alarm system, a console in the pilothouse containing all communications and navigational systems, and an adjustable seat with seat belt permitted one-man operation of a cutter. The living quarters were compact and air-conditioned.

THE VALUE OF AIRCRAFT AND LARGER SHIPS

But there is no type of unit, regardless of its strong points, that can alone prevent infiltra-

tion. There are two ways in which patrol aircraft can assist greatly. On offshore patrols they can spot a single trawler approaching or steaming parallel to the coast. Similarly, they can provide information to plot all merchant ships, and they can spot merchant ships hovering or offloading into smaller craft. Their usefulness inshore in the Gulf of Thailand is less apparent. Aircraft can report concentrations of junks to the area operational commander, but that information is of very limited significance, since there are such concentrations all over the operating area, and it is almost impossible for patrol aircraft to glean any meaningful operational information from them. They can, however, observe unusual incidents and relay them to the operational commander. Whenever they did so, their reports were tracked down religiously, but during the entire first year's operation, none led to the detection of infiltration. Patrol aircraft are valuable, but they are not capable of identifying positively an infiltration attempt.

I remember one instance where aircraft reported that a large junk was anchored offshore and three sampans were relaying loads of something from her to the beach. When this information was passed to the operations center, cutters were immediately diverted to investigate. They found that the junk had been to one of the outer islands where her crew had cut fire wood, brought it back to the coast, and was ferrying it ashore. From the aircraft and to the operations center watch, this innocent operation had all the earmarks of an attempt at infiltration.

In an area such as the Gulf of Thailand, DERs and MSOs also have both strong points and limitations. Shallow waters in much of the Gulf make it impossible for them to get inshore where most of the junk traffic is, and to use them, instead of small cutters, for boarding operations offshore is an expensive way of doing things. However, they do perform a task that cannot be duplicated rapidly by small patrol craft in rough seas: interception of merchant ships or trawlers offshore that have been discovered by aircraft. Small patrol craft do not have the speed needed to intercept ships in heavy weather, nor, if a suspect contact happens to be encountered near the end of a patrol, do they have the endurance to stick with it for a period of days. Also, DERs and MSOs can serve usefully as temporary replenishment ships for patrol craft, and their COs can serve as operational commanders for task elements that are remote from the operation center of the patrol unit commander. More will be said on this subject when the Phase Three operations are discussed.

To the best of my knowledge, closing junks and trawlers to board and search is the only way infiltrators have been positively identified in Market Time operations. It must, however, be recognized that there are limitations on what boarding and searching can do. It is almost impossible to search thoroughly a large junk that is heavy-laden—usually overladen—with cargo. It is impossible to transfer the cargo to a small cutter or Swift boat, and it is impractical to offload it onto a DER or MSO. This means that shoreside port security must ensure that cargoes moving through the government-held villages and towns do not include contraband. In the Gulf of Thailand, all we could do to survey large cargo junks at sea was to check their manifests for form and substance, spot-check their cargoes, and ensure that they were on the trade route between the ports listed on the manifests. We relied completely upon the Vietnamese authorities for port security ashore.

Another thing that boarding and searching cannot do is survey small sampans within small-arms range of the beach. In guerrilla operations it cannot be assumed that a person in a sampan close to the beach is an enemy, but he might be. A sampan can usually see and hear a patrol craft at a considerable distance, and if she is only a hundred yards from the beach, can

easily be in to the beach within a minute or so. Often, it is not possible to tell from a patrol craft three or four miles away whether such action is evasive or is in the normal course of work. If the slope of the bottom is very gradual, an oceangoing patrol craft may never be able to get close enough to the beach to board the sampan and find out. Sampans can also be used to draw patrol craft close inshore where they can be severely damaged by recoilless rifle fire. That risk must be weighed against the chances that a specific sampan is engaged in infiltration before a skipper sends one of his small boats to within point-blank, small-arms range of the beach.

For guidance in cases such as that, the United States has developed rules of engagement that make every effort to protect innocent Vietnamese from being victimized by combat operations, yet permit effective operations against the enemy. These rules require young commanding officers to exercise more judgment than is ordinarily required by officers of the same rank in large ships. Certainly limited war in general requires more command judgment than does conventional war, when identification of the enemy is no problem. The rules, combined with on-the-spot guidance from the patrol unit commander, have been effective in combat operations and in safeguarding noncombatant Vietnamese.

FLASHES OF ACTION

Surveillance patrol consists mainly of long, unrewarding days and nights under way, either taking a beating from the sea, or boarding junk after junk, or both; but there are moments of action which demonstrate the requirement for the patrol and its effectiveness. I will describe three such moments that occurred during Phase Two and that demonstrate both the range and the scope of these operations.

On 19 September 1965, when Division 11

had been deployed in the Gulf of Thailand for some six weeks and we still had no tangible evidence of infiltration, the Coast Guard cutter *Point Marone* was patrolling close inshore near the Cambodian border. Around midnight, her commanding officer, Lieutenant David Markey, observed a very weak radar pip two miles astern, and maneuvered to close the contact. The source of the radar pip turned out to be a 35-foot junk, whose typical after cabin and mast had been removed, apparently to avoid radar detection. At first, the junk attempted to evade and then, as the *Point Marone* closed, her Viet Cong crew opened up with small arms and hand grenades at point-blank range, and dropped what appeared to be mines into the water. The *Point Marone* maneuvered, returned fire with her .50-caliber machine guns and silenced the junk, leaving her dead in the water. While the engagement was going on, two other patrol craft were diverted to the scene. One of them provided illumination, and the other took the enemy in tow, but the junk slowly settled and sank. A patrol aircraft was vectored in to assist in searching for survivors and to spot other craft in the area for further investigation by surface ships.

The next day, the junk was raised by divers from the *Krishna*, towed to that ship, and lifted clear of the water. It was determined that 12 Viet Cong had been on board the junk, 11 of whom were killed; the twelfth was wounded, but he escaped to the beach at Ha Tien, where he was captured later by Vietnamese Regional Forces. The junk contained several rifles, a few hundred rounds of ammunition of Communist Chinese manufacture, a considerable sum of money, and miscellaneous documents and gear. Information obtained indicated that a sizable Viet Cong detachment was operating out of a small river on the northeast coast of Phu Quoc Island—one of the few rocky coasts in the Gulf. Desiring to capitalize on this information, the U. S. Army's Special Forces de-

tachment on Phu Quoc requested naval support to make a small amphibious raid into the area immediately, before word of the sinking of the junk and the capture of one of her crew got back to the Viet Cong on Phu Quoc. In order to preserve the element of surprise, it was reluctantly decided to conduct the raid without advance offshore survey.

Two Coast Guard cutters embarked Vietnamese Special Forces officers, their U. S. advisers, and 30 strikers, together with their arms, ammunition, and assault rafts. A practice landing was made, and then the assault forces, together with a third cutter to supply more gunfire support, proceeded to the area and, just before dawn, off-loaded the troops into the rafts. The platoon paddled ashore, worked south, and started to wade across the small river that was serving the Viet Cong. While it was so exposed, the Viet Cong struck, and a fire fight ensued. When the platoon withdrew to the beach, it came under sniper fire from Hon Mot, a small island offshore. With their .50-caliber machine guns, the Coast Guard cutters suppressed the sniper fire and provided flanking fire on either side of the platoon on the beach, then they used their fire to protect the soldiers as they returned to where the rafts had been left, two miles up the beach. Finally, the cutters saturated the shore line with 81-mm. mortar fire while the assault rafts withdrew.

This raid had no impressive effects, but it was the first of a series of joint U. S.-Vietnamese amphibious operations that increased both in size and effectiveness as experience was gained. In operations of this nature, command relationships are likely to be very different from those worked out by the U. S. Navy and Marine Corps. Even so, as long as it is recognized that the naval commander never has any real control over forces ashore, small, but effective, operations can be conducted.

On 21 October, when a Regional Force pla-

A shell is dropped down the barrel of a Swift boat's 81-mm mortar while the boat provides gunfire support to troops. Unlike similar Army and Marine Corps weapons, naval mortars are not fired as soon as the shell strikes a firing pin at the bottom of the barrel. The gunner behind the weapon decides when he will shoot, and he can fire his weapon at zero degrees of elevation. (Robert D. Corbin, PH1, U.S. Navy)

toon at an outpost near Ha Tien came under night attack by the Viet Cong, we had an example of naval gunfire giving spontaneous support to forces ashore. The outpost sent requests for help to the Vietnamese Special Forces detachment in Ha Tien, who relayed the pleas to their U. S. Special Forces advisers, and they, in turn, relayed to the Coast Guard cutter *Point Clear*, which proceeded to the scene. The *Point Clear* supported the outpost with 81-mm. mortar illumination and .50-caliber machine-gun fire. Then, when the outpost began to run out of ammunition, it requested high-explosive mortar fire, as the only means of saving it from being overrun. This the *Point Clear* provided, driving off the Viet Cong and saving the outpost. With the limited fire-control capability that the cutters have, this type of night firing requires extreme care and considerable skill, and was used only in a desperate situation. On this occasion, the *Point Clear* used tracer ammunition tracks and exploding hand grenades as a point of aim.

Other events during this period included

planned naval gunfire support missions using
the 81-mm. mortar, with spotting provided by
light aircraft; capturing, without meeting resistance, a Viet Cong junk headed for Cambodia; the sinking of a Viet Cong junk about ten
miles south of Ha Tien by the *Point Glover* with
recovery of cargo, guns, and ammunition;
search for a downed Air Force F-100 (aircraft
not found, but pilot rescued by a helicopter);
destruction of a VC junk that evaded ashore,
halfway up the east coast of Phu Quoc (no cargo recovered—perhaps there was none); destruction of certain buildings from which the
Viet Cong were shooting; occasional gunfire
support for junks of Vietnamese Navy coastal
groups which came under fire from the beach,
either on the east coast of Phu Quoc or on the
mainland; and gunfire support in the successful defense of the village of Cua Can when it
was under attack by the Viet Cong.

Phase Three—November 1965

In the fall of 1965, representatives from
OpNav, PacFlt, and Naval Advisory Group met
in Saigon to reevaluate overall requirements
for Market Time operations. At this time, it
was determined that coverage of the entire
coast would require 11 DERs or MSOs on station, enough aircraft to provide two continuously on patrol, plus 26 Coast Guard cutters and some 80 Swifts in-country. Seventeen
of the former were, of course, already on scene,
and the nine additional cutters, which would
form Division 13, would be deployed north and
south from the Mekong Delta. Swifts would be
based and supported along the coast, except
for those in the Gulf of Thailand, which would
be supported afloat. The addition of Swifts in
the Gulf of Thailand and in the Da Nang areas
would release some of the cutters of Division
11 and Division 12 for extended operations
north and south along the coasts to meet the
patrols of the new Division 13, which would
work the central coast of the country. When it

arrived, Division 13 settled at Cat Lo, not far
from Vung Tau. Another ARL, the *Askari* (ARL-
30), was being put into commission to provide
more Market Time support, and LSTs and helicopters were to be used for combined inshore
and river operations in the Mekong Delta.

In November 1965, shortly before it was decided to provide the additional division of
Coast Guard cutters, Chief Naval Advisory
Group requested the Coast Guard to assign
Commander Coast Guard Squadron One/Divi-
sion 11 to his staff for additional duty as Senior
Naval Adviser Fourth Coastal Zone. This step
was taken to consolidate in one person command of both U. S. naval operational and
advisory efforts, and to strengthen coordination between Vietnamese and U. S. naval
forces by making the U. S. and Vietnamese
naval commanders true counterparts. Needless to say, it brought the U. S. operational
commander many new concerns, including the
operational readiness and effectiveness of the
Vietnamese Navy, supply of both the U. S.
advisers and the Vietnamese forces, shoreside
communications, Vietnamese naval planning,
the MAP program, the U. S. advisory compound at Vietnamese Naval Base An Thoi, relations between the Vietnamese Navy and all
official and public segments of the population,
and extensive military construction programs
at An Thoi and Rach Gia. At An Thoi, the major
construction job was a 3,500-foot airstrip; at
Rach Gia, it was a repair base for the Vietnamese Navy's junks. The addition of Division
13 to the squadron made it impractical to
administer the entire Coast Guard squadron
from the remoteness of An Thoi, and it was
decided to move squadron administration to
Saigon. It was also decided to upgrade the
squadron commander billet to captain. The
author stayed in the Gulf of Thailand and retained Coast Guard Division 11 and the advisory, operational, and support commands.

Two Swifts—the first of 17 planned for the

Gulf—arrived in An Thoi on 31 October 1965. It will be remembered that a pontoon causeway and an APL were to augment the support facilities of the *Krishna* when the Swifts arrived. The former, having arrived by the end of October and been set up perpendicular to the beach, was used as a mooring for the Swifts. However, because of high-priority commitments for APLs elsewhere, the one that should have arrived in the Gulf in November to provide messing and berthing facilities for the Swift crews did not arrive until the following June. Only the crews of the first two Swifts and ComPCFDiv 101 and his staff could be berthed in the *Krishna*, so, with the approval of the commander of the Vietnamese naval base, it was decided to establish a tent city ashore in the Advisory Compound of the naval base. Major components for the project were procured and shipped by the Naval Advisory Group staff and, thanks to the considerable ingenuity and technical know-how demonstrated by the people in the *Krishna*, and to the cooperation of all U. S. units in the area, the tent city went into commission 40 days later—just before the next six Swifts arrived in early December.

Since most of the maintenance team for the Swift division was transferred to the *Krishna*, she provided the boats with maintenance and fuel. Swift crews berthed and messed in tents ashore. Many and varied were the problems involved in this operation: a lot of people were cramped in a small area ashore; Swift operating crews, sweltering in tents, found it difficult to get enough rest for the next night's operations; it was difficult to dispose of sewage in a sanitary manner; and the in-country supply system was only beginning to function. To complicate matters further, in December a big camp for RMK-BRJ workmen, who were to rebuild most of the compound, construct a Vietnamese junk repair base, and build the airstrip, was also placed in the Advisory Compound. My five subordinate commanders—

Lieutenant Commander Eugene Rueff, U. S. Navy, CO *Krishna*; Lieutenant Commander Warren Helgerson, U. S. Navy, Assistant Fourth Coastal Zone Adviser An Thoi; Lieutenant Commander Bruce Little, U. S. Coast Guard, Division 11 Chief Staff Officer; Lieutenant Commander James Burpo, U. S. Navy, Assistant Fourth Coastal Zone Adviser Rach Gia; and Lieutenant John Broglio, U. S. Navy, Commander PCF Division 101; plus Mr. Smith, RMK's Project Manager—can take credit for the fact that we managed to solve our biggest problems, and went on to find some more.

THE VIETNAMESE JUNKS

Two attempts to transport Viet Cong and their weapons along the coast and through Cambodian waters had been discovered and the enemy destroyed but, during our first three months of operation, we had uncovered no major attempts at infiltration. Unarmed junks with suspects on board had been captured, or had been destroyed after evading to the beach. Surveillance north of Phu Quoc and along the southern part of the Ca Mau Peninsula was not sufficient to ensure a reasonable probability that infiltration would be detected, and this, obviously, was the reason for deploying the Swifts of PCF Division 101. One thing that had been clearly established, however, was that there was little, if any, movement of junks between Cambodian and South Vietnamese waters. During the entire first year of operations, we recorded no more than ten such instances.

Coordination was difficult because the Vietnamese did not have enough naval officers to man their coastal groups and bases, and to provide liaison officers for U. S. units. Vietnamese supply problems, rapid officer turnover, and the low level of training of the enlisted men in the naval junks, who were integrated into the Navy from what had been, until mid-1965, a paramilitary force, further complicated the problem. On the U. S. side, one-year tours and the shunting of talent to fill new needs in an expanding operation made it difficult for the United States to keep its 40 officer and enlisted advisory billets filled and stabilized—to say nothing of the problem of keeping the people assigned to advisory tasks working on them, rather than on the myriad details connected with operating the crowded Advisory Compound ashore. Each one of the seven Vietnamese coastal groups based at Rach Gia, An Thoi, and Puolo Obi was authorized two U. S. officer and two enlisted advisers. Other officers and enlisted men were assigned to man the U. S. part of the joint Coastal Surveillance Center at An Thoi, and assistant coastal zone advisers were assigned to supervise activities at An Thoi and Rach Gia.

During the early stages of development, Coast Guard cutters had been successful in encouraging the Vietnamese Navy junks to participate in night operations. The cutters would patrol as close to the coast as the depth of the water permitted and, when appropriate, would vector the junks, which were proceeding inside of them, to contacts inshore. When used in a random manner, this procedure proved satisfactory, and it gave some of the coastal groups the confidence to conduct nighttime inshore patrols on their own. The main goal of the advisory effort was to increase the percentage of time that junks operated effectively on patrol, and it was anticipated that consolidation of U. S. commands would improve coordination and assist in that objective.

TESTING THE SWIFTS

Although the Swift crews had been trained at Coronado, and their boats had been shaken down at Subic Bay, the first two to arrive in the Gulf were given one week of operational training and area indoctrination before being placed on patrol. As the boats had never been used in any naval operations, the first few months included considerable testing of their capabilities, through coordinated action of ComPCFDiv 101, ComBoatRon One (Commander Arthur Ismay, U. S. Navy, with headquarters in Saigon), and the operational commander in the Gulf of Thailand. Testing showed that they were ideally suited to steaming continuously for up to 24 hours in calm and moderate seas. The boats were also tested on 36-hour patrols: they would operate for 12 hours, anchor or lie to in the lee of an island for 12 hours, patrol again for 12 hours, and then return to base. This testing was done because many of the patrol areas most suitable for Swift operations were along the mainland coast, some 60 miles away from the base, a trip that could take as long as 8 or 10 hours when it was made in the face of strong northeast monsoons.

Short patrols in nearby waters proved the most effective and the easiest on the crews, because the men could return to base for good food and rest, and the boats did not waste their limited endurance in transit. However, distant patrols were acceptable depending on the weather. Granted that effectiveness is influenced by many variables—fetch of the sea, speed of the boats, relative bearing of the sea, and so forth—the generalization can be made that the Swifts operate satisfactorily in seas up to four feet, but in six-foot seas or higher their capability is limited. If seas are ten feet or more, they might just as well be kept in port.

Areas to be patrolled by the Swifts and the cutters were selected to make maximum use of the capabilities of each. Continued operation at high speed when on patrol reduced endurance drastically and, where there were navigational hazards or many junks to be investigated, it was not feasible in any event. The higher speed of the Swift was useful primarily in proceeding to operating areas. On the other hand, there is a theoretical relationship between area coverage and speed. Therefore, within the constraints discussed, both Swifts and cutters operated at as high a speed as practicable which, in most areas of the Gulf of Thailand, was somewhere between 8 and 15 knots. Swifts were assigned to the areas around Phu Quoc and along the mainland from the Cambodian border to the southern end of the Baie de Rach Gia. Because of their shallow draft, they could operate somewhat farther into the Baie de Rach Gia than could the cutters. By January 1966, eight Swifts and nine cutters were based in the Gulf of Thailand, and this permitted an average of four Swifts and six cutters to be on patrol at the same time, in addition to the DER or MSO which operated offshore.

EXTENDING THE PATROLS

Commander Coastal Surveillance Force was anxious to increase the forces on both the east and west side of the Ca Mau Peninsula, where there were indications of infiltration, and two techniques, both of which proved practical, were developed for that purpose.

First, the range and endurance of the Coast Guard cutters was extended by refueling at sea from the DER, which also supplied emergency repairs and limited provisions. There was always one cutter on patrol along the east coast of the Ca Mau Peninsula, some 100 to 200 miles from the *Krishna*, and that cutter was under the operational control of the DER commanding officer in the area. She could operate close in along this unsurveyed coast, while the DER patrolled the steamer lanes offshore. Using radar, fathometer, and, when there was something to see, visual bearings, the cutters could also chart fairly accurately the alluvial bottom along this barren, jungle-bordered stretch of the Vietnamese coast, which has no harbors, few inlets, limited offshore fishing, and where operations are difficult in the northeast monsoon and not much better in the southwest monsoon.

Second, one Swift boat with two operating crews was placed under the operational control of the DER patrolling in the southern half of the Gulf of Thailand: she also got her support from the DER. Carrying both her crews, the Swift would steam to her assigned area, 60 to 120 miles away from the support base, and one crew would be transferred to the DER. She would then go on patrol, and rendezvous with the DER every 24 hours, at which time the crews would be switched and the Swift refueled and replenished. Sometimes, Swifts and WPBs were refueled from a minesweeper or from another WPB, but that was a very slow process, and refueling from a DER was much better. After several days, that Swift would be relieved on station by another Swift with two crews, and the former and her two crews would return to the support base at An Thoi. Although the DERs performed emergency repairs, maintenance requirements ultimately limited this type of deployment. Nevertheless, the system had advantages: the operating range of the Swifts was extended from approximately 60 miles to 120 miles; DERs and Swifts gained useful experience in working together; and a task element made up of one DER, one cutter, and one Swift functioned much better in the southern area under the DER commanding officer than did a Swift individually controlled from the operations center on the *Krishna*. When the technique first went into operation, the northeast monsoons were blowing and it worked well, but when the southwest monsoons arrived, the Swifts had to pull back to the more sheltered northern half of the operating area.

Coordination between the Vietnamese Army and the Vietnamese Navy, and between Vietnamese and U. S. naval forces, was better during Phase Three than it had been previously. This improvement, plus the additional U. S. forces then available, enabled us to concentrate forces of varying composition, in varying sectors, both at random times and in response to intelligence reports, and thus catch the enemy off guard. The tactic most often used was to have several Vietnamese and U. S. naval units completely surround an area and search every junk in it. At other times, several units would form a line and sweep through an area; or barriers would be established which junks could not penetrate without being boarded. It was considered that these tactics employed over a long period of time, must inevitably lead to the detection of any significant infiltration. To start with, joint operations were planned by the U. S. staff, but as time went on, the Vietnamese Navy became very proficient at preparing operations orders and conducting operations.

DEFENDING AN THOI

The naval base and village at An Thoi, though not particularly well protected, were better off than the other government outposts on Phu Quoc. The small villages of Cua Can and Ham Ninh, for example, were protected only by small groups of civil guards, known as Popular Force platoons. But at An Thoi, there was a platoon of Coastal Force commandos, who manned an outpost to the north of the village. In February 1966, the small Regional Force company recently assigned to protect the airstrip that RMK was building at An Thoi, was joined by a second small company. A Popular Force platoon covered the area slightly to the west. Even so, there were large gaps in the base defenses, particularly on the left flank.

At any time, the Viet Cong could fire small arms into the An Thoi defense perimeter, as they could into Cua Can and Ham Ninh. At Duong Dong, metropolis of the island, the district chief had command of two understrength companies of Regional Forces, who were guarding the perimeter. A U. S. Special Forces detachment of two officers and ten men at Duong Dong acted as advisers to one, and later to two, companies of Vietnamese strikers

under the command of Vietnamese Special Forces. The forces at Cua Can, Ham Ninh, and An Thoi were strictly defensive. Those at Duong Dong, particularly the ones operating with the U. S. Special Forces, were capable of offensive action and were used for deployment out into the surrounding area.

Neither the government nor the Viet Cong were very aggressive between August and November 1965, partly—in the case of our people—because the U. S. and Vietnamese Special Forces were busy training the two striker companies. However, in November 1965 the Viet Cong began sporadic harassment of the naval base at An Thoi. In December and January, they were launching two or three nighttime small-arms attacks per week. The base would go to general quarters and return fire with small arms and mortars. The Regional Force would man its positions and pour small-arms and machine-gun fire into the sector of the perimeter under attack. U. S. naval advisers and Swift support personnel would man the northeast corner of base defenses, and the Vietnamese naval junks in port would get under way and patrol the harbor.

U. S. boats also would get under way: one would steam east, and one would steam west of An Thoi, and a third would moor to the fuel pier offshore. The U. S. naval operational commander would take station with the Vietnamese naval commander at the base because, from there, he could better evaluate the situation and provide for a more appropriate response than if he were afloat. The three U. S. naval vessels would provide illumination with their 81-mm. mortars, or provide harassing and interdicting fire, using high-explosive mortar ammunition, as requested. The detailed operational doctrine that was developed for this firing taxed the capability of the 81-mm. mortar sight to its limit. However, if the seas were calm, and if the position and heading of the vessel were known, the elevation and relative bearing of the mortar could be set to provide the necessary fire even on dark nights. On moonlit nights and when the target area was several hundred yards from the outer perimeter, the outline of a nearby mountaintop provided sufficient point of aim for both illuminating projectiles and for harassing and interdicting fire.

These techniques were developed and tested by simulating nighttime conditions in the daytime, and the vessels became quite proficient at using them. However, the limited nighttime sighting capability of the 81-mm. mortar meant that its use had to be tailored to each threat, and the decision to fire harassing and interdicting high explosive was always made by the U. S. operational commander. We certainly could not allow U. S. naval forces, whatever their fire-control system, to stand by while the village and the base were overrun, but, in making his decision, the commander had to take into account the state of the sea, visibility, the angle of the fire relative to friendly forces, the distance from the outer perimeter, and the extent to which friendly forces were in danger.

OPERATIONS ASHORE

At that time, the only offensive forces on Phu Quoc Island were, as we have seen, the strikers at Duong Dong. In the early days, they would often get ambushed or booby-trapped as they returned from a mission. But the discovery that such traps could be avoided simply by having the patrolling force picked up on the beach by Vietnamese or U. S. naval forces did much to create confidence between the land and naval forces, and led, logically, to the amphibious lift of troops from Duong Dong to Cua Can or An Thoi for offensive or defensive operations. Here again, either Vietnamese coastal or sea forces, or U. S. Swifts or cutters could be used. Coordination finally developed to the point where unopposed amphibious

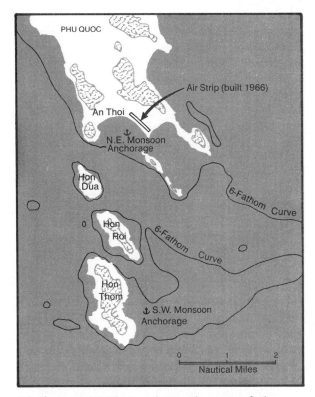

The base at An Thoi at the southern tip of Phu Quoc Island, showing the seasonal anchorages of the Krishna *and the location of the new 3,500-foot airstrip, which became operational in 1966.*

landings all along the west coast of the island were made by forces ranging in strength from a platoon to two companies. Sometimes, these forces would deploy for a few hours, sometimes for as long as ten days. Other times they withdrew to the sea, or swept on down by land to one of the government strongholds. In these operations, Vietnamese and U. S. patrol craft provided appropriate gunfire support. With the U. S. advisory and operational commands centralized, the degree of involvement of the U. S. forces could be tailored to provide a reasonable assurance of success, and Vietnamese naval forces could be used to the maximum of their capability. Under the leadership of Lieutenant Commander Nguyen Huu Chi, the capability of the Vietnamese Navy and its planning staff, and coordination between the Vietnamese Navy and Army increased to the point where almost all aspects of the operations were handled by the Vietnamese, with U. S. naval forces playing a supporting role as appropriate. During the first five months of 1966, the percentage of time the coastal groups devoted to anti-infiltration patrols increased very gradually.

Apart from the differences already discussed, operations during Phase Three were identical to those of Phase Two: that is, continuous patrolling, boarding, and searching; refinement of procedures; special search operations; psychological operations; gunfire in support of missions against Viet Cong strongholds; gunfire support of villages and bases under attack; counterfire when attacks were launched from the beach; search-and-rescue operations; gunfire support of amphibious operations; amphibious transport; and evacuation of casualties.

During Phase Three, the construction company completed the airstrip at An Thoi and began to build a new repair base for coastal groups and quarters for advisory personnel. The airstrip obviated the need for travelers to and from An Thoi, and men shepherding airlifted supplies, to make the 15-mile trip in a junk or patrol craft between An Thoi and Duong Dong, halfway up the island's west coast, where the nearest airstrip formerly was. It meant also, of course, that the junks and patrol craft could spend more time on operational, rather than support, missions. In addition, the two AKLs originally programmed began to bring in supplies from Saigon and Subic Bay, and, for the first time, we were receiving significant in-country supply support.

Another type of unit was added to the mix of forces participating in coastal surveillance operations during this period—the light Army or Air Force "Birddog" O-1 airplanes operating out of Rach Gia. Besides their spotting and ground surveillance missions, these two-place, 90-knot planes flew up and down the coast as often as possible, and communicated any information they gathered to the small ships below. Although they operated only during daylight, their familiarity with the area made them able better to evaluate the significance of unusual activities than were the patrol planes.

SINKING OF THE PCF-4

On 14 February 1966, a Swift boat, *PCF-4*, struck a mine approximately 250 yards off a Viet Cong stronghold north of Rach Gia and sank in about ten feet of water with the loss of four lives. The two survivors were wounded. A Vietnamese Navy junk saw the explosion, proceeded to the scene, and rescued the two survivors from the water. This action undoubtedly saved the two men as well as the guns, ammunition, and classified material on board the Swift from capture. Viet Cong were actually observed in the water en route to the sunken Swift when the Vietnamese Navy junk arrived.

A number of Coast Guard cutters, Swifts, and Vietnamese Navy junks raced to the scene. That night, people from the Swifts and from the Vietnamese junks succeeded in removing most of the ammunition and all of the guns from the sunken craft. Air Force planes provided illumination, and on-scene surface units used .50-caliber machine-gun fire to prevent the Viet Cong from reaching the stricken craft. The next morning, men from the *Krishna* and PCF Division 101 boarded the sunken craft, searched for bodies in the surrounding seas and considered methods of salvaging the boat. The RMK construction company provided an LCM-8 and a crew with a crane. Fire from Viet Cong automatic weapons on the beach hampered salvage operations and forced temporary withdrawal until all air and surface forces could be assembled and coordinated for suppressing fire on the beach. Army helicopters then attacked Viet Cong shore positions with machine guns and rockets, and covered the salvage efforts. Coast Guard cutters, Swifts, and Vietnamese Navy junks were deployed at the same time to provide additional fire.

With RMK, Navy, and Coast Guardsmen aboard, the LCM-8 moved in alongside the sunken Swift and attempted to raise her, but without success. She could not be made watertight and pumped out, because a large section of her bottom had been ripped open. Then, the LCM tried to drag her offshore. This also was unsuccessful. The Coast Guard cutter *Point Mast* moved in and, in tandem, the *Point Mast* and the LCM dragged the wreck offshore about a mile, out of range of Viet Cong guns. Later, a cutter dragged the Swift another ten miles offshore until she was in 30 feet of water, where the *Krishna* raised her, but she was a total loss.

When the PCF-4 struck what was later identified as a booby trap, we had our first indication that there were any mines or booby traps in the Gulf of Thailand. There are many ways of booby-trapping patrol forces, because the very essence of their mission is to investigate any activity out of the normal. After considerable experimenting, we developed techniques whereby possible booby traps could be scooped up and towed to a safe place for inspection. Some of the devices retrieved later broke up before they could be inspected, but none of those that were examined contained explosives.

SUCCESS OF THE POINT GREY

As previously noted, seldom are there any steel-hulled craft operating inshore in the Gulf of Thailand. Thus, the use of a steel-hulled trawler for infiltration in the Gulf would be foolhardy, and during the first year of operations, we did not discover any major attempts to do so. However, on the evening of 9 May 1966, the *Point Grey*, operating on an extended patrol around the hook along the east coast of the Ca Mau Peninsula, did intercept a steel-hulled trawler engaged in infiltration. The *Point Grey* was about four miles offshore when she noted two fires on the beach, and moved in to see what was going on. Some two hours later, a radar contact was picked up approaching the beach. The *Point Grey* closed, challenged, and, finally, illuminated. Maneuverability was restricted in the shallow water, and the contact, a 110-foot trawler, ran aground while still about a thousand yards offshore.

At daybreak, the *Point Grey* closed the stranded trawler and was immediately taken under intense fire by automatic weapons from the beach. She returned fire and withdrew. The USS *Brister* (DER-327), the USS *Vireo* (MSC-205), the USCGC *Point Cypress*, and several Vietnamese naval units all closed to assist the *Point Grey*. Later in the morning, under air cover, the *Point Grey* made two more attempts to board the trawler, but each time she was driven off by fire from the shore. Three of the 11 men in the *Point Grey* were wounded. Increasing winds and seas moved the trawler closer inshore, where the water was too shallow for the cutter to follow. To preclude losing any of the cargo to the Viet Cong during the night, the trawler was again taken under fire, resulting in violent secondary explosions, which ripped the hull in two and set it on fire. Harassing and illuminating fire was provided throughout the night, and the next morning the trawler was boarded unopposed from a shallow-draft Vietnamese Navy junk. Some 15 tons of guns and ammunition were recovered, and the hull was wrecked by more gunfire. Whether the Red crew escaped or perished is not known.

As the arbitrarily defined Phase Three drew to a close in May 1966, it was possible to develop some statistics on operations in the Gulf. At that time, PCF Division 101 had seven Swifts, each on patrol about 55 per cent of the

This steel-hulled trawler (top) was intercepted by the Point Grey *on the eastern side of the Ca Mau Peninsula and was stranded, but proved uncapturable. She was taken under fire by a DER and some smaller ships and blown to pieces,* as shown in the lower photograph. *A Vietnamese Navy command junk is seen recovering guns and ammunition from the bow of the wreck.*

time. The nine cutters of Coast Guard Division 11 had operated on patrol over 70 per cent of the time since their arrival ten months earlier, while at the same time maintaining an average of 24 per cent of the time on five-minute standby and 6 per cent in maintenance status.

Both Swifts and cutters had a maintenance program which would permit operations to be continued at these levels indefinitely. One DER—provided by ComSeventhFlt—was maintained continuously on patrol. Mine-sweepers were no longer in use in the Gulf of

Thailand, as they were smaller and slower than the DERs, had inferior command and control facilities, insufficient room for spare Swift crewmen, and were very slow in refueling Swifts. On one or two occasions, an MSC was assigned to the area, but in addition to, rather than in lieu of, a DER. Ten more Swifts were still scheduled for the Gulf, but by this time allied forces were firmly in control at sea. Additional forces would be used to tighten that control and to expand amphibious and psychological operations.

During the ten months since the arrival of U. S. forces, roughly 80,000 junk sightings were made by the U. S. forces in the Gulf of Thailand, either visually or on radar, and more than half of these were either boarded or inspected. Two Viet Cong junks had been sunk in battle at sea. U. S. operating forces had turned over to the Vietnamese Navy more than 140 Viet Cong suspects along with approximately 30 suspect junks—suspect because of discrepancies in their papers. Boats had engaged in more than 40 gunfire support missions, most of which were unscheduled and in response to hostile fire at bases or villages, or in defense of U. S. or friendly forces under fire from the beach. These support missions resulted in 30 Viet Cong killed in action, more than 10 wounded in action, at least three junks destroyed on the beach, and some 40 buildings either destroyed or damaged.

In May 1966, it was quite apparent that almost no Viet Cong men and materials were infiltrating the Gulf of Thailand. How much had been prevented by Market Time forces cannot be judged. May 1966 was obviously not the end of Market Time, but it was the end of the three phases covered by this essay.

Observations

Since the rationale behind most planning and operational decisions has been discussed in the course of the narrative, it will not be repeated in detail here. But I would like to restate certain conclusions, express some opinions, and identify unsolved problems.

First, operations in the Gulf of Thailand, and to a larger degree throughout all of Market Time, are conducted against an enemy who lacks the normal paraphernalia of naval war. If the enemy could attack our surveillance forces by air, or could infiltrate by submarine, our task would be much more difficult. Second, Market Time deals with infiltration from the sea. Therefore, that is the only aspect of inshore warfare with which this essay deals. It does not address the allied, and very real, problem of infiltration by canal and river.

A mixture of small (Swift), medium (cutters), and large (DER) patrol craft and light (O-1) and patrol (P-2, P-3, or P-5) aircraft is needed if coastal surveillance is to be carried out efficiently. The mix can be altered by various trade-offs, and helicopters might be substituted for the "Birddogs," but, on the basis of Market Time experience to date, I submit that the medium-sized patrol craft—the smallest craft that can mess and berth personnel for long periods of time and can operate in any weather—should be the backbone of a coastal surveillance force. They are certainly the most versatile of all craft, in terms of method of dispatch to the scene, logistic support, and operational capability.

The 82-foot Coast Guard cutters are the patrol craft that meet this description in Market Time operations. They can deploy anywhere in the world as rapidly as merchant ships are available to transport them—or, if underway replenishment is available, they can proceed to the scene under their own power. They can remain in an area of operations for as long as they are wanted. They require a minimum of logistic support, as was proved when Division 12 in Da Nang operated for five months from an LST support ship. As previously noted, they can operate on patrol 70 per cent of the time and can remain on this schedule indefinitely. Even while the cutters undergo their 6,000-hour overhauls and annual dry-dockings, and while the crews go on rest and recreation periods, the schedule is maintained. To my knowledge, such continued operational utilization off a hostile coast, remote from shore support, halfway around the world from the United States, has not been matched, nor is it planned for any other warship in limited war.

In Vietnam, we are using both floating and shore support for small and medium patrol craft. The greater flexibility of floating support was clearly demonstrated when the cutters went into action on short notice and no shoreside support was available. Similarly, floating support can move to where the action is, be it to another area in Vietnam or to a country on another continent. Shore support cannot move rapidly, tends to overburden harbor facilities, and to disrupt the local economy and social structure. I believe that Market Time has proved that the United States should have floating hotel and maintenance facilities available for rapid deployment on coastal surveillance operations.

PROBLEMS STILL UNSOLVED

Not all the problems in the Gulf of Thailand have been solved. Possible Viet Cong activity in the area can be grouped into four categories: infiltration of men, arms, and supplies across the Cambodian border; infiltration of men, arms, and supplies from a large ship or trawler coming in from offshore; infiltration of men, arms, and supplies from point to point along the coast; and harassment and taxation of local fishermen.

Infiltration from across the Cambodian border and from offshore is well under control. Infiltration from point to point along the coast is under control, so far as junks are concerned; however, in favorable weather, small sampans can still work slowly down the coast, if they

operate a hundred yards or so off the beach where U. S. patrol craft and Vietnamese Navy junks cannot pursue. Viet Cong tax collectors present difficulties, for their sampans can work almost at the beach line and can go up the canals. By May 1966, this close inshore problem had not been tackled adequately, because all patrol craft had been required for surveillance farther off the beach line. Additional craft with shallower draft would permit experimentation inshore. In particular, it might be well, as additional Swifts come into the area and as Vietnamese Navy capabilities and coordination improve, to experiment with local sampans working inshore in conjunction with patrol craft offshore. The sampans might be manned either by Vietnamese or U. S.-Vietnamese crews. Further, the use of SEAL teams on missions at selected spots along the nominally hostile coast might produce some interesting results, but it could be that we will not really solve the problem until we control the beaches.

Looking even further into the future, as the tide of war moves in favor of the government of Vietnam, large-scale clear-and-hold operations may be conducted in the countryside along the Gulf of Thailand. Such operations could be coordinated in many ways with the forces of the Vietnamese Navy and the U. S. Navy—prevention of exfiltration, gunfire support, amphibious landings, transport of troops and supplies, and so forth. These tasks could become more important than the prevention of infiltration itself.

WHAT NEXT?

U. S. naval victory must be measured eventually in terms of U. S. naval forces being withdrawn when the threat is under control and the Vietnamese Navy is able—with sufficient well-trained men, sound ships, and timely logistic support—to take over completely all of the naval tasks in the Gulf of Thailand. As the

United States continues to deploy Swifts to the Gulf and as the Vietnamese Navy becomes increasingly capable, there will come a time when the total level of effort is sufficient. If this level is exceeded, forces will begin to get in each other's way, and the complexity of communications, administration, and logistics will increase without any corresponding increase in effectiveness. And the Vietnamese Navy might begin to be overwhelmed by the preponderance of highly trained U. S. forces on modern ships, and could lose its desire to improve. It is most important that we watch carefully for signs that this point has been reached and at that time divert U. S. forces to other areas of need, or withdraw them from the country, so that the Vietnamese Navy is always striving to take the next step toward complete control.

Finally, it was obvious that we were not prepared to deploy a balanced force for surveillance patrol to Vietnam when the need arose. This situation has been remedied. We have converted a concept into a task force, and have developed tactics and support to make it effective. A U. S. coastal surveillance task force that includes both operating units and floating support should be retained on a permanent basis—a task force that is ready for immediate deployment anywhere.

Overseas coastal surveillance is now a U. S. Navy mission, and creation of a permanent task force is a Navy responsibility, but such a force should not rely solely on U. S. Navy capability. As was demonstrated in the deployment of Squadron One, the Coast Guard can rapidly deploy ships and well-trained crews to coastal surveillance operations. If this Coast Guard capability were not made a part of any permanent task force, the Navy would have to duplicate existing facilities and would eliminate the healthy cross-fertilization of Coast Guard–Navy ideas, procedures, and hardware that went into developing a successful Market Time task force. Such coordinated action has proved effective ever since the first cutters sailed to the Caribbean with the Navy squadron in 1799, and it can be effective in the future.

(Naval Review, 1968)

Jackstay: New Dimensions in Amphibious Warfare

Robert E. Mumford Jr., Lieutenant Commander,
U. S. Navy

Operation Jackstay, conducted in March 1966 in the Rung Sat Special Zone, 35 miles south of Saigon, was the first full-scale U. S. amphibious operation of the Vietnamese War to be carried out in a river delta.

The Rung Sat is in the delta of the Saigon River. Just to the south lies the much larger Mekong Delta, whose topography is identical to that of the Saigon Delta: mainly rice fields and swamps, densely filled with mangrove and nipa palm. Water—streams, canals, rivers, estuaries, and marsh—dominates. Very little of the land is more than a few meters above sea level. The tidal range is considerable, and shallows extend miles out into the sea.

Many people believe that, if the Vietnamese War is to be won, it must be won in the Mekong Delta, where more than one-third of South Vietnam's people live. Through Operation Game Warden, with its river patrol boats and "Sea Wolf" helicopters, the U. S. Navy has been operating in the delta areas since the spring of 1966. But, even though the primary means of transportation in the deltas is by water, Game Warden cannot, by itself, beat the Viet Cong. Its mission is to interdict, not to clear. Game Warden's contribution is valuable, but to achieve victory in the delta, ground forces must go on the offensive.

Because Jackstay, carried out by the Marine Special Landing Force (SLF) embarked in the Navy's Amphibious Ready Group (ARG), was also the first such use of U. S. ground forces, it deserves to be studied in detail.

Two parts of the Rung Sat were targeted in the Dagger Thrust amphibious series in 1965–66, but neither was hit; in fact, no serious action against them was contemplated until Viet Cong activities made action mandatory. Interest began to focus on the area in January 1966, when a number of merchant ships proceeding along the Long Tao River to Saigon ran into small-scale ambushes. The Long Tao, a muddy, twisting, tidal river, with few landmarks to aid the navigator, is the primary deep-draft channel into the capital city. The Soi Rap River, to the west, is much wider and is a more direct route from the South China Sea, but it is not extensively used, because of a variety of navigational drawbacks.

With a great deal of the war material arriving in South Vietnam coming through Saigon, it was obvious that neither Washington nor Saigon would accept traffic on the Long Tao being impeded by a sunken ship. Even if traffic could pass the wreck, navigation would be more difficult than ever and ships would be forced close to the shoreline, where they would be more vulnerable to attack: shipping interests were already apprehensive about loss

Up the Vam Sat, deep into the swamp, went the Marine-laden boats from the Merrick *and the* Pickaway.
*First went a couple of river gunboats, and then a pair of minesweeping craft, and then a monitor, all from the
Vietnamese Navy. Next went the landing craft from the amphibious force and salvage vessels and more gun-
boats, all American. A mine exploded nearby, but no one was hurt.*

of or extensive damage to their ships transiting the river. Thus, there were both political and military imperatives to sweep the Rung Sat and remove the hostile forces adjacent to the channel. When the Viet Cong ambushed the SS *Lorinda* in February, an operation became imminent.

What is this Rung Sat like? It is 400 square miles of swamp, bounded on the west by the Soi Rap River, on the south by the South China Sea, and on the east and north roughly by the highway that runs between Saigon and Vung Tau. It is dominated by thousands of interlacing rivers and streams, all affected by tides whose average range is about eight feet. Watercourses that, at low tide, are little more than wet places between the tangled vegetation, become highways capable of floating the largest cargo sampans when the tide comes in. Swamps that can be crossed on foot, albeit with great difficulty, during the ebb, become death traps to the trooper with a heavy pack when the flood water conceals the deep holes.

The Rung Sat is thickly covered by tropical, lowland vegetation, mainly mangrove, with an impenetrable barrier of twisted roots and tightly packed nipa palm. On the river banks and for some distance into the swamp, the foliage appears low, but most of the Rung Sat is hidden by a double canopy of flora, providing secrecy for elements opposed to the law. Indeed, for decades and perhaps for centuries, the Rung Sat has been used as a redoubt by bandits, smugglers, and political insurgents. Despite its proximity to Saigon, it was a Viet Minh bastion during the French-Indochinese War, and the French never penetrated it. Although not known as an agricultural area, the Rung Sat does provide food for those who know its secrets. Its waters teem with marine life, especially large shrimp. There are also alligators, vipers, cobras, and sea snakes.

More than 50 per cent of the estimated 16,000 people in the Rung Sat are Buddhists: most of the remainder are Cao Dai, and a few are Catholics. There are few isolated houses, and the entire population is spread among nine villages, subdivided into 20 hamlets. About 5,000 peasants live on the Long Thanh Peninsula and another 1,000 (at most) in the hamlets on the southeastern bank of the Soi Rap. Can Gio, at the mouth of the Long Tao River, is the largest village. Probably no more than 10 per cent of the inhabitants of the Rung Sat are active Viet Cong, but many more may be sympathizers. The great majority, however, like most Vietnamese peasants, care little for politics, do not understand either the theory or practice of democracy or communism, and merely want to be left alone to tend their crops and raise their families. Almost everyone is engaged in rice farming, woodcutting, or fishing. Rice farming is limited to the shore of the middle and upper reaches of the Soi Rap and the southeast edge of the Long Thanh Peninsula. Woodcutting is restricted by government decree to the areas north and east of the Long Tao. Although wood is plentiful on the western bank of the Long Tao and woodcutters do venture into this area, it is assumed by the government that anyone traveling away from populated districts in the southwestern area is a Viet Cong. There are also certain areas where, if a woodcutter is found by the Viet Cong, he may lose his day's work, his boat, or his life. Fishing is centered in the same villages where rice is farmed.

There are no vehicles, no roads, no telephones, very limited medical facilities, only a few wells, whose water is of questionable potability, and practically no electricity or substantial buildings. In short, the Rung Sat is a primitive, rural region, barely touched by the twentieth century.

In late 1965 and early 1966, it was believed that the area was used as a rest camp for battle-weary V.C. from several nearby provinces. Reports said that medical facilities connected with the camp were supplied with drugs and equipment for treatment of the wounded; that

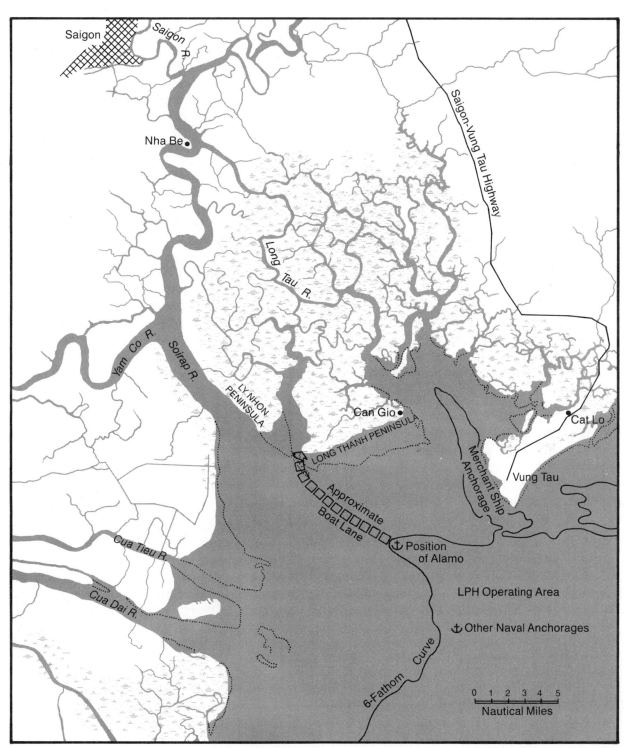

The approaches to Saigon.

there were an arms repair facility and a mine factory a few miles inland from the Soi Rap, and storage areas and caches in various parts of the swamp. Despite these activities, the Viet Cong were not often engaged by the approximately 800 popular and regional forces garrisoned in the villages. Nor did they often seek out the government troops, perhaps for fear that retaliatory raids would threaten their sanctuary.

Occasionally, Viet Cong pressure would be brought to bear against the few tiny villages on the Long Thanh Peninsula and along the Soi Rap, but for the most part military action was limited. From time to time, Vietnamese troops stationed at Nha Be, ten miles below Saigon, would embark in the boats of a nearby River Assault Group (RAG) and conduct small-scale operations on the periphery of the Rung Sat. However, there were areas where these troops would not venture, for fear of strong ambushes, heavy mining, or other dangerous opposition. By the end of February 1966, it was estimated that the enemy in the swamp consisted of infantry, engineers, and various smaller support units, equipped with small arms, automatic weapons, including .50-caliber machine guns, mortars, and recoilless rifles.

Against this backdrop, COMUSMACV had to decide what forces to use in an operation aimed at removing pressure on the Long Tao shipping channel. There were enough Vietnamese troops nearby, but the Vietnamese were committed to many defensive missions in addition to countering Viet Cong attacks. Furthermore, supporting arms would almost have to come from the U. S. forces, since the air and artillery of the Army of the Republic of Vietnam (ARVN) were thinly spread, and there were no Vietnamese naval gunfire ships.

This author who, at the time of Jackstay, was on the staff of Commander Amphibious Squadron One, does not know what factors caused the final decision to use the ARG/SLF, but several pertinent facts can be discussed. First, the terrain, with its severely limited helicopter landing zones, its absence of roads, and its network of waterways that would dictate in such large measure the scheme of maneuver, made an amphibious operation almost imperative. Second, the ARG/SLF, having reformed with a newly re-grouped BLT and three fresh ships, would be available during the latter half of March: an exercise, designed to weld this force into a smoothly functioning team, was scheduled to take place in the Philippines. Finally, few other forces available had the amphibious training that would be needed, and if training had to be given, the delay would be intolerable, considering the threat to the channel. It would have been almost impossible to withdraw a battalion of the Marines from I Corps without providing access for North Vietnamese infiltration. Boats capable of handling the troops involved, and trained coxswains and crews, were, of course, already assigned to the ARG.

Another amphibious operation was in the planning stages, but it was quickly scrapped, and a conference was called at MACV headquarters during the second week of March. It was evident from the beginning that this operation was to be more than just another amphibious raid, and that an unusually large number of ships as well as novel tactics would have to be used.

Captain John D. Westervelt, Commander Amphibious Squadron One and Commander of the Ready Group, was given permission to choose almost any types of ships that could be made available. Most of the ships in the Commodore's own squadron were in their home port of San Diego; no ships from that squadron participated.

It also became evident that a complex command structure would be required. Amphibious doctrine demands that all forces in the

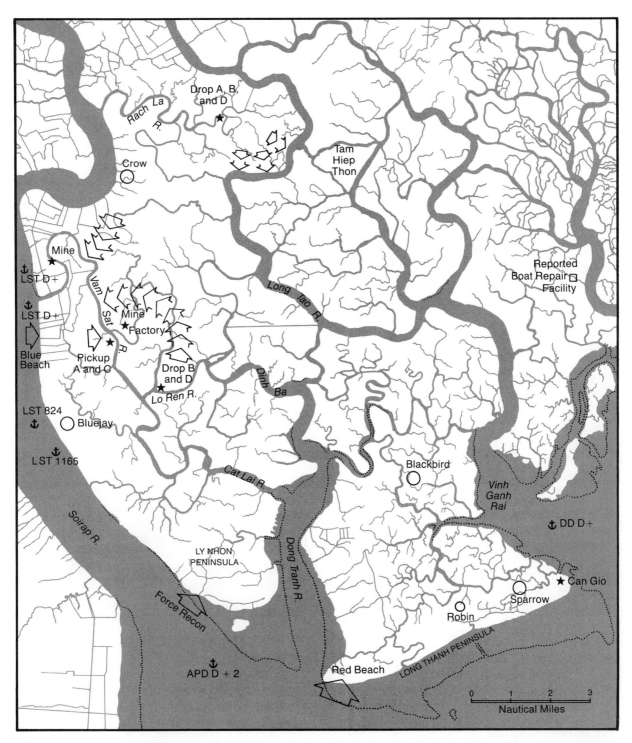

The Rung Sat Special Zone, where Operation Jackstay took place. The map shows how the action was conducted. The main channel is the Long Tau River, but in Jackstay most action was launched and supported from the Soi Rap. (Note: anchorages shown as D+ were those of the DD and LSTs on D + 4.)

Amphibious Objective Area be subordinated to the commander, but because the operation was to take place in the proximity of Saigon, and because of procedures that had been established for the coastal surveillance forces already operating in nearby waters, it was decided that patrol boats belonging to the Chief, Naval Advisory Group, in Saigon, would not chop to the Commander Amphibious Task Force (CATF). Therefore, a delicate liaison had to be established between the two commands: a small staff chosen from the Naval Advisory Group was stationed in the flagship of the Amphibious Task Force, the *Princeton* (LPH-5) and a detachment of that staff was in the *Belle Grove* (LSD-2). The latter was already in the area, working for the Advisory Group. In both ships the Saigon parties had their own radio facilities, which helped speed communications to the small boats. The relationship between Commodore Westervelt and Captain J. T. Shepherd, who headed the Advisory Group staff, was that of equals pursuing a common goal. Orders to the patrol boats were issued by Captain Shepherd, after he had conferred with the Commodore. Thus, a link was forged between Saigon and the flagship.

Planning was done simultaneously in Saigon and in Subic Bay, where lay the ARG/SLF, consisting of the *Princeton* (LPH-5), the *Pickaway* (APA-222), and the *Alamo* (LSD-33) with an LCU, two LCM-8s, HMM-362, and BLT 1/5 embarked. In mid-March, Captain Westervelt dispatched one of his staff officers to the Rung Sat area to gather information concerning friendly and hostile forces, tides (which, because of their wide range, were important factors in detailed planning), and to acquire a grasp of the area. From Vietnam, Captain Larry Ogle, U. S. Marine Corps, and Lieutenant Waldo Rose, U. S. Navy, were sent to Subic Bay to impart to the ARG/SLF the extensive knowledge they had gained during operations

with their Vietnamese counterparts in the swamp. Both men were extremely helpful.

When Captain Westervelt and the Commander Special Landing Force, Colonel J. R. Burnett, U. S. Marine Corps, together, had formulated tentative plans, the Commodore requested additional ships. Because more LCM-6s would be needed than the *Pickaway* could provide, the *Merrick* (AKA-97) was assigned to the operation; and the *Weiss* (APD-135) was added to carry surveillance forces. Rear Admiral D. L. Wulzen, Commander of the Seventh Fleet's Amphibious Force, assigned the *Henry County* (LST-824), with Commander Derwin T. Lamb, COMLANSHIPRON One embarked, and the *Washoe County* (LST-1165). The *Eldorado* (AGC-11) joined the task group to provide communication assistance. From the Service Force came the *Reclaimer* (ARS-42) to take care of any vessels that might be damaged or grounded. The naval gunfire support ship attached for Operation Jackstay was the *Robison* (DDG-12).

Although she was not under the operational control of CATF, the *Belle Grove* was intimately involved in Jackstay. Several weeks prior to D-Day, she had anchored off Vung Tau for training duties. Aboard her were 30 of the new plastic-hulled PBRs and two armed Army HU-1Es from the 145th Aviation Battalion. The crews of the former were neophytes and were not scheduled to participate directly in Operation Jackstay, though they did make some patrols as part of their training; the aircraft, however, were to be on immediate call, and they proved invaluable in covering troop and boat movements. The *Belle Grove* was already servicing the four 57-foot minesweeping boats (MSB) that daily dragged the Long Tao, and the four armed LCPLs (Mark 4) that were the forerunners of the river patrol force. Most of the time during the course of the operation, two 82-foot Coast Guard cutters (WPB) were on patrol in the Soi Rap, and besides the LCPLs, Swift boats (PCF) were on that and the other rivers of the Rung Sat. Although the logistics base for the cutters and Swifts was not far from Vung Tau, they, too, were often to be found alongside the LSD.

Close-support aircraft were to be drawn from the duty CVA at Dixie Station, 80 or 90 miles to the southeast. During the first part of the operation, this was the *Hancock* (CVA-19), and she was relieved by the *Kitty Hawk* (CVA-63). Aircraft (A-1s, A-4s, A-6s, and F-4s) first from one carrier and then from the other, were on station over the Rung Sat almost continually from dawn to dusk each day that Jackstay lasted.

As the bits and pieces of the complex puzzle began falling into place, plans were made for the assault. The Rung Sat had been divided into a series of objective areas, based primarily on intelligence. Both commanders recognized the need to remain flexible because their plans might have to be altered radically. The operation was split into two phases: first, a conventional assault on the face of the Long Thanh Peninsula, where the population was centered; and then, a series of unconventional, company-sized operations by boat and helo into reported V.C. areas. In this way it was hoped to isolate the enemy from possible support in the villages, before hitting him in his own camps. By using separate units for sweeps, the odds of discovering these camps would be markedly increased, and if one became embroiled in a large-scale firefight, the others could be rapidly airlifted or boated in to assist. Swift boats, LCPLs, and Coast Guard cutters would search the waterways to prevent the Viet Cong from massing, receiving reinforcements from the outside, or escaping.

A number of details had to be completed before the force could leave Subic Bay. Because the water at the Amphibious Objective Area was shallow, the boat lane for the initial assault was to be eight miles long, and since the landing was to be made at dawn, a great portion of it would have to be transited in darkness. Boat crews from the APA and AKA had had little recent experience with operations in the dark, and therefore had to be given night training. Using Green Beach in Subic Bay for practice, they became proficient at following compass courses, guiding on a dull beacon on the beach, and using signal flashlights.

Since the Ready Group landing craft had seldom been exposed to enemy fire, their people required training and equipment. Boat crews were provided with body armor as well as the standard helmets, and were instructed in the operation of the machine guns that had been installed on the boats. Although there was little time in which to prepare the crews for combat, they were well indoctrinated in countering hostile action by the time they left Subic Bay.

The Marines were also busy. Company E, a provisional company, was formed from men whose specialties would not be required in this operation—tank crews, for instance—and was given extensive training in the use of small arms.

On 22 March, the *Princeton*, *Alamo*, *Merrick*, and *Pickaway* sortied from Subic Bay. The *Princeton* steamed for Da Nang, the others for Camranh Bay. At Da Nang, two UH-46 helos from HMM-164 and two UH-1E helos from VMO-2 were embarked to provide heavy lift and reconnaissance, respectively, missions not easily performed by the UH-34 flown by HMM-362. When this loading was complete, the LPH steamed to Camranh Bay, to rendezvous with the other three ships and make pre-D-Day transfers. Captain Westervelt and Colonel Burnett, who had flown from Da Nang to Saigon for a last-minute conference with COM-SEVENTHFLT and COMUSMACV, rejoined the *Princeton* when she arrived at Camranh Bay.

On the morning of the 25th, the *Weiss*, carrying UDT 11, arrived at Vung Tau and there embarked more surveillance forces. The same day, the remainder of the task group rendezvoused 25 miles off Vung Tau, and key officers from the ships went aboard the flagship for final briefings. It was strange to think that, though it had no high ground to make it visible, the objective area of the next day's operation lay only a few miles away.

Very early on the morning of 26 March 1966, with the *Alamo* leading the way, the ships of the task group steamed into the Amphibious Objective Area, and anchored. The order "land the landing force" was issued. The *Princeton* remained under way in the LPH operating area, 9 to 15 miles south of the Long Thanh Peninsula. At 0330 the UDT had gone ashore and checked Red Beach, at the western tip of the peninsula, for mines and other obstacles. H-hour had been set at 0630, but it was 0715 when the first troops charged out of their three LCMs into the sea and waded to the beach. A leaking exhaust muffler in one of the boats, discovered and repaired while the boats were partway to the beach, had caused the delay. So critical to this operation was the tide that the 45-minute delay prevented the artillery-carrying LCU from the *Alamo* from driving far enough through the mud flats to discharge her cargo. She did not beach until 1700 that afternoon, when the next high tide occurred.

Pre-H-Hour bombardment by aircraft from the *Hancock* and by the *Robison* was delivered on time, but the schedule for the helicopter waves was also upset. As the helos were readied on the flight deck of the *Princeton*, a violent thunderstorm engulfed the landing zones, and caused a delay of 35 minutes. It was 0720 when the first helicopter wave landed Company C in Landing Zone Sparrow, near Can Gio at the eastern end of the peninsula.

Companies A, B, and D followed, and landed in LZ Robin, approximately midway between Red Beach and Can Gio. One unit was to secure the landing zone and set up defensive positions in the area; another was to move west to link up with the provisional company; a third was to move in the other direction to link up with C to the west of Can Gio. None of the landings was opposed.

Marines on the beach discovered a body, later identified as that of a villager who had been kidnapped by the Viet Cong several days previously. Nearby was a crude sign in Vietnamese which read: "All soldiers: do not follow the U. S. Army. The booby traps are used to kill the Americans. The soldiers who kill U. S. Army love their country."

With no more opposition than sporadic sniper fire, and with the battalion command post firmly established ashore, control of naval gunfire was passed to the Landing Force in the afternoon of D-Day. Control of the air remained in the *Princeton*'s Supporting Arms Control Center throughout the operation. Both air and naval gunfire were directed against structures and strongpoints where Viet Cong had been reported, but airborne observers detected no movement that could be attributed to the enemy.

Naval forces were active on D-Day. Both the *Washoe County* and *Henry County* were on the ramp at Vung Tau, loading Ontos (a Marine anti-tank vehicle armed with six 106-mm. recoilless rifles) and provisions for subsequent up-river operations. Coast Guard WPBs patrolled the objective area to prevent attack on the heavies. In the rivers and waterways, Swift boats inspected local small craft.

Late in the afternoon, Navymen and Marine Force Reconnaissance troops split into 21 four-man teams, and set up surveillance points in the swamp from which they would be able to detect Viet Cong movements during the night. Since there was a curfew in effect, anyone moving outside the villages after sunset was presumed to be an insurgent.

These teams were responsible for the first confirmed enemy casualties in Jackstay; they killed four during the first night's operations. Several teams reported that they were so close to the Viet Cong that they could hear them breathing, but the latter were in such numbers as to preclude an attack. All the teams were extracted by boat, under cover of an armed Huey, at sunrise on the 27th.

American casualties were light on the first day: one Marine was killed by a mine or booby trap, and two were killed when a Viet Cong threw a grenade into night defensive positions. Heat claimed many more victims than did the enemy. During the first day, some 39 men suffered severe heat prostration and had to be evacuated to the *Princeton*, the medical evacuation ship, but most of them were soon returned to duty.

Since the Viet Cong move rapidly when under attack, every source of information on enemy movements was sought. Throughout the operation, Army Mohawk reconnaissance aircraft flying from the airfield at Vung Tau crisscrossed the Rung Sat to detect Viet Cong activity. Information gathered during these missions was forwarded the following morning to the flagship, where it was plotted and made available to the commanders during daily planning.

At the close of the second day—27 March—two companies were ferried to Red Beach by helo, and thence by the *Merrick*'s LCM-6s and the *Pickaway*'s LCVPs to the *Washoe County*, which was anchored offshore. The *Washoe County* and the *Henry County* then followed minesweeping boats up the Soi Rap and anchored in midstream. Two other companies remained at Red Beach during the night, while a third continued to provide security at LZ Robin, where the battalion CP was located.

At 0900 the following morning, D-plus-2, B-

52 bombers flying from Guam dropped their payload on a suspected Viet Cong area, a rectangle a half-mile wide and a mile and one-half deep, between the Soi Rap and the Vam Sat. It had been reported that the Vam Sat was the primary Viet Cong waterway in the Rung Sat, carrying food, equipment, and troops into the interior.

Immediately following the B-52 raid, called Operation Tailwind, Companies A and C embarked in LCM landing craft and proceeded to Blue Beach, located on the Soi Rap, west of the bomb-drop zone. Finding the shoreline unlike any terrain encountered before, Commodore Westervelt who, with Colonel Burnett, was observing the ship-to-shore movement from the *Henry County*, directed the boats to land several hundred yards north of the original "beach." Even at that point, there was a heavy growth of mangrove and nipa palm, through which the coxswains were forced to drive their boats, stopping short of the actual shore and dropping their ramps into the heavy foliage. It was impossible for the troops to charge ashore in the customary manner. This landing was planned to exploit the B-52 strike, but travel through the dense undergrowth proved to be much slower than anticipated and, though the target area was only a mile inland, it was not reached that day.

While Companies A and C were landing to the north, half of Company E was airlifted from LZ Robin to a new landing zone in the rice fields along the Soi Rap, three miles below Blue Beach. Designated Bluejay, this zone was chosen to cover the rifle companies to the north with supporting arms. Therefore, along with Company E went the five 105-mm. howitzers and some 107-mm. howtars. Simultaneously, the other half of Company E was dropped into landing zone Blackbird, one of the few cleared spots in that part of the swamp, about five miles north of Robin. Searches by platoon-sized groups from this landing proved fruitless, and the following day, the troops were airlifted to LZ Crow, a clear area on the bank of the Soi Rap not far from the northern tip of the Rung Sat.

On the night of the 28th, following a day and a half of rest and preparation, the surveillance teams were returned to the swamp in the late afternoon. This time, they went up the Dong Tranh River, a large waterway between the Soi Rap and the Long Tao, separating the Long Thanh and Ly Nhon peninsulas. Again contact was made, this time by a team from Battalion Recon, and three of the enemy were killed and two wounded, with no loss to the Americans.

On 29 March the command post of the BLT was airlifted from LZ Robin to LZ Crow, along with that part of Company E that had been in Blackbird, and Companies B and D. All five companies were then on the western shore of the Rung Sat. The following morning, the *Washoe County* assumed a support position opposite the mouth of the Vam Sat, and the *Robison* moved to the Vinh Ganh Rai (the mouth of the Long Tao) better to cover the new maneuver area. Although even from this position, the two 5″/54 of the latter could not reach the landing beach or the objective area of the second landing, they could reach places from which the Viet Cong could fire mortars on the Marines.

Commodore Westervelt, Colonel Burnett, and Commander Lamb, who was in charge of up-river operations, conferred aboard the *Princeton* and the *Henry County*, and final plans were made for the penetration of the Vam Sat. A boat convoy was to enter the river on the morning of D-plus-5. The night before the assault, Companies B and D left LZ Crow to get a rest and a hot meal aboard the *Washoe County* before embarking on their next assignment.

The operation began shortly after dawn, 31 March, when the *Hancock*'s A-1s and A-4s came wheeling in from Dixie Station to drop over 15 tons of bombs and to fire rockets and 20-mm. at reported enemy positions along the river. Next, the two LSTs fired. The *Henry County* laid down a barrage of 1,500 rounds of 40-mm. and 69 rounds of 106-mm. from the Ontos, and the *Washoe County* added 244 rounds of 3-inch and 43 rounds from her Ontos. This fire was intended to kill any Viet Cong who might be waiting on the banks along the mouth of the Vam Sat to detonate the mines that were reported to be there.

In the meantime, a boat convoy formed near the *Henry County*, with Companies B and D loaded into seven LCMs and two LCVPs in order to minimize casualties in the event of a hit on any one of them. Led by two French-built, Vietnamese-manned FOMs (a V-bottomed boat about the size of an LCVP and much favored by the Vietnamese for its reputed ability to withstand the effects of being mined), the 18-boat convoy entered the Vam Sat. Following the FOMs were two Vietnamese LCVPs rigged with chain drag and grapnels for minesweeping; the minesweepers stayed 100 yards ahead of the LCMs. Heavy fire support was provided by a Vietnamese monitor (an armored LCM-6 armed with both a mortar and a variety of automatic weapons), and additional gunfire support was provided by a pair of the American LCPLs. Troops in all the boats had been directed to recon by fire during the entire transit, except when in the vicinity of their comrades waiting on the bank up-river. As insurance, two U. S. Navy LCM-3 salvage boats were included in the river convoy. To avoid or minimize damage from mines, the boats were spaced 25 yards apart, they followed slightly different tracks, and avoided objects in the water that the Viet Cong might use as sighting marks. Overhead, armed Hueys watched for movement or hostile fire, and some of the *Hancock*'s aircraft were in the sky nearby.

There were few incidents during the inbound trip. About a mile and a half from the Soi Rap, a mine was detonated, but no damage or casualties were sustained. Approximately eight miles up the river (actually, south), the LCMs turned into the Lo Ren River and discharged the troops on a densely covered point of land a few hundred yards from the Vam Sat.

After debarking the troops, the boats reformed the convoy and proceeded back downstream (north). About two miles from the drop point, the LCMs again turned into the shoreline and dropped their ramps. This time, they embarked the weary troops of Companies A and C, who had tramped over from Blue Beach, where they had landed three days before. The remainder of the transit was marked by an increase of small-arms fire from the shore, which was heavily returned, and there were no casualties in the boats. After departing the Vam Sat, the boats, escorted by the *Washoe County*, went to LZ Crow, where the troops were offloaded.

Before the day was over, Companies B and D had discovered a major Viet Cong base area in the dark interior of the Rung Sat. This was our first view of the activity which had been so often reported in the swamp. In the first few hours the Marines were ashore, they discovered 18 carbines and more than 1,000 grenades, together with arms-manufacturing equipment that was so large it was difficult to believe that it had been moved into this watery complex by sampan. Despite its wet environment, the camp was marked by bunkers and numerous tunnels. Marine demolition experts destroyed everything of value in the installations.

Vietnamese sources reported that the Viet Cong were attempting to move out of the area, via the Rach La—the next major waterway to the north of the Vam Sat, and only a few miles above LZ Crow. Since the *Washoe County* was anchored in this vicinity, her gun crews were called upon to harass the enemy. Firing both

3-inch and 106-mm., the LST saturated the banks of the river, but there was no way of evaluating the effects of her fire.

On the following day, 1 April, good fortune continued, as Companies B and D discovered other camps in the same general area. Food, fresh water, uniforms, 105-mm. shell casings, and water mine casings were found and destroyed. Another arms factory, this one so large that special demolitions had to be flown in, was found and destroyed.

Elsewhere, the river patrols had been equally busy. There are few landmarks in that area, and many of the waterways have similar-sounding or identical names, so to help the boat crews indicate their positions to others, an elaborate system of checkpoints, named after vegetables, was set up. Several times, most often at night, Swift boats and LCPLs exchanged fire with the shore, and the *Robison's* five-inchers aided in breaking up enemy attacks on these small boats. Enemy casualties were unknown, since no one went ashore in these small-boat encounters.

Most patrols were concentrated on the rivers in the southern half of the Rung Sat, but some went all the way up to Nha Be at the confluence of the Soi Rap and the Long Tao. They went into all the large rivers—the Dong Tranh, the Cat Lai, the Dinh Ba off the Dong Tranh as well as the Dinh Ba in the Long Thanh Peninsula. Patrols were conducted by day and by night. Some boats patrolled a single point, and others patrolled a stretch of river. Their mission was to stop enemy movement. The continuous boat patrols also prevented the enemy from planting as many mines as he might have, particularly since the only ones he had were of the command-detonated variety, which take a long time to emplace and require a continual watch if they are to destroy a victim.

Also on 1 April, the Vietnamese Marines became active participants in Jackstay, though

Another view of the convoy steaming up the Vam Sat while the Marines "reconnoiter by fire." The big boat at the right is the Vietnamese monitor, converted from an LCM-6. (R. C. Gifford, PH3, U.S. Navy)

they were not under the operational control of the American commanders. Having moved by RAG boats from Nha Be, the Vietnamese Fifth Marine Battalion landed at 0230 at a fortified "New Life" village on Tam Hiep Thon Island, on the other side of the Long Tao, east of LZ Crow. There were reports that the village had been infiltrated by agents of the Viet Cong, so it was cordoned off and the inhabitants were questioned. However, extensive searches by the troops failed to turn up any significant V.C. activity.

Early in the evening of 1 April, two rounds of mortar landed about 100 yards off the star-

board bow of the *Washoe County* and automatic-weapons fire was heard. The LST countered with 3-inch and Ontos. She was unharmed, and the V.C. fire was silenced. The following day, an air spotter over the Rung Sat sighted a mortar pit on the shore with a dead V.C. nearby, which showed that the fire had been effective. Curiously, although the other bank of the Soi Rap was also in hostile hands, occasional sniper fire was all that came from there.

One section of the Rung Sat that had thus far received little attention was the Ly Nhon Peninsula, even though two battalions of Viet Cong engineers had been reported there.

Harassment and interdiction fire had been delivered into this area nightly by the *Robison*, but no evidence of the enemy could be seen from the air: no people, no boats, no smoke. Intelligence reports identified this section as a V.C. strongpoint and marked the lower western portion as the major crossing point of the Soi Rap between the Rung Sat and Go Cong Province to the southwest. Since neither time nor resources permitted a large-scale sweep of this potential hot spot, it was decided to dispatch the Force reconnaissance troops by boat to investigate. If the results of this investigation warranted it, the Jackstay scheme of maneuver could be modified accordingly, or the duration of the operation lengthened to exploit the findings.

On 3 April a team was transported by LCPL to a point close to the alleged crossing, and landed. The terrain, however, was such that the extensive reconnaissance that was planned could not be made. Mud was knee-to-thigh deep, making advance a slow and tortuous process. The small force of Marines was vulnerable to an ambush, particularly since the air cover could not easily follow it. In view of these difficulties, it was decided to restrict the area of search and to extract the men the same day. Some two square miles were covered and the sighting of one man, presumably a V.C., in a tree, was the only event worthy of mention. The impossible terrain encountered emphasized the advantages that the Rung Sat provided to the Viet Cong. If the Marines had known the routes, they probably could have moved inland more easily and might have uncovered significant V.C. activity. Without that knowledge, they were at the mercy of the mangrove.

To the north, the four rifle companies of BLT 1/5 were closing the jaws of a pincer movement around a place where heavy V.C. fortifications had been reported. From LZ Crow, Companies A and C moved south and west along the edges of the brush, rice field, and swamp roughly paralleling the curve of the Soi Rap. To the south of them, Companies B and D moved north and slightly west, paralleling the Vam Sat. On 3 April, Company D entered a Viet Cong base area that had been so recently abandoned that rice was still simmering on the camp fires. Besides being a training area, with 40-by-40-foot log classrooms, it was apparently used to assemble river mines, 200 of which were discovered and destroyed.

As the day grew older it became evident that the camp discovered by D Company was one of many. Other troops found bases where food, arms, ammunition, medical supplies, machinery, and a variety of other war-making materials were stored. Company C was credited with finding the largest of the camps. Primarily a medical center, this one was also apparently used as a rest and recuperation center. It was equipped with electric lights powered by a gasoline generator, a crematorium, medical books, drugs, pain killers, bandages, and operating instruments. Log bunkers, some of which measured 30 by 30 feet, were emplaced for protection. Walkways, raised three feet over the high-water mark and made of felled trees placed in the fashion of a corduroy road, insured that V.C. feet would be kept dry. The complex was so extensive and so well built that EOD and UDT personnel had to be flown in to ensure its timely destruction.

During the midwatch on 4 April, the Viet Cong made three separate attacks on LCPLs patrolling the Dong Tranh and its tributaries near the center of the Rung Sat. Firing recoilless rifles, mortars, and small arms, they tried to sink these 36-foot boats which, though heavily armed, were neither fast nor well armored. They did not succeed, because of skillful maneuvering by the boat skippers, and because the boats rapidly returned fire with their machine guns and mortars. Within minutes of being called, the *Robison* dropped carefully placed five-inch rounds on target, and was instrumental in breaking up all three attacks.

In the meantime, two Vietnamese Marine battalions had launched operations in other parts of the swamp. Troops of the 4th Battalion were embarked in UH-34 helos from HMM-362 and ferried from their base at Vung Tau to landing zones on the Long Thanh Peninsula, in the hope of catching the V.C. as they moved back into this area following the departure of the U. S. Marines. Pre-L-Hour bombardment of the zones was conducted by the *Robison* and the Vietnamese LSIL-229.

Very deep in the swamp, to the north and east, on the Than An "land mass," the 5th Vietnamese Battalion, having embarked from their CP on Tam Hiep Thon Island, had landed from Vietnamese RAG boats. Our UDTs had planned a raid on a reported boat repair facility near their landing point, but the unexpected Vietnamese operation quickly quashed that plan.

Neither the 4th nor the 5th Vietnamese Marine battalion was faced with much more than an occasional sniper round, and neither discovered anything of importance. The following day, both returned whence they had come and by the same conveyances. It was hoped that these local forces could intercept any V.C. who might be fleeing from the U. S. Marines, but if the enemy was present in the Vietnamese zone, he was not identified.

By this time, the U. S. Marines had almost completed their careful search of the wetland immediately east of the Vam Sat, and were moving toward the river for pick-up. Once again, the Ontos and regular mounts on the decks of the LSTs spewed forth their fire towards the mouth of the Vam Sat. And again a convoy led by Vietnamese Navy FOMs and LCVPs wound its way up the Vam Sat to embark the troops. Commander Lamb, assisted by two boat group commanders, one

from the *Merrick* and one from the *Pickaway*, was again in command. On the up-river trip, there was sniper fire, but naval gunfire and airstrikes had saturated the river banks so thoroughly that little opposition was encountered. The Marines of Companies A, B, and D were embarked at three points about three to four and one-half miles up the river. On the down-river voyage, the Viet Cong scored a direct hit with a mortar round on an LCM, but luckily she was a salvage boat, not a troop carrier, and only three men were injured, none seriously. The round did not penetrate the top deck of the boat, and little structural damage was done.

Apart from that hit, the troop withdrawal was conducted without serious incident, and the men were deposited in LZ Crow. Company C was left at the large installation to provide security for the demolition experts who were completing its destruction. While they were waiting, the Marines ambushed a Viet Cong sampan in the river, killing its four occupants and recovering several weapons. The next afternoon, the demolition work finished, the troops were helilifted back to LZ Crow and the following day were flown to the *Princeton*. Meanwhile, Company E was backloaded into the *Princeton* from LZ Bluejay and the artillery was embarked in the *Henry County*.

For the second consecutive day the LSTs were called upon to exercise their gun batteries. For 45 minutes on 5 April, the target was the banks of the Rach La. The third and final convoy of Jackstay was formed, troops embarked from the shore near Landing Zone Crow into the *Merrick*'s and the *Pickaway*'s landing craft, and the boats, 7 LCM and two LCVP, entered the Rach La. About five miles up, the snaky, muddy river splits into three major branches and numerous small streams. Here, the troops debarked and the landing craft returned to the Soi Rap. Although, at high tide, the Rach La is navigable by LCM all the way east to the Long Tao, instead of taking that route the boats returned to the Soi Rap by the route they had come. That choice was made not only because using the eastern exit would have made the journey longer, but also because there were reports that the Rach La's mouth into the Long Tao was heavily mined. The lack of action on the return trip proved that the decision was sound.

Fanning out over a fairly extensive area, the debarked Marines worked their way to the banks of the Long Tao the following morning. The two landing ships had retrieved their anchors early in the day, steamed up the Soi Rap, embarked pilots at Nha Be, then steamed down the Long Tao to pick up the troops. Four LCMs and a salvage boat followed the ships to provide lighterage between them and the banks. When the pick-up had been made, all the ships proceeded down the Long Tao to rejoin the rest of the Amphibious Task Force.

The *Pickaway* and the *Alamo* steamed into the lee at Vung Tau and met the LSTs, there to re-embark their troops and equipment. One by one, the ships and units that had been added to the ARG for the duration of Operation Jackstay were released to their regular operational control, and the operation was concluded. A few days later, the ARG was ready to strike again.

If numbers alone are considered, the results of Jackstay were not impressive. Fifty-three Viet Cong dead were confirmed by body count. The number of wounded could not be accurately judged, in spite of such evidence as quantities of bloody bandages and drag marks. A more impressive aspect of the operation is that many enemy facilities and tons of his material were destroyed or captured. The cost to the United States was low: five men had been killed, 31 wounded, and two were missing when the operation ended. The two missing men were presumed to have drowned while they were crossing a branch of the Rach La during the last maneuver.

Perhaps the most important result of Jackstay was its psychological effects on both sides in this strange war. To the Viet Cong, it proved again that there were no longer any areas in the country that their enemies were unwilling to enter. From this time onward, the Communists would have to resort to mobile operating procedures, and ensure that their equipment, factories, and rest areas could be moved with little warning. No longer could they rely heavily on deep bunkers capable of withstanding air attack, because it takes time to build such facilities. They would have to depend more and more on infiltrated arms and ammunition, since without secure factories they could not hope to meet the demands of a growing war. It would be increasingly difficult for their political cadres to propagandize the "paper tiger" aspect of government forces and their allies.

American troops had learned that they could chase the enemy into his deepest lairs, where the terrain favors the enemy's type of warfare, and emerge as victors. Novel tactics and procedures that best fit the scheme of maneuver to the geography, had been introduced, had been proved worthwhile, and were applicable in other parts of the country.

Further, Vietnamese government forces must have been both impressed and inspired by their American comrades-in-arms who, although not acclimatized to the steaming swamp, with its exhausting mud, had persevered. They had gone where, previously, no friendly troops had dared to venture, and had found the enemy unwilling to fight. Even though the Vietnamese commanders could not hope to accumulate the variety and strength of forces that conducted Jackstay, they and their men, nonetheless, would be reassured by the strength and prowess of their allies.

From the beginning, it was clear to the Jackstay commanders that one battalion operating in the vast swamp for less than two weeks would not be able to clear the area of Viet

Cong. If it could be done at all, it would take a much larger force many weeks to do it. In a guerrilla war, there is no guarantee that the insurgent will not follow right behind his adversaries in a sweep, and re-occupy an area as soon as his enemy has vacated it. What Operation Jackstay did was to disrupt the routine of the Viet Cong, forcing him to regroup, secure new areas, and develop new facilities. His attacks on the Long Tao ship channel could not be renewed until these new tasks had been accomplished. Thus both the political and military objectives of Jackstay were achieved.

For the best understanding and exploitation of Jackstay's lessons, the operation should be dissected into its various parts: naval gunfire, air operations, small craft, logistic support, and intelligence. A brief discussion of each follows.

Naval gunfire was provided by the *Robison*, the *Washoe County*, and the *Henry County*. The destroyer's main battery is the 5"/54, while the two LSTs are fitted with 3"/50 and 40-mm. mounts, respectively. For Operation Jackstay, each LST carried three Ontos equipped with 106-mm. anti-tank weapons, besides her regular armament. Commodore Westervelt and the staff combat cargo officer, Captain Howard E. Knight, U. S. Marine Corps, jointly conceived the novel use of the powerful Ontos that was made in Jackstay. Now that LSMRs are back in service, they, rather than seaborne Ontos, would probably be used under similar circumstances in the future.

A high-trajectory weapon, if accurate, is more effective in flat terrain than one with a low trajectory, particularly against a well dug-in enemy, since the force of the explosion would be directed primarily downward. Hence, when an operation in the delta is planned, significant numbers of reduced-charge shells, which have a greatly increased angle of entry, should be stocked in the gunfire support ships and used whenever ranges permit.

The main advantage of the 5"/54 over its older sister, the 5"/38, in shore bombardment is range (about thirteen miles, rather than eight and one half), not rate of fire. There are few situations in South Vietnam, particularly in the IV Corps Area, where rapid, sustained fire would make the difference between success and failure. But there are many places in the delta where shallows extend far out to sea, making it impossible for the shorter range 5"/38 to hit targets that are not close to the shoreline.

The 3" and 40-mm. did well at the job for which they were employed, namely, direct fire at close-in targets. The great quantity of iron that these weapons put out can prevent a man from rising above ground to detonate a mine, fire a mortar, or fire a machine gun. They can destroy any object above the surface but do not usually penetrate a horizontal surface, so well-dug-in troops are fairly safe from them. Their high rate of fire would have made both these heavy automatic weapons very useful if hostile boats had been encountered, or an ambush had been attempted. The Ontos have the same capabilities and limitations as the 3" and 40-mm., and they were used for the same purposes. The disadvantage of firing Ontos from a deck is that the resultant shock wave is hard on light bulbs, windows, and delicate equipment. Against a fortified bunker—and there are some in the Delta—106-mm. capability would be reassuring.

During Jackstay, the *Robison* anchored in the lower reaches of the Long Tao River. From this position she could cover most of the maneuver area, but she could not reach all the Rung Sat. A destroyer could assume a firing position in the ship channel, and this would assure coverage of virtually the entire swamp; but, besides the awkwardness of her being where so many ships are transiting the river, she would be susceptible to fire from the banks. Although the Soi Rap is wider than the Long Tao and presents a more difficult problem for an attacker, it has not been recently charted, and navigation on it would be somewhat hazardous.

Aviation made a significant contribution to the success of Jackstay. If there had not been the constant cover of aircraft overhead, the convoys in the narrow Vam Sat and Rach La would have been unacceptably hazardous. Armed Hueys, which can hover for long periods in search of enemy movement and can stay directly above a slow convoy, are the most effective craft for this service. Furthermore, Hueys have machine guns on flexible mounts and are not limited to making diving firing runs—they can fire continuously on a target, and do so with greater accuracy than conventional aircraft. Other distinct advantages that these gunships have over fixed-wing aircraft are that they can be based on an LPH, can receive timely briefings from persons familiar with troop movements and plans, and can get to station quickly. It is prudent that the Navy has now acquired some of these aircraft.

Probably the most effective of the aircraft flown from the Dixie Station carriers was the A-1. This is because it can carry a large bomb load, can remain on target for long periods, and has relatively low speed. When nothing but small arms are being fired skywards, the value of speed is outweighed by its disadvantages.

The Air Force assisted greatly by providing airborne spotters flying the tiny O-1 "Birddogs." All the spotters were familiar with the Rung Sat. As was evident in many other facets of Jackstay, the benefits to be derived from knowledge of the locality far surpass the problems involved in establishing liaison and finding mutually satisfactory communications between different services and different organizations.

For moving troops and light equipment, the old UH-34 Marine helo was the workhorse of the operation, but it was obvious that its load limitations when it is working in the low-density air of the tropics impose disadvantages that are burdensome, to say the least. The much newer UH-46 aircraft quickly demonstrated its greater abilities, and the observations of amateurs on deck were corroborated by an operations analyst from Washington who made a study during Jackstay on the relative merits of the two Marine helos.

A great variety of boats was used in the operation. From CTF 115 came the armed LCPLs, PCFs, and the Coast Guard WPBs. From the Amphibious Ready Group came the standard landing craft of the U. S. Navy: the LCVP, LCPL, LCM, and LCU. The Vietnamese Navy RAG provided the monitor, special minesweeping LCVPs, and FOMs. Each type of boat has advantages and drawbacks but, nevertheless, general conclusions can be reached concerning the relative usefulness of each in the riverine environment.

American landing craft are satisfactory for standard, over-the-beach landings, such as were made in World War II, but they are ill-suited for landings in the Delta, where there is a strong likelihood of landing craft being ambushed. One mortar or recoilless rifle round could injure or kill a great number of men in or disembarking from one of our current craft, a risk that makes the employment of such vessels questionable in the Delta or similar environment. The LCM and LCVP used in the Vietnamese RAGs have had both armor and armament added, at the expense of draft, speed, and maneuverability. For boats to be used in the riverine warfare, this "trade-off" is a good one, since the rivers of the Delta are quite deep (particularly at high tide), speed is not usually a paramount requirement, and the turns in the waterways are the lazy curves characteristic of an alluvial basin. The U. S. Navy has recognized the advantages of the modifications made on the Vietnamese craft, and similarly converted a number of LCMs for the use of River Flotilla One, which first went into action about a year after Jackstay, in the Rung Sat. Steel bars have been installed nine inches from the sides of the converted boats, in order to minimize the effects of a direct hit by a projectile from a recoilless rifle.

On both sides of the Pacific, there has been much discussion on the merits of covering an LCM to protect it from mortar attack. The final verdict has certainly not been heard, but the evidence of a U. S. Navy adviser to a Vietnamese RAG would seem to favor cover. That adviser reported that a 60-mm. mortar round was taken directly on top of one of his LCMs, and the only casualties were two skylarkers who were topside when the shell exploded. A disadvantage of cover is that if a boat were mined, the troops might be trapped inside and drowned.

For patrol work, the fast PCF and PBR are much superior to the LCPL. During Jackstay, Swifts were effective in preventing exfiltration and resupply by water. As mentioned earlier, the PBRs did not have trained crews at the time of the operation, and consequently they did not go on patrol. Though neither the PCF nor the PBR has much armor, both can throw out a high enough volume of automatic weapons fire to break up most ambushes, or can use their high speed to get out of contact before sustaining heavy damage. However, both boats are vulnerable to mines. Draft is important in boats used where there is a lot of shallow water: the PCF draws 4½ feet, the LCPL 3½, and the PBR 1½. The WPB draws 6 feet but, being a more stable platform than the smaller PCF and PBR, she is an effective patrol boat for use in deep water.

In Operation Jackstay the *Belle Grove*, the regular home for PBRs, and the two LSTs were all used to support small craft. In a primitive, hostile environment, a mobile base has many distinct advantages over a fixed one, not the least of which are the modern facilities on the naval ships and the high degree of security. The LSD can bring most small craft into her well for repairs at only a few minutes' notice. Except when heavy swells are running, boats can be docked in the well at the same time as helicopters are operating from the super deck.

Logistic support for the ships participating in Jackstay was provided by the regular Service Force shuttle ships that operate up and down the coast of Vietnam. The clear advantage of this system over any other is that no detailed, advanced planning is required: if food, oil, or spare parts are needed, a message request only hours before the rendezvous will usually suffice. One drawback, but decidedly a secondary one, is that it is often impossible for the ships to leave their support areas during an amphibious operation, steam to sea, and conduct underway replenishment. This applies particularly to the LPH, which is usually the refueling point as well as the home for the helicopter squadron, and to the gunfire support ship, which must be ready for instant response. Under these circumstances, replenishment is conducted either by boat or vertically, but neither method is quite as fast as conventional underway replenishment. Vertical replenishment has the advantages of being faster than boating and of being feasible in heavy seas, but it cannot be used unless a helicopter is available and decks are unencumbered to receive the supplies. Further, it is expensive. Replenishment by boat is not very satisfactory when LCVPs have to be used, as was the case in Jackstay, because their capacity is small and they are highly affected by swell action.

Logistic support for the Marines ashore came from all ships, but during up-river operations, it came primarily from the LSTs. The latter provided water, hot meals, short-duration showers, food, and ammunition, the last two having been stored aboard the ships before the first river landing. Fresh water was a constant problem, since much of it was necessary on the beach, and the high silt content of the Soi Rap River interfered with the functioning of the ships' evaporators. To alleviate this problem, *LCU-1497* made daily water runs between the heavies in the anchorage area and the LSTs in the river. As a result of recommendations made after Jackstay, several LCUs are having both their water capacity and their pumping rate increased. These improvements promise to facilitate water resupply in the riverine environment. As an alternative method of supplying fresh water, ships can store river water in settling tanks for a few days prior to distillation, which would probably cause them little difficulty.

Jackstay pointed up once again the need for reliable intelligence. The intelligence provided by COMNAVFORV was essentially correct with respect to installations. The accuracy of that with respect to personnel and units cannot be evaluated, since the Viet Cong did not choose to stand and fight. If complete and up-to-date intelligence had been available, it would have been possible to plan an attack that left no avenues of escape, and the enemy would have had to fight. In all fairness, it must be stated that in a guerrilla war, that kind of intelligence can seldom be provided. Furthermore, the intelligence that was provided prevented the entire twelve days of the operation being spent in a fruitless search of virgin territory—as might well have been the case.

Hand-in-hand with intelligence go security and surprise. Just as it is impossible to evaluate intelligence when there is little contact, so it is impossible to know whether an operation has been compromised. Even if the enemy has notice of an assault, he may elect not to oppose it, either because he judges the landing force too strong, or because he judges its chances of discovering his facilities are small.

Precautions must always be taken to minimize the chance of compromise. Time can be equated with security: the longer the time that elapses between the conception of an operation and its execution, the greater the chances for compromise. Likewise, the more planning that is done, the more people it involves and, consequently, security is diminished. The ideal operation would be one that was both conceived and executed within a few days, with problems solved and persons notified as situations required. Every effort must be made to cut lead time to a minimum, to limit information to those who need it (and harsh judgments must be made on this point), and to have on hand technical intelligence, such as tidal and beach data, so that it does not have to be collected immediately before an operation. Without security there can be no surprise; and in Vietnam, without surprise an operation is not an operation, it is an exercise.

Jackstay accomplished its goals at little cost, struck the enemy a decided blow, and provided lessons for combat operation in an unusual environment. Its success can be attributed to a variety of factors, including all of the elements usually present in a successful operation: thorough planning, aggressive leadership, superb equipment, sound doctrine, and high morale.

But the success of this unique operation can better be attributed to the ability of the commanders to gather and coordinate a highly diversified fighting force made up of all five U. S. services, plus the Vietnamese Navy and Marine Corps, and a wide variety of other organizations. Perhaps most important, the commanders were willing to improvise, to bend doctrine to the situation, to use new tactics in the quest of victory. In an era when helicopter landings are on center stage in amphibious warfare, the commanders of Jackstay were wise enough to realize that in the swamps boating would net higher returns. The fact that the Viet Cong, secure in the knowledge that we could not get there by helicopter, did not dismantle his facilities deep in the swamp, is evidence enough that this tactic was unexpected and was, therefore, successful.

(*Naval Review*, 1968)

River Patrol Relearned

Commander S. A. Swarztrauber, U. S. Navy

A River Patrol Boat (PBR) enroute to a rendezvous with Navy Seals is caught in a Viet Cong crossfire so vicious that only the well-timed arrival of Seawolf helicopter gunships overhead checks certain disaster. A PBR crewman performing the tedious chore of searching an endless series of junks and sampans suddenly discovers the latest in VC booby traps: opening a bilge compartment, he is met by a deadly—and very angry—tropical snake whose tail had been tacked to the keel board. A river minesweeper crewman, throwing a hand grenade at a suspicious-looking floating C-ration box, is startled by a 150-foot geyser of cocoa-colored water; the box was a VC disguise for a floating mine. A pair of PBRs serving as tugs refloat a 10,000-ton merchant ship whose skipper had misjudged a hairpin turn in the sinuous Saigon shipping channel. The crew of another PBR, failing to reach the provincial hospital in time, delivers a Vietnamese baby boy aboard their boat.

These are some of the many faces of river patrol in Vietnam. Beginning in 1966 a group of American sailors who adopted black berets as their trademark learned the skills of earlier muddy-water sailors and became part of the Vietnamese countryside.

The Setting

The countryside is germane to everything that the river patrol sailors do. Although there is considerable high country in Vietnam, the most important area, where most of the people and food are, is the low country, and particularly, the Mekong Delta.

THE MEKONG DELTA

The Delta is a steaming hot, oppressively humid tableland of mud. The Mekong starts in China's Himalayas, and journeys 2,600 miles, gathering silt and mud along the way as it passes through Burma, Thailand, Laos, and Cambodia. Over the centuries, the Mekong has provided in Vietnam one of the most valuable, fertile, and coveted food producing areas in Asia. Upon reaching Vietnam, the Mekong branches out into two and eventually four delta rivers—the Bassac, Co Chien, Ham Luong, and My Tho—and loses its name, Mekong, along the way. (The Vietnamese name for the Bassac River is Hau Giang, "giang" meaning "river." The French name "Bassac" is more commonly used, however.) On a map, these four rivers look something like a huge human hand, with finger tips reaching to the South

A PBR, downstream from Saigon, heads for home at the end of her patrol.

China Sea. Probably half the Republic's people live between these "fingers," and produce most of the national rice crop in the rich mud. The cities and villages "float" on this mud. To build anything of consequence, such as a bridge, requires pile driving down as far as 200 feet in search of bedrock. In no place in the Delta is the elevation as high as ten feet, so the effects of tide on the rivers are felt up to sixty miles inland. Range of tide in the Delta is normally three to four feet. Spring tides can bring a range of ten feet at Can Tho, in mid-Delta.

THE RUNG SAT

The Rung Sat, a delta area produced by several small rivers, and much like the adjacent Mekong Delta, is a twenty-mile square, between Saigon and the South China Sea. It is a swamp of nipa palm, mangrove, and twisted, exposed-root trees, and is laced with myriad canals. Through the Rung Sat winds the

strategically important Long Tau River to Saigon and the larger, but shallower, and less important Soi Rap River.

WATERWAYS AND WATER TRAFFIC

From the air, the countryside of both the Delta and the Rung Sat looks like an elaborate transportation system, blocked out with thousands of miles of roads; except upon examination, these "roads" turn out to be canals and rivers, some natural, some man-made. Waterways and boat traffic in Vietnam are as common as roads and autos in the United States. Roads, on the other hand, are very rare, perhaps no more common than rivers and canals in our country. The average Vietnamese peasant's home fronts on a canal and he has a sampan moored outside.

A boat larger than a sampan is a junk. If the craft is large enough to allow a water buffalo to stand athwartships, she is classified as a junk.

A craft so small and narrow that a buffalo must stand fore and aft is a sampan.

Machinery, glass, lumber, fuel, hardware, fish, rice, bananas, medicine, weapons, ammunition—everything—moves by water. Pigs and chickens go to market in sampans. The doctor, lawyer, teacher, tax collector, all do business by sampan. The public moves in ferries and water taxis. Thus, all Vietnamese, whether loyal to Saigon or to Hanoi, or to neither, rely on the waterways for transportation and passage.

Operation Game Warden

ROOTS OF THE NAVY'S INVOLVEMENT ON THE RIVERS

To win a war in an environment like this obviously requires enough control of the waterways to ensure they are available for our own purposes and to deny their use to the enemy. In the fall of 1963, after the Diem government fell, a group of senior U. S. naval officers was ordered to investigate the waterway situation in Vietnam. They recommended U. S. Navy involvement with, and support of, the Vietnamese riverine units. However, the report did not trigger any immediate U. S. involvement. This was partly because for many years, the Navy had not been assigned a river warfare mission. River money was not a budget item; there were no riverine craft nor any officers and men trained in river warfare concepts or tactics. Moreover, the United States still had not made its major commitment in Vietnam in terms of military and naval strength. That came in 1965.

Specifically, it was not until February 1965, when a 120-foot North Vietnamese supply ship was caught on the coast of South Vietnam delivering arms and ammunition to the Viet Cong, that extensive Navy inshore warfare in Vietnam began to crystallize as a certainty. Immediately, Operation Market Time, the surveillance and interdiction of seaward infiltra-

tion, was commenced by ships and aircraft of the Seventh Fleet under the designation Task Force 71.[1] On 1 August 1965, responsibility for Operation Market Time was shifted to Rear Admiral N. G. Ward, Chief, Naval Advisory Group (CNAG) in Saigon, who forthwith initiated studies to determine the feasibility of expanding Market Time (which, when shifted to Admiral Ward's control, was redesignated TF-115) into the Mekong Delta and the Rung Sat.

These studies noted that the Viet Cong were firmly entrenched in both the Delta and the Rung Sat, using the waterways with impunity to move battalion-size units and their supplies, to levy taxes, and to tie down the Army of the Republic of Vietnam (ARVN). The riverine units of the Vietnamese Navy (VNN) lacked the leadership, resources, and training to dislodge the Viet Cong and to reestablish the necessary government control. Consequently, the studies pointed out a necessity for U. S. Navy involvement, and they proposed that riverine warfare be undertaken, on a joint basis with the VNN, as a secondary mission of Operation Market Time. The Secretary of Defense authorized the Navy to procure the necessary craft and to wage riverine warfare in Vietnam. In September, representatives of the Chief of Naval Operations (CNO), the Commander-in-Chief, Pacific (CinCPac), the Commander-in-Chief, Pacific Fleet (CinCPacFlt), Commander, U. S. Military Assistance Command, Vietnam (MACV), and the Chief, Naval Advisory Group (CNAG), met in Saigon to draft plans for the expanded Market Time force. They recommended the rapid acquisition by the Naval Ship Systems Command of 120 suitable river patrol boats, in time for operations to begin early in 1966.

This, then, is how and why the Navy became involved in river patrol in Vietnam. Much that has since taken place has not been at all as envisioned by those who drew up the plans in September 1965. Eventually, in Vietnam, there were to be two Navy river patrol commands: Operation "Game Warden" in III and IV Corps Tactical Zones (CTZ) and Operation "Clearwater" in I CTZ. The III and IV CTZs are the southernmost tactical areas of the Vietnamese Army, and include the Rung Sat and Mekong Delta areas, while I CTZ is the northernmost, where the U. S. Marines have been since March 1965, and includes the Tonkin Gulf coastal area.

ORIGIN OF GAME WARDEN

Between September and December 1965, it was recognized that the problem of the rivers was sufficiently different from that of the coast to warrant the establishment of a separate task force. Hence, on 18 December 1965, Task Force 116 (River Patrol Force), code-named "Game Warden," was established. Like TF 115, TF 116 was originally an integral part of the Naval Advisory Group, and the Chief, Rear Admiral Ward, was the first Task Force Commander.[2] When CNAG was also made Commander Naval Forces Vietnam (ComNavForV) on 1 April 1966, Game Warden logically shifted to the new operational command rather than remain on the advisory side of the Navy's Saigon headquarters command.

CONCEPT

The original concept called for groups of 10 river patrol boats to operate from bases—some ashore and some afloat. Four old, inactive LSTs were ordered into commission during 1966 to serve as the first afloat bases. Each was to accommodate 10 patrol boats and a fire-support team of two helicopters, and was to anchor in the vicinity of a Delta or Rung Sat river mouth. January and February of 1966 were spent procuring real estate for seven bases ashore, and establishing the operational and logistical framework for Game Warden. A new organization, Naval Support Activity Saigon, was given the task of base support, consisting of supply, personnel, and maintenance support, freeing the Task Force

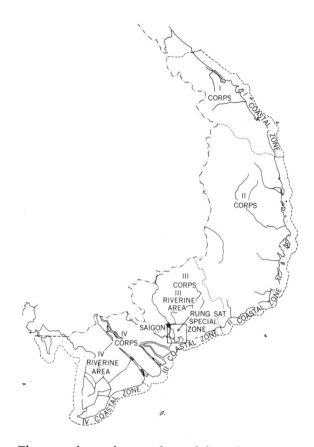

The map shows the complex and dependent nature of the Vietnamese Navy's command structure superimposed on the much greater and dominant Army Command structure. The all-important four corps areas formed the base, of which the VNN Coastal Zones, Riverine Areas, and Special Zones were the subservient appendages. The Allied advisory structure, Army and Navy, naturally conformed to the Vietnamese framework.

commander from all but operational responsibilities.[3] Operations were to be based on two-boat patrols, with tactics to be determined as dictated by the local situation: in other words, they were to be developed from trial and from error. In time, each subordinate task group commander developed his own doctrine and tactics.

A non-self-propelled junk is inspected by the crew of a Mark II PBR in the Long Tau shipping channel.

ORGANIZATION OF GAME WARDEN

In February 1966, the first operation order was promulgated. It organized the Force into two task groups: the Delta River Patrol Group (TG 116.1) and the Rung Sat Patrol Group (TG 116.2). Each task group was made a commander's billet. The task group commander was also an advisor to the South Vietnamese Navy. In the latter role they were called Senior Advisor, Fourth Riverine Area (geographically coincident with the IV CTZ), and Senior Advisor, Rung Sat Special Zone (RSSZ), respectively. (The Rung Sat Special Zone [RSSZ] is a military zone, encompassing the Rung Sat section of III CTZ, and is under the Vietnamese Navy's jurisdiction.) This arrangement stemmed logically from that of the two-hatted parent command in Saigon. Inasmuch as the advisory structure was already in existence, several advisors in both areas had duties with TF 116 added to their advisory missions in order to expedite the inauguration of Game Warden. Eighty of the patrol boats were to operate in the Delta, and forty in the Rung Sat, a two-to-one distribution ratio based on anticipated requirements.

MISSION

The original mission of Game Warden was to conduct patrols on the inland waterways, to visit and search, and to carry on inshore surveillance in order to enforce curfews and prevent Viet Cong infiltration, movement, and resupply in the Delta and Rung Sat. Mine countermeasures were to be conducted in the Rung Sat as required to get seagoing shipping through to Saigon. Compare this with the mission of Market Time, which is to detect and destroy enemy craft attempting infiltration on the coast of the Republic of Vietnam between the demilitarized zone (DMZ) and the Cambodian border. The environmental differences between interdiction on the rivers and interdiction on the high seas have proved to be considerable, and have more than justified the decision to create separate commands for the two missions.

INFANT GAME WARDEN: 1966

The Rung Sat

In 1966 it became clear that the Rung Sat operation was to be essentially one of wresting control of the swamp from the Viet Cong and then of defending it against scores of attempts to recapture it. The Rung Sat, or "Forest of Assassins," is the only gateway from the sea to Saigon, and had been the haven of pirates and criminals for centuries. By 1966, the Viet Cong had established themselves there to train recruits, manufacture munitions, and to hospitalize their casualties. At the end of that year, during which time[4] Operation Jackstay, a major riverine amphibious assault took place, the Viet Cong no longer could claim control of the area. Although they had not been completely evicted, they had to move their training, munitions dumps, and hospitals elsewhere.

The Mekong Delta

During 1966, Game Warden found the Delta to be a "bottomless pit" of opportunity to engage the enemy. The Viet Cong were everywhere, and they did not relish the idea of being routed from their rich, convenient stronghold. It became apparent that 80 boats would never be able to accomplish the mission. The task force commander spent his time reacting to enemy moves and was unable to grasp the initiative. He had to shift his meager assets, repeatedly, between Delta and Rung Sat. This situation prompted him to request additional PBRs and aircraft to support them.

From its austere beginning with four 36-foot steel hull LCPLs working from the Navy Yard at Saigon, Game Warden grew rapidly. In January 1966, the first 15 PBRs arrived at the Amphibious Training Center, Coronado, California, for crew training. Several weeks later,

crew training shifted to the Naval Inshore Operations Training Center, Vallejo, California, because the sloughs of the Sacramento River afforded geography more akin to that of Vietnam. At the same time, 40 more PBRs were ordered so that all crews going to Vietnam could be trained in the United States. This reserve of 40 boats would permit all of the first 120 boats ordered to be deployed for combat in Vietnam. A Seal platoon was assigned to CTF 116 in February. In March, the first U. S. Army UH-1B "Hueys" reported for duty, but the Secretary of Defense directed the Navy to take over all Game Warden helicopter operations as soon as possible and free the Army of that responsibility. Also in March, the LCPL patrols in the Rung Sat were augmented by 82-foot Coast Guard WPBs and 50-foot PCFs ("Swift" boats) from Market Time; four 57-foot minesweepers (MSB) arrived, and the flow of PBRs started to reach Vietnam.

River Squadron Five, a completely separate "type command" for PBRs under the Commander, Amphibious Forces, Pacific (ComPhibPac), was established in Saigon. The first commodore, Commander Kenneth Rucker, reported to CTF 116 for operational control. By April, enough PBRs had arrived to permit dropping the slow (13-knot) LCPLs and to release the Market Time craft. In May, Game Warden got its own task force commander, with Captain B. B. Witham relieving Rear Admiral Ward of that responsibility; but TF 116 remained an integral component of the NavForV organization. That month, PBR patrols commenced in the Delta, operating from Can Tho on the Bassac River, and the first Game Warden afloat base went into operation. In November, Commanding General, IV CTZ, directed his subordinate commanders to provide six English-language-trained National Policemen to each section of 10 PBRs to assist in curfew enforcement and visit-and-search operations. Also in November, three Patrol Air

GAME WARDEN OPERATIONAL CHAIN OF COMMAND*

COMUSMACV

COMNAVFORV

COMNAVSUPPACT Danang	COMNAVSUPPACT Saigon	CTF 115 (Market Time)	CTF 116 (Game Warden)	CTF 117 (MRF)	COM Third Const. Brigade (Seabees)

Bassac River Patrol Group	Co Chien River Patrol Group	My Tho River Patrol Group	Rung Sat River Patrol Group	Upper Delta River Patrol Group
PBR Units	PBR Units	PBR Units	PBR Units	PBR Units
HELO Units	HELO Units	HELO Units	HELO Unit	HELO Unit
SEAL Unit	SEAL Unit	SEAL Unit	SEAL Unit	
SEAL Support Unit	SEAL Support Unit	SEAL Support Unit	SEAL Support Unit	
LST Unit	LST Unit	LST Unit	Mine Counter-measures Unit	

*As of mid-1968. Operation Game Warden, TF 116, had a very flexible, rapidly changing command structure. The above is representative.

Cushion Vehicles (PACVs) were assigned for Game Warden evaluation. By the end of 1966, Game Warden assets included 40 PBRs in the Rung Sat, 80 in the Delta, a Game Warden LST, a minesweeping detachment, three helo detachments, and a Seal detachment.

ADOLESCENT GAME WARDEN: 1967

The year 1967 was one of rapid growth and change. During the year, the number of PBRs rose to 155 (30 in the Rung Sat, the rest in the Delta); the number of helo detachments rose to seven; the number of Game Warden LSTs to four; the number of Seal platoons to six (three in the Delta and three in the Rung Sat). Addi-

tionally, two non-self-propelled floating bases, an APL and a YRBM, were added.

There were also organizational changes. In February 1967, both Market Time and Game Warden were extracted from the ComNavForV organization and set up as separate, individual commands under the operational control of ComNavForV. In the same month, a force level of 250 PBRs was approved, and Task Force 117, River Assault Force, later redesignated as Mobile Riverine Force (MRF), was established.[5] Game Warden was given the additional mission of providing support, on a reciprocal basis, to CTF 117. In September, the mission of TF 116 was liberally interpreted to

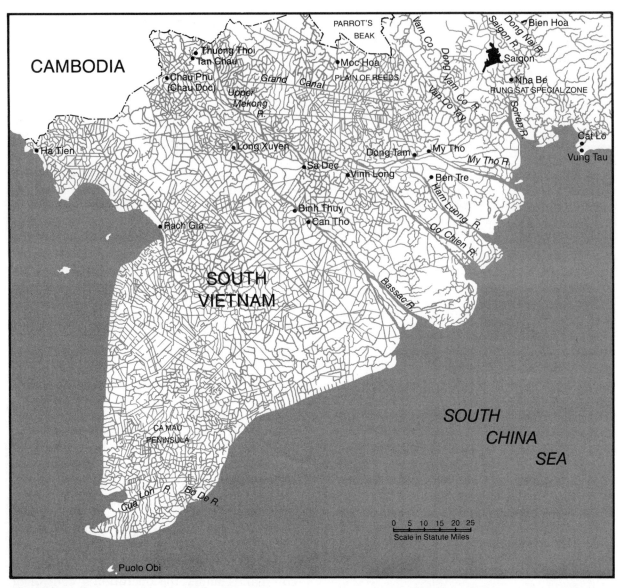

The Mekong Delta, where most of the river fighting in Vietnam took place. Until Task Force 116 was created in 1966, the only craft disputing the Viet Cong for control of these rivers were the worn-out boats of the Vietnamese Navy's River Assault Groups.

include operations in I CTZ, with the sealift of 10 PBRs by a Game Warden LST to the Da Nang area for a one-month operation nicknamed Green Wave. While it was not considered successful because of extensive battle and grounding damage to the boats, the operation proved that PBRs could work the small rivers and lagoons of the north country, if necessary.

Again the mission of Game Warden was modified to include operations on such "rivers as designated by ComNavForV."

Manhood: 1968

In 1968, the expansion and evolution were even more far-reaching. In January, TF 116 was changed from a two-task-group, to a four-task-group, force. It had river patrol task group commands on the Bassac, on the Co Chien, on the My Tho, and in the Rung Sat. In effect, this was a division of the former Delta River Patrol Group into three separate task groups. Each of the four was assigned roughly the same numbers of the same assets (PBRs, helos, Seals, and LSTs), except that the Rung Sat group had no LSTs; it had minesweepers instead.

Only the commander of the Rung Sat Patrol Group retained his advisory role. As advisor, he reported to Senior Naval Advisor in Saigon and as Task Group Commander to CTF 116. In the Delta, a separate billet was set up for the Senior Advisor, IV Riverine Area, reporting to Senior Naval Advisor, and for all practical purposes this billet was outside the Game Warden orbit. The three new Delta task group commanders had no advisory functions.

Initially, all U. S. personnel in Vietnam were advisors, providing advice to their Vietnamese counterparts. However, with the general buildup after 1965, many new operational commands were set up. Flag and general officers who had been only advisors became two-hatted so they could exercise command over the burgeoning operational forces, and still retain command over their advisory structure. Such was the case when CNAG became ComNavForV/CNAG. The same flag officer held both billets and thus commanded all naval personnel in Vietnam, either operationally, administratively, or both. The task force commanders, support activities, and the Seabees report to him in his capacity as ComNavForV, and the Senior Naval Advisor and the Senior Marine Advisor report to him in his capacity as CNAG. The Senior Advisor, IV Riverine Area reports to Senior Naval Advisor, and no one else. CTF 116 reports to ComNavForV. But Senior Advisor RSSZ/CTG 116.4 reports in each of his hats, to both SNA as advisor and to CTF 116 as operator. Another source of complication is the fact that the Navy structure is paralleled by the Army. The IV Riverine Area is a Vietnamese naval area and analogous to a U. S. naval district, and all Vietnamese naval units in it report to the Commander, IV Riverine Area, a naval officer who reports to the Vietnamese CNO in Saigon. The U. S. Navy Senior Advisor, IV Riverine Area, advises him, and reports to Senior Naval Advisor, who is also in Saigon. But the same piece of real estate is also IV CTZ, a Vietnamese Army area, analogous to a U. S. Army military district, and all ARVN units in it report to CG, IV CTZ, an ARVN general, who reports to the ARVN general staff in Saigon. The U. S. Army Senior Advisor, IV CTZ, advises him, and reports to MACV in Saigon.

In April, Game Warden operated for the first time in II CTZ, with another sealift by Game Warden LSTs to Qui Nhon for Operation Maeng Ho II (Fierce Tiger). Game Warden PBRs changed operational commander, coming under control of CTF 115 for one month in order to support Republic of Korea Army troops, who had requested naval support on the waterways in the area of operation.

In late spring 1968, the TF 116 mission was expanded to include the support of the Senior Advisor, IV CTZ, a U. S. two-star general in charge of all U. S. ground and air advisory efforts in IV CTZ. Then, in June, a new task group was formed, the Upper Delta River Patrol Group, charged with the Game Warden tasks on the rivers near the Cambodian border. The same month, another new Game Warden task was added. Increased harassment of Saigon by the enemy led to the Game Warden units being assigned the task of conducting Viet Cong interdiction patrols in the Capital Military District, north of the Rung Sat on the Saigon River and on the Dong Nai River, north to the vicinity of Long Binh. Then, in July, when an Army LCU strayed into Cambodia because of a navigational error and was seized, TF 116's mission was once more expanded, to require surveillance of the upper delta area to prevent that sort of incident from recurring.

In September, because the size of the PBR force had increased, a reorganization plan was implemented, upgrading the administrative unit, River Squadron Five, to flotilla status. Concurrently, CTF 116 assumed command of the new flotilla's assets and henceforth wore two hats: the operational as CTF 116, and the administrative as ComRivPatFlot Five.

During 1968, resources of all kinds almost reached programmed level, except that aircraft deliveries were not completed until 1969. The PBRs reached 230 in number—the remaining 20 of the programmed 250 being assigned to a new task force being formed in I Corps under the name Clearwater. Three non-self-propelled bases arrived; these, in addition to earlier ones, brought the total to five. The Rung Sat minesweepers, formerly detachments of Mine Squadron 11, were reorganized into two mine divisions, 112 and 113. It is interesting to note that the initial Delta to Rung Sat PBR distribution ratio of two-to-one evolved within two years to approximately a six-to-one ratio. The initial disproportionately large commitment to the Rung Sat was occasioned by the fear that the Viet Cong might be able to close the shipping channel to Saigon. But within a year, the Rung Sat was under Allied control, and it became apparent that the major task would be to interdict infiltration in the Delta.

Operation Clearwater

Task Force Clearwater, two years younger than TF 116, is almost a microcosm of its pro-

totype, Game Warden. Consequently, most that is said in describing Game Warden applies also to Clearwater, except size: Clearwater is a Game Warden scaled down to about one-tenth, and in fact was created largely at the expense of Game Warden assets.

AREA OF OPERATIONS

Clearwater operates in the far northern I CTZ and, unlike Game Warden, is tied by mission to a specific geographic area, or the two northernmost provinces within the I CTZ. The I Corps Tactical Zone, commonly referred to as "Eye Corps," consists of five large provinces extending in a line southeast from the DMZ at the 17th parallel. On the east is the Gulf of Tonkin. On the west is the Annam Mountain range, the border with Laos. The coast is characterized by marshes, mud, salt and sand flats, rice paddies, large lagoons, estuaries, and minor deltas created by rivers originating in the Annam range 30 to 50 miles away. About 10 miles inland, the area changes to rolling hills (good for nothing, it is said, except cemeteries and combat bases), then rises to the Annam cordillera. The pattern is broken occasionally by a spur range breaking away from the main Annam range, extending all the way to the Gulf, as is the case just north of Da Nang. About 16 per cent of the South Vietnamese population lives in I CTZ, most of them on the coastal flats, with population centers at Da Nang, the largest city in the north, and at Hue, once the capital of both Vietnams. Because it borders North Vietnam, the source of enemy supply, I CTZ has been hotly contested since the first U. S. Marines landed there in 1965.[6]

OPERATIONAL SITUATION

The northern two provinces, Quang Tri and Thua Thien, have been defended by two or three reinforced U. S. divisions and an ARVN division. Notable battles at Hue, Khe Sanh, and in the vicinity of A Shau Valley, have been fought in the struggle for control of the area.

Charged with supporting all U. S. forces in the two provinces is Commander, Naval Support Activity (ComNavSuppAct) Da Nang,[7] a two-star naval officer, who has the logistic responsibility for all of I CTZ. Approximately 90 per cent of all logistics headed north moves in small vessels from Da Nang up the coast, and then by way of the Perfume River (so named because of the prevailing pleasant scent of various flowers and blossoms) to Hue, in the case of materials destined for forces in Thua Thien Province, or the Cua Viet River to Dong Ha, in the case of Quang Tri Province.

ORIGIN OF CLEARWATER

The two rivers just mentioned are narrow and easily interdicted by mines, rocket grenades, and automatic weapons. Early in 1967, the U. S. commander in I CTZ, Lieutenant General Lewis W. Walt, Commanding General, III Marine Amphibious Force (III MAF), grew increasingly concerned over this kind of enemy action. He requested that MACV assign 30 or 40 new PBRs or ASPBs (TF 117's specially designed Assault Support Patrol Boat) to protect the traffic on these two rivers. The Navy, especially TF 116, was understandably unenthusiastic about such a proposed diminution of its insufficient material assets in the Delta. ASPBs were in even shorter supply than PBRs. Nevertheless, the need in I CTZ was recognized as urgent, and it was decided to construct two mobile support bases for PBRs, one each for the Perfume and Cua Viet rivers, preparatory to redeploying Delta PBRs. The first, PBR Mobile Support Base I (MB I), a complex of nested Ammi barges, designed to provide berthing, messing, repair, command and control facilities for a section of ten PBRs, was ready for deployment in November 1967. River Division 55 was activated at Binh Thuy on 21 November and was deployed to Da Nang on 30 November. River Section 521, then embarked in a Game Warden LST, was deployed to Da Nang on 5 December. Mobile

Support Base I arrived at Da Nang the same week, and all three units were moved to Tan My on the Perfume River and began security patrols on 9 January 1968. Operational command of the PBRs was exercised by ComNavForV/CNAG through CTF 115 and CTG 115.1, who was also the First Coastal Zone Advisor and had Commander I CTZ River Patrol Group/ComRivDiv 55 as his subordinate.

As 1967 drew to a close, enemy pressure continued to mount near the DMZ. General Abrams, then Deputy Commander, U. S. Military Advisory Command (MACV), was dispatched to Phu Bai, near Hue, to establish a special command, MACV Forward, to deal with the situation in Quang Tri and Thua Thien provinces. The siege of Khe Sanh led General Abrams to ask General Westmoreland for still more naval presence, particularly on the Cua Viet. For the last twenty miles, all supplies to that besieged outpost went by air. But until they were airborne the supplies were seaborne, with the transfer point at Dong Ha, about ten miles up the Cua Viet. Because that river was the principal means of resupply for Khe Sanh, ships and boats using it were subjected to intense attack by the Viet Cong and the North Vietnamese Army, both by mining and by river-bank ambush. Even an LST had been sunk on the Cua Viet. But PBRs and ASPBs were still critically few in number, and those that were in Vietnam were needed in the Delta. Because MB II was not yet completed, TF 117's River Assault Division 112, less its ASPBs, was sent instead, and arrived at the Cua Viet in March 1968. This decision was conditioned in part by the fact that the river assault units were far more heavily armored than PBRs, and the Cua Viet, river and base alike, had been under frequent artillery attack.

MISSION OF CLEARWATER

The bitter enemy offensive during Tet 1968, with its concerted campaign against traffic on the Perfume and Cua Viet rivers, again led

General Abrams to ask for expanded naval participation in I CTZ. He requested that a naval task force be established under the command of a senior naval officer, with the mission of protecting traffic, and coordinating all units involved in the movement of logistics craft, on the Perfume and Cua Viet rivers and their adjacent waterways. On 24 February, Task Force Clearwater was established by ComNavForV at Tan My aboard MB I, with just that mission. The first commodore was Captain G. W. Smith, U. S. Navy.

ORGANIZATION OF CLEARWATER

CTF Clearwater (no task force number was assigned) issued a message operation order dividing his force into two task groups: Hue River Security Group (HueRivSecGru) and Dong Ha River Security Group (DongHaRivSecGru), named for the terminal ports on the Perfume and Cua Viet rivers, respectively. HueRivSecGru was headed by ComRivDiv 55 and included 10 PBRs and five minesweepers (locally converted LCM-6s). DongHaRivSecGru was headed by ComRivDiv 112 and included one Command and Communications Boat (CCB), three monitors, and 10 Armored Troop Carriers (ATCs). On 29 February, CTF Clearwater shifted his primary headquarters to Cua Viet, at the mouth of the Cua Viet River, which also became headquarters for ComDongHaRivSecGru.

COMMAND RELATIONSHIPS

CTF Clearwater reported administratively to ComNavForV and operationally to ComUSMACV (Forward), which underwent a name change to Provisional Corps Vietnam, in March, and then again to XXIV Corps in the summer of 1968. XXIV Corps (spoken "Twenty-Four Corps") is commanded by a three-star Army officer.

Fire Support

Army gunship helos were placed on call, "on the pad." Fixed-wing aircraft and artillery were placed at the disposal of Clearwater. The river security group commanders were authorized to carry on direct liaison with the Army and Marine Corps division commanders in their respective tactical areas, for matters involving coordination of artillery, air support, and troop and river craft movement. The ground force commanders in both provinces were charged with the responsibility for security on the river banks.

Logistic Support

ComNavSuppAct Da Nang was given the mission of providing maintenance, supply, and personnel support for the HueRivSecGru by means of facilities at NavSuppAct Detachment Tan My and MB I; and for the DongHaRivSecGru with facilities at the Naval Support Activity detachment Cua Viet.

Clearwater Staff

Clearwater is unusual not only in that it is under the operational control of another service commander, but the Clearwater staff itself consists of Army, Navy, and Marine Corps officers, an Army signal detachment, and a Marine searchlight platoon.

TASK FORCE CLEARWATER EXPANDS

CTF Clearwater was charged with the responsibility for all rivers, lagoons, canals, and estuaries from the coastal mountains at Da Nang north to the DMZ. Before Tet, the PBRs had been performing some of the Game Warden kind of resource and population control operations in addition to their escort and security duties. But Tet changed that. All efforts had to be directed to the protection of the logistic craft. CTF Clearwater directed the formation of convoys, on a 24-hour basis. Even with that, the enemy still managed to sink both logistic and escort craft by means of massive ambushes. This prompted CG III MAF to place an urgent request for additional fast patrol craft for TF Clearwater with which to replace the slow, less-responsive TF 117 craft. Speed was important in reducing the "time-late" of reinforcements, and in providing maneuverability during fire fights, and in the long run proved more important than armor.

The request was honored, and a second section of 10 PBRs was deployed, this time from the Rung Sat. Five PBRs arrived at Cua Viet in May 1968, and five more in June. The PBR commander relieved ComRivDiv 112 as ComDongHaRivSecGru, and the TF 117 unit returned to the Delta, leaving behind six ATCs for use as minesweepers. These were also soon released when replaced by five minesweeping-configured LCM-6s. In mid-1968 the HueRivSecGru was augmented by the three Patrol Air Cushion Vehicles (PACVs) which had been in the Delta. The DongHaRivSecGru was also augmented by eight LCPLs especially equipped and configured for night surveillance duties.

There were no means to provide maintenance support for the PBRs arriving at Cua Viet, which is a very austere place indeed. MB II was still not ready for use. Moreover, Cua Viet was subjected to frequent artillery attacks from the DMZ; building anything there was risky. There were serious questions raised concerning the advisability of mooring MB II at Cua Viet when it did become available. Consequently, it was decided that MB II would be diverted for use in the Delta, and that MB I, 40 miles southeast at Tan My, would be sent more men to take up the load of repairing the Cua Viet PBRs. An ingenious device, nicknamed the "mini-dock" was rigged by NSA Da Nang to transport the PBRs between Cua Viet and Tan My, even during the northeast monsoon. The "mini-dock" was an LCM-8 rigged with PBR skids on the well deck and equipped with special plumbing to enable the craft to ballast and deballast her wingwall tanks, and thus operate like a self-propelled floating dry dock.

By June 1968, the battle to evict the enemy from Hue was history, and the Perfume River had been pacified. Accordingly, CTF Clearwater requested a mission change which would have the command perform the Game Warden sort of functions. This was effected in September by CG XXIV Corps simply by adding to the mission the phrase "... and to conduct riverine operations on the Perfume and Cua Viet Rivers and the adjacent waterways ...," thus opening the door for the conduct of psychological operations, visit and search, cordon and search, amphibious insertions, and for resuming their former resource and population control work. About that time, Clearwater, specifically the HueRivSecGru, went on the offensive, especially on the lagoons, working closely with the 101st Airborne Division, to ferret out the Viet Cong on Vinh Loc Island. On the Cua Viet, the North Vietnamese Army (NVA) launched an increasingly severe mine offensive, burdening the Third Marine Division river bank security units, and forcing the posture of the DongHaRivSecGru to remain essentially defensive. To assist in coping with the increased mine threat, three MSBs from MineDiv 113 were assigned at Cua Viet in early 1969. By this time, it appeared that Clearwater had been outfitted with sufficient assets to carry out its mission successfully.

The River Patrol Assets

The river patrol hardware and the people who operate it are far more interesting than their command structure, mission, and history. Merely to serve with these units, is to be greatly impressed with the men's qualities of

TASK FORCE CLEARWATER OPERATIONAL CHAIN OF COMMAND*

COMUSMACV
|
CG III MAF
|
CG XXIV Corps

CG 3rd MARDIV   CTF Clearwater   CG 101st ABN DIV

Hue River   Dong Ha River
Security Group   Security Group

Patrol Unit   Patrol Unit
(PBR)   (PBR)

PACV Unit   Mine Counter-
                                             measures Unit

Mine Counter-   Surveillance
measures Unit   Unit (LCPL)
                                             |
                                             USMC Searchlight
                                             Platoon Element

*As of mid-1969.

ingenuity, courage, professional skill, and patriotic dedication to duty.

PBRs (PATROL BOAT, RIVER)

Selection of a hull

In September 1965, when NavShips was
asked to procure a "suitable" river patrol craft,
there was no time to design a new boat; yet
they had only a few months to produce a craft
that was to become the "ship of the line" in two
combat task forces. It was fortuitously discovered that several commercial boatbuilders
had already produced what appeared to
be a suitable hull. The design that initially
appealed the most was the "Hatteras" hull,
engineered by the Hatteras Company, High
Point, North Carolina, a stock fiberglass hull.
Consequently, that month NavShips issued
the Circular of Requirements for the proposed
PCR (Patrol Craft, River). Specifications included: high speed (25 to 30 knots); shallow

draft (static 18 inches, cruising 9 inches); light
weight; water-jet propulsion preferred. The
Circular of Requirements obviously made it
considerably easier for the several prospective
bidders who had a "Hatteras-" style hull on
hand. In October, the designation PCR was
changed to PBR. Meanwhile, eight boatbuild-
ing companies bid for the contract, including
such notables as the Chris-Craft Corporation.
In November 1965, the contract was awarded
to the lowest bidder, United Boatbuilders of
Bellingham, Washington, who committed
themselves to deliver 120 boats by 1 April 1966
at a cost of roughly $75,000 each. Essentially,
what United had to do was create a new Navy
superstructure for one of their standard hulls.

PBR Specifications and Characteristics

For main propulsion, General Motors 220-
hp truck diesel engines, already on the shelf,
were selected to provide 2,800 rpm direct drive

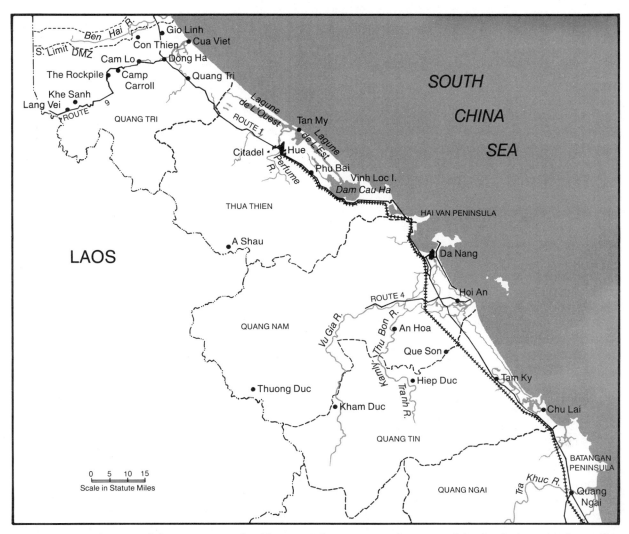

I Corps Tactical Zone. If the Marines and soldiers in I Corps were to be successful inland, their supply routes up the Cua Viet and Perfume rivers had to be made safe. So Task Force Clearwater was created to help accomplish that.

to the Jacuzzi Brothers' water-jet propulsion pumps, also already on the shelf. A Raytheon 1900/N radar and two AN/VRC-46 FM radios were installed as the electronics suit. The armament consisted of a twin .50-caliber machine gun mount forward and a single mount aft. An M-60 (7.62-mm.) machine gun

and a Mark 18 40-mm. grenade launcher were provided for use amidships. The portable Mark 18 was equipped with a pintle mount, so it could be used amidships, either port or starboard, or "piggy-back" on the after .50-caliber. Several small weapons were also included. Ceramic armor, specified to stop a .30-caliber bullet, was installed to protect the coxswain's flat (conning station), and at each of the three machine gun positions.

The final result: the Mark I PBR. She was compact—31 feet long, 10½ feet wide, with a fiberglass hull. She was speedy—28.5 knots at her combat displacement of 14,600 pounds. She was maneuverable—the PBR is steered by turning the water-jet nozzles to the right or left of the centerline by means of Morse control cables. Similarly, reversing is accomplished by dropping U-shaped gates over the water jet which abruptly redirect the water jet flow 180 degrees to straight ahead. PBRs can back with precision, but not very fast. In an emergency, a PBR can reverse course at full speed in her own length, and stop dead in the water in three lengths. (But these maneuvers are a sure guarantee of soaking everyone and everything on board.) She was formidable—bristling with the arms mentioned above, as well as for special missions, a 90-mm. recoilless rifle, a light antitank weapon, and/or a 60-mm. mortar. In 1969, the new, high-velocity automatic Mk 19 40-mm. grenade launcher was introduced, with consideration being given to dropping the manually operated Mk 18. Some PBRs have been outfitted with a 20-mm. cannon in the forward dual mount, paired side by side with a .50 caliber, Mutt and Jeff style.

Suitability

Certainly the PBR is a most suitable type of craft for the mission in the Delta, the Rung Sat, and I Corps. Her lightweight fiberglass hull and water-jet propulsion give her the shallowest possible draft. This is important because PBRs must frequently operate in shoal water, most of it uncharted. In some seasons there is a tremendous amount of floating plant life, especially several varieties of hibiscus, which are dislodged from the fields and bayou banks on spring tides, and then set to drift on the tide. This material is a menace to screw-driven craft. But it also causes concern for PBR skippers, who give it a wide berth. The PBR pump intake grills are designed to reject or, at least, cut up floating materials before ingestion, but they are not infallible.

The Speed Crisis

The PBRs started arriving in Vietnam in March 1966, deck-loaded on Victory ships from Puget Sound, off-loaded at one of three ports in the Saigon-Rung Sat area, and outfitted and shaken down at Cat Lo or Nha Be. Although the PBR propulsion plant and hull have turned out to be surprisingly reliable, rugged, and responsive—probably a lot more so than a metal-hulled, screw-driven craft would have been—it was not always considered so. The boat had been designed for commercial or pleasure use in clean, fresh, and peaceful waters. In Vietnam, it would be shot at, handled roughly, and operated at high speeds in constantly high temperatures and humidity and in muddy water, laden with silt, sand, salt, and debris. There were hardly any replacement parts on hand. Within a month of the arrival of the first boats, a board of investigation convened by ComNavForV predicted that the life expectancy of the PBR "in-country" would be only six months due to premature aging because of hard use, corrosion of machinery, and deterioration of hulls. The board recommended a complete re-engineering. Yet those same boats, off-loaded in March 1966, are still operating in Vietnam. They look as good, if not better, than they did then, and they go faster. Why? It was simply a matter of learning new skills. Maintenance men from the Naval Support Activity, and PBR crewmen themselves, rapidly learned the art of fiberglass repair. Pressure was brought to bear through the supply system to expedite the production and delivery of engine and pump spares and of repair parts.

Before the parts arrived and the repair skills

were learned, however, the maintenance situation was gloomy. By early 1968, the deterioration of the Jacuzzi pumps owing to erosion of impellor blades and wearing rings, had reduced the average PBR speed to about 15 knots, and some boats could make no more than 11.5 knots. A study conducted in the spring of 1968 revealed that the speed loss was also attributable in some measure to excessive displacement caused by waterlogging of the styrofoam (the bow of each PBR was stuffed with block styrofoam, so that the boat would float, bow up, if flooded). The investigators found also that improper loading—carrying extra ammo—was adversely affecting trim. Moreover, poor fiberglass repair had fouled the planing surface. The resultant loss of speed was serious inasmuch as the PBR's best "armor" against the enemy's ordnance was her speed.

By this time, the new Mark II PBRs (all PBRs after the initial 120) had started to arrive. They were essentially the same boat with minor improvements. A few inches wider than the early boats, they present a slightly lower silhouette. Probably the most significant design change is that they have aluminum gunwales, which prevented junks and sampans from tearing up the sides of PBRs when coming alongside for inspection. They also were equipped with a later model, more powerful, water-jet pump. When they arrived in Vietnam, doing 28 knots, they ran circles around the veteran Mark Is.

Speed Crisis Solved

Finally, in mid-1968, two and a half years after the first boats had arrived, the spare parts caught up with the demand. Waterlogged PBRs were hauled out, their styrofoam was dried, and their bottoms were resealed with gel-coating to eliminate the water seepage. It was also discovered that the later model pump, installed in the Mark IIs, could be

adapted for use in the Mark I. Soon the Mark Is were back up to speed, some over 30 knots! Ironically, late in 1968, ComRivPatFlot Five had to issue a directive ordering division commanders to hold the speed of the Mark Is down to 27 knots to prevent possible structural damage, until the necessary compensating adjustments could be made. By this time, the skill of fiberglass repair was also mastered. Now it can be seen that once a force is possessed of the necessary skills, fiberglass is the most suitable hull material, considering weight and maintenance, for this kind of warfare. There is very little the enemy can do to a PBR that cannot be fixed by local maintenance crews.

Overhaul Pool

It was mentioned earlier that a force level of 250 PBRs had been approved. To take full advantage of the in-country maintenance and repair capability, it was decided in mid-1968 not to activate the 25th PBR command, but to earmark the last 10 boats for use as a battle damage and overhaul pool. Although the overhaul program can now prevent PBRs from "wearing out," over the years, more than a dozen boats have been lost and stricken from the register because they were unsalvageable or were damaged beyond economical repair.

THE PBR CREW

The boats are manned by a crew of four. The boat captain is a petty officer first class. Boat captains are selected and trained in the United States. Most are deck ratings—Boatswain's Mate, Quartermaster, Gunner's Mate, and Radarman—but some boat captains are engineers and even cooks and clerical ratings. The crew includes a gunner's mate, an engineman, and a seaman, all of whom become gunners in combat. In fact, each member is trained to navigate and pilot the craft, and to operate the electronics equipment, the engines, and each weapon. Like submariners, PBR sailors discarded the "one-rating mentality." Generally, PBRs operated in two-boat patrols. A chief petty officer or junior officer (warrant officer through lieutenant) serves as patrol officer, or OTC, and positions himself in one of the boats. The Vietnamese National Policeman, when embarked, rides the other PBR. Battle casualties have occasionally necessitated "Fleeting-up" some especially well-qualified first and second class petty officers to patrol officer and boat captain, respectively. They performed ably thus, and in most cases they completed their tours in Vietnam in their new billets.

The PBR Sailor

PBR crewmen have distinguished themselves by making theirs the most decorated naval command in the Vietnamese war. During 1968 alone, a representative year, they earned one Medal of Honor (their second), six Navy Crosses, four Legions of Merit, 24 Silver Stars, 290 Bronze Stars, 363 Navy Commendation Medals, more than 500 Purple Hearts, and scores of other decorations. (One of every three PBR sailors has been wounded during his tour in Vietnam.) Their morale is the highest of any this writer has ever seen in the service. In spite of poor, uncomfortable living and working conditions, rigorously long working hours, and constant personal danger, one out of every five PBR crewmen requests a six-month extension of his tour in Vietnam. Combat pay and special promotion advantages may account for some of this, but the chief reason lies in the enormous responsibility resting on the shoulders of PBR sailors, especially the boat captain, who is called on to make decisions and exercise leadership in a manner virtually non-existent for petty officers elsewhere in the Navy. These collective stimuli of great responsibility, hard work, discomfort, danger, and adventure, accompanied by selective personnel assignment procedures, have developed a remarkably serious-minded and skillful corps of sailors with a keen sense of purpose.

PBR ROUTINE

While there is a great deal of adventure and glamor in this work at times, the biggest danger comes not from the enemy, but from boredom and fatigue, which dull alertness and which can catch one unprepared. This is not so hard to understand when it is realized that the PBR sailor endures demanding and long hours, watching, waiting, searching, and inspecting watercraft. The PBR crewman logs a work week of usually more than 80 hours, and half his time on patrol is at night. Each PBR is under way about 40 per cent of the time, mainly at low speeds. Normally, PBRs operate at full speed only when in contact with the enemy or when proceeding to and from patrol station. Their endurance is about five and one-half hours at full speed. But the nature of PBR patrols is such that after a normal 12-hour patrol, they return with about 25 percent fuel on board. Searching junks and sampans becomes dull work after the first few hundred. Not at all glamorous. The boats search thousands of craft each week. In a typical month, Game Warden's PBRs will detect 200,000 watercraft, board about one-half of them, or 100,000 for cursory inspection, and carefully search about half of those, or 50,000. Certainly, no one knows for sure how many sampans and junks there are in the area. It is safe to say that many craft are detected and perhaps searched two or more times during a month. In most cases, no irregularities are found. The routine of a standard 12-hour patrol is waiting . . . drifting . . . searching . . . verifying cargo manifests . . . checking ID cards against black lists . . . putting on the rain gear . . . taking off the rain gear . . . .

CHARLIE BREAKS UP THE ROUTINE

This tedious routine, which is officially termed "population and resources control," pays concrete dividends in forcing the Viet Cong into hiding and into taking chances that might expose him. The writer had the interesting experience of catching a Viet Cong tax collector moving from one tax collection station to another. What gave him away was the $VN325,000 we found deep inside the cargo of bananas he was hauling as his "front." The enemy had to move his supplies and troops somehow, but he did not want to be caught in the act. Not wishing to have to fight his goods to their destination, he especially avoids direct confrontation with PBRs when he is engaged in logistics operations. His tactic has become one of moving troops, weapons, and supplies across rivers at night, just after a PBR patrol has passed, and before the next one arrives on the scene. He can power a sampan to do 30 knots and dart out of a creek on one side of the river to a creek on the other side. Although most of the Delta area is flat and clear, its waterways are lined with trees, referred to as "tree lines," which provide "Charlie" with excellent staging areas and ambush sites. This environment requires a matching of wits, using deception and stealth. Because PBRs are noisy, "Charlie" can hear them coming. Hence, various tactics have been developed: drifting silently with the tide or current, anchoring, dragging anchor, using a quiet outboard motor, and so forth.

The Viet Cong usually cover a river crossing attempt with a squad or more armed with recoilless rifles, rocket-propelled grenades (B-40, B-41), and automatic weapons such as the AK-47. If he is caught, or thinks he is, "Charlie's" cover troops go into action, and the river bank erupts with fire. "Charlie" fights back fiercely. He may set an ambush, bringing concentrated fire against a passing patrol as a diversion to cover a major troop or logistic movement elsewhere, or to avoid some other disruption of his plans.

PBR TACTICS

The counter-tactic obviously has been to separate the units of the PBR patrol. They generally steam in open column, a "lead" boat followed by the "cover" boat. About 400 to 600 yards' separation provides what is considered an optimum trade-off between radar surveillance coverage and mutual protection.

The rivers are divided geographically into areas of responsibility for the several PBR unit commanders, who in turn, subdivide their individual areas into patrol areas. The patrol areas are not overlapping. Some of these are as far as 90 minutes' steaming from the base. Adjacent PBR patrols, covering their patrol area at random, do not interfere with one another, but occasionally see one another, if they happen simultaneously to approach their mutual border.

At first it was standard operating procedure, when fired upon, to return the fire while retiring from the "kill zone," and radioing for assistance before reentering. The experiences of Tet 1968, however, demonstrated the PBRs to be capable of suppressing enemy fire well beyond expectations. New guidance was issued, extending the option for PBRs to "stand and fight" when attacked, if in the judgment of the patrol officer, it seemed wise to do so.

PBR WEAPONS

PBR weapons have proved to be quite good and suitable for their tasks. Probably their most effective and useful item is the 40-mm. grenade. Captured Viet Cong confirmed its effectiveness and their fear of it. The .50-caliber is a deadly and powerful weapon, but it is difficult to control with any real precision. It is quite necessary, and very good, for fire suppression, driving the enemy back into his hole, but its long-range rounds carry well beyond the target, and this is a problem in densely inhabited areas. The same applies, of course, to the 20-mm. cannon. Fortunately, ammunition supply has been adequate for all PBR weapons.

PBR Psychological Operations

Although the primary mission is that of preventing the enemy from using the rivers for his own purposes, Game Warden and Clearwater PBRs are deeply involved in psychological operations (PSYOPS). When they commenced patrols in 1966, the Viet Cong warned the civilians that PBR sailors would butcher and eat their children, rape their women, and steal their belongings. This was effective; often Vietnamese girls would go into hysterics on the approach of a PBR. It was only through their own counter-propaganda program that PBRs were able to erase this fear. Civic action programs, such as helping to rebuild structures destroyed by the Viet Cong, digging wells, and treating sick and wounded, were undertaken. Leaflets were distributed and loudspeaker programs were broadcast the length of the rivers. Soap, fishing gear, and school supplies were dispensed. Even the tide was used to tactical advantage, by dispensing floating propaganda materials at the mouths of waterways leading to Viet Cong strongholds upstream, just at the beginning of the flood tide. Each PBR was designated as a "Chieu Hoi" station. "Chieu Hoi" is the "Open Arms" program wherein Viet Cong who turn themselves in to the South Vietnamese government are promised amnesty, some job training, and resettlement in an area of their choice.

That PBRs successfuly countered the Viet Cong propaganda barrage can best be illustrated by an incident that took place early in 1968. A Viet Cong soldier, having heard the PBR broadcasts, and having become discouraged with the way the war was going for him, swam out to a PBR in the river and turned himself in. When asked why he surrendered to the PBR rather than to one of the "Chieu Hoi" centers ashore, he replied that "he had heard from the local people that PBR sailors would not hurt him, but would treat him well." Further evidence of the trust developed are several cases in which victims of Viet Cong tax collectors have come to PBRs, reported their experience, and led PBR crews to villages where they fingered the Viet Cong tax collectors.

River Squadron/Flotilla Five

Before moving from PBRs to helicopters, something should be said of the PBR administrative organization. When established in March 1966, River Squadron Five was set up with four subordinate river divisions, commanded by division commanders. Each of these was subdivided into three river sections under officers in charge.

RivRon Five headquarters was moved from Saigon to Binh Thuy in March 1968. Then, when River Squadron Five became River Patrol Flotilla Five on 1 September 1968, the former divisions became squadrons (then five of them), and the sections became divisions (24 of them) with squadron and division commanders, respectively, in command. Some squadrons have five divisions and some have four. Most of the squadron commanders serve operationally as task group commanders; and most of the division commanders serve operationally as task unit commanders, except those division commanders under CTF Clearwater, who serve as task group commanders. The Flotilla Commander is the administrative commander of all PBRs in Vietnam, both those in Game Warden and those in Clearwater. He, in turn, reports administratively to ComPhibPac. Operationally, he reports to himself in his other hat as CTF 116.

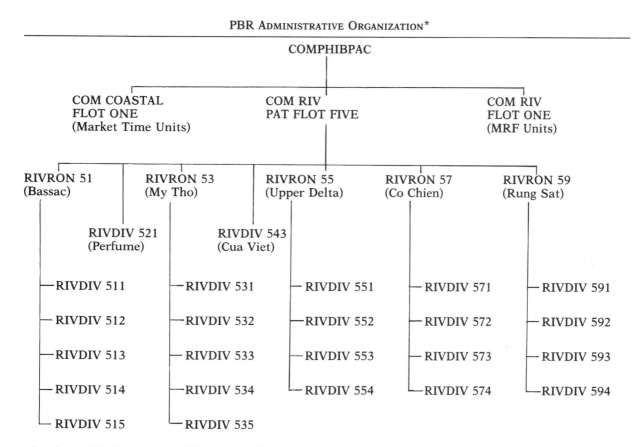

PBR ADMINISTRATIVE ORGANIZATION*

COMPHIBPAC

COM COASTAL FLOT ONE (Market Time Units) — COM RIV PAT FLOT FIVE — COM RIV FLOT ONE (MRF Units)

RIVRON 51 (Bassac) — RIVRON 53 (My Tho) — RIVRON 55 (Upper Delta) — RIVRON 57 (Co Chien) — RIVRON 59 (Rung Sat)

RIVDIV 521 (Perfume) — RIVDIV 543 (Cua Viet)

RIVDIV 511 — RIVDIV 531 — RIVDIV 551 — RIVDIV 571 — RIVDIV 591

RIVDIV 512 — RIVDIV 532 — RIVDIV 552 — RIVDIV 572 — RIVDIV 592

RIVDIV 513 — RIVDIV 533 — RIVDIV 553 — RIVDIV 573 — RIVDIV 593

RIVDIV 514 — RIVDIV 534 — RIVDIV 554 — RIVDIV 574 — RIVDIV 594

RIVDIV 515 — RIVDIV 535

*As of early 1969. The numbering of Rivdiv's 521 and 543 appears inconsistent. These divisions were in ICTZ with TF Clearwater at the time of reorganization, and retained their former River Squadron Five numbers.

RIVER PATROL AIRCRAFT

Although the PBRs are the keystone of both Game Warden and Clearwater, air support has become an integral and indispensable element of the river patrol.

Army Helicopters

While drafting the concept of operations for Game Warden in the winter of 1966, the planners never had any doubts about the need for helicopter gunship support. No other kind of available aircraft was considered suitable for the task envisioned. But the Navy had no heli-copter gunships, and its own ASW helicopters were simply not suitable for adaptation. They were too heavy and too large, as well as being expensive and scarce. The Army, however, had developed tactics for the close air support of airmobile troops using aerial rocket battalions of UH-1 "Iroquois" gunships. Without a great deal of effort, it was believed, these tactics and weapons could be adapted to the support of PBRs. The Army was given the responsibility of providing helicopter gunship support until the Navy could assume the burden. Even before the first PBRs arrived in March 1966, the first two U. S. Army "Hueys," as they are also called, complete with Army crews, reported to CTF 116. Their parent command was the 197th Aviation Company which provided aircraft, crews, and maintenance throughout 1966.

The Light Helo Fire Team (LHFT) made up by these first two "Hueys" got its first operational assignment supporting the PBRs aboard the USS *Belle Grove* (LSD 2), jury-rigged to accommodate PBRs and helos until the Game Warden LSTs could replace her. (The difference between a Light Helo Fire Team and a Heavy Helo Fire Team (HHFT) is one helicopter; three operating together make up an HHFT.)

Navy Assumes Helo Role

In June 1966, the Navy deployed Detachments 25, 27, and 29 of Helicopter Combat Support Squadron One (HC-1), Imperial Beach, California, to Tan Son Nhut Air Base, Saigon. (The detachments were made up of eight officers and eight enlisted men each.) They underwent training at Saigon in helo gunship warfare, provided by the Army's 120th Aviation Company. By the end of 1966, these detachments had learned the trade, and took over all Game Warden flight operations, relieving the Army personnel, but not until after an Army pilot lost his life flying a Game Warden mission in September.

Because the Navy had no gunships of its own, the Army continued to supply "Hueys" and also agreed to perform depot level maintenance, and to provide spare parts and ammunition through its logistics channels. Although the Navy has progressively taken over the maintenance of the UH-1Bs, they are still owned by the Army. The original agreement stipulated an inter-service loan of 22 helos, with replacement of those that were lost. This arrangement was practically as good as outright ownership of the birds. By the end of 1966, the Navy was operating eight Game Warden "Hueys." Two fire teams were embarked

in support ships, and one was based at Nha Be in support of Rung Sat operations. The other two aircraft were in the maintenance pool at headquarters, HC-1 Detachment, Vung Tau, the Army helo maintenance center.

Helicopter Attack (Light) Squadron Three (HA(L)-3) organized

In April 1967, HA(L)-3 was commissioned at Vung Tau, absorbing all the former HC-1 detachments. In September, the strength of 22 helos was reached, with 14 aircraft in seven fire teams, and a maintenance pool of eight located at Vung Tau. Three of the LHFTs were operating from the Game Warden LSTs, and four from fixed bases, at Nha Be, Dong Tam, Vinh Long, and Binh Thuy. HA(L)-3 is commanded by a captain who reports administratively to Commander, Fleet Air, Western Pacific, and operationally to CTF 116. With the completion of the helicopter maintenance facility at Binh Thuy in 1969, HA(L)-3 relocated its headquarters and maintenance crew to Binh Thuy, thus concentrating Game Warden command and control at that location.

HA(L)-3 has provided no helicopters to other commanders; most notably none have been assigned to CTF Clearwater. Early during the Clearwater operation, Army helo gunships were summoned from their pads at Camp Eagle near Hue and Quang Tri City to assist PBRs engaged in fire fights on the Perfume and Cua Viet, respectively. More recently, helicopters have seldom been used by TF Clearwater because of the ready availability and complete coverage of the U. S. artillery installations. Actually, if the pilots are familiar with PBR operations, gunships, Army or Navy, provide better close support for PBRs than the artillery does. But in I CTZ, artillery can be obtained faster than helo gunships, and for this reason, use of helicopters has flagged. (Artillery available to Game Warden is mostly ARVN, and is not as plentiful, and hence is not used as much as in I CTZ.)

SEAWOLVES

HA(L)-3 has adopted the nickname "Seawolves." They call both themselves and their helicopters Seawolves. They, too, wear the black beret of the river patrol forces, and they are a proud assemblage of seasoned combat aviators. It is not unusual for a "Seawolf" to earn as many as 25 Air Medals during his tour in Vietnam.[8] A Seawolf crew consists of a pilot, a co-pilot, and two door gunners, the latter enlisted flight crewmen. Pilots first become qualified as "Seawolves," then they qualify as aircraft commander. The highest qualification is that of fire team leader, analogous to patrol officer of the PBRs on the river below. Seawolves usually operate in pairs, under the command of the "Fire Team Lead," as the fire team leader is called, and who is also the aircraft commander of the lead aircraft.

UH-1B "Seawolf" Characteristics

Although they are being replaced as obsolescent by the Army, Hueys are still remarkably effective weapon systems, especially in the Game Warden environment. Their armament includes a seven-rocket pack of forward-firing 2.75-inch rockets on either side of the aircraft. Similarly fixed 7.62-mm. machine guns (flexguns) are mounted over the rocket packs on each side. Each door gunner—port and starboard—operates a freely-trainable machine gun. The lead helo has one .50-caliber and one M-60 (7.62-mm.). The wing helo has two M-60s. Most "Seawolves" prefer the .50-caliber. Initially it was feared that the airframe could not withstand the stresses of a .50-caliber. Tests proved it could, and now, a .50-caliber is being backfitted into each helo, as weapons become available. Grenades and small arms are also carried. The aircraft patrols at 80 knots. Max-

imum gunship combat load speed is about 90 knots. Endurance at patrol speed is 1½ hours. Length over-all: 53 feet; take-off weight: 8,500 pounds.

Seawolf Operations

The Seawolf mission is two-fold: direct support of PBRs and armed patrol of the river delta areas. The primary mission is to support PBRs in contact with the enemy. Hence they are on a 24-hour alert basis, and can be scrambled within three minutes. They are seldom more than 15 minutes away from—and are usually closer to—the engaged patrol. About 80 per cent of the time is therefore spent standing by to scramble. The rest of the time is taken up by armed reconnaissance patrols and support of planned TF 116 operations.

During patrol, the lead aircraft usually flies about 100 feet higher than the wingman, enabling the latter to fire beneath the lead aircraft in case of trouble. Tree-top flying is dangerous because of the likelihood of being hit by small-arms fire, and is limited to those situations where a close look is required. The principal targets of Seawolf fire are enemy units, or suspected enemy unit positions, in the tree lines. The helo has the distinct advantage of being able to see on both sides of the tree line, and much of what is actually in the tree line itself. Other targets include: sampans, junks, fleeing troops, and bunkers. Upon arrival over the target, the LHFT sets up a circular pattern, each helo alternately engaging the target, the other providing cover.

Their most effective weapon has been the door gunner, particularly the one with the .50-caliber. This is because the door guns can be trained and fired throughout a semi-sphere, and are not limited to firing straight ahead as is the case with the rockets and flex-guns. Operations are conducted both day and night; and all bases, floating and fixed, are rigged and lighted for night operations. Over the target, the fire control problem is simpler at night than in daylight, because the source of enemy fire can be quickly identified and pinpointed. While there is some similarity between Seawolf tactics and those of the Army gunships, the Seawolf tactics are very much original, worked out by trial and error. The essential element of Seawolf tactics is close coordination of fire power, communications, and movement between helo and PBR.

Aircraft Shortage

The most significant Seawolf problem has been the availability of aircraft. The Army is short of gunships. Inasmuch as they are the source of supply, it is a case of robbing Peter to pay Paul each time a Huey is pried out of the Army inventory. If one LHFT cannot be made available to support each PBR section, the next best arrangement would be to have at least one LHFT operating from each PBR base, mobile or fixed, or about 15 fire teams. This has not been achieved, because of the limited Army resources. The "Huey" is no longer in production; however, its successor, the 200-knot Hueycobra or "Cobra" (AH-1G) is currently being delivered to the Army to outfit its airmobile units. As a result, in April 1969, the Army was able to raise the Navy's quota of "Hueys" from 22 to 33.

Fixed-Wing Aircraft Introduced

Even an inventory of 33 was still short of Game Warden's needs. However, a substitute was found in a fixed-wing, short-take-off-and-landing (STOL) aircraft, the OV-10 "Bronco." In April 1969, 16 OV-10s were deployed to CTF 116, eight each at Vung Tau and Binh Thuy. From these two locations, at opposite ends of the operation area, they can range over the entire Rung Sat and Delta.

The Bronco is a two-seat, light armed reconnaissance aircraft, especially designed for counter-insurgency missions. Its armament options include machine guns, bombs, rockets, and missiles, up to a combined payload of 2,400 pounds. The aircraft is powered by twin turboprop engines, which give a top speed of 305 knots with a light load. It requires only 1,130 feet of runway for full-load take-off. As a fixed wing aircraft, the OV-10 has certain advantages over the helicopter. It is faster, with at least twice the speed, therefore there can be less delay in reaching the target. It is larger, and that permits a greater load and more varied weapons mix. But it cannot operate from the mobile PBR bases. Its speed advantage en route to target can work against it once over target; it cannot operate as slowly or maneuver as tightly as a helicopter, a disadvantage when working with PBRs against small or evading targets. It cannot be as precise because its weapons are trainable only by training the whole aircraft. Nevertheless, PBR commanders have become very fond of the greater fire power of the OV-10's 5-inch Zuni rockets and its longer stay time. Ultimately, of course, it would be desirable to replace the Huey Seawolves with the Cobra, if it can be made available while there is still a Game Warden mission in Vietnam.

Patrol Air Cushion Vehicle (PACV)

The "Huey" Seawolves and "Broncos" are not the only "aircraft" that Game Warden has operated. There is also the Patrol Air Cushion Vehicle (PACV), or "Hovercraft" as its manufacturer calls it. The "Pack Vee," as it is usually pronounced, is neither an aircraft nor a watercraft, but rather, both. It is used by both the Army and the Navy, the Army version being designated simply ACV. The craft presently in the inventory were built in Yeovil, England, by Westland Aircraft, Ltd. The U. S. representative is Bell Aerosystems of Buffalo, who calls it the SK-5. The PACVs zoom along, over water, mud, or dry land, up to 60 knots, on a bubble of air about four feet thick, which is developed by a seven-foot lift fan. The bubble is held captive by rubber "skirts." The craft can decelerate quickly and settle down anywhere (large floats are built into the structure for buoyancy). They are powered by a gas turbine engine which drives both the downward-facing lift fan and the aft-facing propeller, which "pushes" the craft like the Florida everglades air boats. They are controlled by elevators and rudders mounted in the slip stream of the propeller. They mount .50-caliber machine guns, 40-mm. grenade launchers, and small arms. They are 39 feet long, 24 feet wide, and 16 feet high. They can clear 4.5-foot waves, 3.5-foot solid walls, 5-foot earthmounds, 6-foot vegetation, and at 20 knots, ditches 12 feet wide by 8 feet deep.

Operation Monster

The PACVs, then of PACV Division 107, first saw duty in Vietnam in May 1966, having been ferried across the Pacific in an LSD. Between May and November they were operated for evaluation in both Game Warden and Market Time environments. Operating from Cat Lo, they performed Game Warden patrols in the Rung Sat, searching junks and sampans. Operating from the well deck of the USS *Tortuga* (LSD-26), they conducted Market Time patrols along the coast. Then, in November and December 1966, there came an opportunity to give the PACVs a comprehensive combat operation test. Operation Quai Vat, as it was named, was conducted on the Plain of Reeds, operating out of Moc Hoa, an ARVN Air Boat Base. Quai Vat is the Vietnamese term for "Monster," the name they have given the PACVs. And no wonder, the PACVs make a terrifying roar, and create a large cloud of mist and/or dust wherever they go. Exploiting this, the PACV sailors have painted slanted cat's eyes and snarling shark's teeth across the front skirt of each PACV. It followed logically that "Monster" soon became the radio voice call.

Operation Quai Vat was described as a suc-

cess. Working with the "Green Berets" of the Moc Hoa Special Forces Camp, the PACVs were credited with 23 enemy dead. Eleven prisoners were taken, and 71 enemy sampans and 71 enemy structures destroyed.

Plain of Reeds

The Plain of Reeds is a 30-mile by 70-mile marsh, north of the Mekong and near the Cambodian border. It is always covered with water. During the dry season it will be covered by a foot or two of water. During the "wet" season, the water level increases six feet or more. Hamlets and trails must be built up to survive the wet season. Canals become meaningless during the wet season, because one can travel anywhere by water, irrespective of the prescribed routes. Rice is the crop; here is found a variety, called floating rice, which thrives no matter whatever the water level; its roots simply develop the length necessary to reach the surface. From the air, the area gives the impression of being a flood disaster area. Straw-like reeds flourish everywhere, and are interrupted only occasionally by a line of trees. Canals can be identified because their greater water depth gives them a contrasting color. A PBR sailor described a bizarre experience on one of those canals: "We came upon this bridge over the canal. The water level was so high it almost reached the bridge itself. A PBR could never have gotten under. So we sounded our way with a boat hook, through the reeds, around the bridge, and back to the canal."

PACV Suitability

In February of 1968, TF Clearwater was clamoring for more resources. It was decided to reassign the PACV unit to Clearwater in I Corps, and let the crews try their craft in a different environment. They arrived in June 1968, and CTF Clearwater placed them under the operational control of ComHueRivSecGru. The huge lagoon, rice paddy, mud, sand, and salt flat area of the Hue River system, where land and water merge almost imperceptibly, was ideally suited for PACV operations. There, the range of tide is only a foot or two so that the height of objects or banks to be hurdled does not change significantly. In operations with the 101st Airborne Division, PACVs were most successful in tracking down, killing, or capturing Viet Cong in cordon and search and in pincer operations, when the Viet Cong would take to the water to escape the pursuing ground forces. Conversely, the PACVs were also able to capture very surprised Viet Cong and North Vietnamese soldiers who abandoned their watercraft and attempted to run away ashore. The paddy berms (dikes) and fish weirs (stake traps) are only about two to three feet high and provide no obstacle to PACVs in that area. They continued to operate with TF Clearwater until mid-1969 when it was decided to retire the Navy's three well-worn and very costly PACVs and to replace them with Army ACVs. Such a move was quite feasible with Clearwater under Army Command.

PACV Versus PBR

While the PACV has no application as a support "aircraft," it can be said that, operationally, the PACV is a reasonably good substitute for a PBR in wide rivers or bays. It can do much that a PBR can do, and it can do it a lot faster. It is less maneuverable, however, and makes much more noise. Its major drawback is its cost. Acquisition, maintenance, and operation are all expensive. At a little less than a million dollars per vehicle, new, it is completely uneconomical when compared with a PBR, which costs about 90 thousand dollars, the cost of the new and improved Mark IIs.

MINESWEEPERS OF THE RIVER PATROL FORCES

Not all the river patrol assets are as sophisticated as PACVs, Seawolves, or PBRs. The minesweeping force includes some of the least

expensive craft in the whole war, the converted LCM-6 (Landing Craft, Mechanized), referred to now as MSMs (Minesweeper, River). At practically no cost, they have been rigged to tow simple minesweeping devices, which no doubt have saved millions of dollars in terms of ship and cargo losses.

The Mine Countermeasure Units

The minesweepers have been in the river patrol force even longer than the PBRs and the Seawolves. The first four 57-foot MSBs (Minesweeping Boats) of Mine Squadron 11 (Detachment Alfa) arrived on the Long Tau on 10 March 1966. Within a year, the number of MSBs on the Long Tau more than doubled. In 1968, after having won a Presidential Unit Citation, that Detachment was commissioned as Mine Division 112, with six MSBs and five MSMs. Also in 1968, Mine Division 113, with the same strength, was organized out of other assets in the Rung Sat, except by that time three of its MSBs were located at NSA Da Nang for sweeping Da Nang Harbor. The Mine Division commanders report to ComMinePac through ComMineRon 11, administratively, and serve operationally as task unit commanders under Commander Rung Sat River Patrol Group (CTG 116.4).

The Vietnamese Navy also operates its own minesweeping launches in the Rung Sat area, under the guidance of the Senior Naval Advisor (CTG 116.4). The U. S. craft, under CTG 116.4, generally sweep from Nha Be south to the ocean, and the Vietnamese craft from Nha Be north to Saigon and Newport.

In I CTZ, there is a mine countermeasures task unit in both the Hue and the Dong Ha River security groups. There are four converted LCM-6s on the Perfume and there are five on the Cua Viet. (As indicated earlier, even ATCs were used as sweeper boats until the LCM-6s became available.) In 1969, ComNavSuppAct Da Nang placed his three MSBs under the operational control of CTF Clearwater for sweeping the LST turning basin at Cua Viet.

The Mine Threat

What is the mine threat? The Long Tau and Cua Viet are absolutely essential in the logistic support of the war effort. They are narrow, and if a major ship were to be sunk in the center of either channel, it could take days, even weeks, to clear the channel and allow the flow of traffic to resume. While Viet Cong and North Vietnamese mines have sunk ships and craft in both rivers, thus far the victims have managed to reach the edge of the channel before going down.

There are other rivers that might be mined. The Perfume is vulnerable, but the enemy has concentrated his efforts on the Cua Viet, 40 miles north, closer to the DMZ, and more important strategically to both sides in the conflict. It is not as big a problem for the North Vietnamese Army to transport mines from the DMZ to the Cua Viet as it would be to get them to the Perfume. At best, neither of these rivers is more than 12 or 15 feet deep.

The My Tho and Bassac rivers are certainly both vulnerable, being similar in characteristics to the Long Tau, with depths of 30 to 60 feet. Yet the enemy has not mounted anything like a serious mine campaign on the Bassac or the My Tho. This is more than likely owing to the fact that while these rivers are not as critical to Allied resupply as are the Long Tau and the Cua Viet, they are vital to Viet Cong logistics.

Because most mines cannot be set to discriminate between friendly and enemy bottoms, the Viet Cong mine campaign in the Delta has revolved essentially around the use of swimmers, carrying limpet mines, against specific ships of TF 117 and the floating bases of TF 116. In November 1967, *YRBM 16*, with a section of PBRs aboard, was heavily damaged

near Ben Tre on the Ham Luong, presumably by a swimmer-carried mine.

The Viet Cong and North Vietnamese Army have waged a continuous mine offensive on both the Long Tau and the Cua Viet. Their tactic has often included the use of rockets and recoilless rifles simultaneously with and in coordination with a mining attack. On the Long Tau, 1966 was a particularly bad year; a number of cargo ships were damaged and several minesweepers were lost. February 1967 was a bad month for the MSBs. In one day *MSB-45* was destroyed, *MSB-49* severely damaged, and two others were hit. Although there has never been a long quiet period, enemy mine activity has gone in spurts. Another major effort was made on both the Long Tau and the Cua Viet in late 1968 and well into 1969.

At the risk of seeming to over-generalize, the enemy's mine operations have favored the use of command-detonated mines on the Long Tau and floating mines on the Cua Viet, though there has been at least one attempt to use a pressure influence mine on the Long Tau, and at least two attempts to use sophisticated magnetic-acoustic influence mines on the Cua Viet. Accordingly, efforts on the Long Tau have concentrated on severing the detonating wires leading from the bank to the mines planted on the river bottom. An effective technique has been the use of MSBs, and later LCM-6s, trailing cutters on chain drags. The MSBs also sweep for influence mines and can sweep for moored mines.

On the Cua Viet, the enemy has developed a remarkably unsophisticated, yet successful, mine that floats just beneath the surface. It can be assembled on the river bank and then set to drift with the tide and current. It is very difficult to see in the muddy water. This one, a simple woven straw basket of explosive slung from the inner tube of a tire, has taken a toll of both Clearwater and NSA logistics craft. The best countermeasure was found to be standard

hand concussion grenades thrown at any suspicious floating object, and also thrown at random out ahead of sweep craft. (In this river, PBRs and logistics craft as well as minesweepers serve as sweep craft on routine patrols and transits.) Using the grenade, sympathetic explosion sweeps the floating mine. This kind of improvisation has been characteristic of the river patrol minesweeping units, and necessarily so, in order to come to grips with and to check the enemy's clever and unorthodox methods.

SEALS (SEA, AIR, LAND)

But the real masters of invention and improvisation are the Seals. These "naval commandos" have found in Vietnam a good place to use their intensive training and manifold professional skills, working under the operational control of CTF 116. They operate clandestinely within enemy-held areas, and in small patrols of from six to ten men. Their mission is counterguerrilla warfare, turning the Viet Cong's own tactics against him. They

At left, *two PBRs of river section 543 out of Nha Be work with members of the Vietnamese 7th Division in Go Cong Province, near the seaward edge of the Delta.* At right, *Seals land in an enemy area along the Bassac River in September 1967. The Seals used a variety of boats, which they modified to suit their purposes.* (R. D. Corbin, PH1, U.S. Navy, and D. S. Dodd, PH1, U.S. Navy)

also have served ably in performing countless intelligence-gathering patrols.

Seals are trained in foreign languages and in the use of all manner of weapons, those of friendly as well as of enemy forces. They are qualified UDT "frogmen"; they are experts in survival, escape, and evasion; they are familiar with explosive-ordnance disposal techniques; and they are parchutists. One of the platoons in the Delta even boasted of having a parachute-qualified German shepherd dog attached. And that dog, during his tour in Viet-

nam, earned a Purple Heart, presented during appropriate ceremony by CTF 116. They never were able to find a black beret that would fit him!

The Seals have been with Game Warden since February 1966, participating in Operation Jackstay in the Rung Sat Special Zone that spring. Game Warden Seals report from both Fleets, Seal Team One, Coronado, and Seal Team Two, Little Creek. Unlike other river patrol personnel, whose tour is a year, their tour in Vietnam is six months. However, Seals repeat their six-month tours, two, three, and more times. They have not operated with TF Clearwater. Army and Marine Corps reconnaissance teams of the 101st Airborne Division (Airmobile) and Third Marine Division perform similar missions along the Perfume and Cua Viet rivers.

Seals have operated throughout the Game Warden area. They are most often "inserted" into and "extracted" from their patrol area under cover of darkness, using small, fast boats provided by Boat Support Unit One, Coronado (and sometimes by PBRs). At first, BSU-1 employed a Boston Whaler style boat, powered by outboard engines, and called the STAB (Seal Team Assault Boat). This boat was phased out after the first of the new LSSC (Light Seal Support Craft) arrived in July 1968. The LSSC, like the PBR, is propelled by Jacuzzi water-jet pumps, except that the LSSC is driven by gasoline engines. They are 24 feet long, are made of aluminum, present a very low silhouette, and do more than 30 knots. Seals have routinely operated from Nha Be, Vinh Long, My Tho, and Binh Thuy, as well as from YRBMs and LSTs.

The Seals have acquitted themselves well in the Delta and the Rung Sat. They work a great psychological burden on the Viet Cong, who fear them. They have made a contribution to the war effort well out of proportion to their numbers.

LCPLs (LANDING CRAFT, PERSONNEL, LARGE)

LCPLs in Operation Game Warden

Seals, Seawolves, minesweepers, and PBRs reported to CTF 116 for duty early in 1966. But even before that, there were the LCPLs, Game Warden's commissioning heritage in December 1965. As early as February 1965, the decision was made to use four PhibRon One, 36-foot, steel-hulled, Mark 4 LCPLs, "pirating" them right out of the skids of ships then deployed to Southeast Asia, under MAP funding,

for river patrol work in Vietnam. The LCPL unit was activated in the Rung Sat in May 1965 to test and evaluate the LCPL for possible use by the Vietnamese Navy for coastal surveillance. By August 1965, the mission was changed to that of evaluating the LCPL for use by the U. S. Navy for river patrol. (This was concurrent with the scramble to come up with a suitable river patrol boat.) LCPL patrols in the Rung Sat under CNAG, the first U. S. river patrols of the war, were commenced on 9 September and lasted until April 1966. Operating from two wooden barges sunk in the mud at the Vietnamese Navy Yard in Saigon, they performed the Game Warden functions of boarding and search, and attempted to prevent Viet Cong river crossings in the Rung Sat. They came under enemy fire 31 times and returned the fire 22 times. With their maximum speed of 13 knots, any Viet Cong crossing the river could easily outrun them; consequently, it was determined that a faster craft was required. The LCPLs were transferred in June 1966 to the Harbor Defense Unit at Vung Tau.

LCPLs in Operation Clearwater

Like the PACVs, which were reassigned several times and were rejected by Game Warden before they found their niche in Operation Clearwater, LCPLs have become an important asset to Clearwater on the Cua Viet. Seven LCPLs make up the Dong Ha River Surveillance Unit. Three types of LCPLs have been used: the fiberglass-hulled Mark XI, the steel-hulled Mark IV, and even earlier wooden-hulled models. They patrol the length of the Cua Viet from dusk until dawn, in order to detect any enemy activity on the banks, particularly mining attempts.

The Clearwater LCPLs no longer look much like LCPLs. They have had a special surveillance platform installed amidships. Such a rig on a smaller, lighter craft, a PBR for instance, would have created stability problems, and that is one reason they were chosen. And there was the even more practical reason that they were available. Speed was not a governing criterion in the surveillance mission planned. For armament, a .50-caliber machine gun has been added on the forecastle and a .30-caliber on the stern. A 24-inch xenon gas infrared searchlight has been mounted atop the special platform. The searchlight is provided by and manned by the First Platoon, First Searchlight Battery, Twelfth Marines, loaned to CTF Clearwater. The LCPL is manned by a crew of six men—two Marines who operate the surveillance equipment, and four sailors who pilot the craft and man the guns. If the LCPLs, in detecting enemy activity, get into a fire fight too big to handle, they can call for the more heavily armed PBRs or for artillery, or both. The Clearwater LCPLs report administratively to Commander, Naval Support Activity Da Nang.

ASPBs (Assault Support Patrol Boat)

It was mentioned earlier that the first Clearwater craft on the Cua Viet were provided by River Assault Division 112 of TF 117. The ATCs and Monitors pinch-hit as patrol boats until relieved by PBRs. These TF 117 craft were LCMs converted for Delta amphibious operations, and were inherently slow at eight knots. There is also the craft that has been specially designed for the MRF and has since 1969 also been employed by Game Warden. That craft is the ASPB (Assault Support Patrol Boat). This boat is 50 feet long, has a speed of 14.8 knots, and is armed with 20-mm., .50-caliber, .30-caliber, 81-mm. mortar, and 40-mm. grenade launcher. The ASPB normally escorts the ATCs of TF 117, and can serve also as a minesweeper. In the spring of 1969, 16 of these craft were assigned to CTF 116 to augment his Game Warden PBRs in the conduct of Operation Giant Slingshot on the Vam Co rivers, west of Saigon. Although they were welcome additions, in the

Game Warden environment the ASPB is not as effective as the more maneuverable PBR.

River Patrol Bases

In the preceding paragraphs, numerous types of boats, aircraft, and equipment have been described. The bases that support them are just as varied. They do, of course, all have some common features: they all provide berthing, messing, and personal services; they all berth PBRs and other small craft, such as the LSSC; all can accommodate Seawolf fire teams or are complemented by a nearby airfield that can accommodate them; all provide command and control facilities for the task force, task group, and task unit commanders they support; and all but the one at Cua Viet provide repair facilities.

Game Warden LSTs

From the time Game Warden was conceived, it was planned to use both afloat and fixed bases. Therefore, four idle LSTs were ordered recommissioned in 1966: the *Garrett County* (LST 786), the *Harnett County* (LST 821), the *Hunterdon County* (LST 838), and the *Jennings County* (LST 846). Each was modified to include four new boat booms, a helicopter landing deck (lighted for night operations), a PBR repair shop on the tank deck, and an entirely new electronics configuration with new radio, CIC, and navigational equipment for river patrol command, control, and navigation.

Interim Game Warden Inshore Support Ship

In the interim, during activation of the LSTs, three Fleet LSDs, the *Belle Grove* (LSD 2), the *Comstock* (LSD 19), and the *Tortuga* (LSD 26) together with a Fleet LST, the *Floyd County* (LST 762) were each equipped with temporary helo decks to provide at least one Game Warden Inshore Support Ship at all times until the first especially equipped Game Warden LST was ready (which was in November 1966). The first LSD ready for operations was the *Tortuga*. In May 1966, she was deployed with PBRs and the Army LHFT to the South China Sea coast between the mouths of the Bassac and Co Chien rivers. She did not enter the rivers. This gave the PBRs a long run to their area of operations, sometimes through heavy seas, and stemmed from a natural reluctance to sail a good-sized ship into scantily charted waters known to have shifting sand bars and mud banks. Moreover, the land between the several river mouths was all Viet Cong dominated. These strongholds, known as "Secret Zones," by adding the very possibility of ambush, compounded the risks of river transit.

The Move Upriver

Nevertheless, the need to bring the war closer to the enemy took priority over these early misgivings, and the Game Warden support ships were soon entering the river mouths and stationing themselves about 10 miles upstream. The Navy now has a small corps of expert river pilots, trained the hard way, who, I am sure, would not fear sailing anywhere. In 1967 a Game Warden LST boldly made a night transit of the treacherous Ham Luong and, by 1968, Game Warden LSTs were routinely transiting all four major Delta rivers both day and night, and occasionally making trips as far north as the Bassac-Mekong crossover near Cambodia. In 1969, in connection with Operation Sea Lords, LSTs took station more than 100 miles inland in the vicinity of the crossover, and in narrow, treacherous, secondary waterways, such as the Vam Co, taking the war to the enemy's logistic "front door" on the Cambodian frontier.

LST Versus Fixed Bases Ashore

Game Warden has four LSTs but uses only three at a time, one always being out of country for a maintenance availability. Each LST

spends about six months on station in the Delta, and then gets an availability of several weeks, usually in the Philippines or Japan. During 1967 and 1968, the four were rotated so as to man continuously the lower Bassac, Co Chien, and Ham Luong. During the early days of Operation Game Warden, when the fixed bases were infants struggling in a hostile environment, the LSTs provided the best PBR bases available in Vietnam; this was "good duty" for a PBR unit. However, in 1968 the PBR repair skills and capability of the fixed bases overtook by a substantial margin that of the LSTs. The LSTs are overcrowded to begin with, having been outfitted with just about everything one could fit into a ship; and there is little room for berthing, stowage, or repair facilities. The bases ashore, on the other hand, had room to develop and expand—for workshops, for stowage, and for creature comforts. Hence, the picture changed, and the "better duty" was found at the NSA bases. Maintenance opportunities among PBR units are equalized by rotating units. After about five months embarked in a Game Warden LST, a PBR division moves upriver and changes places with a PBR unit based ashore.

LST Operations

The LSTs have certainly seen plenty of action. Besides their 24-hour-a-day PBR support role, punctuated by "Flight Quarters" six to ten times, they provide 40-mm. gunfire support for scheduled operations and against targets of opportunity. They have had their moments of glory in gunfire support. For example, in May 1968, the *Jennings County* was credited with 17 enemy killed and numerous Viet Cong structures destroyed during a gunfire mission. But the LSTs also have taken their lumps. Four months later, the *Hunterdon County*, in mid-Delta, was ambushed by Viet Cong rockets and recoilless rifles and suffered two killed, 25 wounded, as well as experiencing considerable damage to her superstructure, her PBR crane, and a PBR.

The LSTs have learned to take the many "unscheduled" groundings in stride. I had the opportunity to observe one of these. After skillfully conning the ship off the sand and mud bar, the OOD remarked coolly, "That shoal wasn't there last week, Captain." The Captain replied calmly, "I know. When you get off watch, write up another one of those competitive Zulu Thirty Alfas, self-observed," referring to the amphibious beaching and retracting exercise.

BASES ASHORE

Unlike the LSTs, which report operationally to CTF 116 and administratively to Commander Landing Ship Flotilla One, all the other river patrol bases report for both operational and administrative control to ComNavSuppAct Saigon (Game Warden bases) and to ComNavSuppAct Da Nang (Clearwater bases), both of whom in turn report for operational control to ComNavForV and for administrative control to ComServPac. There are two kinds of bases in this category, those ashore and the non-self-propelled floating bases.

Selection of Base Sites

Game Warden started out with fixed bases: Cat Lo and Nha Be in the Rung Sat area; My Tho on the My Tho River; Vinh Long on the Co Chien River; Long Xuyen and Can Tho on the Bassac; and Sa Dec on the upper My Tho or Mekong. These bases were picked for three reasons. First, their availability and readiness for use. They were all the site of Vietnamese naval or military installations. All, except Sa Dec, were the site of Vietnamese River Assault Group (RAG) bases. Sa Dec was a Vietnamese Army division headquarters; and within the headquarters compound there was a boat base

site on the Sa Dec Canal which included a primitive marine railway, large enough to haul a PBR.

The second reason was functional. If you recall, in 1965 and early 1966 there was no ComNavForV; CNAG was doubling in brass as CTF 116. The location of Game Warden bases at Vietnamese Navy bases would facilitate carrying out the advisory tasks of CTG 116.1 and CTG 116.2 who were also the senior naval advisors in their respective areas. The third reason was strategic. Looking at a chart of the area, and keeping in mind that there were to be LSTs at the mouths of the Bassac, Co Chien, and Ham Luong, the bases selected provided fairly good area coverage. There were, of course, many other Vietnamese Navy bases to choose from, but those chosen were believed to provide Game Warden with the best opportunities possible to interdict enemy waterborne movements. Again, all the bases selected could be reached by water and air, facilitating logistic support.

Base-Building

As soon as the base site selection was made, the Seabees and civilian construction men went to work dredging and constructing, converting the tent encampments to semi-permanent installations.[9] Steel Butler Buildings and screen and louvered-walled tropical barracks, called "hootches" by their tenants, sprang up overnight. Observation towers and miles of barbed concertina wire provided perimeter security, while millions of sandbags were sculpted into bunkers of various shapes, sizes, and purposes, protecting against "mail call" or "incoming" as enemy ordnance is nicknamed. In some places, such as My Tho, there was no room for a new base, so Ammi barges were towed in to provide mooring facilities, and Vietnamese hotels were leased for living, messing, and headquarters space.

Game Warden Bases

Nha Be is the largest PBR base, accommodating 40 PBRs and more in a pinch. As soon as Nha Be became operational in June 1966, Cat Lo was no longer used for PBRs. It continued operation, of course, as a Market Time base. Nha Be, centrally located, provides adequately for the Game Warden operation in the whole Rung Sat and Saigon area. PBRs did not operate for long from the RAG base at Can Tho. The Vietnamese Navy had decided earlier to move the Can Tho RAG base, which had been in the middle of the city, upriver to Binh Thuy, where greater security could be achieved. So both the U. S. and the Vietnamese navies commenced construction at Binh Thuy. The U. S. Navy moved there even before the new base was completed and operated for several months from a most austere combined shore and floating base arrangement, at Tra Noc, across the road from the Binh Thuy airfield, which was a frequent target of enemy attacks. The new American base was completed in July 1967, the Vietnamese RAG base in mid-1968. Binh Thuy is the second largest PBR base, accommodating 30 boats; if one includes the helo facility, it is the largest of Game Warden's bases.

In 1966, it appeared that Long Xuyen might be an active patrol area. But it proved to be the most pacified area in the Delta. (In fact, it was the only provincial capital not to be attacked during Tet 1968.) So in April 1967, the base there was deactivated, and the PBRs were redeployed to Tan Chau with a floating base, YRBM 16, just below the Cambodian border. Contact with the enemy was light there also, so in July 1967 the YRBM and PBRs were moved south to Binh Thuy, and then in September, to Ben Tre on the Ham Luong River. The fixed base at Vinh Long was replaced by an afloat base in mid-1968. The new afloat base, an activated APL, remained in the Vinh Long vicinity. The move afloat was occasioned by the experi-

ence of Tet 1968. The crews' living quarters were two kilometers from the PBR piers, and when the Viet Cong overran Vinh Long, most of the crews were cut off from their boats. The LHFT that had been based at the Army helo base at Vinh Long, remained at the Army base and did not move afloat with the PBRs.

Clearwater Bases

Clearwater has two fixed bases and a floating one. NSA Detachment Cua Viet is located at the mouth of the Cua Viet River and provides support, but not repairs, for the Dong Ha River Security Group. NSA Detachment Tan My, located on the north side of the Dam Sam (Lagune de l'est), is the base of operations for the Hue River Security Group Mine Countermeasures Unit; and with its seaplane-like ramp, was base of operations for the PACV Unit. PBR Mobile Base I, a few miles from NSA Detachment Tan My, is moored at the mouth of the Perfume and provides headquarters for the HueRivSecGru, a base for the PBRs, and maintenance for all Clearwater PBRs.

Non-Self-Propelled Floating Bases

Game Warden is also served by NSA floating bases, five of them. Logically, it consistently has been the ultimate goal of Operation Game Warden to move afloat as much as possible, retaining only enough shore bases to ensure a high level of maintenance and overhaul support. Afloat bases, by their very nature, afford a great measure of operational flexibility. Too, fixed bases are easier targets for enemy mortars, rockets, and artillery than are mobile ones, provided they move. But, oddly enough, Game Warden's mobile bases, LSTs included, have more frequently been the objects of enemy attack and have suffered greater damage than have its fixed bases, in spite of the fact that the mobile bases do move. Usually they move at night, every night, if only just far enough to deny the enemy the use of mortar-aiming stakes. Defense is also achieved by the use of anti-swimmer nets, random detonation of concussion grenades, security watches manning automatic weapons, and perimeter boat patrols.

Propelling the Non-Self-Propelled Bases

Although they possess no integral means of self-propulsion, clever methods have been devised to move these bases. In some cases, giant outboard motors, with six-foot screws are rigged over the stern; in others, LCM pusher boats are used as tugs. The NSA mobile bases, as far as usable space for Game Warden support is concerned, are much roomier than the LSTs. They even have space for Seal Detachments and Vietnamese National Police. One of NSA's floating bases, the *YRBM 16*, has proven her great flexibility and versatility by serving at various times at Nha Be, Long Xuyen, Tan Chau, Ben Tre, and Binh Thuy.

Base Types

YRBM, the most common designation found among the river patrol floating bases, stands for Repair, Berthing, and Messing Barge (non-self-propelled). The most common use of these barges is support of submarine crews while their submarine is undergoing overhaul. Game Warden has three of them. Task Force 116 also has the PBR Mobile Support Base II, essentially the same as MB I, described earlier, but with a larger and more sophisticated aviation suit, which can accommodate two, instead of only one, helo. There is also the interesting marriage of two dissimilar barges which replaced the fixed base at Vinh Long. The *APL 46* (Barracks Craft, non-self-propelled) is moored with *YR 9* (Floating Workshop, non-self-propelled).

Supporting the Bases

The floating bases, like the fixed bases, are supported by and from the parent commands in Saigon and Da Nang. Reprovisioning runs for bulk and routine supplies are accomplished by LSTs, AKLs, YFs, YFRs, YFUs, and LCUs under the operational control of the naval support activities. MSTS and CTF 76 also provide LSTs for this purpose. High-priority items are delivered by NSA aircraft, helos, and fixed-wing planes, flying out of Saigon and Da Nang. Game Warden and Clearwater men enter and leave the country at Saigon and Da Nang. For administrative purposes men are ferried to and from the various outlying bases by Naval Support Activity aircraft or watercraft, or by being manifested on U. S. Air Force flights, which are also plentiful. Naval Support Activity Saigon also provides logistic support for the Game Warden LSTs. A PBR repair part, urgently required by the LST on the Bassac, would, for example, be taken from the NSA warehouse at Saigon and flown by NSA helo or C-117 from Tan Son Nhut to the Vietnamese Air Force base at Binh Thuy. Binh Thuy's PBRs, in proceeding to patrol station, would carry the part south to the northern boundary of the lower Bassac patrol area, where a PBR from the LST would make rendezvous and pick up the part while patrolling the northernmost leg of his patrol area.

River Patrol Operations

No attempt will be made here to document the heroic exploits and operations of the river patrol forces; rather, a few paragraphs will be devoted to operational procedures, concepts, and statistics, taken together with a few examples.

COMMAND AND CONTROL

Both Game Warden and Clearwater commanders are able to, and do, exercise tight control over their units, with the command and control facilities available to them. Voice and teletype circuits are available to provide them with almost instant communications,

The SS Baton Rouge Victory, *top, is seen after she was mined in the Long Tau on 23 August 1966. She was beached outside the channel and later salvaged. Seven men were killed. The 57-foot MSB 52 is seen chain-dragging near the bank of the Long Tau for the control wires of electrically detonated mines. Several of these wooden boats were sunk or severely damaged. At right,* the men of PBR 121 prepare to tow away a large sampan that had been partially sunk and hidden in a cove upstream from Saigon. The men in the sampan looking for booby traps are soldiers. (T. W. Geren, top, and Ed Nelson, JOCS, U.S. Navy, left)*

not only to their subordinate task group commanders, but also to their operational superiors at Saigon and Phu Bai.

Navy Operations Centers (NOC)

The task force commanders and subordinate commanders are all served by Navy Operations Centers. An NOC is simply a CIC ashore. In the case of Game Warden's LSTs, the NOC is the ship's CIC. All the NOCs are able to communicate with the operations centers of other commands in their respective areas, naval and military, American and Vietnamese. They are manned 24 hours a day by junior officers and radarmen, in most cases on the task force commander's personnel allowance. These NOC watchstanders go through the PBR training course at Vallejo, California. The NOC Watch Officer serves as the commander's representative on duty and controls all assets of the command. The functioning of the NOC can best be illustrated by relating an actual, typical fire fight incident.

At 0740 on 11 December 1966, two PBRs were on patrol near My Tho. They sighted a sampan, containing two green-uniformed occupants, entering the river from a canal. The sampan ignored the PBRs' order to stop for investigation, reversed course, and re-entered the canal. The PBRs followed in hot pursuit. Upon entering the canal, they surprised a large element of a local Viet Cong battalion preparing to cross the river in 40 sampans. The PBRs immediately received automatic weapons fire from a superior force. They retired at full speed, meanwhile returning the fire. At the same time they called the NOC at the Victory Hotel in My Tho, describing the situation, and asked for reinforcements. The fire team on the helo pad at nearby Dong Tam, monitoring the radio circuit, could almost assume it would be scrambled to assist. Air crews manned their planes. Another PBR patrol, about six miles distant, also monitoring the radio, reported its

position to the NOC. The latter directed the LHFT and the second PBR patrol to the scene, and notified the Task Group's other LHFT, aboard the Ham Luong River LST, 20 miles to the south, to stand by for possible action. Within 15 minutes, four PBRs and two Seawolves were ready to re-open the fight. They did, and again they came under fire from what appeared to be an ammunition bunker. As a result of the combined fire power of the PBRs and Seawolves, 15 Viet Cong were killed, 28 sampans were sunk, three sampans were captured, the bunker was destroyed (secondary explosions confirmed it to be an ammunition bunker), and four buildings were destroyed.

Communications

Communications between PBR, helo, and NOC were good from the start. However, communications between bases and with Saigon were not always so rapid and reliable as they are now. Originally, there were delays, long silences, and missed messages. ComNavForV, recognizing the difficulties, undertook a communications get-well program, Project Clarinet Seaward, which produced the present excellent service in the Delta. Essentially, the Project installed more reliable, more secure, and more powerful equipment at the several bases.

In I CTZ, CTF Clearwater is served jointly by XXIV Corps signal units and NSA Da Nang circuits. The Army signal detachment provides communications between CTF Clearwater and other XXIV Corps commands. The Navy provides circuits to naval commands. Both Army and Navy circuits connect Tan My and Cua Viet. This parallel circuitry results in reliable, expeditious service.

Not only are electronic communications excellent, but there is no unit in either task force that cannot be reached personally by the task force commander, or his representative, within an hour by helicopter.

Decision Making

The tight control thus available is not exercised in the sense that most decisions are made at TF headquarters. In fact, the opposite is true. Task group and task unit commanders exercise a great degree of autonomy, far more than tradition would allow, considering their age, experience, and rank: most are lieutenants. Task Force operation orders prescribe general policy, standard procedures, and rules of engagement. All subordinate operations are closely monitored by means of daily situation reports (sitreps) and on-the-spot reports of significant occurrences (spotreps). The task group and unit commanders are authorized, and exercise, close direct liaison with local officials of U. S. and Vietnamese armed forces, with CORDS (Civil Operations and Revolutionary Development Support, the U. S. civilian agency for assistance to the Republic of Vietnam), and with Vietnamese province and district governments. Within the framework of the operational orders, TG and TU commanders routinely arrange joint and combined local operations, make the necessary command decisions, and keep superior operational commanders informed by sitreps and spotreps.

Headquarters

Nerve centers for the two task forces are at Binh Thuy and Cua Viet. CTF Clearwater's primary headquarters is located with the Naval Support Activity Detachment, Cua Viet, under ten feet of sand. He also has an alternate headquarters, with comparable facilities aboard MB I at Tan My. Cua Viet was chosen as the primary headquarters, even though far less comfortable than MB I and exposed to enemy fire, because the Cua Viet River has been the scene of more enemy activity.

During 1966, Game Warden headquarters shifted from Saigon to Nha Be, then to Tra Noc, near Can Tho. Can Tho was also selected as headquarters for CTG 116.1 (Delta River Patrol Group)/Senior Advisor, Fourth Riverine Area. The Can Tho area was the logical choice for the Task Force headquarters, for the city is centrally located in IV CTZ, and, besides being the largest in the Delta, is the most important agricultural, manufacturing, commercial, and military center west of Saigon. It is the headquarters of Commanding General, IV CTZ, ARVN and, hence, of the Senior U. S. Advisor, IV CTZ. It is also the headquarters of the VNN's Fourth Riverine Area, and the site of two air bases, Can Tho and Binh Thuy. On 5 July 1967, with the completion of the Navy base at Binh Thuy, seven miles upriver from Can Tho, CTF 116 moved from Tra Noc to Binh Thuy, where he has been since.

Operational Statistics

Some statistics have already been cited. A few more may help to present a better idea of the scope and magnitude of the river patrol operation. In an average Game Warden month, PBRs will put in about 65,000 to 70,000 patrol hours. Seawolves will fly about 1,500 hours, and Seals will make about 60 missions. There will be about 75 minesweeping patrols and about 20 LST gunfire support missions. The PBRs and Seawolves will engage in some 80 fire fights each. Game Warden units will destroy monthly about 80 enemy watercraft and 125 enemy structures, and every month they will log about 75 confirmed enemy killed. Since the beginning of Operation Game Warden, more than 100 officers and enlisted men of the Force have lost their lives as a result of enemy fire; but this was very costly to the enemy. The ratio of enemy killed by Game Warden units, to those of Game Warden killed by the enemy, has been something on the order of 40 to 1, one of the highest such ratios of all U. S. forces in Vietnam.

During 1968, psychological operations included, among other things, the medical treatment of more than 35,000 sick and injured Vietnamese, and the receipt of 104 Viet Cong returnees who surrendered to Game Warden units under the "Chieu Hoi" program. Additionally, millions of piasters were paid to Vietnamese citizens in exchange for turned-in weapons and ammunition, and for information of intelligence value, under the Volunteer Informant Program.

Tet 1968

As pointed out earlier, it was the massive Tet offensive of 1968 that gave the final impetus to the creation of TF Clearwater, so most of the very hard combat experienced by PBRs in I CTZ, for which they earned a Presidential Unit Citation, was history by the time Clearwater was established in name and fully equipped. But Game Warden was already on the scene, in force, throughout the Delta, when the Viet Cong launched their offensive, so it is useful to examine their reaction to, and the impact of that reaction on, the Viet Cong attack.

The Enemy's Strategy

The Viet Cong's Tet strategy was to provide the push needed to start a general uprising of the population against the Saigon Government. The Viet Cong believed that once their revolutionary activity had been triggered in key locations, the people would join and topple the existing government. The Mekong Delta was especially important to this strategy inasmuch as it accounted for about half the population and most of the food. In implementing this strategy, "Charlie" concentrated his efforts on provincial capitals such as My Tho, Ben Tre, Can Tho, Chau Doc, Sa Dec, and Vinh Long, predicting that once the capital fell, the whole province would soon succumb.

But fate played strange tricks on this strategy in the Mekong Delta. It missed its

mark in two ways: the Viet Cong mispredicted the reaction of their own people, and they failed to envision how fiercely and effectively small numbers of U. S. troops and sailors would fight back.

Importance of Tet

Tet, or the lunar new year, is the period generally regarded by the Vietnamese as that in which whatever befalls them personally, establishes a pattern of events that will affect them and their families for the whole year. For example, they will go to great lengths to ensure that the first visitor who enters their home during Tet is a happy, successful person; it is very important to a Vietnamese to be happy and successful during Tet.

Rather than rallying behind the Viet Cong, the majority of the population were shocked, bewildered, and stunned into activity by the violence and bloodshed occurring during the period traditionally reserved for festivity, family celebrations, and pacific activities. The Viet Cong attackers would have done a lot better to direct their efforts against the U. S. units. But in the beginning they did not. They did not attack the Game Warden forces or bases, and they did not really engage Game Warden units until Seals, PBRs, and Seawolves forced a confrontation. There were several occasions when Game Warden facilities were sorely vulnerable, but they were by-passed by the exuberant Viet Cong in their fervor to influence the local Vietnamese population.

Game Warden Reaction to the Tet Offensive

At the outset of the attack, early on the morning of 31 January 1968, PBR crews manned the boats that were not on patrol, and put out into the river, which was standard operating procedure for any emergency. Fortuitously, Game Warden units were operating in the vicinity of the city of Chau Doc, engaged in Operation Bold Dragon I, which was designed to interdict men and supplies suspected of crossing into Vietnam from Cambodia. PBRs, Seals, and Seawolves saved Chau Doc. A handful of Game Warden sailors sparked the defense of Chau Doc against two very surprised Viet Cong battalions, who had been briefed to expect open arms and waving flags, not resistance.

Likewise, PBRs and Seawolves provided the fire power necessary at Ben Tre, holding back the Viet Cong for 36 hours, long enough for reinforcing ground troops to drive the Viet Cong out of the city. At Vinh Long, where the VC succeeded in temporarily overrunning the city, PBRs and the *Garrett County* evacuated surviving Americans, Koreans, and Vietnamese. Elsewhere, Game Warden units, against ridiculous odds, disrupted Viet Cong plans by bringing their fire power to bear in support of friendly units under attack. The fighting was violent and constant for these TF 116 units for almost two days, until the beleaguered forces were reinforced sufficiently, so that the Viet Cong were forced to withdraw. Then followed the counteroffensive to restore pre-Tet conditions. By 9 April 1968, much of this had been achieved, Viet Cong activity had been reduced drastically, and Vietnamese schools in the Delta were reopened.

Tet losses to Game Warden were only eight killed, but 134 wounded. Many PBRs and helos were damaged, some seriously. But Game Warden accounted for more than 500 confirmed enemy dead. Certainly, Tet 1968 gave us a far greater insight into the Vietnamese national psyche, and it gave us a good feel for what the enemy might attempt during future "truces."

Operation Sea Lords

Later in 1968 and in 1969, the primary thrust of Operation Game Warden was redirected to a large-scale joint operation combining the efforts and forces of Task Forces 115, 116, and 117, called Operation Sea Lords. The name, Sea Lords, is an acronym for Southeast Asia Land, Ocean, River, Delta, Strategy. Its purpose was to make the war even more difficult for the enemy by setting up a barrier from the Gulf of Siam to the outskirts of Saigon, to interdict the infiltration of men and supplies from Cambodia. Headquarters of the "First Sea Lord," Deputy ComNavForV, a flag officer, is at Can Tho.

Ever since Game Warden was set up, river patrol probes have been made into the upper-Delta area, in hopes of catching infiltrators. PBRs operated from the city of Tan Chau during September and October 1966. Again during the late spring and early summer of 1967, using *YRBM 16*, Cambodian border patrols were reinstituted. Still again, in January and February 1968, operating from the municipal wharf at Chau Doc and the Special Forces camp at Thuong Thoi, PBRs patrolled the upper Bassac and Mekong (Operation Bold Dragon I). But none of these efforts yielded results and all were abandoned.

INFILTRATION FROM CAMBODIA

Meanwhile, evidence was mounting that even though it was not coming down the main rivers, a heavy, steady flow of Viet Cong supplies was coming across the Cambodian border. Some were entering Vietnam west of Chau Doc, down the canals, and across the Bassac below Can Tho, to units in the Secret Zones. Some were coming across the Plain of Reeds, especially during the wet season, when reliance on canals was unnecessary. And still more were crossing the border at the "Parrot's Beak," the large projection of the Cambodian border into Vietnam, just west of Saigon. In other words, the supplies were coming in where the Game Warden units were not patrolling.

As a partial remedy, CTF 116 positioned MB

II, with PBRs, helos, and Commander Upper Delta Task Group embarked, at Thuong Thoi, near Tan Chau, when the new base was ready for deployment in July 1968. But even then, as in earlier experimental forays to the north, contact with the enemy was light. This, no doubt, was because the Game Warden coverage was so thin and the Cambodian border was so long that the enemy found no problem in moving his supply boats around Game Warden's fighting boats.

As a result, it was ComNavForV's decision in the fall of 1968 to combine his task forces and "blockade" the border. Accordingly, in November 1968, about one half of Game Warden's forces were shifted north toward the border, taking advantage of the mobility of the LSTs and YRBMs. The blockade consisted essentially of three separate operations, with several supporting operations to the south.

A BORDER BLOCKADE

In the east was Operation Giant Slingshot, taking its name from the fact that the operation is centered on the Vam Co rivers (Vam Co Tay and Vam Co Dong) which straddle the "Parrot's Beak," and form what on a map looks something like a slingshot. Several divisions of PBRs, two Vietnamese Navy river assault interdiction divisions (using river assault-craft), a division of ASPBs on loan from TF 117, minecraft, Seawolves, Army Cobras and artillery, and U.S. Air Force OV-10A Broncos from Tan Son Nhut, and even other units, constituted Operation Giant Slingshot.

In the west, there was the Canal Campaign, covering the network of canals between Rach Gia and Ha Tien on the Gulf of Siam to Long Xuyen and Chau Doc on the Bassac. Swifts (PCFs) of TF 115 patrolled up the canals from the Gulf as far as their four-and-a-half-foot drafts permitted. PBRs and ASPBs patrolled the balance of the canals.

In the center, Operation Barrier Reef

started in January 1969. Again PBRs and boats of the Mobile Riverine Force patrolled the canals through the Plain of Reeds, including the Grand Canal, extending from the Mekong in the west, to the Vam Co Tay in the east, forging the final link in the blockade.

Sea Lords is best described as a Game Warden-type operation, employing elements of task forces 115, 116, and 117, as well as Vietnamese naval craft, along the length of a 200-mile blockade barrier. This concentrated linear deployment is what makes Sea Lords different. Game Warden operations previously were "diluted" throughout the 25,000-square-mile Delta. Continuing month after month, Sea Lords is believed to have been extremely successful, judging from the sharp rise in fire fights and contact with the enemy. Casualties inflicted on the enemy in terms of men, boats, and supplies, similarly attest to the succes of the operation.

Interrelationships with Other Commands

Certainly, the preceding paragraphs dealing with Sea Lords give some idea of the extent that Game Warden is involved with other forces. Some additional facts and examples may be useful in illustrating how Game Warden and Clearwater relate to other commands in the war effort.

Task Force 115 (Coastal Surveillance Force)

It did not take long to discover that PBRs take a real beating in any kind of seaway. The result was that the inshore support ships moved into the rivers. The original line of demarkation between TF 115 and TF 116 was a line drawn essentially from headland to headland across the estuaries of the rivers, meaning PBRs had to patrol in open surf. In September 1967, ComNavForV moved the line upriver about five miles to take advantage of the greater seaworthiness of the PCFs and Coast Guard craft.

Then during Sea Lords, when Game Warden units were shifted north en masse, gaps were created in lower river patrol coverage. ComNavForV changed the TF 115 mission to include operations upriver. TF 115 craft commenced taking over the "big fat" rivers, patrolling upstream 20 miles and more. Also they started patrols in the Ca Mau peninsula, for example, in the very hazardous region of the Song Bo De. But TF 115 and TF 116 craft do not generally operate redundantly in the same waters. Economy in force employment dictates that if TF 115 can handle a portion of the river, the boats of TFs 116 and 117 should patrol elsewhere, in shallower waters. This drain on TF 115 assets was not particularly serious, since that force had long since "pacified" the coast. Now the problem to contend with was infiltration inland. Hence, Operation Sea Lords.

Task Force 117 (Mobile Riverine Force)

Task Force 117 was for all practical purposes a miniature amphibious assault force, complete with minesweeping and gunfire support craft. It worked directly with the U. S. Ninth Infantry Division based at Dong Tam, near My Tho. The Ninth Division had its own air arm, and Task Force 117 units, lifting Ninth Division troops, generally were supported by Army helos, and not by those of TF 116, even though the missions of both 116 and 117 called for mutual support of one another. Mainly, TF 117's mission was to support the U. S. Army in riverine warfare and secondly to supplement the river patrol forces. Such support was provided in Sea Lords in the form of a loan of 16 ASPBs for Giant Slingshot. But there have been frequent joint 116–117 operations such as the one in February 1968 at the Mang Thit-Nicholai Canal, an area jealously defended by the Viet Cong. As part of the Tet counteroffensive, 44 MRF craft and 10 PBRs blockaded an area while troops of the Ninth Division con-

ducted a sweep on the ground. The MRF craft were spaced at 500-yard intervals, with the faster PBRs spaced at random among them. Together, they prevented the escape of the Viet Cong by water during the sweep by the infantry units.

The whole concept of the MRF was borrowed from the Vietnamese Navy, which long before had inherited their RAG units and doctrine from the departing French. Then in mid-1969, with the commencement of the wholesale turnover of TF 117 assets to the VNN, the MRF concept and function for the second time reverted to the Vietnamese Navy. But even after the turnover, some of the boats continued under the American flag as part of Operation Sea Lords.

Vietnamese Navy

Task Force Clearwater works more closely with the Vietnamese Navy than does Game Warden, both for convenience and out of necessity. The Vietnamese operate as many craft in Clearwater's operational area as does Clearwater. The functions of population and resource control on the pacified Perfume were turned over in 1968 to the RAG at Hue, freeing HueRivSecGru craft for offensive operations on the lagoons. Moreover, junks from the coastal groups at Cua Viet, Tan My, and Cua Hai Bay inspect craft entering or leaving the river mouths at those points, relieving Clearwater of that tedious chore.

The Vietnamese Navy has now expanded its operations to include PBRs. They entered the PBR business in June 1968 with the transfer, under the Military Assistance Program, of eight Mark II PBRs from the U. S. Navy. Game Warden sailors provided the training of the new crews.

Both combat and psychological operations are planned and executed jointly by U. S. Navy and Vietnamese Navy river patrol units. In combat operations, the Vietnamese boats

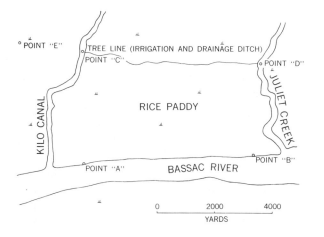

serve usually as blocking forces to prevent an enemy escape by water. In a typical psychological operation, a team of U. S. Navy and Vietnamese Navy hospital corpsmen, transported by PBR, will enter a hamlet and conduct a combined **MEDCAP** (Medical Civil Action Program), with a team of local musical entertainers, U. S. cartoon movies, and candy for the children patients.

Vietnamese Ground Forces

Game Warden operates more with Vietnamese ground forces than with their navy, particularly those forces at the provincial level (Regional Forces, RFs) and at the district government level (Popular Forces, or PFs). The RFs and PFs make sweeps through areas near the rivers that have been the source of fire against Game Warden boats, and are transported to their objective area and inserted by PBRs. It is a small-scale sort of TF-117 type operation.

A typical operation might occur after several days of fire against PBRs from the river banks at Points A and B on the accompanying diagram. A local informant has reported under the Volunteer Informant Program that the fire has been coming from a team of Viet Cong who

have been camping in the tree line running from Point C to Point D. The task group commander arranges with the nearby PF outpost chief to employ 40 of his troops against that tree line. At dawn, two PBRs with 20 soldiers embarked enter the Kilo Canal from the Bassac. Simultaneously, the Game Warden LST commences from Point A, and proceeds towards Point B, firing her 40-mm. battery throughout the length of the tree line, from Point C to Point D, to soften up the enemy, hopefully to dislodge him, and to inflict some casualties. Seawolves at Point E, in orbit at 1,500 feet, serve as spotters for the LST battery, ensuring that the rounds land in the tree line and are not wasted in the paddies. By the time the LST has completed her fire mission, the PBRs have reached Point C, and insert the 20 PFs. Meanwhile, two more PBRs with the remaining 20 PFs embarked, enter Juliet Creek, and proceed toward Point D. The men landed at Point C commence their sweep of the tree line. They have been instructed to kill, capture, or rout out anyone they find, but *not* to leave the tree line. The Seawolves, an LHFT from the LST and one from Binh Thuy, commence following the PFs, an LHFT on either side of the tree line. They take under fire anyone attempting to escape from the tree line into the paddies. Meanwhile, the other 20 PF troops are inserted at Point D as a blocking force to interdict anyone fleeing down the tree line in front of the sweeping force.

Such operations are quite common. While ARVN troops are not generally so employed with PBRs, the ARVN artillery has been placed on call for the support of Game Warden units, just as Game Warden units are always available to assist ARVN, RF, or PF units in a bad situtation.

U. S. Ground Forces

Just as Game Warden PBRs insert Vietnamese troops, Clearwater PBRs insert and extract U. S. Army troops along the Perfume River system, and U. S. Marines on the Cua Viet. Army and Marine Corps artillery frequently support Clearwater units. Game Warden and Clearwater staff intelligence efforts are very closely coordinated with those of Vietnamese IV and U. S. XXIV Corps whenever there is an interface between river patrol and ground units.

U. S. Air Forces

Army and Air Force aviation provide a particularly valuable service to the river patrol boats, that of medical evacuation. When a man is wounded seriously, both the Army "Dustoff's" and the Air Force "Pedro's" are available on radio call for rapid helo evacuation to the nearest hospital. The Pedro has a hydraulically operated winch which can lower a stretcher to a PBR deck, while hovering.

Occasionally, Air Force AC-47 "Puff, the Magic Dragon" or "Spooky" aircraft, with their automatic Gatling-type "mini-guns," or B-52 "arc light" bombing missions, are flown in indirect support of Game Warden and Clearwater by striking base areas from which Viet Cong operate against river craft.

Forward Air Controllers (FACs), flying Army or Air Force O-1 ("Bird Dog") observation aircraft, occasionally will call nearby airborne Seawolves if they have a hot target. They will even request that Seawolves be scrambled if they feel they have a worthwhile target and no Army or Air Force units available to engage it.

Summary, Conclusions, and Recommendation

SUMMARY

Recapitulating what has been presented here, certain significant trends can be identified:

Moving Inland

First, the main thrust of the river patrol operation gradually has moved inland, farther and farther from the "security" of the sea. In 1966, because of uncertainties about a strangely different kind of warfare, PBRs operated cautiously from ships in estuaries. But soon they moved into the river mouths, and were on their way upriver. In 1967, there were several forays up to the Cambodian border and, by 1968, in Operation Sea Lords, Task Force 116 was operating routinely far inland, some units more than 100 miles upriver. The same pattern occurred in I CTZ; within 10 months after Clearwater was established, both river task groups were probing deeply into unfamiliar waterways, throughout the coastal lagoon-canal network, and beyond Dong Ha, wherever the enemy might be found.

Smaller Waterways

Second, the patrol force has progressively moved off the big rivers and into the secondary rivers, canals, and bayous. Initially, PBRs were concerned primarily with establishing control on the main rivers. This they accomplished, making the major rivers safe for friendly forces and innocent civilians to transit. Then, during Tet 1968, PBRs found themselves in fire fights at point-blank range, defending villages and outposts on narrow waterways. They did so well that they have been on the narrow waterways ever since; and the dimensions of the waterways they patrol have steadily decreased. More recently, they were operating on bayous near Cambodia, 40 to 50 feet wide, hardly enough to cast about in. The coastal units of TF 115 have followed the river patrol units inland, taking up the slack, and filling the gaps left in the big rivers and estuaries.

Moving Afloat

Third, the river patrol units have been gravitating from fixed bases ashore to mobile bases afloat. Early in 1967, 88 per cent of the bases were ashore; by 1969, only 36 per cent were.

Reduced Advisory Role

Fourth, the U. S. river patrol units have moved steadily away from their original dual role as advisors and operators to one that became more independent. They were completely oriented toward operations until the rapid turnover of assets and Vietnamization began in 1969.

Going Offensive

Fifth, the river patrol units have shifted from what was essentially a defensive posture to one that has been increasingly aggressive. Although there is still much activity in defending against mines on the Long Tau and Cua Viet, everywhere else the river patrol forces have been seeking out the enemy and bringing the war to him, playing less and less of the sitting and waiting game. PBRs in particular have assumed an offensive stance.

CONCLUSIONS

It must be concluded that:

First, the river patrol forces have done a most creditable job. They saved several provincial capitals during Tet. They have made the rivers safe for passage by innocent civilians and friendly forces. They have eliminated the Viet Cong tax collector as a serious problem on the rivers. They have denied the Viet Cong the option to transit rivers, restricting Viet Cong use of the rivers to clandestine crossings. They have increasingly disrupted and complicated the enemy's logistics efforts, especially since commencement of Operation Sea Lords, contributing directly to a progressive deterioration of the enemy's logistics base and morale. They have steadily advanced on the enemy. Although they have sustained losses, they have inflicted 40-fold losses upon the enemy. They have racked up their brilliant record from a sleeping, not a running, or even a standing, start. Moreover, they have achieved their record with a force small both in men and equipment. Their manpower represents less than one-half of one per cent of the number of Americans in Vietnam. Their principal assets, PBRs and Seawolves, are very cheap, as naval watercraft and aircraft go.

Second, the U. S. Navy has become, for at least the thirteenth time in its history, involved in river patrol operations. The skills and tactics of river warfare have been relearned, and the U. S. Navy has among its ranks, an accomplished, veteran, river patrol force.

RECOMMENDATION

In spite of the Navy's frequent historical involvement in river warfare, there has been a pattern of ignoring river patrol in time of peace. In peacetime, the rivers have been made the province of the U. S. Army Corps of Engineers and the U. S. Coast Guard. Yet, when the chips fell in the present war, as in the past, the Corps of Engineers and the Coast Guard had their hands full elsewhere, and the Navy, although completely unprepared, was given the job in Vietnam.

And while we now have a river patrol force of which we can be justly proud, it must be recognized that it took three years to build it to that level. Who can say how many men died, and how many achievable victories were missed because we were too low on the relearning curve: relearning, by trial and error, the details of combat tactics, relearning how to repair, supply, and otherwise support a river patrol force.

While I would not propose that we maintain a peacetime force anything like the size of the present one, I believe we should maintain a river patrol nucleus on each coast, perhaps a small squadron. Such a squadron, under the amphibious or destroyer type command, and under the guidance of the CNO, could keep alive the procedures, tactics, and lessons learned; it could work on improving concepts and hardware; and it could provide a training and expansion nucleus in the hopefully avoidable event that we ever again have to mount a river patrol campaign. A modest inventory of PBRs and gunships would not be expensive. And, most important, we would not have to start from scratch again. We certainly have learned one thing: not having a river patrol force is no guarantee that we will not have to fight a river war.

(Naval Review, 1970)

Author's note: The river patrol war in Vietnam has proven to be very dynamic. There is little risk in predicting that changes will occur between the time of writing and the time of publication. Writing was completed in June 1969, following my return from Vietnam.

I wish to acknowledge the very valuable research assistance given me by Doctor Dean Allard and Miss Sandra Brown of the Naval History Division, and Lieutenant Commander Detlow Marthinson of the Strike Warfare Division of the Office of the Chief of Naval Operations.

Notes

1. See "Market Time in the Gulf of Thailand," by Captain James A. Hodgman, U. S. Coast Guard.

2. The successive commanders were:
   a. ComNavForV—Rear Admiral N. G. Ward   April 1966–March 1967
      Rear Admiral K. L. Veth   March 1967–September 1968
      Vice Admiral E. R. Zumwalt, Jr. September 1968–present
   b. CTF 116—Capt. B. B. Witham, Jr. May 1966–March 1967
      Capt. Paul N. Gray   March 1967–April 1968
      Capt. Arthur W. Price   April 1968–April 1969
      Capt. J. R. Faulk   April 1969–present

3. See "Naval Logistic Support, Qui Nhon to Phu Quoc," by Captain Herbert T. King, U. S. Navy.

4. See "Jackstay: New Dimensions in Amphibious Warfare," by Lieutenant Commander Robert E. Mumford, U. S. Navy.

5. See "The Riverine Force in Action, 1966–1967," by Captain W. C. Wells, U. S. Navy, which follows immediately.

6. See "Application of Doctrine: Victory at Van Tuong Village," by Brigadier General O. F. Peatross, U. S. Marine Corps, and "Marine Corps Operations in Vietnam, 1965–1966," by Brigadier General Edwin H. Simmons, U. S. Marine Corps.

7. See "Building the Advanced Base at Da Nang," by Captain K. P. Huff, U. S. Naval Reserve.

8. Air Medals can be earned in many ways. A single heroic act in the air could earn one. They can also be earned by accumulating points for combat missions. For example, ten combat missions, each involving a fire fight with the enemy, would earn one Air Medal.

9. See "Civil Engineers, Seabees, and Bases in Vietnam," by Captain Charles J. Merdinger, CEC, U. S. Navy.

A note on pronunciation. The Vietnamese language, although a tonal language and in this respect similar to Chinese, was reduced to writing in the Roman alphabet by Portuguese and French missionaries during the sixteenth century. Hence, if one pronounces the Vietnamese words as if they were Portuguese, he would be much more correct than if he used English pronunciation. To obtain a reasonably acceptable pronunciation of the Vietnamese words in this essay, the following suggestions are made: Pronounce "a" as in "father." The "ai" and "ie" should already be familiar from "Saigon, Vietnam." Pronounce "e" as in "met," except when "e" is the final letter, as the "ay" sound in "pay." The letters "i" and "y" are spoken as the "e" sound in "see." Say "o" as in "ought," unless final, then as in "owe." "Oa" is spoken "wah." Pronounce "u" and "uo" as the "oo" sound in "boot." Pronounce "ui" and "uy" like "we." "Ch" is spoken as in "church," except final "ch" is like the English "k." "Gi" is pronounced like the "y" in "yes." "Nh" is pronounced like the "ny" in "canyon," but final "nh" is simply "n." Pronounce "th" as "t," and "x" as "s." The other sounds are much like English. Thus, "Hue" becomes "who-ay"; "Rach Gia" becomes "rock yah"; "Binh Thuy," "bean twee"; "Long Xuyen" is "Long Swee-en"; and "Nha Be" is spoken "nyah bay."

The Riverine Force in Action, 1966–1967

W. C. Wells, Captain, U. S. Navy

Riverine warfare is not new. The U. S. Marine Corps conducted riverine operations in the Florida Everglades from 1837 to 1842, and in Nicaragua in the late 1920s. The U. S. Navy operated along the Yangtze River in China before World War II. The U. S. Army conducted riverine operations along the James and Mississippi rivers and in the Southern swamps during the Civil War, and in Mindanao in the Philippines in World War II. The British fought along the Nile in 1898, and the Japanese along the Yangtze from 1937 to 1945. More recently, the French fought against the Viet Minh in the Tonkin and Mekong Delta waterways from 1946 to 1954. Since then, units of the Army of the Republic of Vietnam and Vietnamese Navy River Assault Groups (RAGs) have conducted riverine operations against the Viet Cong insurgents along the extensive waterways of the Mekong Delta.

Nor is the idea of a river assault command new. The United States created a riverine group during the Civil War to attain one of its prime objectives: the division of the South. The French used one in Vietnam during their last decade there and called it "Dinassaut" (Naval Assault Division).

The Dinassaut (DNA) were heavily-armed and armored flotillas navigating the rivers of Vietnam for the sole purpose of supporting the ground forces along the rivers. Although some Dinassaut employed as many as 20 vessels, including an LCT (Landing Craft, Tank) with armored vehicles and tanks, as well as reconnaissance aircraft, the average Dinassaut was usually composed of about 12 ships, including an armored LSSL (Landing Ship Support, Large) to serve as the flagship and six to eight LCMs (Landing Craft, Mechanized) to provide fire power, supplies, and troops. Many, if not all, of the French Dinassaut vessels were modified American craft.

The river campaigns of the Civil War were this country's first experience with riverine operations. In May 1861 General George B. McClellan suggested to General-in-Chief Winfield Scott that the Federal troops stationed at Cairo, Illinois, needed gunboats to provide support from the river. Soon thereafter the "inland navy" was born. Its mission was to support and transport advancing armies, and to safeguard navigation of the rivers so new bases could be created to support further advances into hostile territory. Of course, with Federal gunboats cruising the rivers, the Southerners' use of those waterways for logistic support came to an end, save for an occasional furtive crossing.

In January 1862 the first "joint action" riverine operation took place, when Union

Army forces under Brigadier General U. S. Grant joined river gunboats and transports under Commodore A. H. Foote to conduct assault operations on the Tennessee River.

The inland navy, termed the Western Gunboat Fleet and later the Mississippi Flotilla, was initially administered by the War Department, on the theory that although the operations were on the rivers, they were still an inland activity. But in October 1862, Congress gave this river force to the Navy Department. At this time the Mississippi Flotilla was reorganized as the Mississippi Squadron. By late July 1863 every major Confederate waterway was within the patrolling area of the largest shallow-draft navy on inland waters in history. River assault commands played a dominant role in several important actions, including the regaining of Kentucky by the Union, the capture of Vicksburg, the fall of Fort Henry, the victory at Shiloh, and the engagement at Belmont.

Upon cessation of hostilities, the river squadron was disbanded, and for a century the United States had no further need for naval forces on rivers (except those in China), nor for the unique form of joint-service collaboration worked out between the river sailors and the soldiers. Then the country entered the war in Vietnam, and serious consideration was given to the resurrection of riverine warfare, including co-operation between the Army and the Navy. On 1 September 1966, the Navy established River Assault Flotilla One.

Riverine Warfare in Vietnam

The Viet Cong, in their war against the South Vietnamese government, were using the rivers as their primary avenues of assault and of logistic and administrative transportation, and for their best means of evasion, moving along them from one place to another freely, and slipping away from the ARVN forces at night in their sampans. The rivers were also a major source of revenue. Viet Cong tax collectors would set up stations along the rivers and tax the thousands of sampans and junks carrying rice and produce for the markets. The major rivers of the Mekong Delta were under the control of the Viet Cong, and most of the waterways of the Rung Sat Special Zone were enemy-controlled, also. In the Rung Sat the Viet Cong frequently harassed shipping on the Long Tau, the only "safe" river channel connecting Saigon's port with the sea, using mines, guns, and rockets and apparently choosing the time and place of attack at their convenience. Moreover, the arms and munitions being brought in by sea for the rebels, once unloaded from the "trawlers" which carried them, reached the VC fighting units by way of the rivers. All these things were of great concern to Commander U. S. Military Advisory Command (ComUSMACV) in Saigon. This officer, General William Westmoreland, realized that these matters had to be dealt with before the ultimate task of wresting control of the population and land of the Mekong Delta from the Viet Cong could be accomplished.

Action directed against Viet Cong infiltration and Viet Cong control of the waterways in the Delta, and the operations undertaken to ensure the security of the channel to the port of Saigon are, for the purpose of this essay, called "river warfare." The force established to accomplish this is the River Patrol Force (TF 116)—Operation Game Warden. The joint action operations to destroy Viet Cong Main and Local Force battalions in the Delta and the Rung Sat are called "riverine warfare." The force established for this mission is the Mobile Riverine Force, consisting of a reinforced U. S. Army brigade and the Navy's River Assault Flotilla One.

As of January 1968, after one year of "riverine warfare" and two years of "river warfare" conducted in South Vietnam by U. S. forces, a set of definitions, terms, and doctrines for this type of warfare was yet to be generally accepted among the services. Only tentative directives and publications have been issued by the commanders and the services concerned, to provide necessary guidance for the forces involved in both riverine and river warfare in Vietnam.

It is expected that joint publications based on the experience gained over the past two years will be soon forthcoming. Even though they are not as yet jointly accepted, certain terms currently in use in Vietnam ought to be explained.

Riverine Area Environment

This is an inland area with an extensive network of rivers, canals, streams, irrigation ditches, paddies, and swamps extending over a broad, level terrain, parts of which may be inundated periodically or permanently. It may include sparsely populated swamps and forests, places where rivers and streams have steep banks densely covered with bamboo trees, and other places where the terrain is relatively flat and open. A large agrarian population may be concentrated along the waterways. Whether near the ocean or far inland, riverine areas may be affected greatly by the tides.

Riverine Operations

These comprise all military activities designed to achieve or maintain control of a riverine area by restricting or eliminating the enemy's activities or by destroying his forces. Operations are characterized by the extensive use of river assault boats to transport military forces and equipment and to provide close combat support to ground assault forces in the area of operations.

Riverine Warfare

This consists of combat and associated support operations by designated ground and naval forces in riverine areas. This includes operations from the water, the air, and by waterborne and other ground assault forces.

River Warfare

This consists of tasks carried out only by naval components—water patrol, transport, and combat support—as part of the over-all riverine operation.

Land Base

This is a semi-permanent installation where ground and naval combat forces and associated support units may be stationed during a riverine campaign. It includes the immediately surrounding land and water areas required for close-in security.

Afloat Base

This, called in Vietnam *Mobile Riverine Base* (MRB), is a concentration of naval barracks ships, supporting ships, and assault boats easily moved from one to any other of several selected locations for use as a base for riverine operations by both naval and land combat forces and their support units. The base includes the immediately surrounding land and water areas required for close-in security.

Mobile Riverine Force (MRF)

The MRF is a force organized or assembled in order to conduct riverine operations and composed of designated army and naval forces operating from a mobile riverine base.

Riverine Assault Force (RAF)

The naval element of a Mobile Riverine Force is given this title. It is composed of command/control and barracks ships, repair ships, logistic support ships, and one or more river assault squadrons.

RIVER WARFARE

The U. S. Navy began river operations in the fall of 1965, from the Saigon Navy Yard, with four 36-foot armed LCPL-4s. Their mission was

Photographed from a "Seawolf" helicopter, four PBRs steam past Thanh Dinh Island in the Bassac River in January 1968, attempting to draw fire from Viet Cong fortifications they suspect are hidden along the riverbanks. This view, with thick growth along the river and paddies beyond, typifies the Mekong Delta scene. (V. McColley, PHC, U.S. Navy)

to control the VC cross-channel traffic in the Rung Sat Special Zone through which runs the Long Tau shipping channel to Saigon. In addition, the Navy wanted U. S. sailors to take part in such an operation so that they would gain experience for possible future operations. It also wanted to test the concept of waterborne interdiction patrols. The LCPL-4, though slow, was used since it was the only even partly suitable type of boat readily available. The boats were maintained by U. S. naval personnel utilizing facilities of the Vietnamese Navy in Saigon. The operation was under the command of Chief Naval Advisory Group, Vietnam.

In September, 1965, representatives of CinCPac, CinCPacFlt, CNO, and MACV Naval Advisory Group met in Saigon to survey all aspects of waterborne infiltration. This group decided that to carry out the extensive interdiction patrol that was urgently needed on the

major rivers of the Delta and Rung Sat Special Zone, about 120 patrol boats would be required. A 31-foot plastic-hulled pleasure boat was chosen, since its general characteristics were operationally acceptable and it was already in production, hence more readily available than either a newly designed boat or a modified boat from the U. S. naval inventory would have been. The PBR, as this boat came to be known, was preferable to the LCPL-4, which was soon to begin its patrols on the rivers, because it was faster.

Commander Amphibious Force, U. S. Pacific Fleet, was designated the type commander to translate the concept of interdiction patrols (also called "Operation Game Warden") into organizational reality. An administrative organization, River Patrol Squadron Five, was formed to deploy with the crews for the PBRs.

At the U. S. Naval Amphibious Base at

Coronado, California, a training program was inaugurated that relied heavily on the recent experience of the young officers and men who had performed so well in Vietnam as advisors to the Vietnamese Navy Junk Force and River Patrol. Planning had to be closely coordinated with the boat-building project to ensure that the trained crews and their boats arrived in-country simultaneously.

The contract for the PBR Mk. 1 was let on 29 November 1965 and the first boats arrived in-country on 22 March 1966. Operation Game Warden, designated Task Force 116, was established in December 1965. For the time being Chief Naval Advisory Group, Vietnam, was also Commander Task Force 116, with operational headquarters in Saigon. From December 1965 until mid-1967 this officer was Rear Admiral N. G. Ward. While CTF 116 is the operational commander, the commander of the River Patrol Squadron is responsible for the in-country administration of the PBRs and crews assigned and is under Commander Amphibious Force, U. S. Pacific Fleet.

Task Force 116 comprises five river divisions, each of which is composed of several river sections. Normally there are 10 PBRs in each section. Each division is assigned to an area in the Delta or the Rung Sat. The number of sections in the division is determined by the patrol requirements, which are governed by the size of the area assigned. The sections were initially based at existing Vietnamese Navy bases, because of the security and maintenance facilities available there. Several bases were later relocated as the tactical situation changed (for instance, when the VC moved their commo-liaison routes), and as additional maintenance facilities were made ready. Some PBR bases rely on YRBM and APL support craft. At others, such as Can Tho on the Bassac River and Nha Be below Saigon, fixed bases were constructed.

As early as 1962 the old 542-class LST was

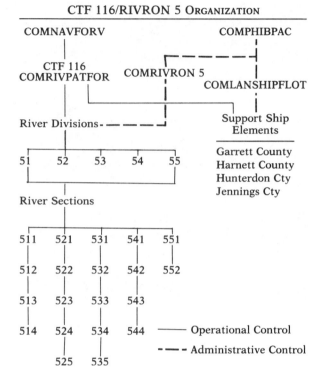

CTF 116/RIVRON 5 Organization

considered for use as a floating base for river operations, and in May 1966 one of that class, the USS *Jennings County* (LST-846) was anchored about ten miles seaward of the Bassac River mouth to serve as the first such base. Because seas were frequently heavy off the Delta river mouths, making it extremely difficult to nest PBRs alongside, and causing the actual loss of one PBR, the *Jennings County* was moved inland to Binh Thuy, five miles upriver from Can Tho. Because the lower Bassac was unsurveyed, she had to steam up the My Tho River, cross over, and then steam down the Bassac—four times the straight-line distance.

The LST has proved to be a fine base for PBR operations, providing command and control facilities, messing and berthing for crews, refueling, repair, and boat berthing. Each LST used as a PBR base serves simultaneously as "mother ship" for two "Seawolf" helicopters and four crews assigned to Operation Game Warden. Currently, the *Harnett County* (LST-821), *Hunterdon County* (LST-838), and *Garrett County* (LST-786) are so employed, in addition to the *Jennings County*. Considerable alteration was necessary to convert these LSTs to PBR tenders: the cargo hatch was enlarged, the crane was removed, and a ten-ton cargo boom was installed for lifting the patrol boats. A 500-square-foot section of the main deck was removed and a flight deck was installed, with appropriate reinforcements and lifting facilities. Communications facilities and the combat information center were expanded. Storage for JP-5 fuel and 2.75-inch rocket magazines were installed.

Meanwhile, specially configured barges were being designed for use in conjunction with the LSTs as mobile PBR bases, and they have since reached their stations. These barges provide berthing and messing for the crews, berthing and logistic support for the boats, and command and control facilities.

Early in 1967, CTF 116 was separated from Chief Naval Advisory Group, Vietnam (who, by this time was also Commander Naval Forces, Vietnam), and the title was given to a separate commander at Binh Thuy in the Delta. The first commander at Binh Thuy was Captain B. B. Witham.

Early in the discussions regarding the need for fast patrol boats to interdict VC movement on and across the waterways in the Delta and the Rung Sat, it became obvious that the patrol boat needed a partner—the armed helicopter. Plans were made to procure suitable helicopters and integrate them into PBR-helo teams. The helo was to gather intelligence on VC sampan and troop movements, to provide eyes aloft for the PBR, to spot clandestine sampan movement, to attack enemy sampans and troops, to provide fire support to the PBR pa-

trols in actions against armed sampans and against ambush positions along the river banks, to provide medical evacuation for injured PBR crewmen and civilians, and to provide overhead fire support for covert operations and for PBR-supported raids against suspected VC concentrations and positions.

At this point, the planners ran afoul of a severe shortage of Navy and Marine helicopters, occasioned by the war. The Army agreed to provide some of their UH-1B helicopters for Operation Game Warden and undertook the necessary training of the Navy helicopter pilots and crewmen who would man the new Helicopter Attack Squadron, Light (HAL-3).

Though its aircraft and crews were working in the Delta months earlier as part of HC-1, HAL-3 became operational in May 1967, with headquarters at the Army airfield at Vung Tau. The squadron is under the operational control of CTF 116 and is administered by Commander Naval Air Force, Pacific. The helicopters, called "Seawolves," operate in support of TF 116 from LSTs and from pads or fields at Dong Tam, Binh Thuy, Vinh Long, and Nha Be, either as a Light Helo Fire Team of two "Seawolves," or as a Heavy Helo Fire Team of three "Seawolves." Early in 1968 there were only 22 helicopters assigned to the squadron, all still provided by the U.S. Army. The number needed for operations in-country is more than this.

TF 116 aims, generally, to interdict the enemy's lines of communications along the waterways of the Delta and the Rung Sat; to deny him secure commo-liaison routes across the rivers (the enemy seldom travels along the axis of rivers); to destroy his tax collection stations along the rivers (which extract taxes from the thousands of sampans and junks transiting the rivers with rice and produce for the markets); to assist the Vietnamese forces in resisting attacks on Regional Force and Popular Force outposts along the rivers; to come to the aid of the Vietnamese people attacked by the enemy; to conduct attacks on suspected enemy positions in conjunction with regular, regional, and popular Vietnamese forces; and ultimately to destroy the Viet Cong infrastructure in the Delta and Rung Sat.

The PBRs form a truly remarkable organization, without precedent in the U.S. Navy. Born of necessity, developed in bitter individual combat, and seasoned by countless examples of courageous and heroic performances by the PBR crews, Operation Game Warden has challenged the Viet Cong in their own environment, and has defeated them— PBRs now patrol where once VC tax-collecting boats worked the rivers. The little gunboats have wrested control of the major rivers from the enemy and have considerably reduced enemy control over the population along the rivers, as well as significantly restricting the movement and concentrations of hostile forces in the Delta and Rung Sat. Seeing the PBRs successfully challenge the Viet Cong in their own backyard, the local population along the main rivers is turning slowly, even reluctantly at times, but surely to the government side, refusing to support the Viet Cong as it has done in the past.

In Game Warden the young ensign, lieutenant junior grade, or petty officer comes of age in conducting individual boat and boat team combat operations. Often a first or second class petty officer is in command during combat operations. The ensign and lieutenant junior grade, as section officers, are just as often fighting their boats in teams or combinations of teams. The Navy can be extremely proud of the young officers, petty officers, seamen, and firemen who have performed so well in the Navy tradition of close combat, which they have revived.

RIVERINE WARFARE

Now let us examine "riverine warfare" as opposed to "river warfare." As we have said,

riverine warfare is conducted by a joint-action force, the Mobile Riverine Force, comprising a reenforced U.S. Army infantry brigade and the Navy's River Assault Flotilla One; the latter is designated the Riverine Assault Force (TF 117).

The mission of the Mobile Riverine Force is to seek out and destroy Viet Cong main and local force units, their resources, and their infrastructure.

The Mekong Delta

The southern third of the Republic of Vietnam, the Mekong Delta region, is exactly described by the term "riverine area environment," as defined above. The Delta is of vital importance to the country's economic and political well-being. Almost nine million people—over half the country's population—live in this flat, poorly drained alluvial plain, which is criss-crossed by one of the densest inland waterway networks in the world. It is a generally accepted fact that the Viet Cong exercise control over about 75 per cent of the predominantly rural people in the Delta.

The area is covered with rice paddies and tall marsh grass. The banks of the waterways are lined with nipa palms and other thick vegetation, while large mangrove swamps stretch along much of the coastline. During the high-water season, from June to November, a large portion of the lowlands are flooded.

More than 80 per cent of the nation's rice is grown in the Mekong Delta, and the VC control or contest almost two-thirds of it. In 1964 South Vietnam produced so much rice that it was able to export a substantial tonnage. After that time the government control of rice production deteriorated, and in 1967 almost one million tons had to be imported to feed the people. Meanwhile, the Viet Cong use the Delta's rice to feed their forces throughout South Vietnam, transporting it on foot and hidden in "friendly," properly registered sampans. Many caches discovered by U. S. forces have contained several tons of rice stored for the use of the Viet Cong. Surpluses accumulated are sold to finance their insurgent effort.

Vietnamese Riverine Forces

Upon the establishment of the government of South Vietnam in 1954, the Delta per se was designated the IV Corps Area, and control was entrusted to the Vietnamese IV Corps Commander. He was, and is, a Vietnamese Army general and has under his command regular Vietnamese Army divisions, and both Regional and Popular Forces, supported by the Vietnamese Navy's river assault groups (RAGs) and by Regional Force river patrol groups. In 1954 most of the RAGs, which were supporting the French campaign in the Indochinese War in the Red River Delta in North Vietnam, were shifted to the IV Corps Area, and the remainder to the adjacent III Corps Area, for support of the South Vietnamese Army.

There were twelve RAGs; eight are presently in the IV Corps Area and four are in the III Corps Area. Each RAG is composed of a balanced force of about 20 boats, including LCM-6s for troop lift; monitors; commandaments (control and command boats); armed LCVPs and French design STCAN/FOM (patrol/minesweeping boats); and the River Patrol Craft (RPC). The RPC, a relatively new boat, was built in the United States to replace the STCAN/FOM.

The RAGs were developed by the French, who also designed the early boats. Of the boats obtained by the Vietnamese from the French, only the U. S.-designed LCVP and the FOM are still in use. The other Vietnamese boats, although armed and armored along French lines, were converted in the United States from U. S. Navy LCM-6s. The current RAG organization is still patterned after the old French units; however, the tactics employed by the Vietnamese Navy have changed considerably. Tactical control of the RAGs is exercised by the corps area commander and his subordinate province commanders, who are also army officers. The mission of the RAGs is close support of the Vietnamese Army and logistic support of outposts and river patrols. Generally, one RAG is designed to transport and support one army battalion.

The Vietnamese Navy assigned the best of their officers and men to the RAGs. U. S. Navy advisors were assigned to the RAGs when our in-country advisory group was formed prior to 1962, and in late 1962 the number of advisors was greatly increased. Now these advisors act mainly as liaison officers with U. S. forces. We drew heavily on the experience of the early advisors in the formation of our river assault flotilla. We employed them not only in the hastily formed training program, but also on the staffs of our squadrons, since some of them remained in Vietnam, or returned there, for a second tour.

The RAGs were extensively and heavily used in the Delta and Rung Sat from 1962 to 1965, but when helicopters were introduced in numbers in 1965, the Vietnamese Army preferred to use them in lieu of the RAGs. A factor contributing to this preference was the enemy's increasing use of heavy weapons in the Delta. The lightly armored RAG boats were no match for the recoilless rifles and rockets fired by the Viet Cong from the banks of narrow waterways, and they were consequently restricted almost completely to operations in the larger rivers and waterways.

Currently, the RAGs are supporting the Vietnamese Army (on a reduced scale), the Vietnamese Marine Corps, and occasionally the U. S. forces. The RAGs are also used extensively for convoying small cargo ships along the waterways of the Delta, in support not only of the Vietnamese Army but also of the U. S. forces and the Revolutionary Development efforts. Perhaps more important is the escorting of native craft carrying rice and charcoal from the Delta to the markets in Saigon, since the Viet Cong can disrupt at will all unescorted movement by water. If the rice convoys to Saigon from the Delta are interrupted, prices in the capital immediately rise, and inflation threatens.

The use of the Vietnamese Navy's RAG bases throughout the Delta and the Rung Sat has made possible operations by U. S. forces that would have been impossible in this riverine area otherwise.

Finally, the RAG intelligence network provides the U. S. forces in the Delta with information on Viet Cong tactics, location, and movements—information which is at times unobtainable elsewhere.

The Regional Force River Patrol Group at the end of 1967 consisted of 22 Regional Force river patrol companies, seven in III and 15 in IV Corps, with support and maintenance companies. More boat companies may be added. Each company is normally assigned armed and armored LCVP- and LCPR-type assault craft organized into platoons and squads.

The mission of the Regional Force boat companies is to assist the province chief in maintaining territorial security. Their tasks include combat in coordination with ground and air units and RAGs, in which the boat companies also lift combat troops and supplies. They conduct waterway patrols, escort other craft transporting supplies and troops to military units and strategic hamlets, and transport in their own boats troops and all classes of military and civilian supplies.

Control of river and waterway traffic is one of the principal missions of the National Police, but control of international traffic on the inland rivers is a mission of the Customs Service. The major waterway in the Delta, the Mekong River, is designated an international waterway within the terms of international law. The National Police and the Customs Service are not military organizations and are, accordingly, trained to operate only in relatively secure areas.

While the size of the National Police and Customs Service and the scope of their operations in the Delta are modest, it is expected that their role and influence will increase. For the present, river traffic is controlled by enforcement of a night curfew and by a series of primary, secondary, and mobile land checkpoints and primary and mobile marine checkpoints.

American Intervention

In 1965, the Viet Cong stepped up their activity and their capability in the Delta, and seemed generally to be gaining control in the region. The South Vietnamese were not making progress, economically or militarily. Since the Vietnamese armed forces had neither enough men nor sufficient assets to mount a successful campaign, plans were made for the introduction of U. S. forces. It had long been apparent to military planners that a riverine force would be necessary to defeat the Viet Cong in the Mekong Delta, and at least six studies since 1961 had cited the need for the development of such a force. There had been serious reservations in many quarters about the idea of committing U. S. ground elements in the Delta in any strength, reservations based on the belief that the Vietnamese government could and should, and in fact did, satisfactorily control the Delta. As the situation continued to deteriorate, however, and the possibility arose that the Viet Cong might soon control the entire area, these reservations diminished, and planning was begun for the actual deployment of U. S. forces to the Delta.

Mobile Afloat Force

Commander U. S. Military Advisory Command, Vietnam, drew up an initial plan in some detail which proposed a brigade-sized Mobile Afloat Force. This concept was elaborated and put in workable form by the Army

A monitor of River Assault Division 92, Mobile Riverine Force, fires in support of troops of the Ninth Infantry Division on 30 June 1967. This would be near Ap Bac, below Saigon. The monitor's main battery consisted of a 40-mm gun and an 81-mm trigger-fired mortar. In 1967 there were ten monitors divided among the Force's four divisions.

and Navy officers on the MACV staff in March 1966.

PLANNING

In studying the means to introduce forces, MACV planners were faced with two major problems. First, there were no tracts of land available which were large enough for a major U. S. base. Ground that stays above water in the wet season is at a premium, and most of it is already heavily populated by Vietnamese. Establishment of a large land base would require relocation of large numbers of people with resultant undesirable economic and political consequences. Second, mobility on the ground was considerably restricted by the thousands of miles of waterways throughout the area.

It was from this dilemma that the idea of the afloat force evolved: a reinforced infantry brigade supported by an artillery battalion and based on the major rivers in U. S. Navy ships.

From such a base, naval assault craft could steam up any of the hundreds of navigable waterways, carrying the riflemen and artillerymen to all parts of the Delta. Moreover, the entire strike force, including its base, would be able to move on short notice to another location.

As planning began for the Mekong Delta Mobile Afloat Force, construction of a major U. S. base on the north bank of the Mekong River five miles west of the provincial capital of My Tho also got under way, but in a fashion which took little of the dry land. Called Dong Tam, it was built on hundreds of acres of abandoned rice paddies, which were filled in with dirt dredged from the river bottom to create solid ground. The base was being built for the sole purpose of giving the riverine force a home ashore in addition to its mobile base afloat. It was, and is, the only shore facility belonging to the riverine force.

THE NAVAL ELEMENT

The MACV plans for the naval element of the force demanded a significant effort from the Navy. An entirely new organization, including assault boats, support ships, supply support systems, and trained crews, had to be created within an extremely short time. Commander Amphibious Force, U.S. Pacific Fleet, was designated as the type commander responsible for delineating the requirements in detail and then making them come to pass—a task similar to, but much more extensive than, that performed in developing the river patrol force.

It was determined that the Chief of Naval Operations would have to establish an entirely new combat organization, River Assault Flotilla One, and a subordinate support organization, River Support Squadron Seven, both under one commander and one staff. The flotilla would consist initially of two river assault squadrons, made up of a mixture of Armored Troop Carriers (ATC), monitors, Command/

Communication Boats (CCB), and Assault Support Patrol Boats (ASPB). The ASPB would be designed especially for the force and the others would be converted from LCM-6 landing craft. The river support squadron would consist of five self-propelled barracks ships (APB), four repair ships (ARL), two support ships (LST), two heavy salvage craft (LHC), two light salvage craft (LLC), two tug boats (YTB), and two harbor clearance teams.

The river assault squadrons would provide the close support to the Army combat assault elements of the force, and the support squadron would provide the afloat base (or Mobile Riverine Base) from which operations would be staged and supported.

This detailed proposal, stating what was needed and when it was needed to implement the concept of the Mekong Delta Mobile Afloat Force, was presented to the Secretary of Defense. It was approved in July 1966, but the Secretary released funds for the construction and conversion of only a portion of the many forces requested, with the provision that if the afloat force proved as effective as advertised, additional funds would be made available later for the remainder of the force. Deleted primarily were three of five barracks ships, and two of four repair ships.

ESTABLISHMENT

Work to put the approved "package" into action accelerated. The concept of the program was new, and many aspects had to be developed specifically for the projected operations: boat design, boat armor and armament, logistic support, training, doctrine, and organization. Determining priorities and requirements involved planners in continual battles with one another, as well as with outsiders. Arrangements had to be made with the Army for handling the difficult logistical problem of supplying the riverine force with the thousands of items it would need that were peculiar to one or the other Service, such as the ammunition for the 2nd Brigade's artillery battalion.

Organizational arrangements also had to be made with the Army. There is no single commander of the Mobile Riverine Force (as the afloat force was later renamed)—the first superior common to both the Army and Navy elements is ComUSMACV. The problems created by the absence of a single commander were solved with the publication of a joint operation order signed by both the Army brigade commander and Commander River Assault Flotilla One. The Mekong Delta Mobile Riverine Force was an unlikely marriage of Army and Navy that violated basic organizational concepts. More often than not, similar arrangements had failed before. Would it work this time?

River Assault Flotilla One/River Support Squadron Seven was established as a unit of the Amphibious Force, Pacific Fleet, on 1 September 1966 at Coronado, California. The two assault boat squadrons were established a month or so later. Close liaison was made with the U. S. Army's Ninth Division, which was being formed in Kansas. One of the Division's brigades, with an artillery battalion in support, was designated the Army element of the afloat force. As can be imagined, the main problems confronted in early conferences concerned logistic support, a responsibility assigned to the Navy element.

It was necessary to find a place in the United States that would provide an environment as much like that of the Mekong Delta as possible, for training of the assault boat crews. Such a site was found at Mare Island, California, where a new training command was established to take advantage of the Delta-like terrain and waterways of the upper San Francisco Bay. The Naval Inshore Operations Training

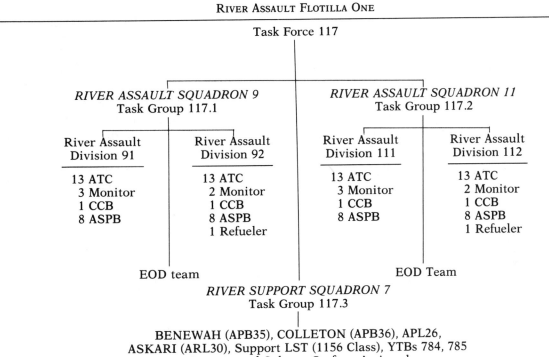

RIVER ASSAULT FLOTILLA ONE

Task Force 117

RIVER ASSAULT SQUADRON 9
Task Group 117.1

RIVER ASSAULT SQUADRON 11
Task Group 117.2

River Assault
Division 91

13 ATC
3 Monitor
1 CCB
8 ASPB

River Assault
Division 92

13 ATC
2 Monitor
1 CCB
8 ASPB
1 Refueler

River Assault
Division 111

13 ATC
3 Monitor
1 CCB
8 ASPB

River Assault
Division 112

13 ATC
2 Monitor
1 CCB
8 ASPB
1 Refueler

EOD team

EOD Team

RIVER SUPPORT SQUADRON 7
Task Group 117.3

BENEWAH (APB35), COLLETON (APB36), APL26,
ASKARI (ARL30), Support LST (1156 Class), YTBs 784, 785
Support and Salvage Craft as Assigned

Center not only provides training for the river assault squadrons but for the PBR boat crews as well.

BOATS AND FACILITIES

While a training program was still being organized, the flotilla "wiring diagram" became definite. It is outlined in our second chart, with a brief list of the boats and support ships and craft of the support squadron.

Assault Craft

Each river assault squadron has 26 armored troop carriers (ATC), to provide the trooplift (normally, a platoon of about 40 men per boat), the resupply, and, until the arrival of the ASPBs, the minesweeping capabilities of the Mobile Riverine Force. The ATCs are armed with one 20-mm. cannon, two .50-caliber machine gun mounts and two Mk. 18 grenade launchers, as well as an assortment of small arms, including M-79 grenade launchers. These are intended for use against an enemy ashore. But should the ATCs be required to operate in an area where they were subject to air attack, they would probably acquit themselves well, since all their weapons are capable of taking an air target under fire. This is true of the other boats, also.

Because they are most likely to meet close-range attack in the narrow, winding streams of the Delta, the ATCs and the other assault craft of the riverine force must be well-armored. The Viet Cong in the Delta use the B-40 and the B-50 rocket anti-tank grenade weapons most often and most effectively against riverine forces. The B-40 (officially, RPG-2) has an effective range of about 120 meters, the B-50 (RPG-7), a range of about 400 meters. Both fire low velocity rounds that are about 82 mm. in diameter. These are one-man weapons, which can be fired from the shoulder, giving the man using them considerable mobility. The enemy also attacks with 57-mm. recoilless rifles—which have an effective range of 1,000 meters, but have a much smaller charge than the B-40 and B-50—and with .50-caliber armor-piercing bullets. The last-named, though encountered frequently, are not very effective. The Viet Cong have 75-mm. recoilless rifles, but cannot always use them, because they are heavy and bulky.

In addition to conventional armor, the riverine force craft have "stand-off" armor to trigger enemy rounds before they hit the conventional armor, and this is particularly useful in providing protection against the 57-mm. recoilless rifle and the .50-caliber. In numerous engagements, the boats have proved their ability to withstand the heaviest of fires and to protect the Army troops they carry.

One significant addition to the force since it commenced operations in Vietnam has been the installation of a helicopter flight deck on the ATCs, capable of supporting UH-1Ds. This platform has a side benefit: it gives additional protection against mortar fire. (Actually, perhaps because of their tactical mobility, to the end of 1967 our boats never came under mortar fire.) The flight decks have proved invaluable for emergency resupply, transfer of personnel and helicopter medical evacuation in the area of operations. Frequently during operations, they provide the only available landing points for the helicopters in the vicinity of the action.

The ATC(H) also serve as battalion aid stations. Each river assault division has one such aid station staffed with a doctor and Army aidmen or Navy hospitalmen equipped to treat battlefield casualties. The aid station team remains afloat in the ATC(H) during operations. In addition, one ATC(H) carrying refrigerated whole blood and an operating table is always maintained in the area of operations to perform emergency surgery when required. The tremendous value of the aid stations was clearly demonstrated on 15 September 1967 when one boat alone treated 56 battle casualties.

Each squadron is also assigned one refueler, which has the same construction as the ATC, but is also capable of providing mogas to small assault boats and avgas (JP-4) to helicopters. Both refuelers have flight decks.

The battleship of the river assault squadron is the monitor with her Navy-type direct-fire 81-mm. mortar, 40-mm., and 20-mm. automatic cannons, two .50-caliber machine guns, and two Mk. 18 grenade launchers. The monitor carries the same heavy armor as the ATC, and can move in and engage the enemy at close range. The monitors have slugged it out several times, often at ranges of no more than 20 yards, with the Viet Cong along the river banks in close support of the troops afloat and ashore. As a gunfire support boat, the monitor has an advantage over the ASPB, which does not carry such heavy armor. Five monitors serve in each squadron.

Two Command/Communications Boats (CCB) assigned each squadron serve as the afloat command post for the battalion commander in the area of operations, in addition to being flagships for the squadron and division commanders. Instead of the 81-mm. mortar, they carry a command and control console installed aft of the 40-mm. cannon, but otherwise the CCBs look much like the monitors. They have the same armor protection as the ATC.

The battalion operations officer and the Navy task group commander are always embarked in the CCB. The battalion commander can divide his time in the area of operations between the CCB and the command and control helicopter as the tactical situation requires, travelling rapidly from one location to another by means of the ATC(H) flight deck. In addition, when he takes part in an operation the brigade commander normally uses one CCB as a forward command post.

The ASPB, the only boat newly constructed for the force, is the riverine minesweeper and destroyer and is equipped with a mine countermeasures chain drag, a Navy-type 81-mm. mortar, a 20-mm. cannon, a twin .50-caliber machine gun, and two or more Mk. 18 grenade launchers. The 16-knot ASPB leads the way on all riverine strike operations, sweeping ahead of the assault formation. She has "stand off" armor protection of a slightly different design from that of the ATC. The ASPB is also employed for escort, counterambush, reconnaissance, patrol, and support of special operations. To improve her performance in all these roles, the ASPB is equipped with a special exhaust system, which exhausts underwater, and, although it has certain engineering drawbacks, makes the boat quieter than any other riverine assault craft in use.

All the assault boats have navigation lights, compasses, and radio transceivers.

The ATCs and the ASPBs carry a crew of seven; the monitors and the CCBs carry eleven. Each boat has a rated gunner's mate or gunner's mate striker on board—the monitors always have a gunner's mate. The boat captain of each assault craft is a chief boatswain's mate or boatswain's mate first class, which means that the senior petty officer is not necessarily boat captain unless he is the boatswain's mate. Although a group of assault craft is usually commanded by an officer, if an officer is not available and the situation dictates, the senior boat captain of a group of assault boats may be placed in tactical command of the group.

Support Craft

The two barracks ships, APBs, were converted from LST-hull barracks ships of World War II. In each case, a helicopter platform was added and the entire ship was air-conditioned, and upon arrival in-country, both were fitted with stand-off armor. Approximately 800 troops can be accommodated in each ship. One, the *Benewah* (APB-35), is configured as a flotilla/brigade command/control flagship. She has extensive communication facilities and a joint operations center to provide both the flotilla commander and the brigade commander with the necessary command/control capability. The other original APB, the *Colleton* (APB-36), is configured to provide a similar arrangement for the river assault squadron commander and the battalion commander. At the end of 1967 the *Colleton* was provided with hospital facilities suitable for lightly wounded men.

In order to embark two infantry battalions and two 105-mm. artillery batteries, we had to use an APL, a non-self-propelled barracks ship. Our particular APL was activated on the West Coast and sent to Vietnam to answer the Riverine Force's need until additional APBs could be made ready. The APL houses approximately 625 men; however, she must be moved by tugs whenever the base is relocated, which necessarily slows down the force and creates a tactical disadvantage. Also, she has no armor and little armament—only .30-caliber and .50-caliber machine guns. These arms normally are sufficient, since the ship stays within the protective envelope of the Mobile Riverine Base.

Repair and maintenance support for river assault craft and ships of the force is the function of the *Askari* (ARL-30), an LST-hull repair ship, which also has space on board for Army maintenance personnel to repair Army

The barracks ship Benewah *with Ammi pontoons in tow is escorted by an armored troop carrier on 18 October 1967. This ship was flagship of the Mobile Riverine Force, serving both CTF 117 and the Commanding General, 2d Brigade, Ninth Division. She carries two 3-inch guns, eight 40-mm guns, and a large number of machine guns. (Ed Shinton, PH2, U.S. Navy)*

weapons, communications equipment, and outboard motors.

One 1156-class LST is assigned to the MRB from the U. S. Seventh Fleet for support of Army and Navy elements. This support ship was chosen specifically for her size, which provides much storage space but is not great enough to cause navigation problems in the rivers. She stores a ten-day supply of ammunition and C-rations, a ten-day emergency back-up supply of dry cargo, and that portion of the APB's basic Army troop support load (primarily ammunition and weapon spares) which cannot be carried in the APB. (To carry so much is beyond the capacity of the LST-542 class.) In addition, the support LST accommodates the brigade helicopter detachment, its four H-23 helicopters, one infantry company, and one river assault division. A second LST is assigned

to supply the mobile riverine base weekly from the port of Vung Tau. This LST, one of the 542 class, delivers all classes of cargo and refuels all of the ships of the MRB.

Pending the approval and deployment of a second ARL, Commander-in-Chief, Pacific Fleet, directed the conversion of a YFNB, a non-self-propelled barge, to a repair and maintenance barge for the river assault boats. The YFNB was sent from the West Coast to be stationed at Dong Tam.

As a result of the success of the Mobile Riverine Force, two more APBs and three more ARLs have since been activated: the *Mercer* (APB-39), the *Nueces* (APB-40), the *Satyr* (ARL-23), the *Sphinx* (ARL-24), and the *Indra* (ARL-37). They provide more mobility to the MRF and do not subject it to the tactical embarrassment the APL caused by having to be towed every time the Force moved. The YFNB (now designated YRBM) and the APL have stayed on at Dong Tam as a permanent repair and housing facility for the MRF. They are cheaper to operate than the self-propelled ships, and since they now form part of a fixed base, engines are not necessary.

Facilities Ashore

The plan for a mobile afloat force in the Mekong Delta required that certain support facilities be provided at the land base at Dong Tam for the Navy element in addition to the facilities for the Army. The support base was approved and at the time of this writer's detachment from command of TF 117, included berthing and messing facilities for one river assault squadron, a boat basin to accommodate berthing for one squadron, waterfront facilities for the resupply of the force by LSTs, drydocks for repair of underwater damage to the boats, alternate command and control facilities for the river assault squadron commander and the battalion commander, and a repair and maintenance support barge for the squadron—the converted YRBM. These facilities made it possible for a river assault squadron and a battalion of the Mobile Riverine Force to operate from a land base, in conjunction with afloat elements. The Dong Tam base does not represent an advantage technically, but is intended to be used when support ships for berthing are not available.

Ammi Pontoons

Finally, while it is neither a ship nor a boat, one of the most vital units of the Mobile Riverine Base is the Ammi pontoon. When the Riverine Force was being organized, no one gave much thought to the embarking and debarking of assault troops from the ships of the MRB, or to berthing for the many assault boats within the MRB. This was a major oversight in the

planning done back in the United States, and it was not until the advance elements of the flotilla and one squadron arrived in-country that the problem was fully appreciated and solved.

Unbeknownst to the planners, a unit construction pontoon called the Ammi pontoon (invented by Arsham Amirikian, the chief engineering advisor at the Naval Facilities Engineering Command) was already being used in Vietnam for a myriad of purposes. It was exactly the right size and shape (30′ × 90′) for mooring alongside the ships of the mobile base to provide an excellent embarkation and debarkation platform and to provide berthing "pier" space and staging for the logistic support of the boats. Moreover, these pontoons could be towed alongside easily, allowing the ships of the base to shift berths quickly. In heavy seas they can be rigged and towed astern. The Riverine Force obtained two such pontoons for each ship of the mobile base, including the support LST.

Thus, the Riverine Force was forced neither to use cargo nets nor to anchor the boats. With the Ammi pontoons alongside it is possible to embark an entire battalion in darkness in less than 30 minutes. Many have said that without the Ammis the Riverine Force could not function—perhaps not; certainly not as effectively as it has.

THE ARMY ELEMENT

The 2nd Brigade, one of three in the Ninth Division, had to be reorganized before it could serve with the Mobile Riverine Force. In preparation, the 2nd Brigade's three infantry battalions (each of which has three rifle companies) dropped their heavy wheeled vehicles, which of course would not be needed on the waterways, and also dispensed with certain heavy weapons, since the assault boats would provide the firepower necessary for close support of the troops. The men who had been assigned to the unneeded vehicles and weapons were retrained as riflemen. However, limited berthing in the Mobile Riverine Base restricted the number of men who could be reassigned in this way.

The concept called for the entire brigade to be afloat in the mobile base, with its attached artillery battalion likewise embarked. The Army would have preferred this arrangement because of the mobility afloat and the living conditions, which were somewhat better afloat than ashore. But barracks ships were available to accommodate only two of the three battalions and two of the three artillery batteries. So, the third battalion and the third battery had to operate from the land base at Dong Tam, pending the approval of the remainder of the Mobile Riverine Force "package."

Each of the three artillery batteries had six 105-mm. howitzers. It was planned that one battery would remain at Dong Tam, while the other two would be loaded in ATCs, transported to the operating area, unloaded, and positioned on firm ground for support of the riverine assault ground operations. The Army learned very quickly once it was in the Delta that no firm ground was to be found, and so it developed another method: the 105s were mounted on barges, which were towed to the area of operations by Army Transportation Corps LCM-8 boats and beached. The guns were then fired from the barges, in support not only of the ground troops but of the movement of the assault boats to the objective area as well. The Army provided the LCM-8s because the Navy had no suitable boats available. The LCM-6 could not have carried the large amounts of 105-mm. ammunition and other support equipment that were required; the LCM-8 could. Although the tide is important for most parts of a riverine operation, it is of little consequence to the fire support barges— when necessary, the barges are simply repositioned on the beach, the batteries reregistered,

and firing continued. The battery at Dong Tam is also located on barges.

Some of the LCM-8s are configured as fire support direction centers, and one as a forward command post for the brigade commander. This boat is always located at the fire support base where the brigade commander spends considerable time, while his CCB remains available to serve as his command post in the area of operations.

Also as a result of experience in the Delta, in July 1967 the Army constructed a barge from Ammi pontoons to serve as a helicopter landing platform for the command and control helicopter and the artillery spotting helicopters. This barge, which can accommodate two Huey (UH-1D) helicopters, is towed with the artillery barges and positioned alongside them at the forward fire support base.

The helicopters which the Army supplies to the Riverine Force do not belong to the 2nd Brigade, but come from the Ninth Division Aviation Company upon request. Plans for helicopter operations have to be made well in advance, so that the proper number of helicopters can be requested and obtained in time.

COMMAND AND RESPONSIBILITIES

Late in 1966, while the River Assault Flotilla and the Ninth Division were preparing to deploy to South Vietnam, both sent advance detachments to Saigon to form an in-country planning team. Their tasks were to prepare for the arrival of the MRF, to develop with in-country commands (USMACV, USARV, Nav-ForV) plans for the organization and employment of the force, to develop procedures and directives governing the relationship between the two service components, and similar organizational duties. Much planning had been done by the Army and Navy commands concerned, but it remained the job of this advance group to develop the actual procedures to be used.

In the fall of 1966, the command relationship setup and the directives for the operations of the Mobile Riverine Force were promulgated by ComUSMACV, initially as a working paper. Each service accepted the directive after some changes were made in the draft. It was at this point that the official name of the force was changed from the "Mekong Delta Mobile Afloat Force" to the "Mekong Delta Mobile Riverine Force."

The Logistic Support Directive was likewise promulgated, but only after considerable staff work by the Service Force, U. S. Pacific Fleet, and Naval Support Activity, Saigon, both working closely in conjunction with the Army Logistic Command in-country and with the flotilla, brigade, and division logistic organizations. The MACV concept required the Navy to give logistic support to the Riverine Force, including the embarked Army element. This was a unique and extensive task for the Navy, and required detailed planning and coordination. A system was worked out before the main elements of the force arrived that has been consistently adaptable to changes occasioned by combat.

The command relations are as shown in the next column.

Aboard the flagship *Benewah*, the flotilla (TF 117) staff and the brigade staff live and work very closely together. For example, the staff N1 and S1, N2 and S2, N3 and S3, N4 and S4, and N5 and S5 share staterooms. The respective offices and operating areas are for the most part located together. A joint operation order is prepared for each operation and signed by the flotilla commander and the brigade commander.

The entire scheme is based on coordination and cooperation, but permits the individual commanders maximum flexibility in attaining effective and workable relationships. The "joint-command" concept violates the principle that command of a military organization,

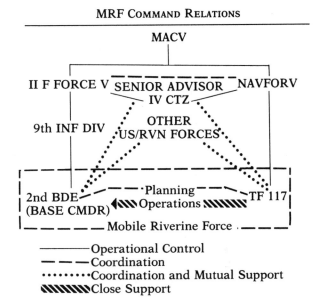

MRF COMMAND RELATIONS

———— Operational Control
– – – Coordination
•••••••• Coordination and Mutual Support
\\\\\\\\\ Close Support

or operation, should be vested in one man, but it works. It gives the element commanders elbow room in their attempts to make a new and untried concept work, and encourages imaginative, individual approaches to difficult combat situations heretofore not experienced. The same arrangement extends down both service chains, with similar relationships at each level, between the battalion commander and the river assault squadron commander, the company commander and the river assault division commander, the platoon commander and the ATC boat captain. (The last-named is also called the assault transport boat commander.) The ground troops and the assault boat crews live together and fight together.

The division of responsibilities initially agreed upon by the Flotilla (CTF 117) and the Brigade and outlined by the MACV directives is as follows:

Army Responsibilities
1. Plan operations in coordination with CTF 117.
2. Conduct tactical operations.
3. Defend the Mobile Riverine Base.

4. Coordinate all supporting fire.
5. Maintain liaison with Vietnamese sectors and districts.

Navy Responsibilities

1. Plan operations in coordination with the 2nd Brigade.
2. Provide close support for 2nd Brigade operations.
3. Assist in defense of the Mobile Riverine Base.
4. Manage logistic support of the Mobile Riverine Force.
5. Escort all movement on the water.

The logistic concept initially agreed upon is very briefly outlined below:

1. The support LST of the Mobile Riverine Base will maintain a 30-day supply of Class I support (provisions: frozen, dry, chilled) and a 10-day supply of all other class support (spare parts, equipage, POL, ammunition).
2. The resupply LST will supply the MRB every seven days from the logistic port of Vung Tau.
3. The Navy's River Support Squadron Seven is responsible for all supplies for the MRF (except certain parts peculiar to the Army).
4. The Navy and Army will jointly manage supply of tactical operations.
5. The Navy manages all water transportation, and the Army all helicopters. (When the troops are operating several miles from navigable waterways, they are supported entirely by helicopters.)
6. Each ATC will maintain a three-day supply of rations, water, and ammunition for the 40 troops embarked.

Commander Service Force, U. S. Pacific Fleet, through his subordinate in-country command, Naval Support Activity, Saigon, provides logistic support to the naval element of the MRF, which in turn supports the entire force. To accomplish this mission, a Navy liaison division of NSA, Saigon, consisting of resident representatives of that command, of the River Flotilla, and of the Ninth Division, was established at Vung Tau. Working in close coordination with the local Army Logistical

MOBILE RIVERINE FORCE
Riverine Assault Force (TF 117)
2nd Brigade 9th Inf. Div.

Mobile Riverine Base

Navy	Army
RIVFLOT ONE Staff	HHC 2nd BDE 9th Inf Div
2 River Assault Squadrons	2 Infantry Battalions
1 River Support Squadron	2 Arty Batteries (105-mm.)
	Det LCM-8 Boat Co
	Combat Support and Combat Service Support Elements

Dong Tam Base

Navy	Army
RIVFLOT ONE Admin Det	1 Infantry Battalion
YRBM-17	1 Arty Battery
	Combat Support and Combat Service Support Elements

Command, the liaison division fills requisitions submitted by CTF 117 for both Army and Navy requirements. It is also the receiving point for supplies coming from overseas for the Flotilla. Each week it assembles all the material requisitioned for the Riverine Force, loads the resupply LST, and sails her to wherever the Mobile Riverine Base may be. Each week the Riverine Force requires some 108 tons of Class I provisions, 65 tons of Class II, 120,000 gallons of POL, and 160 tons of ammunition (mostly 105-mm.).

Even as the current operation is in progress, planning must go forward for the next operation. An operation is likely to last three or four days. There will then be a day or two of preparation for the next one, and this day or two will be the only time the boat crews have for maintaining and repairing their boats.

Mode of Warfare

The operations of the Mobile Riverine Force are characterized as "strike operations" and are conducted following the receipt of hard intelligence of the location of Viet Cong forces. The enemy is mobile and elusive, so the river-

MOBILE RIVERINE FORCE STRIKE OPERATION

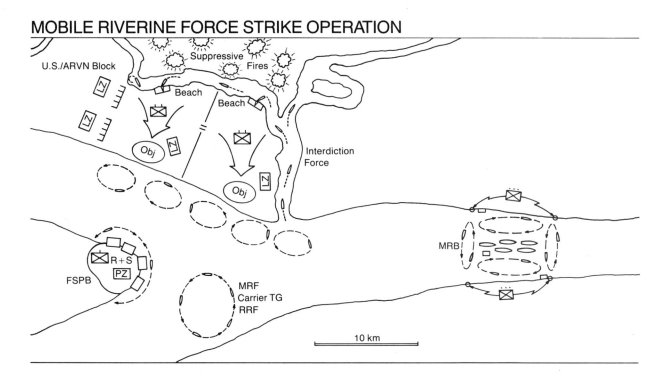

MOBILE RIVERINE BASE DEFENSE

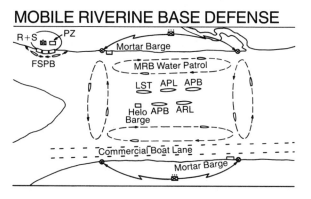

ine units must be fast. The procedure is to gain contact and then to bring in all forces immediately available and any that can be made available on short notice, not only from the Riverine Force, but from any other nearby U. S. or ARVN forces.

The mobility of the riverine base, and even more importantly the mobility of the assault boats, combined with the surprise created by moving at night, enables the force to react swiftly to intelligence, and to make contact quickly. The assault boats can move rapidly to seal off the Viet Cong forces by blocking all waterway escape routes, while helicopters and the MRF armored transports bring in troops, some to establish land blocks and others to seek the enemy. The brigade artillery batteries are positioned to cover the area of operations, to further restrict the movement of the enemy, and to support the troops with their fire. Air strikes are often used in addition to the heavy artillery.

In a region so criss-crossed by waterways, the naval gunfire provided by the assault boats is crucial to the success of the troops ashore. Even the ATCs, once they have disembarked their troops, set up blocking patrols and prepare to support the men ashore with .50-caliber and 20-mm. machine guns. Gunfire support from all the boats is normally adjusted by artillery observers, one of whom serves with each company. Forty-millimeter and machine gun fire is usually limited to a range of 1,000 to 1,500 meters, depending on the thickness of the vegetation along the banks, since both weapons are direct fire guns. Eighty-one-millimeter mortar fire can be called in from as far away as 4,000 yards, however. The troops often push beyond the range of our weapons, but the small craft try to keep as close as possible, taking advantage of the many small waterways, so that they can offer immediate support when it is needed. PBRs can and have been used to augment MRF resources for preventing escape ("exfiltration") on the waterways.

Prior to the coming of the MRF to the Delta, the Viet Cong fought only on their own terms during daylight, and then, mission accomplished or battle lost, they broke contact under cover of darkness and slipped away by sampan. The boats of the Vietnamese Navy RAGs were not sufficiently armored to sustain close-range contact with the enemy in the small rivers and canals, so they were powerless to block this movement. The better armored boats of the MRF can completely seal off waterways, and the force is strong enough to maintain contact with the Viet Cong for several days, and to defeat them.

An integral part of MRF operations is the use of U. S. capability in the air. In almost all riverine operations, waterborne assault is coupled with airborne assault by units of the 2nd Brigade in an attempt to encircle the Viet Cong forces. Moreover, the reported location of the Viet Cong is sometimes in an area that does not lend itself to purely riverine operations. In these cases the operation is primarily an air assault followed by ground action, with the river assault boats transporting troops to helicopter pick-up areas and providing blocking support on suspected Viet Cong communication routes.

In joint air and riverine operations, the "joint command" concept governs the relationship between the commanders of the various forces in combat. The commander of the riverine assault squadron or division is in charge of waterborne movements in the boats, and makes the decisions on boat movements suggested by the Army. The brigade, battalion, or company commander is in command of Army units in the area of operations. The command post is usually in a command and control helicopter over the operating area, but the CCB and the LCM-8 are also available to the commanders.

A typical MRF strike operation is depicted at the top of page 431.

The defense of the Mobile Riverine Base is everybody's concern. The base is most vulnerable to attack by recoilless rifles, but the Viet Cong can also use mortar fire, mines, swimmers, and suicide boats. Fortunately, during the first year of operation no attacks were made. The mobile base locates itself along the rivers of the Delta in support of the MRF, moving at will as the tactical situation dictates.

The base is generally defended as shown in the diagram labeled "Mobile Riverine Base Defense."

Task Force 117

Task Force 117 has two river assault squadrons (each composed of two divisions) committed in close support of three battalions. In an action involving a single battalion, one boat division can provide the escort, minesweeping, trooplift, and close-combat support needed if all boats are available. The other division in the squadron provides the patrols for defense of the base and any reinforcements or replacements of assault boats which may be needed. The squadron commander is embarked with either the battalion commander or the battalion operations officer in the CCB. The boat division commanders are usually designated unit commanders in such an action. The Riverine Force has conducted operations using all three battalions at once, the two battalions afloat joining the battalion from Dong Tam to mount out a brigade-sized operation. In this case, both riverine assault squadrons are used—one division supports each battalion, with the fourth division remaining behind to defend the mobile base.

Assault boats are also provided routinely for escort of the artillery barges and security patrol of the forward fire support base. The boat divisions are rotated to the base defense mission periodically to provide some relief from the continual combat operations in support of the battalions. Likewise, the battalions are rotated periodically from the afloat force to the land base for the same considerations.

MOBILE RIVERINE BASE

River Support Squadron Seven is actually the Mobile Riverine Base, which provides logistic support to the MRF and maintenance repair and supply support to the River Assault Flotilla. One of its most important functions is to provide berthing and support to the sailors and soldiers of the MRF. The command APB houses the flotilla and brigade commanders and their staffs, three Army reconnaissance and surveillance companies, and the mobile base defense element. The latter consists of one river assault division and one of the three reconnaissance and surveillance companies. (The Army company makes security patrols on banks adjacent to the base; the troops are ferried to and from their operating ground by the base defense boat division.) The other APB houses one complete battalion with its supporting boat division, as well as a river assault squadron commander and staff. The APL houses two-thirds of a battalion and staff with its supporting boat division and the other river assault squadron commander and staff. The support LST houses the balance of the battal-

The Askari *(ARL 30), repair ship for the Mobile Riverine Force, is seen in August 1967 with two Ammi pontoons and a number of armored troop carriers alongside. Completed in 1945, the* Askari *had been out of commission for ten years when the need for her developed in 1966. (Ed Shinton, PH2, U.S. Navy)*

ion with one supporting boat division and the Army supply detachment. Engineer platoons and LCM-8 boat companies are berthed in APBs and the APL, with their boats alongside. The two explosive ordnance disposal detachments, and the Army maintenance detachments, are housed in the ARL.

As can be seen, the Army ground elements are embarked with their supporting boat crews. The assault boats are berthed alongside the Ammi pontoons of the support ship.

The support ships provide berthing, messing, and washing facilities for boat crews, as well as laundry services and clothing and small stores. Each operates a ship's store, barber shop, and a small soda fountain, all of which are available to Army personnel as well as the boat crews. Each provides consumable supply support to one river assault division. Some of the consumables stocked for use of the squadron staff and boat crews are paint, cleaning gear, and office supplies. Equipage for each squadron is distributed to the squadron staff by the Flotilla Logistic Office, for further distribution to each boat crew by the squadron.

The assault craft must be watched continuously. When the boats are moored alongside their support ships, at least three men must be in each at all times, and one boat in each nest guards the base defense radio net. Each boat crew is provided with bunks and lockers aboard the support ship or barge to which its division is attached. When not assigned to the boat for watch, a crew member may sleep aboard the support vessel. Crew members mess aboard the support vessel and receive the same services as if they were members of the crew of the support vessel. The watch requirements allow a member of an assault craft crew to spend half his nights sleeping in his boat and half sleeping in the support ship. Many boat crews choose to sleep in their boats almost every night.

Each assault craft is provided with a few standard, folding, Navy frame bunks with canvas bottoms and air mattresses, and each crew member has a poncho liner to use as a blanket. There is no need to have a bunk for each man, nor does any boat have that many.

When a river assault division is based at Dong Tam, bunks and lockers are provided by the NSA detachment at Dong Tam, and each crew is assigned a hut. The same watches are maintained on the assault craft, and a crew member spends every other night in the boat.

During operations, the men live in the boats, eating and sleeping when they can. Standard combat rations are provided for all boats as part of the basic operational load. These are eaten cold, but the sailor may get himself a warm meal by placing his rations on the engine exhaust manifold. The crews of all assault craft that can be rotated back to the fire support patrol base for meals, and of those assault boats assigned to the fire support base for de-

fensive purposes, are fed hot meals there, which are brought in special insulated containers from the mobile base by LCM-8s that supply the fire bases with ammunition.

BOAT CREWS

At first there were only enough crews assigned to operate the boats in the force. There were no extra crews assigned. Extra crews were in training, however, to provide a pool of replacements for casualties. The only time when a boat is not fully manned and active is when she goes into overhaul and the crew is allowed to take leave for rest and recreation. Each boat is scheduled for overhaul and her crew for R&R every six months—the overhaul should be phased to coincide with the mid-point of each crew cycle and the replacement of the boat crews by new crews. Thus, R&R leave for the crew and crew rotation do not interfere with the regular operation of the boats. Although in the first year no one had missed an R&R flight, or failed to return to his boat on time, transportation during the R&R period was an ever-present problem for the crews.

Each assault craft is assigned to a specific boat crew, which is formed prior to the start of training in the United States. Each boat crew is trained to replace the crew of a specific boat currently operating in-country. This system is intended to increase the crew's identification with the unit and the boat, and to provide a basis for planning rotation of boat crews out of the country.

MAINTENANCE AND REPAIR

The riverine assault craft are repaired and maintained at different places, depending on the type of work required. Routine maintenance and repair within the capability of the boat engineer is done by the boat's crew alongside the ship to which the boat is assigned for berthing. Routine maintenance would include

Guns trained port and starboard, minesweeping grapnels streamed astern, assault support patrol boats lead a column of river assault craft up a canal in the Delta. The M-92-1 was a monitor, the most heavily armed and best protected of the river assault craft.

replacing drive belts, cleaning and changing oil and fuel filters, engine adjustments, and minor repair to pumps, injectors, and electrical equipment. It is usually supervised by the squadron maintenance officer, or by a chief engineman or a chief electrician assigned to the squadron. The squadron gunner's mate performs similar services for the boats' ordnance.

All major repair work for the boats, including replacement of engines and underwater hull work, can be accomplished by the ARL. Generally, the ARL repairs unexpected damage, such as battle damage, which occurs between overhauls. Using an "A" frame, she can lift any riverine assault craft, setting the boat on an Ammi pontoon equipped with blocks so work can be done on shafts, screws, rudder, or underwater hull. The ARL maintains a supply of spare parts for the repairs she handles, and for issue to boat engineers performing their own routine maintenance, which consists of 4,100 line items for LCM conversions and ASPBs. The ASPBs require a spare parts supply system separate from that for the LCMs. The ARL also conducts the engine overhaul program. When a boat goes into overhaul (every six months), her engines are replaced with rebuilt engines, while the old engines are removed and returned to the ARL to be completely rebuilt. After an engine has been rebuilt and run in on a dynamometer, it is put into storage on the ARL or sent to the YRBM to be used in a future overhaul.

Every six months, each craft is sent to the YRBM for a complete overhaul and any necessary modifications. Each boat is lifted onto an Ammi pontoon for an underwater hull inspection and treatment with preservatives. All electronic equipment is inspected and repaired or replaced. The YRBM also replaces any engines which are due to be replaced, or which have too few engine hours left to complete another operating cycle.

The YRBM also handles routine maintenance and repair for whatever river assault division may be stationed at Dong Tam, rendering the same service to the assault boats as would the ARL.

Operations

The 9th Division deployed to South Vietnam in December 1966. The first elements of the Flotilla, Commander River Assault Squadron 9, and River Assault Division 91 deployed early in January and joined the Flotilla's advance detachment. Plans had been made for the naval elements to join elements of the 2nd Brigade for training while the balance of the Flotilla's personnel, support ships, and assault craft were arriving and being assimilated bit by bit.

River Assault Flotilla One commenced operations on a modest scale at Vung Tau on 16 January 1967. The *Whitfield County* (LST-1169) acted as a support ship. River Assault Division 91 and the Third Battalion, 60th Infantry (3/60) of the Ninth Infantry Division began basic riverine training together. Until their own boats arrived, they used seven LCM-6 troop carriers and one commandament (command boat) borrowed from the Vietnamese Navy.

A series of four-day riverine warfare training courses was conducted in the southern portion of the Rung Sat Special Zone, each with two infantry companies participating. Troops were given indoctrination lectures to acquaint them with shipboard routine and regulations; with the boats; with their duties and weapons; with mines and mine countermeasures; with embarkation and debarkation; and with survival in the water. Practical training included embarkation and debarkation procedures (wet net and embarkation ladder), firing of installed boat weapons, and day and night assault landings and extractions. As additional sailors and

troops arrived, they were worked into the program.

While training was taking place in the Rung Sat, observer detachments were assigned to Vietnamese river assault groups in the Delta to gain familiarity with the rivers on which they would soon be sailing their own craft. While observing, they developed considerable respect for their Vietnamese counterparts' skillful shiphandling, their knowledge, and their courage. As a result, this program had the additional, unexpected benefit of promoting understanding and friendship between two groups that on occasion would be operating closely together in the months ahead.

By mid-February, 3/60 and 2/60 of the Division's 3rd Brigade had completed basic training, and Navy elements began training with 3/47 of the 2nd Brigade. At this time, the Viet Cong intensified their attacks on ships in the Long Tau. The American minesweeping boats came under particularly frequent and heavy attack, and on 15 February one was sunk by a mine and two others were damaged by recoilless rifle and small arms fire.

As a result, the decision was made to commence battalion-size search-and-destroy operations in the Rung Sat on a full-time basis. On 16 February, 3/47 was committed to these operations, and River Assault Squadron Nine was directed to provide support to the senior advisor in the RSSZ and assigned Army forces.

Support of a battalion-sized operation with the eight borrowed Vietnamese RAG craft would have been almost impossible without the timely arrival of the *Askari* (ARL-30), which arrived only six months after the decision to activate her was made. This was a normal interval for activation among the MRB ships.

On 26 February, ComRivFlot One, Captain W. C. Wells, U. S. Navy, arrived in-country and on 28 February, Task Force 117 (Riverine Assault Force) was activated under his com-

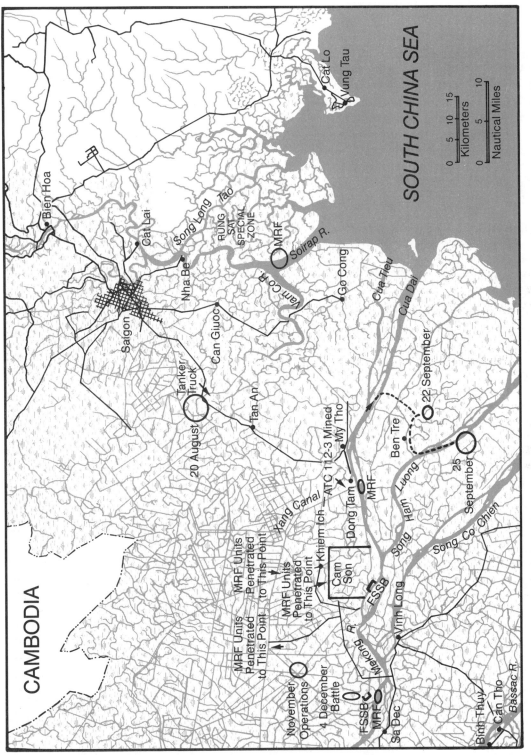

CAMBODIA

SOUTH CHINA SEA

Bien Hoa

Cat Lai

Song Long Tao

RUNG
SAT
SPECIAL
ZONE

Soirap R.

Nha Be

Vam Co Dong R.

Saigon

Can Giuoc

Tanker
Truck

20 August

Tan An

Xang Canal

MRF Units
Penetrated
to This Point

MRF Units
Penetrated
to This Point

MRF Units
Penetrated
to This Point

Khiem Ich

Cam
Son

Dong Tam

ATC 11-2-3 Mined

My Tho

MRF

Ben Tre

22 September

25
September

Song Ham Luong

Song Co Chien

FSSB

Vinh Long

Mekong R.

November
Operations

4 December
Battle

FSSB

MRF

Sa Dec

Can Tho

Binh Thuy

Bassac R.

Go Cong

Cua Tieu

Cua Dai

Cat Lo

Vung Tau

MRF

Kilometers
0 5 10 15

Nautical Miles
0 5 10

Here the Mobile Riverine Force operated during its first year of combat. The rivers and canals are shown in gray, the roads in black. The Delta is a difficult place for travel on foot, and nowhere south or west of Saigon is there enough solid ground to build an airstrip suitable for jet aircraft.

mand. ComRivFlot One/CTF 117 embarked in the *Henrico* (APA-45), which had relieved the *Whitfield County* (LST-1169) as support ship on 26 February. The *Henrico* was anchored at Vung Tau where, with some inconvenience, she did a fine job as an interim support ship.

The men of River Assault Division 92 arrived at Vung Tau on 27 and 28 February and began their indoctrination, advanced training, and participation in the Vietnamese RAG technical observer program.

On 8 March the first three LCM conversions arrived at Vung Tau in the SS *Talkeetna*, a Liberty Ship chartered from the Alaska Steamship Company. These craft, ATCs, had been converted at the Ship Repair Facility, Yokosuka, Japan. They participated in their first combat operation in the Rung Sat Special Zone on 18 March. A monitor on loan from the Vietnamese Navy was added to the force on 20 March. By 8 April, a total of 17 ATCs and one CCB had arrived and had completed outfitting and operational testing.

Riverine operations in the Rung Sat Special Zone resulted in a substantial reduction in Viet Cong attacks on both commercial shipping and U. S. Navy patrol and minesweeping craft. In addition, through these operations numerous enemy base camps and large quantities of mines, ammunition, weapons, documents, provisions, medical supplies, sampans, and tools were discovered and destroyed or captured. On numerous occasions, Viet Cong crossing small streams in sampans were successfully ambushed by ground units. The first mining attempt against units of TF 117 occurred in the lower Rung Sat on 2 April when a CCB on loan from the Vietnamese was almost hit. The resulting vibration exposed considerable structural deterioration in the hull, which required extensive repairs.

On 19 March two companies of 4/47 relieved the men of 3/47 in the Rung Sat. The commanding officer of 4/47 established his command post in the *Henrico*, which was relieved as TF 117 support ship by the *Montrose* (APA-212) on 23 March.

The first deployment of Riverine Assault Force units in the Mekong Delta occurred on 10 April when one CCB and four ATCs steamed from Vung Tau to Dong Tam, a distance of about 50 miles. On the following day nine additional ATCs and the monitor borrowed from the Vietnamese escorted *APL-26* and *YFNB-24*, both under commercial tow, to Dong Tam. At this time, Task Group 117.2 was activated, under the command of Commander C. H. Black, U. S. Navy, operations and plans officer for the Flotilla. The next day, 12 April, Commander Black's task group began riverine operations, staging from Dong Tam, in support of the 2nd Brigade. The first operations were conducted in both Dinh Tuong and Kien Hoa provinces on the north and south banks of the Mekong River and on Thoi Son Island southeast of Dong Tam.

On 15 April the *Kemper County* (LST-854), one of the old LSTs, arrived at Vung Tau to be the first Mobile Riverine Base support ship. On 18 April, the basic inventory for the MRB was loaded aboard her.

The *Benewah* (APB-35) arrived in Vung Tau on 22 April and assumed her duties as permanent flagship for Commander Riverine Assault Force (CTF 117), on 26 April. The *Montrose* (APA-212) was detached on 28 April. The *Colleton* (APB-36) arrived on 2 May.

The 4th Battalion, 47th Infantry, accompanied by a company of 3/39, ended its operations in the RSSZ with a three-day riverine search-and-destroy action on the ninth through the eleventh of May. TF 117 supported the operation with 23 river assault craft while the senior U. S. Navy advisor in the RSSZ (CTG 116.2), at Nha Be, provided 19 Vietnamese RAG craft. River Assault Group 22 contributed seven additional boats. Although several base camps were overrun and destroyed during the three days, and numerous documents captured, only light contact was made with the enemy. The operation was significant mainly because it involved the largest number of TF 117 units to participate in an operation to date and was the first operation in which substantial numbers of TF 117 and TF 116 units participated in support of each other. On 13 May, 4/47 departed the USS *Colleton* at Vung Tau and went to Dong Tam.

By 13 May a total of 39 ATCs, 2 CCBs, and 4 monitors had been received in-country.

15 MAY 1967

On 15 and 16 May Task Group 117.2, supporting the 2nd Brigade, came into heavy contact with the Viet Cong for the first time. Operation Hoptac XVIII began with a search-and-destroy operation conducted in the Cam Son base area of western Dinh Tuong Province, seven or eight kilometers east of the district town of Cai Be. This area was used by the Viet Cong as a marshalling, training, and rest base, and was capable of supporting a Main Force battalion. They controlled all traffic here, and U. S. and ARVN troops would not enter the area except in a well-planned offensive operation. For years the area had been a stopping-off place for enemy troops moving through Dinh Tuong Province. Our purpose in Hoptac XVIII was to engage any enemy in the area and destroy Viet Cong installations, so as to disrupt travel and communications in the area.

The action took place between the Rach Ba Rai and the Rach Tra Tan. It involved the largest number of river assault craft to participate in a riverine operation in the IV Corps Tactical Zone up to that time: 22 ATCs, two CCBs, and two monitors. At about 0800 on 15 May troops of 3/47 and 4/47 were landed on the east bank of the Rach Ba Rai by Riverine Assault Division 91. The Third Battalion was landed at the mouth of the Ba Rai, while the Fourth was landed three or four kilometers up

the river. After unopposed landings, the two groups began moving east and north. Meanwhile, the boats of Riverine Assault Division 92 were moving to set up blocks on the Rach Tra Tan and the Rach Cu La. The blocks were to be on station by 0830. As the boats on the Tra Tan passed through the area where Highway TL 25 crosses the little river, they were fired upon; they suppressed the fire and proceeded to their stations. At about 1015, two ATCs of the blocking force on the Tra Tan came under heavy attack, again at the TL 25 crossing. The two boats cleared the river to the south while air and artillery strikes were called in on the area. One monitor and four ATCs were still on blocking stations to the north of the ambush site. It was apparent by this time that the two battalions on the ground, which had made only slight contact to the west, were forcing the VC to move in order to avoid battle, and that the enemy wanted to clear the Tra Tan in the vicinity of Highway TL 25 so that he could escape across the river.

To prevent this, the four ATCs which had been blocking the Rach Cu La, were called from that station and, with a reconnaissance platoon embarked, fought their way up the Rach Tra Tan to Highway TL 25 to support the craft engaged there. Under heavy RR/B-40 rocket and automatic weapons fire, they closed to within 10 or 15 meters of the dug-in VC and landed the reconnaissance platoon on the east bank of the Tra Tan. After about 20 minutes in close contact, the four ATC were pulled back to the south, and more air and artillery strikes were called in on the enemy positions. When the strikes were lifted, seven ATCs moved against the VC from the south, and they were joined at the highway crossing by the four ATCs and the monitor that had been blocking to the north. This combined force directed heavy fire at the west bank, but was unable to dislodge the VC. During this time, 3/47 and 4/47 were moving east in order to trap the VC

against the naval block on the Tra Tan. The
boats on the Tra Tan, after 20 or 25 minutes of
heavy fighting, once again moved south, after
picking up the reconnaissance platoon. Air and
artillery strikes were repeated, and the boats
returned to reland the reconnaissance platoon
on the east bank and deliver heavy fire on the
west bank. At this point, VC troops were seen
breaking cover and moving off to the west
toward 3/47 and 4/47. They had failed to clear
the naval block, and were being forced to disperse to escape. The riflemen caught and destroyed them. The enemy, estimated to be two
companies in strength, lost about 100 men.
Fourteen men of TF 117 were wounded, and six
craft were slightly damaged.

The battle in the Cam Son base area proved
that our boats could withstand heavy automatic weapons and 57-mm. recoilless rifle fire
at close range. It also showed that the concept
of using the riverine craft as blocking forces
was indeed workable. From this time on, the
enemy could no longer rely on the waterways
as a means of escape and as a means of avoiding contact. Nor could he move his troop units
intact but from now on would have to move in
groups of only three or four.

CORONADO

The *Benewah* and *Colleton* sailed to Dong
Tam with River Assault Squadron Eleven and
all remaining units of River Assault Squadron
Nine on 1 June. The *Askari* and *Kemper County*
remained at Vung Tau to complete the outfitting and operational testing of those LCM
conversions still to be received. The 2nd Brigade headquarters embarked on 2 June and
the Mobile Riverine Force was formed. The
code name "Coronado" was assigned by Com-
USMACV for all Mobile Riverine Force operations. Two days later, on 4 June, Operation
Coronado I was conducted by the force in Dinh
Tuong and Kien Hoa provinces. On 6 June,
ATC 112-3 was acting as minesweeper for a

task unit proceeding north on the Xang Canal
near Dong Tam to insert a platoon-sized patrol, when a mine exploded under her stern. A
.50-caliber machine gun and a Mk. 18 grenade
launcher were blown over the side and the
after part of the boat's hull was damaged extensively. The ATC had to be towed to Dong
Tam for repairs.

The *Tioga County* (LST-1158), the first 1156-
class LST to be assigned to TF 117, arrived at
Dong Tam on 9 June and commenced
embarkation of elements of the 2nd Brigade.
She provided the force with the additional
berthing and logistics capacity needed to support two full infantry battalions afloat.

On 11 and 12 June the Mobile Riverine Base
sailed out of the Mekong and up to Nha Be, just
below Saigon. The mobile base stopped overnight at Vung Tau, where it was joined by the
Kemper County. The force then proceeded to
Nha Be via the Soi Rap River. This river was
not commonly used, but we wanted to see
whether our ships could navigate its length,
from the China Sea to Nha Be, without difficulty. They eventually became familiar enough
with the Soi Rap to operate in it under any
conditions. On 18 June, after five days of operations in the northern part of the Rung Sat Special Zone, the base was again relocated, this
time to the junction of the Vam Co and Soi Rap
rivers. The move was made to shorten the
travel distance for assault craft operating in
Long An Province.

Meanwhile, on 13 June, the *Askari* (ARL-30)
joined at Nha Be, accompanied by *YTB-784*
and *YTB-785*. Both of these harbor tugs were
part of the original program and had sailed
together from Norfolk, Virginia, via the Panama Canal to join the Riverine Assault Force.
The last of the Flotilla's LCM conversions, two
monitors, arrived in-country on 10 June and
were unloaded in Saigon on 15 June. Of the
craft originally allowed, only the 32 ASPBs
were now missing.

With landing craft and supporting monitors beached on both sides of the narrow, twisting stream, aircraft strike an enemy center of resistance a short distance inland. This photo makes clear the soggy nature of the Delta.

The *Holmes County* (LST-836) arrived at Nha Be on 15 June and began the first of the weekly supply runs between Vung Tau and the mobile base. A day later, the *Vernon County* (LST-1161) arrived to relieve the *Kemper County* and *Tioga County* as LST base support ship. Also on 16 June, the last of the riverine craft borrowed from the Vietnamese Navy were returned.

The Mobile Riverine Force commenced Coronado Operation Concordia on the morning of 19 June in eastern Can Giouc District of Long An Province. The area selected for the initial search-and-destroy operation proved to be an important one: troops of the 2nd Brigade, supported by the ARVN 2/46 and the U. S. 2/60, encountered between three and four hundred Viet Cong troops near the hamlet of Ap Bac. The action began when River Assault Division 91 landed 3/47 on the banks of the Song Rach Cac to the west of Ap Bac. The ARVN troops were positioned south of Ap Bac as a blocking force. River Assault Division 92 landed 4/47 to the north of Ap Bac, and that battalion began to sweep south as 3/47 was sweeping east. At about noon, 4/47 came upon the Viet Cong directly east of Ap Bac, dug in with their backs to the Rach Nui River, which was being patrolled by Division 92. When 4/47 came under fire, the river craft were able to aid them with naval gunfire, moving to within 25 or 30 yards of the enemy flanks. The boats received automatic weapons fire, sniper fire, and some RR and B-40 fire during the two days of heavy fighting. Besides providing close fire support and blocking on the rivers, TF 117 also gave extensive medical aid in the field and on board the APBs. The enemy left 250 dead on the battlefield. Forty-six U. S. soldiers were killed in action, and approximately 150 were wounded—the wounded included 15 sailors who were hurt by shrapnel from hits on the boats. Damage to the boats was slight.

Coronado Operation Concordia continued the hunt for the enemy, using riverine assault, search and destroy, and saturation of suspect areas with patrols in southeastern Long An Province and northern Go Cong Province. In addition, each week one company-sized operation was conducted in the RSSZ. Throughout Concordia, the mobile base remained at the junction of the Vam Co and Soi Rap.

A major step forward in increasing the flexibility and versatility of the Riverine Force was taken on 4 July when a small Army helicopter, a three-place H-23, was landed and launched from a pad on an ATC. The following day a UH-1D conducted landings and take-offs from the same platform. This development substantially increased the force's ability to move troops in the area of operations rapidly, to evacuate casualties, and to conduct reconnaissance.

During the month of June, the Mobile Riverine Force accounted for 287 Viet Cong dead, 26 Viet Cong prisoners of war, and 2 Hoi Chanhs. U. S. losses were 47 killed in action. Both sides, of course, suffered wounded, but we had no way to count those of the enemy.

From 1 July through 24 July, the Riverine Force continued Operation Coronado (Concordia II), staging from the junction of the Vam Co and the Soi Rap rivers. On 15 July, at the request of CTF 117, CTF 116 provided PBR support for the first time, when six PBRs from Nha Be were assigned to assist in blocking infiltration of VC during operations in Long An Province. These boats worked hard and well as a blocking force on the major waterways. They are generally unsuitable for blocking work on small waterways and canals, however, because of their vulnerability to close-range fire. Their main protection—speed—cannot be used effectively in the small waterways.

The first helicopter barge was delivered on 22 July, providing the force with a landing area afloat for two helicopters, which in an emergency could refuel the aircraft. In operations conducted in the Can Giouc District during this period, all participating forces made their most effective use of supporting fires to date. Naval artillery and air support was closely coordinated with troop maneuvers, providing maximum protection to ground forces. Only one U. S. soldier was killed, while 31 enemy troops were killed on a single two-day operation. On 24–25 July the Vietnamese Marine Corps participated in Riverine Force operations for the first time. Their 3rd Battalion issued jointly with CTF 117 a movement and embarkation order and River Division 91 lifted the battalion to their area of operations and remained in close support, conducting numerous troop landings and pick-ups as part of a two-battalion operation.

BATTLE ON THE MEKONG AND IN THE RUNG SAT

The mobility of the Riverine Force was put to the test when at mid-day on 25 July, CTF 117 received word that two days hence, the base was to leave the Soi Rap and sail 61 miles to the vicinity of Dong Tam. During the afternoon of 25 July the Vietnamese Marines were picked up and returned to the base as previously scheduled. Movement plans were prepared and promulgated on 26 July, and at 0200 on 27 July riverine assault craft began departing the mobile base, headed for their minesweeping and patrol stations along the track of the base. At 0550 the last ship of the force was under way and proceeding toward the entrance of the Soi Rap. Because of the slow speed of the APL under tow and the fact that the ships were steaming against a flooding tide while proceeding out the Soi Rap River and against an ebbing tide while proceeding up the Mekong River, the move required eleven and a half hours to complete. Normally, the ships of the force preferred to steam with the tide, and the Army groups involved eventually learned also to consider tides in their planning, not only because of the Navy's insistence that they do so, but also because their artillery was mounted on barges.

Despite the adverse tides, strike operations began in Dinh Tuong Province on 28 July as planned. The first boats of TF 117 were under way escorting artillery barges (which were towed by Army LCM-8s) at 0030 that morning. Thus, in just a little over 48 hours from the time of notification, the Mobile Riverine Force was able to relocate a base supporting 3,900 officers and men over a distance of 61 nautical miles and to shift its combat area of operations a total of 85 nautical miles. This relocation proved the ability of the MRF to react rapidly to a changing situation, and through its mobility to redirect its combat power over distances which were substantial in the environment of Vietnam.

Operation Coronado V, a two-battalion action, took place in the Cam Son area of Dinh Tuong Province again, but much farther north than the operation of 15 May. The force staged from Dong Tam at first light on 28 July, and engaged the enemy only briefly during the first day of operation. The boats patrolled the Rach Ba Rai from the beginning of the operation, but received only occasional sniper fire, until suddenly, during the afternoon of 29 July, they were attacked with heavy weapons. Three monitors and three ATCs were struck by 15 rounds of RR/B-40 fire, and 22 U. S. sailors were wounded. Apparently the Viet Cong lulled the boat crews into a false sense of security by allowing them to patrol the area un-

opposed for almost two days, then attacked suddenly in force. The newest addition to the Mobile Riverine Force certainly proved its worth when two of the casualties were evacuated from the miniature flight deck of the *ATC(H) 92-4*. In this and other operations, the ATCs and monitors showed themselves to be well-suited to patrol work in the narrow and winding waterways of South Vietnam. Since patrol areas normally were short, extending only 1,500 to 2,000 meters, the slow speed of these boats did not handicap them.

On 4 August the mobile base sailed to Vung Tau, a distance of 51 nautical miles. Riverine assault craft were positioned beforehand along the route ahead of the force for minesweeping, fire support, and escort. All units of the mobile base anchored on schedule in Vung Tau's inner harbor.

During the period 7–17 August, the Mobile Riverine Force conducted riverine search-and-destroy operations (Coronado III) in the lower portion of the Rung Sat Special Zone in order to reduce the enemy's harassment of shipping on the strategic Long Tau shipping channel.

On 18 August the mobile base returned to the junction of the Vam Co and Soi Rap rivers, and on 20–21 August the assault boats conducted search-and-destroy operations in the Ben Luc District of Long An Province. The most significant fact about this operation was the distance between the area of operations and the base—71 kilometers along narrow, winding streams—the greatest distance to date that operations had been conducted from the mobile base. Even though no heavy contact was made by river assault craft, the operation was noteworthy in several other respects:

(1) During the planning stages, problems in both communications and logistics were envisioned. However, communications between the flotilla and brigade commanders in the *Benewah* and their deployed forces were excellent throughout the operation, both on single

sideband high-frequency radio and VHF FM. Although a CCB was available to serve as a communications "retrans" station, her services were not needed at any time during the operation.

(2) Six ATC were loaded with all classes of supplies, and were positioned within 10 kilometers of the area of operations as a forward supply point for the ground elements of the Riverine Force. These supplies were fully used.

(3) On the second day, the boats were refueled by an Army tanker truck arranged for in advance. Because of the soft mud near the river, the truck could not drive close enough to reach the boats, and was positioned instead on a bridge on Route 4 near Ben Luc with fuel hoses extended over the side of the bridge to the waterline. In spite of a strong current, the boats were able to position themselves under the hose and refuel without incident.

(4) Despite the transit distance involved, no major breakdowns occurred on any of the boats. This operation demonstrated that the Mobile Riverine Force is capable of conducting operations up to 75 kilometers away from their base when the occasion demands.

The Riverine Force continued operations from the Soi Rap and from Vung Tau without significant occurrences through 10 September.

On 11 September, the force sailed to Dong Tam, the major ships getting under way at 0430. The force crossed the Cua Tieu entrance bar at high tide and proceeded up-river against an ebbing current. As a result, the YTBs towing the *APL-26* were able to make good a speed of advance of only 4.5 knots. This was the first time the APL had been towed such a distance against the tide, and consequently the arrival of the Riverine Force at Dong Tam was approximately two and one-half hours later than planned. Standard defensive measures were employed to guard the transit: CCBs, monitors, and ATCs were positioned on

fixed stations along the route. ATCs conducted chain-drag minesweeping of the entire length of the Cua Tieu River and the new base anchorage at Dong Tam. In addition, a new escort technique was used: each major ship of the Mobile Riverine Force was screened by four river assault craft—two off the bow and two off the quarter. It was anticipated that with the arrival of the faster ASPB this tactic would prove even more successful.

Without the ASPBs, however, the Riverine Force was not really hindered by the slow speed of the escorts, for the ATCs could steam just as fast as the base ships could safely move in the rivers. The only check on the movement of the force was the APL, which was two or three knots slower than the APBs. Naturally, the entire force had to move at the speed of the slowest ship.

Operation Coronado V was conducted on 15–16 September in the Cam Son area of Dinh Tuong Province and resulted in the heaviest fighting by our riverine assault craft to that date.

The assault craft came under the heaviest fire they had yet experienced: 57-mm. recoilless rifles, RPG-2 (B-40) and RPG-7 (B-50) AT grenades, automatic weapons, and small arms. One task group, which was reconnoitering by fire along the Rach Ba Rai, was ambushed along a two-and-one-half kilometer stretch from well-prepared positions on the east banks of the river. Eighteen river assault craft were damaged, but not a single boat was placed out of action, and the task group fought its way past the entrenched enemy and landed an infantry battalion in the northern part of the area of operations. In so doing, they inserted a block which prevented the Viet Cong from escaping. This performance, despite the heavy fire and the many hits, was convincing evidence of the boats' rugged construction.

At the same time the large number of

casualties in the boats emphasized the urgent requirement for armor that would successfully protect against the B-40 and B-50 rocket.

NEW ASSETS

During Operation Coronado V, CTF 117 was assigned an H-23 helicopter for tactical coordination of water maneuver. The ability to coordinate operations from the air proved invaluable in alerting task group commanders of imminent danger to their craft and of the location of friendly forces, and in providing a communications relay.

The need for advanced reconnaissance in heavily fortified enemy zones was clearly demonstrated during this operation. If initial fire in preparation for a ground assault is to be sufficient, the enemy's bunkers and other fortifications have to be located and their extent determined in advance. In areas of thick vegetation and overhanging nipa palms, this information cannot be obtained from aerial photography, but must be gathered in other ways.

On 20 September, the first two ASPBs arrived in-country. When, within a few weeks, all these boats were in hand, the Mobile Riverine Force, as approved by the Secretary of Defense, was complete.

On 4 October, the force tested a flame thrower. An M-132-A1 armored personnel carrier fitted with flame thrower was shoehorned into an ATC of River Division 92. With winds blowing at four knots, but gusting higher, the flame thrower was tested on the hostile Kien Hoa shore near the mobile base's anchorage. In the gentle breezes, there was no problem of flames blowing back onto the ATC, even when the thrower fired directly into the wind. In an operation on 5 October the M-132-A1 was demonstrated in an area where Viet Cong were known to be—sufficiently demonstrated, it was hoped, to alert the enemy's intelligence

system to the new capability possessed by the Mobile Riverine Force. It was felt that the psychological effect of the flame weapon would be valuable since, even if the weapon were not employed against manned positions, its demonstration would give the enemy one thing more to consider in planning his opposition to the riverine assault and patrol forces. The Commanding General, Ninth Infantry Division, was asked for four M-132-A1 and associated service units, to be attached to the force for an indefinite period.

OCTOBER THROUGH DECEMBER, 1967

At 0400 on 10 October the mobile base sailed again from Dong Tam to Vung Tau in preparation for Operation Coronado VI (11–18 October) in the Rung Sat Special Zone. The longest part of the move was made along the My Tho and Cua Tieu rivers in darkness. Many merchant ships were anchored along the route, waiting for more favorable tides or to discharge cargo, but no problems were encountered on this, the first night transit of the Mekong by the major ships of the Mobile Riverine Force. The ability of the entire force to move under cover of darkness meant more opportunity to conceal movement and vary its pattern and, therefore, to increase the surprise factor in MRF operations. Minesweeping was conducted in advance of the force, and each major ship was screened by four river assault craft. This arrangement of a moving screen, normal to naval groups operating on the open seas, appears to be the most satisfactory method for protection of the major units of the force during transit through enemy-dominated territory, not only because it affords continuous coordinated defense for each ship, but also because it is a way of giving equal protection to ships of varying speeds, so the faster ships need not be held up by the slower ones.

During October the Riverine Force conducted operations in the Rung Sat Special Zone and in Long An and Go Cong provinces. The objectives were to bring a measure of security to these areas, to prevent the Viet Cong from disrupting local elections, and to protect the Long Tau shipping channel to Saigon. This series of operations saw the first employment of the ASPB, which immediately proved herself to be an outstanding boat. The versatility of this type of boat was demonstrated when on one occasion one was used for high-speed transport of twenty soldiers to a newly installed post under enemy attack.

On 1 November the Riverine Force moved back to Dong Tam in the Mekong Delta to carry out operations in Dinh Tuong Province, their first task being to try to clear out guerrilla forces reported on the My Luong Peninsula in southeastern Giao Duc District between Sa Dec and Vinh Long about 30 miles west of Dong Tam. The area was made a target by ComNavForV because PBRs had been attacked there. In addition, enemy harassment in the form of mortar fire, attacks on Regional Force and Popular Force outposts, and road interdiction had been stepped up in the last two weeks of October. The Riverine Force learned of a 13-man guerrilla unit armed with one Russian carbine, five U. S. carbines, and two U. S. M-1s in a hamlet of My Luong village. The guerrillas were assisted by a local squad armed with hand grenades and knives. Operation Coronado IX began on 2 November with a one-day search-and-destroy operation. No Viet Cong were found, but several enemy bunkers were destroyed.

On 18 November, after several operations in the vicinity of Dong Tam, the mobile base relocated itself 32 miles west of Dong Tam to a spot just east of Sa Dec on the Mekong River, its deepest penetration of the Delta, for the conduct of an important seven-day operation in the so-called 470 VC base area. Three U. S. Army battalions and one battalion of the Vietnamese Marine Corps operated directly with the Riverine Force, and two Vietnamese Army battalions acted as blocking forces. The operation actually started on 16 November with actions by the ARVN Seventh and Ninth Divisions and the 3rd Brigade of the U. S. Ninth Infantry Division. Although our river assault squadrons had staged some 30 to 50 miles west from Dong Tam on several occasions, they had never operated so far from major waterways and so deep in undisputed enemy territory as they now did.

The transit went smoothly with no incidents. River Assault Division 112 with the 5th Vietnamese Marine Battalion embarked departed earlier than the main force from Dong Tam and made an assault at first light on 18 November to secure our entry into the operating area. That day and the next, two additional riverine assault divisions penetrated heretofore untraveled canals, well into the 470th base area, in close support of our two U. S. battalions. The Vietnamese Marines, who had joined the Riverine Force as a third maneuver battalion on 10 November, were being employed for the first time. Their prowess in the field and ability to deploy for as long as five days with the bare minimum in logistic support make them a light infantry assault force well adapted to riverine strike operations. Happily, this battalion liked duty with the Riverine Force and we have continued to cooperate with them. While working with the Riverine Force the Vietnamese Marines have bivouacked in an area near the base at Dong Tam.

Operations continued in the area around Dong Tam throughout the remainder of November without significant occurrences or contact with the enemy.

Operation Coronado IX again pushed into the western part of Dinh Tuong Province on 4 December, to the same general area where the November operations had taken place. This operation equalled in intensity and fierceness the engagement of 15 September (68 were wounded and two killed among the riverine assault craft crews). The operation began during the night of 3 December when the barge-mounted artillery, accompanied by elements of River Division 92, left Dong Tam and set up a fire support patrol base 30 miles up the Mekong River. The artillery was followed by River Division 112 with the 5th Vietnamese Marine Battalion embarked, River Division 111 with 3/47, and River Division 91 with 4/47, in that order.

River Division 112 fought its way through an ambush by Viet Cong armed with B-40s and B-50s, and landed the Vietnamese Marines under fire at 0800 on 4 December about five miles up the Rach Ruong, which is just to the northeast of Sa Dec and ties the Mekong into the canal system north of Sa Dec. The Marines, landing on the flank of the enemy, began a day-long fight with the 520 Local Force Battalion and local guerrillas. The Vietnamese Marines, who accounted for the majority of enemy killed in the action and took the heaviest losses on our side, again displayed tenacity, competence, and aggressiveness.

River Division 112 supported the ground maneuver, taking several hits from recoilless rifles, B-40s, and automatic weapons throughout the day and night. Division 111 was also taken under fire en route to the landing beaches on the Rach Ruong. The troops of 3/47 were placed ashore, however, and the river assault craft continued to provide close support to the battalion throughout the action.

To deceive the enemy, on this occasion the mobile base delayed its relocation until the boats were in the area of operation. At 0630 on 4 December the mobile base got under way from Dong Tam escorted by ASPBs, and with these boats as escorts reduced the transit time considerably for the faster ships. Harassment and interdiction fire was conducted by the ships during the first phase of the transit. Upon arrival in the objective area, Defensive Condition II was set and maintained, since the base had not operated this far west before and there was a concentration of Viet Cong in the area. As a result of this highly successful operation, 266 Viet Cong were killed, 108 suspects were detained, and a large amount of munitions was captured.

AIR CUSHION VEHICLES

Meanwhile, on 5 December, by direction of the Chief of Naval Operations, the Navy's three Bell SK-5 air-cushion vehicles (PACVs) arrived in Vietnam for operations with the Riverine Force. These craft, with their speed and ability to fly across water, land, and rice paddies, had proved themselves to be most valuable the year before in the Plain of Reeds, southwest of Saigon, during the annual high-water season and were expected to enhance the versatility of the force considerably.

A Question Answered

As our narrative of the Mobile Riverine Force operations comes to an end with the close of 1967, some questions may still be unanswered; some facets of the riverine naval war in Vietnam remain yet to be described.

One might ask, for instance: did the Navy enter into riverine warfare in Vietnam with enthusiasm? Was the Army anxious to join the Navy in this venture? The answer to both questions lies in our belief that the defeat of the Viet Cong in the Delta would contribute significantly to a favorable end of the war. The war started in the Delta, it must be fought there, and it must end there. The main source of strength of the Viet Cong—measured both in material resources and in manpower—is the Delta. Both Army and Navy forces in Vietnam felt this to be so.

Creating the naval element of the Mobile Riverine Force required diversion of funds, material, and manpower, already supporting, or earmarked for, vitally needed programs and existing operations. While the Navy may not have been enthusiastic at the outset, it certainly set to the task with dispatch and unstintedly provided all that was needed at the expense of many so-called "blue-water" operations.

On 1 September 1966, River Assault Flotilla One/River Support Squadron Seven consisted of the commander, one yeoman, and one desk. A brief review of the preceding narrative will refute any charges of "reluctance" on the part of the Navy to engage in riverine warfare. The Army can show equally dramatic examples of extraordinary support of the Mobile Riverine Force concept. The number of men from each service serving in the Riverine Force has about doubled during 1968.

One can say that the unlikely "marriage" of the Army and the Navy in the joint endeavor has been a satisfactory one. Certainly it has been a productive one: the combat record of the Riverine Force is exceeded by no other organization in Vietnam.

It is a proud record, and is the work finally of the assault boat crews, who with raw courage and professional skill, fought their boats against heavily fortified and bunkered firing positions along the banks of the narrow waterways at point-blank ranges—against heavy anti-tank rockets and heat rounds at ranges of 20 and 50 feet. Those men can truly claim to be combat sailors.

It is a proud record, too, that has been achieved by the Army's combat infantrymen, fighting under conditions that are as uncomfortable and dangerous as those in any previous war. These soldiers are often immersed in slime and water for days on end, fighting an elusive enemy on his terms and in his environment.

Whatever success the Mobile Riverine Force and the Game Warden operations have had can be directly attributed to the perseverance of our young men, to their adaptability to conditions that appear impossible, to their dedication in performing a task that is sometimes not fully understood or appreciated, and to their belief in themselves and in their responsibility to each other.

(*Naval Review*, 1969)

Naval Logistic Support, Qui Nhon to Phu Quoc

Herbert T. King, Captain, U. S. Navy

For a command which spans five-sixths of South Vietnam, from the northern edge of II Corps Tactical Zone to Phu Quoc Island in the Gulf of Thailand, the title U. S. Naval Support Activity, Saigon, is not very accurate. In the southern Delta the command, known more simply as NSA, Saigon, stretches inland as far as Tan Chau, near the Cambodian border, 120 miles up the Mekong River from the South China Sea. Three-fourths of the command's officers and men are scattered among the dozen or so naval bases located in the II, III, and IV Corps areas of the Republic of Vietnam.

Beginnings

The command was born during the chaotic spring of 1966. The Army and Marine troop buildup in the Republic of Vietnam was well under way. The Navy's role in the II, III, and IV Corps areas had already changed from merely advising the Vietnamese Navy to full-fledged combat in Operations Market Time and Game Warden.

The Naval Support Activity had a predecessor, the Headquarters Support Activity (HedSuppAct), which, as the Navy representative under the worldwide system of service responsibilities, was responsible before 1966 for providing logistic support to the U. S. forces in-country. The latter consisted primarily of a few thousand advisors from all services. The decision to do more than simply advise the Vietnamese resulted in another decision—because of the massive buildup of its forces, the U. S. Army would relieve the Navy as the primary support agent in the II, III, and IV Corps areas of South Vietnam. The Navy had already accepted such responsibility in I Corps Area, where the Marines were operating ashore in considerable numbers. It was agreed that Headquarters Support Activity would turn over all functions and all assets to the Commanding General, U. S. Army, Vietnam. The Navy decided that the Support Activity could then be disestablished.

MARKET TIME AND GAME WARDEN

Meanwhile, a crash program in the States was culminating in the production of two new Navy boats (new to the Navy, but each a version of a commercial boat): the PCF (Patrol Craft Fast or "Swift" as it came to be called), a 50-foot, aluminum-hulled boat to be used for inshore surveillance; and the PBR (Patrol Boat River), a 31-foot, plastic-hulled boat with waterjet propulsion to be used in river operations. Convinced that enemy men and supplies were being infiltrated from the sea as well as the land contiguous to South Vietnam, the Navy's plan was to conduct a coastal surveil-

Sailors load ammunition aboard the YFR 890, *which will carry it to U. S. bases in the Mekong Delta. The* YFR 890 *is one of several small supply ships belonging to Naval Support Activity, Saigon. (John M. Sperling, PH3, U.S. Navy)*

lance operation, code named Market Time, to prevent this infiltration. The coast to be covered ran from the seventeenth parallel in the northeast to the Cambodian border in the southwest. Meanwhile, Operation Game Warden would prevent the infiltration of personnel and supplies across the major inland waters of South Vietnam, especially in the Delta where the dominant feature of the landscape and the primary means of communication was the ex-

tensive network of interconnecting rivers, canals, and lesser waterways.

Market Time forces included not only Swift boats, but also destroyer escorts, radar picket ships, ocean minesweepers, and Coast Guard patrol craft. All of the oceangoing ships received their support from sources outside Vietnam, though many were later to receive considerable assistance from the USS *Tutuila* (ARG-4), a repair ship under the operational control of the Commander, NSA, Saigon. Patrol planes, either P-2 "Neptunes" or P-5 "Marlins," covered the coast under Commander Task Force 115 (Market Time). The Neptunes operated from Tan Son Nhut, and were essentially self-supporting, at least in regard to maintenance. The Marlins, working from a tender anchored at Con Son Island or Camranh Bay, were also essentially self-supporting. (More recently P-3 "Orions" have come into use, flying from an air facility at Camranh Bay.) The operation of small boats close inshore was another matter. Although it was planned that some support should be provided by the ships of the Seventh Fleet's Underway Replenishment Group (Task Force 73), most of it had to come from means not yet in existence. Since the problem was one of maximizing time on station for boats which were short-legged, bases for them had to be developed close to their operating areas. Consequently, a number of locations were examined by naval advisors already on hand and selected by the Chief, Naval Advisory Group. The main criteria were the security of the spot and its proximity to the operating areas. One difficulty was that the long expanse of coast from Vung Tau to the Cambodian border was not under our forces' control. Except for An Thoi on Phu Quoc Island, the places chosen were near Army bases, which was helpful for both defense and logistics. At An Thoi, the Vietnamese Navy had a small base. Action taken to acquire land on which to construct facilities usually included efforts by both the Navy and the Army, to say nothing of local authorities. The basic planning for shore facilities was done by officers of the Service Force, the Naval Advisory Group, and the Pacific Division of the Bureau of Yards and Docks. The most important decisions concerned the location of the bases and the responsibilities of each. Detailed plans were drawn by Pacific Architects and Engineers. The construction usually was by Raymond-Morrison-Knudsen (RMK).

With the arrival of the first Swift boats in October 1965, close-in surveillance commenced and bases at Qui Nhon, Camranh Bay, Cat Lo (near Vung Tau), and An Thoi were activated. (In I Corps, Da Nang served as headquarters for these activities.) While base facilities were being prepared, support at Camranh Bay was provided by the *APL-55*, a barracks ship which had been towed from Japan. An afloat base was planned for An Thoi, and support was provided by the USS *Krishna* (ARL-38), which came from Little Creek, Virginia. As forces expanded and facilities ashore at Camranh Bay became ready in July 1966, the *APL-55* was moved to An Thoi to assist the *Krishna*. At that point, the Market Time personnel, who had been living in tents at An Thoi, moved into the APL. In addition to the Swifts, the Cat Lo and An Thoi bases each supported eight or nine Coast Guard patrol craft (WPBs). Unlike the crews of the Swifts, the crews of the air-conditioned, 82-foot Coast Guard cutters lived aboard their own boats.

Game Warden operations opened early in 1966 with arrival of the PBRs, concentrated first in the river approaches to Saigon. Support was provided by Cat Lo, which served both Market Time and Game Warden operations, and Nha Be, located just south of Saigon. Nha Be was used by the Vietnamese as a base for two river assault groups. The first American naval force to use it was the detachment of 57-foot minesweeping boats which began

sweeping the approaches to Saigon in March 1966. Criteria for establishing Game Warden bases were much the same as those for Market Time.

Berthing, messing, and limited boat repair were provided at these locations. Personnel assigned to them were on the rolls of Chief Naval Advisory Group, Rear Admiral Norvell G. Ward. This officer's responsibilities were expanded on 1 April 1966 when he assumed the title Commander U. S. Naval Forces, Vietnam (ComNavForV). He was also assigned responsibilities as area coordinator, and he retained his old advisory title and tasks.

Pre-establishment Support

With no support activity on the scene earlier, just how were units supported? Market Time forces in I Corps were getting support from NSA, Da Nang, but the situation in the three southern corps areas was more complex. Fortunately, however, the channels of support had been set forth in December 1965 in a logistic plan prepared by Commander Service Force, Pacific Fleet (ComServPac), Rear Admiral E. B. Hooper. Moreover, the Army buildup was such that the naval forces at Qui Nhon, Camranh Bay, and Cat Lo could get supply items common to both services from the Army supply depots that were located near each base, and Nha Be could draw from Saigon. The support of An Thoi was a special problem. The only other U. S. unit on Phu Quoc Island, a small Special Forces group at Duong Dong, about 15 miles up the island's west coast, itself needed support. The solution was to have ships of the Seventh Fleet's mobile logistics group make periodic stops, though it required them to steam a great distance from their regular routes. Sometimes, helicopter lift from a passing supply ship was sufficient. (This procedure continued even after the establishment of NSA, although requirements for it were considerably reduced.) In the meantime,

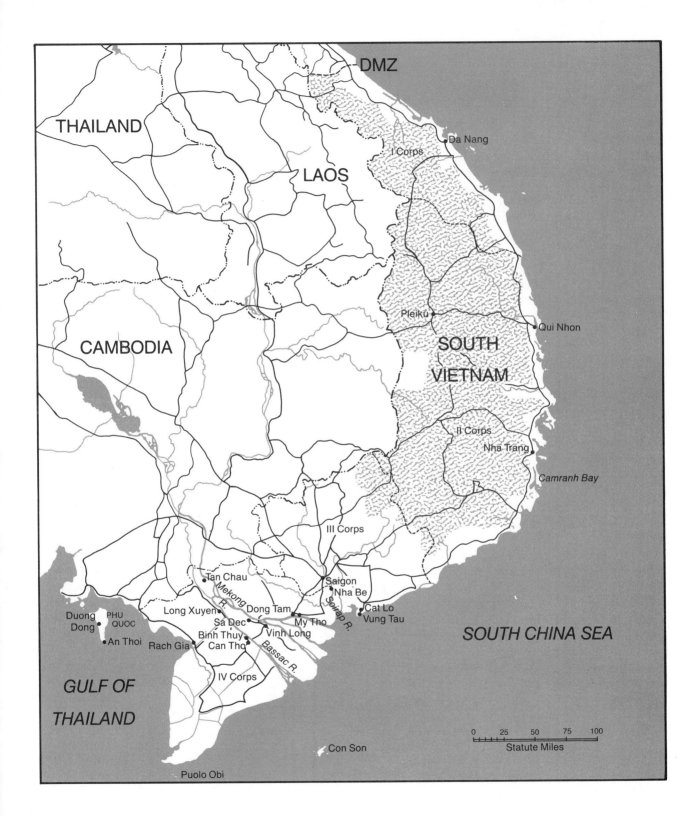

DMZ

THAILAND

LAOS

I Corps

Da Nang

CAMBODIA

Pleiku

Qui Nhon

SOUTH
VIETNAM

II Corps

Nha Trang

Camranh Bay

III Corps

Tan Chau

Saigon
Nha Be

Mekong
R.

Long Xuyen

Dong Tam

Soirap R.

Cat Lo
Vung Tau

Duong
Dong

PHU
QUOC

Sa Dec

My Tho

SOUTH CHINA SEA

An Thoi

Binh Thuy

Vinh Long

Rach Gia

Can Tho

Bassac R.

IV Corps

GULF OF

THAILAND

Con Son

0   25   50   75   100

Statute Miles

Puolo Obi

because of the time involved in supporting An Thoi by ship (or by air to Duong Dong and then by boat to An Thoi), a 3,500-foot runway of pierced steel planking was built there by RMK, working for the Navy's Officer in Charge of Construction at Saigon. It was completed in April 1966.

Providing Navy-peculiar items, primarily boat repair parts, was not an immediate problem, since most of the boats were new and had not yet experienced a great number of casualties. But it was recognized in the planning stages that eventually large numbers of spare parts would be needed. At first the Naval Supply Depot at Subic Bay was charged with the responsibility of providing boat spares. Each activity ordered parts as it needed them from Subic Bay. Small parts were generally delivered by U. S. air mail; heavy or bulky items were forwarded by surface freight, sometimes by air freight, and at times by the ships of the mobile logistics support group. The USS *Mark* (AKL-12) and USS *Brule* (AKL-28), which had been in the Marianas and Philippines, were transferred to ComServPac in the summer of 1965. At first these small ships sailed directly from Subic Bay to the Market Time bases awaiting their cargo before visiting Saigon. Following approval by ComServPac of a request to move the boat spares to Saigon, in the fall of 1966, sailings to and from Subic Bay were no longer necessary. All loadings were then handled from Saigon. Upkeep of the *Mark* and *Brule* was taken care of by the *Tutuila*, anchored at Vung Tau. Mail delivery provided the fastest response to in-country needs, but even so a one-week delay was not unusual, since there were often too few airplanes at Saigon to haul the volume of mail. Spare parts

replenishment was to be a matter of constant concern for NSA.

DECISION TO ESTABLISH A SUPPORT ACTIVITY

One thing was certain from the beginning: supporting Navy operations in-country was going to be difficult. In November 1965 ComServPac was made responsible for the planning and execution of services and supply support of Market Time operations. Early in 1966 the Chief, Naval Advisory Group, expressed the need for a naval support organization to fill the gap left by the abolition of HedSuppAct. The requirements greatly exceeded the local capabilities, making it all the more obvious that the Naval Advisory Group was a staff organization and should not be in the logistics business. Study was given by the Naval Advisory Group staff to the possibility of supporting the effort from the Seventh Fleet, and from other sources, such as Subic Bay, but none made so much sense as having a support activity in-country, especially in view of a recommendation from ComServPac that support of all U. S. naval forces in II, III, and IV Corps tactical zones be handled by one command. The result was that on 5 March Commander-in-Chief, Pacific Fleet, made ComServPac responsible for the plans, programs, and directives for providing shore-based Navy support to the Chief, Naval Advisory Group. In April CinCPacFlt approved establishment of the U. S. Naval Support Activity, Saigon, under the command of ComServPac and under the operational control and area coordination of ComNavForV, Admiral Ward.

This decision set the wheels of planning in motion, but no one realized that the establishment of NSA was less than two months away.

All U.S. naval forces in the II, III, and IV Corps areas of South Vietnam depended for their logistic support on Naval Support Activity, Saigon. To the north, in I Corps, Naval Support Activity, Da Nang, served mainly the III Marine Amphibious Force and secondary local naval forces.

One immediate concern, that of establishing a personnel allowance, was not to result in an authorizing document until after NSA was already in existence. In the meantime a "hold" was placed on everyone serving with Headquarters Support Activity who had completed less than a year's tour, and some of ComNavForV's people were assigned on temporary additional duty. These would provide the nucleus of the new command until new personnel could be ordered in. The ComNavForV staff was unable to pay much attention to the details of the new organization. The ComServPac staff was busily engaged in finding people to staff the new command and in drafting directives of its general responsibilities. HedSuppAct personnel were doing some planning for the new command, but most of their effort was funneling into the disestablishment of their own activity. New concepts were involved, far different from the methods and responsibilities of HedSuppAct. Consequently, NSA, Saigon, came on the scene with the benefit of suitable over-all plans but without enough detailed plans, and its capabilities would lag behind requirements for some time to come. No one could be accused of poor planning in the face of the rapidly changing situation and our increasing involvement in Vietnam. Nothing was quite so common as "change," even after establishment; supporting U. S. naval forces in Vietnam simply meant fighting many "fires" in the daily course of events.

Establishment

And so it was that on 17 May 1966 the U. S. Naval Support Activity, Saigon, was established, with the present writer as its commanding officer, twelve days after his arrival from Key West. HedSuppAct was disestablished in the same ceremony. The few remaining turnover functions of the old Activity became the responsibility of NSA. As it happened, HedSuppAct had already turned over to the Army most of its assets, primarily warehouse space, the materials therein, shop space, and vehicles. Not having these things naturally hindered the new command. The personnel situation was complicated, since it involved managing men reassigned from the preceding command and men of still another command on temporary additional duty. Jobs to be done flowed in at an unrelenting pace: it did not matter that NSA was just getting a toe hold—as the expansion of U. S. forces in South Vietnam continued, the tasking came anyway.

What kind of tasking? First, the Activity had to assume the responsibilities, which had originally belonged to the staff of the Naval Advisory Group, of operating the bases. Because jobs came faster than people, base personnel were very much on their own, trying to get their bases set up, and the boats and crews, to a great extent, had to support themselves.

According to its charter, NSA was to do all the supporting, with the result that the boat operators, who were anxious to get on with operating, placed great pressure on each NSA detachment to take over support. It was, of course, not immediately possible.

Everyone wanted spare parts. Everyone wanted vehicles of all types. Everyone wanted communications gear, and men to use it, and maintenance people to keep it working.

Everyone wanted berthing and messing facilities. And as their jobs grew, and the number of men under them grew, their demands on Naval Support Activity for these things also grew.

Commander Task Force 115 wanted facilities for "Stable Door"—that part of his force responsible for harbor protection and control. He also wanted Naval Support Activity to set up a radar surveillance site on Con Son, a mountainous little island about 100 miles from the southern tip of South Vietnam. And the Coast Guard wanted logistic support for its loran station in that same isolated spot.

There were other tasks, too. All the new bases in the Delta had to be planned and once planned, established. The interservice support agreements (ISSA) had to be negotiated with the Army. U. S. Navy ships entering Saigon had to have port services. The indoctrination program, which told newcomers about Vietnam, the enemy, living conditions, and so on, had been handled by the Army; now the Army had more than enough of its own people to indoctrinate, so this job, too, was given to Naval Support Activity, Saigon.

MISSION

Organization means different things to different people, but basically it can be said to be the analysis and grouping of all activities necessary to the objectives of any undertaking so as to provide a structure of duties and responsibilities. The objectives of NSA, Saigon, appeared clear enough: "to support the U. S. Navy in II, III, and IV Corps Tactical Zones." The addendum, "to provide such other support as may be directed," meant there would be no limit, either in variety or size, to the demands the new command could expect to face. The forces to be supported were diverse: the staff of the Commander, Naval Forces, Vietnam; Task Force 115 (Market Time); Task Force 116 (Game Warden); the naval advisors to Vietnamese forces; the Officer in Charge of Construction, Vietnam; and the Military Sea Transportation Service personnel in the area. The task was to build a structure to fit the Navy's operational plans in South Vietnam, which consisted primarily of rapidly expanding in scope and intensity coastal surveillance and river patrol while continuing to serve in an advisory capacity with the Vietnamese Navy. A headquarters staff was set up in Saigon to plan and direct the efforts of NSA people in the field and to support an increasing number of boat bases which would be established as new boats arrived.

ORGANIZING

The headquarters staff in Saigon and the detachments were organized along functional lines. A short summary of duties and responsibilities is included in the next several paragraphs.

Detachments

With the inheritance of five bases (then called facilities), namely Qui Nhon, Camranh Bay, Cat Lo, Nha Be, and An Thoi, the question of whether to decentralize the command was not something to be decided; the only question was to what extent we should decentralize. Neither was it a question that required much study, since it was simply necessary to provide service as near to the area of operation as possible, to permit the boats to carry out their operations with minimum interruption. With each base operating at a bare level of existence and with an overall shortage of personnel, the detachments, as they were now called, were organized to concentrate on services to the boats and crews, leaving routine administrative tasks to be assumed in Saigon. Otherwise, the organizational structure at detachments took the same form as the headquarters staff, except that the public works function was absorbed in the repair department. Basically, the detachments rendered complete logistic support: berthing, messing, supply, disbursing, maintenance, communications, recreation, laundry service, transportation, water, fuel, security, and a multitude of other services—no small responsibility for the sparsely staffed and equipped detachments.

Relationships between the local detachment officer-in-charge and the local operational commander were much the same as might be the case at any naval station regularly visited by operating ships. The detachment's main responsibility was to support the boat operations, but there was no chain of command linking the two groups, nor should there have been.

Operations Department

In contrast to the command structure, the majority of the operations lent themselves to centralization: communications coordination, surface and air operations, ordnance coordination, and registered publications services. Again, the extreme shortage of personnel, in this case electronic and cryptographic repair technicians, made necessary the establishment of a headquarters repair pool, which would repair equipment components and dispatch repairmen to the field for larger or more urgent jobs as required. Besides coordinating ordnance requirements, the headquarters facility maintained an armory in Saigon from which were issued all personal weapons and field gear. Finally, according to report, the Naval Support Activity, Saigon, held more registered publications than any other naval activity.

Surface and air operations are discussed later under sections covering air and surface assets.

Supply Department

The inheritance of three dilapidated warehouses (one several miles from the other two and none close to either the quays or Tan Son Nhut Airport) and some 3,000 line items of general-use material was certainly an austere beginning for NSA's supply department. As good facilities were nowhere available in Saigon, the command just had to live with what was available, making repairs as necessary to keep the buildings usable. Providing or arranging for material support was another matter. As we have seen, action was taken early to move the boat repair stocks from Subic Bay to Saigon, to check the load lists against the usage data available, to establish new load requirements, to implement a full-

time in-country screening procedure so that urgent requirements could be filled as quickly as possible, and in general to improve the supply support of some 400 assorted surface craft and several thousand officers and men of the operating forces. The limited general stock expanded to include about 27,000 line items, principally repair parts, during the first year of operation. In addition, requisite types and quantities of boat repair parts were maintained with considerable success at each detachment, on the basis at first of lists prepared in the States, and then on the basis of lists revised by experience. Saigon became the supply center for in-country activities, handling all requests for Navy-peculiar material and for general-use material not available at Army supply depots.

Centralizing disbursement in Saigon was proven unsatisfactory. At first the pay agents from field locations picked up pay checks, military payment certificates, and piasters; went back to their units to hold payday; then returned to Saigon with cashed checks and unused money. Besides requiring a large number of officers to make two trips to Saigon each month, the system could not answer the many inquiries of personnel in the field. An increase in the Activity's allowance of supply officers permitted the assignment of deputy positions at Qui Nhon, Camranh Bay, and Cat Lo, and the transfer of pay accounts to these detachments. The men at An Thoi were paid by the *Krishna*, and the Nha Be detachment, near Saigon, continued to be paid by agent. A roving disbursing team was established to hold staggered monthly paydays at the detachments in the Delta. Teams armed with pay records, as well as weapons, journeyed by air, either by our own "Air Cofat" (about which, more shortly) or in Army helicopters, to each detachment, where in addition to holding payday, they discussed pay matters in detail with any payee having a question. Although their mission made them prime targets for the enemy, during the writer's tour of duty they went about their job unmolested. These innovations provided a responsive and personalized disbursing service and surely contributed much to good morale.

Repair Department

While some departments were centralizing activities, the repair department followed more closely the "centralized direction and decentralized action" theme. NSA's boats arriving in-country were checked and prepared for service at the Vietnamese naval shipyard in Saigon by our repair department personnel, but most boat repairs were carried out in the field, either at the repair departments of the individual detachments or by assigned repair ships. Repairs to component parts that were beyond the capability of one base were coordinated by the repair department in Saigon, which arranged for the damaged equipment to be shipped to another activity in-country, or out of country (Japan or Subic Bay) when major repair was necessary. The immensity of the repair responsibility can best be appreciated by thinking of the number of individual pieces of equipment and machinery involved in the upkeep of over 400 assorted craft operating in widely dispersed areas. The repair department was the only department reorganized significantly during the first year of operation, shifting from groups specializing in components such as hull, machinery, or electronics, to units organized and assigned for repair of an entire boat type. The object was to specifically tie down responsibilities and work toward the readiness of each boat as a whole.

Public Works Department

Envisioned in pre-establishment planning as a small engineering consultant firm, the public works department was, in fact, to become involved in major construction projects at a number of outlying bases. Common service support expected from the Army and discussed later in this paper, failed to materialize to the degree expected. As a result, this department needed many more people than originally planned. Sudden reductions in military construction funds and the cancellation of military construction planned at some of the Delta bases brought about the greatest demands, for the construction tasks now fell to NSA personnel, namely those of the public works department. More people were quickly requested, and in December 1966 ComServPac directed NSA, Da Nang, to provide 100 Seabees, who eased the tight situation immensely. They stayed with NSA, Saigon, for several months. Still, there always remained a backlog of tasks to be performed as bases expanded and our stock of equipment multiplied. Of all NSA functions, those of public works least resembled the early picture of what the responsibilities and tasks would be.

Administrative Department

Because of the shortages of personnel and the need to relieve the detachments of many routine and time-consuming duties, effort was initially concentrated on the centralization of many functions in Saigon. Among the first things done was the establishment of a central office to handle all personnel matters and to maintain the relevant files. One major task was the processing of all personnel in and out. This included the important indoctrination of people arriving in-country and the arrangement of transportation both within and out of country. The educational branch coordinated the training program and administered the Navy-wide competitive examinations, including the "field waiver" program. The waiver of a competitive examination was one of the more attractive and sought-after benefits of service in Vietnam, for it meant automatic promotion, even to chief petty officer, for those who had previously passed the chief exam. The special services branch provided normal recreational services, administered the popular R&R program for all Navy personnel and Navy-connected civilians in the II, III, and IV Corps areas, and in addition maintained a central accounting office to handle all detachment open mess accounts—a $3,500,000-a-year business until the cost of living allowance was cancelled and food service at all detachments was converted to general mess.

Special Assistants to the Commander

Special assistants to the Commander included a legal officer, a protocol officer (also responsible for public affairs), and four chaplains—three Protestant and a Catholic. All had one or more enlisted assistants, of course, and eventually each section got more help. Their functions were coordinated by the Commander. All public information releases were prepared by staff personnel who made field trips to gather their material. This section was responsible also for the publication of the *Jackstaff News*, a newspaper for the U. S. naval forces in II, III, and IV Corps areas, concerning the activities of these forces. The legal staff provided our people with legal aid and handled any disciplinary cases which exceeded the authority of Article 15 of the Uniform Code of Military Justice, an authority vested in the officer-in-charge of each detachment. Additionally, the Commander, Naval Support Activity, acted as commanding officer of enlisted men for the purposes of establishing Article 15 jurisdiction for headquarters staff personnel; the staff of Commander, Naval Forces, Vietnam; naval advisors; and naval personnel on the staff of the Commander, U. S. Military Assistance Command, Vietnam. Visits to the command were coordinated by the protocol section, usually working closely with personnel of ComNavForV. The senior

officer in each locality was responsible for coordinating local arrangements. The chaplains provided religious services to the command and to other activities as requested. Because the command was so scattered throughout South Vietnam, the chaplains could truly be called "circuit riders."

Common Item Support

When the U. S. Army assumed logistic responsibilities in Vietnam, it also assumed responsibility for providing common support to the other services. Interservice support agreements (ISSAs) arranged for this support between the interested services. The procurement of general supplies under this arrangement has already been discussed. Other areas of common interest include ammunition support, maintenance support, and fuel arrangements.

Without a doubt the quality of the ammunition support provided through Army channels to the Navy was exceptionally good. The Army used our reports of usage to anticipate requirements, and although some types of ammunition were in short supply at times, there was no occasion known to the author when units failed to receive the ammunition requested, or a suitable substitute (such as point detonating ammunition if armor piercing were unavailable). Initially, the only problem in providing ammunition support concerned An Thoi, since the other detachments then in existence were close to Army ammunition supply points. (During the buildup phase, naval units had to get their ammunition from these supply points.) An Thoi was successfully supported by means of the mobile logistic support group, the *Mark* or *Brule*, or by occasional emergency lifts by Air Cofat. The delivery problem worsened when Delta operations commenced, because there were no ammunition supply points in the Delta. Again the solution was to use the *Mark* and the *Brule*, and Air Cofat in those areas where landings were possible. Sometimes a special airlift was requested. While basic ammunition support continued in this manner, later the Army did undertake delivery of ammunition to the Delta bases as requested, by "Caribou" and occasionally by helicopter.

The initial staffing of the NSA public works department was based on the assumption that, because of the overwhelming presence of the Army, maintenance of facilities and equipment not peculiar to the Navy would be accomplished through ISSAs. This often fell short of what was desired, for the Army was having problems caused by its own expansion. The Army was not unwilling to do maintenance work for the Navy; it was simply not able, at the time, to shoulder a greater load. Consequently, Navy repair crews at the detachments were required to maintain the local transportation and base utilities. Repairs beyond the capacity of the detachments were accomplished by a roving team of public works repairmen. As the number of men available increased, it was possible to assign maintenance ratings to the detachments. By early 1967, the Army, through contracts with civilian groups (American firms, generally employing foreign nationals, especially Koreans and Filipinos), began providing both maintenance and operating support at the Navy's base power plants. Maintenance and operation of the smaller, portable plants remained a responsibility of the Navy.

Vehicle maintenance turned out to be a "peculiar" problem. Whereas the Army's equipment is mainly tactical, Navy trucks and automobiles are generally commercial types. Consequently, the Army did not stock spares for most of the equipment in the Navy inventory. The net result was that NSA entered the vehicular maintenance business, for detachments simply could not afford idle vehicles. Another reason compelling NSA to take up automotive repair was that the Army had few maintenance facilities in the vicinity of the naval bases newly established in the Delta, and therefore could not have assumed the responsibility for repair even had it had the parts and mechanics to use them.

POL

The expression, "It is a peculiar war," is one heard often in Vietnam. Into this category must fall POL support, a peculiar animal indeed! While the Army depots at Camranh Bay and a few other places provided the Navy with some fuel, the U. S. Navy in Vietnam seldom got its fuel directly from the Army. In general, fuel was provided by civilians, through Army contracts with Shell, Caltex, or Esso. These companies made truck deliveries to the naval bases from storage centers in much the same manner as home deliveries of heating oil are made in the States, though not always with the same punctuality. Weekends, holidays, flooded roads during the rainy season in the Delta, and strikes all served to create local fuel shortages. One could always contact the Army, which would contact the contractor, who would contact the agent, but this is an odd way to fight a war. Since we had neither a backup fuel supply nor any but the barest means to move it (except for a few Army fuel barges and tugs which operated unescorted in the rivers and coastal waters, filling emergency requests only, there was only the small carrying capacity of the AKLs), the Navy was at the mercy of the local civilians. One solution of course was to increase the storage capacity at each base. Another was to acquire a YOG to carry fuel. Both were done, but they took some time, and many crises occurred in the interim. Happily, no operation ever was curtailed because of lack of fuel. Before the Tet offensive in January 1968 the tank farms and fuel trucks seemed to be immune to VC attack, leading to the popular belief that they were protected by payment of the VC "tax." Since the Tet offensive the tank farm at Nha Be, for one, has been attacked fairly frequently.

Taking Stock

ASHORE IN SAIGON

When the Army took over responsibilities for military logistics and housekeeping in Saigon, the Navy's status in that city changed tremendously. Instead of controlling all leased property, the Navy was now only a tenant. Almost all the facilities once operated by Headquarters Support Activity were turned over to the Army, and the few remaining were earmarked for occupancy by other forces on the assumption that the Navy would move out. Among the facilities still in hand when NSA was born were spaces in the Cofat Compound for the commander, the chief staff officer, and the administrative, operations, supply, and repair departments. The Cofat Compound, named for the French cigarette company which had occupied the quarters earlier, is located in Cholon, a large Chinese city adjoining Saigon. The public works department occupied offices in the Post Engineer Building, about ten minutes by car from the Cofat Compound. Disbursing was located in the Seventh Finance Building across the street from ComNavForV in downtown Saigon (three miles from the Cofat Compound), and each supply warehouse was located in a different section of the city. Eventually Headquarters, NSA, Saigon, was transferred to the Seventh Finance Building, but the supply officer and his staff remained in the Cofat Compound.

COMMUNICATIONS

To make the problems created by the dispersion of NSA sections all over Saigon and throughout the Delta even worse, communications were not the best. We could usually expect to get a priority message delivered from Saigon to an outlying base within 12 hours, but a routine message took 24 and sometimes 48 hours to be delivered. There were three telephone systems available—Tiger, PTT, and Arvin—none of them good. Waiting for connections to be made, even within Saigon, was often frustrating. To assure oneself the dubious convenience of a telephone conversation within the city, connections had to be made on all three systems. Otherwise, even endless patience was no help in reaching a person whose telephone was on a different system.

All Air Cofat flights carried guard mail, and its delivery was consequently fairly fast, but the delivery of U. S. mail from Saigon to the detachments depended on the volume of mail received in Saigon, and took from one to five days.

The form of communication which was most commonly used, and which was most reliable, was the teletype. The system was considered secure.

SHIPS AND BOATS

Upon the establishment of ComNavForV, the operational control of ships engaged in in-country support operations was transferred from Commander Seventh Fleet to ComNavForV who delegated it to Commander NSA, Saigon. These included the repair ship USS *Krishna* (ARL-38), at An Thoi, and the small cargo ships USS *Mark* (AKL-12) and USS *Brule* (AKL-28). The *Mark* and the *Brule* had been employed primarily in shuttle runs between Subic Bay and the coastal ports, including Da Nang. With the transfer of supplies to Saigon and the reduction of the role of Subic Bay as a repair parts base and the establishment of supply channels direct to Naval Supply Center, Oakland, California, there was a diminishing requirement for trips to Subic. But the two ships occasionally ran from Saigon or Vung Tau to Da Nang, when there was a full load of cargo to be transported. Once the USS *Tutuila* (ARG-4) had come to Vung Tau, primarily to support in-country operations as part of NSA, the *Mark* and *Brule* could undergo maintenance work in-country, thereby saving the transit times to Subic. We adopted the procedure of staging these two light cargo ships out of Saigon. At the time of establishment, only one other craft was in inventory, the *APL-55*, which was used first at Camranh Bay, and later at An Thoi, as living space for boat crews.

While these ships and craft met the initial needs of the command, a study of requirements of the bases already existing and those soon to be established indicated that additional craft would be needed at an early date, since there were no Army logistics facilities in the Delta. Four YFNBs were available in the Philippines, and after considerable correspondence with ComServPac Maintenance Section concerning alterations to these craft, it was decided that two would be moved into the Delta immediately, to serve basically as warehouses and repair spaces at Game Warden detachments, where there was a great shortage of temporary facilities. The other two would go to Japan for modification to permit their use as afloat bases. The first two craft came to the Delta essentially stripped of equipment. One was stationed at Nha Be and the other at Can Tho. To each were added extra generators (they did have generators on arrival) and machinery from the Advanced Base Functional Component (ABFC) equipment, and then offices, storerooms, and repair shops were fashioned. The barge at Can Tho already had 35 berths, but because of overcrowded living conditions ashore at Nha Be, a screened berthing area was constructed on the upper deck of the *YFNB-16* there. All this was considered temporary, while the construction of permanent base facilities ashore was under way. ComServPac, always on the alert for unused resources, determined that two refrigerated lighters, *YFR-889* and *YFR-890*, were available, and offered them to Saigon and Da Nang. Saigon requested one to meet anticipated re-

Tan Chau, on the Mekong, is near the Cambodian border. The mobile base, a YFNB, served most of the purposes of the river patrol force. Hence, the U.S. Navy required little of the scarce, highly valued solid ground. Here, as at Binh Thuy, the base was situated at the confluence of river and canal, with a road nearby.

quirements in the Delta, and several months later requested the second to support forthcoming riverine operations. The YFRs were outfitted at Subic and brought from there under tow. Because an overflow of riverine force personnel was expected at Dong Tam, an APL was requested, and one was made available from Seattle.

None of the ships and craft in the NSA inventory was constructed specifically to support Vietnam operations. The immediate needs for them actually allowed no time for a construction program, even had funds for new construction been available. On the other hand, the *YFNB-21* and *YFNB-24*, which were modified in Japan and were then stationed at Tan Chau and Dong Tam, were configured specifically to support the operation of river patrol boats. Except that they had no propulsion plant for emergency moves in a hostile environment, these craft fitted requirements quite satisfactorily. They had modern command and control spaces, up-to-date messing and berthing areas, a wardroom, air-conditioning in messing, berthing, office, and communications spaces; binned storerooms; good workshops; and sufficient boom lifting capacity.

The working craft at the various bases, originally numbering some 24, were LCM-3s. Larger craft, up to and including LCUs, would have been preferred in many cases, but LCM-6s and LCM-8s were not immediately available. Eventually the command received five LCM-6s. The larger craft could have been used in the river movement of bulky cargo, most advantageously between Cat Lo and Saigon. If the Activity had moved to Nha Be as planned, the larger craft would have been indispensable. As it was, several LCMs were usually kept at Saigon and extra ones at Nha Be, from where they could easily be brought to Saigon. The LCMs presented another supply problem, since the store of repair parts in-country for these World War II workhorses had long since been exhausted. Happily, some parts were in Vietnamese Navy inventories and could be borrowed, some parts of the LCM engine, the GM 671, were common to other diesel engines, and the use of LCMs by the Mobile Riverine Force in the Delta was bringing new spares into the supply system.

The remaining two craft requested and acquired by ComNavSuppAct, Saigon, during the first year of operations were a YW and the YOG already mentioned. These two craft were to be partial solutions, at least, to two serious and continuing problems faced by the detach-

ments and ships operating in the river waters. Even if there weren't a continuous threat of fuel exhaustion at Delta bases, a YOG was well suited to replenishing the LSTs operating in the rivers and river mouths in support of Game Warden operations. As for the YW, "Water, water, everywhere, Nor any drop to drink," describes many sections of Vietnam quite well. While shallow wells produced good water in some areas, in other areas neither shallow nor deep wells (to 500 feet) produced any but salt water. Purification plants which performed perfectly in the upper rivers were useless in the lower rivers and coastal waters because of the salt content of the water. Surprisingly, the salt water incursion line from tidal waters reached as far as My Tho, 30 miles up the Mekong. Even at Can Tho, 40 miles from the sea, the tidal range approached ten feet. Shipboard distilling plants, which worked well at sea, soon clogged and were much less efficient in river waters because of the suspended sediment in the water. The solution to the water shortage both on ships and at bases appeared to be a YW operating from Saigon, where the water supply was supposedly adequate (though water taken by ships from outlets along the waterfront was often contaminated after running through the city's piping).

Both the YOG and the YW traveled the rivers in comparative safety during the day, and although they were frequently fired upon, they suffered no casualties in the first year of operations, to the writer's knowledge.

AIR COFAT

Among Navy assets not turned over to the Army were three airplanes: one C-47 that had been used by HedSuppAct, an HU-16 amphibian that was maintained for ComNavForV, and a C-45J maintained for the proficiency flying of some 30 or 40 naval aviators in the Saigon area. It was immediately obvious that these

aircraft were ill-suited to the anticipated lift
requirements of NSA. The amphibian was
down awaiting parts a good portion of the
time, and with completion of the runway at An
Thoi, an amphibian was no longer needed. The
C-45 had little cargo capacity, leaving the C-47
as the only aircraft with a useful lift capability.

A study of requirements resulted in a
request for two C-130s to replace the one amphibian. However, instead of C-130s, two additional C-47s were approved. Although the
C-130s would have provided much greater lift
and short runway capabilities, the few owned
by the Navy were committed to support of
operations in the Antarctic, and the Navy was
not permitted to buy more. But the C-47s permitted regularly scheduled flight service to or
near all detachments. A flight north to Da
Nang beginning at Tan Son Nhut in the morning and returning to Tan Son Nhut in the afternoon, covering a total of 1,012 miles, and a
second, shorter flight south and southwest to
An Thoi and return, a total of 651 miles, were
both scheduled three days each week. Aircraft
from the Naval Support Activity, Da Nang,
flew round trip to Saigon on two days of the
week, to provide a total of five days' service to
naval personnel and to accommodate the flow
of visits between members of the Da Nang staff
and the staffs of Commander Naval Forces,
Vietnam, and Military Assistance Command,
Vietnam, in Saigon, and the traveling of people
involved in Task Force 115. Often cargo intended for NSA, Da Nang, ended up in Saigon,
and it, too, had to be flown to Da Nang.

The southern circuit, which was a seven-
hour trip from Saigon, had stops at Vung Tau,
Binh Thuy (Can Tho), Rach Gia, An Thoi, Rach
Gia (for advisors and Vietnamese naval personnel who preferred the plane to the boat ride
from An Thoi), Binh Thuy, Con Son (which was
supported mainly by special flights), Vung
Tau, and return to Saigon. Additional flights

were scheduled as required; normally two aircraft would be flying and one would be held in
readiness at Saigon to handle emergency lift
requirements.

The airfield distances in statute miles
follow:

From	To	Distance
(*North*)		
Saigon	Phan Thiet	97
Phan Thiet	Camranh Bay	105
Camranh Bay	Nha Trang	23
Nha Trang	Qui Nhon	107
Qui Nhon	Da Nang	174
(*South*)		
Saigon	Vung Tau	45
Vung Tau	Binh Thuy	97
Binh Thuy	Rach Gia	43
Rach Gia	An Thoi	76
Binh Thuy	Con Son	108
Con Son	Vung Tau	118
Saigon	Vinh Long	64
Saigon	Long Xuyen	88
Saigon	An Long	85

Space assignment was a matter of priorities, with naval personnel and tactical cargo
receiving first allocation of space, followed by
men and cargo of the other services, Vietnamese naval personnel, and other people authorized passage by ComUSMACV directives.
Every attempt was made to utilize available
space in the airplanes, to the point of notifying,
on approach, the operations office at each
airfield how many seats would be available for
the next leg, or to the terminal point. Although
most passengers were U. S. Navy people, as
might be expected, Vietnamese naval personnel were heavy customers, since the Vietnamese Navy had no airline or any other
scheduled means of transportation between
bases. Vietnamese cargo, other than personal
effects, was not normally hauled; however,
flights departing An Thoi were expected to car-

ry an interesting, highly prized, and even "po-tent" cargo in limited quantities. This was "Nuoc-Mam," the piquant and—to some—highly appetizing sauce prepared from sun-dried fish. This sauce is the most distin-guishing thing about a Vietnamese meal, and Nuoc-Mam produced at An Thoi is considered the very best in all Vietnam. Careful handling was in order, for one broken bottle of Nuoc-Mam in an aircraft could flavor it for months.

Air Cofat, named for the Navy headquarters compound, was, and is, a hard-working outfit. Its early personnel ran the gamut of experi-ence, from pilots who were veterans of World War II and the Korean War to those who had recently earned their wings. Among them were three who had retired as lieutenant command-ers and agreed to continue serving the Navy on two-year contracts. Whatever their back-ground, they were all eager to give that little bit extra. Days were long, often lasting from 0400 to 2000, and flying was hazardous. Planes were frequently fired upon during approach and takeoff at most of the airfields used, and the aircraft bore evidence of the fact. As haz-ardous as ground fire were the conditions of some of the airfields. In general the runways were oriented northeast-southwest, because of the monsoons, but often there were cross winds. All of the runways north of Saigon, and at Binh Thuy in the Delta, were hard-surfaced and long enough to suit our needs, but most of the other runways were unimproved, surfaced only with packed crushed coral, and short (about 3,000 feet—a fully-loaded C-47 needs 3,000 feet for take-off, 2,500 for landing), pre-senting a challenge to even the most qualified of the pilots. Communications at the better fields were not good at any distance, and Long Xuyen, Rach Gia, and An Thoi had no radio towers. The USS *Krishna* helped out at An Thoi, but at the first two fields, there were no communications facilities at all. Later, por-

table communications equipment was pro-vided to An Thoi.

Operating for most of the first year from what was known as the "mud bowl/dust bowl," an unpaved area between taxi strips at Tan Son Nhut which was muddy during the wet season and stifling with dust in the dry season, Air Cofat personnel accepted adversity as part of the job. They loved what they were doing, and what was of equal consequence, they could see their contribution to the war effort. They realized the importance of the material they were transporting, and they were anxious to keep both men and material moving. All aviators flew more than 100 hours per month, and some logged as many as 140 hours in a single month.

Two of the three retired lieutenant com-manders were lost when a wing fell off their C-47 near Phan Rang on the northern circuit. The wing floated down almost completely in-tact, but the aircraft and all 28 persons aboard were lost.

The aircraft were maintained and repaired by the Air Cofat maintenance gang working in the dust and mud at Tan Son Nhut, without repair facilities, relying on their pack-up kits and whatever equipment could be begged, bor-rowed, or otherwise acquired from the Air Force, the China Airlines (a contract activity at Tan Son Nhut), or anyone else. Under these conditions, the number of flying hours logged each month, 150 per aircraft, represented much hard work and not a little ingenuity.

Often the NSA repair crew had to go to an outlying airfield to repair or replace engines on an aircraft stranded with engine trouble. Perhaps the most notable repair job was accomplished at Phan Thiet, a stop on the northern leg, where one of the Air Cofat craft lost a wing in landing. A replacement wing was brought in, a difficult task in itself, but once there, the problem was to attach it properly to the plane without the assistance of the sophisticated equipment found at large repair activities where such a job is normally done. The men used a fork lift to place the wing in approximate position and then adjusted the wing's position using sand bags on top of fuel drums to support it while completing the attachment. The plane was test flown to Saigon, and then on to Sangley Point in the Philippines, where the experts declared it a perfect repair job.

For periodic calendar checks, the planes were flown to Sangley (except the C-45J, which was checked by China Air), which kept them out of service for at least a week each time.

The C-47s, though adequately serving a number of bases, could service none in the Delta, except Can Tho and later Binh Thuy, five miles away, when the field there was opened. Vinh Long and Long Xuyen did have airfields; however, these were only 3,000 feet long and were not used except under ideal wind and load conditions. Tan Chau and Sa Dec had no airstrips, only soccer fields (rush cargo for Tan Chau was flown to An Long, then shipped by LCM to its destination; cargo for Sa Dec could be brought from Vinh Long, by road or water), and the runway at My Tho was only 1,600 feet long. A further study resulted in the request for some H-46 helicopters to satisfy the emergency requirements of My Tho, Vinh Long, Long Xuyen, Tan Chau, and Sa Dec. It was envisaged that the helicopters would also provide an excellent emergency backup for requirements which might be generated by Riverine Force operations. Although the Army's "Caribou" would have been an ideal aircraft for these bases (except Tan Chau and Sa Dec), there were none in Navy inventory or otherwise available to the Navy. Two H-46s have since been assigned to NSA, Saigon.

As better aircraft replaced the original ones, the facilities improved at Tan Son Nhut.

Obtaining property on that field was a real struggle, as had been expected, but the larger problem was obtaining clearance from the U. S. Air Force and then permission from the VNAF, which managed all of the field except the commercial terminal area, to use land and again to construct buildings on the land obtained. After many delays, four quonset-type buildings were constructed to house the entire Air Cofat operation. It was anticipated that upon relocation of the Navy's P2V patrol plane operation to Camranh Bay, the parking areas used by these aircraft would then be made available to Air Cofat by the Vietnamese Air Force. The move took place in the early summer of 1967, and Air Cofat was able to leave the mud bowl/dust bowl for the vacated parking area. The hardships of operating an airlift in Vietnam continued, but every day the wherewithal and the know-how for accomplishing the job were improving.

Operations

MATERIAL HANDLING

Once the boat repair parts had been transferred to Saigon from Subic Bay, the naval supply channel was direct from the Naval Supply Center, Oakland, to Saigon, thence to the detachments. Except for small items which could be mailed direct from Oakland to the individual detachment, most naval material flowed through the Saigon port into the Navy's warehouses in that city. Occasionally material consigned to detachments at Qui Nhon, Camranh Bay, and Cat Lo (Vung Tau) was unloaded at those ports, but this was rare. Navy cargo comprised only a fraction of the overall volume of military material entering the Saigon port; in fact, it would be only a small part of the cargo carried by any individual ship entering the port. The bulk of materials arrived in Vietnam in MSTS or commercial hulls, although every conceivable means of transportation was utilized. High-priority items were lifted across the ocean by military or contract flights into Tan Son Nhut.

The U. S. Army was responsible for the port operation, including the unloading of ships. Material for the Navy might either be delivered by the Army to naval warehouses or be picked up by the Navy at the wharf. Much has been written about thievery in the dock areas; this was not the Navy's problem. NSA was primarily concerned with the security of material in warehouses. Several break-ins were attempted, and at least one group of thieves (known as "cowboys") was accosted after they had broken in. Security forces consisted of U. S. naval personnel and "Nung" guards, local mercenaries who were considered both competent and honest. Naval material being moved from the warehouses to Tan Son Nhut or to ships in the port was always carried by the Navy's trucks in the custody of naval personnel.

RESUPPLY METHODS

While it might be expected that within any country supplies would mainly be trucked overland, this was not so in Vietnam, for a number of reasons. Many bases were inaccessible by road, especially those in the Delta, where waterways are the most common means of communication. Except for Nha Be, the Delta bases were supplied almost exclusively by water or air. Occasionally men from a Delta base would join Army units in convoy for limited resupply from Saigon, but only after careful security arrangements, including air cover, had been made. The narrow, potholed road running the eight miles between Saigon and Nha Be was the lone overland route considered relatively secure—and that only during daylight hours.

The "Southern Shipping Company," the Activity's resupply force consisting of the *Mark, Brule, YFR-889,* and later the *YFR-890,*

divided its responsibilities into three itineraries: a northern coastal trip to Qui Nhon and on to Da Nang if required; a southern coastal trip that made only two stops, at Cat Lo and An Thoi; and a Delta river trip that reached as far upstream as Tan Chau on the Mekong. Each trip took roughly ten days. The one stop common to all three was Cat Lo.

The LSTs anchored at the mouths of the rivers as tenders for the PBRs and "Seawolf" helicopters were to have been served by the ship on the southern coastal trip, but bad weather forced the LSTs into the rivers, so they were not served on the southern run. Seaborne supplies for Con Son Island or Poulo Obi (six miles south of the southern tip of Vietnam) would have to be brought in by boat, for there is no deep water at Con Son and no kind of harbor at all at Poulo Obi. For this reason, both islands are served by air. Con Son has an airstrip, but Poulo Obi has only enough flat space for helicopters.

Because of their limited seakeeping ability, the YFRs (draft, 10 feet; maximum speed, 10 knots) were restricted, when they arrived, to the river route, relieving the AKLs (draft, 12 feet; maximum speed, 12 knots) for the coastal runs, though the AKLs continued to make occasional trips into the Delta as necessary.

Along the river route, ships anchored or moored in the vicinity of bases at night; no night transits were attempted, because, though the river charts were reasonably reliable, navigational aids were inadequate for nighttime use, and because the danger of enemy attack at night was too great. Even with this schedule, days were long and trying; crews remained at general quarters during transit to be ready for the occasional enemy fire from the shoreline. Most trips up the broad rivers, with their low, uninteresting jungle-bordered banks, were uneventful, but engagement was always a possibility. The men of the USS *Mark* would attest to this, for on one return trip to

Nha Be early in 1967. Until the new barracks were completed, American officers lived in a converted warehouse (facing the PBR pier) and American sailors lived in tents in the middle of the compound. A Vietnamese river assault group was berthed out of the picture to the right. In the foreground are four of the 57-foot minesweeping boats used to keep the channel to Saigon clear of mines.

Saigon along the Soi Rap River, they found themselves in the middle of a running battle between some minesweepers and the VC that lasted about thirty minutes and covered a six-mile stretch of river. As protection, the AKLs carried .30-caliber and .50-caliber machine guns, 4.2-inch mortars, and grenade launchers.

Probably more menacing than the VC were the rivers themselves. Delta trips would not have taken ten days if it had not been neces-sary to schedule them so that the ships could cross the bar between Cat Lo and the Delta rivers at high tide, and if the ships had not had to play the currents and the tides to be sure that they would get to port before nightfall. The treacherous currents, especially in the so-called "banjo ditch" northwest of Long Xuyen, where the ships crossed over from the Mekong to the Bassac, and the changing contours of the rivers always presented a tremendous chal-lenge to these ships. During the flood period, the rivers overflowed banks and the entire countryside became a lake, making it very hard to find midstream. Ships and crew were equal to the challenge, and overcame every obstacle in accomplishing their tasks. The skippers of the AKLs and YFRs, mustang lieutenants and boatswain's mates first class, respectively, became more familiar with the rivers than the Vietnamese pilots themselves—after the first couple of trips they dispensed with the pilots. The AKL skippers during the first year of operation were on two-year tours of duty, since their home port was Subic Bay.

Adventure marked many transits. On one, the *Mark* navigated the lower reaches of the Bassac River from Can Tho to the sea, the first ship of her size to do so in over ten years. Although this section of the Bassac was unmarked and considered VC territory, the *Mark* demonstrated that passage was feasible. This would eventually mean a trip of 140 miles instead of 185, and would save two days out of the ten for the Delta transit, once the route was marked by the Vietnamese Bureau of Navigation. The procedure to this time was to steam up the Mekong River, cross over into the Bassac, and proceed downstream to Can Tho, and then to backtrack along this route for the return trip.

The Southern Shipping Company ran a continuous, as opposed to a regular, schedule. Upon return to Saigon, the ships were reloaded as quickly as possible, and turnaround time was often as short as twenty-four hours. Our goal was to keep the Saigon warehouses empty of material that was needed at the bases. Because of the shortage of berths at Saigon it was often necessary to load out in midstream using the ship's lifting gear, which was in fact the usual method of unloading at the various bases. When alongside berths were available in Saigon, loading was accomplished using a truck-crane. Good working relationships with

Army personnel who controlled the majority of dock space usually contributed to early assignment of space and expeditious loading. Until the arrival of the Riverine Force and its two supporting LSTs (one of which was assigned to NSA Saigon's operational control), there were no beaching ships in the command. In the early stages of development of the bases, LST types would have been too large, but as the scale of operations increased, they would have been useful, had they been available to us.

Through Army contracts, NSA, Saigon, occasionally had the use of civilian tugs and barges for water delivery and sludge removal during salvage operations, and a tug with some refrigerated storage was also available to us at times, under MSTS contract, mostly for transport between Saigon and Cat Lo.

The allotment of material for surface transport or airlift in Vietnam was controlled by priority and by size and weight. The U. S. Army Transportation Management Authority (TMA), which assigned Army and Air Force vehicles to carry material to a particular destination, worked on a priority system. Because items which were high priority to the Navy were usually low in the TMA system, the Navy generally asked TMA to move only those items which were very large or too heavy to be handled by the cargo booms of NSA's ships. Otherwise, Air Cofat moved high-priority cargo of limited weight (if it could be loaded through the doors of a C-47), and NSA's ships moved the remaining cargo, up to and including trucks. The system worked extremely well to keep incoming cargo moving with a minimum storage period in the warehouses.

Cargo moved for the most part in one direction only, however, and NSA, anxious to use its ships more fully by carrying material to as well as from Saigon, offered space to TMA and the other services. Even so, the resupply ships generally made their return trips empty, and carried no cargo either for the Vietnamese services or for the U. S. Air Force and only occasionally for the Army—chiefly frozen foods from Vung Tau to Saigon. The Army in the Delta (the Ninth Division at Dong Tam) was supported by ships contracted for by the Army, since there were not enough trucks to support the base overland as had been planned—even had security of the trucks along the 30-mile trip from Saigon presented no problem. Naval Support Activity, Saigon, was responsible for the support of Army units deployed in the Navy craft of the Riverine Force, and a joint Navy-Army office was set up at Vung Tau to provide a staging base for materials going to the mobile force. This material was loaded into the resupply LST at Vung Tau (the one under NSA Saigon's operational control) for delivery into the Delta.

The Activity was not responsible for the logistic support of the U. S. naval advisors to the Vietnamese Navy—they were to be supported by the Army—a sensible arrangement, since many of them were in remote locations inaccessible to the Activity's craft. Nevertheless, NSA gave them considerable support: facilities and material at all detachments were available to them, NSA handled their records and their pay, transported them by Air Cofat, at their request repaired some of the Vietnamese equipment, and gave them other assistance at the detachments and in Saigon.

SECURITY

Central to the problem of security of bases and facilities is the matter of defense perimeters. But what does one do when both the outer and inner defense perimeters are at the back door? Protecting the boat bases was of vital concern, yet the problems associated therewith were staggering. For the most part, the detachments were located within the boundaries of cities and towns, often immediately adjacent to main thoroughfares. Closing traffic on these thoroughfares might

have been an intelligent security move, but in some cases it was impossible because there were no alternate routes for civilian traffic, and in other cases because closing a road would have been a sign of military weakness to city officials in their supposedly secure cities. In effect, living among "friendlies" subjected bases and personnel to the constant possibility of attack in just about any form. Surprisingly few attacks occurred during the first year of operation, and few casualties were sustained. The VC attacks of early 1968, which included an attack on Vinh Long and severe damage to the *YFNB-21* at Ben Tre, have demonstrated the extreme vulnerability of such forces and bases, yet operations must continue and there is a limit to the number of men who can be assigned to guard duty.

"MOOSE"

When NSA, Saigon, was established, the focal point for both incoming cargo and personnel was that city, and since some facilities were already available there, no other place was seriously considered initially for a headquarters. Even so, diplomatic pressures had already begun to mount to hold down inflation and to return Saigon to the people through moving the U. S. military establishment out of the city. A moving project was initiated, called MOOSE (move out of Saigon earliest). Three areas were considered in the search for a new home for NSA: Camranh Bay, Vung Tau, and Nha Be. The most serious drawback to Camranh Bay was its northern location, away from the Delta bases which would be requiring more and more support. Vung Tau would have been ideal except for lack of property and the uncertainty that it could become a deep-water port. Because of its proximity to Saigon (Vietnamese civilian employees could be brought by bus from the city and materials could come either by road or by river) and the property available there, Nha Be was chosen and the move was tentatively scheduled for the summer of 1968. But in the meantime, NSA acquired additional space at Newport, the Army's new port east of Saigon, making an immediate move to Nha Be unnecessary.

PIONEERING

Establishing the new Delta detachments was an early task of the command. The Chief of Naval Personnel selected detachment officers, many of whom were limited-duty officers chosen because of their engineering background. In some instances these officers arrived on scene early enough to assist in establishing detachments; otherwise, officers chosen from the Naval Advisory Group in Vietnam were employed in a temporary additional duty status. An advance team of one or two officers and approximately twenty men underwent an indoctrination period in Saigon, including, for the officers, visits to established detachments to observe methods and procedures for supporting the operating forces and for dealing with the multitude of problems. As many advance preparations as possible were completed, and materials were gathered for truck convoy to site (it would have been simpler to move all material by ship, but when most bases were being set up, the AKLs had not yet begun their trips into the Delta). Where roads did not exist, materials were cached, to be picked up later by LCMs and moved to site. Material for My Tho was brought by truck convoy, and much material for other bases was staged into My Tho by truck and moved from there by LCM.

Some six weeks before operations were to begin, the advance teams moved out to set up shop. Like the American pioneers, these officers and men often suffered the inconveniences of primitive living conditions and the dangers of a hostile environment. Surviving on warmed C-rations and living in tents, they went about the laborious chore of preparing bases for operation, making arrangements for berthing, messing, boat repairs, armory and ammunition requirements, piers, boat ramps, concertina security fences, bunkers, fuel, water, communications, transportation, and a variety of other matters. Typical of the work was the construction of the boat ramp at Nha Be. Using dunnage lumber from the ammunition ships unloading at the anchorage a few hundred yards away, and working with hand tools, the men constructed a wooden ramp, in spite of the action of the tide, which rapidly eroded the river bank and made this a most difficult job.

Seabees included in some advance teams were invaluable in supervising other men on construction work. At Vinh Long, Sa Dec, Can Tho, and Long Xuyen, they helped build piers by covering and connecting several Army-type boat pontoons. Rubber fuel cells from Advanced Base Functional Component (ABFC) stocks made available by the Naval Facilities Engineering Command were used for fuel storage. ABFC techniques and stocks were exploited fully, and the value of this system was demonstrated time and again. The fact that some equipment included in long-stored components was obsolete was but a minor irritation when balanced against the overall good of the system.

Directly associated with base establishment was property acquisition, an interesting and often frustrating task. The Vietnamese Navy made waterfront facilities available at some bases, but in no case were such facilities adequate to handle requirements, especially those for the berthing and messing of personnel, and space in the Delta was always limited, making expansion difficult. The selection of land, facilities, and locations was influenced by an effort to minimize the disruption of normal civilian activities. As a result, property acquired was often less than desirable, when suitable areas were not offered to us. Even so, lease negotiations were usually time consuming, as initial "asking" prices exceeded the amounts authorized. When, as sometimes happened, property under negotiation was owned by several persons, the difficulty of arranging the meeting of all the owners also created frustrations. Once property was acquired, it had to be improved to meet operational requirements, which at Nha Be, Binh Thuy, and Dong Tam meant hauling in fill dirt or dredging from the river or nearby abandoned paddies to raise the land acquired above water level.

SUPPORT OF RIVERINE OPERATIONS

Support of various activities, such as the U. S. Coast Guard loran station on Con Son Island and the Task Force 115 harbor defense units at the major ports (Operation Stable Door), were handled routinely as the operations of NSA, Saigon, expanded. Far from routine, however, was the Activity's task of supporting the riverine forces. Since Task Force 117 involved both Army and Navy units, the Navy, in discussions with the Army command in Vietnam, arrived at a plan for the establishment of a joint support group, whose responsibility it would be to arrange and provide for the replenishment of the deployed riverine forces, staging from Vung Tau. While this in itself was a major job, NSA also had to prepare to support units attached to TF 117 but not deployed.

Although TF 117 was designed to be a mobile group, it was plain to NSA, when some of the APBs requested in the original program were not approved, that a number of boats and men assigned to the Task Force could not be deployed afloat, and would have to be based ashore. Consequently, it was decided that an NSA detachment should be established at Dong Tam, five miles up the Mekong River from My Tho, for support of these ashore units.

Dong Tam was chosen because it was to be the land base for the U. S. Army Ninth Division, the army component of the riverine force. While it was still only a plan, representatives of NavForV and NSA, Saigon, negotiated with the Army for joint occupancy of the base. The Army was given command at the Dong Tam base, and the responsibilities of the two services were clearly delineated well in advance of its occupancy.

The Army had done considerable planning for the establishment of a base in the Rung Sat Special Zone to accommodate the Ninth Division while the base at Dong Tam was still being built. The terrain of the Rung Sat is similar to that of the Delta, and would have made an excellent training ground for both army and naval units. However, the facilities at Dong Tam were completed earlier than scheduled, and the boats to be used in training arrived late, so the Rung Sat base idea was abandoned, and the Army moved directly into Dong Tam. The NSA detachment established itself there at the same time.

"NAVY PECULIAR" SUPPORT PROBLEMS

Supply

Responsible primarily for items used by the Navy only ("Navy peculiar"), NSA concentrated at first on mastering the spare parts situation. Usage data from which future requirements might be projected were available, but for some equipment, particularly that associated with the new boats, stocks of repair parts were completely exhausted. Obviously, provisioning was grossly inadequate in such instances. For example, it was reported, though never verified, that provisioning was based on data drawn from civilian use of similar boats, there being no statistics in existence for actual naval operation. Unlike their civilian sisters, the naval boats were used almost continuously upon arrival in-country, accumulated engine hours much faster than had been anticipated, and needed overhauling before spare parts were scheduled to arrive.

The compilation of revised load lists for the ships bringing parts from out-of-country only initiated procurement actions. The parts themselves were far down the pipeline—often at the end of new contract negotiations in those cases where earlier contracts had been filled. Because as soon as this situation was recognized every effort was made to obtain spare parts as quickly as possible, even by air, a crisis was averted. For the most part, required parts were on hand shortly after the first major engine overhaul cycle was due, before any of the boats had to be sidelined (overhauls were dependent upon cumulative engine hours, except when major repair work was required, in which case engines were overhauled regardless of engine hours). It was to ease the parts shortage that the existing stocks of spares were moved from Subic Bay to Saigon. From Saigon they could be delivered to any detachment within 24 hours of a requisition's arrival in that city. In addition, a casualty report screening system was implemented: if a part was not on hand in Saigon, a message was sent to all the detachments, asking them to check their stocks for the item.

Ordinary items not in Army stocks, such as housekeeping and office supplies, were quite often ordered through the Navy system and thereby became in effect Navy-peculiar items. Procurement times for these items, usually of low priority, were extremely long, so long that the ordering unit usually found a suitable substitute, borrowed from another unit or service, or simply learned to live without the item. Urgently needed items often fell victim also to lengthy procurement times, resulting in the usual, though undesirable, action of increasing their priority to ensure air shipment.

Personnel

Few commanders will admit that they have enough officers and men to accomplish their assigned tasks, yet they usually do accomplish those tasks with the talent available. Beginning with 40 officers and 300 enlisted men, many of whom were temporary duty personnel, and expanding to 120 officers and 1,800 men by the end of the first year, NSA, Saigon, was always behind the personnel "power" curve. Tasks always arrived well in advance of approval for more men. The most critical shortages were in the electronics technician and engineman ratings, making it necessary to pool the electronics talent in Saigon and to delay assumption of the full responsibility for boat repair at the detachments. These two ratings remained in critically short supply during the first year of operation as demands for this type of talent increased. Not only were they needed badly by NSA, but also by the growing Market Time and Game Warden forces and then by the new Riverine Force. The men for the new base at Dong Tam and for the attached *YFNB-24* were also slow in arriving. Otherwise, by year's end, May 1967, most billets had been filled.

Repair

The major repair problems involved getting people and parts to do the job, as already discussed. Equipment to do heavy jobs was lacking at most places, and many makeshift arrangements resulted. At My Tho, for example, an A-frame was mounted on the bumper of a truck, and a chain-fall was attached to lift boat engines; and at Long Xuyen, a similar arrangement was installed on the pier. Another principal problem was that of making underwater repairs to the boats. The PBRs could be lifted on a boat trailer over ramps constructed by detachment personnel, or by crane onto the deck of a YFNB, but the heavier PCFs, and the still heavier Coast Guard WPBs, were another problem. The *Krishna* at An Thoi could lift PCFs, but the lift capabilities planned for the other Market Time bases were not being produced stateside. For bottom paint work, the WPBs were at first sent to Bangkok. Later they went to Sasebo or Yokosuka, traveling as deck cargo on freighters. Under ComServPac's push, procurement officers flushed out and shipped three tractor cranes and one floating crane, all worth their weight in gold to men at the awaiting bases. In the meantime, a small Navy pontoon dock was installed at Camranh Bay and use was made of a larger Army dock, also at Camranh Bay. At the time of this writer's relief, in late April 1967, a portable dock badly needed for lifting MSBs at Nha Be had not yet arrived. When it did, it would fulfill the immediate lift requirements. Then, besides the multitude of minor problems, only the task of maintaining some 400 craft operationally ready remained.

Relationships with other Commands and Services

Singleness of purpose was the mark of relationships between NSA, Saigon, and ComNavForV, and this contributed greatly to an understanding between the two commands. Continuous contact at the headquarters level in Saigon precluded any surprises and contributed to NSA's readiness to conduct new operations. Although poor communications caused some difficulties within the command relationships, especially between NSA headquarters in Saigon and the individual detachment commander who had a job to be done immediately, sometimes before he could obtain approval from Saigon, they were always resolved. Headquarters encouraged the boat operators to make known their requirements well in advance of the actual operation. For example, if the operating forces asked the officer-in-charge at an NSA detachment to provide a fuel cache 50 miles up the river within a day or two, the trip could be made, with PBRs providing security, but had Headquarters been notified in advance, perhaps a better or an easier solution might have been found.

Except for the fact that both were under the command of Commander Service Force, U. S. Pacific Fleet, and the operational control of Commander Naval Forces, Vietnam, NSA, Saigon, and NSA, Da Nang had little in common. Da Nang did support Market Time PCFs and WPBs, and there was an exchange of assistance between the two commands, but basically, their operations were different. Whereas Da Nang was mainly supporting a large land campaign in I Corps, Saigon was supporting one naval campaign in the Delta and another up and down the long coast, and nearly every base supported by NSA, Saigon, was, in effect, on an island, for overland communications were almost nonexistent.

Commander NSA, Saigon, was responsible for providing logistic support to ComNavForV and his subordinate commands, primarily CTF 115 (Market Time) and CTF 116 (Game Warden). Although directly responsible only to the Commander Naval Support Activity, the task of each detachment was to be responsive to the needs and requirements of all units being supported. The U. S. Coast Guard units of CTF 115 received support on an equal basis with naval units and were completely integrated with the command, including the spare parts control system.

Relationships with U. S. Army commands and the U. S. Air Force were on a cooperative basis. It happened that there were few formal agreements with the Air Force, but the opposite was true with the Army. In these agreements, the Navy was usually on the receiving end of services. People of the Navy and Army worked very closely in resolving problems which arose as each service expanded its operation. Difficulties between the two services stemmed largely from differences in system and procedure, organizational communications barriers, and marginal capabilities at certain locations. The Army insisted on using its own system of accounting for supplies, so the Navy, as the receiver, learned the Army's way. Even though all requirements were not met, a spirit of co-operation existed, and the Army logistics commands were anxious to provide completely satisfactory support within their capabilities.

Dealings with the Vietnamese occurred at almost every level of the command. In Saigon, they usually concerned U. S. use of facilities at Tan Son Nhut or the Navy yard and its facilities. It was at the detachment level, however, where U. S. Navy personnel shared Vietnamese Navy facilities, that the closest association occurred between the two services. Here there was joint concern for base security and for boat operations; other functions were generally conducted separately. Vietnamese personnel did not normally share berthing and messing arrangements, except for those Vietnamese sailors and National Police who participated in U. S. Navy boat patrols. In such cases berthing and messing were shared to help make them feel a part of the crew. Vietnamese nationals employed as mess cooks were also permitted the use of messing facilities, so that they would not have to bring aboard food, which might either conceal weapons or cause health problems. Detachment and headquarters personnel were involved in a variety of civic action projects, which brought them into contact with all phases of Vietnamese life.

In relationships with the Vietnamese, there were no command lines; there was a sharing of certain responsibilities at those bases jointly used, there was a limited amount of mutual support rendered, there were employer-employee relations, but most of the thousands of daily contacts were those made by individuals in an unofficial capacity. That there was only an occasional disagreement or flare-up is a tribute to the people of both nations, for cooperation didn't just happen: it was the result of efforts by both sides to keep relationships on the highest plane, so that everyone could concentrate on the tasks at hand.

Within our own chain of command, ComServPac and his staff did not only support ComNSA Saigon fully—often they were ahead of us, and our every request brought quick, positive action. Our primary contacts with the ServPac staff were with officers of the planning and advance base divisions, the fleet and force supply office, and the fleet maintenance office.

Reflections

The first several months of operation were certainly months of "fighting fires" for NSA, Saigon. To be sure, in many areas tasks exceeded capabilities. The problem was to determine requirements and establish the necessary capabilities as expeditiously as possible, a process which in a war can never be fast enough. Little, if any, precedent existed in American naval history for the support of small-boat operations at isolated advance bases in a hostile environment. Consequently, there was much trial and error, but more important, there was much ingenuity and proficiency in improvisation demonstrated by American sailors in accomplishing what at times appeared to be almost insurmountable tasks. The work that went into keeping Air Cofat's planes in the air without the benefit of sophisticated repair facilities was only one instance of this effort. Advances were rapid, and after six months of operation it was obvious that much stability had come to the organization and that refinement was in order. All "fires" were by no means extinguished, but a multitude of problems had been solved or were in the process of being solved.

The overall shortage of personnel and of certain critical ratings in particular persisted. This was not at all good, considering that the fighting man deserves every ounce of support necessary for his well-being, but naturally people cannot be added to a command overnight.

Nor is it possible to determine requirements in detail in an ever-changing environment. At times there were long delays before approval could be obtained, but the Bureau of Personnel did its best to make available to NSA, Saigon, the men needed, even prior to approval.

As already mentioned, our ships and non-commissioned craft were adequate, but experience did indicate that in one area, craft of the YFNB type would have proved more practical than the ships used. In any event, because of the difficulty of acquiring land and of establishing facilities in the field, it was apparent that mobile afloat bases were often the best solution, and particularly those organized around the barges, which offered more space for all the necessary support activities than a ship of comparable size. However, such craft were not available in the early phase of operations. The two YFNBs that were modified in Japan and later employed in support of both Game Warden and riverine operations, demonstrated the extreme utility of a small-boat support craft and the advantages of having such craft ready for use when and if the Navy must again establish coastal or river bases in support of small boat operations. Of course, propulsion plants in such craft would make them much more maneuverable members of the mobile base, but they take up a great deal of space, require maintenance, and call for extra personnel. What was needed in the Delta and along the coast was working space, storage space, lifting capacity, fuel capacity, and berthing, messing, and communications facilities suitable to the needs of the operating forces. Non-self-propelled craft are well suited to these purposes. In fact, new barges designed specifically to meet these needs have now become operational in Vietnam. The base built around a barge has an important drawback—one mine could put the entire base out of business.

Interservice support agreements provided a great service to the command and, for the most part, proved effective. Yet, to depend entirely on ISSAs is to court disaster. In its pre-establishment planning, NSA, Saigon, relied heavily on such agreements, but in some instances, such as maintenance, the Army was simply not ready to support another service. To have relied solely on the other services for air and surface lift would certainly have reduced the effectiveness of the organization. Judging from our experience in the first year of operation, it is essential that some organic capability for air and surface transport be permanently maintained.

The advanced base section of the Service Force has gained invaluable experience in this war, and should make sure that it is put to good use, by updating its plans for establishing bases in the future and by reorganizing its stock of materials, beginning with the ABFC package.

Once the war in Vietnam is over, the small-boat support ships, such as the *Krishna*, will naturally be stationed with whatever small boats remain in the Navy, which means that those formerly with the amphibious forces will be returned to that duty. Commander Service Force, Pacific, employs them (and the many service craft) in an operation that is a Service Force responsibility in this particular war. In future operations, we may never see quite the same situation take shape again.

An interesting observation related to living conditions at the various detachments was that morale was inversely proportional to the quality of living conditions. Most personnel arrived in Vietnam fully expecting to endure hardships. Where hardships existed, such as tent living, there was a feeling of sacrifice, a feeling of giving more of oneself to the war effort. Once improvements were made (new barracks built), there was a tendency not to give more but to expect more, to concentrate more on the improvement of living conditions than on the tasks at hand. With every improvement came increased maintenance requirements, also, and further drains on personnel. Typical were the PBR crewmen at Nha Be who lived in tents for their entire one-year tour. Temperatures in these tents exceeded 100° (even with pedestal fans), but when they were offered the opportunity to move to more comfortable quarters topside on the *YFNB-16*, they refused. As new barracks ashore neared completion, the sailors laughed when this writer mentioned that it appeared they would be forced to move from the tents. Their reply was, "No, it will never happen to us, our tour will be completed first." Officers were as reluctant, and dragged their feet in moving from surely as primitive a BOQ as was ever occupied by naval officers. "Roughing it" was very much a measure of contribution for the individual.

Most rewarding to those involved in establishing Naval Support Activity, Saigon, was the association with dedicated men whose energy was tireless and who were determined, in the face of the boundless problems and shortcomings of equipments and supplies, to provide outstanding service and support to the operating forces. Many tasks were no different from a stateside or shipboard support job, yet the nearness to the war spurred men to better performance. Knowing that those supported were facing the enemy daily, and witnessing the results of their encounters, gave the people in the command a real sense of responsibility and a desire to provide everything needed or desired by those being supported. Among the many examples of the extra effort seen everywhere, only a few can be mentioned.

The Nha Be personnel were responsible for activating both the *YFNB-16* and the *YFNB-9*, a job which is normally assigned to a repair activity for accomplishment. This was quite an undertaking with the limited equipment available.

The men at the Qui Nhon detachment made

a marine railway for the PCFs by getting the 50-foot boats onto a set of logs, which, as the tide fell, could be rolled onto dry ground, the men replacing the logs in front of the boats from those left behind as they proceeded to higher ground. Often, when underwater repairs to a boat were required, she was moored so that at low tide she would be aground, and then furious work took place to repair the boat before the next tide refloated her. This became a standard practice for repairing the PBRs.

At My Tho, a Vietnamese LCM ran over one of our PBRs and actually rode up on the bow, crushing the entire forward section, the cabin area, radar, and other raised portions. The repair crew at My Tho rebuilt this boat (by hand of course) so completely that only close inspection revealed that she had ever been damaged. This was accomplished at a time when the boats were in short supply and every boat was badly needed for patrol.

Our landing party on Poulo Obi consisted of several Seabees under the direction of a Civil Engineer Corps lieutenant. They were to clear a hilltop for a helo landing pad and to prepare some accommodations in anticipation of establishing a radar surveillance station there. There being no roads up the very steep slopes and through dense brush, the group jumped from the helo, which had no place to land. The lieutenant broke his leg in the jump. While clearing the brush, one Seabee cut his leg to the bone with a chain saw. The group established good relationships with the local inhabitants, and the cut leg was treated with Vietnamese remedies to keep down infection. The lieutenant had a makeshift splint. This group did not yell for help; they accomplished their mission even in the face of these obstacles, and it was only when they returned days later that we learned of the injuries. Hospital doctors found both of the injured men to be in good shape, all considered.

The people of Naval Support Activity,

Saigon, were equal to every task, regardless of the difficulties encountered. Theirs is an experience which cannot be duplicated, nor will those who follow appreciate the hardships experienced by their predecessors. Nor should they necessarily. They will face a new set of problems. The first year in the life of NSA, Saigon, was interesting and rewarding, to say the least; there was certainly every reason for the command to be proud of a job "Well Done."

(Naval Review, 1969)

The Merchant Marine:
The Last Satisfactory Solution?

For a time there were over half a million Americans in South Vietnam, and hardly any of them stayed more than a year or so. Soldiers stayed 12 months, Marines 13. Some of them went to Vietnam by sea. Most went by air.

Whichever way the people went, their things, their arms, ammunition, food, fuel, and all sorts of supplies, went almost exclusively by sea, and almost always in civilian-manned privately operated ships.

That vast fighting force in Vietnam depended utterly on a few thousand seamen, mostly middle-aged, sailing a few hundred ships, mostly old. As Lane C. Kendall makes plain, there were enough ships to be found, either in active commercial employment or lying in idleness in one of America's large coastal rivers or bays. But, as he tells us, because "the shrinking of the merchant fleet" had "discouraged any large number of men from making careers as merchant seaman . . . the basic pool of American seafarers was small. . . ."

Not only was the pool small, but for a time the Department of Defense thought better use could be gotten from the few young mariners we had if they were drafted into the Army than if they were left where they were. In any event, sometimes shorthanded and sometimes with watch-standing mates in their seventies, the ships sailed.

In July 1965, when the war began to require a lot of shipping, the privately owned American merchant marine consisted of 965 active ships of many different types: general cargo ships, coastal traders, bulk carriers, refrigerator ships, passenger ships, and tankers. Moreover, in the idle fleets the federal government owned another 400 usable freighters. By the beginning of 1967, over 160 of those old ships had been put back into service.

Twenty years have since gone by. The active U. S.-flag merchant marine numbers not 965 ships, but 400, more or less. The government-owned inactive fleet consists of about 230 ships, including some of those that in 1965 were already old. The middle-aged men who manned those ships in the 1960s have become old men. And even though of necessity sometimes it was done, it is not wise to depend on old men to run ships, especially ships that themselves suffer the ailments of age.

Numbers are part of our current problem. Types of ships and their sizes are other parts. Modern merchant ships are much larger than those of a generation ago, which means they cannot get into some of the ports their predecessors entered with ease. Because most of them carry their cargo in containers, modern freighters can be loaded swiftly and efficiently. But if their port of arrival lacks cranes with which to lift those containers (either because they never were there or because they were destroyed by enemy action), the ships must use their own cranes. Unfortunately, most modern container ships have no cranes of their own. Modern roll-on roll-off ships are also susceptible to unloading problems, while most current tankers are far too big and can enter only a very few very deep ports. Their cargo can reach the fighting forces only if there are sufficient smaller tankers or adequate overland routes to distribute it.

Fortunately, most modern merchant ships are designed to operate with crews much smaller than those required by older ships. But this is partly because more versatility is demanded of modern mariners than of those who went to sea earlier in this century. Whether in an emergency men long retired from the sea could adequately meet the wider variety of demands placed on them by the new ships is at least worth questioning. Further, while most retired marine engineers are skilled in steam, most modern ships are driven by diesel engines. In light of these facts, the urge to man old ships broken out from reserve with old men returned from retirement could be overwhelming.

What about the ships flying the flags of friendly foreign countries? Most U. S.-owned flag-of-convenience ships are large tankers, suited for what they do now, but for little else. Moreover, the need in this country for the oil they can carry would be as great in war as in peace, for in war homes, offices, and factories will be as dependent on heat, cooling, and power as they are in peace. In war as in peace, without fuel autos, buses, trucks, trains, aircraft, and ships do not move.

As for the famous old merchant fleets of Great Britain, the Netherlands, France, and our other allies, our story is their story: they all possess much smaller fleets of much larger ships than before, all of them generally less well suited for the crude demands of war than were their predecessors. Recently the decline in these fleets has been so fast that, for example, almost none of the merchant ships that made possible the successful British military campaign in the Falkland Islands in the spring of 1982 were still manned by British seamen and sailing under the British flag in the spring of 1985. To a great extent, the trade of the world today is carried in ships manned by crews from, and under the flags of, the "Third World."

In the United States the Military Sealift Command has done and is doing a great deal to alleviate the problems an inadequate merchant fleet would cause at the beginning of a new war. But the solutions for the long haul must be found elsewhere. Whether they will be found by a country that is not anxious to find them is in doubt. Free-enterprise businessmen and politicians have no sympathy for an industry that, in order to survive, needs cartels and government subsidies. Those who wish to expand (or at least not contract) the government's social activities favor no competition for federal funds from any sort of business, much less one important mainly for foreign trade, defense, or war. People fascinated by the slick world of computers, satellites, jet aircraft, and intercontinental nuclear weapons are repelled by such archaic things as steel freighters that are run adequately by men of little formal learning and that can take weeks to cross an ocean. Even the Armed Forces, with their own institutional pressures, quickly lose interest beyond a certain point. The current marvel is that they have pressed that point as far as they have.

Hence, the basic problem of how to ensure that the United States can move and sustain large forces across a wide ocean, a problem that was solved satisfactorily in every war up through the one in Vietnam, in Vietnam may have been solved satisfactorily for the last time.

U. S. Merchant Shipping and Vietnam

Lane C. Kendall

Headlines daily proclaim the activities of American soldiers and sailors in Vietnam; photographs show the amazing variety of equipment they use; news stories reflect the ways they use all these things, from clothing to explosives. Occasionally, there is a comment about the problems caused by crowded ports and about the numbers of merchant ships observed in anchorages. Rarely, however, does a reporter differentiate between ships supporting the civilian economy of Vietnam and those carrying the equipment and supplies of the military and naval forces.

Let us, therefore, begin by defining the merchant marine and explaining its close relationship with the military establishment.

The American merchant marine is the collection of ships and managers which provides transportation on the ocean trade routes linking the United States with overseas markets. About one-third of those ships receive direct subsidy from the U. S. government. When the military—including the naval services—requires it, the merchant marine provides sealift for troops and their supporting equipment by augmenting the organic capability of the Mili-

tary Sea Transportation Service (MSTS)*, the single agency of the Department of Defense charged with providing non-tactical logistical transportation by sea. ("Sealift," a manufactured word of recent origin, includes not only the movement of goods across the oceans but the planning for and the management and procurement of every mode of carriage that uses the sea-lanes.)

Basic to this proposition is the concept that ships of the American merchant marine are available to the military in peace, or in time of emergency short of war, only to the extent that their owners voluntarily offer them to MSTS. The authority to requisition ships is included in the broad war emergency powers of the President of the United States, but he alone can direct the use of those powers. Throughout the Vietnam experience, the unchanging policy of the White House has been to conduct business in the normal pattern, and not to invoke the emergency powers. Ships for support of operations in Vietnam have, therefore, been obtained entirely from voluntary offerings.

The American merchant marine industry, be it said to its credit, has been consistently willing to offer its ships to MSTS. Chief among the variety of factors responsible for that willingness are:

*Now called the Military Sealift Command, or MSC. (Editor)

—The fleet operated by MSTS has been kept small, expressly in order that private industry might participate profitably in the transportation of military cargo.

—The nature of military cargo is such that, usually, the ocean freight rates paid on it are attractive to American shipowners.

—Much of the military cargo is of a type similar to that moved in normal waterborne foreign commerce, and therefore can be carried in the average merchant ship.

Despite the above, military cargo possesses characteristics which distinguish it from commercial cargo:

—The quantity (i.e., the tonnage) in which it moves is very large, especially as compared with the cargo shipped by individual commercial traders.

—It usually must be delivered by specified, urgent dates.

—It is impossible to attach a monetary value to military cargo, since there is no known way to forecast priorities. That is to say that, at a given time and place, the shortage of one item might have a much more serious effect upon the efficiency or morale of combat troops engaged in a critical assignment, than would the shortage of another.

—Priorities for the delivery of goods are subject to change between the date of loading and the time the ship arrives in the overseas port of destination. This is particularly true in situations such as those which arise in Vietnam, where barbed wire might be desperately needed one week, and the next week, because the forces suddenly had gone on the offense, demolitions might become the commodity in critical supply.

—The places where military cargo is needed often bear no relation to commercial trade patterns.

On 1 July 1965, the American merchant marine, privately owned and in active opera-

tion, consisted of the following numbers and types of ships:

General-cargo ships		538
With speeds over 20 knots	67	
With speeds of 18.0 to 18.5 knots	40	
World War II C-4s of 17 knots	7	
World War II C-3s of 16.5 knots	127	
World War II C-2s of 15.0 to 15.5 knots	167	
Victory ships of 16.5 knots (AP-3 type)	37	
Victory ships of 15 knots (AP-2 type)	19	
C1-A and C1-B types of 14 knots	11	
World War II Liberty ships of 10 knots	28	
Others, most with speeds under 15 knots	35	
Bulk carriers		73
Refrigerator ships		18
Coastal ships		11
Passenger ships (including combination passenger-cargo ships operated primarily on cargo routes, but with capacity to carry up to 125 passengers each)		34
Large tankers		255
Other types of tankers		36
Total number of ships		965

This fleet was divided into three parts of approximately equal size. One part comprised the tankers, almost all of which were engaged in carrying oil between ports in the United States, in which service they were not subject to the competition from much-lower-cost foreign tankers. A few of them were being used to haul grain, to India or Pakistan, for instance. Almost the only tankers carrying oil to foreign ports were those under charter to MSTS. Another part was the subsidized fleet of ships in berth service. These 314 ships, which included the newest and fastest ships under U. S. registry, were all assigned to essential foreign-trade routes serving American importers and exporters. The third part, of 360 ships, con-

A C-2 freighter of Lykes Lines stands down the Saigon River, with Saigon on the starboard hand and, to port, territory dominated by the Viet Cong. The three nearest ships are a Waterman C-2, an MSTS Victory ship, and a United Fruit refrigerator ship. The square, white building in lower center is the MSTS office, Saigon.

sisted of the unsubsidized berth operators, the domestic carriers, and about 115 ships in the tramp trade. About 90 of the tramp steamers were considered satisfactory for carrying general cargo. Except for one bulk carrier, all 360 ships in the third group dated from World War II; some had been modernized, but none was faster than 17 knots.

In the eyes of the military, this American-flag commercial fleet had certain notable deficiencies:

—None of its 965 ships had beaching characteristics, with operable bow doors.

—None of its ships had heavy-lift booms, that is, those capable of lifting more than 80 tons.

—None of its ships had deck space to permit

carrying Landing Craft, Utility (LCU), which are about 120 feet long, weigh 180 tons, and are essential for lighterage and beaching operations.

—Except for one converted World War II C-4 under charter to MSTS, none of its ships could handle roll-on/roll-off cargo.

Nevertheless, this fleet had some substantial assets:

—About 130 of its 965 ships had been built since 1946, and approximately 100 of these new ships could cruise at a speed of 20 knots or better.

—The new ships were capacious, with big hatchways, making them particularly suitable for modern military equipment.

—Many of the new ships had booms of 70 to 75 tons' capacity, adequate to lift tanks and the newest type of Landing Craft, Mechanized, the LCM-8. Wartime freighters had 30- or 50-ton booms at best.

This, then, was the merchant marine on which MSTS, as the logistical, water-transportation agent for all military services, was able to rely for augmentation of its own organic sealift capability when, in mid-July 1965, President Johnson announced to the United States and to the world that the First Cavalry Division (Airmobile) was to be sent to Vietnam, and that additional troops would follow if they were needed. There were troops already in Vietnam, but they had gone there in such small groups that either a single troopship or even airplanes had been able to handle the load. Marines, of course, went in amphibious ships.

The President's announcement came as no surprise to the commander and staff of MSTS in Washington. On 18 April, Vice Admiral Glynn R. Donaho, U. S. Navy, Commander Military Sea Transportation Service (COMSTS), had been alerted to the plan to send the First Cavalry Division into combat, and he had assigned to his planning office the complex task of developing ways and means to carry out the anticipated presidential directive.

Necessarily, the intelligence passed to COMSTS was highly classified and, for weeks, only concepts could be discussed. The basic plan that emerged from those discussions was to move the troops by MSTS transports, and to carry essential impedimenta in cargo ships programmed to arrive at the discharge port not earlier than five days before, and not later than two days after, the transports. This "unit lift" concept was predicated on the closest coordination between all concerned. Cargo was to be called forward well in advance of the troops, because the difference in ship speeds was to be made up by sailing the slower cargo-carriers before the transports took the troops aboard.

As plans were developed, it became obvious that major adjustments in MSTS operations would have to be made. The six transports, which had been shuttling between Brooklyn and Northern Europe with dependents and troops, would have to be reassigned to lift combat troops to Vietnam. The three ships operated in the MSTS roll-on/roll-off service between Brooklyn and Bremerhaven would be used to lift the First Cavalry Division's heavy wheeled and tracked equipment to Vietnam, and then would remain in the Pacific. Finally, the planning showed that major augmentation of the MSTS fleet would be essential for the indefinite future.

Carrying out the plans, insofar as they concerned MSTS ships, presented no problems. These ships, operated by MSTS for the sole purpose of carrying the people and property of the services, had no commercial commitments, and were available, on COMSTS' order, to meet the changed requirements. Consequently, the six transports were quietly phased out of the shuttle to Northern Europe and shifted to Charleston, South Carolina; Savan-

nah, Georgia; and Mayport, Florida. The roll-on/roll-off ships were directed to move to these same ports. All ships were informed that they would be retained indefinitely in the Pacific. Not until January 1967 did any of them return to the Atlantic. Meanwhile, most of the Division's 434 helicopters were sent to Vietnam aboard the USS *Boxer* (LPH-4), a ship both larger and faster than any possessed by MSTS.

Procurement of additional ships from commercial sources was a different matter, since the White House policy of "business as usual" was interpreted to mean that there was to be no requisitioning of American merchant ships. The alternative was to seek, without publicity, voluntary offers of ships. This was done by enlisting the cooperation of the Maritime Administration, which briefed the shipowners, in two separate groups, early in June.

As it happened, about 100 ships belonging to the subsidized operators and based on the Atlantic and Gulf coasts lay idle because of a labor-management dispute. When the Maritime Administrator, Mr. Nicholas Johnson, appealed for ships, the response was immediate and subject only to the qualification that the unions agree to man ships carrying military cargo exclusively. When the unions were informed of the impending requirements, they promptly gave assurance that no military cargoes would be delayed because of their dispute with the operators.

Negotiations to charter these ships began on 13 July, and by 1 September the strikebound operators on the Atlantic and Gulf coasts had made a total of 47 subsidized ships available for use in support of operations in Vietnam. Subsidized operators on the West Coast, who were not affected by the labor dispute, offered no ships. The West Coast berth line ships which were already serving Vietnam were being used to nearly their full capacity, and little additional space would have been gained by chartering them.

In fairness to all concerned, MSTS established charter rates per day for the different types of ships, as follows:

American Challenger class	$4,628
Louise Lykes class	4,399
Mormacargo class	4,628
Mormacpride class	4,187
C3-S-37 class	3,980
Old C-3	3,213
Old C-2	2,880
Victory AP-3	2,880
Victory AP-2	2,825
Liberty	2,330

Concurrently with the chartering of the subsidized liners, negotiations were carried on with the unsubsidized berth operators and tramp shipowners, most of whose ships were World War II C-3s, C-2s, and Victory class. By 1 September 1965, MSTS's time-chartered, American-flag fleet consisted of 47 subsidized ships, 6 unsubsidized liners, and 12 tramps.

In spite of the strike, the unions lived up to their assurance, and provided crews for the ships, on the condition that only military goods were carried. Friction between the management of Lykes Lines and the Marine Engineers' Beneficial Association over the complement of licensed engineers to be carried in the highly automated *Louise Lykes* delayed the provision of crews for some Lykes ships presenting in Gulf ports, but when the problems eventually were solved, the Lykes ships served as effectively as any others.

Even with the cooperative spirit manifested by the American shipowners, it was apparent that more ships would be needed than could be provided from the active merchant fleet. The National Defense Reserve Fleet, maintained by the Maritime Administration, was the only source of additional capability, and its numerical inventory suggested a tremendous potential:

Transports	89
Naval auxiliaries	263
Tankers	65
Diesel-engined refrigerator ships	13
C-3s	8
C-2s	22
C1-As and C1-Bs	55
Victory AP-3s	31
Victory AP-2s	135
Experimental Liberty ships (1 diesel, 1 turbine, 2 gas-turbine-powered)	4
Z-EC-2 type Liberty ships, with four hatches and extra-long holds	20
Standard Liberty ships (EC-2 type, with five hatches)	726
British Liberty	1
Diesel-propelled, 6,000-ton-dead-weight C1-M-AV-1	44
N-3 coastal cargo ships, 3,000 tons deadweight, 10 knots	6
Others	2
Total	1,484

Analysis of the fleet, however, showed that the usable resources in the cargo-ship category were limited. Only about 250 ships with speeds of 14 knots or more, and 150 Liberty ships, were susceptible of activation. The diesel-powered ships had to be discounted because there were so few engineers qualified to operate them. Most of the Liberty ships were in fair-to-poor condition, due to the rugged service they had seen during World War II and the Korean War, and the minimum maintenance they received during their years in the reserve fleet.

Since the days of the Korean War, the Maritime Administration had continued to use the concept of "general agents" of the National Shipping Authority (NSA), a division of the Maritime Administration. "General agents" were steamship companies which NSA had found qualified to assume responsibility for all aspects of ship operation: they had posted (and, in many cases, had maintained since the end of the Korean campaign) performance bonds, and were prepared to assume the active management of ships for NSA, when directed. Compensation to cover the services of a general agent was 100 dollars per day per ship until 1 September 1966, when it was increased to 125 dollars. All operating expenses incurred in behalf of the ship were reimbursed to the agents by NSA. To reduce even further the burden imposed on a general agent, NSA advanced working capital to each agent at the rate of 100,000 dollars per ship, but not more than 500,000 dollars for any one agent, regardless of the number of ships he might handle under his agreement.

On 16 July 1965, pursuant to instructions from the Secretary of Defense, COMSTS requested the Maritime Administration to activate 14 ships from the National Defense Reserve Fleet, and to place them under general agency for the purpose of transporting military cargoes. The request stated that the cost of activation, operation, compensation of general agents, and expenses of administration incurred by NSA would be reimbursed by MSTS. At first, the reimbursement of activation costs (i.e., withdrawal from the reserve fleet, drydocking, and preparation for sea) was financed through the Navy Industrial Fund under the cognizance of MSTS. But, after 50 ships had been activated, it was decided that future activations should be financed from appropriated funds, while the operating costs would be paid out of MSTS's Navy Industrial Fund.

By the end of August 1965, 50 ships were in the process of being activated. As of 1 January 1967, 40 general agents were operating a total of 172 activated ships:

Victory AP-2 types	114
Victory AP-3 types	22
C-2s	11
C-3s	4
Steam-turbine-propelled Liberty	1
C1-Bs	15
C1-M-AV-1	3
C-2 refrigerator ships, which have been operated under general agency for MSTS for many years	2

Of these 172 ships, 161 were taken from the reserve fleet and activated by shipyards on all coasts at a cost of about 549,000 dollars per ship. No particular pattern of cost was established, since the availability of shipyard and ship-repair facilities and the law of supply and demand seemed to be the dominant factors.

Nine ships were assigned to operate under general agency on slightly different terms. Six ships had been traded in as partial payment on new construction or conversion of ships under the Ship Exchange Act, and had been placed under so-called "use charter agreement" with the original owner, in order to permit him to maintain his service until replacement ships were delivered by the shipyard. The law required that, when the replacements were delivered, the traded-in ships be surrendered to the Maritime Administration, which normally put them into the reserve fleet. However, in view of the need for ships at this time, it was decided to transfer traded-in ships from service under "use charter agreement" to service under general-agency agreement, and to assign them immediately to MSTS.

There is an interesting footnote to this procedure that is worthy of inclusion in this essay. The SS *Winged Arrow*, a Victory ship operated under "use charter agreement" by the Central Gulf Steamship Company of New Orleans, was being made ready for service under general agency when Hurricane Betsy devastated the port of New Orleans. The *Winged Arrow* was damaged so badly that it was deemed uneconomical to repair her. She was relegated to the reserve fleet without repair, and a replacement for her was taken from the reserve fleet. The cost of making the replacement ship ready, over and above what the "use charterer" had to pay, was for the account of MSTS, and therefore represented an out-of-pocket loss to the government.

For many years, in order to cope with its need for extra capacity during the summer months, the Alaska Steamship Company had been bareboat-chartering three C1-M-AV-1-type ships from the Maritime Administration. These motor ships are 339 feet long, 50 feet in beam, draw 23 feet of water, and have a speed of 10 knots. Each year, when they had filled the company's need, the ships were laid up in Seattle. However, in the fall of 1965, and again in the fall of 1966, instead of following that routine, they and their regular crews remained with the Alaska Steamship Company for operation under general-agency agreement. Each time that procedure was followed, the ships were made available to MSTS for a period of six months.

The two C-2 refrigerator ships listed above have been in operation across the Pacific Ocean since the days of the Korean conflict. Among other purposes which their operation under general agency served, was that of keeping the NSA organization alive in the period between shipping emergencies and, thus, when the reactivation program was instituted almost overnight in July 1965, demonstrating the value of such a "housekeeping" arrangement.

The National Shipping Authority is the office of the government officially designated to deal with steamship companies that manage ships under general-agency agreement. Although all costs eventually are paid by MSTS, the ships are only "controlled" by MSTS; the full responsibility for operation remains with NSA. Ships under general-agency agreement are recognized internationally as public vessels; they are owned by the United States and carry only government cargoes. The management and the crews, however, are civilian and are not in the direct employ of the government. An interesting technicality exists in the case of seamen crewing these ships. The master is appointed by the agent with the express permission of the NSA, and therefore is considered legally to be a "government employee"; since the seamen sign the shipping articles with the master, they also are considered "government employees" for the purpose of establishing the status of the ships as public vessels.

As mentioned previously, when the privately owned ships were chartered by MSTS in July 1965, the strike against owners on the Atlantic and Gulf coasts was in effect. By agreement, the duration of the charters was fixed at from three to six months, with the government having the option to retain the ships for the longer period. When the strike was terminated the following September, the companies began to press for release of their ships, particularly the new and fast ones, as quickly as possible so that they could resume their normal commercial trading. But the government's need for ships had not diminished after the arrival in Vietnam of the First Cavalry Division, and replacement tonnage had to be found.

On 2 November 1965, COMSTS called a meeting at his headquarters, and all segments of the industry and representatives of the Maritime Administration and the Department of Defense attended. At that meeting, the need for continued support from the active merchant marine was emphasized, and it was acknowledged that older and slower ships were acceptable to the military. Consequently, predominantly old tonnage was offered, and the resultant deficiency in carrying capability was made up by additional activations from the reserve fleet. As of 31 December 1966, a total of 202 separate charters had been negotiated since the meeting of 2 November 1965, and the number of ships on charter at the end of 1966 was 33 subsidized liners (including 12 new ships of 18.5 knots speed or higher), 32 unsubsidized berth liners, and 73 tramps, for a total of 138. In addition, there were, on charter to MSTS, 14 refrigerator ships out of a total supply of only 18 such ships, all owned by the non-subsidized United Fruit Company, and five bulk carriers engaged in hauling coal to Northern Europe. Coal is sent to Europe from the United States for Defense Department account, and is used, rather than locally mined coal, to help reduce the gold outflow and to provide more employment in depressed areas at home.

Early in the buildup, supplying the large quantities of ammunition needed in Vietnam became a major problem. The Air Force first, and then the Navy, asked for and obtained the assignment of ships to "Special Express" service carrying ammunition exclusively, and loaded for selective discharge. The ships were to be used as mobile depots, providing the right ammunition at the right time and the right place. On 31 December 1966, there were 23 ships so assigned and making regular runs from ammunition depots on the West Coast, principally Concord, California, and Bangor, Washington, to Camranh Bay, Nha Be, and other points, as required by the tactical and logistical situation.

All the ships used were of World War II variety, the preferred type being the C-4, because of its numerous compartments and its seven hatches. Next in acceptability was the C-3, and then the Victory, which the Navy used exclusively for its express ammunition ships. In last place was the C-2. The actual count of "Special Express" ships on 31 December 1966 was: 4 C-4s, 6 C-3s, 10 Victory, and 3 C-2s. Twelve of the group were operated under general-agency agreement, and the balance were time-chartered. In January 1967, the concept of a "Special Express" fleet was abandoned by the Air Force because, by that time, port facilities

One of the nation's 16 troop transports in 1968, the USNS General N. M. Walker, at anchor at Vung Tau, South Vietnam. These were the ships that carried the majority of troops to Vietnam during the first year of the war. In the background, landing craft are being offloaded from a foreign-flag bulk carrier. There were no bulk carriers such as that pictured under the American flag. (J. T. Luscan, PH1, U.S. Navy)

having improved and storage facilities ashore having caught up with the need, MSTS could provide adequate shipping without specifying individual ships for the carriage of ammunition.

From its inception, MSTS has relied heavily upon American berth-line operators, both subsidized and unsubsidized, to provide service to many ports of military interest on schedules which permit maximum flexibility and convenience to transportation officers and logisticians of the Army, Navy, Marine Corps, and Air Force. The onset of the Vietnam operation intensified the use of these less-than-shipload carriers, but it did not change the patterns. Several of the unsubsidized companies chartered foreign-flag ships to fill the gaps in their berth services created by chartering their American-flag ships to MSTS. Occasionally, therefore, it came about that foreign ships were placed on berth by American carriers and were made available for any cargo the military might wish to book to them. If no American ships were at hand, these foreign ships were used in order to let the cargo be shipped to its destination without delay.

It was under these circumstances that the much-publicized episode concerning *El Mexicano* took place during the late summer of 1965. The ship, of Mexican registry, was chartered by an unsubsidized American operator for worldwide trading. She was placed on berth in the company's regular service, and offered, as a routine matter, to MSTS for such cargo as might be in need of transportation. The charterer announced no restrictions on the ship's ability to perform under the proposed schedule, which included Saigon as a port of call. The Mexican government's ruling that national law forbade dispatch of a Mexican ship to the combat zone was not published until several thousand measurement tons of military goods had been loaded into the ship. But as a result of it, the cargo was removed from *El Mexicano* and booked to a Greek ship chartered by the same American operator. When the Greek crew learned that the destination of the cargo was Vietnam, they refused to sail the ship, even though a substantial cash bonus was promised. The cargo was booked once more, this time to an American ship, and

although it reached Saigon several weeks late, there were no more incidents.

Expanding requirements of the military forces in Vietnam, coupled with the long turnabout time at ports in that area, made shipping particularly critical during the late summer and fall of 1965, and in the course of trying to provide sealift to urgently required material, COMSTS chartered the *Marilena P*, a Greek-flag ship, for a single voyage from Seattle to Saigon. The owners of the *Marilena P* were aware of her proposed destination, and apparently assumed that the crew would interpose no objection. However, on 27 August 1965, when the ship presented, pursuant to the terms of the charter, the seamen announced that they would not carry military cargo to Vietnam. After several days of discussion with the owners, the charter was cancelled on 2 September, on the ground that the contract had been breached through non-performance. In the meantime, an American-flag ship had become available and, as in the case of the cargo for *El Mexicano*, this cargo also went under the American flag.

These are the only occasions on which foreign ships have not provided satisfactory service. Nevertheless, the chartering of foreign ships is kept to the absolute minimum. Between 1 July 1965 and 31 December 1966, COMSTS took only 27 foreign ships, of which but 15 were assigned to the Southeast Asia/ Vietnam run, the rest being used to move military goods between Northern Europe and the East Coast of the United States.

For many years, foreign-flag ships have supplemented American shipping capability, and their use has increased somewhat since the build-up began in Vietnam. But, even so, during fiscal year 1966, only 5 per cent of U. S. military cargo was carried in foreign-flag ships, compared with 3 per cent during the preceding fiscal year.

Aside from the day-to-day difficulties of matching ships with cargoes, and meeting schedules imposed by circumstances far beyond the purview of COMSTS, there was a major problem that everyone concerned with shipping to the war zone had to face: the provision of seamen to man the ships as they were reactivated. For a number of years, the shrinking of the merchant fleet has discouraged any large number of men from making careers as merchant seamen. Consequently, the basic pool of American seafarers was small, and each ship activated meant that another 45 qualified men, give or take a few, had to be found.

The maritime unions generally gave thoroughgoing support to the supplying of crews. Typical of their support was the practice of withholding assignments of seamen to new, well-equipped, and comfortable ships on short runs until the Vietnam-bound ships had been staffed to at least the minimum requirements of the Coast Guard. These requirements are below the union manning scales: in a ship where the union scale calls for a master and four mates, the Coast Guard requires a master and only two mates. The hard fact was that there were not enough men to meet the union levels, so the unions waived their own contract terms and left the Coast Guard to decide what size the crew should be. Shortages of both licensed and unlicensed mariners are directly responsible for many of the ship delays experienced since mid-1966.

Service to Vietnam was not, and is not now, popular with seamen. The climate is not good; liberty conditions in the ports to which American ships are routed are poor, if they exist at all; accommodations for both licensed and unlicensed mariners in the reactivated ships are markedly below the minimum standards demanded by the unions; the round trip is long; often, ships are kept for days or weeks in "holding" ports, while waiting for a berth in the Vietnamese harbor; mail service is erratic; and boredom and personal privation are integral parts of the whole picture. Moreover, ships are subject to attack, either by mine or gunfire, and several have been hit in the approaches to Saigon.

Some of these problems are being solved. For instance, specifications for the latest activations include air conditioning of the officers' wardroom and crew messrooms. As ships already in service return to the United States and as the work can be performed by shipyards, they will receive the same improvement. Mail service has been ameliorated by assignment of a special zip code in the Navy mail system. Liberty launches, converted from LCM-3 and LCM-6 landing craft, have been shipped out to the Vietnamese ports, and are being operated by a civilian contractor. These launches service the MSTS and general-agency ships on a priority basis, and commercial ships as space is available in the launches. A program supported jointly by MSTS, the Maritime Administration, and the United Seamen's Service is providing motion pictures. Finally, the United Seamen's Service has opened a simple but quite spacious center for merchant seamen at Camranh Bay, and it plans to install similar facilities in other ports as soon as funds and equipment are made available.

Although personnel problems have received attention at the highest levels and the situation in Vietnam is better than it was in 1965, there is still room for improvement.

To offset the manpower shortage, meantime, the Maritime Administration advanced the graduation dates of the classes of 1966 and 1967 at the U. S. Merchant Marine Academy, and the five state maritime colleges shortened their courses, in order to make licensed deck and engineer officers available to meet the needs of the Vietnam service. The unlicensed unions opened training schools to assist their members to improve their qualifications and to prepare themselves for licensed status. The licensed unions instituted upgrading programs to aid their members to obtain higher licenses. The Coast Guard approved the rating of "apprentice engineer," which permits a recruit to spend a year in study ashore and a year at sea under tutelage, at the end of which period he is eligible to take the examination for a third assistant engineer's license. This arrangement shortens from three years to two the period of sea service required before an engineer can qualify for a license.

Despite these measures, which have resulted in a substantial output of qualified men, ships have been sailed with less than the full complement. Shortages have been critical in engineer billets, but have appeared among the ranks of the deck and radio officers as well. All American-flag ships have suffered from shortages: MSTS ships have been unable to find full complements, and berth-service ships to all parts of the world have been delayed by lack of people to sail them.

As one means of increasing the number of seamen to staff the ships sailing from U. S. ports, COMSTS decided that MSTS ships permanently based in Far Eastern waters and under the operational control of Commander Military Sea Transportation Service, Far East (COMSTSFE), should be converted to Japanese or Korean manning. The 25 Landing Ships, Tank (LST) operated by COMSTSFE at the outbreak of the campaign in Vietnam had been Japanese-manned for many years before 1965. When this fleet was increased to 37 ships, the additional LSTs were home-ported in Pusan, and Korean officers and unlicensed crews were recruited to man them. Finally, in the closing days of 1966, five ships—three deep-draft and two coastal types—were converted from American to Korean manning. Ships so converted undergo little change, and

they could easily be manned again by Americans, if it were so desired.

The three deep-draft ships were the *Provo*, *Cheyenne*, and *Phoenix*, Victory ships which had been converted from standard cargo carriers into specially equipped Forward Floating Depots. They were loaded with the heavy equipment needed by an armored regiment, stationed at Subic Bay, and participated in Army maneuvers in 1964. In early 1966, they were directed to discharge their cargoes in Vietnam, and were assigned to conventional point-to-point transportation duties in the Far East. Since they will not be returned to the continental United States for years to come, and since there is a manpower shortage in the United States, it was appropriate to substitute Asian crews for the American seamen. The other two ships affected by this policy were the C1-M-AV-1 types *Bondia* and *Short Splice*, the former a refrigerator ship in use as a floating warehouse in Vietnamese waters.

The American seamen in these five ships were civil service—"civil marine"—personnel of MSTS, and they were returned to the United States and assigned to other ships of the MSTS fleet, without loss of seniority or pay. It is appropriate to note, in this regard, that MSTS civil marine personnel are hired by the operational command, rather than for a particular ship, as is the custom in the merchant marine, and are subject to rotation and reassignment, as are shore-based career employees of the government.

As the sealift agency for the Department of Defense, MSTS is responsible for cargo from the time it is stowed in a ship at the loading port until the stow is broken at the destination. It does not operate the terminals either in the United States or overseas. Problems of ports, however, cannot be ignored by MSTS, since the efficiency with which cargo is handled affects markedly the turnaround time of the ships. From the time it began, the build-up in

Vietnam posed a series of problems ranging from those inherent in a small port suddenly being required to process several times its normal capacity, to those related to converting virgin areas into military waterfront complexes. The biggest problems faced may be summarized:

—Warehouses and transit sheds were inadequate, both in size and in number, to accommodate the suddenly increased amount of cargo.

—Equipment for efficient movement of cargo in and around the terminals either was not available or was not kept in operating condition by the local labor force.

—Waterfront labor was not accustomed to the high-speed procedures required by the expensive American ships, all of which were paying their crews 100 per cent bonuses for the time they were in the war area.

—Lighterage to work ships from berths in the stream, as at Saigon, or at anchor, as at Camranh Bay, was insufficient in number and size of individual craft to provide satisfactory service.

—Confusion between military and commercial interests, as each tried to obtain priority in use of the insufficient wharf space, often frustrated both parties and kept both types of ships waiting.

In the early days of the buildup, the plan was to hold ships in Vietnamese waters, or those of nearby countries, and use them as floating warehouses, from which individual items would be unloaded as needed. As facilities for storage of military goods were improved, enlarged, and put into operation, the necessity for this procedure was reduced significantly. At the end of 1966, there were two reasons for ships being held in ports outside the combat zone: one was that war-zone bonuses were not paid while ships were in the holding ports; and the other was that the number of ships in Vietnamese ports could be con-

trolled, and there was some sort of assurance that when a ship was called forward, she would be handled with reasonable dispatch.

Lighterage for Saigon and Camranh Bay was a critical problem from the beginning, and in the first 18 months, many Army LCUs were shipped in from the United States to alleviate this condition. However, in all Vietnam, there is no crane powerful enough and no American ships have booms heavy enough to lift a 180-ton LCU. Consequently, from time to time, it has been necessary to engage foreign-flag ships with extra-heavy-lift gear to provide some of the transportation. Other LCUs have been stowed on the decks of barges, held in place by steel bars, and towed from ports on all coasts of the United States to various destinations in Vietnam. For example, in September 1966, MSTS signed a contract with a Pacific Coast towing company for the latter to move six units of two "piggy-backed" barges each from Charleston, South Carolina, to Saigon. The tow started on 12 October 1966, and the two tugs and their tows of three tandem barges arrived safely in Saigon on 15 January 1967. The contract price for the job was 372,000 dollars.

Building up the new facilities involved moving a number of patented De Long piers from the United States and Japan to Vietnam. The first of these 300-foot-long, 90-foot-wide structures was towed from Charleston to Camranh Bay via Suez. Fueling stops were made in the Azores, at Gibraltar, Port Said, Aden, and Ceylon. This route—rather than one through Panama—was selected because the distance saved was equal to two days of towing time; also, refueling points were located at more convenient distances on the Suez route. The big tow was delivered in 80 days, and its condition on arrival in Camranh Bay on 30 October 1966 called forth no complaints. Other port units, such as heavy-lift cranes, barges, and tugs, were towed out from the United States.

Between July 1965 and December 1966, the staff of COMSTS negotiated 11 contracts for the towing of floating equipment to South Vietnam.

The critical shortage of lighterage and towing services in Vietnam prompted the award in December 1965 of a contract to Alaska Barge and Transport, Inc., of Vancouver, Washington, to provide lighterage, towing, and complete stevedoring in Vietnamese ports, as well as coastwise delivery between the ports. A fleet of tugs of various sizes was assembled in the Pacific Northwest. As the flotillas were formed, the big tugs were ordered to tow the barges, which carried on their decks the smaller tugs and barges. Service covered by this contract was provided to Camranh Bay, Qui Nhon, Nha Trang, and Vung Tau. Collateral assignments were made to the same company, and in the summer of 1966, it was chosen to operate the liberty launches in Vung Tau and Qui Nhon. This activity was one means of alleviating the poor recreational conditions that seamen had to endure in the ports of Vietnam.

Because of the confusion between commercial and military cargoes in the port of Saigon, and the resultant delays to ships, the Department of Defense and the Agency for International Development (AID) agreed on 29 August 1966 to integrate AID cargo for Vietnam into the Department of Defense transportation system. By ending the distinction between the two types of cargo sponsored by the U. S. government, insofar as assignment of berthing facilities was concerned, delays in unloading could be reduced. This was a step forward, but not a big enough one. The only way to deal efficiently with the problem of trying to fit too many ships into too few berths is to appoint a port operations authority with power to direct the utilization of all facilities in Vietnam. Establishment of such an authority is, of course, a matter to be handled between the chiefs of the states involved.

In April 1966, the Maritime Administration set up a two-man office in Saigon, staffed by an operations expert and a marine engineer/ repair supervisor. Their mission was to coordinate the activities of the general-agency ships; to deal with the commercial shipping companies, the ships' masters, and their crews; to supervise local repair and salvage work on American merchant ships; to reduce port delays in Vietnam, not only for the general-agency ships, but for all American merchant ships; and to serve as a liaison between the merchant marine and the military. Housed in the MSTS office in Saigon, the Maritime Administration office worked closely with MSTS. A "Traffic Management Agency," under the chairmanship of the senior MarAd-V representative, was created in May 1966, and consisted of all U. S. officials concerned with shipping as well as of the civilian coordinators for the individual steamship companies. That body proved to be an effective tool for developing better understanding of mutual problems, was beneficial in reducing delays to American ships, and helped to assure more effective use of the available facilities.

Because of the large number of American-flag commercial ships in Vietnamese waters, it was found desirable to assign a specialist officer of the U. S. Coast Guard to the Vietnam area. The first such officer reported for duty in late November 1966, and his specific mission was to supervise, within Coast Guard cognizance, all merchant ships in the area. He devoted all his time to handling the numerous and intricate details of ship safety, seaworthiness, and inspection; crew qualifications; and enforcement of discipline aboard American merchant ships. His authority extended to all Vietnamese ports and was intended to assure that, at all times, American ships and seamen met the minimum standards of the Coast Guard. From the day he took over, there was the closest coordination between the Coast

Guard, MSTS, and MarAd-V, and the active and aggressive exercise of Coast Guard supervision in Vietnamese waters aided materially in improving operations.

The biggest problem of shipping to Vietnam has been the turnaround of ships. In the early days of the buildup, dozens of ships were to be seen congregated at the various anchorages in Vietnam and in the "holding" ports, and persons qualified to object, as well as those who were not, complained at length about the lack of efficiency in ship management that this situation demonstrated. Since the breaking of this bottleneck involved many factors, ranging from inter-governmental relations down to the distribution between transit sheds of palletboards and fork-lift trucks, it required patience and diplomacy as well as technical competence to bring about a businesslike atmosphere. In the course of seeking and developing solutions, various new concepts were considered and several of them were adopted.

In the fall of 1965, representatives of specialized commercial steamship operators and the president of the International Longshoremen's Association, independently, proposed that general cargo destined for Saigon and Camranh Bay, and ammunition consigned to Nha Be, about ten miles below Saigon, be moved in large containers, similar to those used by carriers in the coastwise trade of the United States. The container concept is a commercially successful device which assures prompt handling of large tonnages of cargo, but it depends upon the availability of a large marshalling area for parking containers and tractor trucks, and on adequate berthing space. Satisfactory roads for inland distribution of the containers are also of prime importance in accomplishing the ultimate objective of container service, which is delivery to consignee or ultimate consumer without rehandling. Since none of these requirements could be met at that time, it was decided that large containers

(8 feet wide, 8 feet high, and from 20 to 40 feet long) could not be accepted in Vietnam until facilities had been constructed at Newport, just above Saigon. When new berths and support areas became available in December 1966, the subject of containerization of cargo for Vietnam was reopened for discussion.

An alternative that was available was to use Okinawa, some 1,800 sea miles from Vietnam, as a staging base for cargo moving in large containers, measuring about 8 feet cube and known as Conex boxes. The idea was that cargo in containers could be delivered to this island, and then smaller units, filled with specific items requisitioned by consumers in Vietnam, could be prepared by the depots in Okinawa. Conex boxes and Army trailers would be carried to Vietnam in the roll-on/roll-off ships, USNS *Comet*, USNS *Taurus*, and SS *Transglobe*, shuttling between Okinawa and Saigon and Camranh Bay. Since those three ships already were assigned to COMSTSFE for the intra-theater lift, the concept was approved, and COMSTS was directed to negotiate a contract with a container carrier to provide the transpacific service from the West Coast of the United States to Okinawa. Sea-Land Service, Incorporated, of Elizabeth, New Jersey, was awarded a two-year contract of affreightment to transport each month, in converted T-2 Mission-type tankers, approximately 1,000 containers, each measuring 8 feet wide, 8.5 feet high, and 35 feet long, and with a capacity of about 42 measurement tons, from Oakland and Seattle to Okinawa. This container size, though not of the international standard, was derived from the standard over-the-road trailer used by truckers on the East Coast of the United States. Prompt dispatch of the big T-2 tankers was assured; the Army, as the receiving agency, agreed to pay demurrage if the ships were held in port longer than 24 hours. Five sailings in two months were required under the contract. The first ship sailed in this coordinated service in July 1966, and regular departures from the West Coast have been maintained ever since.

At the same time as the discussions with Sea-Land Service were going on, MSTS negotiated time charters for a fleet of 12 ships from Seatrain Lines of Edgewater, New Jersey. These ships, some of which had just been withdrawn from an unprofitable trade, were obtained with worldwide trading privileges— that is to say, they could be sent anywhere MSTS desired—and were under direct control of MSTS. Five of them had been built as railroad-car-carriers, but had been adapted so that, in addition, they could transport containers, wheeled and tracked vehicles, and package or general cargo. The other seven were Mission-type tankers which were being rebuilt to carry, not oil, but containers and vehicles, with complete flexibility as to how the cargo was stowed. If desired, a whole shipload of vehicles might be moved; with no structural change, all space might be filled with containers; or the entire reach of the ship might be used for package cargo. These ships were accepted under charter on a progressive basis; the first ship presented in June 1966, and the last was programmed for delivery in mid-summer 1967.

The ships of both Sea-Land Service and Seatrain Lines are self-sustaining, and are, therefore, not dependent upon shore facilities to handle their cargoes. Sea-Land Service's ships were procured for indirect support of operations in Vietnam; Seatrain Lines' ships can be sent directly to the combat zone.

In mid-1966, a combination of steamship operators and helicopter manufacturers proposed an imaginative new concept, under which containerized cargo would be delivered by ship to ports in Vietnam, and lifted off by CH-54 high-capacity helicopters, which would carry the containers to the marshalling yard. The virtue of the scheme, its proponents stated, was that the containers, which might weigh a gross of ten tons each, would be transported *over* the congested waterfront and local city traffic to the receiving point, thus eliminating the bottleneck of terminal facilities. Problems of practicality, however, have beset this concept. The availability of the high-capacity helicopters is, of course, critical. When carrying a full load, the aircraft would have to be refueled every 40 miles or so; hence, marshalling yards close to the waterfront would have to be found. Containers would have to be stuffed absolutely tight, so that no shifting would occur while in flight and cause a crash. Alternatively, accordion-like containers, which could be made small enough to fit tightly around any cargo, could be made, but that course has shortcomings, too. Finally, the high cost of the system had to be weighed against the military advantages.

Less spectacular than the developments of container traffic have been the efforts to enlarge the American merchant marine, particularly the unsubsidized part of it. The terms of the Ship Exchange Act of 1966 permit ships that are more than 17 years old to be exchanged for ships in the National Defense Reserve Fleet which, though equally old, have had less use and, therefore, should be able to perform more economically. This law has been invoked to secure the release of a number of Victory ships, all of which have been chartered by MSTS.

In July 1966, the Secretary of the Navy released to the Maritime Administration, for exchange under the above law, 25 C-4 transports that had been built during World War II. A condition of the release was that after the ships had been converted to cargo-carriers, their new owners must offer them to COMSTS for charter at reasonable rates. Fifteen of the 25 were released in November 1966; four were to be converted into heavy-lift ships with booms of 125 to 200 tons' capacity, and 11 were to be made into general-cargo carriers. The rest of them were awarded early in 1967 for conversion into container ships. A board, consisting of representatives of the Navy, MSTS, and the Maritime Administration, made recommendations on the allocation of the ships, and the Secretary of the Navy approved the recommendations before they were announced.

Other possibilities for improving the American merchant marine lie in the release of 122 Victory ships. Nineteen of these are of the AP-2 class, which were converted into troop transports during World War II, and could probably be restored to commercial-cargo configuration for between 600,000 and 750,000 dollars each. They have had less than six years of operational service, so their work potential is considerable. The other 103 Victory ships are of the AP-3 type which, during World War II, were made into transports for the Navy's amphibious force and designated VC2-S-AP5. If these ships were converted into standard cargo-carriers, they would provide faster and, theoretically, more competitive transportation than the AP-2 troopers, but the cost of such conversion was estimated variously at between 2,600,000 and 4,300,000 dollars per ship. Whether unsubsidized shipowners would be interested in acquiring old tonnage at these prices remains to be seen.

In its reporting on merchant marine support of the Vietnamese campaign, the public press has given more attention to dry-cargo ships than it has to tankers, but this does not mean that the latter have not been important, or that there have been no problems concerning them. Obviously, the increased activity of aviation units and the large number of Navy ships in the Pacific have combined to multiply the requirements for petroleum, oil, and lubricants (POL). For example, on 1 July 1965, MSTS had 22 tankers under charter, whereas by 16 December 1966, it had 53 such ships.

Many of the problems that beset the dry-cargo carriers are also experienced by the tanker fleet. There is a limited number of American-flag tankers, and those whose size is most satisfactory for military supply—the 16,500-ton T-2s—are disappearing because they are no longer commercially economical to operate. Because the chartering activity of MSTS has decreased the number of general-cargo ships available to the shipping public, there has been a demand for tankers to move grain to countries receiving massive donations of American wheat under the AID program. Consequently, from time to time, it has been necessary to charter foreign-flag tankers to meet military requirements. Between 1 July 1965 and 31 December 1966, the total of such charters was 24, and until October 1966 the use of non-American tankers was no more than the occasional exception to the rule that only ships registered in the United States shall be used to carry military cargo. Foreigners that have been used have been chartered for the outbound voyage only and routed to destinations other than Vietnam, in order to free American ships to service the combat zone, if necessary. Much of the POL lift is destined for Japan, Guam, Okinawa, and the Philippines. It is difficult, therefore, to state specifically how many tankers are supporting the campaign in Vietnam, but it is clear that much of the cargo delivered is used directly or indirectly for the military campaign.

A survey of the foreign tankers chartered by COMSTS shows that only four of them were registered in Liberia or Panama, and one of these is American-owned and considered to be a member of the "effective U. S. control" fleet of foreign ships. The largest supplier of tankers has been Norway, with 12 ships; Britain came next with three; Panama, Liberia, and Greece each provided two ships; and Denmark and West Germany supplied one tanker each.

American tankers controlled by MSTS are used on many different kinds of supply missions. For example, on 16 December 1966, six small coastal tankers, operated with MSTS civil service crews, were assigned to the operational control of COMSTSFE; three T-2 type tankers were performing duty as floating storage in Vietnamese waters; 8 were steaming towards Vietnam; 28 were en route to destinations in the Far East, other than Vietnam; 31 were directed to ports outside the Far Eastern area; one was in the Mediterranean on shuttle service; and one was operated out of Honolulu to islands in the Pacific. This total of 78 ships was made up of five ships operated directly by MSTS, 20 deep-draft tankers owned by MSTS but operated by three experienced American contractors, 44 ships on long-term, consecutive-voyage charters, 8 tankers on time charter, and one on bare-boat charter. Many of the chartered tankers had been driven out of the oil trade some years before by the Colonial Pipeline which runs from Texas to Long Island, and their owners had been able to keep them busy only by having them carry grain to India under the AID program. Most of them are war-built T-2s and are near the end of their operational lives.

Manpower shortages have caused fewer delays for the tankers than they have for dry-cargo ships, probably because there has been little, if any, increase in the number of tankers, and seamen who sail tankers tend to seek employment only in tankers.

Mechanical difficulties resulting from operating old ships have caused some delays, but no more than the history of operating ships of this type and trade would lead us to expect. The average loss of time, up to the end of 1966, was 3.2 days per ship.

All the time that operations in Vietnam have been in progress, MSTS has maintained its regular water-transportation links with all the other military bases overseas. Stations in the Antarctic and in the Eastern Arctic were supplied, as usual, by MSTS-operated cargo ships and tankers. The radar stations scattered along the coast and on the islands of Alaska received their food, fuel, and other necessary material, by means of ships and barges chartered by MSTS from American operators with long experience in these waters. As always, regular American berth-line services have provided most of the required sealift to Europe, the Mediterranean, the Caribbean, and the Far East outside of the war zone. The military services' dependence on the American merchant marine increased as the tempo of combat quickened in Vietnam, and the controlled ships—that is, the MSTS blue-and-gold ships, the chartered ships hauling military cargo exclusively, and the general-agency ships—became less available to carry goods to peaceful ports.

The impact the build-up in Vietnam has had on MSTS is indicated by the statistics, given in thousands of measurement tons in the table on the opposite page.

Use of the American merchant marine to support the operations in Vietnam has served to point up significantly:

—The value of having a substantial fleet of operating ships. How promptly the American merchant marine could react to an emergency was not proved in the summer of 1965, because of the maritime strike on the East and Gulf coasts, but the willingness of operators and unions to provide ships and crews in a minimum of time was demonstrated, and merits both attention and commendation.

—The need for ships to support a large overseas military campaign. Despite the tremendous growth in the capabilities of aircraft, about 97.5 per cent of all the cargo delivered to Vietnam moves in ships. Such cargo could not be handled without hundreds of merchant ships and thousands of merchant seamen.

—That ships still provide transportation at a fraction of the cost of air delivery. The Military Airlift Command estimated in December 1966 that the cost of transporting a short ton of

	January 1965	June 1965	December 1965	Year 1965	June 1966	December 1966
Cargo to Vietnam	86.5	284.2	396.3	4,197.7	790.8	945.8
Cargo worldwide, other than Vietnam	748.1	1,055.2	1,073.0	12,543.1	1,162.4	1,000.1
Total	834.6	1,339.4	1,469.3	16,740.8	1,953.2	1,945.9
Percentage of total destined to Vietnam	10.4	21.2	27.0	25.1	40.5	48.6

cargo in a C-141 cargo aircraft from Dover, Delaware, to Tan Son Nhut, Vietnam, is 709 dollars. The ocean freight rate from an East Coast port of the United States to any port in Vietnam for a similar quantity of cargo is approximately $73.50, exclusive of stevedoring costs.

—That assuring a dependable source of shipping to augment MSTS becomes a problem of the first magnitude when the size of the present American merchant marine is taken into account. The disruption to commercial routes which results from the large-scale diversion of ships to non-commercial activity has effects which may endure for many years after the military emergency has passed. Both subsidized and unsubsidized lines are committed to providing their peacetime customers with regular, dependable sailings using the most modern ships they can afford. Sudden reductions of these sailings are likely to alienate permanently many shippers who otherwise would support the American merchant fleet. Furthermore, the loss of American dollars to overseas interests cannot be overlooked. Adoption of the obvious alternative—restricting the military to using American-flag tramp ships because the latter have no long-term commitments either to shippers or to trade routes—may weaken to an unacceptable degree the nation's ability to meet military emergencies. Since the obsolescence and mechanical exhaustion of its present ships make the continued existence of the tramp fleet uncertain, the practicality of that alterna-

tive is very much open to question. The military services, therefore, face the dilemma of how, in time of emergency short of mobilization, to provide the essential augmentation of MSTS's sealift capability.

—That the National Defense Reserve Fleet is now an asset of only limited value. When operations in Vietnam began, it consisted of about 400 usable ships, including 150 ten-knot Liberty ships. While 161 of the usable ships have been reactivated, and many of these will have undergone substantial upgrading as a result of their service, some will have to be scrapped at the end of their present tours of duty. The speed, slow by current standards, relatively small size, and other limitations of the Victory ships reduce their value for any future military transportation requirements.

—That finding seamen to crew ships, not only those activated from the National Defense Reserve Fleet, but also those that have just been built, is a serious problem. The present privately owned merchant marine is small, employment opportunities are limited, and prospects for advancement and security in the career have been discouraging up to this time. Enlargement of the MSTS sealift capability is a basic concept of strategic planning, but unless there are seamen to operate the ships, it cannot be realized.

—That, in spite of all the delays and disruptions caused by inadequate port facilities, operations to Vietnam have been carried on without serious interference by the enemy. One ship, the *Baton Rouge Victory*, was sunk by a mine, but she was raised and later sold for scrap. A foreign-flag cargo carrier, the *Eastern Mariner*, loaded with cement, also was mined and sunk, but she was not working for MSTS. A few other ships have been damaged by bombs attached to their hulls, or by fire from recoilless rifles or machine guns. It is obvious that the strain on the American merchant marine would have been much greater, and almost, if not entirely, unbearable, had there been serious attrition as a result of hostile action.

—The validity of the concept of the general-agency agreement for operating government-owned ships to transport military cargoes. It is still the most effective method of obtaining steamship management skills in times of "business as usual." There is every reason to believe that it will be equally valuable in the future, and therefore the machinery should be kept in some form of ready-reserve status.

—That the use of old, slow, small ships to provide logistical support is not necessarily in the best interest of the nation. The cost in money, manpower, and resources is high, when compared with that of such ships as the new Constellation, Master Mariner, and Challenger classes. However, the characteristics that make the new ships valuable for logistic support also make them particularly valuable to their owners for commercial operation. Especially when the nation is not placed on a war footing, the conflict between the interests of the nation and those of the shipowner seeking to earn a reasonable profit on his investment and to protect his position for the future, could be disastrous to the military. If the owners do not make a profit, there will not be more such ships for the military to call on.

—That there is a need for the development of new techniques of cargo-handling and new patterns of ship design. It is in the interest of the United States not to permit relaxation of present efforts to solve the problems being experienced in support of operations in Vietnam. The only way to meet future military requirements for sealift is to develop truly modern methods now.

In an atmosphere of "business as usual," plagued with shortages of manpower as well as of modern ships, torn between the patriotic desire to assist the national military effort and the pressure to earn revenues and to obtain a permanent role in the transportation program of the future, the American merchant marine has done a professional and commendable job in finding ways to meet its obligations to the United States and still remain actively in the international and domestic transportation business. It is in special recognition of the triumph over these difficulties that an accolade may be awarded:

"Well done."

(*Naval Review*, 1968)

About the Authors

Vice Admiral Malcolm W. Cagle, USN, a graduate of the U. S. Naval Academy in 1941, was director, aviation programs division, in the office of the Deputy Chief of Naval Operations for Air in 1965–1968 and then made two deployments to the war area as Commander Carrier Division One. Currently he is, among other things, owner of a Lynchburg, Va., meat company, a cattle farmer, senior vice president Naval Aviation Museum Foundation, and editor of the naval aviation journal, *Foundation*.

Commander Frank C. Collins, Jr., USN, was graduated from Louisiana State University in 1949. In 1966–67 he was operations officer at Naval Support Activity Da Nang. Recently retired from the Navy in the rank of rear admiral, he is vice president for quality for a highly diversified international conglomerate with revenues of over six billion dollars a year.

Captain James A. Hodgman, USCG, was graduated from the U. S. Coast Guard Academy in 1944. In 1965–1966 he was concurrently Commander Coast Guard Division 11 and Coast Guard Squadron One. Since his retirement he has been a ship pilot in Alaska.

Captain K.P. Huff, USNR, a graduate of the University of New Hampshire in 1939, was in 1965–1966 Commander Amphibious Logistic Support Group, Seventh Fleet (CTG 76.4) and then Commanding Officer Naval Support Activity Da Nang. After retirement from active duty he became project manager for a large shipbuilding company, a position from which he has only recently retired.

Lane C. Kendall was graduated from Tulane University and in 1935 entered the shipping industry. During World War II he served in the Marine Corps and is a colonel, USMCR (Retired). During the Vietnam war he was Commercial Shipping Advisor to the Commander Military Sea Transportation Service. Now in retirement, he continues to write on shipping matters.

Captain Herbert T. King, USN, was commissioned at Northwestern University in 1945 and earned his baccalaureate from George Washington University in 1968. He was Commanding Officer Naval Support Activity Saigon in 1966–1967. He has since retired from the Navy.

Commander F.O. McClendon, Jr., MSC, USN, is a graduate of the Naval School of Hospital Administration. From 1963 through 1966 he was Officer-in-Charge Naval Medical Administration unit, Tripler Army Medical Center, Hawaii, and, in 1970 he was special assistant to the Surgeon General of the Navy for management information. He is now retired from the Navy.

Lieutenant General Keith B. McCutcheon, USMC, a graduate of Carnegie Institute of Technology in 1937, was Commanding General First Marine Air Wing and Deputy Commander III Marine Amphibious Force in 1965–1966. In 1970 he served as Commanding General III MAF and then was selected to become assistant commandant of the Marine Corps, but died before he was able to assume office. He was promoted to four-star rank upon retirement.

Captain Charles J. Merdinger, CEC, USN, was graduated from the U.S. Naval Academy in 1941. In 1967–1968 he was public works officer Naval Support Activity Da Nang. Retired from the Navy, he served as president Washington College, vice president Aspen Institute, deputy director Scripps Institution of Oceanography, and director AVCO Corporation.

Lieutenant Commander Robert E. Mumford, Jr., USN, a graduate of the University of Rochester in 1957, was intelligence officer for Amphibious Squadron One in 1966. Now retired as a captain, he has his own management consulting firm and also is engaged in professional photography.

Brigadier General O.F. Peatross, USMC, was graduated from North Carolina State College and commissioned in the Marine Corps in 1941. In 1965 he was a colonel commanding the 7th Marines. He is retired now as a major general.

Commander R.L. Schreadley, USN, a graduate of Dickinson College in 1955 and the Fletcher School of Law and Diplomacy in 1972, was special assistant to Commander Naval Forces Vietnam in 1969–1970. Now retired from the Navy he is executive editor of *The News and Courier* and *The Evening Post* in Charleston, S.C.

Brigadier General Edwin H. Simmons, USMC, was graduated from Lehigh University in 1942. As a colonel he served in Vietnam in 1965–1966 first as the operations officer for III Marine Amphibious Force and then as Commanding Officer 9th Marines. During his second Vietnam tour, 1970–1971, he was, as a brigadier general, the assistant division commander, 1st Marine Division. He is Director, Marine Corps History and Museums.

Commander Sayre A. Swarztrauber, USN, was graduated from Maryville College in 1952. During the Vietnam war he was successively Commander River Squadron Five, chief staff officer to Commander River Patrol Force (TF 116), and Commander Task Force Clearwater. Recently retired from the Navy in the rank of rear admiral, he is Superintendent Maine Maritime Academy in Castine, Maine.

Captain Wade C. Wells, USN, a 1937 graduate of the Georgia Institute of Technology, was Commander River Assault Force (CTF 117) in 1966–1967 and Navy component commander of the joint Army/Navy Mobile Riverine Force. Since retirement from the Navy he has, as a director of an international firm, been a consultant to developing countries in Africa and the Far East in establishing rapid reaction force capabilities.

Index